Identity, Mission and Community

Biblical Hermeneutics Rediscovered

The Series as the name suggests will focus on Biblical Hermeneutics, i.e., literary works concerned with methods of interpreting the Old and New Testaments of Bible via different stream of topics like Literature & Poetry, Indigenous Philosophizing, Ethical response towards Ecology, Health & Healing, Science & Technology, Feminist Theology, Sociological approach towards Human Rights, Law & Politics, Arts, History of Ideas, Ancient Civilizations, Cultural Contiguity, Religious Cosmologies & Mysticism, Appraisal of various Theologians, World Peace & Harmony, Global Capitalism, Network Marketing, Cybertheology, Population & Demographics, Epigraphic Studies, Contextualized Education, and many others. We welcome a Mss. on any topic/s mentioned, whether they are original works, scholarly monographs, collections of conference papers, revised dissertations, or translations of historical documents. Through the Series we, the Publishers, are striving to put forward published works that may help Institutions, Academic Bodies, Researchers, Scholars and the World at large in furthering their respective knowledge and understanding on the concerned subject. We welcome your comments on our efforts and further suggestions on how we can enshrine new ray of analysing & explaining the written Texts through our upcoming books.

Biblical Hermeneutics Rediscovered - 11

Identity, Mission and Community

A Study of the Johannine Resurrection Narrative

Asish Thomas Koshy

CWI

Christian World Imprints™

First Published in 2018 by

Christian World Imprints™
Christian Publishing & Books from India
H-12 Bali Nagar, **New Delhi-110015**
info@christianworldimprints.com
www.ChristianWorldImprints.com
Phone: +91 11 25465925

ISBN: 978-93-5148-252-9 (HB) ISBN: 978-93-5148-253-6 (PB)

Cataloging in Publication Data--DK
Courtesy: D.K. Agencies (P) Ltd. <docinfo@dkagencies.com>

Koshy, Asish Thomas, 1971- **author.**
Identity, mission and community : a study of the Johannine resurrection narrative / Asish Thomas Koshy.
pages cm. -- (Biblical hermeneutics rediscovered ; 11)
Originally presented as the author's dissertation (doctoral)--Serampore College (University).
Includes bibliographical references.
ISBN 9789351482529 (HB)
ISBN 9789351482536 (PB)

1. Johannine school. 2. Bible. John, XX--Criticism, interpretation, etc. 3. Jews in the New Testament. 4. Judaism--Relations--Christianity. 5. Christianity and other religions--Judaism. I. Title. II. Series: Biblical hermeneutics rediscovered ; 11.

LCC BS2615.52.K67 2018 | DDC 226.506 23

Printed in India

Contents

Foreword

By connecting the Resurrection narrative in John and the mission of the post-Apostolic Church, Dr. Asish Koshy has done an excellent monograph, which, I am sure, will be a creative contribution to the New Testament scholarship in India. Since, the work was done primarily as a D.Th thesis, he has systematically revised the same for wider readership as a book entitled *Identity, Mission and Community: A Study of the Johannine Resurrection Narrative,*an excellent articulation of the early history of Christianity using contextual hermeneutical tools. It is not an easy task for a researcher to enter into the world of the Johannine community as there are many complexities involved in the origin and development of the Johannine community.

Dr. Asish has painstakingly analysed the issues and concerns debated within the community of John in terms of identity and mission of the early church. In a postmodern world, the issue of identity is very significant as neo-colonial powers dominate the socio-political systems of our time. It is very interesting to observe how the Johannine community carried out the mission of the church in a dedicated manner within the challenging frame and structures of the Post-resurrection communities. Dr. Asish could further thus evaluate the contribution of mainstream Johannine scholars as well as other significant voices in the field in order to construct a world of the Johannine community.

I am indeed fascinated by the way in which Dr. Asish could combine the issue of identity with the post-Apostolic concerns of Christian mission. It is noted that how significant was the miracle of resurrection and its historicity in defining the identity of the early Christian church. The study will continue to remain as a model forconstructing the contours of Christian mission by empowering communities, those that are engaged in Christian mission. It will also offer to clarifythe various dimensions of Christian identity by giving us a possibility of locating the spaces and opportunities for mission in a postcolonial world.

I am sure this book will be a welcome addition to this field of New Testament scholarship. I wish and pray that Dr. Asish Thomas Koshy will contribute more books to strengthen the Christianministry.

Rev. Dr. C. I. David Joy
Professor, NT
UTC, Bangalore

Preface

This book, originally submitted as a doctoral dissertation to the Senate of Serampore College (University), attempts to look at the identity and mission of the Johannine community as described in the resurrection narrative of John 20. Steps to define the identity was an inevitable necessity in the context after the destruction of the Jerusalem Temple. Different groups within Judaism, especially Formative Judaism took efforts to define their identity and this resulted in conflict with the Johannine community that also tried to express their identity in relation to Christ. In this regard, the resurrection narrative succinctly presents the identity and mission of the Johannine community, which is central to the identity and mission of the Fourth Gospel.

This study was generally conducted not in isolation but it surfaced from a pool of resources and it attempts to enrich and contribute to it. It includes not only published sources but also people who have had a role in it. Therefore, it is only fitting to acknowledge some of them, though there are many others who have facilitated the smooth progress of the research. I acknowledge the Almighty's enabling hand from the beginning to the end of my research.

I acknowledge with deep gratitude the help of H.G. Dr. Yuhanon Mar Demetrios Metropolitan, my supervisor, for his observations, suggestions, corrections, and valuable advice. It would have been impossible to complete this research without his help and encouragement throughout the process.

My thanks to the FFRRC (Federated Faculty for Research in Religion and Culture, Kottayam) fraternity, which includes the administration and faculty members of the associated seminaries. I appreciate the contribution of the faculty members and staff of Union Biblical Seminary, my family members and the extended family.

Abbreviations

2nd ed., 3rd ed	second edition, third edition
AB	Anchor Bible
AJR	American Journal of Archaeology
ALGHJ	Arbeiten Zur Literatur Und Geschichte Des Hellenistichen Judentums
AnBib	Analecta Biblica
APB	Acta patristica et byzantine
BBET	Beiträge zur biblischen Exegese und Theologie
BBR	Bulletin for Biblical Research
BECNT	Baker Exegetical Commentary on the New Testament
BETL	Bibliotheca ephemeridum theologicarum Lovaniensium
BI	Biblical Interpretation
Bib	Biblica
BibBh	Bible Bashyam
BibThBul	Biblical Theology Bulletin
BInS	Biblical Interpretation Series
BIS	Biblical Interpretation Series
BJRL	Bulletin of the John Rylands University Library of Manchester
BJS	Brown Judaic Studies
BSR	Biblioteca di scienze religiose
BZNW	Beihefte zur Zeitschrift für die neutestamentliche Wissenschaft
CBQ	Catholic Biblical Quarterly
CBQMS	Catholic Biblical Quarterly Monograph Series
CBR	Currents in Biblical Research

CE	Common Era
CH	Church History
Chap., chaps.	Chapter, chapters
comp., comps.	Compiler, compilers
ComViat	Communio Viatorum
ConBNT	Coniectanea Biblica New Testament Series
CRINT	Compendia Rerum Iudaicarum ad Novum Testamentum
CurTM	Currents in Theology and Mission
ed., eds.	Editor, editors, edition, editions
EDNT	Exegetical Dictionary of the New Testament
EJL	Early Judaism and its Literature
EncJud	Encyclopaedia Judaica
ERT	Evangelical Review of Theology
et al. (et. alit)	and others
etc. (et cetra)	and others of the same class, and so forth
EuroJTh	European Journal of Theology
ExpT	Expository Times
f., ff.	and the following page (s)
f.n.	foot note
HTR	Harvard Theological Review
HTS	Harvard Theological Studies
HUCA	Hebrew Union College Annual
i.e.,	that is to say
IndJT	Indian Journal of Theology
Int.	Interpretation
IRM	International Review of Mission
ITQ	Irish Theological Quarterly
IVPNTC	Inter-Varsity Press New Testament Commentary
JAAR	Journal of the American Academy of Religion
JBL	Journal of Biblical Literature
JES	Journal of Ecumenical Studies
JETS	Journal of Evangelical Theological Society
JQR	Jewish Quarterly Review
JRAS	Journal of the Royal Asiatic Society
JSJ	Journal for the Study of Judaism
JSJSup	Journal for the Study of Judaism, Supplement Series
JSNT	Journal for the Study of the New Testament

JSNTSup	Journal for the Study of New Testament, Supplement Series
JSOTSup	Journal for the Study of the Old Testament, Supplement Series
JTS	Journal of Theological Studies
LEC	Library of Early Christianity
Lit.	Literally
NCB	New Century Bible Commentary
NCBC	The New Cambridge Bible Commentary
NCCR	National Council of Churches Review
NDCT	New Dictionary of Christian Theology
NEA	Near Eastern Archaeology
NICNT	The New International Critical Commentary on the New Testament
NIDNTT	New International Dictionary of New Testament Theology
NovT	Novum Testamentum
NovTSup	Supplements to Novum Testamentum
NSBT	New Studies in Biblical Theology
NTS	New Testament Studies
PBM	Paternoster Biblical Monographs
PBTM	Paternoster Biblical and Theological Monographs
RelSoc	Religion and Society
RevExp	Review Expositor
RSV	Revised Standard Version
SacPag	Sacra Pagina
SBL	Society of Biblical Literature
SBLSS	Society of Biblical Literature Symposium Series
SBT	Studies in Biblical Theology
SJLA	Studies in Judaism in Late Antiquity
SJT	Scottish Journal of Theology
SNTA	Studiorum Novi Testamenti auxilia
SNTS	Society for New Testament Studies
SNTSMS	Society for New Testament Studies Monograph Series
SNTW	Studies of the New Testament and its World
SPB	Studia Postbiblica
StVTQ	St Vladimir's Theological Quarterly

SubBi	Subsidia Biblica
SWJT	Southwestern Journal of Theology
TCS	Text Critical Studies
TDNT	Theological Dictionary of the New Testament
TDOT	Theological Dictionary of the Old Testament
TGST	Tesi Gregoriana Serie Teologia
ThDiss	Theologische Dissertationen
Trans.	Translator, translated by
TrinJ	Trinity Journal
TS	Theological Studies
TW	Theologie und Wirklichkeit
TynBul	Tyndale Bulletin
UBS	United Bible Socities
v. vv.	verse, verses
VigChr	Vigilae Christianae
vol., vols.	volume, volumes
WBC	Word Biblical Commentary
WUZNT	Wissenschaftliche Untersuchungen Zum Neuen Testament
YJS	Yale Judaica Series
ZNW	Zeitschrift für die neutestamentliche Wissenschaft

Months of the Year

Ja.	January
Feb.	February
Mr.	March
Apr.	April
My.	May
Je.	June
Jl.	July
Sep.	September
O.	October
Nov.	November
Dec.	December

Books of the Bible

Old Testament		New Testament	
Gen.	Genesis	Matt.	Matthew
Exod.	Exodus	Mk.	Mark
Lev.	Leviticus	Lk.	Luke
Num.	Numbers	Jn.	John
Dt.	Deuteronomy	Act.	Acts of the Apostles
Jos.	Joshua	Rom.	Romans
Judg	Judges	1 Cor.	1 Corinthians
Ruth	Ruth	2 Cor.	2 Corinthians
1 Sam	1 Samuel	Gal.	Galatians
2 Sam	2 Samuel	Eph.	Ephesians
1 Kgs	1 Kings	Phil.	Philippians
2 Kgs	2 Kings	Col.	Colossians
1 Chr	1 Chronicles	1 Th.	1 Thessalonians
2 Chr	2 Chronicles	2 Th.	2 Thessalonians
Ezra	Ezra	1 Tim.	1 Timothy
Neh	Nehemiah	2 Tim.	2 Timothy
Esth	Esther	Tit.	Titus
Job	Job	Phm.	Philemon
Ps	Pslams	Heb.	Hebrews
Prov	Proverbs	Jas.	James
Eccl	Ecclesiastes	1 Pet.	1 Peter
Song	Song of Songs	2 Pet.	2 Peter
Isa	Isaiah	1 Jn.	1 John
Jer	Jeremiah	2 Jn.	2 John
Lam	Lamentations	3 Jn.	3 John
Ezek	Ezeliel	Jude	Jude
Dan	Daniel	Rev.	Revelation
Hos	Hosea		
Joel	Joel		
Amos	Amos		
Obad	Obadiah		
Jon	Jonah		
Mic	Micah		
Nah	Nahum		
Hab	Habakkuk		
Zeph	Zephaniah		
Hag	Haggai		
Zech	Zechariah		
Mal	Malachi		

Introduction

Identity of Jesus is one of the prominent motifs in the Fourth Gospel.[1] Jesus often describes himself as the one who is sent by the Father (4:34; 5:24, 30, 37; 6:39, 44; 7:16, 28; 8:16, 18, 26, 29; 9:4; 12:44, 45, 39; 13:20; 14:24; 16:5) to fulfill the mission of the Father. At the same time, the mission of Jesus is related to his identity. Thus, identity of Jesus is derived from his mission and his mission authenticates his identity.

There is another dimension that the FG brings out in relation to identity and mission of Jesus. This is connected with the identity and mission of the Johannine community. There exists an analogical relationship between the story of Jesus and the Johannine community. This has prompted several scholars[2] to conclude that Jesus' story in the FG can also be termed as a story

---

[1] Hereafter referred to as FG.

[2] The approach significantly developed in the mid 1960s in the first edition of the commentary by C. K. Barrett (1955) where the use of ἀποσυνάγωγος (9:22; 12:42; and 16:2) is seen in relation to B*irkat ha-Minim* (a benediction framed against the heretics). C. K. Barrett, *The Gospel according to St. John: An Introduction with Commentary and Notes on the Greek Text* (London: SPCK, 1955). Later on it received detailed expression in J. Louis Martyn's *History and Theology in the Fourth Gospel* (Nashville: Abingdon Press, 1979). Martyn proposed that the FG is written as a two level drama simultaneously reflecting both the period of Jesus' ministry and the conflict between the Johannine community and the synagogue. *Birkat ha-Minin* is cited as the chief reason for the expulsion. Martyn, *History and Theology*, 30. In this regard, John K. Riches observes that Martyn's two-level drama could be misleading. Martyn seems to give the impression that the composition of the FG itself must be located at a particular point in the history of the Johannine community when in fact the interaction between the story and the community-experience is an ongoing process. John K. Riches, *A Century of New Testament Study* (Cambridge: The Lutterworth Press, 1993), 187. Another work of Martyn is *The Gospel of John in Christian History: Essays for Interpreters* (New Jersey: Paulist Press, 1979). Raymond E. Brown proposed that the gospel developed in a number of stages over a lengthy period of time. Raymond E. Brown, *The Gospel according to John (i-xii)*, AB Series 29 A (New York: Doubleday & Company, Inc., 1966), xxxiv-xxxvi. Detailed expression of his views is seen in *The Community of the Beloved Disciple: The Life, Loves, and Hates of an Individual Church in New Testament Times* (New Jersey: Paulist Press, 1979). The other works in this approach include: R. Alan Culpepper, *The Johannine School: An Evaluation of the Johannine-School*

of the community.[3] The FG presents the story of Jesus as well as the history of the community simultaneously — its struggles and search for meaning and identity, in the midst of opposition. A detailed study of the gospel reveals that the community has a long and complex history, accounting for a unique presentation of the person and work of Christ, different from that of the synoptic gospels. In this regard, John Painter states, "…the most significant factor in shaping the Johannine tradition was the relation to the synagogue, a relationship which began with dialogue, became a conflict and ended in mutual execration."[4] The Johannine community was forced to define its identity and mission after being expelled from the synagogue.

The dual aspect of identity and mission of Jesus and the Johannine community is best illustrated in the resurrection narrative of the FG (Jn. 20). But some of the Johannine scholars seem to have neglected the resurrection narrative and given prominence to the crucifixion/exaltation motif. Craig F. Evans confirms this view when he states that the 'ascent' rather than 'resurrection' is the key word to describe the subject of Jesus' life and ministry (Jn. 3, 6; 12:32).[5] He opines, "Strictly speaking, there is no place in the Fourth Gospel for resurrection stories, since the ascent or exaltation has already taken place."[6] On this basis, Evans concludes that the resurrection narrative in the FG is an appendage, and therefore something that must be glossed over.[7] However, a careful study of the resurrection narrative in the FG proves

---

Hypothesis Based on an Investigation of the Nature of Ancient Schools (Montana: Scholars Press, 1975), Oscar Cullmann, *The Johannine Circle*, translated by John Bowden (London: SCM Press Ltd, 1976). For Cullmann, the FG has considerable affinity with heterodox Judaism (non-conformist Judaism), a group or groups in the earliest church in Jerusalem who came from this Judaism and after their conversion stood apart from the other followers of Christ, who were adherents of official religion. Unlike the other scholars discussed earlier, Cullmann opines that at the unredacted stage the FG was as early as the synoptics or even earlier than the earliest of them. John Painter, *The Quest for the Messiah: The History, Literature and Theology of the Johannine Community*, 2nd ed. (Edinburgh: T & T Clark, 1993).

[3] Brown, *The Community of the Beloved Disciple*, 17. Also see Painter, *The Quest for the Messiah*, 68.

[4] Painter, *The Quest for the Messiah*, 61.

[5] Craig F. Evans, *Resurrection and the New Testament*, SBT, second series 12 (London: SCM Press Ltd., 1970), 116.

[6] Evans, *Resurrection and the New Testament*, 116.

[7] Evans also sees in the resurrection narrative traditional elements being added with what is characteristically Johannine. Evans, *Resurrection and the New Testament*, 116. Bultmann also echoes the same position. Rudolf Bultmann, *The Gospel of John: A Commentary*, translated by G. R. Beasley-Murray (Philadelphia: The Westminster John Knox Press, 1971), 635. N. T. Wright disagrees with Evans and also with John Macquarie who states, "…though John includes resurrection stories, their significance is reduced." John Macquarie, *Jesus Christ in Modern Thought* (London: SCM Press, 1990), 413 cited by N. T. Wright, *The Resurrection of the Son of God* (London: SPCK, 2003), 665. However, there is nothing in the crucifixion narrative which

otherwise. In fact, the themes discussed in the earlier part of the FG such as the descent-ascent motif and the promise of a Paraclete, are drawn to a climax in the resurrection narrative. This implies that the resurrection narrative is an indispensable part of the FG, and is unique in its presentation from the rest of the gospels. The Johannine community's identity is clearly defined in the words of Jesus in Jn. 20:17 where, for the first time, the disciples are called the brothers of Jesus and also have a relationship with the Father. Further, the disciples are called to participate in the mission of Jesus: just as the Father had sent Jesus, so now Jesus sends the disciples to the world. What evolves here is a new understanding of the world, far from the bitter animosity that the Johannine community had experienced earlier.

A few monographs have discussed the resurrection narrative exclusively in the FG. They have concentrated on viewing Jn. 20 as an example of faith. One such example is the study undertaken by R. Mahoney.[8] A deviation from Mahoney's point of view is a study done by J. Riley.[9] He makes a significant contribution to the study of traditions about the resurrection of Jesus. His study defends the relationship between the FG and literature connected with Thomas – the *Gospel according to Thomas*, the *Book of Thomas the Contender*, and the *Acts of Thomas*. Over a decade earlier to Riley's study, Osborne undertook a study on the resurrection narratives of the four gospels.[10] He uses the tools and methodology of tradition critics in order to authenticate rather than deny the resurrection accounts. In Chapter 5, Osborne deals with the FG's resurrection narrative. Here, he affirms that the FG's resurrection narrative forms a kind of harmonious unity that is not as evident in other synoptic accounts.[11] The resurrection narrative develops on the themes of ecclesiology, discipleship, and witness of martyrdom.[12] Osborne seems to fail to state the criteria for distinguishing tradition from redaction and for making historical judgments. The study also leaves out the role of the Johannine community in shaping the resurrection narrative in the FG.

---

supports the conclusion that the crucifixion is after all the point at which a theme of glorification reaches its goal. Wright, *The Resurrection of the Son of God*, 673.

[8] Robert Mahoney, *The Two Disciples at the Tomb: The Background and Message of John 20:1-10* (Frankfurt: Peter Lang, 1974). Grant R. Osborne echoes R. Mahoney when he views the resurrection narrative as demonstrating four types of faith. The presentation of faith is seen in a kind of descending spiral from the highest type of faith (BD) to the lowest or most meager kind of faith (Thomas) between the extremes is Mary. Grant R. Osborne, *The Resurrection Narratives: A Redactional Study* (Grand Rapids, Michigan: Baker Book House, 1984), 147.

[9] Gregory J. Riley, *Resurrection Reconsidered: Thomas and John in Controversy* (Minneapolis: Fortress Press, 1995).

[10] Osborne, *The Resurrection Narratives*, 147.

[11] Osborne, *The Resurrection Narratives*, 191.

[12] Osborne, *The Resurrection Narratives*, 192.

Another work that could be of interest is a study taken up by Sandra M. Schneiders on Jn. 20. [13] This work too does not seem to address the community aspect behind the resurrection but rather sees its implications for deriving spirituality.

In addition to these monographs, articles have dealt with the faith motif, Mary Magdalene, and other such issues. The faith motif is discussed by Byrne[14] where he defines the role of the Beloved Disciple[15] as the 'point of insertion' for the later generations into the pivotal events and experiences attested in the gospel. The later generations, according to him, can believe in Jesus through the signs recorded in the gospel, just as the BD came to believe through the sign given at the tomb. Brown also discusses the faith motif.[16] Brown takes Jn. 20 as five different reactions to the risen Jesus – reactions of faith. These include the BD, Mary Magdalene, the disciples, Thomas, and finally those who believed without seeing Jesus' garments or his bodily presence. According to Brown, the interest of the evangelist is in the fifth reaction. Finally, Kelly O'Brien argues that the BD is not the ideal disciple and believing in the FG is a process.[17]

Several articles have also discussed the role of Mary Magdalene in Jn. 20. Gerald O' Collins and Daniel Kendall in their work[18] postulate a synthesis that does not deny the authority of Peter but rather argue for the complementary roles of women, Peter, and the other disciples as witnesses to the risen Christ. They

---

[13] Sandra M. Schneiders, *The Johannine Resurrection Narrative: An Exegetical and Theological Study of John 20 as a Synthesis of Johannine Spirituality* (Ann Arbor, Michigan: University of Microfilms, 1982). In another work- Sandra M. Schneiders, *Written that You May Believe: Encountering Jesus in the Fourth Gospel* (New York: The Crossroad Publishing Company, 1999), she traces the line of the argument. She states, "…the primary purpose of chapter 20 is not to tell the reader what happened to Jesus after his death but to explore, through the paradigmatic and foundational experiences of the disciples, the meaning of believers for Jesus' glorification. Elsewhere I have suggested that there are two sides to the paschal event in John: *glorification* is what happens to Jesus on the cross; *resurrection* is the communication to Jesus' disciples of his paschal glory through his return to them in the Spirit." The latter part of the quotation is taken from her work – *The Johannine Resurrection Narrative…*, 97-141, cited in *Written That You May Believe…*, 190. This work as like the other works discussed also does not seem to address the community aspect behind the resurrection but rather sees its implications for deriving spirituality.

[14] Brendan Byrne, "The Faith of the Beloved Disciple and the Community in John 20," *JSNT* 23 (Fall 1985): 83-97.

[15] Hereafter, referred to as BD.

[16] Raymond E. Brown, "The Resurrection in John 20- A Series of Diverse Reactions," *Worship* 64/3 (My. 1990): 194-206.

[17] Kelli S. O'Brien, "Written that You May Believe: John 20 and Narrative Rhetoric," *CBQ* 67/ 2 (Apr. 2005): 284-302.

[18] Gerald O' Collins and Daniel Kendall, "Mary Magdalene as Major Witness to Jesus' Resurrection," *TS* 48/4 (Dec.1987): 631-646.

point that among the female recipients of the appearances, Mary Magdalene shares a primary role. Sandra M. Schneiders' article[19] proposes that the BD is a textual paradigm of ideal discipleship which is realized diversely in several characters in the text. Further, she assumes that women were more significant in the leadership of the Johannine community than has been recognized in the past. Finally, Teresa Okure's article[20] focuses on the commission given to Mary Magdalene and asserts that the commission includes promotion of life and responsibility to one's brother and sister.

All of these studies tend to deal with Jn. 20 in terms of different strands or characters such as BD, Thomas, Mary Magdalene, and so on. There seems to be a lack of orientation from the Johannine community's perspective. None of these studies have considered this from the view of the identity crisis the community faced, or how it altered the community's perception of the world. In other words, the social context of the Johannine community is set aside and the individual characters seem to be highlighted in these studies. Thus, this study endeavours to look at the identity and mission, in terms of the Family of God, that emerges out of the struggles the Johannine community faced as reflected in the resurrection narrative of the FG.

The study makes use of various hermeneutical approaches in order to bring out the identity and mission aspects of Jesus and the Johannine community in Jn. 20. The Historical Critical Method (Source Criticism, Form Criticism, and Redaction Criticism) helps to identify the differences in the resurrection narratives of the FG and the synoptics. This could provide a clue to identify the community behind the FG. Sociological Criticism is used to outline the trajectory of the Johannine community. Finally, narrative criticism helps in tracing the literary devices in the text. All of these hermeneutical approaches are valuable in arriving at the best possible meaning of the text.

The study is organized into four chapters excluding the introduction and conclusion. Chapter one discusses the context before and after 70 CE, which were periods of considerable diversity and sets the context of the Johannine community. There were different reactions to the Roman administration and the ruling class of Judea. Some of these reactions were anti-establishment and others in the form of passive resistance. The reaction crystallized in the form of the first revolt which was the result of interwoven factors such as socio-economic, political, and religious factors. The context after 70 CE era witnessed a movement towards defining identity in Judaism and Christianity, which gave way to rivalry, conflicts, and so on, though these were still in

---

[19] Sandra M. Schneiders, "'Because of the Woman's Testimony...": Reexamining the Issue of Authorship in the Fourth Gospel," *NTS* 44/4 (O. 1988): 513-535.

[20] Teresa Okure, "The Significance Today of Jesus' Commission to Mary Magdalene," *IRM* 81/322 (Apr. 1992): 177-188.

their formative stages. Both were involved in defining their relationship with each other and their own respective identities. The measures to keep their boundaries could have sparked off inter-Jewish conflicts in the synagogues where the Christian communities belonged. The *Birkat ha-Minim* could be taken as one such effect on the ever growing separation between Judaism and Christianity. The Johannine community was forced to look at its identity and mission in relation to Christ.

The next chapter, chapter three evaluates the reconstructions of the Johannine community discussed by various scholars. The study emphasizes that the Johannine community consisted of Jewish Christians, Samaritan Christians and the Gentiles. It seems to be clear, however, that the Johannine community did go through expulsion but probably expulsion in terms of an intra-Jewish dispute, and not a general expulsion. The christological formulations of the Johannine community played a part in it and the community continued to express its identity in terms of christology; these put the community in opposition to the Jewish synagogue at Ephesus.

Further aspect of this study, chapter four, deals with the resurrection narrative in Jn. 20. The resurrection narrative in Jn. 20 draws together varied events of disclosure such as disclosure to the BD, Mary, the disciples and Thomas; but these are not to be pitted against each other. Resurrection is a sign, a sign revealing the identity of Jesus as well as the identity of the disciples. Essentially, the resurrection describes the effect of Jesus' incarnation to the disciples. The line of relationship is redrawn and a relationship is established.

The last chapter, chapter four proposes the family identity as the expression of the identity of the community and this identity is seen in relation to the identity of Jesus, who is also described as belonging to the family. There are three families represented in the Fourth Gospel: a) Divine Family, b) Earthly Family, and c) Metaphorical Family. There is an interaction between these families and this creates conflict. The first makes possible the third. If the identity of the Johannine community was the Family of God then the mission of the Johannine community is to witness to the works of the Divine Family.

Chapter 1

Formative Judaism and Early Christian Communities after 70 CE
Situating the Context of the Johannine Community

Introduction

Christianity took shape as a religious movement[1] within the Second Temple Judaism and was very much a part of Judaism in the mid-first century CE; nevertheless, it did retain differences in some areas.[2] If this assumption is correct, then, the factors that affected Judaism, consequently, had a bearing on its relationship with Judaism, especially along the lines of identity. In this regard, a study of the first century Judaism, especially Judaism post 70 CE, could throw light on the factors that went into the identity formation of both Judaism (Formative Judaism[3] to be precise) and Christianity. Further, such

---

[1] The question of whether early Christians can be termed as sectarians has been a matter of discussion in the recent times. Regev is of the view that early Christians were not sectarian as the definition of the term 'sect' was narrower in its definition. Eyal Regev, "Where the Early Christians Sectarians?," *JBL* 130/4 (Winter 2011): 771-93.

[2] Burkett in this connection notes, "Many people today do not think of Christianity as a sect of Judaism but in the beginning that is precisely how it was regarded, both by those inside and those outside." Delbert Burkett, *An Introduction to the New Testament and the Origins of Christianity* (Cambridge: Cambridge University Press, 2002), 57.

[3] This term is coined by Neusner. Jacob Neusner, "The Formation of Rabbinic Judaism: Yavneh from A.D. 70-100," in *Aufstieg und Niedergang der römischen*, 19.2, 3-42, edited by H. Temporini and W. Haase (New York: de Gruyter, 1979), cited in J. Andrew Overman, *Matthew's Gospel and Formative Judaism: The Social World of the Matthean Community* (Minneapolis: Fortress Press, 1990), 35. This term refers to the fluid nature of Judaism, a state of consolidating, organizing and obtaining a structure for its existence. For Sim, formative Judaism is "...the reorganization and consolidation of Judaism in the period after the first Jewish war which was

a study would help to understand the context in which the FG took shape, especially, the Johannine community, as most scholars would agree that the FG was written towards the end of the first century CE.[4] This chapter details the context in which the Johannine community took shape i.e., events leading to the first revolt, destruction of the Jerusalem Temple, Formative Judaism, and Jewish-Christian relations.[5]

1.1. Events Leading to the First Jewish Revolt (66 – 73 CE)

The destruction of the Jerusalem Temple as well as the city of Jerusalem can be better ascertained by looking into events that led to the first Jewish revolt. Some of the important questions worth discussing are: Why did the Jews revolt? What were the factors that influenced the Jews to revolt against Rome? Was there decadence in the Roman as well as the Jewish administration? If so, how did this degeneration in the political and religious climate affect the common people? How did the agrarian community in Palestine react to the decadence in the socio-economic situation?

---

led by a coalition of the pre-70 Pharisees and those belonging to the scribal profession, but in which other groups participated as well." David C. Sim, *Apocalyptic Eschatology in the Gospel of Matthew*, SNTSMS 88, edited by Margret E. Thrall (Cambridge: Cambridge University Press, 1996), 183.

[4] James D. G. Dunn, "The Question of Anti-Semitism in the New Testament Writings of the Period," in *Jews and Christians: The Parting of the Ways A. D. 70 to 135*, edited by James D. G. Dunn (Grand Rapids, Michigan: William B. Eerdmans Publishing Company, 1992), 199. Harold W. Attridge, "Christianity from the Destruction of Jerusalem to Constantine's Adoption of the New Religion: 70-312 CE," in *Christianity and Rabbinic Judaism: A Parallel History of their Origins and Early Development*, edited by Hershel Shanks (London: SPCK, 1993), 167.

[5] Understanding the first century context is beset with difficulties. One of them being, the available literary data conceals apologetic motives. Alexander points out that Christians tend to prove that Christianity transcended or transformed Judaism and for Jews, Christianity was an alien form of Judaism that transgressed the true path. He also points out two lopsided approaches - a. retrojecting Rabbinic Judaism into first century Pharisaism and b. determining the essence of first century Judaism. Philip S. Alexander, “"The Parting of the Ways" From the Perspective of Rabbinic Judaism," in *Jews and Christians: The Parting of the Ways A. D. 70 to 135*, edited by James D. G. Dunn (Grand Rapids, Michigan: William B. Eerdmans Publishing Company, 1992), 2. Nickelsburg also attests to this problem. According to him, the New Testament writings are "thoroughly confessional, substantially apologetic, and significantly polemical." He further warns against the uncritical use of rabbinic texts as the dating of any given passages can be extremely problematic even when it is ascribed to a known and datable rabbi. George W. E. Nickelsburg, *Ancient Judaism and Christian Origins: Diversity, Continuity, and Transformation* (Minneapolis: Fortress Press, 2003), 25.

1.1.1. Political, Socio-Economic and Religious Factors[6]

1.1.1.1. Political Factors

From 6 to 66 CE, the Palestinian Jewish society came under direct Roman rule. During this time, it witnessed a period of extensive agitation and occasional disturbance.[7] The deterioration in the political situation, especially the malfunctioning of the Roman administration, had a telling effect on the Jewish people which led to many upheavals against the Roman administration. Though it could be said that the Romans were sensitive to Jewish religious feelings, they stumbled at certain times, raising occasional provocations that ignited the situation.[8] It is said that Pontius Pilate's tyrannical rule (26-36 CE) left an indelible mark on the nation's memory due to two critical incidents: a) he forced the people to accept the images of Caesar;[9] b) he constructed dedicated shields or plaques apparently in honour of the emperor in Herod's palace which resulted in a massive protest by the Jews.[10] Pilate also made use of funds from the sacred treasury in the Temple to pay for the construction of a conduit to bring water into Jerusalem. When the Jews protested, he killed many of them.[11]

---

[6] In effect, the political, economic, social and religious factors should have been dealt together as they are inseparably conjoined together and inevitably what affects one affects the other. This is confirmed by Saldarini, when he states, "...in the Roman Empire and Jewish Palestinian society, religion was engrained in the political and social fabric of the community."Anthony J. Saldarini, *Pharisees, Scribes and Sadducees in Palestinian Society: A Sociological Approach*, The Biblical Resource Series (Grand Rapids, Michigan: William B. Eerdmans Publishing Company, 2001), 5. But for the sake of a better clarity, these factors are dealt separately.

[7] Richard A. Horsley and John S. Hanson, *Bandits, Prophets and Messiahs: Popular Movements in the Time of Jesus* (Pennsylvania: Trinity Press International, 1999), 35. However, the Roman rule of Palestine stretched over several years. Edwards notes, "Pompey's conquest of the Near East in 63 BCE made it official that Rome controlled Palestine for the next 350 years with periodic interruptions." Douglas R. Edwards, "Constructing the World of Roman Palestine: An Introduction" in *Religion and Society in Roman Palestine: Old Questions, New Approaches*, edited by Douglas R. Edwards (New York: Routledge, 2004), 1.

[8] Horsley and Hanson, *Bandits, Prophets and Messiahs*, 35.

[9] Flavius Josephus, "The Wars of the Jews," in *The Works of Josephus: Complete and Unabridged in one Volume*, translated by William Whiston, (Peabody: Hendrickson Publishers, 1987), 2:9:2; Horsley and Hanson, *Bandits, Prophets and Messiahs,* 38.

[10] Philo states, ""But when he steadfastly refused this petition (for he was a man of a very inflexible disposition, and very merciless as well as very obstinate), they cried out: 'Do not cause a sedition; do not make war upon us; do not destroy the peace which exists. The honour of the emperor is not identical with dishonour to the ancient laws; let it not be to you a pretence for heaping insult on our nation." Philo, "On the Embassy to Gaius: The First Part of the Treatiseon Virtues," *The Works of Philo Complete and Unabridged*, translated by C. D. Jonge (Peabody: Hendrickson Publishers, 1993), VI (38).

[11] Flavius Josephus, "The Antiquities of the Jews," in *The Works of Josephus*, 18:3:2.

There was a change in the Roman administration after Agrippa's death in 44 CE, and Judea came under the procurators.[12] The change did not improve the situation for the Jews because the procurators incited the people through vindictive cruelty. The situation worsened in the time of Cumanus (48-52 CE) with the Roman administration becoming increasingly callous and unyielding, especially with procurators Albinus[13] and Gessius Florus.[14] Both of them were known for their insensitivity and clumsiness and were blamed for the Jewish uprising.[15]

Along with the repressive rule by the procurators, there existed also Jew-Gentile nexus particularly during the mid-first century as pointed out by Josephus.[16] The condition was such that the high priestly families, Herodians, and much of the affluent nobility, resorted to enhance their coactions with the Roman administration to gain dominance over Palestine.[17] The unholy alliance between the high priests, Herodians and Roman administration only left the common people at the mercy of circumstances. Instead of maintaining social order, the high priestly families[18] and Herodians[19] had their own group of ruffians who were engaged in internal battles, which clearly aggravated the disintegration of the social order.[20]

Thus, it is quite clear that the Roman administration lacked sensitivity to Jewish sentiments and its rule was oppressive. The Jewish administration did

---

[12] Josephus, "The Wars of the Jews," 2:12:1.

[13] Albinus plundered public and private funds, accepted bribes, and also allowed the *sicarii* to be ransomed from prisons. Josephus, "The War of the Jews," 2:14:1. George W. E. Nickelsburg, "Revolt-Destruction- Reconstruction," in *Jewish Literature between the Bible and the Mishnah: A Historical and Literary Introduction*, 2nd edition (Minneapolis: Fortress Press, 2005), 264.

[14] Florus retaliated savagely when the Jews could not endure his irritating treatment. Josephus notes, "...called out aloud to the soldiers to plunder that which was called the Upper Market Place, and to sly such as they met with. So the soldiers, taking this exhortation of their commander in a sense agreeable to their desire of gain, did not only plunder the place they were sent to, but forcing themselves into every house, they slew its inhabitants; ..." Josephus, "The War of the Jews," 2:14:8.

[15] F. F. Bruce, "Roman Administration," *ABD*, vol. 5, edited by David Noel Freedman (New York: Doubleday, 1997), 98.

[16] Josephus, "The Antiquities of the Jews," 20:8:9.

[17] Horsley and Hanson, *Bandits, Prophets and Messiahs*, 42. Josephus notes an incident where the high priests took away the tithes due to which the priests and the poorer priests died of want. Josephus, "The Antiquities of the Jews," 20:8:8.

[18] Josephus notes of how Ananias, the high priest, used his riches to gain supporters. Josephus, "The Antiquities of the Jews," 20:9:4.

[19] Josephus points that they used violence with the people. Josephus, "The Antiquities of the Jews," 20:9:4.

[20] Horsley and Hanson, *Bandits, Prophets and Messiahs*, 42.

not help the cause of those burdened by the Roman yoke. Rather, the nexus between the Romans and the ruling Jewish elite only drove more nails into the coffin. However, these political factors need to be understood in congruence with the socio-economic factors.

1.1.1.2. Socio-economic Factors

Together with political pressure, socio-economic factors played a vital role in precipitating the circumstances that led to the Jewish revolt. Palestine in the first century CE was predominantly a peasant community. The peasants became miserable, as they bore the brunt of a devastating famine of 48 CE along with the oppressive taxation by the procurators.[21] The Jewish agricultural producers were subjected to double taxation, in all likelihood totalling to more than 40 percent of their yield.[22] In addition to accepting their primary and traditional obligation of tithes and other dues to support the priesthood and temple apparatus, Roman tribute was superimposed on the tithes and other taxes owed to the temple and priesthood. It was seen by the peasants as a major drain on their resources. The high priests did not reduce their own taxation even though they no longer needed it to maintain military forces and political administration for an independent state.[23] Over and above this double taxation, the requirements of the Roman civil war occasioned the need for special levies of taxes, and huge amounts of money were collected immediately.[24]

Class tensions also prevailed allowing the rich to get richer and leaving the rest in dire poverty. The accrual of assets by the mighty priests and Herodians only increased the peasants' debts, dispossession of land and huge estates.[25] In addition to this, higher interest loans given to the needy peasants out of the surplus wealth that came and accumulated in Jerusalem from the contribution

[21] L. I. Levine, "Jewish War (66-73 CE)," *ABD*, vol. 3, edited by David Noel Freedman (New York: Doubleday, 1997, 1992), 839. Josephus reports of several famines: Famine in Judea in the 13th year of Herod's reign "The Antiquities of the Jews," 15:9:1.; another famine in the reign of Claudius, "The Antiquities of the Jews," 3:15:3, 20:2:6, 20:5:2; and famine in Jerusalem "The War of the Jews," 5:10:2.

[22] Horsley and Hanson, *Bandits, Prophets and Messiahs*, 56. Josephus notes of how in addition to the paying tithes to Hyrcanus, the Jews were asked to pay a tax for the city of Jerusalem. Josephus, "The Antiquities of the Jews," 14:10:6.

[23] Horsley and Hanson, *Bandits, Prophets and Messiahs*, 55-57.

[24] Josephus describes how Cassius demanded tribute of the cities and went to the extent that the Jews were not able to pay. Josephus, "The War of the Jews," 1:11:1.

[25] Horsley and Hanson, *Bandits, Prophets and Messiahs*, 60. Horsley notes of how the fertile area to the south of Galilee was in the hands of Herodian families, the ruler in Jerusalem or the Roman soldiers. Richard A. Horsley, *The Covenant Economics: A Biblical Vision of Justice for All* (Kentucky: Westminster John Knox Press, 2009), 91.

sent by the poor diaspora Jews to the temple, only led the poor peasants to losing their ancestral property to those to whom they owned money.[26]

The end result was the uprisings from the peasant communities. One of the ways the peasants reacted to the paralyzing situation around them was by getting involved in 'social banditry.'[27] Reactive movements surface when the state or local rulers become selfish and unbearable in their actions.[28] The bandits had the support of the Jewish peasants. The peasants not only supported and protected the bandits, but also held them in high esteem.[29]

The political and socio-economic situation presents a grim picture. Divisions and group orientations thrived on the disparate and appalling conditions of those not part of the aristocracy. These divisions split across the Jewish religious groups as well with some taking a passive stance (non-involvement), others supporting the Roman administration, and still others vehemently standing against all those in power and position, backed by the peasants and the common people. All of these religious groups had their own affiliations and thus were divisive. Importantly, the divisive elements ripped apart the integral aspect of the Jewish people. Not only was this seen as a dark blot in the events leading to the revolt, but it was also considered as something to be taken special note of by those who were involved in the formation of Judaism after the destruction of Jerusalem and the Temple.

1.1.1.3. Religious Factors

Prior to the destruction of the Temple in Jerusalem, there was a great deal of diversity as groups, sects, lived side by side with different levels of hostility in their relationship with each other.[30] In this regard, Saldarini rightly describes Jewish society as one filled with "…groups, coalitions, factions and interest groups who varied in practice, view point and strategy on major social issues."[31] The general atmosphere seems to have been conducive to it, especially at a time when the religious authorities worked hand in glove with the Romans. Sectarianism did greatly affect the unity in Judaism, and this was

---

[26] Horsley and Hanson, *Bandits, Prophets and Messiahs*, 55-60.

[27] This term is used by Horsley and Hanson to refer to those that were forced off their land by economic pressures, or who came into political trouble with the ruling groups banded together into "self-help" groups. Horsley and Hanson, *Bandits, Prophets and Messiahs*, 246. Josephus calls this group as 'robbers.' Josephus, "The War of the Jews," 2:12:2.

[28] Horsley and Hanson, *Bandits, Prophets and Messiahs*, 49. Josephus, "The Antiquities of the Jews," 20:5:1-2 and Josephus, "The Wars of the Jews," 2:12:2.

[29] Horsley and Hanson, *Bandits, Prophets and Messiahs*, 49.

[30] Goran Forkman, *Limits of the Religious Community: Expulsion from the Religious Community within the Qumran Sect, within Rabbinic Judaism and within Primitive Christianity*, translated by Pearl Sioelamder, ConBNT 5 (Sweden: CWK Gleerup Lund, 1972), 87.

[31] Saldarini, *Pharisees, Scribes and Sadducees*, 202.

an impediment to an orderly prosecution of a war against Rome. After 70 CE, sect[32] formation should be seen as a form of deviance, and in a society that included many interpretations of the prevailing system of belief, much of social activity involved conflicting social groups which often labeled one another deviant. Sects are not to be categorized as withdrawn protest groups but as active agents in society that kindle reactions among other groups and are often instrumental in creating changes in society. They, as Saldarini notes, made use of "...political protest and action and the exercise of power and influence and made allowance for several responses to social and cultural pressure."[33]

1.1.2. Sectarianism[34] in Judaism

The period between 165 BCE – 100 CE in Palestine was fluid and diverse. There emerged during that time a number of groups: Hasidim ("the pious"),

---

[32] Wilson created a working typology of seven kinds of sects, based on the group's relationship with its host society: a) the *conversionist* – look for the emotional transformation now. With salvation presumed to follow in the future after evil has been endured. Because of the alienation a new community is formed (Early Christians); b) the *revolutionist*- awaits the destruction of the social order by divine forces (ex. Apocalyptic groups); c) the *introversionist* – withdraws from the world into a purified community (ex. Essenes); d) the *manipulationist* – seeks happiness by a transformed subjective orientation which will control evil –ex. Gnostics; e) the *thaumaturgical response*- seeks relief from specific ills by special not general dispensations (ex. Magicians and healers); f) the *reformists* – seeks gradual, divinely revealed alterations in society (ex. Pharisees and Jesus could fit); g) the *utopian*- seeks to reconstruct the world according to divine principles without revolution. B. Wilson, *Magic and the Millennium: A Sociological Study of Religious Movements of Protest among Tribal and the Third-World Peoples* (London: Heinemann, 1973), 23-26.

[33] Saldarini, *Pharisees, Scribes and Sadducees*, 74-75.

[34] A "sect" is an organized group which separates itself from the community and asserts that it alone has religious truth. It must have authority figures, membership requirements, and various regulations. It must separate from the majority. The separation can be physical or merely ideological. Only its authority figures are authentic and only its teachings are true. It validates its claims internally and authenticates itself by a revelation or tradition unknown to outsiders. A sect usually has a ceremony of admission by which it clearly distinguishes members from non-members. Members are righteous, pure and destined for eternal bliss and non-members are wicked and destined for eternal damnation. Shaye J. D. Cohen, "The Significance of Yavneh: Pharisees, Rabbis, and the End of Jewish Sectarianism," *HUCA* 55 (Jan. 1984): 29-30. Blenkinsopp also notes "A sect is not only a minority, and not only characterized by opposition to norms accepted by the parent-body, but also claims in a more or less exclusive way to be what the parent-body claims to be. Whether such a group formally severs itself, or is excommunicated, will depend largely on the degree of self-definition attained by the parent body and the level of tolerance obtaining within it." Joseph Blenkinsopp, "Interpretation and the Tendency to Sectarianism: An Aspect of Second Temple History," in *Jewish and Christian Self-Definition*, vol. 2: *Aspects of Judaism in the Greco-Roman Period*, edited by E. P. Sanders, Albert I. Baumgarten, and Alan Mendelson (Philadelphia: Fortress Press, 1981), 1-2. Overman notes some of the characteristics of a sect, particularly, the use of dualistic language where the group refers to itself as 'the righteous' and those outside the sect are denounced as 'the wicked'

Sadducees, Pharisees, Essenes, Zealots, Sicarii ("the swordsmen"), and others. Some of them, including the Qumran community, thrived on the polemic against the Temple. Cohen notes "...a common feature of Jewish sectarianism is the polemic against the Temple of Jerusalem: its precincts are impure, its cult profane, and its priests illegitimate."[35] Further, the sects claimed exclusivity in identifying themselves as the unquestionable abode of God and those who understood the will of God and obeyed the Law rightly.[36] This period also witnessed widespread rejection of the Jewish leadership and there developed an antagonism between the Jewish authorities and the various groups. In such a context, obedience to the Law attained great implications; one such implication was that it helped them to be members of the covenant community.[37]

1.1.2.1. The Pharisees

The Pharisees, in a technical sense, cannot be categorized as a sect for they did not separate from society.[38] The etymology of 'Pharisee' is disputed.[39] The term Pharisees is used only by outsiders, Josephus and the New Testament.[40] The term Pharisees[41] is used only by outsiders (Josephus and the New Testament)

---

and this antithetical usage has a specific function of setting boundaries and identifies the nature of the insider and outsider. Overman, *Matthew's Gospel and Formative Judaism*, 17.

[35] Cohen, "The Significance of Yavneh:" 43.

[36] One of the aspects that appealed in favour of the sectarian group was the general understanding that the Second Temple seemed to be inauthentic as it was built by the support of a gentile king and without direct signs of divine grace. Cohen, "The Significance of Yavneh:" 43.

[37] Overman, *Matthew's Gospel and Formative Judaism*, 23-24.

[38] Joachim Jeremias, *Jerusalem in the Time of Jesus: An Investigation into the Economic and Social Conditions during the New Testament Period*, translated by F. H. and C. H. Cave (Philadelphia: Fortress Press, 1969), p. 230, n. 36. Saldarini in this regard notes that Josephus has been misinterpreted as arguing for Pharisees and Sadducees as sects. The reason for misunderstanding pertains to the use of the term *hairesis* which meant a way of life or a particular school of thought. Saldarini, *Pharisees, Scribes and Sadducees*, 123.

[39] Albert I. Baumgarten, "The Name of the Pharisees," *JBL* 102/3 (Summer 1983): 411-412.

[40] Wenham and Walton note that unfortunately the gospels present the Pharisees as "'bad guys'" which is was not how they were understood; they were rather understood as pious Jews. David Wenham and Steve Walton, *Exploring the New Testament: A Guide to the Gospels & Acts*, vol. 1 (Illinois: InterVarsity Press, 2001), 39. Basser notes that in order to portray Jesus as the revolutionary, the gospels show that Pharisees have a hidden interest in persecuting and killing Jesus. Herbert W. Basser, *Studies in Exegesis: Christian Critiques of Jewish Law and Rabbinic Responses 70-300 CE*, The Brill Reference Library of Ancient Judaism, vol. 2, edited by Jacob Neusner (Leiden: Brill, 2000), 16.

[41] The name seems to come from the Hebrew and Aramaic root *prš* which means "separate" and "interpret." The most common etymological interpretation of Pharisees is "separate ones," though separate from whom or what is disputed. Rabbinic literature uses the term in two ways – a. those separated from normal Jewish society or from gentile society in order to observe Jewish law (purity, tithing?) more rigorously; b. it would also mean sectarians or heretics, that

though Pharisees belonged to a prominent group that existed before the destruction of the Temple, and also played a pivotal role in the absence of the Temple. [42]

It must be noted that the tannaitic authors do not identify themselves as Pharisees.[43] A historical description of the Pharisees remains a distant possibility as the sources are unclear.[44] For Horsley,[45] the Pharisees' origin can be traced to the Hasidim;[46] they were those that did not join the Qumran community, but still reacted differently to the handling of political and religious authority by the Hasmoneans.

The Pharisees are first mentioned by Josephus in the reign of John Hyrcanus, which was a period of conflict.[47] It is probable that they had some kind of internal organization. Josephus[48] describes this condition of the Pharisees. He notes that they wanted Hyrcanus to relinquish the high priesthood because

---

is, people who separated themselves illegitimately from society at large because of beliefs and practices judged illegitimate. Another meaning of the name is "interpreters;" this would comply with the understanding in Josephus and the New Testament where Pharisees had their own interpretation and were considered accurate interpreters of the law. Saldarini, *Pharisees, Scribes and Sadducees*, 221.

[42] Saldarini states, "It is very likely that the pre-70 Pharisees contributed to the emergence of the post-70 rabbis, but evidence is not abundant." Saldarini, *Pharisees, Scribes and Sadducees*, 8.

[43] Cohen, "The Significance of Yavneh:" 37. In this regard Gafni states, "To be sure, the Sages usually refrain from referring to themselves as 'Pharisees', using this name preferably in connection with their Sadducean adversaries. They clearly preferred the title 'Sages'; moreover, in drawing the chain of rabbinic tradition they preferred to designate persons rather than groups or parties." Isaiah Gafni, "The Historical Background" in *The Literature of the Sages*, Part One, CRINT 3, edited by Shmuel Safari (Philadelphia: Fortress Press, 1987), 8.

[44] Rivkin notes, "Josephus is both explicit and hazy, the New Testament hostile and blurring and the tannatic sources tantalizingly obscure." Ellis Rivkin, "Defining the Pharisees: the Tannaitic Sources." *HUCA* 40-41 (1969-1970): 205. Neusner also agrees that describing the Pharisees is not easy. The Jews tend to praise the Pharisees as the source of wisdom and learning because the Jews also trace their religious traditions to the Pharisees. Protestants emphasize the legalism of the Pharisees. Therefore, much that is said about the Pharisees by way of historical narratives (Josephus) or the biographical traditions about Jesus reflect the situation, interests and point of view of the author. Jacob Neusner, *Judaism in the Beginning of Christianity* (London: SPCK, 1984), 45-47.

[45] Horsley and Hanson, *Bandits, Prophets and Messiahs*, 26.

[46] Hasidim was a Jewish sect that fostered the maintenance of the Jewish ritual and the discipline of the Torah. David Solomon, "Pharisees," *EncJud*, vol. 16, edited by Fred Skolnik (New York: Keter Publishing House, 2007), 30. This view is also espoused by Brownlee. William Hugh Brownlee, "The Wicked Priest, the Man of Lies and the Righteous Teacher- the Problem of Identity," *JQR* 73/1 (Jl. 1982): 24.

[47] Samuel Sandmel, *Judaism and Christian Beginnings* (New York: Oxford University Press, 1978), 159.

[48] Josephus, "The Antiquities of the Jews," 13.9.1-10.3.

he was from a non-Zadokite family. For this reason, Hyrcanus rejected the Pharisees as clients and allies and accepted the Sadducees in their place. The consequence was great for the Pharisees; Hyrcanus got rid of the regulations peculiar to the Pharisees and punished those who observed them. The people who followed the Pharisees eventually came to hate Hyrcanus and his sons.

Things changed for worse under the reign of Alexander Jannaeus (104-76 BCE) when many of the Pharisees had to flee the country and remain in exile until his death.[49] Alexander, however, in his final speech to his wife, admits that his conflict with the people was partly caused by his mistreatment of the Pharisees, who had the ability to hurt or help people by influencing public opinion, though sometimes they acted out of envy. He asks her to promise him that she will not take any action, while she rules, without the consent of the Pharisees.[50] Thus, during the time of Alexandra, the Pharisees returned to power and played a role in the governing council. The queen gave the Pharisees legal support for their particular interpretation of Judaism and some direct power to run internal affairs. The Pharisees used their power to attack their rivals, the old governing class. Saldarini notes that after the death of Alexandra, the Pharisees disappeared from the scene but occupied a significant position in Herod's court and received support from him. [51]

The Pharisees were known for their religious piety, especially their penetrating influence among the common masses with ardour of holiness and total allegiance to both the written and oral Law.[52] The positive aspect of the pharisaic community consisted in conducting organized fellowships where the followers observed the rules of tithing and ritual purity[53] and the study of the Torah. In this regard, Forkman notes that though they were comprised of the laity, they reacted against all those who flouted the rules they observed

[49] Josephus, "The Antiquities of the Jews," 13:14:2.

[50] Josephus, "The Antiquities of the Jews," 13.15.5.

[51] Saldarini, *Pharisees, Scribes and Sadducees*, 95. Jacob Neusner is of the view that the Pharisees ceased to be politically active group, and left the political arena during the time of Herod and the Romans and took on a more sectarian characteristic. Jacob Neusner, *From Politics to Piety: The Emergence of Pharisaic Judaism* (New Jersey: Prentice-Hall, Inc., 1973), 65-66. But Saldrini disagrees with Neusner on the count that this separation of the political and religious is too sharp. Also, the fact that the Pharisees were a politically and religiously based group in a complex society and were always interested in political power and always a factor in society at large. That the Pharisees did survive after the reign of Herod as a political force is attested to by the presence of Pharisees among the Jerusalem leaders at the beginning of the war with Rome and on the delegation sent from Jerusalem to Josephus in Galilee. Saldarini, *Pharisees, Scribes and Sadducees*, 132-133.

[52] Solomon, "Pharisees:" 30. Josephus notes, "…Pharisees have delivered to the people a great many observances by succession from their father, which are not written in the law of Moses…" Josephus, "The Antiquities of the Jews," 13:10:6.

[53] Forkman, *Limits of the Religious Community*, 87.

meticulously. In the context of the importance given to rules of purity, it is reasonable to suppose with Forkman that the Pharisees practiced banning but these applied only within the pharisaic fellowships.[54] The leaders of the pharisaic community were the scribes who appointed the guidelines for contacts with others.[55] Further, they sought to replicate the altar of the Lord in their table fellowship[56] which remained the high climax of the community's existence.[57] However, they always sought to modulate with the governing class and were dependent on the rulers for their position in society.[58]

The Pharisees believed in free will coupled with predestination, resurrection of the dead as well as reward and punishment in this life and the next.[59] For Rivkin, the Pharisees' teaching helped in protecting the Jewish way of life in the Greco-Roman period from falling out and promised individual life beyond death.[60] The Pharisees pursued good dealings with everyone, treated with respect their traditions and elders, and thus were able to garner a great many followers.[61] Newman notes that there are two terms that are often associated with the Pharisees - *paradosis* and *akribeia*. He notes, "These terms imply accuracy and excellence in interpreting and observing the *mitzvoth*."[62]

To conclude, as Saldarini points out, the Pharisees probably functioned as a "...social movement organization seeking to change society."[63] Thus, if the Pharisees are taken to be a sect, they need to be taken as a group which was religiously centered yet did not brush aside its public involvement in the

---

[54] Forkman, *Limits of the Religious Community*, 103.

[55] Forkman, *Limits of the Religious Community*, 88.

[56] Cohen, "The Significance of Yavneh:" 44.

[57] Howard Clark Kee, "The Transformation of the Synagogue after 70 CE: Its Import for Early Christianity," *NTS* 36/1 (Jan. 1990): 6.

[58] They were not monastic as a community or as a withdrawn sect which demanded primary and total commitment from every member. It is most likely that Pharisees were bound together by certain beliefs and practices and by endeavors to influence social change. A member of the Pharisees retained his family and territorial allegiances, his roles in society and occupation, his friends and network of associates. Saldarini, *Pharisees, Scribes and Sadducees*, 39.

[59] Solomon, "Pharisees:" 30.

[60] Ellis Rivkin, "Defining the Pharisees:" 205-249. Rivkin has been criticized by Saldarini for grouping together texts that come from rabbinic sources spanning several centuries. In his analysis he takes each Pharisees-Sadducees text as historically reliable and takes no account of the kind of collection it comes from, nor place, nor date. Saldarini, *Pharisees, Scribes and Sadducees*, 230.

[61] Saldarini, *Pharisees, Scribes and Sadducees*, 122.

[62] Hillel Newman, *Proximity to Power and Jewish Sectarian Groups of the Ancient Period: A Review of Lifestyle, Values and Halakah in the Pharisees, Sadducees, Essenes and Qumran*, edited by Ruth Ludlam, Brill Reference Library of Judaism 25, edited by Allen J. Avery-Peck and William Scott Green (Leiden: Brill, 2006), 54.

[63] Saldarini, *Pharisees, Scribes and Sadducees*, 95.

society.[64] The active role of the Pharisees continued into the second century without violence, and they helped their followers to live according to the Torah.[65] They also had their belief centered on eschatology-the coming of the descendant of God.[66]

1.1.2.2. The Sadducees[67]

The end of the relationship between the Pharisees and Hyrcanus signaled the emergence of Sadducees. Jonathan the Sadducee was instrumental in bringing the Sadducees to power under John Hyrcanus.[68] The sect was formed in the second half of the Second Temple period, about 200 BCE.[69] Unlike the Pharisees, the Sadducees considered the Law as sufficient for social existence, i.e., the written Law without the oral law and therefore excluded the legal interpretation popularized by the Pharisees.[70]

The term 'Sadducees' comes from the Greek name Σαδδουκαῖοι and the Hebrew *Ṣaddûqîm* (with variant forms), which do not lend any perception of their identity.[71] Only a negligent number of Sadducees were present in the governing class, yet they had the recognition of a well accomplished group among the first century Jews.[72] They exerted a great deal of influence in the

---

[64] Anthony J. Saldarini, "Pharisees" *ABD*, vol. 5, edited by David Noel Freedman, (New York: Double Day, 1992), 302.

[65] Solomon, "Pharisees:" 30.

[66] D. Mendels, "Pseudo-Philo's *Biblical Antiquities*, The "Fourth Philosophy," and the Political Messianism of the First Century CE" in *The Messiah: Developments in Earliest Judaism and Christianity*, edited by James H. Charlesworth, et.al. (Minneapolis: Fortress Press, 1992), 265.

[67] Though, Sadducees are dealt as a part of sectarianism in Judaism, in a strict sense they cannot be called a sect as the Sadducees represented a sub-group of the governing class and interpreted on how society should run.

[68] Saldarini, *Pharisees, Scribes and Sadducees*, 105.

[69] Menahem Mansoor, "Sadducees," *EncJud*, vol. 17, edited by Fred Skolnik (New York: Keter Publishing House, 2007), 654.

[70] Horsley and Hanson, *Bandits, Prophets and Messiahs*, 28. Porton brings an interesting comment in this regard, the issue of contention between the Sadducees and Pharisees centered on the issue of purity. Gary G. Porton, "Sadducees," *ABD*, vol. 5, edited by David Noel Freedman (New York: Doubleday, 1992), 893.

[71] Saldarini, *Pharisees, Scribes and Sadducees*, 225-226. Two explanations of the name have been proposed. The more popular explanation recently has been to connect the term Sadducee with the Sadokites, the high priestly family which traced its ancestry to David's high priest, Sadok. Thus, Sadducees would be either the Sadokites priests or partisans of the Sadokites. However, the forms of the name extant in Greek Hebrew and Aramaic do not give clear support to this hypothesis. The other hypothesis is that the name is descriptive and characterizes this group as the "just" or "righteous," either as a positive or ironic description. No explanation has been definitively proven.

[72] Saldarini, *Pharisees, Scribes and Sadducees*, 302.

councils of the Jews and were generally wealthy. Their influence is seen in their hand-in-glove role with the Roman power, and this they did in order to insure themselves under the Roman rule.[73] In a certain sense, they had a catalytic function in the first Jewish revolt. Thus, they were weary of the revolutionaries who were against the establishment.

In their doctrines, the Sadducees conceived that God acted independently.[74] God was understood not as transcendent but in "anthropomorphic terms."[75] They anchored their belief system on God's covenant and the covenantal provision but emphasised human intervention in the affairs of existence. They echoed an attitude of aloofness of God from the affairs of this world. As Josephus notes, "...they take away fate ...they suppose that all our actions are in our own power, so that we are ourselves the cause of what is good, and receive what is evil from our own folly."[76] This prompted them to preserve the state of affairs as it is and work against any change in the situation.[77] However, they valued the sacrificial cult and held sway over the affairs of the Temple.[78]

1.1.2.3. The Scribes

The scribes were not a well-coordinated group, different from their presentation in the synoptic gospels (to mention a few references - Matt. 2:4; 5:20; 7:29; Lk. 5:21, 30; 6:7; Mark 8:31; 9:11, 14).[79] They did not belong to a religious sect or a political party but rather represented the professional class.[80] In rabbinic literature, the scribes are presented as those who were the teachers of Israel prior to the rabbis. They were also copyists.[81]

The Hebrew word for scribe, *sôfēr*, participle form of the root *spr*, denotes 'to count' and is a likely cognate to Akkadian *šāpiru*, meaning "secretary, official."[82] Another term used in this connection is *shoṭer*, a derivative of the cognate Akkadian *šatāru*, "to write," and is used in Hebrew to mean *sheṭar*,

---

[73] David Wenham and Steve Walton, *Exploring the New Testament*, 41.

[74] Saldarini, *Pharisees, Scribes and Sadducees*, 122. They rejected the idea of resurrection and took to believing that souls end with the bodies. David Wenham and Steve Walton, *Exploring the New Testament*, 40. Josephus notes, "But the doctrine of the Sadducees is this: That souls die with the bodies..." Josephus, "The Antiquities of the Jews," 18:1:4.

[75] Mansoor, "Sadducees:" 654.

[76] Josephus, "The Antiquities of the Jews," 13:5:9.

[77] Saldarini, *Pharisees, Scribes and Sadducees*, 304.

[78] Mansoor, "Sadducees:" 655.

[79] Saldarini, *Pharisees, Scribes and Sadducees*, 241.

[80] Robert H. Gundry, *A Survey of the New Testament*, 4th edition (Grand Rapids, Michigan: Zondervan Publishing House, 2003), 67.

[81] Saldarini, *Pharisees, Scribes and Sadducees*, 241.

[82] Aaron Demsky, "Scribes," *EncJud*, vol. 18, edited by Fred Skolnik (New York: Keter Publishing House, 2007): 212.

"a written document" (Job 38:33).[83] The Greek word for scribe, *grammateus*, means written letters.[84]

In terms of social involvement, the scribes represent a broad segment. They worked for the king, the Temple, and the establishment, and were drawn from the Priests, Levites,[85] Pharisees,[86] aristocrats as well as the people.[87] The scribes played an important role in wisdom writings, the prophetic writings and the Pentateuch. They occasionally concurred with priestly and apocalyptic association.[88] It is noted that, until the end of the Second-Temple period, the title *grammateus* was interpreted as having definitive rendering of the Scriptures and proficiency in the Law.[89]

What role did the scribes play? The scribes do not constitute a class by themselves and had several roles ranging from the village to the palace and the Temple,[90] and so were reckoned neither a political nor a religious force.[91]

1.1.2.4. The Qumran Community

Unlike the others discussed earlier, the Qumran sect was more exclusive in their approach. Horsley and Hanson assume that the Essenes,[92] the group from

---

[83] Aaron Demsky, "Scribes:" 212.

[84] Saldarini, *Pharisees, Scribes and Sadducees*, 241-242. Schams reasons the partial portrait of the scribes in Josephus, synoptics, Mishna, Tosefta, and Targumim to the interests of the authors and compilers of these sources. Christine Schams, *Jewish Scribes in the Second-Temple Period*, JSOT Sup 291, edited by David J. A. Clines and Philip R. Davies (Sheffield: Sheffield Academic Press, 1991), 311.

[85] Schams is of the view some of the scribes were drawn from either Priests or Levites. Schams, *Jewish Scribes in the Second-Temple Period*, 323.

[86] The scribes of the Pharisees made specific examples of the general laws of the Torah and one example of this is seen in defining of what constituted work on the Sabbath. Burkett, *An Introduction to the New Testament*, 46.

[87] Saldarini, *Pharisees, Scribes and Sadducees*, 273.

[88] Saldarini, *Pharisees, Scribes and Sadducees*, 273.

[89] Schams, *Jewish Scribes in the Second-Temple Period*, 325.

[90] Anthony J. Saldarini, "Scribes," *ABD*, vol. 5, edited by David Noel Freedman (New York: Doubleday, 1992), 1014.

[91] Saldarini, *Pharisees, Scribes and Sadducees*, 276.

[92] Josephus describes their manners, rites and doctrines thus: a. all the best things are attributed to God; b. they teach the immortality of the souls and also hold highly the rewards of righteousness; c. they offer their own sacrifices according to their approved purity ritual; d. Josephus uses the phrase "addict themselves to virtue" to describe their religiosity; e. they had an institution of holding all things in common so as to remove any inequality; f. they do not marry nor keep servants in order to avoid them being unjust, rather they minister to each other; g. stewards are appointed to collect their income and the fruit of their labour. Josephus, "The Antiquities of the Jews," 18:1:5; g. they are Jews by birth and esteem exercise self-constraint in sexual matters; h. though they overlook wedlock, they do not deny fitness of marriage; i. they

which the Qumran community emerged and withdrew to the wilderness,[93] and the Pharisees surfaced from the Jewish group called the Hasidim during the time when Hasmoneans founded their illegitimate high priesthood and kingship.[94]

There were many reasons for the withdrawal of the Qumran community to the wilderness. The first was a direct response to the unlawful institution of

---

consider oil as defilement; j. they do not buy or sell to one another as everyone is allowed to take whatever they want from the other; Josephus, "The War of the Jews," 2:8:2ff.

[93] The first hypothesis that the Qumran community was part and parcel of the wider Essene movement was proposed by Eleazar L. Sukenik, Megillot Genuzot: Mi-tokh Genizah Kedumah she-Nimtseah be-Midbar Yehudah vol. 1 (2 vols.; Jerusalem: Bialik, 1948), 16 cited in Kenneth Atkinson and Jodi Magness, "Josephus' Essenes and the Qumran Community" *JBL* 129/2 (Summer 2010): 317. Burkett gives two reasons why those that living at Qumran were Essenes: a. Pliny (23-79 CE) notes that the Essenes lived in that place during his time; b. the beliefs and practices described in the scrolls coincide with the description of Essenes. Burkett, *An Introduction to the New Testament*, 48. The deduction of Essenes to Qumran is not without its share of problems. The Qumran community did not call themselves as Essenes nor is the name Essene mentioned in the manuscripts. Humbert notes that the deduction can be stated on three counts: "ancient authors, manuscript and site." Jean-Baptiste Humbert, "An Essene Identity at Qumran" in *NEA* 63/3 (Sep. 2000): 174. Those who oppose the view such as Stoutenburg who note that the archaeological and textual basis are not congruent with sectarian community detailed in the scrolls. There are two reasons for this: a. The War Scrolls describe the strategies, imposition, etc., but Essenes are noted for peace loving nature; b. Palm trees are associated with the Essenes which becomes impossibility with regards to the background of the Dead Sea Scrolls. She notes that the similarity between Essenes and Qumran is due to the climate of the Second Temple period. Dennis Stoutenburg, review of *Qumran and the Essenes: A Re-Evaluation of the Evidence, Texte und Studien zum Antiken Judentum 60*, by Lena Cansdale, Διδασκαλία 13/2 (Spring 2002): 109. There are others who go beyond the Essene hypothesis; Boccaccini is of the view that the Qumran community was influenced by the "Enochic Judaism." Eckhard J. Schnabel, review of *Beyond the Essene Hypothesis: The Parting of the Ways between Qumran and Enochic Judaism*, by Gabriele Boccaccini, *JBL* 120/2 (Summer 2001): 372-373. Broshi and Esher after having discussed twelve theories on the identity of the Qumran Community (these include: Essene monastery, Christians, *Forgery*, Pharisees, Qaraites, Sadducees, Zealots, agricultural establishment, A Caravanserai and a commercial entrepot, A Fort, Papyrus processing plants, Agnostics) conclude that the identity of the authors and the owners of the Dead Sea Scrolls are inconclusive. Magen Broshi and Hanan Esher, "Qumran and the Dead Sea Scrolls: The Contention of Twelve Theories" in *Religion and Society in Roman Palestine: Old Questions, New Approaches*, edited by Douglas R. Edwards (New York: Routledge, 2004), 162-169. How then is one to conclude on the relation between Essenes and the Qumran Community? The persuasive arguments proposed by Atkinson and Magness, who draw the relation between Josephus, scrolls and archaeological evidences and thus argue for the Essene *hypothesis*, seems to provide the best solution. Evidences are noted in several areas by them, and these include: ragged clothing, spitting, community meals, Sabbath Observance, toilets and toilet habits, oil and bathing. Atkinson and Magness, "Josephus' Essenes:" 317, 326-341.

[94] Horsley and Hanson, *Bandits, Prophets and Messiahs*, 23-24.

the high priesthood by the Hasmoneans,[95] so they could organize themselves for the coming kingdom of God.[96] The community anticipated a time when the members could celebrate the cult, the offerings, and the sacred calendar in the temple that would be erected by God. However, the community considered the sect itself as the temple.[97] The second is somewhat related to the first. The community's aspiration to establish a legitimate kingdom of God focused on the Jerusalem Temple as it was subsumed and thus the community sought to mobilize a "legitimate" priesthood centered on a "Righteous Teacher."[98] The community, through its writings, objurgated the leadership in Jerusalem and looked for divine vindication through a holy war. If this happened, the faithfulness of the community would find vindication while the apostasy of the priests and religious leadership would suffer punishment.[99]

The Qumran sectarians followed a combination of the law and sectarian regulations which set themselves against the outsiders. The legal laws operated as sociological boundary markers.[100] In the Qumran *halakhah*, the law was distinguished in terms of *nigleh* and *nistar*, which defined the sectarian aspect of the community.[101] The former refers to the written Torah which contains laws available to all Jews while the latter is the 'hidden' law revealed only to the sectarians through divinely inspired study sessions as part of the progressive revelation of God's will.[102] Thus, one of the primary features of the sectarian outlook is that the accurate knowledge of the will of God is the possession of only the members of the group. This understanding is linked with their understanding of eschatological expectations. As members of the *new* covenant, they were always in a state of readiness.[103] The final fulfillment involved three principal eschatological agents – the coming of the prophet and the anointed (ones) of Aaron and Israel.[104] According to them, the rest of the people of Israel were predestined for doom as they lacked the teachings of

---

[95] Michael O. Wise, "Dating the Teacher of Righteousness and the Floruit of his Movement," *JBL* 122/1 (Spring 2003): 86.

[96] Horsley and Hanson, *Bandits, Prophets and Messiahs*, 24.

[97] Cohen, "The Significance of Yavneh:" 44.

[98] Horsley and Hanson, *Bandits, Prophets and Messiahs*, 24-25.

[99] G. Vermes, *The Dead Sea Scrolls in English*, 2nd ed. (New York: Penguin, 1975), 96.

[100] Lawrence H. Schiffman, "Halakhah and Sectarianism in the Dead Sea Scrolls," in *The Dead Sea Scrolls in their Historical Context*, edited by Timothy H. Lim et al. (London: T & T Clark International, 2000), 131.

[101] Schiffman, "Halakhah and Sectarianism," 133.

[102] Schiffman, "Halakhah and Sectarianism," 133.

[103] As a mark of preparation for the coming of the kingdom of God, they observed regular ritual bathing and regularly conducted the eschatological ritual of a messianic banquet. Horsley and Hanson, 26.

[104] Horsley and Hanson, *Bandits, Prophets and Messiahs*, 102-103.

the sectarian law, making them inadequate to participate in the eschatological banquet occasioned for them. Thus, the *halakhah*, sectarianism and eschatology are invariably connected with the Qumran sectarians.[105]

1.1.2.5. The Fourth Philosophy[106]

The Fourth Philosophy was a group that aligned with pharisaic characteristics with the exception of martyrdom, i.e., "God is to be their only Ruler and Lord"[107] and therefore nothing else matters. Horsley and Hanson note[108] that their resistance to Rome was based on four interconnected aspects: a) to pay taxes to Rome was considered as slavery for the Jews; b) this was because they believed that their existence was under the dominion of God; c) they also believed that all things depend on God's providential guidance, yet did not deny human responsibility; d) finally, they had a particular eschatological thinking - by obeying the eschatological will of God that they could be a catalyst in the arrival the Kingdom of God. Josephus does not mention anything about them being engaged in actions of violence or revolution. Rather, they prepared to suffer violence and death as a result of their resistance.[109]

1.1.2.6. The Sicarii

Josephus describes the emergence of the Sicarii with the arrival of Festus in Judea.[110] They were called so as they made use of Roman *sicae* to strike many people.[111] Their goal was similar to that of the Fourth Philosophy. They wanted to erase the Roman rule from Palestine, yet they also targeted the Herodian fortresses and the Jewish ruling elite – the priestly aristocracy, the Herodian families and other notables. They did this because of the nexus between the Jewish elite and the Roman imperial system that only led to increased oppression of the common people.[112] In their attempts to rid the injustice done to the common people and get their support, they

---

[105] Schiffman, "Halakhah and Sectarianism," 133.

[106] The term is assigned by Josephus to denote the fourth sect of Jewish philosophy that was championed by Judas, the Galilean. The group figures fourth in the list of sectarians. The others are Pharisees, Sadducees, and Essenes. Josephus, "The Antiquities of the Jews," 18:1:6.

[107] Josephus, "The Antiquities of the Jews," 18:1:6.

[108] Horsley and Hanson, *Bandits, Prophets and Messiahs*, 192-194.

[109] Josephus, "The Antiquities of the Jews,"18:1:1.

[110] Josephus, "The Antiquities of the Jews," 20:8:10. Horsley and Hanson are of the view that they began operation in the fifties in Jerusalem. Horsley and Hanson, *Bandits, Prophets and Messiahs*, 200.

[111] Josephus, "The Antiquities of the Jews," 20:8:10.

[112] Horsley and Hanson, *Bandits, Prophets and Messiahs*, 205.

burned the archives that contained the record of debts.[113] Horsley and Hanson note that the Sicarii made use of three strategies:[114] a) "selective, symbolic assassinations" seen in the case of the assassination of the high priest Jonathan who was considered as the symbol of the Jewish nation, but was the one who joined hands with Roman administration and oppressed the people; b) they targeted those who supported the Roman aristocracy, especially the powerful members of the Jewish society, and ruined their property; c) kidnapping the servants of Ananias's servants in order to secure the release of their own members in prison.[115] Though this was the case, the Sicarii played a passing and limited role in the actual revolt as they did not initiate it but only joined the rebels who had captured the Jewish elites.[116] It was not the Sicarii who captured the fortress of Masada from the Roman garrison there. In fact, the deed can be attributed to a number of "rebels" and "revolutionary" groups who were active in the summer of 66 CE.[117]

1.1.2.7. The Zealots[118]

From the accounts of Josephus,[119] one can assume that the Zealots came to power in response to Roman conquest of Judea in 67-68 CE.[120] They were an

[113] Josephus notes, "…set fire to the house of Ananias, the high priest, and to the palaces of Agrippa and Bernice; after which they carried the fire to the place where the archives were reposited, and made haste to burn the contracts belonging to their creditors, and thereby dissolve their obligations for paying their debts; and this was done, in order to gain the multitude of those who had been debtors, and that they might persuade the poorer sort to join in the insurrection…" Josephus, "The War of the Jews," 2:17:4.

[114] Horsley and Hanson, *Bandits, Prophets and Messiahs*, 205-206.

[115] Josephus notes, "… for the robbers perpetually contrived to catch some of Ananias's servants; and when they had taken then aloe, they would not let them go till they thereby recovered some of their own *sicarii*…" Josephus, "The Antiquities of the Jews," 20:9:3.

[116] Josephus, "The War of the Jews," 2:17:5.

[117] Josephus, "The War of the Jews," 2:17:1-2.

[118] The identity of the "Zealots" remains a bone of contention for the historian: It is not clear whether they refer to the Jewish revolutionaries in general who waged war against the Romans or one of the groups, in particular, who were actively involved in the resistance movement against the Romans. Going with Rhoads, it can be said that Zealots were one of the many subversive groups active in the Jewish revolt. David Rhoads, "Zealots," *ABD*, vol. 6, edited by David Noel Freedman (New York: Double Day, 1992), 1045, 1047.

[119] Horsley and Hanson have rightly noted the prejudice of Josephus in narrating the role of Zealots. Zealots are portrayed by Josephus as history's most wicked groups and this is because they attacked Chief Priests and Pharisees including Josephus. Horsley and Hanson, *Bandits, Prophets and Messiahs*, 217. Rhoads too gives three reasons why Josephus' account of the Zealots is faulty. See Rhoads, "Zealots," 1046.

[120] Josephus, "The Wars of the Jews," 4:3:2-4.

alignment of armed and bandit groups.[121] Zealots were peasants who were hard pressed by the Roman legions and, since they were devoid of any alternatives, formed an organized coalition.[122] Josephus mentions two reasons for the Zealots assailing the ruling class of Judea. The first reason had to do with the class conflict that was taking a toll on the Jewish society while[123] the other reason could be that the nobles were betraying the city to the Romans.[124] They formed their central office in the temple and had an egalitarian administration.[125]

1.1.3. Other Movements in Palestine

It is clear that there was a mushrooming of different groups in Palestine during the Roman rule. The early Christian communities were also seen as sects within Judaism, so were included among the rest such as Pharisees, Sadducees, Zealots, and so on.[126] Overman and Green[127] are of the view that the time of turmoil in Palestine saw the rise of many popular leaders who were referred to by various terms such as "king,"[128] "prophets," and "messiah."

---

[121] Josephus, "The Wars of the Jews," 4:3:3-4. There seems to be disagreement among the origins and goals of the alignment of the Zealots. One groups of scholars such as G. Baumbach, M. Stern, D. Rhoads argue for the origin as a continuation of the priestly group under Eleazar son of Ananias and the Zealots as those who desired to cleanse the city and the temple. The other group of scholars, R. Smith and R. Horsley, note that the Zealots were refuges and bandit groups who ran away to Jerusalem at the conquest of Vespasian. Their goal was establishing an "egalitarian leadership." Rhoads is right when he states that possibly the Zealots are a combination of both these views, that is, they were a combination of the Eleazar forces and the refuge groups from Judea. Rhoads, "Zealots," 1049.

[122] Horsley and Hanson, *Bandits, Prophets and Messiahs*, 241.

[123] Josephus, "The Wars of the Jews," 4:5:4. Horsley and Hanson rightly understand this in terms of the exploitation of the Herodian nobles on the weaker sections of the Jewish society. Horsley and Hanson, *Bandits, Prophets and Messiahs*, 225.

[124] Josephus states, "Before these was Zacharias accused of a design to betray their polity to the Romans, and having traitorously sent to Vespasian for that purpose." Josephus, "The Wars of the Jews," 4:5:4.

[125] Rhoads, "Zealots," 1048. Horsley and Hanson are of the view that the Zealots were not priests but knew their sacred traditions. Horsley and Hanson, *Bandits, Prophets and Messiahs*, 241.

[126] George M. Smiga, *Pain and Polemic: Anti-Judaism in the Fourth Gospel* (New York: Paulist Press, 1992), 5.

[127] J. Andrew Overman and William Scott Green, "Judaism in the Greco-Roman Period," *ABD*, vol. 3, edited by David Noel Freedman (New York: Doubleday, 1992), 1044-1045.

[128] Josephus notes in "The War of the Jews," 2:17:8 – "In the meantime one Manahem, the son of Judas, that was called the Galilean (who was a very cunning sophister, and had formerly approached the Jews under Cyrenius, that after God they were subject to the Romans) took some of them and retired to Masada…and returned in the state of a king to Jerusalem." The same is said of Anthronges, "…but one in all respects been a shepherd only, and was not known by anybody; yet because he was a tall man, and excelled others in the strength of his hands, he was so bold as to set up for a king." Josephus, "The Antiquities of the Jews," 17:10:7.

More importantly, the rise of prophetic, messianic and apocalyptic movements did affect the situation in Palestine. However, it must be said that the popular movements were not the reasons for the revolt but rather indicators of the degenerating political and socio-economic condition.[129]

1.1.3.1. Prophetic Movements[130]

Popular prophetic movements took on special features during the time of unrest in the first century CE in Palestine.[131] The prophets articulated the message that, in spite of being the people of God, they had gone away from following the Laws of God and have incurred upon themselves impending judgment. Their message also stressed the hope of exoneration and restoration.[132] Josephus describes Theudas who was a prophet of God but was captured and beheaded by Fadus, the governor of Judea.[133] He also mentions another Egyptian prophet who, in his opinion, was a false prophet;[134] he rallied about thirty thousand men to overthrow the Roman garrison but was defeated by Felix, at the end of which he sped away.[135]

The followers of these prophetic movements came primarily from the peasants and these movements arose from dissatisfaction among the common

---

[129] Horsley and Hanson, *Bandits, Prophets and Messiahs*, 255.

[130] Horsley calls the prophetic movements as distinct ones. He states, "…these prophets, while also messengers of God, do not simply announce the will of God but (a) lead actions of deliverance; (b) involving "revolutionary changes;" (c) in accord with God's "design;" and (d) corresponding to one of the great historical formative acts of deliverance led by Moses or Joshua." Richard A. Horsley, ""Messianic" Figures and Movements in First-Century Palestine," in *The Messiah: Developments in Earliest Judaism and Christianity*, edited by James H. Charlesworth (Minneapolis: Fortress Press, 1992), 282.

[131] Horsley notes that these prophetic movements were distinct in several ways: a. their actions/events need to be understood not their intentions; b. they were leaders of movements; c. signs are the vital aspect of these movements; d. they participated in the God's action. Richard A. Horsley, "Popular Prophetic Movements in the time of Jesus: their Principal features and Social Origins" *JSNT* 26 (Feb. 1986): 3, 5-10.

[132] Saldarini, "Judaism in the Greco-Roman Period," 1045.

[133] Josephus calls Theudas a magician whose head was cut off and carried to Jerusalem. Josephus, "The Antiquities of the Jews," 20:5:1.

[134] Horsley notes in this regard, that though Josephus caricatures the prophets as false and cheats, yet he uses language with reference to them that assumes seriousness in terms of their message and movements. He further notes, "He portrays the first-century prophets in exactly the same terms as he portrays Moses: just as Moses did signs of liberation (σημεία της ελευθερίας) in accordance with God's providence (πρόνοια του θεού), so did the first-century prophets (cf. *A* J. 2.286, 327, and 20.168; *BJ.* 2.259)… Josephus not only writes the speeches which he places in the mouths of certain main actors in his histories, but he himself portrays and characterizes actors and events according to his own point of view." Horsley, "Popular Prophetic Movements in the time of Jesus:" 4-5.

[135] Josephus, "The War of the Jews," 2:13:5.

people regarding the social situation of Palestine during the Roman rule.[136] They saw the divine hand in opposing established groups and rulers.[137] The opposition was met with brutality by the Roman governors.[138]

1.1.3.2. Messianic[139] Movements

Messianic movements, like the Prophetic movements, did not emerge from a vacuum but from periods of unrest, like the other popular movements. In this regard, Lenowitz rightly notes, "Messianic events take place at points of pressurized confusion. They tend to run into each other—chronologically or geographically; religion does not cause them but only provides them with an expressive mode."[140] What is interesting is that Josephus avoids the term "messiah" when he discusses these popular movements.[141] There was the expectation of an anointed king, and the widespread hopes became acute as the first Jewish revolt drew closer.

Horsley notes of large followers of three popular figures - Judas, Simon, and Anthronges - who were from the peasant community.[142] Josephus describes Simon thus: "Simon ...relying on the handsome appearance...put a diadem upon his own head...he went about with the company of robbers that he had gotten together."[143] This note suggests that, according to Josephus, Simon proclaimed himself as the Messiah and his followers were robbers who were in a desperate situation before joining his movement. These popular movements

---

[136] Horsley, "Popular Prophetic Movements in the time of Jesus:" 13.

[137] Horsley, "Popular Prophetic Movements in the time of Jesus:" 14.

[138] Josephus describes Felix's action, "...he ordered his soldiers to take their weapons, and came against them with a great number of horsemen...He slew four hundred of them, and took two hundred alive." Josephus, "The Antiquities of the Jews," 20:8:6. Tacitus also mentions this: "Most people held the belief that, according to the ancient priestly writings, this was the moment at which the East was fated to prevail: they would now start forth from Judaea and conquer the world." *Tacitus the Histories*, vol. II, translated with Introduction and Notes by W. Hamilton Fyfe (Oxford: Clarendon Press, 1912), 5.13.

[139] The term Messiah recurs very few times in the Second Temple Jewish literature and the expectations of a Messiah were of no interest to the dominant literary group consisting of the scribes and the sages. R. A. Horsley, ""Messianic" Figures and Movements," 280. de Jonge states, "the term "anointed" restricted to remarkably few instances, but it is also clearly not an essential designation for any future redeemer." Marinus de Jonge, "The Use of the word 'Anointed' in the time of Jesus" *NovT* 8/2-4 (Apr.-O.1966): 147.

[140] Harris Lenowitz, *The Jewish Messiahs: From Galilee to the Crown Heights* (Oxford: Oxford University Press, 1998), 8. Horsley also argues for this, when he states, "And the concrete messianic movements can be at least partly explained as a reaction to these circumstances." Richard A. Horsley, "Popular Messianic Movements around the Time of Jesus" *CBQ* 46/3 (Jl. 1984): 10 (471-495).

[141] Saldarini, "Judaism in the Greco-Roman Period," 1045.

[142] Horsley, "Popular Messianic Movements:" 15.

[143] Josephus, "The War of the Jews," 2:4:2.

were also better organized supposedly than other movements. For example, Josephus notes of Athronges: "They were every one of them also commanders; but, when they came to fight, they were subordinate to him and fought for him…all things were done according to his pleasure."[144]

The messianic movements had two aims according to Horsley. First, they wanted to set themselves free from the nexus between Rome and Herod. Second, they wanted to constitute a structure that favoured equality.[145] These goals are vividly presented by Josephus in his description of the acts of Simon: "He burnt down the royal palace at Jericho, and plundered what was left in it. He also set fire to many others of the king's household in several places of the country...and permitted those that were with him to take what was left in them for prey…"[146] These messianic movements reached sizeable proportions in terms of their strength and opposition against the Roman troops which is seen in the steps taken by Varus, the president of Syria: "…he was afraid for the legions he had left there; so he took the two other legions (for there were three legions in all belonging to Syria), and four troops of horsemen, with the several auxiliary forces which either the kings or certain of the tetrarchs…"[147] These movements were also "massive movements" consisting of Jewish peasants drawn from the towns of Bethlehem, Emmaus, and Sepphoris.[148]

Many scholars hold the view that the popular messianic movements arose out of distress over the socio-economic condition in Palestine. Mendels suggests that these movements[149] also had a political aspect which resulted in a terrible disaster for the Jews. One could extend this view and say that not only the popular messianic movements but also sectarianism in Judaism emerged out of the Roman imperial rule.

---

[144] Josephus, "The Antiquities of the Jews," 17:10:7.

[145] Horsley, "Popular Messianic Movements:" 486. This view of Horsley is a reinstatement of Hengel's view, which argues for a common messianic vision of these groups, "It is indisputable that a distinction has to be made between the various bands and groups, but it is equally certain that they all had the same aim: the liberation of the people of God from the Roman yoke and the purification of the Holy Land from all transgressors of the law and all traitors." Martin Hengel, *The Zealots: Investigation into the Jewish Freedom Movement in the Period from Herod I until 70 A.D.*, translated by David Smith (Edinburgh: T & T Clark, 1989), 387. This view has been questioned by L. J. Levine, "*Megamoth Meshihiot Besof Yemei Habait Hasheni*," in *Messianism and Eschatology,* edited by Z, Baras (Jerusalem, 1983), 135-52 [Hebrew]; D. M. Rhoads, *Israel in Revolution 6-74 CE* (Philadelphia, 1976), esp. 54-93 cited in D. Mendels, "Pseudo-Philo's *Biblical Antiquities*," 261.

[146] Josephus, "The Antiquities of the Jews," 17:10:6.

[147] Josephus, "The Antiquities of the Jews," 17:10:9.

[148] Horsley, "Popular Messianic Movements:" 487.

[149] Mendels here refers to the Zealots and Sicarii. D. Mendels, "Pseudo-Philo's *Biblical Antiquities*," 274-275.

Along with all these movements, Jewish literature during this period, especially the Testaments and Apocalypses, reflected the context of the first century Palestine. Overman rightly notes, "The role of political domination and the impact of Roman imperial power and rule should not be underestimated in evaluating the shape and nature of various Jewish movements and literature in this period. The Testaments and Apocalypses, along with several of the groups mentioned above, are powerful testimony to this reality within Judaism in the Greco-Roman period."[150]

Was the Jewish revolt caused by a single factor or a combination of factors? Josephus seems to argue for two important reasons for the revolt throughout his works: the mismanagement by the Roman procurators and criticiszing the reactions of the Jewish groups, especially the Fourth Philosophy.[151] The latter reason stated by Josephus reflects his bias. However, the Jewish revolt was caused by a combination of political, socio-economic, religious, sectarianism, and popular movements. Rhoads clearly brings out this aspect:

> The war was caused by the accumulative effect of a variety of factors over a long period of time … Every social, economic, political, and cultural issue was at the same time a thoroughly religious issue... it was also a "social revolution," a "peasant rebellion," a "quest for holiness," a "clash of cultures," a "millenarian movement," a "national war for freedom," and much more. Only by the use of several depictions can we adequately characterize the complexity of events comprising the Roman-Judean War.[152]

1.2. The Great Revolt (66-73 CE) and the Destruction of the Jerusalem Temple

Divisions were prevalent in Judea with groups having different responses to the situation. The war with the Romans consisted chiefly of two groups in broad terms – the moderates and the radicals/revolutionaries.[153] The moderates were supported by the Roman administration, whereas the radicals were not

---

[150] Overman, "Judaism in the Greco-Roman Period," 1051-52.

[151] Susan Sorek, *The Jews against Rome: War in Palestine AD 66-73* (London: Continuum, 2008), 28. Josephus does not seem mention the entire history of the revolt of the Jews. Smallwood notes that Josephus fails to mention Judas of Galilee, who refused to pay the tribute money to Rome and also opposed the Census. But this was significant as it lead to the formation of a nationalistic party against the Romans. E. Mary Smallwood, *The Jews under Roman Rule: From Pompey to Diocletian*, SJLA 20, edited by Jacob Neusner (Leiden: E. J. Brill, 1976), 153.

[152] Rhoads, "Zealots," 1052. Levine too notes, "Given this chaotic situation, in which many different groups, each with its own ideology, leadership, and composition, were competing with one another, it is no wonder that to speak of an underlying cause of the revolt is misleading." Levine, "Jewish War," 840.

[153] Levine, "Jewish War," 840.

supported and were vehemently against Rome. The moderates consisted of the high priestly families including the Sadducees, some Pharisees, the Herodian family and the urban aristocracy. On the other hand, the radicals, who were not part of the ruling class, comprised of a number of different groups. These groups not only fought with each other, but also targeted the Romans and the moderates.[154] It is interesting to note that Josephus describes the moderate stance of the aristocracy who were more interested in peaceful settlement with Rome rather than a conflict. Josephus points out that Ananus "...preferred peace above all things."[155] Josephus also mentions that the wealthy ran away from their houses and took shelter under the Romans.[156] Much of the perspective of the moderates had to do with the benefits they were receiving and hoped to receive from the Roman rule. Ananus in his speech praises the Romans, "How then can we avoid shedding of tears, when we see the Roman donations in our temples, while we withal see those of our own nation taking our spoils, and plundering our glorious metropolis,... from which enormities those Romans ...would have abstained."[157]

1.2.1. Conflict of Interests between Moderates and Radicals

The radical camp comprised of two factions - one led by a priest, Eleazar,[158] son of Ananias, and the other group the Sicarii led by Manahem,[159] a descendant of Judas, the Galilean. Manahem captured Masada in 66 CE[160] while Eleazar was instrumental in the decision to cancel the sacrifices on behalf of the emperor. This act was very crucial, for according to Josephus, "...this was the true beginning of our war with the Romans; for they rejected the sacrifice of Caesar on this account."[161] However, the moderates continued their support to Rome. They urged Florus and Agrippa to send troops to the city to crush the rebellion.[162] With the support of the moderates, the Romans held the upper city, but the Lower city, including the Temple Mount area, was in the hands of revolutionaries. After a week of clashes, the Jewish rebels took control of

[154] Levine, "Jewish War," 840.

[155] Josephus, "The War of the Jews," 4:5:2.

[156] Josephus, "The War of the Jews," 4:7:1.

[157] Josephus, "The War of the Jews," 4:3:10.

[158] Josephus describes Eleazar as a "bold youth." Josephus, "The War of the Jews," 2:17:2.

[159] Josephus does not describe him in a good light: "...very cunning sophister, and had formerly reproached the Jews under Cyrenius, that after God they were subject to the Romans." Josephus, "The War of the Jews," 2:17:8. This statement of Josephus probably comes out his prejudice.

[160] Josephus,"The War of the Jews," 2:17:2.

[161] Josephus, "The War of the Jews," 2:17:2.

[162] Josephus, "The War of the Jews," 2:17: 4.

the Upper city also.[163] They seemed to gain success in the beginning but lost ground in course of time.[164] In the meanwhile, Manahem slew Ananias the high priest and adorned himself with royal clothes.[165] This incited jealously from the followers of Eleazar who attacked Manahem which resulted in an intergroup conflict and thus forced him to flee to Masada.[166] Josephus notes that Eleazar's followers trapped, tortured and killed Manahem.[167] Horsley calls this uprising essentially a revolt by the peasants, a situation arising out of being hard pressed on all sides - politically and socio-economically.[168] As discussed earlier, this is only one of the dimensions of the revolt. Certainly, the religious aspect also played an important part, if one supposes that Jewish life was through and through religiously oriented.

The revolt lends itself to greater proportions in terms of the Jew-Gentile conflict. It is said that the rebels annihilated the Roman garrison in Jerusalem which resulted in a chain reaction. The Gentiles in Caesarea slaughtered close to 20, 000 local Jews.[169] The backlash was seen in the Jewish retaliations throughout the country. Jews attacked the Gentiles in Syrian villages, Philadelphia, Heshbon, Gerasa, Pella, Scythopolis, Gadara, Hippos, and the Golan, as well as in other places along the Phoenician coast from Tyre to Gaza.[170] These attacks were fashioned by local leaders. The Gentiles retaliated and many Jewish communities were greatly affected.[171]

1.2.2. Intervention of Gallus

As the conflict between the moderates and radicals escalated, there was surprisingly a period of silence on the part of the Romans, which was finally broken with the decision of Cestius Gallus, the Roman governor of Syria, to march to Jerusalem and put an end to the rebellion in its early stage.[172] On October 66 CE, with a force of 30,000 men in Antioch, Gallus ran through

---

[163] Josephus, "The War of the Jews," 2:17:6.

[164] Part of the rebel's success had to with the victory over Herod's army. Josephus, "The War of the Jews," 2:17:8.

[165] Josephus, "The War of the Jews," 2:17:9.

[166] Josephus, "The War of the Jews," 2:17:9.

[167] Josephus, "The War of the Jews," 2:17:9.

[168] Horsley and Hanson, *Bandits, Prophets and Messiahs*, 43.

[169] Josephus notes that the 20,000 Jews were slaughtered in about an hour. Josephus, "The War of the Jews," 2:18:1.

[170] Josephus, "The War of the Jews," 2:18:1.

[171] Josephus' description of the conflict presents a sad picture: "It was then common to see cities filled with dead bodies, still lying unburied, and those of the old men, mixed with infants, all dead, and scattered about together with women lay amongst them..." Josephus, "The War of the Jews," 2:18:2.

[172] Josephus, "The War of the Jews," 2.18.9.

Ptolemais and Caesarea, torched Lydda and approached Jerusalem via Beth Horon. When he realized he would need a larger force than the one he had, he suddenly retreated and withdrew northward.[173] The rebels, seizing the advantage, slew soldiers and gathered a good portion of Roman arms. The moderates united and set up a provisional government to manage the city for a year. The defeat of Gallus ended any hopes of negotiation with Romans. The rebels set up a revolutionary government in Galilee.[174]

As the revolt broke out, there were already several large groups of brigands active in Galilee. The action to suppress the rebellion only served to multiply the number of brigands. The bandit groups constituted a dominant force in Galilee because of their military strength, the sympathy and respect that the peasantry had for social bandits[175] and their alliance with other rebel forces. For these reasons, the brigand groups were the most important insurrectionary force in Galilee.[176] In Galilee, the common people were not inclined to fight while those who had a liking for revolution were consumed by factionalism.

1.2.3. Destruction of Jerusalem

Plagued by the disastrous defeat of Cestius Gallus, Nero appointed one of his noted generals Vespasian to fight the Jews. Apart from a few places (Jotapta, Gamala, and Tarichear) that offered some resistance, the rest was smooth sailing. Their campaign of 67 CE closed with the capture of Jamnia and Azotus[177] and resumed in the early months of 68 CE. By the spring of 68 CE, all of Judea including Perea and Idumea had been occupied and only Jerusalem was remaining. The passing away of Nero[178] and the acknowledgement of Vespasian as the new ruler delayed the campaign till December 69 CE.[179]

Meanwhile, there was anarchy in Jerusalem between 67-70 CE.[180] With the capture of Judea in late 67 CE, refugees flowed into Jerusalem and the social,[181] political, and religious problems compounded.[182] John of Gischala arrived in

---

[173] Josephus, "The War of the Jews," 2:19:1-9.

[174] Josephus, "The War of the Jews," 2.20.3.

[175] Josephus, "The War of the Jews," 4:84.

[176] Horsley and Hanson, *Bandits*, *Prophets and Messiahs*, 79.

[177] Josephus, "The War of the Jews," 4.3.2.

[178] Josephus, "The War of the Jews," 4:9:2.

[179] Josephus notes that Vespasian put off his entry into Jerusalem waiting for the replacement of Nero. Josephus, "The War of the Jews," 4:9:2.

[180] Josephus notes that there was confusion and civil war in every city. Josephus, "The War of the Jews," 4:3:2.

[181] Josephus describes the barbarity of the people and it went to the extent that "...it seemed to be much lighter thing to be ruined by the Romans than by themselves." Josephus, "The War of the Jews,"4:3:2.

[182] Levine, "Jewish War," 843.

Jerusalem.[183] In the beginning he identified himself with the moderates[184] but secretly supported the Zealots and took steps to conspire against Ananus.[185] The Zealots consisted of the lower-class priests and refugees from the Judean countryside. At the request of John, the Zealots sent for the Jews of Idumea[186] who joined them. The Zealots along with the Idumeans plundered and killed the high priests including Ananus, the high priest.[187] Soon a conflict broke out within the Zealot coalition; later John broke with the Zealots and was followed by some of the Idumeans.[188] In the spring of 69 CE, John and the Zealots joined together and held the Temple,[189] while the Idumeans and the remnants of the moderate party along with the Jerusalem populace laid siege to it.

Vespasian handed over the campaign of Jerusalem to his son Titus.[190] By the time Titus approached Jerusalem in the spring of 70 CE for his final campaign, the situation was more than easy for him.[191] The Romans, having successfully broken the outer wall,[192] found themselves in the narrow streets of the city. Taking advantage of their knowledge of the neighbourhood,[193] the

---

[183] Josephus reports, "…upon John's entry into Jerusalem the whole body of the people were in uproar, and ten thousand of them crowded about every one of the fugitives that were come to them…" John also noted the weak condition of the Romans and boasted of his own power. Josephus, "The War of the Jews," 4:3:1.

[184] Josephus notes that he shared a good relationship with Ananus but gave away the secrets to the Zealots. And he did in fact take an oath and would help in overthrowing those that attacked them. Josephus, "The War of the Jews," 4:3:13.

[185] Josephus, "The War of the Jews," 4:4:1.

[186] At the counsel of John, the Zealots wrote a short letter stating, "That Ananus had imposed on the people and was beteraying their metropolis to the Romans; that they themselves had revolted from the rest and were in custody in the temple, on account of the preservation of their liberty." Josephus, "The War of the Jews," 4:4:1.

[187] Josephus reports, "…but they sought for the high priests, and the generality went with the greatest zeal against them; and soon as they caught them they slew them, and then standing upon their dead bodies…" Josephus goes on to praise Ananus, the high priest, and states, "… for he was thoroughly sensible that the Romans were not to be conquered." Josephus, "The War of the Jews," 4:5:2.

[188] Josephus, "The War of the Jews," 4:7:1.

[189] John also held the part adjoining it, Ophla, and "the Valley of Cedron." Josephus, "The War of the Jews," 5:6:1.

[190] Josephus, "The War of the Jews," 3:1:3.

[191] Josephus notes that Titus was informed of the condition when he arrives at Jerusalem: "the people who were fallen under the power of the seditious and the robbers were greatly desirous of peace; but, being tooweak to rise up against the rest, they lay still." Josephus, "The War of the Jews," 5:2:1.

[192] The first attempt to break the wall was not successful. Josephus, "The War of the Jews," 5:6:4.

[193] They had great knowledge of the narrow lanes which were unknown to the Romans and thus were able to inflict casualty on the Romans. Josephus, "The War of the Jews," 5:8:1.

Jewish rebels imposed heavy causalities, and as a result the Romans were forced to retreat out of the city.[194] In spite of this, the Romans eventually destroyed the entire second wall and took part of the city.[195] The difficult part of the siege was the Antonia fortress.[196] But after repeated efforts, the Romans overran Antonia and proceeded to the Temple where they were faced with the forces of John.[197] Unable to dislodge the walls of the Temple, the Romans set fire to the gates and porticos of the Temple.[198] The Jews were driven into the confines of the Temple's inner court.[199] The Temple was destroyed on August 30, the 10th of Ab, 70 CE.[200] They then quickly took the Upper city, and victory was achieved.[201] Jerusalem was in the hands of the Romans once again. After a mass slaughter, a fire broke out and the city was entirely destroyed.[202]

1.2.4. Capture of Masada

Following the fall of Jerusalem, the Jewish rebels continued to hold three fortresses: Herodium, Machaerus and Masada.[203] The first two were taken by the legate, Lucilius Bassus, with relative ease.[204] After seeing the wall burnt down by the Romans and with no signs of victory, Eleazar, convinced his comrades that suicide was an honourable course of action.[205] There was a mass

---

[194] Josephus also notes that the city was struck with famine. Josephus, "The War of the Jews," 5:8:1.

[195] Josephus, "The War of the Jews," 5:8:2.

[196] The reason for the difficulty according to Josephus had not only to do with the Jews standing on a higher ground but also the skill in using their weapons. Josephus, "The War of the Jews," 5:9:2. Josephus also notes that he was sent by Titus to the Jews to exhort them to surrender to the Romans. Josephus, "The War of the Jews," 5:9:2-4.

[197] Josephus, "The War of the Jews," 6:1:7.

[198] Josephus is of the view that the fire was ignited by the soldiers and not with the order of Titus, who on the contrary instructed to quench the fire. Josephus, "The War of the Jews," 6:4:6.

[199] Josephus, "The War of the Jews," 6:5:1.

[200] Sandmel, *Judaism and Christian Beginnings*, 34.

[201] Josephus, "The War of the Jews," 6:8:5.

[202] Josephus, "The War of the Jews," 6:9:4. Harold W. Attridge, "Christianity from the Destruction of Jerusalem," 151.

[203] Josephus, "The War of the Jews," 7:8:1.

[204] Josephus, "The War of the Jews," 7:6:1.

[205] The narration of the speech of Eleazar certainly has a degree of slant and a lot of questions remain unanswered. Josephus, "The War of the Jews," 7:8:6. Sorek notes some of the discrepancies in the accounts of Josephus and the archaeological findings in Yadin: a) the defenders of Masada were not just revolutionaries as Josephus time and again argues but also religious indicated by the house of study, Bible scrolls, etc.; b) the mass suicide seems only a distant possibility because of the narrowness of the ridge, and the less possibility of rallying for mass suicide when the battle was going on. Sorek, *The Jews against Rome*, 150, 152. Varneda in

suicide leaving only two women and five children.[206] The Romans who entered the fortress were shocked at the sight of the mass suicide.[207] In 73 CE, the Romans captured the last of the Judean fortresses, Masada and this marked the end of the rebellion.[208]

1.3. Fall Out of the Destruction of Jerusalem and the Temple

The effects of the destruction of Jerusalem and the Temple on the Jews were numerous and varied:[209] political, social, religious and economic. Jerusalem was totally destroyed and only the three towers and remnants of the western city wall remained intact. The high priesthood and Jerusalem's aristocratic class, which had so far dominated the Jewish religious and political life of the Second Temple period, were rooted out. Judea paid a heavy price for its revolt.[210] It is probably fair to express with Goodman that the destruction of the Temple not only affected the Jews in Palestine but also the Diaspora.[211]

1.3.1. Political Condition

Before the war, the Roman rule in Judea was limited by the incompetent governors and insufficiency of armed forces.[212] These loopholes were plugged in after the war. One of the changes was that Judea's status as a Roman province was elevated. Unlike the period before the war, Judea was now governed by a

---

analyzing the historical method of Josephus seems to rationalize this, when he states, "It has also been said that the historian is the measure of history, and, moreover, it is he who qualifies the events he narrates. Consequently history is, in a sense, what the historian himself wants it to be. Therefore, Flavius Josephus cannot remain indifferent to this reality, and throughout his works certain moments and viewpoints may be perceived which answer more to the very personal vision of the historian." Pere Villalba I. Varenda, *The Historical Method of Josephus*, ALGHJ 19 (Leiden: E. J. Brill, 1986), 278.

[206] Josephus, "The War of the Jews," 7:9:1.

[207] Josephus, "The War of the Jews," 7:9:2.

[208] Sandmel, *Judaism and Christian Beginnings*, 34.

[209] Here, one has to disagree with Cohen. Cohen notes that "…not all Jews of the first century felt the trauma in the same way or treated all elements of the catastrophe equally." For this evidence is drawn from tannaitic literature. Cohen, "The Significance of Yavneh:" 27. What has to be borne in mind is that the tannaitic literature is also subjective in that it does convey the triumph of the Yavnean sages. So the account of the sages also has to be looked at critically.

[210] Lee I. A. Levine, "Judaism from the Destruction to the End of the Second Jewish Revolt: 70 -135 CE," in *Christianity and Rabbinic Judaism: A Parallel History of their Origins and Early Development*, edited by Hershel Shanks (London: SPCK, 1993), 125.

[211] Martin Goodman, "Diaspora Reactions to the Destruction of the Temple" in *Jews and Christians: The Parting of Ways A.D. 70 to 135*, The Second Durham- Tübingen Research Symposium on Earliest Christianity and Judaism, edited by James D. G. Dunn (Michigan: William B. Eerdmans Publishing Company, 1999), 28.

[212] Martin Sicker, *Between Rome and Jerusalem: 300 Years of Roman-Judaean Relations* (London: Praeger, 2001), 167.

legate of a senatorial rank who was directly responsible to the emperor, with legionary troops under his command.[213] Also, as the Romans expected an uprising in Jerusalem, the majority of the legion was posted in Judea rather than in the remote administrative capital at Caesarea.[214]

1.3.2. Economic Condition

On the economic front, taxes were levied upon all Jews in the Roman Empire as punishment for the war of 66-70 CE.[215] Vespasian taxed Jews on the privilege of religious freedom of both Jews in Palestine as well as in the Diaspora and the funds were used for the temple of Jupiter Capitolinus, who was supposed to have triumphed over the God of Israel. The collection of taxes was a grim reminder of the humiliation suffered by Jews at the hand of Romans.[216] Economic difficulties were also caused by the carnage or incarceration of an enormous magnitude of people and the deprivation of central establishments of the state.[217] Most importantly, for the Jews the destruction of the temple meant the loss of the symbolic focus of God's unique presence among his people. There was an end to the Temple, the priesthood, the Temple liturgy, the animal sacrifices, indeed to a whole system of cult and law which was bound up with the Temple, without the slightest hope that the Temple and its cult could be rebuilt or resumed in the foreseeable future.[218] Combined with this was the threat to the integrity of the Jewish people that was represented by the attacks on them under Gaius and Claudius.[219]

1.3.3. Social Condition

On the social side, people were in shock at the massacre of large segments of the population.[220] Land and property were confiscated by the Romans.[221] The Jewish community in the land of Israel no longer had a recognized social elite or establishment, and the Jews of the Diaspora no longer had a center that

---

[213] Bruce, "Roman Administration," 99.

[214] Sicker, *Between Rome and Jerusalem*, 167.

[215] Shaye J. D. Cohen, "Crossing the Boundary and Becoming a Jew," *HTR* 82/1 (Ja. 1989): 14.

[216] Sicker, *Between Rome and Jerusalem*, 167.

[217] Cohen, "The Significance of Yavneh:" 28.

[218] Hans Küng, *Judaism: The Religious Situation of Our Time*, translated by John Bowden (London: SCM Press Ltd., 1992), 130.

[219] Kee, "The Transformation of the Synagogue:" 6.

[220] Nickelsburg, "Revolt-Destruction- Reconstruction," 280.

[221] Shaye J. D. Cohen, "The Emergence of Rabbinic Judaism," in *From the Maccabees to Mishnah*, LEC 7, edited by Wayne Meeks (Philadelphia: The Westminster John Knox Press, 1987), 215.

bound them together.[222] A large number of Palestinian Jews were killed or sold into slavery. Some were paraded through the Roman Forum, and then forced to build the Colosseum.[223]

1.3.4. Religious Condition

The Jerusalem Temple had an indispensable role in defining all that mattered to Jewish life and society. Neusner very clearly brings out the pivotal role of the Jerusalem Temple when he notes[224] that the Temple stood at the very center of the order of Israelite society with the cult being the primary means of atonement and reconciliation with God.[225] The political basis of the Jewish community life rested on the Temple administration and the religious life of the people centered on the sacrificial cult. For the majority of the people, the Temple represented the relationship between heaven and earth.[226] Neusner further states, "God revealed the laws to Moses and these laws were kept in the Temple where daily sacrifices and the exact sacrificial technology represented a primary means by which Israel served its father in heaven."[227] In this regard, Dunn rightly notes that the Temple was the political, economic and religious centre of Israel's national and religious life pre 70 CE.[228]

The Temple was not only the place where the Jews worshipped but more importantly, it was the place where God was said to be present.[229] Schremer clearly notes the crisis situation when he opines, "A political and military defeat of the magnitude of the destruction of the Second Temple must be religiously and existentially troublesome for the community of believers."[230] Further, Schremer accentuates that Jewish literature in the first and third century period stresses a crisis of faith among the Palestinian Jews and the crucial question

---

222 Cohen, "The Emergence of Rabbinic Judaism," 221.

223 James H. Charlesworth, "Christians and Jews in the First Six Centuries," in *Christianity and Rabbinic Judaism: A Parallel History of their Origins and Early Development*, edited by Hershel Shanks (London: SPCK, 1993), 309.

224 Jacob Neusner, *Ancient Israel after Catastrophe: The Religious World View of the Mishnah* (Charlottesville: University Press of Virginia, 1983), 12.

225 Neusner, *Ancient Israel after Catastrophe*, 14.

226 Wiliam Scott Green, "What's in a Name?- The Problematic of Rabbinic "Biography,"" in *Approaches to Ancient Judaism: Theory and Practice*, edited by William Scott Green (Montana: Scholars Press, 1978), 78.

227 Neusner, *Judaism in the Beginning of Christianity*, 47-48.

228 James D. G. Dunn, *The Parting of the Ways: Between Christianity and Judaism and their Significance for the Character of Christianity*, 2nd ed. (London: SCM Press, 2006), 42-44.

229 E. P. Sanders, *Judaism Practice and Belief 63 BCE-66 CE* (London: SCM Press, 1992), 70.

230 Adiel Schremer, *Brothers Estranged: Heresy, Christianity, and Jewish Identity in Late Antiquity* (Oxford: Oxford University Press, 2010), 26.

was : "Where was, and where *is,* God?"[231] The defeat of the Jews at the hand of the Romans also led to the understanding (among some Jews) that the God of Israel was not powerful.[232]

Many of the Jewish sects that had played a key role in Jewish religious life pre 70 CE disappeared: the Sadducees, centered around the Jerusalem priesthood in the days of the Temple, lost their base of political and religious authority; the Qumran community was destroyed in 68 CE; members of the various pre 70 CE revolutionary movements (Sicarii, Zealots, followers of John of Gischala and Simon Giora) either were killed, taken captive, fled to North Africa or went underground.[233]

An important development during this period was the spurt of apocalyptic literature which attempted to deal with the religious turmoil and gauge the cause for the destruction of the Temple. While on one hand, the literature reasoned that the cause of the destruction of the Temple was the wickedness of the Jewish people, on the other hand, there was a positive orientation to the need of studying the Law. In this regard, Rowland notes, "…the debacle of 70 does not appear to have lessened the impact of these beliefs, and there is evidence to suppose that the years between the two revolts continued to be full of eschatological hope."[234] The first aspect can be seen in *The Apocalypse of Abraham*, which predicts a grim picture regarding the future: "A heathen people went out from its left side and they captured those who were on the right side: the men, women and children. And some they slaughtered and some they held with them."[235] But the reason for this state is "…all that you have seen will happen because of your seed who will provoke me, because the idol and the murder which you saw in the picture in the temple of jealousy."[236] However, the apocalyptic literature also forecasted good times if the Law was

---

[231] Schremer, *Brothers Estranged*, 26.

[232] Schremer, *Brothers Estranged*, 27.

[233] Levine, "Judaism from the Destruction," 125.

[234] Christopher Rowland, "The Parting of the Ways: the Evidence of Jewish and Christian Apocalyptic and Mystical Material" in *Jews and Christians: The Parting of Ways A.D. 70 to 135*, The Second Durham- Tübingen Research Symposium on Earliest Christianity and Judaism, edited by James D. G. Dunn (Grand Rapids, Michigan: William B. Eerdmans Publishing Company, 1999), 221.

[235] Alexander Kulik, *Retroverting to Slavonic Pseudepigrapha: Towards the Original of Apocalypse of Abraham*, TCS 3, edited by James R. Adair (Atlanta: SBL, 2004), 27, 1-2. The same idea is seen in *4 Baruch* "…For we have not been found worthy to guard them, because we became unfaithful trustees." *4 Baruch*, translated by Jens Herzer, edited by Abraham J. Malherbe (Atlanta: SBL, 2005), 4, 4.

[236] Kulik, *Retroverting to Slavonic Pseudepigrapha*, 27, 7-8.

given importance, and this was certainly their message in the wake of the destruction of the Temple.[237] Baruch brings the focus back on the Law:

> "Hear, O sons of Israel, see how many you are who remain of the twelve tribes of Israel. 77.3 For to you and to your fathers, above all nations, the Lord gave the Law. 77.4 And because your brothers transgressed the commandments of the Most High, he brought vengeance upon you and upon them. And he did not spare the former, but he also gave the latter into captivity. And he did not leave a remnant of them. 77.5 And behold, you are here with me. 77.6 If, then, you make your ways straight, you also will not depart as your brothers departed, but they will come to you. 77.7 For he who you worship is merciful, and he in whom you hope is gracious and true, so that he will do good to you and not evil…"[238]

The importance of the Law was also stated in *4 Ezra*.[239] This does reiterate that the role of the Law took great importance post 70 CE.[240] The Jewish community that took over after the catastrophe of 70 CE had to deal with the problem of a disintegrated Jewish community. Most importantly, the need of the hour for Judaism was a process of consolidation and collaborative

[237] It must also be stated that the apocalyptic literature also presents the eschatological redemption. *2 Baruch* brings this out in its totality with the description of the victory over Satan and the descent of heavenly Jerusalem. Rivka Nir, *The Destruction of the Jerusalem Temple and the Idea of Redemption in the Syriac Apocalypse of Baruch*, EJL 20, edited by John C. Reeves (Atlanta: Society of Biblical Literature, 2003), 197.

[238] Daniel M. Gurtner, *Second Baruch: A Critical Edition of the Syriac Text with Greek and Latin Fragments, English Translation, Introduction and Concordances*, Jewish and Christian Texts in Contexts and Related Studies, edited by James H. Charlesworth (New York: Continuum International, 2009), 77, 2-7.

[239] *4 Ezra* 3:17-20: "[17] And when thou didst lead his descendants out of Egypt, thou didst bring them to Mount Sinai. [18] Thou didst bend down the heavens and shake the earth, and move the world, and make the depths to tremble, and trouble the times. [19] And thy glory passed through the four gates of fire and earthquake and wind and ice, to give the law to the descendants of Jacob, and thy commandment to the posterity of Israel. [20] "Yet thou didst not take away from them their evil heart, so that thy law might bring forth fruit in them.

[240] Jones rightly notes the significance of 4 *Ezra* in the context of post 70 CE. He points out, "The author's purpose is to change attitudes towards Rome. He detects in the Josephan hypothesis a weakening of appreciation for the special relationship that exists between God and his chosen people. The consequence of such thinking is the erosion of a healthy devotion to the Law and divine commandments. The same is the case with *2 Baruch* where the writer instructs the readers to give up the interest in Rome and consider the Jewish aspects, especially the following of the Law. Kenneth R. Jones, *Jewish Reactions to the Destruction of the Jerusalem Temple in A.D. 70: Apocalypses and Related Pseudepigrapha*, JSJSup 151, edited by Hindy Najman (Boston: Leiden, 2011), 77, 109.

efforts where the fragmentation of Jewish community had to be minimized. This is clearly expressed in the history of *halakhah*.[241]

Saladarini's statement is quite relevant to this discussion: "The loss of the Temple, of the Jerusalem leadership and of the political identity that went with them resulted in a major adjustment to the Jewish understanding of the world as well as its symbolic system, behavioral patterns and values."[242] Thus, the Jewish revolt against Rome removed institutions that were central to Jewish identity. The situation necessitated a search for identity within Judaism. Charlesworth notes that this period was a time in which "Judaism" and "Christianity" each developed a coherent self-definition.[243] The post 70 scenario was a period of consolidation wherein both Judaism and Christianity looked to build their own identities.

1.4. Towards Establishing their Respective Identities: Formative Judaism and Early Christian Communities

1.4.1. Synagogue Judaism

On a positive note, the lack of a focal point, the Temple, facilitated an enhanced role for the synagogue.[244] The leadership also passed to a great extent from priests to sages. As the Temple was not rebuilt, the nature of reconstruction had to be radically changed.[245] After 70 CE, the synagogue helped to fill the gap in Jewish religious life left by the destruction of the Jerusalem sanctuary.[246] Synagogue Judaism in a real sense arose or found its directing guidelines from Pharisaism. Synagogue Judaism survived and emerged after this as the replacement of the Temple and was reasonably developed at that time.[247] The destruction of the Temple in 70 CE ended the sacrificial cult and the priestly system.[248]

Levine details three features of synagogues after 70 CE.[249] First, the synagogue of Roman Palestine continued to serve as a communal institution

---

[241] What is undeniable is the crucial role of the first generation sages following the destruction in overcoming the initial trauma, as well as redefining and passing on to subsequent generations much of what is recognized as historic post-temple Judaism. Gafni, "The Historical Background," 30-31.

[242] Saldarini, *Pharisees, Scribes and Sadducees*, 8.

[243] Charlesworth, "Christians and Jews," 309.

[244] Gafni, "The Historical Background," 27.

[245] Nickelsburg, "Revolt-Destruction- Reconstruction," 280.

[246] Nickelsburg, *Ancient Judaism and Christian Origins*, 158.

[247] Sandmel, *Judaism and Christian Beginnings*, 34.

[248] Neusner, *Judaism in the Beginning of Christianity*, 47.

[249] Lee I. A. Levine, "The Nature and Origin of the Palestinian Synagogue Reconsidered," *JBL* 115/3 (Fall 1996): 444-447.

par excellence. Rabbinic literature makes it perfectly clear that the synagogue belonged to the community; members of the town managed its affairs. Second, it was rapidly developing prayer liturgy. Though there was the continuation of pre-destruction religious practices such as the reading of the Torah and its accompanying activities, there was also significant development in the introduction of public communal prayer. Third, it had an increasingly religious profile. The synagogue began to be perceived as a holy place. The events of the year 70 CE – the destruction of the Temple and the vacuum created in its wake – had a significant influence on the status of the later Palestinian synagogue.[250]

There came a realization that divisions within the people had made the orderly prosecution of the war against Rome and the Temple had fallen as a result. Therefore, only in unity could the people and the land be rebuilt. Since only the Pharisees had survived the destruction, it was thought that Pharisaism, with its flexibility in adapting the Halakah to new circumstances, would be best fit to deal with the new realities after the unsuccessful revolt and destruction of the temple.[251] It was clearly the time for the entire nation to unite behind the Tannaim, the inheritors of the pharisaic approach to Judaism.

Most importantly, the destruction of the Temple made a difference in the relation of Jewish Christians to the Jews. The two had worshipped together in the Temple.[252] The social context for these changes was the factionalism within Judaism and the struggle for self-identification by Christians and Jews.[253] The destruction of the Temple ended the possibility of seeing the early Jewish Christian community as an integral part of the Jewish people. The Jewish Christians were seen as pursuing a religious and common agenda different from the Jewish community.[254]

1.4.2. Formative Judaism

The current scholarly discussions[255] note that the post 70 CE contexts gave rise not to Rabbinic Judaism but to Formative Judaism.[256] Rabbinic Judaism as an entity probably emerged only in the second century. Therefore, it is necessary to understand Formative Judaism before proceeding further.

---

[250] Levine, "The Nature and Origin of the Palestinian Synagogue:" 444-447.

[251] Lawrence H. Schiffman, "At the Crossroads: Tannaitic Perspectives on the Jewish-Christian Schism," in *Jewish and Christian Self-Definition*, vol. 2: *Aspects of Judaism in the Greco-Roman Period*, edited by E. P. Sanders, Albert I. Baumgarten, and Alan Mendelson (Philadelphia: Fortress Press, 1981), 148.

[252] Canon Sell, *The Talmud, Mishnah and Midrash* (Madras: SPCK, 1928), 74.

[253] Charlesworth, "Christians and Jews," 312.

[254] Levine, "Judaism from the Destruction," 129.

[255] For further discussions refer Overman, Sim, Neusner and others cited in this chapter.

[256] Rabbinic Judaism as an entity probably emerged only in the second century.

Sim defines Formative Judaism as "...the reorganization and consolidation of Judaism in the period after the first Jewish war."[257] It is a step to redeem the Jewish faith from the damages of the war and absence of the Temple by a "coalition of forces."[258] However, Formative Judaism should not be equated with Rabbinic Judaism.[259] Judaism after 70 CE was in a fluid stage and there were many forms of Judaism, including Christian Judaism, which competed for supremacy at that time.[260] There were also apocalyptic movements in many communities as attested by *2 Baruch*, *4 Ezra*, and the *Apocalypse of Abraham*. Also, the revolutionary option retained considerable appeal and resistance. Formative Judaism was involved in the process of self-definition and consolidation in a society that was fragmented and divided.[261] Overman states, "Formative Judaism was involved in a process of social construction and definition. Formative Judaism was in the process of becoming."[262]

The most prominent feature in the period after 70 CE was the Pharisees; they centered on the household and the study of the Torah independent from the temple cult. Tithing, Sabbath observances, and Torah study were also essential features of the movement. During this time, Jewish groups looked to the pharisaic system.[263] Neusner points out that the beliefs and organizational structure of the Pharisees made them the most viable option for acceptance among many of the Jews after 70 CE.[264] He further adds that the purity laws provided a social structure for the sect and guided the life of the sect and its members in that they provided a means of group definition, restricted contact with outsiders, and regulated the internal life of the community.[265] Other

[257] David C. Sim, *The Gospel of Matthew and Christian Judaism*, SNTW, edited by John Barclay, Joel Marcus, and John Riches, (Edinburgh: T & T Clark, 1998), 113.

[258] Sim, *The Gospel of Matthew*, 113.

[259] Formative Judaism does not belong to what later stylized and idealized rabbinic accounts claim, immediately upon the founding of the rabbinic academy at Yavneh. It was many hundreds of years before rabbinic Judaism emerged as the dominant type of Judaism and gained control over the synagogue. Nor should it be identified with the Jewish religion. Sim, *The Gospel of Matthew*, 114, 146 and Overman, *Matthew's Gospel and Formative Judaism*, 2.

[260] Sim, *The Gospel of Matthew*, 146.

[261] Overman, *Matthew's Gospel and Formative Judaism*, 3.

[262] Overman, *Matthew's Gospel and Formative Judaism*, 2.

[263] Overman, *Matthew's Gospel and Formative Judaism*, 36.

[264] Jacob Neusner, *A Life of Yohanan Ben Zakkai Ca. 1-80 CE*, 2nd ed. (Leiden: E. J. Brill, 1970), 198f.

[265] Jacob Neusner, "The Fellowship in the Second Jewish Commonwealth," *HTR* 53/2 (Apr. 1960): 125.

than the Pharisees, Formative Judaism also consisted of scribes who were representatives of the priesthood and the nobility.[266]

The major focus of Formative Judaism was the Torah. This was a legacy of its predominantly pharisaic heritage. Pharisaism before 70 CE had a concern for the Law and the accuracy[267] of its interpretation–observances of the rules of purity and impurity, the Sabbath and the holy days, laws of agricultural elements (tithes)[268]– which served Formative Judaism well in this initial period of formation and definition following 70 CE.[269] The Pharisees acknowledged that the ancient Law requires constant reinterpretation in the light of changes in society; they developed an oral tradition[270] known as the tradition of the elders, which supplemented the written Law, and updated it when necessary. Neusner states that the temple cult was replaced by the study of the Torah.[271] One of the claims of Formative Judaism was that what they believed and practiced was not new but passed on from their ancestors. This helped them to attain the reputation of being the most accurate interpreters of the law in order to legitimize the role of the leaders of the people in the period after 70 CE. Initially, these claims created competition and conflict.[272]

1.4.2.1. The Yavnean Period (70–130 CE)

The sages of Yavneh laid the foundation for Rabbinic Judaism.[273] The rabbis preserved the pre 70 CE pharisaic traditions and developed the legal corpus which guided Judaism forward.[274] In the city of Yavneh, on the Mediterranean coast, Rabbi Yoḥanan ben Zakkai gathered an assemblage of scholars and students around him and began the process of crystallizing the tradition which led to a new definition and interpretation.[275] The sages at Yavneh under the

---

[266] Sim, *The Gospel of Matthew*, 113.

[267] Josephus, "The Antiquities of the Jews," 17:2:4.

[268] Newman, *Proximity to Power*, 72.

[269] Overman, *Matthew's Gospel and Formative Judaism*, 68.

[270] They claimed that the oral tradition was in reality a compilation of ancient laws which had been passed on through the generations by word of mouth. The tradition of the elders therefore had the utmost authority because of its ancient pedigree. Sim, *The Gospel of Matthew*, 114.

[271] Jacob Neusner, "The Formation of Rabbinic Judaism: From the Mishnah's Philosophy to the Talmud's Religion," *ComViat* 44/1 (2002): 38.

[272] Overman, *Matthew's Gospel and Formative Judaism*, 71.

[273] Neusner, *From Politics to Piety: The Emergence of Pharisaic Judaism*, 97.

[274] The other achievements of the Yavneans include: laying down the main outlines of the Judaic Prayer book, the *iddur*; - shaping Judaic piety; - the important elements of doctrine, theology, and ethics of Rabbinic Judaism. The period of Yavneh formed the seedtime of classical Judaism. Neusner, *From Politics to Piety: The Emergence of Pharisaic Judaism* 97.

[275] Nickelsburg, "Revolt-Destruction- Reconstruction," 280. It must be mentioned here that there exists a groups of scholars who question the very existence of the Council of Yavneh.

leadership first of Yoḥanan ben Zakkai, and later Gamaliel II, began the process of rebuilding centered around the Torah, defining Judaism against other groups of the Second Temple Judaism including Christianity.[276] The presiding head, *nasī* ("Prince") or "patriarch," Gamaliel II, named by Rome, was a descendent of Hillel, and from 90 CE onwards the Academy exerted decisive leadership in religious matters.[277] The local aristocracies, especially in the cites, were not going to subject themselves voluntarily to the hegemony of a new power group; the priests still thought of themselves as the leaders of the people; and the masses were indifferent to many aspects of rabbinic piety.[278]

What was the identity of the rabbis? Where did they draw their resources from? It is a fact that the rabbis could not emerge from a vacuum, especially if one were to consider the initiatory steps that they undertook towards consolidation. In this regard, Cohen maintains that the rabbis saw themselves not as "Pharisees" but as "sages of Israel."[279] But almost all modern scholars agree that the rabbis of the Mishnah were closely related to the Pharisees. Some assume that the two groups were identical in all but in nomenclature, while others admit that the relationship is more complex.[280] However, it seems to be clear that no other Jewish group of importance was in a situation to

Cohen states, "All that is known of the "synod" of Yavneh is based on the *disjecta membra* of the Mishnah and later works, all of which were redacted at least a century after the event." Cohen, "The Significance of Yavneh:" 29. Boyarin discusses his own view in relation to Cohen's: I would, therefore, substitute for Cohen's prospective "creation," a retrospective and utopian "imagination." Daniel Boyarin, "A Tale of two Synods: Nicaea, Yavneh, and Rabbinc Ecclesiology" *Exemplaria* 12/1 (2000): 29. Boyarin takes a step further to argue that both Nicaea and Yavneh are fabricated.

[276] Christian *minim* were held guilty of the "two powers heresy" and abandoning the unity of God. Dunn, "The Question of Anti-Semitism," 199.

[277] Sandmel, *Judaism and Christian Beginnings*, 35. Though, they had the authority of decisive leadership on religious matters their authority was restricted. One tends to agree with Overman when he states "Only gradually did rabbinic schools become authoritative for Judaism. The legendary symbol of Yavneh reflects the *beginning* of the task of social reconstruction in the wake of the destruction of Jerusalem. Yavneh gives the impression that an authoritative body suddenly appeared which was able to impose orthodoxy, on the various groups and factions within Judaism. The formation and establishment of guidelines and authoritative figures or bodies would be part of a lengthy process of social construction within Judaism." Overman, *Matthew's Gospel and Formative Judaism*, 41.

[278] Cohen, "The Emergence of Rabbinic Judaism," 215, 221.

[279] Cohen, "The Emergence of Rabbinic Judaism," 226.

[280] Cohen, "The Significance of Yavneh:" 36. E. P. Sanders notes that the Pharisees and Rabbis cannot be simply equated. *Paul and Palestinian Judaism* (Philadelphia: Fortress Press, 1977), 60-62. A few scholars who doubt the pharisaic-Rabbinic connections altogether are J. Bowker, *Jesus and the Pharisees* (Cambridge: Cambridge University, 1973); P. Sigal, *The Emergence of Contemporary Judaism I. The Foundation of Judaism from Biblical Origins to the Sixth century AD* (2 vols; Pittsburgh: Pickwick, 1980, 377-413, 21-23). At no point in antiquity did the rabbis clearly see themselves either as Pharisees or as the descendants of Pharisees. The

claim leadership other than the Pharisees. The Pharisees skillfully maintained a balance through the stages of political conflict by keeping the confidence of the people as well as winning over the Romans. Further, they benefited from the fact that their religious programme was neither tied to Jerusalem nor to the Temple. Thus, it goes without saying that the Pharisees did have a definite role to play in the consolidation period of the Yavnean sages.

There were certain changes that took place in the pharisaic community after the events of 70 CE. The coalition that emerged from the events of 70 CE took on the task of unifying Jewish society and constructing institutions to maintain society. There may well have been a gathering at Yavneh following the destruction of Jerusalem. Formative Judaism then began to reorganize the social, religious and communal life of the Jewish community.[281] The Yavnean period lasted for about 60 years (70 -130 CE).[282]

1.4.2.1.1. The Sages

The Yavnean sages palliated the disaster of 70 CE by offering alternate means of religious expression in the absence of the Temple. They affirmed that the Torah still remained as the will of God stand unvanquished despite the destruction of the Temple. Even if the Temple no longer existed, it did not mean that Israel had lost all ways of serving God; the way shown by the Pharisees traced back to Sinai while looking forward to the reformation at Yavneh.[283] The oral Torah revealed by Moses and passed on from the prophet to the scribe, sage and rabbi was still in the hands of Israel.[284]

1.4.2.1.1.1. Rabbi Yoḥanan ben Zakkai[285]

The Pharisees of Jerusalem, who survived the Jewish revolt, assembled at Yavneh under the leadership of Yoḥanan. He offered an alternative in the absence of the Temple which was essentially reconciliation through the deeds

---

rabbis refer to themselves as "sages of Israel," "sages," "rabbis," etc., rather than "Pharisees" and do not acknowledge their sectarian origins. Cohen, "The Significance of Yavneh:" 40-41.

281 Overman, *Matthew's Gospel and Formative Judaism*, 43.

282 Levine, "Judaism from the Destruction," 133.

283 Neusner, *Judaism in the Beginning of Christianity*, 48

284 Neusner, *Judaism in the Beginning of Christianity*, 48.

285 Hereafter Rabbi Yoḥanan ben Zakkai is referred to as Yoḥanan. The rabbinic Judaism gives immense importance to Yoḥanan. In fact he is considered as the sole person who helped in the survival of Judaism after the first revolt. Gary G. Portion, "Yohanan Ben Zakkai," *ABD*, vol. 6, edited by David Noel Freedman (New York: Doubleday, 1992), 1024. One of the difficulties in tracing the involvement has been that there is a lack of information concerning his life and career and even the information available in the texts are dissimilar. Neusner notes that in the Tannaitic Midrashim, "...we hear nothing about Yoḥanan's dramatic escape from Jerusalem." The reason he gives is that the Tannatic Midrashim did not know of his escape. Jacob Neusner, *Development of a Legend: Studies on the Tradition Concerning Yohanan Ben Zakkai*, SPB 6

of loving kindness.[286] The Academy[287] established by Yoḥanan at Yavneh, along with his prominent disciples, Eliezer ben Hyrcanus and Joshua ben Hananiah, continued its relationship with the previous Sanhedrin at Jerusalem.[288] There he introduced a number of laws that were passed *(takkanot)* but avoided any form of extremes.[289] Yoḥanan was able to shift the Academy from Jerusalem to Yavneh signaling change from "…Temple religion to Synagogue Judaism."[290] The Romans gave a free hand to him except for one restriction

(Leiden: E. J. Brill, 1970), 35. Portion is skeptical about whether one is able to construct precise historical portrait of Yoḥanan's intellectual activity. Portion, "Yohanan Ben Zakkai," 1024.

[286] Simeon mentions about Yoḥanan: "Once as Rabban Johanan ben Zakkai was coming forth from Jerusalem, Rabbi Joshua followed after him and beheld the Temple in ruins. "Woe unto us!" Rabbi Joshua cried, "that this, the place where the iniquities of Israel were atoned for, is laid waste!" "My son," Rabban Johanan said to him, "be not grieved; we have another atonement as effective as this. And what is it? It is acts of loving-kindness, as it is said, "*For I desire mercy and not sacrifice*" (Hos. 6:6)." "Sayings of Simeon the Righteous," in *The Fathers according to Rabbi Nathan*, YJS 10, translated by Judah Goldin (New Haven: Yale University Press, 1955), 34.

[287] There are four sources that describe the legend about Yavneh and the establishment of the school there by Yoḥanan. They are: *The Fathers according to Rabbi Nathan*, one version from A and another from version B; another version from the Babylonian Talmud (*Babylonian Talmud Gittin* 56 a and b); and the fourth version from *Lamentations Rabbah* (*Lam. Rabbah* 1:5, 31). Overman, *Matthew's Gospel and Formative Judaism*, 39. Just before the destruction of the Temple, Rabbinic sources narrate that Yoḥanan, escaped from the disaster of Jerusalem by the pretense of having died, with his disciples being permitted to carry his casket outside the city. Yoḥanan received the right to the little town of Yavneh (in Hebrew Yavneh) on predicting to the general that Vespasian would soon become the Emperor of Rome.. Cohen, "The Emergence of Rabbinic Judaism," 227. It is also said that he received from Vespasian permission to establish a new center of an autonomous religious community in Yavneh, a Judean town, designated by the Romans as a detention center. Asher Finkel, "Yavneh's Liturgy and Early Christianity," *JES* 18/2 (Spring 1981): 231. *The Fathers according to Rabbi Nathan* notes, "Art thou Rabban Johanan ben Zakkai?" Vespasian inquired; "tell me, what may I give thee?" "I ask naught of thee," Rabban Johanan replied, "save Jamnia, where I might go and teach my disciples and there establish a prayer [house] 29 and perform all the commandments." "Go," Vespasian said to him, "and whatever thou wishest to do, do."" *The Fathers according to Rabbi Nathan*, 36. Schafer considers the establishment of a school as the "foundational myth of rabbinic Judaism." P. Schaefer, "Die Flucht Johanan b. Zakkai aus Jerusalem und die Gründung des "Lehrhauses" in Jabne" in *Aufstieg und Niedergang der römischen Welt* 2/19/2, edited by H. Temporini and W. Haase (Berlin, 1979) cited in Portion, "Yohanan Ben Zakkai," 98.

[288] Neusner, Jacob. *From Politics to Piety*, 98. The difference was the older Sanhedrin was body of the elite, the wealthy, the aristocrats; its successor at Yavneh was a body of scholars. Sandmel, *Judaism and Christian Beginnings*, 139.

[289] Levine, "Judaism from the Destruction," 133-134.

[290] Sandmel, *Judaism and Christian Beginnings*, 138. The question of when did the synagogue begin is disputed by scholars, chiefly because the clinching evidence is not to be found.

on the Academy.[291] The new center, according to Finkel, assured the survival of Judaism through: a. the consolidation of Torah legislation, in particular the oral traditions, despite serious differences; b. the centralization of prayer service, despite the destruction of the Temple; and c. the promotion of "love deeds" in contrast with the sacrifices of old. Yavneh's academy pursued Hillel's direction, "Consolidate in the time of scattering."[292] Yoḥanan, who headed the Academy, offered a provisionary assurance, that is, salvation certainly follows penitence[293] and good deeds will atone as sacrifices once did.[294]

To what extent did Yoḥanan have control over the Jews? Unfortunately there is no evidence that Rome recognized Yoḥanan's leadership or of any kind of recognition by the Jews generally, or by communal heads.[295]

1.4.2.1.1.2. Rabban Gamaliel II[296]

After Yoḥanan, Gamaliel II took over Yavneh and during his tenure the center attained widespread acknowledgement from both the Jewish and non-Jewish community. Further, the Yavneh at this time dealt with Halakhic matters

---

[291] In the time of Yoḥanan, Hillel's great grandson, Rabbi Gamaliel II, should have presided at Yavneh. The Romans vetoed this designation fearing that leadership by a supposed Davidic descendant would possibly induce insurrection. Thus, Yoḥanan's was allowed to assume leadership on a substitute basis. The title which, according to Rabbinic tradition, Gamaliel II would have borne was *nasi* ("prince"). Under the nasi there was an actual presiding chairman, the *Ab Bet Din* ("father of the Court"). It was this latter title that Yohanan bore, but he never had the title *nasi*. Sandmel, *Judaism and Christian Beginnings*, 139.

[292] Finkel, "Yavneh's Liturgy:" 232.

[293] Neusner, *Judaism in the Beginning of Christianity*, 93.

[294] Levine, "Judaism from the Destruction," 136.

[295] Levine, "Judaism from the Destruction," 136.

[296] Alon maintains that Gamaliel assumed leadership some 10-15 years after the destruction. Alon, G. *The Jews in their Land in the Talmudic Age*, vol. *I. Jerusalem*, 1980, 119 cited in Gafni, "The Historical Background," 29. Hereafter Rabban Gamaliel II will be referred to as Gamaliel II.

even from parts of "Asia."[297] Gamaliel II had a high prestige[298] and was more authoritative than Yoḥanan.

Gamaliel II understood his task as revitalizing the center through "... uniting the people around Torah, promoting academic and patriarchal authority, and introducing definitive measures for the preservation of the Jewish community in the areas of socio-economic and public liturgical life."[299] One of the prominent developments during Gamaliel II's period was that private and communal prayer became more or less codified as also the basic arrangement of the Jewish prayer.[300] It is at the instruction of Gamaliel II that the Eighteen Benedictions was composed at Yavneh by Shmu'el ha-Qatan against the *minim*.[301] Gamilel II was one of the most prominent supporters

---

[297] Levine also mentions that Gamaliel II, accompanied by other sages, often traveled to cities and towns throughout the country to visit colleagues, supervise religious practices and dispense halakhic advice (Tosfeta *Terumot* 2:13). He notes that Gamaliel II visited Jericho, Lod and Ashkeol in Judea (Tosfeta *Berakhot* 4:15); Narbata and "Samaritan towns" in Samaria (Tosfeta *Demai* 5:24); Kefar Ithnai (Legio) in the Jezreel Valley; as well as Tiberias, Acco, Akhziv and the "Ladder of Tyre" in the Galilee (Tosfeta *Shabat* 13:2). One rabbi (Rabbi Joshua be Hanniah, traveled to Alexandria to discuss various halakhic issues (Babylonian Talmud *Niddah* 69b-71a); another (Rabbi Akiva) ventured to Arabia, Africa, and Medea (Mishnah *Yevamot* 16:7). Gamaliel traveled to Rome on a number of occasions). Levine, "Judaism from the Destruction," 137.

[298] Gamaliel's high prestige had to do with: a) internal- his great grandfather was Hillel the elder, who held a leading positioning in first century Jerusalem, and a prominent figure in the Sanhedrin in the 30s, when the priests and Sadducees contemplated bringing the early Christians to trial (Acts 5:34-39) and his father, Rabbi Simeon ben Gamaliel, played an active revolt in the moderate leadership of Jerusalem during the early stages of the revolt; b) Rome recognized him as the spokesman and leader of the Jewish community in Palestine, *de facto* if not *de jure*. The precise nature of authority is not spelled out. The Romans gave the recognition as they were simply following their long-established policy of seeking ht support among the local aristocracy in order to maintain their rule over conquered provinces. This prestige and authority was probably conferred on Gamaliel some time close to the turn of the century. Levine, "Judaism from the Destruction," 137-138.

[299] Finkel, "Yavneh's Liturgy," 232.

[300] Sandmel, *Judaism and Christian Beginnings*, 147.

[301] Bavli Berakhot 28b-29a:

A. "Our Rabbis taught:

B. Shimʿon ha-Paqoli arranged the Eighteen Benedictions in order before Rabban Gamaliel at Yavneh

C. Rabban Gamaliel said to the Sages: 'Is there no-one who knows how to compose a benediction against the heretics (*minim*)?

D. Shmu'el ha-Qatan stood up and composed it.

E. Another year he forgot it and tried to recall it for two or three hours, yet they did not remove him." Alexander also notes the danger of giving too much importance to Bavli Berakhot 28b-29a as the precise connection of *Birkat ha-Minim* with Shmu'el ha-Qatan and the editing of the synagogue liturgy at Yavneh at the time of Gamaliel finds attestation only in the later Rabbinic literature. As cited in Alexander, ""The Parting of the Ways" From the Perspective,"

of unity.[302] The shift from the earlier period is clearly visible. At that time, holiness was given prominence, but now the thought of Israel's unity takes center stage.

The role of the Yavnean authorities needs to be understood in the context of the climate of the Jewish-Christian relationship post 70 CE, especially in terms of the relationship they shared and the factors that affected the relationship with one another.

1.5. Formative Judaism and Jewish-Christian Relationship in the Post 70 CE

1.5.1. Diversity and Conflict

The assumption that Rabbinic Judaism was normative in the first century Palestine has been questioned by Neusner who uses the plural term "Judaisms,"[303] instead of the singular, "Judaism"[304] to describe Judaism in the first century CE. Segal[305] affirms the diversity in Judaism. There has also been a shift in the Christian descriptions of Judaism especially in the second half of twentieth century. This has to do with asserting the diversity in religious expression in both the Second Temple Judaism and first-century Christianity.[306] Nevertheless, the aspect of diversity in both Judaism and first century Christianity does not insulate against situations of conflict. There were certain factors that probably drove a wedge in the Jewish-Christian relationship and one of them certainly

---

6. Levine notes that it is probable that some sort of public prayer had previously existed and that Rabban Gamaliel and his colleagues may have added some material during the editorial process. Levine, "The Nature and Origin of the Palestinian Synagogue Reconsidered:" 445. It was probably composed by Samuel the Little at the request of Rabban Gamaliel II at the end of first century CE. Pieter W. van der Horst, "The *Birkat Ha-Minim* in Recent Research," *ExpTim* 105/12 (Sep. 1994): 363. Bickerman notes that the wording of the Tefillah remained free and fluid even after the fixation of its schema by R. Simeon ben Gamaliel. Elias J. Bickerman, "The Civic Prayer for Jerusalem," *HTR* 55/3 (Jl. 1962): 169.

302 Forkman, "*Limits of the Religious Community*," 108.

303 The terms "Jews" and "Judaism" are difficult terms in the first century context. Mason remarks that there is no category of Judaism as such in the Graeco-Roman world. Steve Mason, "Jews, Judaeans, Judaizing, Judaism: Problems of Categorization in Ancient History," *JSJ* 38/4-5 (Nov. 2007): 457-512.

304 Neusner notes that just as there are various expressions of Judaism so it is also with Christianity. Jacob Neusner, "Preface" in *Judaism and their Messiahs at the Turn of the Christian Era*, edited by Jacob Neusner, William Scott Green, Ernest S. Frerichs (Cambridge: Cambridge University Press, 2003), xi.

305 Alan Segal, *The Other Judaisms of Late Antiquity*, BJS 127 (Atlanta: Scholars Press, 1987).

306 Martin Goodman, "Modeling the "Parting of the Ways" in *The Ways that Never Parted: Jews and Christians in Late Antiquity and the Early Middle Ages*, edited by Adam H. Becker and Annette Yoshiko Reed (Minneapolis: Fortress Press, 2007), 185.

concerned the identity of Jesus and his relationship to the Mosaic Torah.[307] Hurtado argues, "Whatever the intention of the Christian Jews…it may well be that the Jewish religious opponents saw earlier and more clearly than the Jewish Christ-devotees themselves that this Christ-devotion was a significant 'mutation' in the Jewish monotheistic practice."[308] It is necessary to examine the diversity as well catalysts that precipitated the conflict.

1.5.1.1. Diversity in Judaism and Christianity

After 70 CE one did not witness an end to Jewish sectarianism, instead it continued in Jerusalem. The writings of *2 Baruch* and *4 Ezra* written towards the end of the first century testify to this view.[309] The destruction of the Jerusalem temple in 70 CE (*2 Baruch and 4 Ezra*) was interpreted as confirmation of the beliefs of the community concerning God's rejection of the parent group. Towards the close of the first century CE *4 Ezra* (righteous 7:17, 51, 11; 9:14ff; the wicked 8:48, 15:1-8, 23) and *2 Baruch* (chapter 15-18, chap. 84) also reflect some of the sentiments and convictions. Both these writings use the language of sectarianism, especially the two terms that are characteristic of these sectarian communities, namely, "lawless" and "righteous." 4 Ezra uses the term "righteous" to designate Ezra's faithful community while the majority are contrasted and termed as wicked and ungodly (8:48; 15:23). In 2 *Baruch* it is the righteous who will be rewarded (85:3-5) and saved (2 *Baruch* 75:1-77:26).

Diversity characterized not only Judaism but also Christianity after 70 CE,[310] and thus one could even speak of 'Christianities' prevalent during this time. Here the term 'Christianities' means different expressions of Christian theology. Goodman is of the view that the Second Temple Judaism and first-century Christianity were diverse in their religious outlooks.[311] Meeks opines, "…the diversity of both the forms of Judaism and the forms of Christianity in

---

[307] Goodman notes that towards the second century Christians claimed "…the exclusive eschatological revelation concerned the identity and activity of Jesus of Nazareth." Goodman, "Modeling the "Parting of the Ways,"" 195.

[308] Hurtado argues that opposition to Christians was prevalent also in the pre-70 CE. Larry W. Hurtado, "Pre-70 CE Jewish Opposition to Christ-Devotion," *JTS* 50/1 (Apr. 1999): 58.

[309] Isaiah Gafni, "The Historical Background," in *Jewish Writings of the Second Temple Period: Apocrypha, Pseudepigrapha, Qumran Sectarian Writings, Philo, Josephus*, edited by Michael E. Stone (Philadelphia: Fortress Press, 1984), 28.

[310] It is interesting to note that Barker argues for pluralism existing in Judaism after the exile which continued into the first century. The tradition of a second God that existed in Judaism was interpreted by the Gnostics, the Church Fathers and the writers of the NT. She attempts to locate the high Christology for Jesus in the early Jewish tradition. Margaret Barker, *The Great Angel: A Study of Israel's Second God* (Kentucky: Westminster John Knox Press, 1992), especially 213-232.

[311] Martin Goodman, "Modeling the "Parting of the Ways," 185.

the first-century …is now generally conceded, at least in principle."[312] In this regard, Brown notes that early Christianity probably cannot be conceptualized only in terms of a clash between "Jewish Christianity" (Torah observing) and "Gentile Christianity" (against the Law), but rather "types of Jewish/Gentile Christianity."[313] Lüdemann terms the Jerusalem church's flight to Pella as a myth thereby adding scepticism over the view that there was a demise of apostolic Jewish Christianity in the first Jewish revolt.[314]

The representation of Christianity in the form of Jewish Christianity,[315] which was also seen as a sect within Judaism,[316] did help in finding a middle ground in the conflict in Jewish-Christian relations. Gager talks about "Dangerous Ones in Between" to denote the Jewish Christians who observed the Torah. Mainstream Jews and Christians considered them as threats to

---

[312] Wayne Meeks, "Breaking Away: Three New Testament Pictures of Christianity's Separation from the Jewish Communities" in *"To See Ourselves as Others See Us:" Christians, Jews, "Others" in Late Antiquity*, edited by Jacob Neusner and E. S. Frerichs (California: Scholars Press, 1985), 108.

[313] Raymond E. Brown, "Not Jewish and Gentile Christianity but Types of Jewish/Gentile Christianity," *CBQ* 45/1 (Ja. 1983): 74-79.

[314] Eusebius was the first to state this: "…the people of the church in Jerusalem were commanded by an oracle given by revelation before the war to those in the city who were worthy of it to depart and dwell in one of the cities of Perea which they called Pella." E. Capps, ed., *Eusebius: The Ecclesiastical History*, The Loeb Classical Library, vol. 1, translated by Kirsopp Lake (London: William Heineman, 1926), III. v. 3. Gerd Lüdemann, "The Successors of Pre-70 Jerusalem Christianity: A Critical Evaluation of the Pella-Tradition," in *Jewish and Christian Self-Definition*, vol. 1, *The Shaping of Christianity in the Second and Third Centuries*, edited by E. P. Sanders (Philadelphia: Fortress Press, 1980), 161-73. Palumbo is of the view that the evidence from the Dead Sea Scrolls "…the actual mass of exodus of the New Covenant to the land of Damascus (AD 65-66) was the source of alleged emigration of the pre-war Jerusalem church to Pella." Arthur E. Palumbo, *The Dead Sea Scrolls and the Personages of Early Christianity* (New York: Algora, 2004), 271.

[315] Taylor opines that the terms "Jewish-Christianity" and Judaeo-Christianity are treated as synonyms in modern scholarship. It was used to refer to a supposed religious phenomenon which spans the period from the very beginnings of Christianity to some time in the fifth century, when it is perceived to be extinct. Jewish-Christians are generally understood to have been marginalized, accepted neither by church nor by synagogue, because they intended to be both Jewish and Christian at one and the same time." Joan E. Taylor, *The Holy Places: The Myth making Jewish-Christian Origins* (Oxford: Clarendon Press, 1997), 18. She also notes that the attempt to define Jewish-Christianity by theology presumably is a futile exercise as "Christianity is the child of Judaism. The very idea of a Christ is a Jewish one. The Christian God is the Jewish God…" Taylor, *Christian and the Holy Places,* 22.

[316] Here is where one would disagree with Cohen who seems to envisage an idealistic situation. Cohen states that Jewish sectarianism ceased after 70 CE, which is not true. Cohen is correct when stating that the war of 66-7- CE weakened many sects. It is also that the war also removed one of the focal points of sectarianism. Cohen, "The Significance of Yavneh:" 31-36 and Cohen, "The Emergence of Rabbinic Judaism," 226. But the weakening of sects need not mean the end of sectarianism.

observing the boundaries between Christianity and Judaism.[317] The reason for this prolonged relationship between Judaism and early Christianity was due to the part played by Jewish Christianity, an intermediary. However, Rabbinic Judaism prevailed later on because of the failure of Jewish Christianity.[318]

Between 70-135 CE, there was a movement towards defining Jewish identity. Inspite of the process of self-definition by the rabbis and the attempt to rabbinize Judaism by their successors, there was still a Jewish-Christian group that continued the relationship between both beyond this period.[319] Nonetheless, one cannot visualize an idealistic situation between Judaism and Christianity in the first century CE as one devoid of conflict. There were certainly occasions of conflicts, which are expressed in the texts of the New Testament as well that of the Church Fathers.[320]

1.5.1.2. Conflict[321] *in Jewish-Christian Relations*

Ceratin texts in the New Testament describe a situation of conflict which is also documented by Justin Martyr and others. How does one deal with texts such as Matthew 23 and 27:25, Jn 9:22, 12:42, 16:2; 8:44 where there seems to be a polemic against the Pharisees and "the Jews?" According to Stanton, Matthew's community parted with Judaism and the community viewed itself as '*extra muros*.'[322] This interpretation of Stanton has been under scrutiny in recent scholarship, which views the parting of ways as a phenomenon that took

---

[317] John G. Gager, "Jews, Christians, and the Dangerous Ones in Between" in *Interpretation in Religion*, edited by Shlomo Biderman and Ben-Ami Scharfstein (Leiden: E. J. Brill, 1992), 249-257.

[318] Alexander, """The Parting of the Ways,""" 5.

[319] James D. G. Dunn, "Concluding Summary," *Jews and Christians: The Parting of Ways A.D. 70 to 135*, The Second Durham- Tübingen Research Symposium on Earliest Christianity and Judaism, edited by James D. G. Dunn (Grand Rapids, Michigan: William B. Eerdmans Publishing Company, 1999), 368.

[320] Of course here the researcher takes the view that texts mirror reality are not just examples of rhetorics; this is a fundamental presupposition of sociological interpretation.

[321] Taylor argues for the inadequacies of the conflict-theory. She notes, "The sense with which anti-Judaism was a theological choice, built into the church's vision of itself and of the world, and intrinsic to Christian teaching, is dissimulated by the "conflict theory"." Miriam S. Taylor, *Anti-Judaism and Early Christian Identity: A Critique of the Scholarly Consensus* (Leiden: E. J. Brill, 1995), 196. But Taylor's view that conflicts were based on theological ideas and did have nothing to do with the context has been criticized by Kinzig. For him, Taylor is just regurgitating the view of Harnack. Wolfram Kinzig, review of *Anti-Judaism and Early Christina Identity: A Critique of the Scholarly Consensus* by Miriam S. Taylor *JTS* 48/2 (O. 1997): 649 (643-649).

[322] Graham N. Stanton, "Gospel of Matthew and Judaism," *BJRL* 66/2 (Spring 1984): 273, 264-284.

place much later.[323] Nevertheless, there were hints of conflict visible in the Christian interpretation of scripture.

The texts in the New Testament argue for the Christians' right to be called Israel and for the right interpretation of Scripture.[324] The interpretation of the Scripture had two aspects. First, Judaism as an Old covenant is now superseded (Lk. 22:20; Hebrews 8:8-13). Second, Jesus as the fulfillment of what was promised in the Bible (Matt. 5:17; I Cor. 10:1-11).[325] In this regard, Yuval notes, "Even before the Christianization of the Roman Empire, Christians saw the Destruction of the Temple and the subjugation of Jews to Rome as a proof of the blessing "the elder shall serve the younger."[326] Other than Scripture, there were other instances of conflict, which include Christology, Temple, Gentile inclusion, and apocalypticism.

Christology, especially in terms of high Christology, was one of the important factors that created differences.[327] The Jewish side had its primary focus on the Law whereas in the Christian texts, the stress was on the centrality of Christ, and also the perception that the final revelation was in and through Christ.[328] The Christology of the FG is another aspect to be reckoned here. It moves beyond the synoptic gospels especially in terms of the Father-Son relationship, the descending and ascending Son of man, and so on;[329] this conception of Christ suffered difficulty in accommodating the monotheistic stance of the Second-Temple period.[330] There also probably existed assertions

---

[323] A discussion on the question of parting of the ways is taken up later in this chapter. However, one tends to agree with Dunn when he notes that for Luke, Matthew and John the separation was not over and "Judaism was not yet solely rabbinic Judaism. Christian Judaism was not yet simply Christianity." He also notes that the parting aspect probably was understood from the point of view of the opponents and not so with the evangelists because there seems to be ample evidence of Christianity trying to see it in relation to Judaism. Dunn, *The Parting of the Ways*, 212, 214.

[324] Marc G. Hirshman, *A Rivalry of Genius: Jewish and Christian Biblical Interpretation in Late Antiquity*, translated by Batya Stein (Albany: SUNY Press, 1996), 2.

[325] Edward Kessler, *An Introduction to Jewish-Christian Relations* (Cambridge: Cambridge University Press, 2010), 27-28.

[326] Israel Jacob Yuval, *Two Nations in Your Womb: Perceptions of the Jews of Christians in Late Antiquity and the Middle Ages* (California: University of California Press, 2008), 15.

[327] Alexander, ""The Parting of the Ways,"" 19.

[328] Rowland, "The Parting of the Ways," 236.

[329] Lindars states, "The central aim of the Johannine christology is to expound the intimate relationship of Jesus and God. For this purpose John takes over the idea of the Son of Man, already current in the gospel tradition. He works creatively on this basis in full view of the primary tex in Dan. 7, and in the light of developments from it in Jewish apocalyptic." Barnabas Lindars, "The Son of Man in the Johannine Christology" in *Essays on John*, SNTA 17, edited by Christopher M. Tuckett (Leuven: Leuven University Press, 1992), 49.

[330] Dunn, *The Parting of the Ways*, 234.

and counter assertions between Jews and Christian leaders regarding Christ. Stanton is of the view that, in response to the claims of Jesus as the Son of God by the members of the Matthean community, the Jewish leaders laid charges of his being a sorcerer and deceiver.[331] In the FG, the claim of Jesus as the Son who shares a relationship with the Father probably sparked off dispute with the Jewish leaders.[332] An important aspect in the conception of Christology had to do with the interpretation of death and resurrection of Christ.[333]

Another element that led to conflict was the concept of the Temple. Stephen's speech is widely seen as an extreme critique of the Temple in the early Christian movement.[334] Dunn notes, "Stephen affair and the Hellenist outreach from Jerusalem marked a development from and a growing breach with Temple-centered Judaism."[335] In the wake of the destruction of the Temple, the Temple was seen as replaced by Christ.[336] Paul regards the location of the presence of God not in the Temple but rather in the *body of Christ*, the communities of faith; this was quite contrary to the view of 'Temple-centered Judaism.'[337] This identification probably goes to a period earlier than Paul and is seen in different layers of the Christian tradition.[338] However, this concept had three benefits: the presence of God now made visible in the community, importance of holy living, and opening of an avenue to incorporate the Gentiles

---

[331] Stanton also notes that these accusations refer back to the time of Jesus. Graham N. Stanton, "Matthew's Christology and the Parting of the Ways," in *Jews and Christians: The Parting of Ways A.D. 70 to 135*, The Second Durham- Tübingen Research Symposium on Earliest Christianity and Judaism, edited by James D. G. Dunn (Grand Rapids, Michigan: William B. Eerdmans Publishing Company, 1999), 101. Also refer G. N. Stanton, "Early Christian-Jewish Polemic and Apologetic," *NTS* 31/3 (Jl.1985): 377-92.

[332] Stanton, "Matthew's Christology," 99.

[333] Stuhlmacher notes this aspect, when he adumbrates that the cause for the split between Christians and Jews goes back to the passion and resurrection of Jesus. Peter Stuhlmacher, "Understanding of Christ in the Pauline Tradition: A Sketch" in *Jews and Christians: The Parting of Ways A.D. 70 to 135*, The Second Durham-Tübingen Research Symposium on Earliest Christianity and Judaism, edited by James D. G. Dunn (Grand Rapids, Michigan: William B. Eerdmans Publishing Company, 1999), 174.

[334] Acts 7:1-53.

[335] Dunn, *The Parting of the Ways*, 98.

[336] The redactional passages in Matthew (Matt. 1:23; 18:20; 28:20) emphasize the presence of Jesus with the disciples and further Matt. 12:6 states Jesus' claim of being greater than the Temple. This certainly was counter to the Jewish understanding of God's presence. Graham N. Stanton, "Matthew's Christology," 115. Also refer Andreas J. Köstenberger, "The Destruction of the Second Temple and the Composition of the Fourth Gospel," *TrinJ* 26/2 (Fall 2005): 205-242.

[337] Dunn notes that with such a view "*…at least there was a pulling apart and a parting of the ways at a very early stage.*" Dunn, *The Parting of the Ways*, 101-103, 126.

[338] Timothy Scott Wardle, *Continuity and Discontinuity: The Temple and Early Christian Identity*, PhD dissertation (Duke University, 2008), iv.

into the people of God.[339] This view is seen in the FG where Jesus overshadows the Temple (Jn. 2:21) and also in the passages of other New Testament writers who note that with the coming of Jesus, the Temple and its cult do not hold relevance.[340]

Inclusion of the Gentiles did create embers that turned into a conflagration. As the Church became more and more Gentile, it resulted in a conflict with those who advocated keeping of the Law by the Gentiles.[341] Cohen too notes that the Church becoming more and more Gentile only escalated the conflict between Jews and Christians.[342] Goodman also notes, "…it disavowed the Mosaic Torah as the hallmark for a righteous life, and it claimed that salvation and God's blessing were possible only through faith in Jesus… it excommunicated the native children of Israel who maintained the traditional criterion of Israelite identity, adherence to the Mosaic Torah."[343] Together with the inclusion of Gentiles, was also the spurt of Jewish nationalism that did not die down after the first Jewish revolt but continued to gain strength as seen in the second Jewish revolt. Nationalism was intertwined with the zeal for the Law and took on a messianic colouring.[344]

Apocalypticism also played a role in Jewish-Christian relations. Rowland notes that apocalypticism probably had a role in the growth and sustainment of the early Christian communities.[345] He highlights that it asserted the promise of God's reign wherein injustice and oppression would be removed. Moreover, he says that it also encouraged a spirit of separation, in terms of a dualistic conception of the world.[346] Chester in a similar vein notes, "It is clear that the yearning of God to intervene and bring about his kingdom on earth …that concern for the restoration of Jerusalem and the Temple was often bound with this… Fervent messianic and eschatological hopes survive the catastrophe of 66-70 CE."[347] The apocalyptic movement operates not in terms of change but in

---

[339] Wardle, *Continuity and Discontinuity*, iv.

[340] Dunn, *The Parting of the Ways*, 125.

[341] Alexander, ""The Parting of the Ways,"" 23.

[342] Cohen, "The Emergenec of Rabbinic Judaism," 220.

[343] Goodman, "Modeling the "Parting of the Ways," 195.

[344] Alexander, ""The Parting of the Ways,"" 22.

[345] Rowland, "The Parting of the Ways," 213.

[346] Rowland, "The Parting of the Ways," 215, 218.

[347] Chester notes that the coming of the messianic kingdom and the consequent judgment was an important theme of 4 Ezra and 2 Baruch. Andrew Chester, "The Parting of the Ways: Eschatology and Messianic Hope" in *Jews and Christians: The Parting of Ways A.D. 70 to 135*, The Second Durham-Tübingen Research Symposium on Earliest Christianity and Judaism, edited by James D. G. Dunn (Grand Rapids, Michigan: William B. Eerdmans Publishing Company, 1999), 252-253.

valuing the things received and a keen incentive to continue.[348] It is interesting to note that the third of the 18 Benedictions longs for God's interference and the refurbishment of the Temple or the messianic kingdom.[349] Though there was a great deal of apocalyptic emphasis in Jewish and Christian texts and its commonality, "...the way the eschatological hopes and messianic promises are in many cases given their fulfillment in the Christian community serves to deepen and harden the division."[350]

Thus, there were catalysts that created conflicts in Jewish-Christian relations though it could be argued that diversity was a noted feature of Judaism post 70 CE. Lieu's comment on the Christian identity in the Jewish and Greco-Roman world holds significance here; she notes, "Jewish self-definition was evolving within the wider context of the Graeco-Roman world in the late Second Temple period and beyond. This would invite not just opposition but also assimilation or expropriation... The diversity within Judaism extended into diversity in her interactions within the complexity of the wider world. 'Christian' identity-making was taking place in the same context."[351] There were not just situations of conflict but also expressions of conflict.

1.5.1.3. Expressions of Conflict

Two expressions of conflict are worth discussing: the Benedictions and evidence from the Church Fathers.

1.5.1.3.1. Benedictions

The two central prayers in Jewish liturgy were the '*Amidah* and the *Shema*.'[352] The recitation of the Shema is followed by the prayer, Tefillah, in the synagogue. It consists of a series of 'Benediction,' named after the responses at the end of each petition: "Blessed art thou, O Lord."[353] It is assumed that Simeon ha-Paḳuli, at the behest of Rabbi Gamaliel II at Yavneh, ordered the eighteenth benediction.[354] It was obligatory for everyone to repeat the Eighteen

---

[348] Rowland, "The Parting of the Ways," 236.

[349] Chester, "The Parting of the Ways," 254.

[350] Chester, "The Parting of the Ways," 306.

[351] Judith M. Lieu, *Christian Identity in the Jewish and Graeco-Roman World* (Oxford: Oxford University Press, 2004), 19-20.

[352] Levine, "The Nature and Origin:" 444.

[353] George Foot Moore, *Judaism in the First Centuries of the Christian Era: The Age of the Tannaim*, vol. 1 (Cambridge: Harvard University Press, 1950), 291. Instone-Brewer locates the *Birkat ha-Minimi* before 70 CE and the curse of the *minim* from the period of Gamaliel I. David Instone-Brewer, "The Eighteen Benedictions and the *Minim* Before 70 CE," *JTS* 54/1 (Apr. 2003): 25-44.

[354] There are two types of berakoth in Jewish tradition. The first type is a brief formula and is composed merely of a praise-thanksgiving and accompanies every action of the pious Jew

Benedictions. R. Gamaliel was disturbed by the rampant heterodoxy in the Jewish community and demanded a prayer for the heretics, which was rendered by R. Samuel the Small between 85 and 95 CE.[355]

1.5.1.3.1.1.The Text of the XII Benediction

Birkat ha-Minim (Palestinian Recension)[356]

A. For apostates (*mešummadim*) may there be no hope,[357]
B. And the arrogant kingdom (*malkhut zadon*) uproot speedily in our days
C. May the Christians (*noṣerim*) and the heretics (*minim*) perish in an instant
D. *May they be blotted out of the book of living,*
And may they not be written with the righteous (Ps. 69:29).
E. Blessed art Thou, O Lord, who humblest the arrogant."

1.5.1.3.1.2. Origin and Composition

There seems to be difficulty in tracing the oldest or the original version[358] of this benediction as there are more than ten versions of it in the publication on the *Shemoreh Esreh*.[359] In several of these versions the heavy hand of Christian

---

from morning to evening. The second type is more developed formula in which the supplication has its place but in the context of "blessing" and has its place either in the Synagogue service or in the meal prayers. In the *Birkat ha-minim*, one is dealing with the second type. Louis Bouyer, *Eucharist: Theology and Spirituality of the Eucharistic Prayer*, translated by Charles Underhill Quinn (London: Notre Dame Press, 1968), 50.

[355] Steven T. Katz, "Issues in the Separation of Judaism and Christianity after 70 CE: A Reconsideration," *JBL* 103/1 (Mr. 1984): 63.

[356] Jacob Mann, "Genizah Fragments of the Palestinian Order of Service," *HUCA* 2 (Jan. 1925): 306f. The Talmud is a two-stage compilation of the laws of Synagogue Judaism – the first stage is the Mishnah and the second stage is Gemara. The Gemara has been transmitted in two versions which are called "recensions" once compiled by Babylonian Jews about 500 CE ("the Jerusalem Talmud") and the other by Palestinian Jews about 450 CE ("the Palestinian" Talmud). Sandmel, *Judaism and Christian Beginnings*, 103.

[357] Fragment no. 7 has the important addition that for apostates there be no hope 'if they do not return to Thy Torah.' Kaufmann Kohler, "The Origin and Composition of the Eighteen Benedictions with a Translation of the Corresponding Essene Prayers in the Apostolic Constitutions," *HUCA* 1 (Jan. 1924): 387-425; Mann, "Genizah Fragments of the Palestinian Order:" 296.

[358] What makes matters worse is that the text differs not only in the various medieval rituals, but even in manuscripts of the same prayer book, such as that compiled by R. Amran Gaon in the ninth century CE. Bickerman, "The Civic Prayer:" 164.

[359] D. J. van der Sluis *et. al.*, *Elke morgen nieuw: Een inlieidung tot de Joodse gedachtenwereld aan de hand van de Sjemoneh* Esreh (Hilversum, 1978), 393-396 cited in der Horst, "The *Birkat ha-Minim*:" 363. Further, Christian censorship in the Middle ages or later is another factor that one has to contend with. van der Horst, "The *Birkat ha-Minim*:" 363.

censorship is obvious. The most erstwhile manuscripts available are the two Geneziah manuscripts published by Solomon Schechter.[360] Though these manuscripts have the phrase, 'May the *nostrim* and the *minim* perish speedily,' it is still unclear whether the original version contained the phrase.[361]

A number of scholars have been persuaded that the Genizah's wording, '*Noztrim* and the rest,' is the original formula[362] while some others disagree. A major obstacle in resolving this issue is the unavailability of the original version of the Yavenan malediction.[363] However, what can be retraced is the original meaning of the benediction.[364] Bouyer notes in connection with this aspect, "…the Jewish prayers had a content, a structure and key terms that were perfectly defined from the outset."[365] The term word *minim* was a part of the original version as this could be the only rationale for its usage in the Rabbinic and patristic writings.[366] Further, it has been pointed that all the versions seem to attest two different motifs with one common objective: a

---

[360] Solomon Schechter's discovery of a different rendition of the blessing in the Cairo Genizah, the Genizah fragment reads: For apostates (*meshumaddin)* let there be no hope, and the dominion of arrogance do Thou speedily root in our days; and let Christians (*ve-ha-Notzrim*) and *minim* perish in a moment, let them be blotted out of the book of the living and let them not be written with the righteous." S. Schechter, "Genizah Specimens," *JQR* old series 10/4 (Jl. 1898): 654-659.

[361] van der Horst, "The *Birkat ha-Minim*:" 363.

[362] According to Ashton the theory of the relation between the proceedings of Yavneh and the FG goes back at least as far as 1861 to M. von Aberle's article in *Theologische Quartalschrift* 42 (1861) cited in John Ashton, "The Identity and Function of *IOYΔAIOI* in the Fourth Gospel," *NovT* 27/1 (Ja. 1985): 74. Davies argues that if *ha-Nozrim* is removed from Samuel's prayers then the structure of the prayer is disturbed. W. D. Davies, *The Setting of the Sermon on the Mount* (Cambridge: Cambridge University Press, 1964), 276. The others who hold the same view are R. Wilde, *The Treatment of the Jews in the Greek Christian Writers* (Washington, DC: Catholic University of America Press, 1949); J. T. Townsend, "The Gospel of John and the Jews," in *Antisemitism and the Foundations of Christianity*, edited by A. Davies (New York: Paulist Press, 1979), 72-97; Marcel Simon, *Verus Israel: A Study in the Relation between Christians and Jews in the Roman Empire (135-425)*, translated by H. McKeating (Oxford: Oxford University Press, 1986), 236. These scholars are cited in Katz, "Issues in the Separation:" 64.

[363] Katz is of the view that the Yavnean text did not include an explicit reference to *Notzrim*. In all probability addresses itself to "outsiders" *(perushim),* "heretics" (*minim*), and the "arrogant of the nations" (*zedim*). Katz, "Issues in the Separation:" 68-69. J. Heinemann, *Prayer in the Talmud* (Berlin: de Gruyter, 1977); L. Hoffmann, *The Canonization of the Synagogue Service* (Notre Dame: University of Notre Dame Press, 1979) and others point that the process of standardizing the liturgy into a relatively uniform text was a long and complex, reaching in culmination only at the end of late antiquity or in the early Middle ages. The above works are cited in Levine, "The Nature and Origin of the Palestinian Synagogue:" 445.

[364] Elias J. Bickerman, "The Civic Prayer:" 164.

[365] Bouyer, *Eucharist*: *Theology*, 53.

[366] der Horst, "The *Birkat ha-Minim*:" 363.

request for the destruction of the "arrogant kingdom" and prayer for a verdict on the *minim*.[367]

Instone-Brewer opines, "The origins and original wording of the Eighteen are now impossible to construct, though their form goes back before the first century, because very similar ideas and wording is found in various sources especially Ben Sira 36:1-17; 51:21-35 (Hebrew) and 2 Macc. 1:24-29."[368] Whether there is a veiled or explicit reference of the *minim* in this benediction is a concern that needs to be examined.

1.5.1.3.1.3. Birkat ha-Minim (XII Benediction)

Before proceeding to the discussion on *Birkat ha-Minim,* it is necessary to place the twelfth benediction in its proper context. The daily prayer of the synagogue, Tefillah or Amidah, was a request for well being and comprised of eighteen sections and each ended with the saying: "Blessed be thou, YHWH."[369] The twelfth *berakhah* in the Jewish *Shemoneh Esreh* was commonly titled the *Birkat ha-Minim* (the blessing of the heretics), an indirect expression to anathemize the outsiders.[370] The structure of the petition was assumed to have been fixed toward the end of the first century CE, but the exact wording was not fixed. Since the Amidah was in the oral stage, they were recited differently in the synagogues.[371]

Out of the Eighteen Benedictions, the last six were eschatological petitions concerned with the hope of Israel, especially in light of the fall of Jerusalem and probably reflected Yavneh's solution.[372] Perhaps what is seen here is that sages at Yavneh attempted to formulate the eschatological concern in terms of its own "self-understanding."[373]

---

[367] Alexander, "The Parting of Ways,"" 7.

[368] Instone-Brewer, "The Eighteen Benedictions:" 27.

[369] Bickerman, "The Civic Prayer for Jerusalem:" 163.

[370] van der Horst, "The *Birkat ha-Minim*:" 363. Ehrlich states, "Worded more like an imprecation (see *Tanḥuma* [Buber ed.], *Vayikra* 3), in its invocation of divine wrath against internal enemies to Jewish integrity and against external enemies of the Jewish people, it differs from the other petitions." Uri Ehrlich, "BIRKAT HA-MINIM" in *EncJud*, edited by Fred Skolnik, vol. 3, 2nd ed. (New York: Thomas Gale, 2007), 711. The tradition ascribes the origin and sequence of the Eighteen Benedictions to men of the Great Synagogue. Scholars are united that the Eighteen Benedictions existed earlier but difference of opinion whether they were innovated on a single instance or grew to eighteen by accumulation. Sandmel, *Judaism and Christian Beginnings*, 148.

[371] Bickerman, "The Civic Prayer:" 164.

[372] Finkel, "Yavneh's Liturgy:" 245.

[373] Finkel, "Yavneh's Liturgy:" 246.

1.5.1.3.1.3.1. The Term Minim

A *min* was defined as one who broke a covenant and was thus a traitor to the belief of the fathers and to the tenets of Israel's God.[374] In this limited sense, it could stand for Jewish Gnostics, Jewish Christians,[375] and Christians. However, the term *minim* was not confined to Christians but could be applied to heretics in general.[376] There are other disapproving terms, like minim, found in the various versions of the benediction.[377]

There are three main theories[378] concerning the term *minim*. The first is that it was directed against those who violated the pharisaic regulations; groups such as Jewish gnostics, Jewish Christians, Essenes and others were included in this. Another possibility is that it referred to the Jewish Christians. The third proposal was that it concerned those other than the Jewish community who posed a threat to Jewish existence, even a reference to Rome.[379]

The first theory can be seen in the way Rabbinic Judaism looked at those who did not accept its authority. Alexander states, "…a *min* in Rabbinic terms denotes a Jew who does not accept the authority of the Rabbis and rejected the Rabbinic halakhah." Further, the heretic not only forfeits the covenantal blessings in the present but also in the future and thus does not belong to the

---

[374] Sell, *The Talmud*, 72.

[375] Reuven Kimelman, "*Birkat Ha-Minim* and the Lack of Evidence for an Anti-Christian Jewish Prayer in Late Antiquity," in *Jewish and Christian Self-Definition*, vol. 2: *Aspects of Judaism in the Greco-Roman Period*, edited by E. P. Sanders, Albert I. Baumgarten, and Alan Mendelson (Philadelphia: Fortress Press, 1981), 228.

[376] Kimelman notes the meaning of the term *minim* different in the tannatic and amoraic literature. Kimelman, "*Birkat Ha-Minim*," 228.

[377] "Wicked" (*reša'im*), "sinners" (*poše'im*), "slanderers" (*malšinim*), "informers" (*moserim*), "apostates" (*mešummadim*), "renegades" (*perušim*) but these terms are general and do not carry the quarreling meaning that *minim* carries. Alexander, """The Parting of the Ways,""" 8.

[378] Horbury has a slight variation of this: a. directed against the Gentile government and as well as heretics, b. or against Christians especially or c. a combination of these. William Horbury, "The Benediction of the *Minim* and Early Jewish-Christian Controversy," *JTS* 33/1 (Apr. 1982): 33.

[379] Katz, "Issues in the Separation:" 69.

"*Kelal Yiṣra'el* (community of Israel)."[380] This would mean a change to stricter forms from the liberal attitudes in the Second Temple period.[381]

The third theory is elucidated by Finkel[382] who argues that the *minim* refers to "dualistic Gnostics." His argument is that *min* is related to *genos*, which means 'type' and in the post-temple period pertained to "libertine and ascetic gnostics and antinomians."[383] Finkel also mentions Jewish dissenters but has overlooked the fact that Jewish Christians did figure prominently in the post-Temple scenario.[384]

The second theory seems to be the most plausible. Kimelman, after having surveyed the tannaitic literature, amoraic literature of Palestine and Babylonia confirms that *minim* denoted a Jewish sectarian group and not the Gentiles in Palestinian literature.[385] Further, there seems to be no reference to non-Jews in the tannaitic literature before 135 CE. It seems best to agree with Katz when he notes, "The argument favouring the association of the *minim* of the *Birkat ha-Minim* primarily with the Jewish Christians is more widely held and considerably more plausible, if not without problem of its own."[386] Though the term *minim* could refer to Jewish Christians, there still remains the problem of defining the meaning of the term *noṣrim*.

---

[380] Rabbis used various terms to describe those outside the community: *minim* ("heretics"); *mešummadim* ("apostates"); *ḥiṣonim* ("outsiders"); *Kutiyyim* ("Samaritans"); *'ovedei kokhavim* ("heathens": lit. "star-worshippers"). Jewish Christians were ostracized in social and also commercial life. Tosefta Ḥullin 2:20-21 states that a piece of meat found in the hand of the *minim* is forbidden to derive any benefit and the meat which comes out of the house of a *minim* is considered as meat of sacrifices to the dead. So also nothing is sold to a *minim* and nothing is bought from them. Rabbinic Jews were not allowed to eat with Jewish Christians. Alexander, ""The Paring of the Ways,"" 5, 6, 15.

[381] Alexander, ""The Paring of the Ways,"" 9. Here one tends to disagree with Cohen who states that after the destruction of the temple the emergence of the ideology of pluralism arose to replace the monism which previously characterized the temple and the sects. Cohen, "The Significance of Yavneh:" 45. The use of the term *minim* clearly disowns this understanding.

[382] Finkel, "Yavneh's Liturgy:" 238-239.

[383] Finkel, "Yavneh's Liturgy:" 239.

[384] Kimleman affirms this when he notes that one of the prominent groups which could be included in the term *minim* was Jewish Christians. Kimelman, "*Birkat ha-Minim* and the Lack," 232.

[385] Kimelman, "*Birkat ha-Minim* and the Lack," 230. Schiffman notes that a number of restrictions directed against *minim* clearly refer to the early Jewish Christians as seen from their date and content. Schiffman, "At the Crossroads: Tannaitic Perspectives on the Jewish-Christian Schism," 149.

[386] Katz, "Issues in the Separation:" 69-70.

1.5.1.3.1.3.2. The Use of the Term Noṣrim

As stated earlier, a number of witnesses from the Cairo Geniza and elsewhere specify that the term *noṣrim* refers to Christians.[387] Here, Schürer's caution needs to be taken into account.[388] Scholarship seems to be divided on whether the term *noṣrim* was part of the original text. Krauss argues that the term was included on the basis of Epiphanius' mention of Jews cursing Nazarenes.[389]

Kimelman[390] clearly brings out the different views related to the term *noṣrim*. Geneziah text was part of the original text, which had the term *noṣrim*.[391] The patristic writers dwell on the Jewish exercise of cursing Christians and thus *noṣrim* was a component of it. The underlying supposition here is that *noṣrim* is akin to Nazarenes.[392] Still others are of the view that since Christians are not directly mentioned, *noṣrim* must be the original.[393] Many are of the view

---

[387] Horbury, "The Benediction of the *Minim*:" 19.

[388] Schürer warns against the assumption that the Genziah text-form was already current in the end of the first century. Emil Schürer, *A History of the Jewish People in the Time of Jesus Christ*, translated by Sophia Taylor and Peter Christie, vol. 2, Second Division (Edinburgh: Hendrickson, 1998), 89.

[389] Though, he recognizes that the benediction could have undergone changes, it did include Nazarenes as Epiphanius mentions it. He answers his critics on the non-occurrence of the term in the Talmud due to "medieval censors." S. Krauss, "The Jews in the Works of the Church Fathers," *JQR* old Series 5/1 (O. 1892): 131-132. Katz refutes Krauss as his reading of Notzrim is post-tannaitic in origin. Katz, "Issues in the Separation:" 70.

[390] Kimelman, "*Birkat ha-Minim* and the Lack," 232-233.

[391] One of the advocates of this view is K.G. Kuhn, *Achtzehngebet und Vaterunser und der Reim*, Tübingen , 1950, pp. 18ff cited in Kimelman, "*Birkat ha-Minim* and the Lack," 232.

[392] Advocates are – Krauss, "The Jews in the Works of the Church Fathers:" 130ff. J. Louis Martyn's *History and Theology in the Fourth Gospel* (Nashville: Abingdon Press, 1979), 58. W. D. Davies, The *Setting of the Sermon on the Mount*, 1966, 278f.; J. T. Townsend, 'The Gospel of John and the Jews: The Story of a Religious Divorce,' *Antisemitism and the Foundation of Christianity*, edited by W. D. Davies, (New York: Paulist Press, 1979), 72-79 cited in Kimelman, "*Birkat ha-Minim*," 233. Kimelman does not agree with this assumption and proposes that Jerome is pointing to a group of Jewish Christians who are called Nazoraeans. He notes that they are associated with Minaeans and are cursed by the Jews. Further, nosrim does not denote Christians, but rather Nazoraens, a Jewish sect whose existence is vouched for at least two fourth-century sources. The Hebrew original *naṣrim* is more assonant with Nazoraeans. This proposal does not warrant any consideration. Schiffman notes that Jerome is also wrong in seeing *nostrim* and *natsrim* are identical – the former are Nazarenes and the latter are Nazoreans. Lawerence Schiffman, *Who was a Jew? Rabbinic and Halakhic Perspectives on the Jewish Christian Schism* (Hoboken, 1985) cited in van der Horst, "The *Birkat ha-Minim*:" 367. van der Horst also agrees with Schiffman and opines that Jerome certainly knew the difference between Nazoreans and Nazarenes. der Horst, "The *Birkat ha-Minim*:" 367.

[393] Townsend, "The Gospel of John and the Jews" cited in Kimelman, "*Birkat ha-Minim*," 233.

that *noṣrim* was a later addition. The chief reason being that *noṣrim* makes the reading hard as well repetitive because it has the same functions as *minim*.[394]

The last view presents a case. It is a theory that *noṣrim* was not part of the *Birkat ha-Minim* but added later.[395] Other than the fact that the addition of *noṣrim* would hinder a smooth rendering, there are persuasive arguments as well. One of them is that it gives space for the historical developments in the growth of the Christian community. The growth was from an exclusively Jewish group to a stage where the addition of Gentiles grew more and more, consequently there was a reduction in the Jews.[396] This development prompted an addition of the term *noṣrim* in the *Birkat ha-Minim* in order to differentiate between the Jewish Christians (*minim*) and the Gentile Christians (*noṣrim*).[397] There are other arguments presented by scholars that strengthen the thesis that term *noṣrim* was added later in the *Birkat ha-Minim.*[398]

Thus far it has been argued that the *minim* referred clearly to the Jewish Christians and the later addition of the term *noṣrim* in the *Birkat ha-Minim* had to do with the historical development of Christianity. Having said this, there is a crucial aspect that needs attention: what function did the *Birkat ha-Minim* play in the synagogue? This aspect gets attention in the next section.

---

[394] J. Jocz, *Jewish People and Jesus Christ* (London 1949), 56ff cited in Kimelman, "*Birkat ha-Minim* and the Lack," 233.

[395] As with regards to the rest of the views: the first view that Geneziah text was part of the original text has long been overridden as it difficult to recover an ur-text; the second one is also feasible as Justin and Origen does not mention it, only Epiphanius and Jerome mention it and this could be argued for a later addition; the third view does not hold good as *mnim* would certainly denote in late first century context, Jewish Christians.

[396] Kimelman notes, "Epiphanius and Jerome wrote about a century and half after Origen and by then much happened within between Judaism and Christianity in the meanwhile. It is only they who make clear references to Jews, Nazoraens, and cursing during the prayers thrice daily. Kimelman, "*Birkat ha-Minim* and the Lack," 237.

[397] One would tend to go with Schiffman who states that in the final decades of fourth century Christians were cursed under the name of nostrim in the synagogues unlike in the final quarter of the first century the Tannaim saw the Jewish Christians as a threat to the unity of the Jewish people and they cursed them together with other *minim* by expanding the already existing twelfth *berakhah* of the *Amidah*. Later, somewhere between 150 and 350 CE when Christianity had become predominantly non-Jewish Christianity, the term *nostrim* was added to include the gentile Christians (as they cannot be called *minim*). Schiffman, *Who was a Jew?...* cited in van der Horst, "The *Birkat ha-Minim*:" 367. Finkel adds another reason: the poetic structure of six verses with three beats in each. Nazarenes would appear in the text as an addition. Finkel, "Yavneh's Liturgy:" 238.

[398] Kimelman notes two reasons: a. if *noṣrim* were present originally in the Talmudic literature, the nomenclature would have been *birkat ha- noṣrim*; b. if it had been used as a part of statutory liturgy from first century then the term *noṣrim* should have become a common term in rabbinic literature. The term does not appear in tannaitic literature. Kimelman, "*Birkat ha-Minim* and the Lack," 233.

1.5.1.3.1.3.3. The Function of the Birkat ha-Minim

As in the earlier case, scholarship has taken different positions concerning *Birkat ha-Minim*. Contemporary scholarship concedes that while these pharisaic leaders were putting things in order, they set up fences against the flourishing influence of early Christianity. Judaism, in its quest for survival, was apparently threatened by Christianity. In its response, Yavneh not only formulated a negative view of Christianity, but purposely aimed at the exclusion of Christians from Jewish services. An act of excommunication was enforced by Yavneh's missionary activities. This widely accepted thesis has been developed further by Christian scholars.[399] These scholars more or less recognize that a definite breach had occurred between Jews and Christians during the early years of the Yavneh period and the *Birkat ha-Minim* played an important part in it.

This conjecture of the 'parting of ways' is beset with various problems. It is problematic because synagogues, at least in the first century, were not run by a centralized authority; further, even if the rabbinic authorities had power, it was limited to a particular region.[400] Finally, there is a lack of evidence of a general ban against Christians.[401]

---

[399] G. Bornkamm, "Die Binde und Lösegewalt in der Kirche des Matthäus," in *Geschichte und Glaube* II (Munich: Kaiser, 1971), 37-50; P. F. Ellis, *Matthew: His Mind and Message* (Collegeville: Liturgical Press, 1974); J. P. Meier, *Law and History in Matthew's Gospel* (Rome: Biblical Institute Press, 1976); S. van Tilborg, *Jewish Leaders in Matthew* (Leiden: Brill, 1972); K. Stendhal, *The School of St. Matthew*, 2nd ed. (Lund: Gleerup, 1968); D. Hare, *The Theme of Jewish Persecutions of Christians in the Gospel according to St. Matthew* (Cambridge: Harvard University Press, 1967). There are others who express caution R. Hümmel, *Die Auseinandersetzung zwischen Kirche und Judentum in Matthäus-evangelium*, 2nd ed. (Munich: Kaiser, 1966) and H. von Campenhausen, *Die Enstehung der christlichen Bibel* (Tübingen: Mohr, 1968). These scholars are cited in Finkel, "Yavneh's Liturgy:" 233. Krauss also argues for this position. Krauss, "The Jews in the Works of the Church Fathers:" 122-157. There are others who hold this view: Adolf von Harnack, *Judentum und Judenchristentum in Justins Dialog mit Trypho* (TU 39, Leipzig, 1913), 80, 91; Marcel Simon, *Verus Israel* 2nd ed. (Paris, 1964), 234-236 cited in Horbury, "The Benediction of the *Minim*:" 20. Frend states, "From the Jewsih point of view the separation was now complete." W. H. C. Frend, *Martyrdom and Persecution in the Early Church: A Study of a Conflict from the Maccabees to Donatus* (Grand Rapids, Michigan: Baker Book House, 1965), 179.

[400] Cohen, "The Emergence of Rabbinic Judaism," 227. Alexander also echoes this view when he states, "But it would be wrong to imagine the Yavneh was in any position to force it upon the synagogues of Palestine, let alone of the Diaspora." Alexander, ""The Parting of the Ways,"" 10. Several studies bring out the limitation of such a proposal. Katz, Steven T. "Issues in the Separation:" 43-76; Anthony J. Saldarini, *Pharisees, Scribes and Sadducees*," 207-208; Cohen argues that the separation between Judaism was a process not an event; this is in regard to the role of *Birkat ha-Minim*. Shaye J. D. Cohen, *From the Maccabees to Mishnah*, 2nd ed. (London: John Knox Press, 2006), 220.

[401] Katz also points that there is no clarity of an existence of a general use of the ban against Christians. He goes on to mention two types of ban. Two types of ban mentioned in rabbinic

Another view that has gained scholarly support is that the primary function of *Birkat ha-Minim* was to exclude Christians from responsible posts in the synagogue, such Jews who formed a threat to the unity of the people.[402] In other words, the aim was to identify Jewish Christians while they served as precentors during the synagogue liturgy. Kimelman points out that it is unlikely that in any case they would be invited to lead the service.[403] Yet another approach is by Maier,[404] who notes that the *Birkat ha-Minim* did not have the aim to remove heretics from the synagogue, but rather served the Jewish self-definition and the establishment of self-consciousness.

Given the different views on the function of *Birkat ha-Minim,* the theory that is most viable seems to be that the malediction was a curse against the heretics. As Katz points out, the *Birkat ha-Minim* was not necessarily a ban but a "filter"[405] that made it difficult for people to take part, which eventually led to dissenters moving out of the community.[406] However, Katz goes on to state that the issue of "cursing" is ambiguous in tannaitic literature.[407] Kimelman notes that there are only vague grounds of Jews cursing Christians in their prayers. On the contrary there is a large evidence of Christians being received in the synagogue.[408] However, the latter view need not be taken as a benchmark. Horbury rightly rejects this view of Kimelman, as "...Christians were

sources: *Niddui* was a means of communal discipline against stubborn resistant members (a temporary, revocable ban, usually of at least thirty days, which was leveled against those who threatened the pharisaic halakhic process as much as against those who threatened halakhic decision, example of R. Eliezer ben Hyrcanus) , especially sages, of the community; the second is *Ḥerem* connotes a permanent exclusion from the community, only after 200 CE. The full excommunication from Judaism and the Jewish community have a post-mishnaic provenance. *Ḥerem* made not one an excommunicant, but an excommunicant Jew. There seems to be no concrete evidence that R. Gamaliel II and the sages of Yavneh necessitated a *Niddui* or *Ḥerem* on the Jewish Christians. Katz, "Issues in the Separation:" 48-50. Cohen argues that those who embraced faulty beliefs were corrected or refused a part in the future world or were hushed up but not expelled. Cohen, "The Significance of Yavneh:" 42.

[402] Schiffman, *Who as a Jew?...* cited in van der Horst, 366.

[403] Kimelman, "*Birkat ha-Minim* and the Lack," 227.

[404] Johann Maier, *Jüdische Auseinandersetzung mit dem Christentum in der Antike* (Darmstadt, 1982) cited in van der Horst, 365.

[405] Katz, "Issues in the Separation:" 51.

[406] Katz, "Issues in the Separation:" 51.

[407] He states it is obscure because it could be a "curse" on the heretic or the heresy. Both the meanings are possible according to the sources. He also states that there is no official anti-Christian policy at Yavneh. Katz, "Issues in the Separation:" 75-76.

[408] Kimelman, "*Birkat ha-Minim* and the Lack," 244.

welcomed in the synagogues in situations before and after, separate Christian and Jewish worship had become normal."[409]

1.5.1.3.1.4. Birkat ha-Minim : An Evaluation

How does one evaluate the function of the *Birkat ha-Minim* in terms of Jewish-Christian relations? There are a few aspects that can be deduced from the scholarly discussions.

a) It is difficult to conceive of a wide implementation of the ban by the Yavenean authorities. Overman is right when he states that the gap between Jews and Christians was a protracted one and did not take place at a specific time.[410] Thus, it is also difficult to surmise that the Yavneh could consolidate so quickly so as to issue a general ban to be implemented in all the synagogues. Even if they had the authority to execute a ban, the scope would have been definitely limited.
b) Stemberger is of the view that *minim* could not have transpired in Judea for the paucity of Jewish Christians and Gentiles in this region.[411] This need not be taken as a major hurdle as there is ample evidence of conflict in different texts of Scripture. According to der Horst, [412] it seems definite that the development of relations between Judaism and Christianity in the first two centuries was one of "… increasing enmity that created a climate in which mutual curses are a distinct possibility."[413]
c) Dunn notes that there is a strong possibility that the relationship between Jews and Christians continued,[414] especially with the Jewish Christians. Thus, the "*clear cut or final parting of the ways at 70 CE is distinctly premature.*"[415] Here Dunn seems to be contesting

[409] William Horbury, *Jews and Christians in Contact and Controversy* (Edinburgh: T & T Clark, 1998), 48.

[410] Kimelman, "*Birkat ha-Minim* and the Lack," 244; Overman, "Matthew's Gospel and Formative Judaism," 49.

[411] Günther Stemberger, "Die sogennante 'Synod von Jabne' und das frühe Christentum," *Kairo* 19 (1977): 14-21 cited in Daniel Boyarin, "Justin Martyr Invents Judaism," *CH* 70/3 (Sep. 2003): 430 (427-461). Meeks terms *Birkat ha-minim* as the "red herring in Johannine research." Meeks, "Breaking Away: Three New Testament Pictures," 102.

[412] van der Horst, "The *Birkat ha-Minim*:" 367.

[413] van der Horst, "The *Birkat ha-Minim*:" 367.

[414] Dunn calls attention to different Jewish as well as Christian writings during this period that seem to suggest this aspect. Refer Dunn, *The Parting of the Ways*, 311. Stanton also notes that 70 CE should not be taken as water shed in Jewish-Christian relationship as there were interactions between Jews and Christians even in the second century. Refer Stanton, "Aspects of Early Christian-Jewish Polemic:" 377-392.

[415] Dunn, *The Parting of the Ways*, 311.

the view that *Birkat ha-Minim* was a watershed in terms of Jewish-Christian relations, which probably is true. Meeks rightly describes *Birkat ha-Minim* as "…a red herring in Johannine research."[416]

d) Recent scholarship has strongly emphasized that diversity did not disappear after 70 CE but rather continued, and this is seen as a drawback to the understanding of *Birkat ha-Minim*. In this regard, the withdrawal of Judeo-Christians to Pella on the arrival of Titus in Jerusalem does not seem to be a possibility.[417] This would then mean the diversity continued even in Christianity. However, the proposition of the *Birkat ha-Minim* was founded on the hypothesis that after 70 CE Judaism lost its diversity and the only other group that Christianity had to deal with was Rabbinic Judaism. But as seen earlier, diversity was a feature before as well as after 70 CE. Harnack bolstered the concept that after 70 CE Christianity succeeded Judaism as the true world religion. In other words he advocated Christianity as replacing Judaism. He notes,

> By their rejection of Jesus, the Jewish people disowned their calling and dealt the death-blow to their own existence; their place was taken by Christians as the new People, who appropriated the whole tradition of Judaism, giving… All that Gentile Christianity did was to complete a process which had in fact commenced long ago within Judaism itself, viz., the process by which the Jewish religion was being inwardly emancipated and transformed into a religion for the world.[418]

This view of Harnack is lop-sided as there was a considerable amount of diversity after 70 CE. Even so, the diversity did not mean that there was no conflict. In fact, to state there was no conflict between Jews and Christians probably idealizes the situation. There are scholars who do argue that the conflict continued. Simon points out the relations between Jews and Christians as one of debate and conflict.[419] He notes, "The problem of Jewish-Christian

---

416 Meeks, "Breaking Away: Three New Testament Pictures," 102.

417 Parkes mentions about the flight to Pella and the rabbinic leadership going to Jabne. James Parkes, *The Conflict of the Church and the Synagogue: A Study in the Origins of Anti-Semitism* (New York: The Word Publishing Company, 1961), 77.

418 Adolf von Harnack, *The Mission of Early Christianity*, translated by J. Moffat, vol. 1 (New York: G. P. Puttnam's Sons, 1908), 69-70.

419 Marcel Simon, *Verus Israel*. Baumgarten highlights the contribution of Simon in the understanding of Jewish history. Albert I. Baumgarten, "Marcel Simon's *Verus Israel* as a Contribution to Jewish History" *HTR* 92/4 (O. 1999): 465-478. Simon's conflict theory has drawn criticism from Taylor. She notes, "the "conflict theory" also proves inadequate as a theory of theological explanation. Not only does it contain inherently denigrating ideas of ancient

relations in the ancient world is a real one…Judaism, did not cease to trouble the Church."[420] Shoemaker also notes, "Significant Jewish populations were scattered throughout the early Byzantine Empire, and interreligious contact was an unavoidable consequence of the late ancient city's cramped quarters."[421]

Finally, it is possible to conclude that *Birkat ha-Minim* probably was not a universal ban but the possibility of an intra-Jewish conflict that could still exist. It does not do away with the fact that local synagogues did dispense with those who were a threat to the community. There seems to be no ruling out of the possibility of an intra-Jewish conflict that ended up in expulsion of some of its members. The Christian communities could be a part of the expulsion. Further, diversity post 70 CE need not necessarily imply there was no conflict in the Jewish-Christian relations. In addition, *Birkat ha-Minim* is not a watershed in Jewish-Christian relations. In other words, as Meeks puts it, "…the massive confrontation between "apostolic Christianity" and "normative Judaism," which even now haunts the imagination of students of Christian origins, never happened."[422]

Expressions of conflict are not limited to the *Birkat ha-Minim* but can also be seen in the texts of the Church Fathers. Though these discussions do not pertain to the first century CE, they still describe instances of conflict as well as contact in the Jewish-Christian relations.

1.5.1.3.2. Evidence from Church Fathers

Scholars have argued back and forth regarding the evidence that can be gathered on *Birkat ha-Minim.* In this regard, it is crucial to determine how much value can be attached to early Christian evidence.

1.5.1.3.2.1. Justin

Justin's *Dialogue*[423] was probably written between 155 and 160 CE.[424] There are in all eleven passages which are relevant to the present study. Out of these,

---

Judaism, but it obscures the role of anti-Judaism in Christian theology, fails to understand it as a phenomenon of enduring significance, and fails in its supposed aspirations to address the questions so essential to any genuine attempt at theological reevaluation." Taylor, *Anti-Judaism and Early Christian Identity*, 5.

[420] Simon, *Verus Israel*, 369.

[421] Stephen J. Shoemaker, "Let Us Go and Burn her Body:" The Image of the Jews in Early Dormition Traditions" *CH* 68/4 (Dec. 1999): 785.

[422] Meeks, "Breaking Away: Three New Testament Pictures," 115.

[423] Justin Martyr, "Dialogue with Trypho," in *The Ante-Nicene Fathers*, vol. 1, edited by Alexander Roberts and James Donaldson (Grand Rapids, Michigan: William B. Eerdmans Publishing Company, 1996).

[424] Adolf Harnack, *Judentum und Judenchristentum in Justins Dialog mit Trypho* (TU 39, Leipzig, 1913), 281 cited in Horbury, "The Benediction of the *Minim*:" 24.

there are four texts that call for attention: two texts which mention cursing of Christians in the synagogue (xvi, xcvi),[425] one text that notes of anathematization of Christ in the synagogues (xlvii), and one more on mockery of Christ taught by *archisynagogi* after the prayer (cxxxvii).[426]

There are two major questions discussed among scholars in relation to Justin's comments.[427] First, Justin does not mention Jewish Christians who are the concern of *Birkat ha-Minim*, but rather mentions Christians, a general term; second, Justin mentions mockery of Christ in the context of prayer only once and even that is only after prayer.

In relation to the former, H. Graetz,[428] Israel Abrahams[429] and others,[430] point that Justin made a mistake in supposing the curses to apply to Christians in general whereas only those of Jewish descent were meant in the prayer. Horbury refutes their claim and states that Justin was right in supposing that both Jewish and Gentile Christians were cursed in the synagogue.[431] He also

---

[425] xvi – "Accordingly, these things have happened to you in fairness and justice, for you have slain the Just One, and His prophets before Him; and now you reject those who hope in Him, and in Him who sent Him—God the Almighty and Maker of all things—cursing in your synagogues those that believe on Christ. For you have not the power to lay hands upon us, on account of those who now have the mastery. But as often as you could, you did so." xcvi -"For you curse in your synagogues all those who are called from Him Christians; and other nations effectively carry out the curse, putting to death those who simply confess themselves to be Christians; to all of whom we say, You are our brethren; rather recognise the truth of God." Martyr, "Dialogue with Trypho," xvi, xcvi.

[426] Horbury, "The Benediction of the *Minim*:" 24.

[427] Kimelman takes only the text that has a reference to prayers – cxxxvii -"Assent, therefore, and pour no ridicule on the Son of God; obey not the pharisaic teachers, and scoff not at the King of Israel, as the rulers of your synagogues teach you to do after your prayers: for if he that touches those who are not pleasing to God, is as one that touches the apple of God's eye, how much more so is he that touches His beloved! And that this is He has been sufficiently demonstrated." He further notes the problems related to it. First, there is no mention of Christians in this verse. Second, he uses here the term e]piskwyntepote (=scoff) a term inappropriate for *Birkat ha-minim*. Third, it takes place after prayers while *Birkat ha-minim* takes place in the middle of statutory prayers. On this basis states Justin clearly proves inadequate for posting the existence of statutory Jewish prayer which cursed Christians. Kimelman, "*Birkat ha-Minim* and the Lack," 235-236. Though these problems are noteworthy, there are some limitations in Kimelman as well. He seems to leave out the other references (xvi, xlvii, xcvi, cxxxvii,) that do mention Christians being cursed in the synagogues. The use of phrase "cursed in the synagogues" is still open and this does not disprove that is was not in the context of prayers.

[428] *Geschichte der Juden,* iv, 2nd edn., (Leipzig, 1866), 105f. cited in Horbury, "The Benediction of the *Minim* and Early Jewish-Christian Controversy," 20.

[429] *A Companion to the Authorized Daily Prayer Book* (3rd edition, London, 1932), lxiv cited in Horbury, "The Benediction of the *Minim*:" 20.

[430] van der Horst, "The *Birkat ha-Minim*:" 367.

[431] Horbury, "The Benediction of the *Minim*:" 59.

notes that from the second century onwards an imprecation on Christians was pronounced in synagogues.[432]

With regard to the latter question regarding mockery in the context of prayer, Horbury points out that Justin's reference to the cursing and mockery of Christ alludes to a separate practice.[433] It would probably be right to agree with Horbury who states that though Justin does not mention Nazarenes, credit can still be given to his complaint that Christians in general were being cursed.[434] Harnack counts the cursing of Christians and the mockery of Christ after prayer as one of the reliable pieces of detailed information in the *Dialogue*.[435] J. Jocz,[436] after looking into all the objections to Justin's remarks, concluded that the *Birkat ha-Minim was* newly created after 70 CE with special reference to Hebrew Christians and holds this benediction to be one of the marks of resistance to the Christian movement within the synagogue.

1.5.1.3.2.2. Origen

Origen comments that Jews cursed Christ everywhere up to the present time (Origen *hom.* II.8 in Ps. 37). There are other comments that accuse Jews of cursing and blaspheming Jesus and plotting against those who believed in him (*Homilies on Jeremiah* 10.8.2; 19.12.31; 12.13.20-23).[437] de Lange states that Origen's claim is suspiciously general. In a recent study it has been both rejected and accepted as evidence for an anti-Christian curse in the Eighteen Benedictions.[438] Further, Origen makes no mention of Christians being cursed or any connection to the prayers of the Jews.[439]

1.5.1.3.2.3. Tertullian

The comments of Tertullian are mainly referred to in two places. The first is Tertullian against Marcion iv.8.1: "The Christ of the Creator had to be called a *Nazarene* according to prophecy; whence the Jews also designate us, on that very account, *Nazerenes* after him."[440] The second is in *De Spectaculis* xxx:

---

432 Horbury, "The Benediction of the *Minim*:" 27.

433 Horbury, "The Benediction of the *Minim*:" 27.

434 Horbury, "The Benediction of the *Minim*:" 28.

435 A. Harnack, *Judentum und Judenchristentum in Justins Dialog mit Trypho* (TU 39, Leipzig, 1913), 78-81 cited in Horbury, "The Benediction of the *Minim*:" 24.

436 *The Jewish People and Jesus Christ* (London, 1949), 51-57 cited in Kimelman, "*Birkat ha-Minim* and the Lack," 21.

437 Kimelman, "*Birkat ha-Minim* and the Lack," 236.

438 N. R. M. de Lange, *Origen and the Jews* (Cambridge, 1976), 86 cited in Horbury, "The Benediction of the *Minim*:" 24.

439 Kimelman, "*Birkat ha-Minim* and the Lack," 236.

440 Tertullian, "Tertullian against Marcion," in *The Ante-Nicene Fathers*, vol. 3, edited by Alexander Roberts and James Donaldson (Grand Rapids, Michigan: William B. Eerdmans

"...to fix a gaze insatiable on those whose fury vented itself against the Lord. "This," I shall say, "this is that carpenter's or hireling's son, that Sabbath-breaker, that Samaritan and devil-possessed."[441] The testimony of Tertullian, like Origen, is general and cannot be used as evidence.

However, apart from Justin, Origen and Tertullian, Epiphanius and Jerome do make clear references to Jews, Nazoraens, and cursing during the prayers in the synagogues thrice daily.

1.5.1.3.2.4. Epiphanius

It is to be noted that Epiphanius and Jerome wrote about a century and half after Origen, and by then a lot could have transpired between Judaism and Christianity.[442] Epiphanius says of the Jewish-Christians 'Nazoraeans:' 'the sons of the Jews...standing up at the morning and midday and about evening, three times a day when they complete their prayers in the synagogues curse and anathematize them, saying three times a day "God curse the Nazoraeans."[443] Epiphanius clearly takes Nazoraeans to be Jews and notes that they are cursed thrice daily. Epiphanius also notes that proclaiming that Jesus is the Christ resulted in malediction.[444] Graetz[445] held that Epiphanius knew of the benediction and rightly understood it to refer to the Jewish-Christian Nazarene sect. Epiphanius also notes that the words of the curse were uttered thrice daily.

1.5.1.3.2.5. Jerome

Jerome goes further than Epiphanius and mentions the names *Minaei* and *Nazaraei*, who are cursed by the Jews.[446] Kimelman, however, states that there is a conflict in the testimonies of Epiphanius and Jerome. Unlike Epiphanius, Jerome refers to the Nazoraeans as the ones who believe in Christ, but wanted to be Jews even though they embraced Christianity.[447] Schiffman states that Epiphanius makes a mistake in stating that the *berakhah* was directed against

---

Publishing Company, 1996), 354.

441 Tertullian, "The Shows, or De Spectaculus," in *The Ante-Nicene Fathers*, vol. 3, edited by Alexander Roberts and James Donaldson (Grand Rapids, Michigan: William B. Eerdmans Publishing Company, 1996), 91.

442 Kimelman, "*Birkat ha-Minim* and the Lack," 237.

443 *Panarion*, xxix. 9 reprinted in Strack, p. lxvi and A.F. J. Klin and G. Reinink, *Patristic Evidence for Jewish-Christina Sects* Supplements to *NovT* xxvi (Leiden: Brill, 1973), 172-175 cited in Horbury, "The Benediction of the *Minim*:" 25.

444 Kimelman, "*Birkat ha-Minim* and the Lack," 238.

445 H. Graetz, *Geschichte der Juden*, vol. 4, 2nd ed. (Leipzig, 1866), 434f. cited in Horbury, "The Benediction of the *Minim*:" 25.

446 Kimelman, "*Birkat ha-Minim* and the Lack," 238.

447 Kimelman, "*Birkat ha-Minim* and the Lack," 235-238.

the Jewish Christian group or Nazoraeans and that Jerome is right in referring to Christians in general.[448]

Does the mention of cursing in the synagogues by Justin as early as middle of the second century suggest that there was a parting of the ways between Judaism and Christianity? Or was there a parting of the ways at the end of the first century CE? It is necesassary to analyze this parting of the ways and its significance in the first century CE.

1.5.2. The Parting of the Ways between Christianity and Judaism

'The parting of the ways' is a model used by scholars to discuss the separation between Judaism and Christianity with the aim of comprehending the cause and its date.[449] The parting of the ways between Christianity and Judaism was probably first proposed by Parkes.[450] Parkes notes "…it is possible to conclude that the definite separation into two religions took place towards the end of the first century."[451] He further states, "…the evidence of the epistles and Apocalypse is adequately accounted for, and that so far as the Roman evidence is concerned, the end of the first century is the time of the definite emergence of Christianity as a new religion."[452] However, he notes that the move to separation did not result in the emergence of Judaism and Christianity. Parkes notes, "The fourth century marks a decisive moment in the history of both Judaism and Christianity. Though neither were born in this century, yet both owe more to its outstanding leaders than to any other similar group of contemporaries, and both are to this day, in many ways, fourth century religions."[453]

---

[448] Lawrence Schiffman, *Who was a Jew* cited in der Horst, "The *Birkat ha-Minim*:" 366-367.

[449] Judith Lieu, ""The Parting of the Way:" Theological Construct or Historical Reality?," *JSNT* 56 (Dec. 1994): 101-119.

[450] Parkes, *The Conflict of the Church*. Lieu notes the precursor to this study in F.J. Foakes Jackson (ed.), *The Parting of the Roads: Studies in the Development of Judaism and Early Christianity* (London: Arnold, 1912) cited in Judith Lieu, ""The Parting of the Ways:"" 101. There are others who discuss this aspect in books and articles. Reed and Becker discusses on some of them: Abraham Cohen, *The Parting of the Ways: Judaism and the Rise of Christianity* (London: Lincolns-Prager, 1954); Robert Murray, "The Parting of the Ways," *Christian-Jewish Relations* 20 (1987): 42-44. These works are cited in Annette Yoshiko Reed and Adam H. Becker, "Introduction: Traditional Models and New Direction," in *The Ways that Never Parted: Jews and Christians in Late Antiquity and the Early Middle Ages*, edited by Adam H. Becker and Annette Yoshiko Reed (Minneapolis: Fortress Press, 2007), 10.

[451] Parkes, *The Conflict of the Church*, 91.

[452] Parkes, *The Conflict of the Church*, 92. Though he states this, he also concedes, "While, therefore, we may correctly date the actual separation from the end of the first and the beginning of the second century, we should be wrong to assume that the distinction which we can now observe between Christians and Jews represents the situation as it appeared to those living at the time." Parkes, *The Conflict of the Church*, 95.

[453] Parkes,*The Conflict of the Church*, 153.

Parkes' theory has influenced the view on the separation of Christianity from Judaism, but as having taken place in the fourth century and not in the first century.[454] However, Parkes' views have been misread by scholars who use them to argue for an early split between Judaism and Christianity.[455]

1.5.2.1 Different Time Periods of the Parting of the Ways

There are several proposals by scholars as to when the parting of the ways between Judaism and early Christianity occurred. A few of them are worth examining.[456] The first one is c. 28-30 CE, referring to the time when Jesus started his ministry, consisting of a new vision in the midst of hostilities. The second one estimates the parting of ways in c. 50, when the Pauline churches imagined themselves as distinct from the other synagogue communities in the Diaspora. Another one dates it as c. 70 CE, when the destruction of the Jerusalem Temple gave rise to the detachment from Jewish regulations. The third one is in c.135 CE, when the Jews were not allowed into Aelia, and the leadership moved on from Jewish to Gentile Christians. The fourth one is in c. 200 CE,[457] which witnessed the Jewish persecutions of the Gentile Christians. The fifth one was a recent addition to the above views to situate it with the

---

[454] Reed and Becker state regarding Parkes contribution, "...his argument for a first-century "separation" already contained the seeds for recent critiques of this model, which frequently point to the fourth century as the critical era for Jewish and Christian self-definition." Reed and Becker, "Introduction: Traditional Models," 17. Stemberger is of the view that Parkes observation that Judaism and Christianity are religions of the fourth century, may sound exaggerated but is of vital importance for understanding the development of Christianity. Günter Stemberger, *Jews and Christians in their Holy Land: Palestine in the Fourth Century* (Edinburgh: T & T Clark, 2000), 1.

[455] Reed and Becker, "Introduction: Traditional Models," 17.

[456] The categorization of the different views followed here is borrowed from Paula Fredriksen, "What was the "Parting of the Ways"? Jews, Gentiles, and the Ancient Mediterranean City," in *The Ways that Never Parted: Jews and Christians in Late Antiquity and the Early Middle Ages* edited by Adam H. Becker and Annette Yoshiko Reed (Minneapolis: Fortress Press, 2007), 35-36.

[457] Dunn is of the view that in the second century there are signs of parting of ways between conventional rabbinic Judaism and Christianity. Refer Dunn, *The Parting of the Ways*, 314. Dix takes the view that there was a parting of ways in the end of the first century or the beginning of the second and this led to break in relationship between Jews and Christians. George Dix, "The Ministry in the Early Church" in *The Apostolic Ministry: Essays on the History and Doctrine of Episcopacy*, edited by K. E. Kirk (London: Hodder & Stoughton, 1946), 228 cited in Annette Yoshiko Reed and Adam H. Becker "Introduction: Traditional Models and New Directions" in *The Ways that Never Parted: Jews and Christians in Late Antiquity and the Early Middle Ages* edited by Adam H. Becker and Annette Yoshiko Reed (Minneapolis: Fortress Press, 2007), 1. Meeks also opines that the separation took place by the beginning of the second century. See Meeks, "Breaking Away: Three New Testament Pictures," 115.

period of Constantine or to Theodosius, which saw the rise of Christianity as a state religion.[458]

Of the various proposals traced above, the third approach had large recognition until the beginning of the twentieth century.[459] In this connection, Goodman states that the Christian depiction of Judaism in the scholarly writings, especially those in the nineteenth and first half of the twentieth century, point to the difference between early Judaism and early Christianity.[460] This view is mostly connected with *Birkat ha-Minim* and its role in creating the separation between Judaism and Christianity. All the same, this has been questioned by various scholars in recent times. Horbury notes, "It was not decisive on its own in the separation of church and synagogue, but it gave solemn liturgical expression to a separation effected in the second half of the first century through the larger group of measures to which it belongs."[461]

1.5.2.2. Limitations of the Parting of the Ways Model

The first limitation is vividly described by Lieu. According to her, specific and local aspects of Judaism and Christianity were given universal colouring. She notes, "The problem with the model of the 'parting of the ways' is that, no less than its predecessors on the pages of Harnack or Origen, even while fully acknowledging that variety, it operates essentially with the abstract or universal conception of each religion, Judaism and Christianity, when what we know about is the specific and local."[462] Lieu further notes that in terms of social reality one could only perceive of "…a crisscrossing of muddy tracks which only the expert tracker, or poacher, can decipher."[463] She rightly notes that the best approach is to look for interaction at "social and popular religious level."[464] Reed and Becker in a similar vein argue for the universal conception when they note that primary assumption has been "…: the equation of rabbinic

---

[458] Fredriksen proposes that the Parting of the Ways took place probably between the fifth and seventh centuries when a gradual wearing away of civic patterns and an ideology of separation was built in line with *contra Iudaeos*. She also notes that the judgment on when the Parting of the Ways would depend on what evidence was considered. She adds that there are evidences of separation in the mid-century writers as well as pointers that interactions continued as seen in the sermons, letters, commentaries and conciliar canons. Paula Fredriksen, "What "Parting of the Ways"?," 35-64, especially 61.

[459] Dunn, *The Parting of the Ways*, 302.

[460] Martin Goodman, "Modeling the "Parting of the Ways,"" in *The Ways that Never Parted: Jews and Christians in Late Antiquity and the Early Middle Ages*, edited by Adam H. Becker and Annette Yoshiko Reed (Minneapolis: Fortress Press, 2007), 185.

[461] William Horbury, *Jews and Christians: In Contact and Controversy*, 110.

[462] Lieu, ""The Parting of the Ways:"" 108.

[463] Lieu, ""The Parting of the Ways:"" 119.

[464] Lieu, ""The Parting of the Ways:"" 119.

Judaism and proto-orthodox Christianity with "Judaism" and "Christianity" in a global sense."[465]

Dunn presents another limitation of the parting of the ways. For Dunn, Christianity emerged out of Judaism and so this image is not acceptable.[466] The parting of the ways was an ongoing process[467] and differed according to locations; further, there was overlapping of Judaism and Christianity that delayed the process of separation.[468] Becker and Reed note that the literary and archaeological information points to a complex situation in the first century and not a simplistic view of the turn of events.[469] In addition to this, they note that the developments took place in both Jewish and Christian traditions and there was a mutual sharing of cultural contexts.[470] They note,

> Rather than approaching Judaism and Christianity as monolithic entities that partook in a single act of separation, we here attempt to illuminate the broad range of regional and cultural variation in the encounters between different biblically-based religious groups - including Jews and Christians, but also those so-called

[465] Becker and Reed "Introduction: Traditional Models," 19.

[466] Dunn, "Concluding Summary," 368.

[467] Dunn goes on to note that the Parting of the Ways "was very "bitty," long drawn out and influenced by a range of social, geographical, political, as well as theological factors." Dunn, "Concluding Summary," 368. Alexander is of the view that the Parting of the Ways cannot be understood as a "decisive moment" but as a consequence of "an ever-widening rift" occasioned by the radical aspects of the Christian message. In other words for him, the progressive rabbinic influence of the Palestinian Jewish society that resulted in the separation of Judaism and Christianity. Philip S. Alexander, ""The Parting of the Ways,"" 3. Dunn disagrees with Alexander when he notes, "…we must beware of thinking of a clear or single "trajectory" of either Christianity or Judaism; … avoid using imagery … implies an ever widening gap between Christianity and Judaism." Dunn, "Concluding Summary," 367. See also in this regard, Cohen, *From Maccabees to Mishnah*, 220; Richard L. Rubenstein, "What was at Stake in the Parting of the Ways between Judaism and Christianity?" *Shofar* 28/3 (2010): 78.

[468] Dunn, *The Parting of the Ways*, xi, xiii, xix.

[469] Reed and Becker, "Introduction: Traditional Models," 2.

[470] Reed and Becker, "Introduction: Traditional Models," 2. There are others who also have a similar opinion. Yuval discusses on how the traditions concerning Jacob and Esau were used by the Jews and Christians, especially on how "The Christians countered the Jewish equation of Jacob=Jews, Esau=Romans with the opposite equation: Jacob=Christians, Esau=Jews." Yuval, *Two Nations in Your Womb*, 14. Hirschman states, "We must note that the Jewish and Christian battle for supremacy, for the right to be called *Israel*, for the ownership of Scripture and its true interpretation, was not waged in isolation. Pagans attacked both religions for their pretense that only one of them was privy to the authentic revelation. Pagan thinkers were appalled by the insolence of both Jewish and Christian claims to ascendancy and closeness to God, when their real life situation, at least in political terms, was at its lowest ebb." Hirshman here argues that the Jewish and Christian tradition emerged out the same Roman context. Hirshman, *A Rivalry of Genius*, 2.

> "Jewish Christians" and "Judaizers" who so strain the dichotomous definitions of modern scholarship. In the process, we hope to highlight the value of studying Judaism and Christianity as traditions that continued to impact one another, in constantly changing but consistently meaningful ways, throughout Late Antiquity and into the Middle Ages.[471]

Rutgers, based on the archaeological evidence, argues that Jews in the Jewish Diaspora in Late Antiquity interacted with Gentiles and Christians.[472] Kinzig also notes that in terms of 'popular piety' there was a great deal of convergence between the church and the synagogue at any rate until the fourth century and probably beyond as well.[473]

Still another reason for not considering this model is that in the first century CE, the boundaries were in the process of construction and there was a lack of clarity on the terms 'Judaism'[474] and 'Christianity.' Boyarin insists that the name "*Ioudaios*" primarily referred to an ethnic aspect, i.e., Judean, and though the term "*Ioudaismos*" existed before the Christian era, it had a different connotation to what is called Judaism.[475] The second century and its later period did not provide the boundaries between identities of Jews and Christians, so also this is another reason for the lack of clarity with the term "Jews" and "Christian."[476] Kraft is also against a "unilateral development model" where Judaism and Christianity separated in clear terms because

[471] Reed and Becker, "Introduction: Traditional Models," 3. Goodman mentions some of the common traditions such as: worship of a common God as seen in the authoritative scriptures and God calling them to live accordance to the divine will. He further notes, "Yet the child broke away from it mother (Judaism)." Goodman, "Modeling the "Parting of the Ways,"" 193.

[472] Leonard Victor Rutgers, "Archaeological Evidence for the Interaction of Jews and non-Jews in Late Antiquity," *AJA* 96/1 (Jan.1992): 101-118.

[473] Wolfram Kinzig, "'Non-Separation:' Closeness and Co-operation between Jews and Christians in the Fourth Century," *VigChr* 45/1 (Mr. 1991): 29 (27-53). Contrary to this view, Martin conceives that the snapping of ties between did not take place later but at the very beginning though it took about a century when the separation became final. Vincent Martin, *A House Divided: The Parting of the Ways Between Synagogue and Church* (New York: Paulist Press, 1995), 1.

[474] Dunn also notes, "*Judaism was a term or concept whose reference was in some dispute, whose range of application was shifting, whose identity was in process of developing.*" Dunn, *The Parting of the Ways*, 212, 189.

[475] Daniel Boyarin, "Semantic differences; or, "Judaism"/"Christianity,"" in *The Ways that Never Parted: Jews and Christians in Late Antiquity and the Early Middle Ages*, edited by Adam H. Becker and Annette Yoshiko Reed (Minneapolis: Fortress Press, 2007), 67.

[476] Becker and Reed, "Introduction: Traditional Models," 2.

historically it is not definite whether the terms "Jewish" or "Christian" had an exclusivist connotation.[477]

1.5.2.3. Alternative to the Parting of the Ways Model

Instead of conceptualizing the relationship between Judaism and Christianity as the parting of the ways, there have been different images proposed to assert their defining relationship. Boyarin is of the view that Christianity and Judaism were two sisters (religions) who "rivaled each other, learned from each other, fought with each other perhaps even sometimes love each other."[478] He further notes that they consisted of one "complex family, twins in a womb" and though contested with each other for priority, yet they belonged to the same source.[479]

How does one read this into the development of parting of ways in contemporary scholarship? Did the ways actually part at all? Reed and Becker argue for the position that Judaism and Christianity never parted ways, to use their terminology, "The Ways that Never Parted;" rather they argue that traditions intertwined much after the revolts against Rome.[480] Notwithstanding this, most of the scholars would state that there was some sort of divergence in the fifth century CE[481] but not so in the first century CE. They propose model

---

477 Robert A. Kraft, "The Weighing of the Parts: Pivots and Pitfalls in the Study of Early Judaisms and their Early Christian Offspring," in *The Ways that Never Parted: Jews and Christians in Late Antiquity and the Early Middle Ages*, edited by Adam H. Becker and Annette Yoshiko Reed (Minneapolis: Fortress Press, 2007), 92.

478 Daniel Boyarin, *Dying for God: Martyrdom and the Making of Christianity and Judaism* (Stanford: Stanford University Press, 1999), 5-6. Georgi opines that early church can be taken as a "variant within Judaism." But he also notes that at the end of first century CE Jews and Christians belong to develop their own identities in terms of opposing each other and also looking for ways to come to grips with the Roman establishment. Georgi, "The Early Church: Internal Migration:" 65.

479 Boyarin, *Dying for God*, 6. Segal opines, "It is startling truth that the religions we know today as Judaism and Christianity was born at the same time and nurtured in the same environment. Like Jacob and Esau, the twin sons of Rebecca and Isaac, the two religions fought in the womb…As was the case of Rebecca's children, the conflict between Judaism and Christianity molded their characters and determined their destines." Alan F. Segal, *Rebecca's Children: Judaism and Christianity in the Roman World* (Cambridge: Harvard University Press, 1986), 1. The same view seems to be echoed by Lieu, when she notes, "Yet alongside the reconstruction of the 'other' there is also, co-existing with discontinuity, a continuity of boundaries claimed…" Judith Lieu, "'Impregnable Ramparts and Walls of Iron': Boundary and Identity in Early 'Judaism' and 'Christianity,'" *NTS* 48/3 (Jl. 2002): 313.

480 Becker and Reed, "Introduction: Traditional Models," 3.

481 Boyarin states, "It was in the Catholic Church period that there rabbinic Judaism emerged as Jewish orthodoxy and both these (rabbinic Judaism and Christianity) became autonomous children of Rebecca." Boyarin, *Dying for God*, 6.

of "parting and joining and parting and joining," which continued like this for centuries after the second century.[482]

1.5.3. Birkat ha-Minim and the Parting of the Ways Model: An Evaluation

While it can be argued that the parting of the ways was not a general parting of ways of these two religions, this does not rule out the possibility of conflicts taking place in different local situations in the post 70 CE scenario.

There could be several factors that led to the conflicts. One of them was the movement towards nationalism which, though it was prevalent in the pre 70 CE, certainly did not die down but rather escalated and was seen in the second Jewish revolt. This would mean that the Christian position did come in the way of nationalist feelings rampant in this situation. Another factor was the movement towards defining Jewish identity, especially seen in the messianic movements and others. The presence of diversity did not mean that stringent measures were not taken against dissenters when such measures were needed. More importantly, conflict stemmed from perceived differences in terms of "...cohesion, identity, and boundaries."[483] One of these had to do with how Jews and Christians looked at the destruction of the Jerusalem Temple. For the rabbinic leaders, this was a punishment for the sins of the people. The Judeo-Christians viewed this as a "final departure of the scepter from Israel."[484] A third factor that contributed to conflicts was the existence of a group that can be called Jewish Christians, who mediated Jewish-Christian relations, but even this group was faced with defining its identity.

The *Birkat ha-Minim* and its implementation do not signify the parting of the ways between Judaism and Christianity. Nevertheless, the *Birkat ha-Minim* as a sign of intra-Jewish conflict still remains a possibility, and there were conflicts existing in the Jewish-Christian relations in after 70 CE. One of the weaknesses of the parting of the ways model is its failure to acknowledge the local aspects of the conflicts in Jewish-Christian relations. There is a possibility that the relations were not the same in any given locality. The reaction to the conflict also differed according to the location. Cohen notes, "In some places, the Jews expelled the Christians; in others, the Christians left on their own accord."[485] Here again, space needs to be given for different responses, and not a unilateral action.

---

[482] Reed and Becker, "Introduction: Traditional Models," 23.

[483] Meeks, "Breaking Away: Three New Testament Pictures," 108.

[484] Parkes, *The Conflict of the Church*, 77.

[485] Shaye D. Cohen, *From Maccabees to Mishnah*, 220. Meeks is of the view – "*Archontes* of the Jewish community in John's location had simply made up their minds to get rid of these trouble making followers of a false Messisah." Meeks argues for this view even though he

Conclusion

The periods before and after 70 CE had considerable diversity. Diversity certainly helped in weathering the gruesome period before the revolt, especially because it diversified expressions of reactions. Some of these reactions were anti-establishment while others were in the form of passive resistance. All the same, eventually the diversified expressions also led to a building of animosity towards forces that crippled common people's existence. Thus, the first revolt was the result of an interweaving of socio-economic, political and religious factors. However, as far as Jewish society was concerned, the religious factor played a pivotal role and defined the rest of the factors. One good example of this is the messianic movement which garnered support from the common people.

The period after 70 CE witnessed a continuing diversity, but had its own significant developments as well. The absence of the Temple meant the loss of the cultic centre, a binding factor of the Jewish community. This occasioned two reactions. The first was a retrospective deliberation on what caused the destruction of the Jerusalem Temple. There are evidences of this in the apocalyptic writings. There were spurt of explanations for what could have caused the destruction. Along with the Jewish reactions that came from different quarters, there were reactions from the Christian side. The presence of diversity did not mean that stringent measures were not taken against dissenters when such measures were needed too; and this possibly made further inroads into the already strained Jewish-Christian relationship. The destruction of the Jerusalem Temple also meant that there needed to be a centre in the absence of the Temple, which had earlier acted as the center. So, the second significant development of this period was that the Law was taken as a substitute and facilitated in defining the cohesiveness of the Jewish community.

On the other hand, the Christians in the wake of the absence of the Temple articulated christological positions that did not augur well for the Jewish-Christian relations. Thus, there was in all likelihood a movement towards defining identity which gave way to rivalry and conflicts, though these were still in a formative stage. Hence, the notion of a wider ban or excommunication coming from a normative Judaism seems to be out of question. It was a difficult time for both Judaism and Christianity. Both were involved in defining their relationship with each other and their own respective identities. In the process of consolidation, any group was bound to take measures to define one's boundaries, though there is much truth in arguing for a fluid stage in the post 70 CE context. These measures to keep the boundaries could have sparked off inter-Jewish conflicts in the synagogues where Christian communities existed.

---

rejects the view that *Birkat ha-Minim* resulted in a wide ban. Meeks, "Breaking Away: Three New Testament Pictures," 103.

Though there is not enough evidence to argue for a generalized ban, one can safely say that each localized synagogue had its own rules. The *Birkat ha-Minim* had its effect on the ever growing separation between Judaism and Christianity, and the testimonies of the Church Fathers add to the evidence about the growing divide.

Chapter 2

The Trajectory of the Johannine Community

Introduction

The previous chapter focused on the first century CE and the context from which the Johannine community emerged. It was an environment in which intra-Jewish conflicts took place in the synagogues, especially because there were forces at work trying to bring together different streams that divided after 70 CE Judaism. The search for identity was clearly witnessed in Judaism after the destruction of the Temple and this could have necessitated reformative steps. At the same time, early Christianity was required to look at its own understanding of its identity in the light of these developments.

This chapter traces the possible history of the community behind the FG, the Johannine community. In doing so, it makes use of the indicators in the FG and evaluates the discussions on various reconstructions of the Johannine community to make a more viable reconstruction of the Johannine community. A reconstruction of the Johannine community is of paramount importance if there has to be a meaningful interaction with the text. Further, it seems to be one of the best solutions to some of the ambiguities in the FG. Ringe in this regard notes, "…while the Gospel writer's focus is on Jesus' life and ministry, the point of that story is not a neutral report or the product of the individual creativity of the author, but rather a demonstration of the significance of Jesus for the life of the community from and to which the Gospel was written."[1]

---

[1] Sharon H. Ringe, *Wisdom's Friends: Community and Christology in the Fourth Gospel* (Louisville: Westminster John Knox Press, 1999), 10.

2.1. Pointers to the Johannine Community[2] in the FG

Before looking at the various reconstructions of the Johannine community, it is worthwhile to look at some of the reasons for exploring a community behind the FG. Not all the Johannine scholars subscribe to the Johannine community hypothesis, though a majority of them argue in support of it.

2.1.1. Objections to the Johannine Community Hypothesis

The discussion on the Johannine community has figured in the recent literature on the FG. While some would find it reasonable to assume a community behind the gospel,[3] some others reject it. Richard Bauckham has been a recent advocate of the latter.[4] He rejects the community hypothesis of the FG on two grounds.[5] First, the FG is not a text written for an isolated Johannine community, rather it envisages a wider readership than perhaps any other NT text. Further, in the early Christian movement, communities regularly communicated with each other.[6] Second, the FG does not have a developed special language as such and the literary constructions of this gospel show that the FG's special language and symbolism would be accessible to outsiders.[7] Bauckham bases

---

[2] The early expression of the Johannine community goes back to 1820, when Karl Gottlieb Bretschneider wrote, "The Fourth Gospel ...is more an apologia than a work of history...which concerned controversies not between Jesus and the Pharisees but between Christians and Jews of the second century." K. G. Bretschneider, *Proababilia de evangelii et epistularum Joannis, apostolic indole et origine* (Leipzig, 1820), 118-119 cited in John Ashton, *Understanding the Fourth Gospel* (Oxford: Clarendon Press, 1991), 10.

[3] Scholars who argue for the Johannine community model are J. Louis Martyn, R. E. Brown, R. Alan Culpeper, John Painter, Oscar Cullmann, and others; some of them are discussed below.

[4] Richard Bauckham, "The Audience of the Fourth Gospel," in *Jesus in Johannine Tradition*, edited by Robert T. Fortna and Tom Thatcher (London: Westminster John Knox Press, 2001). Hengel's has also produced a work independently of Bauckham, which seems to be similar in orientation. He is of the view that the gospels were related with the church's worship and liturgy and were used in the churches as a means of persuasion. Further, the four gospels were presented as one gospel. Martin Hengel, *Four Gospels and One Gospel of Jesus Christ: An Investigation of the Collection and Origin of the Canonical Gospels* (London: SCM Press, 2000). Bauckham's view has the support of Bird. Mike Bird, "Bauckham's *The Gospel for All Christians* Revisited," *EuroJTh* 15/1 (Apr. 2006): 5-13, especially 11. Bird is of the view that Gospels were composed for a wider community and "…the Gospels were written to tell the story of Jesus for Christians in the Greco-Roman world."

[5] Bauckham, "The Audience of the Fourth Gospel," 111.

[6] Bauckham, "The Audience of the Fourth Gospel," 107ff.

[7] Bauckham gives three reasons for this proposition: a. FE sometimes explains explicitly the meaning of figurative or enigmatic sayings of Jesus (Jn. 2:21) b. Misunderstandings by Jesus' hearers frequently have the literary function of leading Jesus to explain the image he has used or to develop in ways that clarify its meaning (Jn. 3:3-8). c. The FG has riddles which are part of a larger literary strategy that drives readers both to think about their meaning and to read in hope of learning their answers. Bauckham, "The Audience of the Fourth Gospel,"

his first argument on the genre of the gospel. Even so how much of this can be applied to the gospels, in its total meaning, is something that one needs to be skeptical about?[8] With regard to the second argument, it is true the Johannine community interacted with other communities,[9] and so it is highly improbable to categorize the Johannine community as a sect.[10] However, the community understood itself as different from those surrounding it; the use of special language,[11] the ambiguous presentation of Jews, and the denigration of others all testify to the uniqueness of the FG and a community behind it.[12] The FG

107-110. Gary M. Burge also agrees with Bauckham and states that it is better to acknowledge widespread mobility and communication channels as being available in the first century. Gary M. Burge, "Situating John's Gospel in History," in *Jesus in Johannine Tradition*, edited by Robert T. Fortna and Tom Thatcher (London: Westminster John Knox Press, 2001), 41.

[8] Sim criticizes the view of Bauckham. David C. **Sim**, "The Gospels for all Christians? A response to Richard Bauckham"*JSNT* 84 (Dec. 2001): 3-27, especially 18.

[9] There is every reason to suppose that the Johannine community interacted with the community of John the Baptist, followers of Peter and host of others. But the FG also presents evidence of these communities being downplayed at the cost of asserting the community's Christology. Ringe is also of the view the FE shared relationship with other Christian communities. Ringe, *Wisdom's Friends*, 11.

[10] Wayne A. Meeks was probably one of the first New Testament scholars to give the title 'sectarian' to the Johannine community using some of the aspects of a sociological 'sect' model. Wayne A. Meeks, "The Man from Heaven in Johannine Sectarianism" *JBL* 91/1 (Mr. 1972): 44-72. Lindars seems to agree with Meeks. He states, "Johannine church is a beleaguered sect, alienated from the local society, intensely loyal internally, but hostile to those outside. The command to love one another (13:34) gives a splendid example but it does not extend to the opponents." Barnabas Lindars, "John," in *The Johannine Literature*, edited by Barnabas Lindars, Ruth B. Edwards and John M. Court (Sheffield: Sheffield Academic Press, 2000), 73. Brown evaluates Meeks and finds the term inappropriate since the picture of the community presented in the FG was a community not totally isolated from the general Christian movement (Jn. 21). Raymond E. Brown, *The Community of the Beloved Disciple* (New York: Paulist Press, 1979), 162.

[11] Here, the researcher would like to differ with Bauckham; there are clear evidences of a special language and the underlying notion that the Johannine community through the BD understood better than the disciples of Jesus (Jn. 2:22). The use of the special language is commented by Petersen. He notes that the narrator and Jesus use the grammar and vocabulary of everyday language, but differently which results in misunderstanding and partial understanding among those who speak everyday language. The two uses of language contribute to the plot of John's story. For him, the narrator uses everyday language in a special way that is both implicitly and explicitly contrasted with everyday usage. Norman R. Petersen, *The Gospel of John and the Sociology of Light: Language and Characterization in the Fourth Gospel* (Valley Forge: Trinity Press International, 1993). Also refer, Philip Francis **Esler**, "Community and Gospel in Early Christianity: A Response to Richard Bauckham's *Gospels for All Christians*," *SJT* 51/2 (1998): 235-248, especially 247.

[12] Fulgseth rightly notes that to include the Johannine community in a general audience results in a failure to explain the peculiarities of the FG. He further adds, "A 'general Christian audience' is a vague and imprecise notion for a gospel like John. The quest for the existence of a community must not be confused with the quest for its social nature." Kåre Sigvald Fuglseth,

seems to have had a specific purpose (Jn. 20:31) for a specific community. Bauckham also critiques the concept of the FG written to cater to the needs of the Johannine community in another work.[13] The central argument is that the parenthetical descriptions in Jn. 3:24; 11:2 were inserted for those who were already familiar with Mark's gospel,[14] thus arguing that the FG was not written only for a limited audience.[15] All the same, these insertions more possibly deal with the structure of the FG and the distinct presentation of the FG.

In a previous work,[16] Bauckham[17] rejects the community perspective of all the gospels, not just the FG. He challenges the view that each evangelist addressed the specific context and concerns of his own community. He states that it is probable that the gospels were written for general circulation around the churches and so envisaged a very general Christian audience. The

---

Johannine Sectarianism in Perspective: A Sociological, Historical, and Comparative Analysis of Temple and Social Relationships in the Gospel of John, Philo and Qumran, NovTSup 116, edited by M. M. Mitchell and D. P. Moessner (Brill: Leiden, 2005), 69. Richard Last too finds that the 'communal practices of writing' does not comply with the idea of 'all Christians.' Richard Last, "Communities that Write: Christ-Groups, Associations, and Gospel Communities," *NTS* 58/2 (Apr. 2012): 173-198. Thus, Bauckham's view that gospel genre was intended for a wider audience does have its limitations.

[13] Richard Bauckham, "John for Readers of Mark," in *The Gospels for All Christians: Rethinking the Gospel Audience*, edited by Richard Bauckham (Grand Rapids, Michigan: William B. Eerdmans Publishing Company, 1998).

[14] He notes, "If we find evidence that the Gospel is designed to accommodate such readers (i.e., readers of Mark), while not excluding others, and if there is no similar evidence that readership already familiar with specifically Johannine Gospel traditions is in view, this will be a significant confirmation of the argument that John was written, not for the "Johannine community," but to circulate generally among the churches." Bauckham, "John for Readers of Mark," 149, 151.

[15] North objects to the arguments of Bauckham. Some of these objections include: a) Bauckham's argument that the note in Jn. 11:2 refers to 12:1-8 is not sustained as it more possibly refers to a story already known to the reader; b) Jn. 11:2 is not an explanation as Bauckham conceives but is a reminder to the Johannine readers what Mary did; c) North rightly notes that the connection of Mk. 14:3 is more possible with Jn. 12:3 rather than with Jn. 11:2 as supposed by Bauckham; d) the concluding argument of North is the most persuasive of all- if it is supposed that the FG was written for all not just for the Johannine community, then one would have to suppose that the Gospel was against all Jews. Wendy E. Sproston North, "John for Readers of Mark? A Response to Richard Bauckham's Proposal," *JSNT* 25/4 (Je. 2003): 449-468, especially 455,459, 464,468.

[16] *The Gospels for All Christians: Rethinking the Gospel Audience* has several articles but the persuasive among them, are the two articles of Richard Bauckham: "Introduction" and "For Whom Were Gospels Written?," in *The Gospels for All Christians: Rethinking the Gospel Audience*, edited by Richard Bauckham (Grand Rapids, Michigan: William B. Eerdmans Publishing Company, 1998).

[17] Rowe supports Bauckham's view from the perspective of Luke-Acts. C. Kavin Rowe, "Literary Unity and Reception History: Reading Luke-Acts as Luke and Acts," *JSNT* (Je. 2007) 29/4: 449-457.

implied readers were not specific but every Christian community in the late-first-century Roman Empire.[18] He notes, "...the evangelist writing a Gospel expected his work to circulate widely among the churches, had no particular Christian audience in view, but envisaged as his audience any church ... to which his work might find its way."[19] He further states, "...any reader who finds the argument of this chapter convincing should cease using the terms Matthean community, Markan community, Lukan community, and Johannine community. They no longer have a useful meaning."[20] Bauckham seems to agree with one view but does not seem to agree with the finer aspects of the same view. For example, he agrees that there is a historic context for the gospels but does not agree on the context of the Fourth Evangelist's[21] community.[22] Another example of Bauckham's contradictory views is that he agrees on the diversity of the gospels. Here again, the diversity of gospels goes against the proposition of the gospel writers responding to the general context. Other

---

[18] Bauckham, "Introduction," 1.

[19] Bauckham, "For Whom Were Gospels Written?," 11. In the latter part of the article, Bauckham gives six descriptions of the early Christian movement: 1) the Roman society was conditioned as such that there was frequent relations between spread across the empire; 2) the early Christian was "a worldwide movement;" 3) almost all the early Christian leaders "*moved around*;" 4) the early Christian movement maintained contact through letters; 5) he notes that there are "...concrete evidence for close contacts between churches in the period around or soon after the writing of the Gospels;" 6) finally, he notes, "...the evidence for conflict and diversity in early Christianity supports my picture of the early Christian movement as a network of communities in constant communication." Bauckham, "For Whom Were Gospels Written?," 32-44. Though the interaction between the communities seems to be true, this does not rule out the possibility of gospels being addressed to particular audience and the particular community emphasis of each of the gospels.

[20] Bauckham, "For Whom Were Gospels Written?," 45.

[21] Hereafter the abbreviated form FE is used.

[22] Here he differs by stating that the historical context is the "early Christian movement in the late first century" i.e., "the political, social, economic, religious, and ideological constructs."Bauckham, "For Whom Were Gospels Written?," 46.

scholars who have voiced criticism on Bauckham's views include Sim,[23] Esler,[24]

---

[23] Sim presents the evaluation of Bauckham with the following views: a) the evidence cited by Bauckham does not deal with the internal evidence from the gospels; b) in the midst of factionalism in the early Christian movement, Sim rightly considers Bauckham's picture of the early Christian movement as one unified movement as highly improbable; c) Sim agrees that the Greco-Roman context provided a network of communication but in terms of rival groups it only resulted in hostility; d) Sim responds to Bauckham view -that since Matthew and Luke knew Mark, it implies that their Gospels were not just for their communities- by stating that the gospel writers were concerned how the readers perceived the significance of Jesus and the ethical result of it; e) to the question of whether the gospel genre implied a wider audience, Sim is of the view that it is possible that the gospel envisaged a limited readership; f) Sim also responds to Bauckham's criticism of historical and sociological approaches, by noting that Bauckham fails to give an alternative approach that explains the diversity of the Gospels and their distinctive characteristics. Sim's arguments against Bauckham's views seem convincing specially in stressing the fact that the existence of the gospel communities does reiterate the diversity and distinctive characteristics of each of the gospels. Sim, "The Gospels for all Christians?:" 3-27.

[24] Esler's criticism of Bauckham begins with the statement, "Bauckham mounts his argument confidently, but this confidence is of a recently converted." He notes this as until 1993 Bauckham espoused the view that he now attacks concerning the FG. Esler is referring to the view of Bauckham in Richard Bauckham, "The Beloved Disciple as Ideal Author," *JSNT* 49 (Mr. 1993): 21-44, especially 30 where Bauckham notes the view that the FG was intended for churches beyond the Johannine community as extremely doubtful. Esler responds to the argument by Bauckham basing on Markan priority – since Mark envisaged a wider audience, the same applies to Matthew and Luke and therefore these gospels also were not restricted to a limited audience. Esler notes that Bauckham's argument fails to take into consideration the alterations made by Matthew and Luke to Mark, that is, alterations in order to make the gospel relevant to their audience. Thus, if the respective gospel were prone to be changed according to new situations, Bauckham's view that the gospels were addressed to 'all Christians' does is not valid. Esler concludes by noting the view of Bauckham and others does not take into account the complex relations "…between text and context, and community and gospel." **Esler**, "Community and Gospel in Early Christianity:" 235-248, especially 236, 241, 248. Bauckham responds to the critique of Esler. Bauckham criticizes Esler for using the anthropological model of Malina. Richard **Bauckham**, "Response to Esler," *SJT* 51/2 (Jan. 1998): 249-253, especially 249. But the central argument against Esler seems to be the view of Bauckham that the there is difference between expected audience of the Gospel and the influence of the evangelist's context on his writing. This view of Bauckham is debatable as one cannot really distinguish the former from the latter as both are intertwined. Thus, it seems that Esler arguments are more plausible than Bauckham's. There are some scholars who take a middle path, ie., they argue that the evangelists had a specific community in view but also wanted the gospels to be read widely. A. T. Lincoln, *Truth on Trial: The Lawsuit Motif in the Fourth Gospel* (Peabody: Hendrickson Publishers, 2000), 264-265 cited in Edward W. Klink III, "The Gospel Community Debate: State of the Question," *Currents in Biblical Research* 3/1 (O. 2004): 77 (60-85). See also Philip F. Esler and Ronald A. Piper, *Lazarus, Mary and Martha: A Social-Scientific and Theological Reading of John* (London: SCM Press, 2006); Margaret M. Mitchell, "Patristic Counter-Evidence to the Claim that the 'The Gospels Were Written for All Christians," *NTS* (Jan. 2005) 51/1: 36-79. Blooberg states, "Nothing in the Fourth Gospel requires knowledge of any other document in order to understand John's text, but numerous features of his narrative read as if trying o allufe to events in Mark for those who are famililar with them." Craig L. Blomberg, *The*

Frey,[25] and Kazen.[26]

Other than Bauckham, Kysar[27] has also questioned the reconstruction of the Johannine community in two areas. He explains, "*The first problem has to do with the evidence for such a hypothetical construction as the Johannine community;*"[28] and he goes on to say, "*The problem is further aggravated when we ask how we might go about testing the veracity of the proposed Johannine community.*"[29]

When he talks about the first problem, Kysar questions the possible meaning offered to the expulsion texts (9:22; 12:42; 16:2) by the advocates of the Johannine community hypothesis. These texts could mean that the event of expulsion did not occur but could be an anticipation of what could happen in the future.[30] Further, unlike the common understanding of the hostilities faced by 'the Jews,' Kysar explores the possibility of the hatred coming from the author of the FG himself.[31] The ascent-descent motif is a myth created by someone else and not the community as such.[32] Lastly, Kysar presents the lack of extra-biblical evidence for such a community experience behind the gospel.[33]

Historical Reliability of John's Gospel: Issues and Commentary (Downers Grove: InterVarsity Press, 2001), 48.

[25] Frey notes, "Though it might be correct that the gospels were not written for a small local community but for a wider audience which he had in mind when they wrote their works; it is a broad consensus that the Fourth Gospel and the Johannine epistles primarily refer to a circle of Christian communities influenced by a certain type of theological reflection and proclamation." Jörg Frey, "Eschatology in the Johannine Circle," in *Theology and Christology in the Fourth Gospel: Essays by the Members of the Society for New Testament Study Johannine Writings Seminar*, BETL 184, edited by G. Van Belle, J. G. Van der Watt and P. Maritz (Leuven: Leuven University Press, 2005), 56, f.n. 31.

[26] Kazen criticisms of Bauckham are: a) there seems to be a lack of evidence for the view that the gospel authors were constant travelers; b) the 'in-group culture' to which the gospels belong suggests that they reflect the community's ideas and attitudes rather than just individual mind; c) Bauckham mixes up the "...*purposes* of the gospel authors with the *premises* for the reception of these texts." Thomas Kazen, "Sectarian Gospels for Some Christians? Intention and Mirror Reading in the Light of Extra-Canonical Texts," *NTS* 51/4 (O. 2005): 563-564.

[27] Robert Kysar, "The Whence and Whither of the Johannine Community," in *Life in Abundance: Studies of John's Gospel in Tribute to Raymond E. Brown*, edited by John R. Donahue (Minnesota: Liturgical Press, 2005), 71-76.

[28] Kysar, "The Whence and Whither," 71.

[29] In addition to the two problems mentioned, Kysar also notes of the limitations of historical criticism and the emergence of new methods of interpretation. Kysar, "The Whence and Whither," 72, 75-76.

[30] Kysar, "The Whence and Whither," 71.

[31] Kysar, "The Whence and Whither," 72.

[32] Kysar, "The Whence and Whither," 72.

[33] Kysar, "The Whence and Whither," 72.

With regard to the second problem, Kysar asks the question, "*Simply because a hypothesis illumines the possible meaning of a passage does not necessarily prove that the hypothesis is true.*"[34] For Kysar, sectarianism in the FG could result from familiarization with "Gnostic-like Christian views."[35]

How does one respond to the Kysar's scepticism? Kysar has noted that the reconstruction of the Johannine community is hypothetical, which is true. Even so, this hypothesis is not without certain evidence; the reconstruction of the Johannine community is not a 'bolt from the blue.' The community behind the FG is far more attestable than the construction of other communities such as Lukan or Matthean, for that reason that there exists a body of literature—the Johannine letters are an example —to attest this aspect. Klauck responding to the views on Kysar notes, "In principle, letters are not simply self-referential, but refer to an external context."[36] This means the letters do speak of a community and the context in which they were composed and read.[37] The Johannine community has a reference point in the Johannine epistles. Further, the incident in Jn. 9 does seem to suggest an action that has already been decided and not a proleptic one. Kysar has suggested that there is certainly room for the author of the FG giving a biased presentation of 'the Jews,' but this is again not a satisfactory point because it can be argued both ways. With regard to the problem of "testing the veracity of the proposed Johannine community," Kysar is possibly right in noting that a hypothesis cannot be proved only on the basis of its usefulness in interpreting the text. Still there is evidence, other than in the FG, which notes a conflict between proponents of Judaism and Christians, especially the Pauline letters and Matthew's gospel.

The criticism on the reconstruction of the Johannine community necessitates the need to look further at some of the pointers in the FG that suggest a possible community behind the FG.

2.1.2. In Support of the Johannine Community Hypothesis

Many contemporary scholars argue for a community behind the FG.[38] Fugsleth opines, "The existence of a Johannine community or a group 'of one or another

---

[34] Kysar, "The Whence and Whither," 73.

[35] Kysar, "The Whence and Whither," 73.

[36] Hans-Josef Klauck, "Community, History, and Text(s): A Response to Robert Kysar" in *Life in Abundance: Studies of John's Gospel in Tribute to Raymond E. Brown*, edited by John R. Donahue (Minnesota: Liturgical Press, 2005), 84.

[37] Klauck draws attention to some of the features in I Jn. that point to the process of communication in the Johannine community: a) the differentiation between "we" and "you" (plural); b) the address "children;" c) the "we" texts. Klauck, "Community, History, and Text(s)," 84-85.

[38] It should be mentioned that while many would comply with the idea of a community evidenced in the FG, differences still persist on the historical background, the nature of the

kind' has not been a matter of dispute."[39] Lieu also attests to the fact that there is a defined sense of identity that underlies a community of Christians.[40] Meeks is of the view that the existence of a community or "group of communities" is richly apparent in the making of the Johannine writings.[41] Barrett attributes one of the reasons for such a consensus to the existence of at least two different Johannine groups exemplified in the Johannine epistles.[42] In addition to these scholars, there are a host of others who argue for a communitarian view of the FG.[43] The basic proposition for supposing a Johannine community has to do with the peculiarities of the FG and some of these lend themselves to a notion of a community.[44]

---

community, and its involvement in the production of the text. This is taken up in the section on the trajectory of the Johannine community.

[39] Fuglseth, *Johannine Sectarianism*, 67.

[40] Judith M. Lieu, *The Theology of the Johannine Epistles* (Cambridge: Cambridge University Press, 1991), 103.

[41] Meeks, "The Man from Heaven:" 49.

[42] C. K. Barrett, "School, Coventicle, and Church in the New Testament," in *Wissesnchaft und Kirche*, Texte und Arbeiten zur Bibel 4, edited by K. Alan and S. Meurer (Bielefeld: Luther-Verlag), 96-110 cited by Fuglseth, *Johannine Sectarianism*, 67.

[43] D. Moody Smith notes that it is difficult to equate the Johannine discourse as the creation of the mind of a single theological genius. D. Moody Smith, "Johannine Christianity: Some Reflections on Its Character and Delineation," *NTS* 21/2 (Jan. 1975): 231. Kysar is of the view that the Gospel reflects a highly organized group and the ejection from the synagogue becomes the rationale of John's peculiarities. Robert Kysar, "The Gospel of John," in *ABD*, vol. 3, edited by David Noel Freedman (New York: Doubleday, 1992), 918. Oscar Cullmann describes the existence of a Johannine circle "wohl kaum zu bestreiten ist" (probably is best guessed). Oscar Cullmann, *Der Johanneische kreis. Sein Platz im Spätjudentum, in der Jüngerschaft Jesu und im Urchristentum. Zum Ursprung des Johannesevangelium* (Tübingen: Mohr, 1975), vii, cited by Fuglseth, *Johannine Sectarianism*, 68. Martin Hengel, *The Johannine Question* (London: SCM Press, 1989). Udo Schnelle, *Antidocetic Christology in the Gospel of John* (Minneapolis: Fortress Press, 1987). R. Alan Culpepper, *The Johannine School: An Evaluation of the Johannine-School Hypothesis Based on an Investigation of the Nature of Ancient Schools*, SBL Dissertation Series 26 (Montana: Scholars Press, 1975).

[44] Barton rightly notes, "one of the reasons for the distinctiveness of John is that it mirrors the experiences of a predominantly Jewish Christian community radically estranged, not only from the wider society, but also from the society of the synagogue, even perhaps from the society of other Christian groups." Stephen C. Barton, "Christian Community in the Light of the Gospel of John" in *Christology, Controversy and Community: New Testament Essays in Honour of David R. Catchpole*, NovTSup 99, edited by David G. Horrell and Christopher M. Tuckett (Leiden: E. J. Brill, 2000), 281.

2.1.3. Evidence for the Johannine Community in the FG

Several implicit references to a community can be gleaned from the FG.[45] Firstly, the use of language, especially the plural reference, could constitute a reference to a community. There are four such references, namely, 1:14 (ἐθεασάμεθα);[46] 1:16 (ἡμεῖς);[47] 3:11(οἴδαμεν);[48] 21:24 (οἴδαμεν). Barrett notes that the plural reference in 1:14 means 'church' or 'Christians.'[49] Hengel is of the view that the plural references in 1:14, 16; 21:24, may refer to a Johannine community or someone in the Johannine milieu.[50] The plural references in 1:14 and 21:24 betray a community involvement, especially 20:24 where it seems the BD's[51] testimony is being authenticated by a community. Pamment rightly notes, "Far from emphasizing individualism to the exclusion of the community, the Gospel uses community as the dominant idea in characterizing both the life of God (i:1f.; xiv:16f.; xv:26; xvi:13ff.) and that of the disciples (x:16; chap. xvii)."[52] The plural language also continues to dominate in the Johannine epistles, and this lends weight to the idea of a Johannine community behind the FG.

---

[45] The researcher has made use of some of the aspects mentioned by Fuglseth, *Johannine Sectarianism*, 72-85.

[46] Εθεασάμεθα - verb indicative aorist middle deponent 1st person plural of *θεάομαι* see, look at. Smith rightly notes, "If the Johannine community which produced the Gospel saw itself in traditional continuity with Jesus, we are in a position to perceive in the 'we' of the prologues of both Gospel and Epistle, not the apostolic eye-witness *per se*, but a community which nevertheless understood itself as heir of a tradition based upon some historical witness to Jesus...'we have beheld his glory' has part of its meaning the obvious one: at the beginning of the community and its tradition stands someone who has seen Jesus." Smith, "Johannine Christianity: Some Reflections:" 236.

[47] ἡμεῖς - noun pronoun nominative 1st person plural; occurs eighteen times in the FG.

[48] Οἴδαμεν - verb indicative perfect active 1st person plural of οἶδα know, understand, perceive; other than this verb, there are other plural verbs in Jn. 3:21- λαλοῦμεν, έωπάκαμεν, μαρτθροῦμεν.

[49] C. K. Barrett, *The Gospel according to St. John: An Introduction with Commentary and Notes on the Greek Text* (London: SPCK, 1965), 143.

[50] Martin Hengel, *Die johanneische Frage. Ein Lösungsversuch (Mit einem Beitrag zur Apokalyse von J. Frey)*, Wissenschatliche Untersuchungen zum Neuen Testament 67 (Tübingen: Mohr, 1993), 225, cited in Fuglseth, *Johannine Sectarianism*, 72.

[51] Hereafter referred to as BD. The very term BD presents the possibility of a community referring to the leader of the community as the BD. Cullmann rightly notes, "If the evangelist introduced himself into the narrative in the person of the disciple, it is hard to understand how he could describe himself as 'the one whom Jesus loved'...These two passages (i.e., 18:25 and 20:2) make it seem very plausible that all the passages relating to this disciple ...was the redactor who first added the workds 'the one whom Jesus loved'." Oscar Cullmann, *The Johannine Circle*, translated by John Bowden (London: SCM Press Ltd, 1976), 73.

[52] Margaret Pamment, "The Son of Man in the Fourth Gospel," *JTS* 36/1 (Apr. 1985): 58.

Secondly, in connection with the plural use of language,[53] the editorial comments can be seen as an indication that the gospel was written long after the events. Some of the notable ones are 1:15, 2:22, 11: 49ff., and 12:16. The remark about the disciples in 2:22 and 12:16 not being able to understand Jesus' words which would later be brought to remembrance signals a function of the Paraclete after his resurrection, and emphasizes the community's involvement. Here, as elsewhere in the FG, the disciples represent a wider group unlike the references to the disciples in the synoptic gospels. A clear example is Jn. 6:66 where many of the disciples are said to have left Jesus because of Eucharistic language used by Jesus. In the next verse (6:67), Jesus then asked the twelve whether they too wished to go away. This implies that the disciples are a larger group and not just the twelve.

---

[53] Lincoln also alludes to this view. Lincoln, *Truth on Trial*, 264-265 cited in Klink, "The Gospel Community Debate:" 77.

Thirdly, there is an implicit reference to a group, though it is not a straight forward one. The Jews[54] in 9:22 had already (ἤδη)[55] decided to put out of the synagogue those who confessed Jesus to be the Messiah.[56] The instance of ἀποσυνάγωγος and the Christological basis suggest the existence of a specific group in the FG.[57] There are other texts in the FG typifying group dynamics.

---

[54] The term oi` VIoudai/oi occurs 194 times in the New Testament out of which 70 and 79 in the FG Gospel and Acts of the Apostles respectively (75% of the total usage in the New Testament and mostly in the plural form "Jews"). James D. G. Dunn, "The Question of Anti-semitism in the New Testament Writings of the Period," in *Jews and Christians: the Parting of the Ways A. D. 70 to 135*, edited by James D. G. Dunn (Grand Rapids, Michigan: William B. Eerdmans Publishing Company, 1992), 182. In the FG, the opponents of Jesus are primarily described as "the Jews." Out of the many occurrences of the term "the Jews," von Wahlde notes that in forty instances it conveys a sense of hostility. Urban C. von Wahlde, "The Terms for Religious Authorities in the Fourth Gospel: A Key to Literary-Strata?," *JBL* 98/2 (Ja. 1979): 233. Schnackenburg distinguishes the occurrence of the term "the Jews" thus: a) "Jew" or "Jews" used as an ethinic term by non-Jews – 4:9; 18:33, 35, 39; 19:3cf. 19:19, 21; b) "Jews" conveying a historical aspect or in the narrative- 3:25; 4:22; 11:19, 31, 33, 36; 18:20; 19:20; c) more or less with the above meaning but the FE detaches from them – 2:6, 13; 3:1; 5:1; 6:4; 7:2; 11:55; 19:21, 40, 42; d) having the implied meaning of "unbelieving" – 6:41, 52; 7:11, 15, 35; 8:22, 31; 10:19; 11:45, 54; 12:9, 11; 13:33; e) Jews as referring to a hostile group consisting of Pharisees and religious authorities- 5:10, 15, 16, 18; 7:1, 13; 8:48, 52, 57; 9:18, 22; 10:24, 31, 33; 11:18; 18:12, 14, 31, 36, 38; 19:7, 12, 14, 31, 38; 20:19. Rudolf Schnackenburg, *The Gospel according to St. John*, vol. 1, translated by Kevin Smith (Kent: Burns & Oates, 1990), 287. However, the FG seems to allude to any sort of categorization. For example in Jn. 8:31, "the Jew" are described as those who believed in Jesus but as the dialogue proceeds they offer strong resistance to him. A pertinent question arises here: Who are "the Jews" referred to in the FG? Some of the possibilities suggested by scholars are noted here. They are a) The expression could be a reference to Judeans as opposed to Galilean Jews. Malcolm Lowe, "Who were IOYΔAIOI?," *NovT* 18/ 2 (Apr. 1976): 101-130. This view has major difficulties especially when one substitutes Judeans for "the Jews" in all its occurrences. Lowe also does not explain why the Evangelist should have such hatred for the Judeans. John Ashton, "The Identity and Function of IOYΔAIOI in the Fourth Gospel," *NovT* 27/ 1 (Jan. 1985): 70. b) The religious leaders of the Judaism contemporaneous to the Evangelist. Urban C. von Wahlde, "The Johannine 'Jews': A Critical Survey," *NTS* 28/1 (Jan. 1982):33-60. c. For Brown, it is a technical title for the religious authorities, particularly those in Jerusalem who are hostile to Jesus. Raymond E. Brown, *The Gospel according to John*, vol. 1, AB 29A (London: Geoffrey Chapman, 1966), lxxi. The view taken in this research is that the term relates more with the Johannine community's experience of fractured relationship with the synagogue.

[55] D. A. Carson takes h;dh in 9:22 as a reference to an instance that could have taken place in Jesus' life time and therefore there is no question of this incident having taken place after the resurrection. D. A Carson, *The Gospel according to John* (Grand Rapids, Michigan: William B. Eerdmans Publishing Company, 1991), 369-372. Fuglseth rightly argues that the differences between John's version and the synoptic strengthen the proposition that the incident took place after Jesus' death. Fuglseth, *Sectarianism*, 78.

[56] A detailed discussion is taken up while discussing the Johannine community.

[57] Fuglseth notes, "The anachronistic use of ἀποσυνάγος is without doubt the most telling evidence." Fuglseth, *Johannine Sectarianism*, 79.

The Farewell Discourse (13-17) begins in the second part of the gospel and illustrates this aspect; the petition of the prayer takes on a plural dimension[58] and it extends well beyond the visible community to those who would be part of the community in the future (17:20b). The prayer for unity (17:11)[59] also underscores the feature of a group that is involved in the context of Jesus' imminent departure from them; it also highlights the hatred the disciples had received from the world (17:14),[60] and it seems that here is a possible indication that what is referred to is an incident after Jesus' death. The reason is that there seems to be no visible hatred of the disciples stated either in the synoptics or the FG.

There are also ecclesiological metaphors and allusions that strengthen the community aspect. The use of collective terms such as φίλοι (15:14), τεκωία (13:33), ἀδελφῦς (21:23), αὐλῆς, ποίμνη, ποιμήν (10:16), ἄμπελος, κλήματα (15:5). Fuglseth opines that this does not provide conclusive arguments for the existence of a community as the focus of these metaphors is not ecclesiology but rather ethics.[61] However, though this may be the case, the ethics is linked to christology which finds expression in the context of a community. In support of the community hypothesis, Ashton notes, "The community's concern for its survival found its expression in a series of allegories (door, shepherd, and vine) which are eloquent testimonies ...total commitment to Jesus."[62]

Fourthly, there are references to the later life of a community. These include: the confession of Peter on behalf of the disciples (6:69, especially the plural form - καὶ ἡμεῖς πεπιστεύκαμεν καὶ ἐγνώκαμεν), the concern for apostasy (6:60ff.), the question of believing without seeing (20:29) and the declaration of the sending of the disciples (17:18 καθὼς ἐμὲ ἀπέστειλας εἰς τὸν κόσμον). The needs of a later time seem to figure in these texts, especially, as Ashton has pointed out, the Farewell Discourse and the prayer in chapters 14-17.[63] Fuglseth also mentions that along with this aspect there is an occurrence of future tense

---

[58] 17:3- Ἵνα γινώσκωσίν σε, vs. 6 σοὶ ἦσαν κἀμοὶ αὐτοὺς ἔδωκας, vs.7 νῦν ἔγνωκαν; and similar traits are seen in vv. 8, 9, 10, 11, 12, 13, 14, 15, 16, 17, 18, 19, 20, 21, 22 23, 24, 25, 26. Thus the prayer is through and through a petition involving a group.

[59] Rolff views 17:11 as an indication to consolidate the community. J. Rolff, *Die Kirche im Neuwn Testament*, Grundrisee zum Neuen Testament, Das Neue Testament Deutsch Ergänzungsreihe 10 (Göttigen: Vandenhoeck & Ruprecht, 1993), 308-309 cited in Fuglseth, *Johannine Sectarianism*, 79.

[60] Ἐμίσημεν- verb indicative aorist active 3rd person singular of μισέω hate, despise; disregard, be indifferent to; signifying an incident in the past.

[61] Fuglseth, *Johannine Sectarianism*, 81.

[62] John Ashton, *Understanding the Fourth Gospel*, 2nd ed. (Oxford: Oxford University Press, 2007), 114.

[63] Ashton, *Understanding the Fourth Gospel*, 2007, 27.

in the FG.[64] These together point to a time when the FE is attempting to relate to the situation of the readers.

Fifthly, the impression of a community in the FG can be seen in the reference to the Paraclete, especially in terms of functions. Martyn notes that through his Paraclete, Jesus is present in the community after his death but not in an identical manner.[65] Some of the functions of the Paraclete include: to teach (14:26), to bring to remembrance the words of Jesus (14:26), to bear witness to Jesus (15:26), to be a guide to the truth (16:13) and to declare the things that are to come (16:13). In this regard, Burge notes that these references allude to the life of an 'anointed' Christian community.[66]

Sixthly, there are instances of the polemics of Judaism presented in the FG and these certainly argue for the existence of the Johannine community. Ashton rightly opines in this regard, "The most important reason for believing that the Johannine group was no longer attached to the synagogue at the time the Gospel was written is the uncompromisingly bitter tone of the exchanges between Jesus and 'the Jews' in chapters 5, 8, and 10."[67]

Lastly, there is the point raised by Esler in order to disprove the theory of Bauckham that the gospels, including the FG, was written for 'all Christians.' Esler notes that the FG's use of the phrase, 'the disciple whom Jesus loved' (13:23; 19:26; 20:2; 21:20) to refer to an anonymous but an important character highlights the fact that this character was known to the Johannine churches.[68]

The cumulative evidence does point in the direction of the existence of a community. Martyn notes, "…the literary history behind the Fourth Gospel reflects to a large degree the history of a single community which maintained over a period of some duration its particular and rather peculiar identity…

---

[64] Fuglseth mentions of 170 different instances of the future tense (in addition other constructions representing a future meaning - μέλλω followed by infinitive and others). The occurrence of future tense are of three main types: a) references to the ministry of Jesus in future (1:39, 42, 51; 4:25; 6:64; 11:12; 13:21; 26, 28); b) words referring to the time after Jesus' death (2:17, 19, 20; 5:28f.; 11:48; 13:7; etc. Two examples of major importance are 14:26 and 16:2); c) forms that retrospectively may be read as a reference to a later community, school (1:50; 3:12; 4:13, 21, 23; 5:25, 43, 45, 47; 6:27, 35, 54; 7:35; 8:12; 10:5, 9, 16; 12:25f.; 13:35; 14:13; 15:26). Fuglseth, *Johannine Sectarianism*, 83.

[65] J. Louis Martyn, *History & Theology in the Fourth Gospel* (Nashville: Abingdon Press, 1968), 148.

[66] Gary M. Burge, *The Anointed Community: The Holy Spirit in the Johannine Tradition* (Grand Rapids, Michigan: William B. Eerdmans Publishing Company, 1987), 8.

[67] John Ashton, *Understanding the Fourth Gospel*, 2007, 22. Dunn notes, "Johannine distinctive as a development of the Jesus tradition designed to express the truth of Jesus as understood within the Johannine circle." James D. G. Dunn, "Let John Be John: A Gospel for Its Time," in *The Gospel and the Gospels*, edited by Peter Stuhlmacher (Grand Rapids, Michigan: William B. Eerdmans Publishing Company, 1991), 321.

[68] Esler, "Community and Gospel in Early Christianity:" 246.

to draw form the *Gospel's literary history* certain conclusions about the *community's social and theological history*."[69]

2.2. A Critical Survey of the Reconstructions of the Johannine Community History[70]

Several scholars[71] have attempted to reconstruct the history of the Johannine community. Some of these reconstructions are relevant for evaluation.

2.2.1. J. Louis Martyn

Martyn has proposed an influential view that οἱ Ἰουδαῖοι were not just the Judean leaders in Jerusalem at the time of Jesus, but also symbolize the opponents of the Johannine community, who are primarily identified as the leaders of the emerging Rabbinic Judaism.[72] This view of Martyn can be found even in

---

[69] J. Louis Martyn, *The Gospel of John in Christian History: Essays for Interpreters* (New York: Paulist Press, 1978), 91.

[70] The expression "the Johannine community" was first used by Adolf Bühner in its present connotation. Jean-Adolf Bühner, *Der Gesandte und Sein Weg im 4. Evangelium*, WUNT 2nd ser. 2 (Tübingen: J. C. B. Mohr, 1977), cited in Robert Kysar, "The Whence and Whither," 67.

[71] There are other reconstructions of the Johannine community proposed by Johannine scholars. Wayne A. Meeks' article, "The Man from Heaven in Johannine Sectarianism" did impact the views on the Johannine community, especially in terms of in-group language. B.W. J. de Ruyter, *The Community of John the Evangelist: Its Polemic and Its History* (Delft: Eburon, 1998). Ferreira's Johannin community hypothesis is as follows – "a distinguished disciple, an influential figure in a specific region, constructed the gospel on the basis of a sign source which had a definite missionary purpose. The writing of the gospel was occasioned by a crisis that the Christians in his region faced, namely, conflict with a synagogue (or several synagogues). Later, a group of disciples gathered around this individual to form a community or a school. After he passed away the community was faced with other needs or crises, internal ones, which occasioned the need to make additions to the community's gospel." Johan Ferreira, *Johannine Ecclesiology*, JSNTSup 160 (Sheffield: Sheffield Academic Press, 1998), 31. Chennattu has discussed the Johannine community from the perspective of covenant-discipleship motif. She states, "Amid the sociopastoral and theological identity crises of the Johannine community perceived as a deviant group within synagogue Judaism of post-70 CE, the paradigm of discipleship as a covenant relationship redefines the community as the chosen people of God and consolidates the group as a distinct social and religious community." Rekha M. Chennattu, *Johannine Discipleship as a Covenant Relationship* (Massachusetts: Hendrickson Publishers, 2006), 211. Due to constraints of space, it is not possible to discuss in detail all the different views. A very different perspective is offered by Karris. He is of the view that the Johannine community was expelled from the synagogue for including the marginalized in the community of God's people and the FG offers peace and justice to those who are marginalized. Robert J. Karris, *Jesus and the Marginalized in John's Gospel*, Zacchaeus Studies: NT, edited by Mary Ann Getty (Collegeville: The Liturgical Press, 1990).

[72] The two major works of Martyn on the history of the Johannine community include: *History & Theology in the Fourth Gospel* and *The Gospel of John in Christian History*.

previous scholarship.[73] Though the association of *Birkat-ha-Minin* with the FG dates back before Martyn, it is he who makes use of this theory in his detailed analysis of Jn. 9. He proposes that layers of literary strata can be distinguished from each other.[74] His central proposition is that the FG presents a two-level drama which not only describes the Jesus' story (*einmalig*[75] level of the story), but also illustrates the contemporary situation of the Johannine Christians.[76] Martyn uses this to explain the healing in Jn. 9. He notes that the text "...witnesses on two levels: (1) witness to an *einmalig* event during Jesus' earthly lifetime... (2)...events experienced by the Johannine church."[77] Martyn postulates three periods in the Johannine community history, namely, the Early Period, the Middle Period, and the Late Period.[78]

2.2.1.1. The Early Period (till 80 CE)[79]

In the Early Period, the Christian missionaries came and preached[80] to the Jews in the synagogue and this consequently led to the formation of a messianic group. There was a good response to the proclamation.[81] But the Jewish

---

[73] Grässer mentions several scholars who have already stated this view of the FG. They are J. Josz, K. L. Carroll, L. Goppelt, G. Baum. Erich Grässer, *Text and Situation: Gesammelte Aufsätze zum Neuen Testament* (Gütersloh: Gütersloher Verlagshaus Gerd Mohn, 1973), cited in Raimo Hakola, *Identity Matters: John, the Jews and Jewishness*, NovT Sup 118, edited by M. M. Mitchell and D. P. Moessner (Leiden: Brill, 2005), 11.

[74] Martyn, *The Gospel of John in Christian History*, 90.

[75] Martyn, *History and Theology*, 30.

[76] This view of Martyn is rejected by Reinhartz, who is of the view that there is no external evidence to support this view. She goes on to argue that the negative portrayal of 'the Jews' in the FG does not have to do with the historical situation but a part of the self-definition process and the rhetoric that is used to present it. Adele Reinhartz, "The Johannine Community and Its Jewish Neighbors: A Reappraisal," in *"What is John?,"* vol. 2: *Literary and Social Readings of the Fourth Gospel*, SBL Symposium Series 7, edited by Fernando F. Segovia (Georgia: Scholars Press, 1998), 115-118, 137. The same view has been argued by Hakola. Hakola, *Identity Matters*, 22.But according to the researcher, this view also has its share of problems. How does one differentiate between historical situation and self-definition as one is the movement of the other? Self-definition is important because it suggests that one cannot understand religious texts only as reflection of historical reality but also and perhaps primarily as a reflection of how writers understand themselves in relation to that reality.

[77] Martyn does go on to state that the two levels cannot be deciphered with lucidity. Martyn, *History and Theology*, 30.

[78] Martyn, *The Gospel of John in Christian History*, 6-7.

[79] Martyn, *The Gospel of John in Christian History*, 93-102.

[80] Martyn conjectures that the sermon preached by the missionaries included Jn. 1:35-49, the passion and resurrection narrative, as well as the miracle stories. Later on it resulted in a signs source that was used in the proclamation. Martyn, *The Gospel of John in Christian History*, 97-98.

[81] Martyn, *The Gospel of John in Christian History*, 98.

group remained in the synagogue fellowship and lived within its theological, social and cultural boundaries.[82] Martyn is also of the view that the group also observed the Torah and as such the understanding of Christology was not a threat to monotheism.[83] Thus, for Martyn, the early period stands in precise continuity with the synagogue.

2.2.1.2. The Middle Period[84]

During this period, part of the group experiences two traumas which result in the birth of a separate community.[85] The two major traumas are excommunication from the synagogue and martyrdom. The authorities grew uneasy about the rapid growth of this messianic group and call for an exegetical proof of their proclamation thus leading to a number of midrashic debates. Further, the authorities take a radical step to stem the flow of converts into the group.[86] In such a situation, the re-worded *Birkat ha-Minim* is introduced in the synagogue service for the task of identifying and excommunicating those who confessed Jesus as Messiah (9:23, 24); thus, the messianic group within the synagogue separated into a community outside.[87] The authoritative body reached a formal decision regarding messianic faith in Jesus.[88] Those who confessed were separated from the synagogue. Members of John's church were Jewish excommunicates.[89] Benediction against heretics was reworded around 85 CE, and Jn. 9:22 corresponds to the already agreed action taken by Gamaliel II to reword the *Birkat ha-Minim* to make it an effective means for detecting Christian heresy.[90] Thus, Jews in Jn. 9:22 are to be taken as a reference to the *Jamnia* Academy and the events described in the FG concerning Jesus also find their correlation in the Jewish Christians during the FE's time.

Martyn is also of the view that the *Jamnina* authority imposed the *Birkat ha-Minim* over a "wide geographical area."[91] The excommunicated experienced social disruption as well as estrangement from the synagogue and even became

---

[82] Martyn, *The Gospel of John in Christian History*, 99.

[83] Martyn, *The Gospel of John in Christian History*, 102.

[84] Martyn, *The Gospel of John in Christian History*, 102-107.

[85] Martyn, *The Gospel of John in Christian History*, 102.

[86] Martyn, *The Gospel of John in Christian History*, 103. One of the drawbacks of Martyn's approach in the Middle period is the lack of explanation concerning the development of 'high Christology.'

[87] Martyn, *The Gospel of John in Christian History*, 103.

[88] Martyn, *History and Theology*, 38.

[89] Martyn, *The Gospel of John in Christian History*, 104.

[90] Martyn, *History and Theology*, 56-57.

[91] Martyn, *The Gospel of John in Christian History*, 119.

the enemy of the synagogue members.[92] This occasioned dualistic patterns of thought of the world and alienation.[93] Some of the evangelists who left the synagogue underwent trial and execution (10:28f; 15:18) as they were noted as *Messithim* (seducers), and ditheists for directing the other Jews to the worship of another god besides *Adonai*.[94] The expulsion from the synagogue instigated the need for a mature interpretation and led to new Christological formulations; in this process they ceased to be "Christian Jews" and became instead "Jewish Christians;" from then on they were no longer "Jews" like Nathaniel.[95]

2.2.1.3. The Late Period[96]

The late period is envisaged as a movement toward firm social and theological configurations. The first and second editions of the FG were written at this time.[97] The Johannine community formulated its theology not only in relation to the synagogue but also in connection to other Christian groups from which it emerged.[98] Martyn supposes that there was a group who remained "Christian Jews" and were not willing to take the risk of being separated from the synagogue; rather they took the role of informers.[99] There is another group according to Martyn, which the FG addresses, that is, the Jewish Christians who had been scattered by the implementation of *Birkat ha-Minim*. The phrase "other sheep" (Jn 10:16) refers to those who are disjointed like the Johannine community. Thus, the vision of the Johannine community is to bring together all those dispersed Jewish Christians.

By the time the FG was written, the Johannine community found itself in a complex social situation as there were several groups that existed side by side. Besides themselves, there was the synagogue and its "Jews." To them, they were the "alien" world. There were also the Christian Jews who did not sever their relationship with the parent synagogue. Finally, there were other groups of Jewish Christians who were expelled but with who the Johannine community looked forward for a time of reunion.[100]

---

[92] Martyn, *The Gospel of John in Christian History*, 104.

[93] Martyn, *The Gospel of John in Christian History*, 104.

[94] Martyn, *The Gospel of John in Christian History*, 105.

[95] Martyn, *The Gospel of John in Christian History*, 107.

[96] Martyn, *The Gospel of John in Christian History*, 107-121.

[97] Martyn, *The Gospel of John in Christian History*, 107.

[98] Martyn, *The Gospel of John in Christian History*, 107.

[99] Martyn, *The Gospel of John in Christian History*, 114.

[100] Martyn, *The Gospel of John in Christian History*, 120.

2.2.1.4. Evaluation

There are several valuable insights brought out by Martyn's proposal of the Johannine community. Firstly, Martyn's two-level reading has helped in unearthing the great richness to the understanding of the FG. In this regard, Adele Reinhartz notes that the two-level reading has become "axiomatic in Johannine studies."[101] Secondly, Martyn's hypothesis has also highlighted the conflict dimension between "the Jews" and the Johannine Christians. He further notes that the evidence of conflict is continued in several other communities. R. Alan Culpepper also supports the view of Martyn when he states "… the FG reflects an intense and violent conflict between Jews and Johannine Christians."[102] There are several other scholars who have also echoed Martyn's contribution to the understanding of the FG. Hakola notes that the general picture of Martyn's community still dominates the Johannine studies.[103] Smith observes, "…his vehicle may not have been perfect but it has proven good enough to maintain itself and stand correction."[104] Rensberger terms this work as the 'cornerstone' of Johannine research.[105] However, Martyn's attempt to pin down the context of the community with the Jamnia Academy has thrown open widespread criticism from Johannine scholars.[106] In this connection, Boyarin assesses the *Birkat ha-Minim*, "This hardly constitutes reliable evidence or indeed evidence at all. The aroma of the legend hovers over this entire account."[107] Another criticism of Martyn could be that one wonders whether layers of literary strata can be distinguished from one another.[108] He has also

---

[101] Adele Reinhartz, "The Johannine Community and Its Jewish Neighbors," 69. Hägerland rejects the two-level reading because of the lack of any ancient parallel. Tobias Hägerland, "John's Gospel: A Two-Level Drama?," *JSNT* 25/3 (Mr. 2003): 309-322.

[102] R. Alan Culpepper, "Anti-Judaism in the Fourth Gospel as a Theological Problem for Christian Interpreters," in *Anti-Judaism and the Fourth Gospel: Papers of the Leuven Colloquim, 2000*, edited by Reimund Bieringer, Didier Pollefeyt, and Frederique Vandecasteele-Vanneuville (Assen: Royal van Gorcum, 2001), 69.

[103] Hakola, *Identity Matters*, 17.

[104] D. Moody Smith, "The Contribution of J. Louis Martyn to the Understanding of the Gospel of John" in *The Conversation Continues: Studies in Paul and John in Honour of J. Louis Martyn*, edited by R. T. Fortna and Beverly R. Gaventa (Nashville: Abingdom Press, 1990), cited by Hakola, *Identity Matters*, 17.

[105] David Rensberger, *Overcoming the World: Politics and Community in the Gospel of John* (London: SPCK, 1989), 22.

[106] The criticism of Martyn and the constructions of the Johannine community of those that follow are taken up in the section on evaluation.

[107] Daniel Boyarin, "The *Ioudaioi* in John and the Prehistory of "Judaism,"" in *Pauline Conversations in Context: Essays in Honour of Calvin J. Roeztel,* edited by J. C. Anderson *et.al.* (Sheffield: Sheffield Academic Press, 2002), 220.

[108] Ashton notes, "…the Gospel does not display its strata one on top of the other in a given order: there is nothing in the text itself to inform us which came first." Ashton, *Understanding*

been criticized for methodological defects especially focusing much on Jn. 9 for his theoretical framework.[109] He also seems to have glossed over the role of the Gentiles in the Johannine community.[110]

2.2.2. Raymond E. Brown[111]

Brown too orients the construction of the Johannine community with the two-level reading of Martyn.[112] The importance of Brown in the reconstruction of

the Fourth Gospel, 2007, 14.

[109] This point has been rightly brought out by Kierspel, who also notes two other flaws- a) Martyn disconnects words from a coherent system of language by making a single word *aposynagogos* (and *Ioudaioi*) the key to the interpretation of the text;" b) "Martyn's historical analysis depends too much on Fortna's form critical isolation of a narrative source that underlies the FG." Lars Kierspel, *The Jews and the World in the Fourth Gospel* (Tübingen: Mohr Siebeck, 2006), 172.

[110] Raymond E. Brown, "Johannine Ecclesiology: The Community's Origins" *Int.* 31/4 (O. 1977): 392.

[111] Raymond E. Brown proposes his theory regarding the use of Johannine traditions in the first volume of his two volume commentary on the FG – *The Gospel according to John.* In it he detailed a five stage development, which would account for the literary and stylistic unity of the gospel as well as the presence of different styles, duplicate discourses, and interruptive passages. Stage 1: The existence of a body of traditional material pertaining to the words and works of Jesus was independent of the synoptic tradition. Stage 2: The material developed in Johannine patterns. For over several decades the traditional material was sifted, selected, thought over and moulded into the form and style of individual stories and discourses that became part of the FG. This process was probably accomplished through oral preaching and teaching. Written forms of what was preached and taught took shape. Though the units betray minor differences, probably they are the result of a close-knit school of thought and expression and the principal preacher of the school was responsible for the main body of Gospel material. Stage 3: The organization of the above material led to the first edition of the FG as a distinct work. Brown refers to the master preacher as the "evangelist." The first edition was in Aramaic. There is a basic cohesiveness in the first edition of the Gospel. The first edition was a selection of the Johannine material coming for the evangelist's preaching. Stage 4: The second edition was done by the evangelist and 1:19-34 convey traces of editing. This addition took place to answer the objections or difficulties of several groups – disciples of John the Baptist, Jewish Christians who left the Synagogue. Stage 5: A final editing or redaction was done by someone other than the evangelist and whom Brown calls the redactor. The redactor was a close friend or disciple of the evangelist and part of the general school of thought. The redactor inserted the duplicate discourses often side by side with the form of the discourse that existed in the earlier edition ex. 6:51-58 next to 6:35-50. This collection was added to the Last Supper Discourse of Jesus in chs. 15-17. The redactor also added the material in chs. 11 and 12 to the Gospel outline. Thus, for Brown the original ending of the public ministry came in 10:42-43. Raymond E. Brown, *The Gospel according to John (i-xii)*, xxxiv-xxxvi. Thirteen years later, Brown offered a more comprehensive presentation of the history of the Johannine community in *The Community of the Beloved Disciple* where he rejects the view that the BD is John son of Zebedee and takes the view that the BD was a disciple of John the Baptist. Brown, *The Community of the Beloved Disciple*, 34.

[112] Brown does differ from Martyn and Richter's proposals of the Johannine community. Refer Brown, "Johannine Ecclesiology:" 379-393.

the Johannine community has been clearly described by Kysar, who notes, "His appeal to a single community to which the gospel was directed attempts to take into account the peculiar features of the document by references to several events in the community's life. *Consequently, the community concept grew out of Brown's efforts to explicate the peculiarities of the gospel.*"[113]

For Brown, the FG is a narrative of Jesus and the community's expression of the faith in him.[114] The latter holds more prominence for Brown as, according to him, the FG chiefly concerns itself with how the FE thought of and communicated Jesus to a community of Christians in the last part of the first century CE which offers indirect pointers to the community's existence at the time the gospel was composed. This is important for Brown as only the works and discourses of Jesus that are relevant to the members of the community find their place in the FG.[115]

Brown breaks down the history of the communityinto four phases.[116] Phase one deals with the period before the FG was written, especially describing the relationship between the community and "mid-first century Judaism."[117] Phase two discusses the period when the FG was composed.[118] Phase three deals with the divided Johannine community which relates to the context of the epistles.[119] The last phase dwells on the breakup of the community into various groups such as, Docetism, Gnosticism, Cerinthianism, and Montanism.[120]

2.2.2.1. Phase One (50s to 80s CE)

Brown is of the view that some of the originating group of "Christians Jews"[121] (Jews who believed in Jesus) included the disciples of John the Baptist,[122] and

---

[113] Kysar, "The Whence and Whither," 68.

[114] Brown, *The Community of the Beloved Disciple*, 17.

[115] Brown, *The Community of the Beloved Disciple*, 18.

[116] Brown, *The Community of the Beloved Disciple*, 22.

[117] Brown, *The Community of the Beloved Disciple*, 22.

[118] Brown, *The Community of the Beloved Disciple*, 23.

[119] Brown, *The Community of the Beloved Disciple*, 23.

[120] Brown, *The Community of the Beloved Disciple*, 23. The last two stages do not seem to have much importance with the research and therefore is not discussed below.

[121] Not just that but also had the messianic understanding like the twelve disciples. Brown, *The Community of the Beloved Disciple*, 32.

[122] Brown bases this view on John the Baptist's acknowledgement of Jesus' pre-existence. Thus for him, some members of the Johannine community came from John the Baptist movement while others from those stated in the synoptics. Brown, *The Community of the Beloved Disciple*, 29.

the BD[123] is seen as the unnamed disciple of John the Baptist.[124] The Johannine community began with a relatively low Christology,[125] but at a later stage embraced a high christology that brought the community into acute conflict with the synagogue. Unlike Martyn, who tides over the reason for the shift in Christology, Brown attributes this shift to the entrance of the anti-temple Jews and their Samaritan converts which occasioned a different Christology, opposition to the Temple cult, and Samaritan elements.[126] According to Brown, the Samaritans group mobilized, "...the Johannine community towards a theology of descent from above and pre-existence."[127] The second group brought in a Christology that was not centered on a davidic messiah; and more importantly, this precipitated the suspicion and hostility of the synagogue leaders.[128] The Johannine Christians were seen as proclaiming a second God, so they were violating the basic principle of Israelite identity (Deut. 6:4), and the sacred cultic institutions of Judaism were relegated to a position of insignificance for those who believe in Jesus.[129] The reason for Brown's conjecture is that after Jn. 4, the conversion of the Samaritans, the gospel concentrates on the rejection of Jesus by "the Jews."[130] Brown agrees with Martyn while stating that the term "the Jews" is a reference to "the Jewish authorities of Jesus" time and the hostile inhabitants of the synagogue in his own time.[131] The new situation reinterpreted the old understanding even as

[123] For Brown, the BD is an "idealized" person but also "...a historical person and a companion of Jesus." He further notes that he was not among the twelve disciples. This is a change in the position earlier held by Brown (Anchor Bible Commentary) where he had noted that the BD was John, son of Zebedee. Brown, *The Community of the Beloved Disciple*, 33-34.

[124] Brown, *The Community of the Beloved Disciple*, 32.

[125] By "Low" Christology Brown means the use of titles taken from the OT or intertestamental expectation such as Messiah, prophet, servant, lord, Son of God, the titles that do not have any implications of divinity. Brown, *The Community of the Beloved Disciple*, 25.

[126] Brown, *The Community of the Beloved Disciple*, 38-39. Brown draws support from others to affirm this point of view: Wayne A. Meeks, *The Prophet-King Moses Traditions and the Johannine Christology*, NovTSup 14 (Leiden: Brill, 1967), 318-319. Freed states of three aspects of influence of Samaritan theology on the FG: a) the "I am" as divine name; b) the love motif; c) developed belief in the resurrection of the body. Edwin D. Freed, "Did John Write His Gospel Partly to Win Samaritan Converts?" *NovT* 12/3 (Jl. 1970): 252-254 (241-256). Purvis is of the view that Samaria is the place where many Johannine traditions developed and Johannine Christianity emerged from the "...heterogeneity of Palestinian intellectual history." James D. Purvis, "The Fourth Gospel and the Samaritans" *NovT* 17/3 (Jl. 1975): 162.

[127] Brown, *The Community of the Beloved Disciple*, 45.

[128] Brown, *The Community of the Beloved Disciple*, 44.

[129] Brown, *The Community of the Beloved Disciple*, 47.

[130] Brown, *The Community of the Beloved Disciple*, 40.

[131] Brown, *The Community of the Beloved Disciple*, 41. Martyn, *History and Theology*, 47ff.

the cross is reinterpreted as "lifting up" (12:31-32).[132] Brown moves beyond Martyn in adding a third group[133] that joined the Johannine community-the Gentiles. For Brown, the evidence for this view is in the explanation of terms such as "Messiah," "Rabbi;" the arrival of Greeks in 12:20-23; and citation of Isa. in Jn. 12:37-40, a text used for explaining the reason for turning to the Gentiles.[134]

2.2.2.2. Phase Two[135]

Brown notes that ca. 85 those who embraced a high Christology faced expulsion from the synagogue with the possible execution of Jewish Christians.[136] However, he seems to retract from his earlier position of associating the 18th benediction to expulsion, when he notes that one does not know how soon and the extent to which the curse was adopted.[137] The Gentiles joined the community; and in an event such as this, there was no strife, as the community was already outside Judaism.[138] The aspects of dualism and universalistic outlook appealed to the Gentiles.[139] This view differs from Martyn, who holds the view that the Gentile mission took place at phase three.[140] At the same time, Brown rightly points out that the development of Christology did not lead the community to an introverted position. On the contrary, the community engaged with other groups such as the crypto Christians[141] (Christian Jews who remained within the synagogue), the Jewish Christians (churches of inadequate

[132] Brown, *The Community of the Beloved Disciple*, 54.

[133] The other two being: Jewish Christians, and Jewish Christians of anti-Temple orientation and their Samaritan converts. Brown, *The Community of the Beloved Disciple*, 55.

[134] Brown, *The Community of the Beloved Disciple*, 55.

[135] Brown notes the Second Phase as surviving many decades. Brown, *The Gospel according to John (i –xii)*, xxxvi.

[136] Brown, *The Community of the Beloved Disciple*, 66-67.

[137] Brown notes, "...we do not know how quickly and widely this curse was adopted. The inclusion of Christians among the deviants may have come considerably later than the composition of John." Raymond E. Brown, *An Introduction to the New Testament*, AB Reference Library, edited by David Noel Freedman (Bangalore: TPI, 2009), 374, f.n. 102.

[138] Brown rightly notes that the concept "world" in the FG is much wider and includes both Jews and Gentiles. He is of the view that the opposition against the Johannine community shifts from "the Jews" to Gentiles at later stage. Brown, *The Community of the Beloved Disciple*, 63.

[139] Brown, *The Community of the Beloved Disciple*, 55.

[140] Martyn, *The Gospel of John in Christian History*, 120.

[141] Brown, *The Community of the Beloved Disciple*, 71-73.

faith (8:31; 7:3-5)),[142] and the Christians of apostolic churches (Peter and the great Church).[143] At a later stage, ca. 90 CE, the gospel was written.

2.2.2.3. Evaluation

Brown's reconstruction has certain merits. First, he rightly notes that the Johannine community was not a sect but was in communication with other groups. Second, he also has backtracked from his earlier position of relating expulsion with *Birkat-ha-minim*, a position that is favoured in recent scholarship. However, there seems to be some drawbacks to his approach. Brown precisely notes several editions of the FG and the occasions related to it. It is important to tread cautiously here since reconstruction of several editions of the FG is a difficult proposition.[144] The other being, Brown's conjecture of preciseness of several groups that interacted with the Johannine community has also difficulties with it, especially, the view that Samaritans joined the community later has also difficulties because there is no reason why they could not have joined earlier.

2.2.3. John Painter

Painter in his work entitled *The Quest for the Messiah: The History, Literature and Theology of the Johannine Community* (1993), also agrees with Martyn in pointing out that the evangelist fused together the story of Jesus with the story of the community. But, unlike Martyn, he is of the view that it is impossible to state the line of separation.[145] Like others, he opines that the Johannine community was born out of a bitter schism between Jewish believers in Jesus and the synagogue. Johannine literature is the product of the Johannine School which is different from the Johannine community who is the intended audience.[146] Painter also describes different periods for the composition of the gospel.[147]

---

[142] Brown, *The Community of the Beloved Disciple*, 74-81.

[143] Brown arrives at this conclusion from the texts in the FG that contrasts Peter with the BD. Brown, *The Community of the Beloved Disciple*, 82-83.

[144] Cullmann, *The Johannine Circle*, 12.

[145] John Painter, *The Quest for the Messiah: The History, Literature and Theology of the Johnnine Community* (Edinburgh: T & T Clark, 1993), 24.

[146] Painter, *The Quest for the Messiah*, 33.

[147] The shaping of the Johannine tradition went on in Palestine until 60s. The evangelist and his group of disciples migrated to a place in the Diaspora perhaps in Ephesus and in the last decade of the first century while the tradition continued to be shaped by the evangelist and finally published by a member or members of his school. The writing of the FG was done over a lengthy period and was revised and added to earlier "drafts" of the evangelist's work before his contribution was completed. There were three editions to the FG. In the first edition, the tradition was shaped by an open dialogue concerning the messiahship of Jesus which stopped after the Jewish war. The second edition took place at the experience of expulsion from the

2.2.3.1. Evaluation

The community reconstruction of Painter seems to follow Martyn, Brown and others even though he takes the reason for the expulsion as the movement from Formative Judaism to Jewish orthodoxy and not *Birkat ha-minim*. The difficulty seems to be that one is not sure whether the Jewish orthodoxy had developed at this stage. Further, one is not sure whether the Jewish orthodoxy had a wide impact. Another difficulty of Painter's view is the preciseness with which he delineates the different editions of the FG; this again is only a hypothetical reconstruction and the nature of the FG seems to resist clear demaracations.

2.2.4. R. Alan Culpepper

Painter's use of the term Johannine School echoes R. Alan Culpepper's usage. Culpepper[148] makes a study of the essential characteristics of ancient schools[149] and sums up nine characteristics[150] that the Johannine community shared with them.[151] - First, the Johannine community was at the beginning a fellowship of disciples but later the BD became the teacher who instructed and construed the traditions of Jesus; Second, the community was formed around the BD and drew its roots from the BD, the founder.Third, the community gave much importance to the teachings and traditions of the BD. Four, the community members were followers or students of the BD. Five, the community engaged in teaching, learning, studying, and writing. Six, the Johannine community celebrated a fellowship meal. Seven, the community also had its stipulations

---

synagogue and contains the tradition of dispute and conflict leading up to the expulsion. Painter rejects Martyn's proposal of *Birkat ha-Minin* as the chief reason for expulsion. The situation could have been for him the movement from Formative Judaism towards the development of Jewish orthodoxy which led to exclusion of the Jewish believers who confessed Jesus to be the Christ from the synagogue. The third edition came up as the result of the growing schism within the Johannine community. Painter, *The Quest for the Messiah*, 66.

[148] Culpepper, *The Johannine School.*

[149] The schools include the Pythagorean school, the Academy, the Lyceum, the Garden, the Stoa, the school at Qumran, the House of Hillel, Philo's school and the school of Jesus. Culpepper, *The Johannine School*, 38, 250.

[150] The nine characteristics of the ancient schools are 1) consisted of groups of disciples that stressed on φιλία and κοινωνία; 2) the drew their ancestry to the founder who was thought of as a wise or a good man; 3) they considered of great importance the teachings and tradition relating to him; 4) the members were disciples or students of the founder; 5) most of the activities in the school were teaching, learning and studying; 6) common supper was celebrated in remembering the founder; 7) regulations were observed with regards to entry, continuance of membership and furtherance in membership; 8) they maintained aloofness from the society; 9) they also had an organizational structure to ensure their continuance. Culpepper, *The Johannine School*, 259.

[151] Culpepper, *The Johannine School*, 287-289.

for membership and importance was given to belief in Jesus as the Christ, the Son of God (Jn. 20:21), and baptism (Jn. 3:5; I Jn. 2:19). Eight, the community remained aloof from the society. Nine, the community also followed organizational structure for its continuance. Based on the above, Culpepper concludes that the Johannine community can also be referred to as a school.[152]

2.2.4.1. Evaluation

Culpepper's reconstruction of the Johannine construction is meritorious as he attempts to define the Johannine community in relation to the ancient schools. His reconstruction does have limitations. First, the ancient schools which were of varied backgrounds cannot be compared to a community in the late first century CE. Moreover, it is highly doubtful whether the Johannine community had an organizational structure. The FG does lend the view that the community was more fluid in its organizational structure, especially in light of the fact that Jesus calls his disciples his friends.

2.2.5. Oscar Cullmann

Oscar Cullmann's work *The Johannine Circle*[153] is an important contribution to the Johannine community hypothesis. It was supposed to be a part of the introduction to the commentary on the FG.[154] Instead of arguing for different sources for the FG, Cullman prefers to argue for "special Johannine *traditions*."[155] He further notes that the evangelist of the FG was in the knowledge of "a *separate tradition*," which he received from "the *particular circle*" he came from; this tradition did go through development before the FG was composed.[156] According to him, the purpose of the evangelist is to strengthen those who believe in Christ by relating the life of "*incarnate* Jesus" with the Johannine church.[157] However, by doing so does not deny the FG's historical value.[158] Cullmann notes that the evangelist belonged to

[152] Culpepper, *The Johannine School*, 289.

[153] Cullmann, *The Johannine Circle.*

[154] Cullmann, "Preface" in *The Johannine Circle*, ix.

[155] Cullmann, *The Johannine Circle*, 7.

[156] Cullmann is also of the view that the language and style of the FG were shaped by the Johannine circle in its particular context. Cullmann, *The Johannine Circle*, 7, 28.

[157] Cullmann also adds that the evangelist was concerned for the "*unity*" of the church and that is why Peter is not at all attacked in the FG. Cullmann, *The Johannine Circle*, 14-15.

[158] Cullmann notes categorically, "For him the narrative of what happened once is not an outer garment which could be stripped from the Gospel. In this case *history, facts*, are the *object* of theological consideration." Cullmann, *The Johannine Circle*, 21.

a circle, i.e., a Judaism that belonged to the fringes.[159] For Cullmann, there existed a "Johannine circle," while the author was alive and the author had an important role[160] in it.[161] For Cullmann, the FG has a considerably close connection not just with heterodox Judaism[162] (non-official Judaism),[163] but also with the "*Hellenists in Jerusalem*,"[164] who too have had their foundation in heterodox Judaism.

Cullmann describes the relationship between these in terms of a triangle. He notes, "The apex of the triangle is represented by heterodox Judaism, in which Samaria plays a predominant role, but only *alongside* other analogous tendencies."[165] He posits two points of contact with 'marginal Judaism:' the origin of the community itself and Transjordan or Syria after the community's flight from Jerusalem before 70.[166]

After having dealt with the origin of the FG,[167] Cullmann deals with his view on the evangelist of the FG. For Cullmann, the evangelist comes from the Jewish circle, unlike the mainstream Judaism, and considers the era of the Temple cult as over.[168] The evangelist is supposed to have come from Judea, based on the emphasis of the FG's narrative in Judea, but was not one of the

---

[159] Cullmann uses several terms to describe this: "'non-conformist' or even 'heterodox Judaism,' 'marginal Judaism." He adds, "…this non-conformist Judaism has numerous roots in the pagan syncretism of its environment." Cullmann, *The Johannine Circle*, 24, 32.

[160] Cullmann considers the author as a "towering personality" who "shared the theological foundation for it (the work) with the whole his circle." He further adds that the evangelist was guided by the Paraclete in remembering the words of Jesus (2:22;12:16) and "the risen Christ speaks through the evangelist" in the case of the Nicodemus episode. Cullmann, *The Johannine Circle*, 10-11, 18.

[161] Cullmann argues that after the death of the author a redactor or a group of redactors who were influenced by the author composed the whole of the FG. Cullmann, *The Johannine Circle*, 8, 10.

[162] Cullmann is of the view, "…Jesus himself is not a stranger to marginal Judaism." Cullmann, *The Johannine Circle*, 91.

[163] In this category Cullmann also includes "*pre-gnostic* features," and the Gnosticism of the pseudo-Clementines, "*Samaritan*" religion, the Qumran community, the John the baptist movement, Gnostic Ebionitism. Cullmann, *The Johannine Circle*, 35-36, 60.

[164] Cullmann states three similarities: a) theological understanding, which includes christology, liturgy and worship; b) concern for the mission to Samaria; c) similar aspects of Stephen's speech in the FG and the Samaritan theology. Cullmann, *The Johannine Circle*, 43.

[165] Cullmann, *The Johannine Circle*, 52.

[166] Cullmann, *The Johannine Circle*, 59.

[167] Cullmann identifies three stages in the origin of the FG, they are: the oral tradition, along with portions of it being written; the written gospel by the evangelist who was involved in the framework and the theological focus of the gospel; and a redactor or a group of redactors who completely revised the gospel. Cullmann, *The Johannine Circle*, 64.

[168] Cullmann, *The Johannine Circle*, 66.

twelve disciples.[169] He was a disciple of John the Baptist, later a disciple of Jesus, and was present with Jesus in his ministry in Jerusalem.[170] The evangelist had access to the common tradition as well as to the special collection from Galilee.[171] Further, the evangelist represents a tradition different from the synoptics and Paul.[172] The BD is not the apostle John who is the author of the FG.[173] The evangelist was an eye-witness in a limited number of events, and thus also made use of other traditions.[174] Unlike the other scholars discussed earlier, Cullmann opines that at the unredacted stage of the FG was "…as early as the Synoptics or even earlier than the earliest of them."[175] The difference between the FG and the synoptics is because Jesus had two different styles of teaching.[176]

2.2.5.1. Evaluation

Cullmann is different from the reconstructions seen so far, especially his view on the Johannine circle to which the evangelist belonged. He views the varieties of Judaism present in heterodox Judaism as coming from the Johannine circle. This is unlike Brown, who sees different groups as joining the Johannine community at different stages. Cullmann goes further in stating that the disciples of Jesus consisted of two groups, one from the mainstream Judaism and the other from the fringes. He is possibly pushing the hypothesis to an extreme view. There seems to be no evidence of Jesus using different styles of teaching to these two groups. Though Jesus' disciples were drawn from different backgrounds, it is not possible to conclusively say whether he offered different styles of teaching.

2.2.6. Martinus C. de Boer[177]

de Boer divides the history of the Johannine community into four phases, and though his views share some similarities with Martyn and Brown, he does differ from them.

---

[169] Cullmann, *The Johannine Circle*, 66-67.

[170] Cullmann, *The Johannine Circle*, 78.

[171] Cullmann, *The Johannine Circle*, 67.

[172] Cullmann, *The Johannine Circle*, 67.

[173] Cullmann, *The Johannine Circle*, 78.

[174] Cullmann, *The Johannine Circle*, 80.

[175] Cullmann, *The Johannine Circle*, 97.

[176] Cullmann would attribute the different styles of Jesus' teaching to the two groups that Jesus had- the one from mainstream Judaism and the other from the fringes; though he notes these two groups were not completely separate. Cullmann, *The Johannine Circle*, 93-94.

[177] Martinus C. de Boer, *Johannine Perspectives on the Death of Jesus* (Kampen: Kok Pharos Publishing House, 1996), 43-82.

In the first phase, the context is the mission to fellow Jews. The death of Jesus, the Messiah, by crucifixion was a note of embarrassment and the Johannine response was to present it as the fulfillment of Scripture and prelude it to the resurrection. It became a divinely foreshadowed event leading to resurrection from the dead, a climatic messianic sign.

In the second phase, the community was expelled from the synagogue ca. 85 CE. The Samaritans became part of the community after the Johannine community separated from the synagogue. de Boer, unlike Brown, says that the community was expelled simply for confessing Jesus to be the earthly Messiah (9:22). The high Christology was developed after the decree of expulsion.

In the third phase in ca. 90 CE the martyrdom for high Christology took place in the community, and Gentile converts were added. The community also developed contact with other Christian groups.

Finally, in the fourth phase, a schism developed in the community ca. 100 CE, after which time the epistles were written. This was followed by the dissolution of the Johannine Christianity.[178]

2.2.6.1. Evaluation

de Boer's reconstruction differs from Brown, especially his view that the Samaritans joined after the expulsion. de Boer's reconstruction is unique as he gives importance to the death of Jesus in the Johannine community in the first phase. However, de Boer's view that the community was expelled for its belief in the earthly Messiah does present its share of difficulties; especially as there seems to be no reason why the community should be expelled for confessing faith in the earthly Messiah at a time when several messianic movements existed.

All of the above reconstructions seem to delve into the specifics of the Johannine community. But there has been a significant change in the contemporary discussion on the Johannine community; scholars tend not to go into the particular details of the community, unlike Martyn and Brown. This is a notable change even though the general framework still plays an invaluable part in the understanding of the FG. One of the recent constructions of the Johannine community is worth considering.

---

[178] de Boer reconstructs four editions of the FG corresponding with four different perspectives on the death of Jesus in the FG. He notes, "While Johannine writer 'recontextualized' previous perspectives in rewriting the gospel under the pressure of changing communal situations, they did not themselves attempt, or at least did not themselves achieve, a synthesis." de Boer, *Johannine Perspectives*, 314-315.

2.2.7. Celestino G. Lingad[179]

Lingad opines that John, as a young man, grew up within the bosom of Judaism eagerly expecting the Messiah. He was a follower of John the Baptist and witnessed Jesus' miracles, stood at the foot of the cross and himself encountered the risen Lord.[180] Later, he became close to John son of Zebedee and Philip, and was thrown out of the synagogue for confessing his faith in Jesus as the Messiah. Thus, he departed from Palestine and stayed on in Asia Minor, at Ephesus.[181] He brought together a group of disciples, which eventually became a school with its centre at Ephesus. He became the elder of the school, the inspiration for its life and doctrine.[182] After many years of involvement in the community in terms of teaching and preaching, he brought out a gospel putting together the traditions of Jesus' deeds and his teachings. This gospel was independent of the synoptics.[183] Another edition of the gospel took place later when a member, after his death, made a final redaction of the gospel, which included chiefly Jn. 21.[184]

2.2.7.1. Evaluation

Lingad differs from Martyn and Brown since he placed, the expulsion in Palestine. In doing so, he glosses over the question of whether expulsion could have taken place in the Diaspora. Further, he also delinks the traditions in the FG as coming from John, the son of Zebedee. In fact, for him, John, the son of Zebedee, is only an acquaintance. Here again, this hypothesis tries to answer why John, the son of Zebedee, finds less significance in the FG.

2.2.8. Johannine Community Reconstructions: An Assessment

Different propositions such as the Johannine Community, Johannine School and Johannine Circle attempt, to deal with the aporias and other inconsistencies in the FG. Cullmann's suggestion of heterodox Judaism having influenced Jesus is historically inaccurate according to Brown.[185] Cullmann's oversimplification of the differences between the synoptics and the FG on the basis of different

---

[179] Celestino G. Lingad, *The Problems of Jewish Christians in the Johannine Community*, TGST 73 (Rome: Gregorian University Press, 2001).

[180] Lingad, *The Problems of Jewish Christians*, 186.

[181] Lingad, *The Problems of Jewish Christians*, 186.

[182] Lingad, *The Problems of Jewish Christians*, 186.

[183] Lingad, *The Problems of Jewish Christians*, 187.

[184] Lingad, *The Problems of Jewish Christians*, 188.

[185] Brown, *The Community of the Beloved Disciple*, 178. However, Brown's criticism of Cullmann for stating that the FG was written by an eyewitness is a misreading of Cullmann. As stated above, Cullmann does not state that FG in total does come from an eyewitness record, only partially.

speech styles coming from Jesus is unacceptable.[186] Thus, the supposition of a Johannine Circle behind the FG does not seem viable.[187]

The suggestion of a Johannine School behind the writing of the FG is also distraught with difficulties. Ashton states the great Greek schools were academic and their purpose was intellectual while the Johannine School was primarily a religious body.[188] Culpepper assumes that the Johannine School, like the other academic schools, was deeply academic in nature; second, the BD is supposed to be a teacher, but in the FG the BD is portrayed as a listener and one who received teachings from Jesus.

Though the community hypothesis seems to have many supporters among Johannine scholars, yet the advocates of this hypothesis do not share consensus on several areas. Firstly, there is no unanimity on the base material at the earliest stage of evolution. For Brown, the Johannine tradition began with a body of oral traditional material relating to the words and works of Jesus.[189] Painter posits three major stages in the development: a base oral tradition, three written editions published by FE, and a final redaction of FG. Painter points that the oral tradition cannot be deduced from the present text. Martyn argues that the written sign source underlies all subsequent editions of FG.[190] The second area that lacks unanimity concerns the role of the BD. For Brown, the BD plays a decisive role in handing over the traditions concerning Jesus to the community whereas for Martyn, the BD is not a historical person and did not play any such role. The third area of contention is the reason for the shift from lower Christology to higher Christology in the FG. For Brown, the reason for the shift occurred when the Jews of anti-temple bias and the converts of Samaria entered the group. This led to a pre-existence Christology, debates with Jews and expulsion from the synagogue. Painter raises a few questions concerning Brown's hypothesis of a Johannine community.[191] Besides these disagreements, the very cornerstone of Martyn's proposal, which is the use

---

[186] Brown, *The Community of the Beloved Disciple*, 178.

[187] Kysar also notes, "The concept of school provides us with a number of important features of the community, but it is not to be equated with the whole community." Kysar, "The Whence and Whither," 66.

[188] John Ashton, *Understanding the Fourth Gospel*, 195.

[189] Brown, *The Gospel according to John (i -xii)*, xxxiv-xxxv.

[190] Martyn, *The Gospel of John in Christian History*, 28-32.

[191] The issues raised are a. There is no good reason for delaying the development of "higher" Christology. It could have been a contribution of the evangelist in the context of dialogue with the synagogue. b. The break with the synagogue almost certainly opened the Johannine Community with the Gentiles; c. The 'redactor' clearly is responsible for 21:24 and the added the whole chapter 21 including the reference to the BD. Painter, *The Quest for the Messiah*, 67.

of *Birkat ha-minim* at Yavneh, has been questioned by some.[192] The case for expulsion resulting from an inner conflict does seem to present a possibility.[193] Judith Lieu[194] states that it is not possible to precisely delineate the history of the Johannine Community from the FG. Adele Reinhartz[195] asserts that the expulsion texts and anti-Jewish language serve to pacify any ambiguity associated with the choice to follow Jesus.

2.3. Possible Johannine Community Reconstruction

The precise details of the Johannine community are elusive but these do not prevent one from charting out the contours of the Johannine community. The researcher has attempted below such an enterprise.

2.3.1. The Contours of the Johannine Community

The seminal works of Martyn and Brown have enriched and broadened the horizon of Johannine interpretation. All the same, as rightly noted by Judith Lieu, the attempt to sketch the details of the history of the Johannine community eludes one's grasp. There seems to be a consensus among scholars on a basic proposition, which is the concerned community suffered conflict with the

---

[192] Aune states that Heinrich Graetz is the author of the Javneh myth. David E. Aune, "On the Origins of the "Council of Javneh" Myth," *JBL* 110/3 (Fall 1991): 491-493, especially 491. Instone-Brewer note that the origin is before 70 CE and a critique of the Sadducean priesthood. David Instone-Brewer, "The Eighteen Benedictions and the Minim before 70 CE," *JTS* 54/1 (Apr. 2003): 25-44. Beutler notes, "Exclusion of Christians by the Synod of Jamnia cannot be proved, it is disputable whether they had authority over all the Jewish community of the Mediterranean." Johannes Beutler, *Judaism and the Jews in the Gospel of John*, SubBi 30 (Rome: Editrice Pontifico Instituto Biblico, 2006), 29. However, Marcus supports Martyn's reconstruction arguing on the basis of the rabbinic control in the early Christian centuries. Joel Marcus, "*Birkat Ha-Minim*: Revisited," *NTS* 55/4 (O. 2009): 523-551.

[193] John T. Townsend, "The Gospel of John and the Jews: The Story of a Religious Divorce" in *Antisemitism and the Foundation of Christianity*, edited by A. Davies (New York: Paulist, 1979), 72-79; Hartwig Thyen, "Das Heil kommt von den Juden" in *Kirche: Festchrift für Günther Bornkamm zum 75 Geburtstag*, edited by D. Lührmann and G. Stecker, (Tübingen: Mohr siebeck, 1980), 177, 180-182; Kikwo Matsunaga, "Christian Self-identification and the Twelfth Benediction" in *Eusebius, Christianity and Judaism*, edited by H. W. Attridge and G. Hata, 355-371. Leiden: Brill, 1992. Stefan Schapdick, *Auf dem Weg in den Konflikt: Exegetische Studien zum theoligischen Profil der Erzählung vom Aufenthalt Jesu in Samrien (John 4:1-42) im kontext das Johannesevangeliums*. BBB 126 (Berlin: Phico, 2000). These scholars are cited in Kierspel, *The Jews and the World*, 167. Culpepper argues for the expulsion process of the Jesus-believing Jews from the synagogue. R. Alan Culpepper, "The Gospel of John and the Jews," *RevExp* 84/2 (Spring 1987): 273-288, especially 281.

[194] Judith Lieu, *The Second and Third Epistles of John: History and Background* (Edinburgh: T & T Clark, 1986), 168. She also states that the separation of John's community from the synagogue is not traced in John as often supposed. Judith Lieu, "Temple and Synagogue in John," *NTS* 45/1 (Ja. 1999): 51.

[195] Reinhartz, "The Johannine Community and its Jewish Neighbors," 111-138.

synagogue.[196] The unclear aspects are the precise details of the history of the Johannine community. It seems virtually impossible to unearth the different editions of the FG from the present gospel.[197] Cullmann rightly expresses the difficulty in trying to retrieve the sources and the various redaction stages of the FG.[198] Therefore, it is only possible to make an attempt to draw the general contours of the community.

The community began with the disciples of Christ,[199] who were formerly disciples of John the Baptist.[200] The disciples here refer to a broad category and are not to be restricted to the twelve disciples. Samaritans were also included. Cullmann rightly addresses this aspect, he notes, "… the Twelve do not play any essential role anywhere in the Fourth Gospel (they appear only once, in 6:70), and that on the contrary we find other intimate disciples like Nathaniel and Lazarus close to Jesus."[201]

---

[196] Ashton is of view that the FG gives one version of the break from the synagogue but other side of the version, that is, from the Jews is not available. Despite this fact, Ashton concludes that the Jesus group had broken from "the Jews," not to return again. Ashton, *Understanding the Fourth Gospel*, 2007, 32.

[197] It seems to be a futile exercise too. Kierspel states in this connection, "The confidence of going behind the text in order to find individual sources or multiple editions has largely eroded." Kierspel, *The Jews and the World*, 45.

[198] Cullmann, *The Johannine Circle*, 12.

[199] The researcher is skeptical about the view of a sign source being part of the proclamation in the Early Period as suggested by Ashton. Ashton, *Understanding the Fourth Gospel*, 2007, 110. For one, the existence of a sign source is debatable. The other reason being, it is difficult to trace such a source in the FG as the whole of FG can be seen from the perspective of the sign, including the resurrection.

[200] This view is espoused by Brown as seen earlier in Brown's reconstruction of the Johannine community. Brown, *The Community of the Beloved Disciple*, 29.

[201] Cullmann, *The Johannine Circle*, 75-76.

The view that the Johannine community consisted of Jewish Christians,[202] Samaritan Christians,[203] and the Gentiles[204] is plausible although it may not be possible to accurately pinpoint when they joined the community. As part of the synagogue, they began a dialogue with the other fellow Jews. The dialogue crystallized into a development of Christology. The confession of Jesus being the Messiah in the synagogue included the aspects of Christology. The confession of Jesus as the Messiah in ordinary terms would not have been a matter of offense as there were many messianic movements in Judaism; all

---

[202] The term Jewish Christians has been widely interpreted: a. with the emphasis on nationality, the term could refer to the practice of Christian faith by those who belong to the Jewish race; b. it could also refer to the Christological orientation, i.e., the group of Jews who understood Jesus in terms of a Jewish Messiah and not as Son of God (Ebionites); c. another possibility is that it could refer to Jews who have separated from Jewish affiliation but understood themselves in categories borrowed from Judaism; d. Jewish Christians could also mean in the historic sense, i.e., those Jewish Christians who lived in Palestine between the resurrection of Jesus and the Second Jewish Revolt. After having described the four possible categories, Lingad espouses the last view. Lingad, *The Problems of Jewish Christians*, 19-21. The term 'Jewish Christians' is difficult to define as noted by Paget, who discusses three difficulties pertaining to it. He does discuss three ways of defining 'Jewish Christianity' such as – a) an ethinic definition; b) a praxis-base definition; c) ideological and doctrinal definitions. J. Clarenton Paget, "Jewish Christianity," in *The Cambridge History of Judaism*, vol. 3: *The Early Roman Period*, edited by W. Horbury, W. D. Davies, and J. Sturdy (Cambridge: Cambridge University Press, 1999), 731-732, 733-739. The researcher understands the term 'Jewish Christians,' as applied to the Johannine community, referring to the Jews, who confessed their faith in the messiahship of Jesus and this confession resulted in opposition from those who disregarded messiahship of Jesus. Thus, the FG uses Jewish categories to define its identity but yet distinguishes itself from it. Identity is expressed in relation or in opposition to something. This is where one tends to disagree with Hakola, who rejects the Johannine community as not consisting of Jewish Christians because identity is not constructed in terms of opposition. For Hakola, the Johannine community does not consist of Jewish Christians as the motivation for new identity was not the result of external pressure. In other words, he states, "The believers defined themselves anew, not only in continuity with but also in opposition to basic matters of Jewishness." Raimo Hakola, "The Johannine Community as Jewish Christians? Some Problems in Current Scholarly Consensus," in *Jewish Christianity Reconsidered: Rethinking Ancient Groups and Texts*, edited by Matt Jackson-Mc Cabe (Minneapolis: Fortress Press, 2007), 192. Ringe gives evidence of Jewish Christians existing in the community: a) recourse into the Jewish Scriptures; b) the reference to participation in the synagogue; c) Semitic aspects of the Greek. Ringe, *Wisdom's Friends*, 14.

[203] The Samaritan acceptance of Jesus in Jn. 4:39-42 suggests that they were a part of the community. So also the possible hint of this is seen in Jn. 8:48. Freed goes to the extent of arguing that the writer of the FG was written to appeal to the Samartians and was influenced by Samaritanism. Freed, "Did John Write his Gospel:" 256.

[204] Kierspel states, "Being most likely written towards the end of the first century, the Gospel has also been preached to the Gentiles and the text shows ample evidence of their presence in and around the Johannine community (7:35; 12:20; 4:42; 21:18-19) and use of common Aramaic words into Greek terms as Ραββῖ (1:38; 20:16) and Μεσσίας (1:41; 4:25)" Kierspel, *The Jews and the World*, 41.

of these movements were accommodated. The intense development in the understanding of Christology[205] in messianic terms, especially in terms of the Father-Son relationship was seen as unacceptable to the other Jews in the synagogue.[206] The conflict escalated and led to a separation from the synagogue. Painter rightly notes, "Christology leads to conflict and the consequences of conflict contribute to the shaping of the Johannine community. Development of Christology led to conflict out of which Johannine community was born."[207] Segal also notes this view when he states, "...Christianity shared the experience of expulsion from the synagogue for violating the doctrine of monotheism."[208] It is quite possible that those who viewed Jesus' messiahship in Christological terms faced action from the synagogue. As pointed out in the previous chapter, this incident cannot be termed as a general ban but an intra-synagogue problem.

---

[205] Painter highlights the importance of Christology in the FG. He states, "…christology is also the ground of unity- unity of the Father and the Son (5:17; 10:30-33); unity of the believer with the Father through the Son (17:20-33); unity of the believers is dependent on a certain separation from the world (17:16); unity is an expression of the mission of the sent one on behalf of the sender (17:3-4, 6-8, 21-23, 25)." John Painter, "The Point of John's Christology: Christology, Conflict and Community in John," in *Christology, Controversy and Community: New Testament Essays in Honour of David R. Catchpole*, NovTSup 99, edited by David G. Horrell and Christopher M. Tuckett (Leiden: Brill, 2000), 232. Piper also states in a similar vein – "It is hardly an exaggeration to claim that everything in the fourth gospel revolves around christology." Ronald A. Piper,"Satan, Demons and the Absence of Exorcisms in the Fourth Gospel," in *Christology, Controversy and Community: New Testament Essays in Honour of David R. Catchpole*, NovTSup 99, edited by David G. Horrell and Christopher M. Tuckett (Leiden: Brill, 2000), 253. Culpepper also argues, "Christology not dualism is the real focus of each of the Johannine writings. Dualism is merely the conceptual context in which christology and the appeal to respond in faith are developed." R. Alan Culpepper, "An Introduction to the Johannine Writings," in *The Johannine Literature*, edited by Barnabas Lindars, Ruth B. Edwards and John M. Court (Sheffield: Sheffield Academic Press), 2000.

[206] Brown rightly notes, "The battle between the synagogue and the Johannine community was, after all, a battle over christology." Brown, *The Community of the Beloved Disciple*, 43.

[207] Painter, "The Point of John's Christology," 231.

[208] Alan Segal, *Two Powers in Heaven: Early Rabbinic Reports about Christianity and Gnosticism* (Leiden: Brill, 2002), 255.

The term ἀποσυνάγωγος[209] does denote some form of expulsion.[210] As discussed in the previous chapter, *Birkat ha-Minim* as having wider impact has been questioned, but this does not imply that expulsion did not take place.[211] The

[209] The meaning of the term has been widely contested by scholars. Boyarin takes this to mean- "…thrown out of the synagogue and not excommunication from the synagogue." Boyarin, "The *Ioudaioi* in John," 227. Ashton objects to this view and states that this does not just signify removal from the synagogue but rather excommunication from it for all those asserted Jesus as the Messiah. Ashton, *Understanding the Fourth Gospel*, 2007, 74. Meeks notes in relation to Jn. 16:2, "It speaks of being put out of the synagogue. All we have to assume is that the *archontes* of the Jewish community in John's location had simply made up their minds to get rid of these trouble making followers of a false messiah." Wayne A. Meeks, "Breaking Away: Three New Testament Pictures of Christianity's Separation from the Jewish Communities," in *"To See Ourselves as Others See Us": Christians, Jews and "Others" in Late Antiquity* edited by Jacob Neusner and Ernst Frerichs (California: Scholars' Press, 1985), 103. Davis is of the view that it is highly impossible that in the first century CE Jews practiced expulsion and therefore notes that the evangelist borrowed it from scripture to argue that Christian community is totally unrelated to the Jewish community. Margret Davies, *Rhetoric and Reference in the Fourth Gospel*, JSNTSup 69 (Sheffield: JSOT Press, 1992), 291-301. There are many scholars who support the expulsion theory and these include: Severino Pancaro, "The Relationship of the Church to Israel in the Gospel of John," *NTS* 21/3 (Apr. 1975): 396-405, especially 401-402; C. K. Barrett, *The Gospel of John and Judaism*, translated by D. M. Smith (Philadelphia: Fortress Press, 1975); John Ashton, *Understanding the FG*, 1991; J. D. G. Dunn, "The Question of Anti-semitism," 199-200; Painter, *The Quest for the Messiah*, 30; de Boer, *Johannine Perspectives on the death of Jesus*; James F. McGrath, *John's Apologetic Christology: Legitimation and Development in Johannine Christology*, SNTMS 111, edited by Richard Bauckham (Cambridge: Cambridge University Press, 2004), 44; Fréderic Manns, *John and Jamnia: How the Break Occurred between Jews and Christians ca. 80-100 A.D.*, translated by Mildred Dual and Marina Riadi (Jerusalem: Franciscan Printing Press, 1988), 25, 53. Kysar is of the view of ἀποσυνάγωγος is , "The Jewish Christians *may have felt* the leaders of their synagogue had kicked them out of the community...The feelings expressed by the Johannine Christians may have been much like some discontent Christians or Jews today who claim the particular congregation "drove them out." Kysar seems to argue that the text only presents one aspect of the story and the other side to it is the polemic aspect of the FE. Robert Kysar, "The Expulsion from the Synagogue: The Tale of the Theory," in *Voyages with John: Charting the Fourth Gospel* (Texas: Baylor University Press, 2005), 240. For Ling, "'Banished from the synagogue' (9:22; 12:42; 16:2) do not necessarily indicate a defining social schism." Timothy J. M. Ling, *The Judean Poor and the Fourth Gospel* (Cambridge: Cambridge University Press, 2006), 155.

[210] Wilson notes in this regard, "It is accepted that the Johannine Christians were at one stage expelled from the Jewish community, there must have been a time before when they lived within it and a time after when they did not…It is not essential to connect the expulsion from the synagogue with the *Birkat-ha-minim*. Christians were forcibly expelled, whether or not by the use of liturgical curse, need not be doubted." Stephen G. Wilson, *Related Strangers: Jews and Christians 70-170 CE* (Minneapolis: Fortress Press, 1995), 73. There are many scholars who support the view that church-synagogue conflict led to expulsion. Vallianippuram give a list of 24 scholars who prescribe to this view and 6 scholars who are uncertain. Refer Thomas Vallianippuram, *New Society in John's Gospel* (Thrissur: National Printing Press, 2008), 326-329.

[211] Rensberger, *Overcoming the World*, 26.

separation led to the emergence of the Johannine community. Dunn rightly notes that the FE operates in the context of an "intra-Jewish factional dispute."[212]

Christology further developed in terms of expressing the self-understanding of the community.[213] It is not possible to differentiate the aspects of Christology into separate layers. Christology led to conflict and this conflict propelled further development of Christology.[214] Here it is important to note that the separation from the synagogue created a crisis in identity. Towards solving the issue of identity, the Johannine Christology redraws its own Christology. But the Johannine community also redraws its identity in familial lines. The prologue at the beginning of the gospel makes this aspect succinctly clear. The children of God are termed as not belonging to the flesh. In Jn. 19:25-27, at the foot of the cross, familial lines are redrawn too. It is not the flesh and blood members who are now part of the family. This probably echoes the climate of the community where identity of the family has to be fused with adoption. Also, the resurrected Jesus' conversation with Mary further establishes this point. The Johannine community reframes family boundaries. However, this redrawing need not be seen as a sectarian feature because the community still had openness to those outside. To put it in the words of Ashton, the Johannine community "...looks both outwards and inwards... addressing the world and hiding itself away from the world."[215] The loss suffered is compensated with the eschatological hope and assurance of sharing a place in the Father's house (14:2-3).

Brown[216] rightly explains that the community was also involved in the mission to the Gentiles.[217] But in which provenance did the Johannine

[212] Dunn, 'The Question of Anti-semitism," 203.

[213] Boring is of the view that 'Christian prophetism' influenced the development of the Johannine community. M. Eugene Boring, "The Influence of Christian Prophecy on the Johannine Portrayal of the Paraclete and Jesus," *NTS* 25/1 (O. 1978): 113. Culpepper attributes the "anti-Jewish tone" and language of the FG to expulsion and the conflicts that followed with the synagogue. Culpepper, "The Gospel of John and the Jews:" 284.

[214] The proposal by Pryor seems difficult to comprehend. He states, "So, opposition did not create the theology, but an earlier theology was eventually rejected, and this in turn led to further definition and the exclusiveness of the sectarian claims over against the parent body." John W. Pryor, *John Evangelist of the Covenant People: The Narrative and Themes of the Fourth Gospel* (London: Darton, Longman and Todd, 1992), 167. Many aspects seem to be unclear: Why was the earlier theology rejected? What was the reason for their rejection?

[215] Ashton, *Understanding the Fourth Gospel*, 2007, 115.

[216] Brown, *The Community of the Beloved Disciple*, 63.

[217] Cullmann notes that Jn. 12:24 points to the mission to the Gentiles after the death of Jesus. Cullmann, *The Johannine Circle*, 16.

community take shape?[218] Ephesus does seem to present a possibility.[219] Swanson brings out why Palestine is probably not a possibility when he states,

> Since the Johannine sect probably did not have recent or direct roots in Palestine, "Samaritans" and "*Iudaioi*" would have worked structurally, or metaphorically, as the contrast terms for construing the possible non-Johannine stances towards spaces presently occupied by neighbouring communities. It was only against these present representatives of the Samaritans and *Iudaioi* from the mythic past that Johannine Christians living in a quite different place and time could act out their identity as sparks of light recalled

---

[218] Ringe notes the possibility of the community residing in the Jewish Diaspora, especially as the FG presents an "immigrant language" i.e., it shows aspects of a community in change. Ringe, *Wisdom's Friends*, 12.

[219] There are different places suggested on the origin of the FG. Among these include Ephesus, Syria or Antioch and Alexandria. As far as Syria is concerned Ashton leaves this place out as the language spoken there was Aramaic, not Greek. Ashton, *Understanding the Fourth Gospel*, 2007, 135. However, Becker argues for this as according to him, the language spoken at that time was Koine Greek. J. Becker, *Johanneisches Christentum* (Tübingen: Mohr Siebeck, 2004), 80 cited in Ashton, *Understanding the Fourth Gospel*, 2007, 135. Arguments in favour of Antioch or Syria are that Ignatius of Antioch makes use of the FG, especially the relation between FG and *Odes of* Solomon. But these arguments are not convincing. Brown, *The Gospel according to John (i -xii)*, CIII. Alexandria is excluded as the evidence comes only from "large number of papyrus fragments discovered in Egypt." Ashton, *Understanding the Fourth Gospel*, 2007, 135. In support of Alexandria: it is the place of Philo, writers of Hermetic Corpus, and Gnostic Valentinus thought. Brown, *The Gospel according to John (i -xii)*, CIII. The objection to Ephesus has been that there is no Pauline influence on the Johannine works. The researcher agrees with Schnackenburg who holds that the vastness of Ephesus could allow for isolation of communities. R. Schnackenburg, "Ephesus: Entwicklung einer Gemeninde von Paulus zu Johannes," *Biblische Zeitschrift* (BZ) 35 (1991): 60, cited in Ashton, *Understanding the Fourth Gospel*, 2007, 135. Müller does accept the unreliability of patristic evidence. However, there are other factors that favour Ephesus- a) Acts 19:1-7 describe the followers of John the Baptist at Ephesus, who share close ties those mentioned in the FG. U. B. Müller, "Die Heimat des Johannesevangeliums" *Zeitschrift für die neutestamentliche Wissenschaft* (ZNW): 44-63, cited Ashton, *Understanding the Fourth Gospel*, 2007, 135, f.n. 69. b) The existence of Hellenistic groups and a prominent group of Jewish community. Lindars, "John," 77. c) The relation between the FG and Revelation, as there are indications that Revelation originates from Ephesus, especially "anti-synagogue polemics" in Asia Minor. Brown, *The Gospel according to John (i -xii)*, CIII. Keener after studying various possibilities places for the Johannine community concludes, "Roman Asia (most likely Ephesus or Smryna) and Syro-Palestine (most likely Galilee or Antioch) remain the most likely, and widely accepted, sites for the Johannine community." He goes on to take the former location, i.e., Roman Asia. Craig S. Keener, *The Gospel of John: A Commentary*, vol. I (Massachusetts: Hendrickson Publishers, 2003), 149. The researcher also would go in line with Keener in taking Ephesus as the place for the Johannine community.

from the darkness of their schismatic homelands into an unmediated fellowship with the One.[220]

The early witnesses attest to Ephesus.[221] One of the major reasons for favouring Ephesus[222] over other places is that Ephesus, being one of the major cities of Asia Minor, could have housed many groups, a feature seen explicitly in the FG.[223] In addition, Ephesus probably had Pauline communities by the time the Johannine community originated. The Christological development in the FG could also be seen in the same way. Ephesus also gave emphasis to women, an aspect seen very clearly in the FG; the gospel begins with the

---

[220] Tod D. Swanson, "To Prepare a Place: Johannine Christianity and the Collapse of Ethnic Territory," *JAAR* 62/2 (Summer 1994): 257-258.

[221] Irenaeus states, "Afterwards, John, the disciple of the Lord, who also had leaned upon His breast, did himself publish a Gospel during his residence at Ephesus in Asia." Irenaeus, "Irenaeus Against Heresies," in *The Ante-Nicene Fathers: The Writings of the Fathers Down to A.D. 135*, vol. 1: *The Apostolic Fathers*, edited by Alexander Roberts and James Donaldson, Reprint (Grand Rapids, Michigan: William B. Eerdmans Publishing Company, 1996), 3.1.1. Irenaeus also states, "And these are borne witness to in writing by Papias, the hearer of John, and a companion of Polycarp…" Irenaeus, "Irenaeus Against Heresies," 5.33.4. Eusebius resonds to this statement by Irenaeus, by stating, "But Papias himself in the preface to his discourses by no means declares that he was himself was a hearer and eye-witness of the holy apostles, but he shows by the words which he uses that he received the doctrine of the faith form those who were their friends." Eusebius, "The Church History of Eusebius," in *Nicene and Post-Nicene Fathers*, vol 1, edited by Philip Schaff and Henry Wace, Reprint (Massachusetts: Hendrickson Publishers, 1999), 3.39.2. Brown discusses the difficulty of Irenaeus' view: a. Irenaeus places John at Ephesus. However, there is no New Testament evidence for John son of Zebedee being at Ephesus; b. It has been suggested that Irenaeus was wrong about Polycarp's relation to John as in other instances; c. It has been suggested that Irenaeus and the other early writers confused John son of Zebedee with another John residing at Ephesus. Brown, *The Gospel according to John (i -xii)*, lxxxviii - xc. Smith presents another possibility of Ephesus being the place from which the gospel was written, he notes, "…the Gospel could have been published in Ephesus without its tradition having originated there." Smith, "Johannine Christianity:" 237.

[222] For Brown the attack on the synagogues in Asia Minor at Smryna and Philadelphia (Rev. 2:9; 3:9) makes Ephesus location appealing. Brown, *The Community of the Beloved Disciple*, 67.

[223] Koester notes that variety of groups existed in Ephesus, they are, disciples of John the Baptist, a groups affiliated to Apollos and Paul, and a sect called the Nicolaites. Helmut Koester, "Ephesos in Early Christian Literature," in *Ephesos: Metropolis of Asia: An Interdisciplinary Approach to Its Archaeology, Religion and Culture*, HTS 41, edited by Helmut Koester (Valley Forge: Trinity Press International, 1995), 133. Trebilco states that the church grew rapidly at Ephesus. There was also the presence of Jewish community at Ephesus, which kept the Sabbath and maintained continuity with the Temple at Jerusalem. Paul Trebilco, *The Early Christians in Ephesus from Paul to Ignatius*, WUZNT 166, edited by Jörg Frey (Tübingen: Mohr Siebeck, 2004), 1, 38-40; Trebilco also notes of several aspects of Jewish identity observed at Ephesus such as, " …a commitment to the synagogue, to the Temple tax, to the Sabbath, to food laws and to living in accordance with their tradition." Paul R. Trebilco, *Jewish Communities in Asia Minor*, SNTS 69, edited by G. N. Stanton (Cambridge: Cambridge University Press, 1991), 19, 34.

involvement of a woman, Jesus' mother and also a ends with Mary Magdalene being the harbinger of Jesus' resurrection.[224] There is also a possibility of conflict arising in Ephesus.[225] Casey notes, "The authors of the Fourth Gospel intended to rewrite the story of Jesus in accordance with the needs of the Johannine Community at Ephesus in the late first century."[226]

2.3.2. The BD and the Johannine Community

It is supposed that the BD was an authority figure of the Johannine community, who made the invaluable link between Jesus and the community. The quest for the identity of the BD seems to be an unending one; there are various suggestions and some of them are farfetched. Robinson prefers the traditional view that the BD was John, son of Zebedee. He finds fewer objections to common authorship than to the alternatives.[227] D. A. Carson[228] also supports the traditional view. He rejects the view that distinguishes BD and the evangelist and favours the view of Morris[229] and Robinson.[230] The two are one and the same person.[231]

---

[224] Tilborg notes, "Women do not escape completely the male cultural supremacy, but they are presented as persons with some independence. This position in John runs parallel with that happens in Ephesus with and around women. Ephesus like that in the whole of Asia Minor is visible regard to the prominence of women in the first two or three centuries AD." Sjef van Tilborg, *Reading John in Ephesus* (New York: E. J. Brill, 1996), 154. Kanagaraj states, "… John unreservedly portrays a woman (Mary) in the very beginning of his Gospel and this would have been impossible for him unless the Johannine community had already instituted women as leaders in key areas." Jey J. Kanagaraj, "The Profiles of Women in John: House-bound or Christ-bound?," *ERT* 27/1 (Ja. 2003): 30.

[225] Trebilco notes, "Jewish communities were very much part of the 'foreground' for the local Christian churches. Consequently, Christians would often be forming and preserving their identity in a context in which significant Jewish communities were visible and attractive. These Christians would be confronted with Jews in their own cities who would be rival interpreters of the Jewish tradition which Christians now claimed as their own." Trebilco, *Jewish Communities in Asia Minor*, 189.

[226] Maurice Casey, *The Solution to the 'Son of Man' Problem* (New York: T & T Clark International, 2009), 276.

[227] John A. T. Robinson, *The Priority of John* (London: SCM Press Ltd, 1983), 106.

[228] Carson, *The Gospel according to John*, 75.

[229] Leon Morris, *The Gospel according to John*, NICNT, edited by Ned B. Stonehouse, F. F. Bruce, Gordon D. Fee, revised edition (Grand Rapids, Michigan: William B. Eerdmans Publishing Company, 1995), 5.

[230] Robinson, *The Priority of John*, 106. The view of Wescott can also be noted here. Wescott states, "*a. The Author was a Jew…. b. The Author of the fourth Gospel was a Jew of Palestine…. c. The Author of the fourth Gospel was an eyewitness…; d. The Author of the fourth Gospel was an Apostle…. e. The Author of the fourth Gospel was the Apostle John…*" B. F. Wescott, *The Gospel according to St. John* (Grand Rapids, Michigan: William B. Eerdmans Publishing Company, 1959), v-xxii

[231] Carson, *The Gospel according to John*, 75.

There have been other names proposed for the BD: Lazarus,[232] John Mark,[233] Gentile Christianity,[234] the elder who wrote II & III Jn.,[235] and an ideal symbolic figure.[236] Thatcher gives a different proposal. The BD functions in the Johannine tradition in three different ways at once: as a character in the story about Jesus, as the narrator of the story about Jesus,[237] and as the foundation for the community's claims for historical credibility of the story about Jesus.[238] Thatcher enumerates different stages.[239]

The recent proposal for identity of the BD is Thomas, which is discussed at length by Charlesworth.[240] The first argument is that the BD was at the foot

---

[232] The reasons for favouring Lazarus are a. Lazarus is the only person in the FG of whom it is specifically mentioned that Jesus loved him – Jn. 11:3, 11, 36; b. all the texts that describe about the BD come after the raising up of Lazarus; c. the BD could recognize Jesus because it was Lazarus who had gone through this experience. However, there are reasons for not favouring it: a. it is hard to understand why Lazarus is anonymous in chap. Chap. 13-21 and is mentioned only in Chaps. 11 & 12; b. BD is introduced as a new character in Jn. 13: 23; c. the ancient church does not identify BD as Lazarus. Brown, *The Gospel according to John (i -xii)*, xcv.

[233] The reasons for supposing are a. John Mark was not one of the 12 disciples but was from Jerusalem; b. John Mark was a cousin of Barnabas who was a Levite and therefore the possibility of knowing the high-priest. But the second century sources clearly identify John Mark with Mark the evangelist. R. Alan Culpepper, *John: The Son of Zebedee: The Life of a Legend* (Columbia: The University of South Carolina, 1994), 78.

[234] Bultmann opines that the BD is not a historical figure but an ideal figure, a symbol of the Gentile Christendom. Rudolf Bultmann, *The Gospel of John: A Commentary*, translated by George R. Beasley-Murray (Philadelphia: The Westminster John Knox Press, 1971), 483-485.

[235] Hengel's thesis is that the FG and the Epistles of John were composed by a towering theologian who was not the apostle but John the Elder. Hengel, *The Johannine Question*, ix.

[236] Barnabas Lindars states, "a creation of the evangelist in order to serve a function…He represents true discipleship…He is thus a foil to Peter." Barnabas Lindars, *The Gospel of John* (Grand Rapids, Michigan: William B. Eerdmans Publishing Company, 1972), 22. Bauckham opines that the BD is an ideal author. Bauckham, "The Beloved Disciple:" 21-44.

[237] Lincoln is of the view that the BD is a narrative device. Andrew T. Lincoln, "The Beloved Disciple as Eyewitness and the Fourth Gospel as Witness," *JSNT* 24/85 (Jl. 2002): 3-26.

[238] Tom Thatcher, "The Legend of the Beloved Disciple," in *Jesus in Johannine Tradition*, edited by Robert T. Fortna and Tom Thatcher (Lousiville: Westminster John Knox Press, 2001), 97.

[239] Stage 1 – The real person who first performed the materials underlying the current FG was the original source of the Johannine tradition. This person's name and identity have been effaced by the tradition and may have been unknown to the final redactor of Jn. 21. Stage 2: The "BD" a character in the Johannine community who witnessed events that is critical to the Johannine understanding of Jesus. At this stage, the source is integrated into the narrative as a legendary figure, functioning as both character and narrator. Stage 3: The Johannine performance tradition, embodying the values encoded in the presentation of the BD. Reference to the BD supports validity and authority of the continuing witness. Thatcher, "The Legend of the Beloved Disciple," 97-98.

[240] James H. Charlesworth, *Beloved Disciple Whose Witness Validates the Gospel of John?* (Valley Forge: Trinity Press International, 1995), 168. Patty opines that it is possible to

of the cross and had seen the wound on Jesus' side, the only unique wound that Jesus suffered. This piece of information is unique to the FG which implies Thomas is the BD.[241] The other argument is the relationship between Judas and Thomas. By the principle of Johannine dualism, the author portrays Judas as the betrayer and his antithesis is the BD;[242] The third reason why Charlesworth argues for Thomas as the BD is because he appears as the hero of the gospel drama, next to Jesus, in three important phases of the story (Jn. 11:16; 14:5; 20:24-29). The overall structure of the FG draws to a climax in the confession of Thomas "My Lord and my God" (20:28).[243] Sandra Schneiders suggests that Thomas' three appearances (11:16; 14:5-6; 20: 24-29) in the FG provide an effective picture of the journey of true discipleship.[244] Patty too argues that the BD is the personification of Thomas, and though Peter was the originator of the Petrine tradition, Thomas was the main stay of the "Johannine" tradition.[245]

Another recent proposal is by Schneiders, who states that the BD is a kind of textual paradigm and concretely represents the corporate authority of the Johannine School. The BD in the text is a prism refracting the ideals of discipleship into a number of characters such as Nathanael, Mary and Lazarus of Bethany, Mary Magdalene[246] and Thomas the twin, and each realizes the paradigm of Johannine discipleship.[247] The proposal of Schneiders seems forthcoming. But if the inclusion of the term BD is to affirm the testimony of the FG, then this argument does hold good. It is possible, as pointed out by others, that the term BD was redacted into the gospel to affirm the testimony of the FG.

The issue of authorship still eludes a conclusive solution. Brown and Schnackenburg changed their positions from BD as John the son of Zebedee

---

infer from Jn. 2:20 that Jesus showed his hands and the side to other disciples and they shared with Thomas. Paul Patty, "The Beloved Disciple and Apostle Thomas," *BibBh* 27/3 (Sep. 2001): 169.

[241] Charlesworth, *Beloved Disciple*, 168. Patty opines that it is possible to infer from Jn. 2:20 that Jesus showed his hands and the side to other disciples and they shared with Thomas. Patty, "The Beloved Disciple, 169.

[242] Charlesworth, *Beloved Disciple*, 168.

[243] Charlesworth, *Beloved Disciple*, 170.

[244] Sandra M. Schneiders, *Written that You May Believe: Encountering Jesus in the Fourth Gospel* (New York: The Crossroad Publishing Company, 1999), 226.

[245] Patty, "The Beloved Disciple," 172.

[246] Ringe hints at the possibility that the BD could have been a woman as in the FG women take important roles in the the FG such as Jesus' mother, Samaritan woman, Mary and Martha, etc. Ringe, *Wisdom's Friends*, 16-17.

[247] Schneiders, *Written That You May Believe*, 231.

to one of the unnamed disciples.[248] For Barrett, the evangelist was not an eye-witness[249] of the events he narrates. The gospel was written, edited and published by those who had no personal historical contact with Jesus and certainly not by an apostle.[250] Lindars also argues against apostolic authorship when he states, "The attribution of the author of the Fourth Gospel to John the Apostle is not well founded. The BD is neither the author nor even a person who could have supplied eye-witness information, in spite of 21:24."[251]

There seems to be no consensus on the identity of the BD. However, it is possible to delineate some information about the BD drawn from the FG. The BD was a Palestinian Jew[252] well acquainted with the religious-philosophical thought of the time and gives a fair amount of historical details.[253] The BD is certainly a historical figure[254] and not an ideal figure as evidenced in Jn. 21. It is also possible that the BD passes away before the final writing of the gospel (Jn. 21:23). The passing of the BD gave rise to the role of the Spirit, who leads the community into all truth (Jn. 16: 13).

The role of the BD in the community seems to be the link between Jesus and the community. A closer look at the FG confirms that the BD seems to be redacted into different texts for the reasoning of affirming the testimony of the BD. The texts are redacted at crucial stages in the FG (Jn. 13:23; 19:26;

---

[248] Brown states, "The FG gives the impression that he was an outsider to the group of best-known disciples." Brown, *The Community of the Beloved Disciple*, 33-34.

[249] Dewey gives a different definition of eye-witness. He points, "For FE history was not something given and finished. Instead the presence of the Paraclete allowed FE to see the concussive effect of event and tradition. An eyewitness is one who has made the connection. The historical interest was found in the creative chemistry of remembrance." Arthur J. Dewey, "The Eyewitness of History: Visionary Consciousness in the Fourth Gospel," in *Jesus in Johannine Tradition*, edited by Robert T. Fortna and Tom Thatcher (Louisville: Westminster John Knox Press, 2001), 70.

[250] Brown, *The Gospel according to John (i -xii)*, 106-107.

[251] Lindars, *The Gospel of John*, 34.

[252] Ingo Broer opines that the FG seems to show the knowledge of the places and customs of Palestine. Ingo Broer, "Knowledge of Palestine in the Fourth Gospel?" in *Jesus in Johannine Tradition*, edited by Robert T. Fortna and Tom Thatcher (Louisville: Westminster John Knox Press, 2001), 84.

[253] Martin Hengel states in this regard, "...astonishingly accurate geographical, historical and religious details, and ...interesting information about Jewish customs and festivals." Hengel, *The Johannine Question*, 110. Brown too points to the historical facts in the tradition behind the FG in Brown, *The Gospel according to John (i -xii)*, xlii. Francis J. Moloney opines that the FG cannot be dismissed out of hand as a possible source for the reconstruction of the earliest period in the public life of Jesus. Francis J. Moloney, "The Fourth Gospel and the Jesus of History," *NTS* 46/1 (Ja. 2000): 58.

[254] Hengel argues that the BD is not a fictional figure. He also gives an elaborate possible sketch of the life of the BD, which remains hypothetical. Hengel, *The Johannine Question*, 77, 133-135.

20:8). There seems to be a parallel between the roles of BD and Jesus. The noun κόλπος occurs only in two places in the FG (1:18; 13:23) and both signify intimacy. The former refers to the intimacy Jesus shares with the Father, and the latter to the intimacy of the BD with Jesus. As far as the community is concerned, the BD was the link between the traditions of Jesus and the community. The community shared contacts with the other communities but clearly differentiated themselves from others in their understanding of Christology.

Conclusion

The FG seems to have been shaped by the Johannine community's struggle with the synagogue. While the reconstructions of the Johannine community do have their own share of problems, the researcher is of the view that the Johannine community consisted of Jewish Christians, Samaritan Christians and also the Gentiles. A clear demarcation of when the various groups became part of the Johannine community is difficult to arrive at. So, is the possibility of identifying the different editions of the FG. It seems to be clear, however, that the Johannine community did go through expulsion but probably an expulsion in terms of an intra-Jewish dispute, and not a general expulsion. The Christological formulations of the Johannine community played a part in the expulsion and the community continued to express its identity in terms of Christology which kept it in opposition to the Jewish synagogue at Ephesus. The conflict further gave rise to a Christological understanding of Messiah and the separation further affirmed this understanding. In defining their identity, the community retraced its traditions to the BD who served as a link with Jesus. The traditions of Jesus have been intertwined with the self-understanding of the community; therefore, it is needless to separate the tradition from self-understanding.

Chapter 3

An Exegetical Study of John 20
The Johannine Disclosure of Identity and Mission

Introduction

The previous chapter discussed the characteristics of the Johannine Community. Having done so, the research attempts to study the resurrection narrative in Jn 20 in relation to the Johannine community. The resurrection narrative offers certain unique features, especially in terms of dialogue with the wider circle of disciples that throw light on the interpretative activity of the Johannine community. However, such an exegetical study is not in isolation from the rest of the gospel and the New Testament. This makes it necessary to look at the resurrection in Paul and synoptic gospels before considering the FG.

3.1. Resurrection in Paul and Synoptics[1]

The resurrection accounts in Paul and synoptics are briefly studied here, though there seems to be a wide consensus that the FG makes use of separate traditions to a large extent.

[1] Recent studies of the resurrection accounts in Paul and the synoptics have neither considered tracing the tradition nor the history and development of the tradition. The focus is on the unique nature of the resurrection accounts with the aim to highlight their distinct understanding. It is virtually impossible to dissect the tradition with its distinct emphases of the writers and thus arrive at the formation of the resurrection tradition.

3.1.1. Resurrection in Paul[2]

The earliest available tradition concerning the resurrection is traced to I Cor. 15: 3-8. Paul makes use of a tradition but ambiguity lies over the time and origin of the tradition.[3] The language used in the tradition,[4] especially ἐγήγερται (I Cor. 15:4) translated as "was raised," echoes the Jewish apocalyptic language[5] evident in the OT (Isa. 26:19; Dan. 12:2).[6] More importantly, for Paul, the resurrection of Christ begins the eschatological process of resurrection. There are five appearances listed by Paul: Cephas, the Twelve, the + 500, James and all the apostles. Marxsen draws attention to the order of the tradition which states the appearance was first to Peter followed by the twelve.[7] The tradition informs us that Peter was the first to believe. The central focus is on seeing.[8]

The intention of Paul in tracing the tradition is to "...trace back the later functions and the later faith of the church, as well as the later leadership of James, to a single root: the appearance of Jesus.... For Peter, seeing Jesus resulted in mission."[9] Paul uses the tradition of the resurrection appearances as an argument for the reality of the future resurrection resurrection. Jesus' resurrection is not a mere resuscitation but rather a 'radical transformation.'[10]

---

[2] The understanding of resurrection in Paul's letters is diverse and there seems to be no systematic view; rather the context seems to define Paul's articulation on resurrection. Due to the constraints of time and space a thorough going study of concept of resurrection in Paul is not possible. Thus, the focus is on I Cor. 15 where Paul cites the resurrection tradition. Calvin J. Roetzel summarizes the concept of resurrection in Paul's letters. Refer Calvin J. Roetzel, "As Dying, and Behold We Live:" Death and Resurrection in Paul's Theology," *Int.* 46/1 (Ja. 1992): 6-7.

[3] Some of the suggestions include a. Antioch before 50 CE; b. Damascus before 40 CE; c. Jerusalem ca. 36 CE; R. H. Fuller, *The Formation of the Resurrection Narratives* (New York: The Macmillian Company, 1971), 10. d. Aramaic speaking community. J. Jeremias, *The Eucharistic Words of Jesus* (New York: Charles Scribner's Sons, 1966), 102-3, cited in Fuller, *The Formation of the Resurrection*, 10.

[4] Fuller conceptualizes the tradition into 4 formulae- a. Christ died; b. "he was buried"; c. "He was raised up on the third day according to the Scriputres"; d. a list of appearances. Fuller, *The Formation of the Resurrection*, 14.

[5] Fuller states, "The apocalyptic understanding of resurrection emphasizes on a transformed existence, not just raising from the dead." Fuller, *The Formation of the Resurrection*, 18.

[6] Gerald O' Collins supposes that the Jewish Christians in Antioch made this formula in Greek, which betrays Semitic influences. The use of "I handed over to you..." points to the transmission of the early church's creed, which could provide for a Palestinian/Jerusalem origin. Gerald O'Collins, *The Resurrection of Jesus Christ* (Pennsylvania: Judson Press, 1973), 5.

[7] Willi Marxsen, *The Resurrection of Jesus of Nazareth*, translated by Margaret Kohl (Philadelphia: Fortress Press, 1972), 82.

[8] Marxsen, *The Resurrection of Jesus*, 86.

[9] Marxsen, *The Resurrection of Jesus*, 95. Fuller categorizes the resurrection appearances in I Cor. 15 as "Church founding appearances." Fuller, *The Formation of the Resurrection*, 34.

[10] O'Collins, *The Resurrection of Jesus*, 10.

There are several notable features in the resurrection narratives of the gospels that do not figure in I Cor. 15. Some of these are the empty tomb and witnesses of the women which have led to a questioning of the resurrection accounts in the gospels.[11] Even so, this need not be so, for Paul's theology of resurrection developed out of the crises in the churches, which were a guiding factor and not the resurrection tradition as such;[12] though it was also founded on the tradition as cited by Paul in I Cor. 15:1.

3.1.2. Resurrection in the Synoptics

The canonical gospels do not record the resurrection proper.[13] Only the empty tomb and the resurrection appearances are detailed, which attempt to convey the outcome of the resurrection.[14] The resurrection accounts differ in many ways and one among them is the location of these appearances. Fuller notes the differences in terms of appearances in Galilee – implied in Mark, Matthew and Jn. 21, and the appearances in Jerusalem – Luke and Jn. 20. Further, the appearance as of a "spiritual" kind unlike in Luke and in Jn. 20 where the corporal aspect is stressed.[15]

3.1.2.1. Resurrection in Mark's Gospel

Unlike Paul, Mark and the other synoptics have a reference to the empty tomb.[16] However, the resurrection appearances are not narrated in Mark;[17] rather, the

---

[11] Fuller opines that the empty tomb narrative is a later legend, which Mark introduced in the resurrection narrative. The reasons are Paul does not mention the empty tomb, its difficulties faced in relating the empty tomb with the burial story, and the lack of familiarity with the Jewish burial tradition in Mark. Fuller, *The Formation of the Resurrection*, 52.

[12] Roetzel, ""As Dying, and Behold:" 6. Marxsen tries to reconcile the appearance aspect in I Cor. 15:3-8 and the empty tomb aspect in Mark by stating that in the pre-gospel traditions there existed one story concerning the empty tomb (handed down by Mark) and another story about the appearance to the disciples and several additional stories such as Emmaus story, Thomas story, etc. Marxsen, *The Resurrection of Jesus*, 73. Neill Q. Hamiliton is right when he states, "The empty is a logical and traditional prelude to appearances in his body." Neill Q. Hamilton, "Resurrection Tradition and the Composition of Mark," *JBL* 84/4 (Dec. 1965): 416.

[13] Thomas L. Brodie, *The Gospel according to St. John: A Literary and Theological Commentary* (New York: Oxford University Press, 1993), 556.

[14] Charles H. Talbert, "The Place of Resurrection in the Theology of Luke," *Int.* 46/ 2 (Ja. 1992): 20.

[15] Fuller, *The Formation of the Resurrection*, 5.

[16] Fuller, *The Formation of the Resurrection*, 52.

[17] The lack of appearance stories in Mark has led to the terming the resurrection in Mark as a 'translation.' One of the advocates of this view is Hamilton. Hamilton, "Resurrection Tradition and the Composition of Mark:" 416-420. Peter C. Bolt defines 'translation:' "A person is granted the privilege of avoiding death, which implies there is no mention of a grave, let alone an empty grave, like Enoch and Elijiah and they are concluded to have become gods." Bolt rightly notes that 'translation' cannot be applied to the Markan narrative as the verb ἠγέρθη

resurrection account ends[18] with the angel's message and a description of the reaction of the women. Despite this limitation, the Markan narrative certainly has a significant role. The narrator highlights the unexpectedness of Jesus' resurrection (v.3), and there is also the stress on divine involvement in the rolling of the stone from the entrance.[19] The narrative draws to the climax with the angelic message.[20] This does imply that in Mark "…the certainty of resurrection rests totally upon the word of revelation."[21] The reaction of the women to the revelation is unique: καὶ ἐξελθοῦσαι ἔφυγον ἀπὸ τοῦ μνημείου, εἶχεν γὰρ αὐτὰς τρόμος καὶ ἔκστασις· καὶ οὐδενὶ οὐδὲν εἶπαν· ἐφοβοῦντο γάρ. (Mar 16:8). It does suggest that they understood the significance of the empty tomb, and fear in the gospel is mostly a response to the "disclosure of Jesus' transcendent dignity (4:41; 5:15, 33, 36; 6:50; 9:6, 32)."[22] The phrases οὐδενὶ οὐδὲν εἶπαν and ἐφοβοῦντο γάρ, can be seen as a "christological affirmation."[23]

3.1.2.2. Resurrection in Matthew's Gospel

Matthew's account of the resurrection event has several notable features which pertain to his theological framework, apart from the difference in details from Mark.[24] The apocalyptic presentation of Jesus' resurrection is a unique motif

---

dissuades this theory. Peter G. Bolt, "Mark 16: 1-8: The Empty Tomb of a Hero?," *TynBul* 47/1 (My. 1997): 34, 37.

[18] There has been a great deal of discussion among scholars concerning the ending of Mark. The "shorter" as well as "longer" endings are seen as what was added later. Robert H. Stein, *Mark,* BECNT, edited by Robert W. Yarbrough and Robert H. Stein (Grand Rapids, Michigan: Baker Academic, 2008), 727. Knox investigates the ending in both Jewish and Gentile popular narrative and concludes that there are no parallels found. Wilfred Lawrence Knox, "The Ending of St. Mark's Gospel," *HTR* 35/1 (Ja. 1942): 22-23. Boomershine and Bartholomew conclude that the ending in Mark was "unintentional" and "accidental." Thomas E. Boomershine and Gilbert L. Bartholomew, "The Narrative Technique of Mark 16:8," *JBL* 100/2 (Je. 1981): 213.

[19] Stein, *Mark*, 730.

[20] The angelic message focused on the crucified Jesus as the risen one from the tomb and that he is going to Galilee where the disciples are to meet him and they are to tell this to Peter and the disciples. Stein, *Mark*, 737. The significance of Galilee according to Perrin has to do with the Gentile mission of the early Christian church. Norman Perrin, *The Resurrection Narratives: A New Approach* (London: SCM Press Ltd, 1977), 29. Fuller views that Mark has made the resurrection narrative distinct from the tradition stated in I Cor. 15:3-8, i.e., from 'church -founding' to 'mission- innagurating.' Fuller, *The Formation of the Resurrection*, 67.

[21] William Lane, *The Gospel of Mark*, NICNT, edited by Ned B. Stonehouse, F. F. Bruce, and Gordon D. Fee (Grand Rapids, Michigan: William B. Eerdmans Publishing Company, 1974), 589.

[22] Lane, *The Gospel of Mark*, 591.

[23] Lane, *The Gospel of Mark*, 591.

[24] Both Perrin and Fuller take them as redactional elements. Perrin draws attention to three major redactional changes in Matthew: a. the young man in Mark and details concering the

in this gospel. There are two aspects[25] that signify this: the earthquake[26] (28: 2, 4 which was earlier described in 27:51-53) and the description of the angelic interpreter.[27] The angel rolling the stone away is the closest that the gospel accounts arrive at describing the resurrection event.[28] Here, the narrator tries to materialize the resurrection event. Angels play a crucial role in that they announce both the birth and the resurrection of Jesus (Matt. 1:20; 2:19).[29] While the women are on their way in obedience to the angelic instruction, they experience a Christophany and they respond in worship. Bauckham observes, "...this is a prominent feature: it climaxes the Matthean theme of the worship of Jesus that began with the magi in 2:11."[30] Importantly, the response of the women represents Matthew's high Christology.[31] In his instruction to them, Jesus calls the disciples as brothers (12: 49-50; 23:8; 25: 40), a kinship metaphor.[32] The appearance of Jesus to the women along with the story of the guards[33] authenticate that Jesus' body has not been stolen, but rather that Jesus

---

rolling away of the stone; b. supposes that women fulfilled their responsibility; c. the story of the guards is added. Perrin, *The Resurrection Narratives*, 47. Fuller notes minor changes: Joseph of Arimathea is noted as a disciple of Jesus (27:57); the number of women at the grave is limited to two only (to avoid contradiction between the names of the women at the burial and those at the tomb); the motive of the women's visit is "to see the sepulchre," "and Peter" is removed from the angel's charge to the women (v. 7); and the cross reference (Mark 14:28 "as he told you) is removed from Mark in order to prepare the charge by the risen Jesus in v. 10. Fuller, *The Formation of the Resurrection*, 76-77.

[25] In addition to these, the bestowal of God's authority on Jesus echoes Dan. 7: 13-14, 18, 22, and 27. David L. Turner, *Matthew*, BECNT, edited by Robert W. Yarbrough and Robert H. Stein (Grand Rapids, Michigan: Baker Academic, 2008), 689.

[26] Weaver draws attention to the divine origin of the event seen in the earthquake and the appearance of the angel. Dorothy Jean Weaver, "Matthew 28: 1-10," *Int.* 46/4 (1992): 400.

[27] Daniel J. Harrington, *The Gospel of Matthew*, SacPag 1, edited by Daniel J. Harrington (Minnesota: Liturgical Press, 2007), 411.

[28] David Wenham, "The Resurrection Narratives in Matthew's Gospel," *TynBul* 24 (Ja. 1973): 21.

[29] Turner, *Matthew*, 681.

[30] Richard Bauckham, *Gospel Women: Studies of the Named Women in the Gospels* (Grand Rapids, Michigan: William B. Eerdmans Publishing Company, 2002), 278. Fuller describes this as the first occurrence of 'materialization of apperances' in the resurrection narrative and Matthew has changed angelophany to Christophany. Fuller, *The Formation of the Resurrection*, 77. One cannot be sure if Matthew has changed it or probably it was there in his source or tradition because John also mentions of it, though there are differences.

[31] Turner, *Matthew*, 682.

[32] Turner, *Matthew*, 682.

[33] Perrin righlty notes that this addition has to do with the context in which the gospel was written, i.e., "...in strong dialogue with the Jewish community." Perrin, *The Resurrection Narratives*, 48.

has risen and he is going ahead of the disciples to Galilee.[34] The climax of the narrative is commissioning of the risen Jesus (vv. 16-20).[35] Not all of the disciples believe the appearance of risen Jesus.[36] But it is in vv. 18-20 that the Christology of Matthew fully blossoms[37] and there is a broadening of mission that was earlier restricted to "the lost sheep of Israel" (Matt. 10:6).[38]

3.1.2.3. Resurrection in Luke's Gospel

The resurrection narrative in Luke's gospel, like the other synoptic gospels, also has distinct materials which offer significant Lukan motifs.[39] An important addition to the Lukan empty tomb narration is the "prophecy fulfilment

---

[34] Harrington notes that Galilee is chosen because Matthew and his opponents were located in Galilee and this would add to the interest of the reader. Harrington, *The Gospel of Matthew*, 413. Turner is probably right when he states that Galilee was earlier associated with Gentiles (4:14-16) and this goes well with the mission to all nations. Turner, *Matthew*, 687.

[35] Kingsbury notes that Matthew composed vv. 16-20 in order to reinforce his Son of God Christology. He further notes that this is wholly redactional and not traditional. Jack Dean Kingsbury, "The Composition and Christology of Matt 28:16-20," *JBL* 93/ 4 (Dec. 1974): 582. But this view stands to be questioned as the commissioning aspect figures in all the gospels. Fuller notes that the commissioning element is incipent in Mk. 16:1. Fuller, *The Formation of the Resurrection*, 80.

[36] Turner notes that this goes along with the weaknesses of the disciples presented in the passion narrative. The FE too mentions this in the Thomas episode. A good deal of discussion exists on the interpretation of οἵ δϵ in Matt. 28:17. Some of these discussion include Kenneth Grayston, "The Translation of Matthew 28:17," *JSNT* 21 (Jae. 1984): 105-109; Kenneth L. McKay, "The Use of *hoi de* in Matthew 28:17: A Response to K. Grayston," *JSNT* 24 (Ja. 1985): 71-72. van der Horst rightly notes that it cannot represent all the disciples but only some of the disciples. Pieter W. van der Horst, "Once More: The Translation of οἱ δὲ in Matthew 28:17," *JSNT* 27 (Ja. 1986): 29.

[37] Harrington lucidly presents the prominent themes in vv. 16-20: "a. The Father has given supreme and universal authority; b. the disciples are to share their discipleship not only with their follow Jews but also with non-Jews; c. The spirit of the risen Jesus will guide and protect the Church unitl God's kingdom comes in its fullness." Harrington, *The Gospel of Matthew*, 416-417.

[38] Schuyler Brown sees the universal dimension as occasioned by the controversy in the evagelist's community and this is done "...to heal the divisons within the community which had arisen over the issue." Schuyler Brown, "The Matthean Community and the Gentile Mission," *NovT* 22/ 3 (Jl. 1980): 221.

[39] It has to be said that apart from these, there are differences in the details from Mark's gospel. This could suggest a redactional element or Luke is following an independent source or tradition. These include a. list of women mentioned at the end and the inclusion of Joanna; b. the women by themselves find the tomb empty; c.the appearance of Jesus is not in Galilee but in Jerusalem and the passion predicton as in Mk. 9:31; d. the young man in Mark becomes two men in dazzling apparel; e. Luke has no resurrection appearance to the women. Fuller, *The Formation of the Resurrection*, 95.

motif."[40] In addition to stating that Jesus has risen, the angels remind them of the teachings of Jesus in Galilee as well as the predictions he had made.[41] There is a string of infinitives put together in the angelic instruction: παραδοθῆναι, σταυρωθῆναι, ἀναστῆναι (Luk 24:7). This is done to stress the fact that the resurrection is part of God's ordained plan (the theme of fulfilment is seen Lk. 24:25-26, 32, 44-47; 2:38-39; 4:14; 7:18-19) and "movement of divine history."[42] Therefore, the resurrection needs to be devoid of any astonishment. The "fulfillment motif" is further reiterated in the Emmaus episode and Jesus' appearance to the disciples as a group. The Emmaus narrative[43] presents further evidence of the report of the women. It also deals with the motifs of "journey, hospitality, table fellowship[44] and scriptural fulfilment."[45] Luke, unlike Matthew, also has Peter visiting the tomb.

The Emmaus narrative is followed by the appearance to the disciples. There is a considerable emphasis on sight here.[46] The narrative eliminates the view of resuscitation or resurrection in Hellenistic terms. Jesus discloses his resurrection in many ways: through an invitation to touch him, eating in front of the disciples confirming his real presence[47] and also through the fulfilment of scripture. Jesus' interpretation of the scripture has three elements. The first is that the messiah has to suffer, followed by resurrection from the dead on the

---

[40] Luke Timothy Johnson, *The Gospel of Luke*, Sac Pag 3, edited by Daniel J. Harrington (Minnesota: Liturgical Press, 1991), 391.

[41] Joel B. Green, "Seeing the Kingdom of God: NICNT, edited by Need B. Stonehouse, F. F. Bruce, and Gordon D. Fee (Grand Rapids, Michigan: William B. Eerdmans Publishing Company, 1997), 836.

[42] Darrell L. Bock, *Luke 9:51-24:53*, BECNT, edited by Mosés Silva (Grand Rapids, Michigan: Baker Academic, 1996), 1888, 1894-1895.

[43] Johnson clearly draws the literary and religious features of this incident: "a. the story gives a transition from empty tomb to Jesus' appearance to the collective disciples; b. Luke has used this to put together different stories into one narrative; c. Luke also describes the discussion that goes in the community; d. the aspect of reciting and reflecting these experiences not only builds a "community narrative" but also a forms a community." Johnson, *The Gospel of Luke*, 398-399.

[44] Charles H. Talbert relates table fellowship with "ecclesiological ramifications." He further states, "…the resurrection functions in Luke to clarify the nature of the Eucharist as meak time with Jesus – meals with sinners (5: 29-32), with Pharisees (7: 36-50); with disciples (22: 19-20), etc. Talbert, "The Place of Resurrection:" 26. Johnson rightly notes that Jesus is being revealed in the "community fellowship." Johnson, *The Gospel of Luke*, 398.

[45] Green, *The Gosple of Luke*, 844. Fuller opines, "Christ's suffering as the pathway to glory, and the prophecy of the suffering-glory pattern in the scriptures." Fuller, *The Formation of the Resurrection*, 106. Perrin observes, "...the passion has become an apotheosis." Perrin, *The Resurrection Narratives*, 68.

[46] R. Alan Culpepper, "Seeing the Kingdom of God: The Metaphor of Sight in the Gospel of Luke," *CurTM* 21/6 (Nov. 1994): 434-443.

[47] Johnson, *The Gospel of Luke*, 404.

third day. The third and final element is repentance and forgiveness preached to all nations starting from Jerusalem."[48] The narrative ends with the ascension of Jesus.

Talbert rightly notes that the earliest Palestinian Jewish Christianity that stressed the three aspects concerning the resurrection of Jesus such as "his victory over death, his removal from human time and space into another dimension (that of God), and his new function as cosmic Lord (I Cor. 15:3-5)."[49] It is Luke who separates the three aspects in different time frames: resurrection (Lk. 24:1-11) - the ascension (Lk. 24:51) - the exaltation (Lk. 22:69).[50]

The ascension forms the high point of Luke's gospel and is placed as a distinct event from the resurrection itself.[51] John F. Maile[52] draws out the significance of ascension for Luke: a) ascension takes place before the sending of the Spirit; b) ascension forms the basis for mission; c) ascension is the assurance of the return of Christ; d) ascension narratives are in accordance with the exaltation proclamation of the New Testament.[53]

There are certain elements that are common in the resurrection accounts. First, the accounts describe the motif of unexpectedness, the empty tomb (only in the gospels). Second, they state the presence of angels at/near the tomb. Third, they deal with the appearance tradition. Fourth, they note the element of doubt on the part of the disciples. Fifth, they detail the corporal aspect of the risen Jesus (Luke). Sixth, resurrection leads to belief. Lastly, they end with the commissioning aspect. The commonalities suggest a common pool of tradition and do not affirm the development of a resurrection tradition.[54]

---

[48] Green, *The Gosple of Luke*, 856. Perrin notes the significance of this, when he states, Luke-Acts presents, "... the life of Jesus as a sacred time, a time of fulfilment, blessing and revelation." Perrin, *The Resurrection Narratives*, 72.

[49] Talbert, "The Place of Resurrection:" 23-24.

[50] Talbert, "The Place of Resurrection:" 24.

[51] Perrin, *The Resurrection Narratives*, 74. Fuller notes that Luke has "...separated the two events to conform with his scheme of resurrection- appearances- ascension- Pentecost... integrated the resur rection narratives into his scheme of salvation-history...Jesus' earthly ministry (Luke) and the church (Acts)." Fuller, *The Formation of the Resurrection*, 119-120.

[52] John F. Maile, "The Ascension in Luke-Acts," *TynBul* 37 (Ja. 1986).

[53] Maile, "The Ascension in Luke-Acts:" 58-59.

[54] Marxsen on the contrary argues for a development of the resurrection tradition and in this regard notes that the synoptics developed a seeing and mission aspects from Paul's account of resurrection. Marxsen, *The Resurrection of Jesus*, 84, 86. Collins states that the accounts were drawn from three traditions: a. tradition of Peter meeting Christ; b. tradition of the other disciples also meeting Christ; and lastly c. tradition of women discovering the empty tomb. O'Collins, *The Resurrection of Jesus Christ*, 29. All of these remain as hypothetical constructions and can never be proved as particular theologies of the evangelist, which played a significant role in shaping these narratives. Bauckham, *Gospel Women: Studies*, 266-267.

The resurrection narrative in the FG is frequently compared with the resurrection narratives in the synoptics, but this does not imply that the FE borrowed from the synoptics. This is an unlikely hypothesis; a common tradition in any case cannot be ruled out. Jerome H. Neyrey[55] notes the difference in the understanding of resurrection in the synoptic gospels and the FG. In the former, the resurrection is God's vindication of Jesus, that is, removing the shame and restoring Jesus to a new role and status. The FG seems to convey that there is no vindication by God but rather "Jesus' own power effects his resurrection;[56] there is also the other side to it, namely, the Son participates in the life given by the Father (Jn. 5:26). Another difference in the resurrection narrative is that in the FG, as noted by Catchpole, it is "...a journey from earth to heaven, not form Jerusalem to Galilee..."[57] However, retracing the exact tradition in the FG is an impossible task,[58] for the tradition and the interpretative role of the Johannine Community are intricately woven together into one complex web.

3.2. Passion and Resurrection in the FG

The passion and the resurrection in the FG share some unique elements and have been a subject of discussion among scholars, and there is a tendency to dampen the significance of the resurrection in the light of what figured at the passion.

3.2.1. The Passion of Jesus in the FG

The FG shares both the similarities and dissimilarities with the synoptics in accounting the passion of Jesus as it is uniquely patterned and presented. One of the prominent aspects is the absence of the terminology of suffering; in fact, Jesus is said to be in control of the situation (19:11). Bultmann equates Jesus' death to departure, which can also be termed as "elevation" and "glorification" and Jesus' return to pre-existent glory.[59] The FG uses the language of exaltation-

---

[55] Jerome H. Neyrey, *The Gospel of John*, NCBC, edited by Ben Witherington III (Cambridge: Cambridge University Press, 2007).

[56] Neyrey, *The Gospel of John*, 316-317. However, it needs to be noted that there is the reference to Jesus' righteousness in Jn. 16:8-11, where the context is the ministry of the παράκλητος. But here, righteousness is associated with Jesus going back to the Father and there seems to be only a veiled reference to his vindication. Futher, Kysar has rightly opined that in the passion narrative Jesus is not presented as a 'victim' but "...as Lord of the situation." Robert Kysar, "Christology and Controversy: The Contribution of the Prologue of the Gospel of John to New Testament Christology and their Historical Setting," *CurTM* 5/6 (Dec. 1978): 354.

[57] David Catchpole, *Resurrection People: Studies in the Resurrection Narratives of the Gospels*, Sarum Theological Lectures (London: Darton, Longman and Todd Ltd., 2000), 157.

[58] D. A. Carson, *The Gospel according to John* (Grand Rapids, Michigan: William B. Eerdmans Publishing Company, 1991), 41.

[59] Rudolf Bultmann, *Theology of the New Testament*, translated by Kendrick Grobel, vol. 2 (London: SCM Press Ltd, 1955), 52-53.

glory-glorification to describe the death of Jesus. Loader[60] notes that the Son's return to the Father is "one of the complex varieties of images used in the gospel to express the significance of Jesus' death."[61] Käsemann[62] opines that "departure" is the characteristic description of Jesus' death in the FG.[63] This view has been supported by other scholars such as R. E. Brown,[64] Rudolf Schanckenburg,[65] Lindars,[66] and Moody Smith,[67] all of who do not give much importance to the resurrection narrative in the FG. Brown observes that on the cross Jesus had already started the process of exaltation and glorification; therefore, the resurrection does not fit into the theology of crucifixion.[68] He further notes that, unlike the synoptics where Jesus predicts his resurrection three times, the Johannine Jesus describes himself as being lifted up. So, Brown concludes that the resurrection was not excluded from the FG as it was part of the Christian tradition.[69] Bultmann also has this same view, "If Jesus' death on the cross is already his exaltation and glorification, *his resurrection* cannot be an event of special significance… For the cross itself was already triumph over the world …There is not a word in John of the idea that not until the resurrection and exaltation after his death was Jesus made Lord."[70]

These views of scholars seem to present a scathing criticism against the significance of resurrection in the FG. However, considering the fact that the FG was written from the perspective of the resurrection (2:22ff; 1:18; 3:13; 12:16) and that resurrection guided the understanding and interpretation of the life of Jesus in the early Christian thought, the view held by Brown and other scholars on the perspective of resurrection requires further study. Does the

---

[60] William Loader, *The Christology of the Fourth Gospel: Structure and Issues*, BBET 23, edited by Jürgen Becker and Henning Graf Reventlow (New York: Peter Lang, 1989).

[61] Loader, *The Christology of the Fourth Gospel*, 29.

[62] Ernst Käsemann, *The Testament of Jesus: A Study of the Gospel of John in the Light of Chapter 17*, translated by Gerhard Krodel (London: SCM Press Ltd, 1968).

[63] Käsemann, *The Testament of Jesus*, 17-18.

[64] Raymond E. Brown, *The Gospel according to John (xiii-xxi)*, 1013.

[65] Rudolf Schnackenburg, *The Gospel according to St. John,* vol. 3, translated by David Smith and G. A. Kon (New York: The Crossroad Publishing Company, 1982), 301.

[66] Lindars states, "The death of Jesus thus turns out to be the decisive factor in the whole argument just as it is the climax of the narrative structure of the Gospel as a whole." Barnabas Lindars, *John*, NT Guides (Sheffield: JSOT Press, 1990), 81.

[67] Smith states, "The description of Jesus' death as exaltation and glorification is a way underscoring its revelatory character." D. Moody Smith, *The Theology of the Gospel of John* (London: Cambridge University Press, 1995), 121.

[68] Raymond E. Brown, *The Gospel according to John (xiii-xxi)*, Anchor Bible 29B (New York: Doubleday & Company, Inc., 1966), 1013.

[69] Brown, *The Gospel according to John (xiii-xxi)*, 1013.

[70] Bultmann, *Theology of the New Testament*, 56.

concept of 'lifting up' on the cross exhaust the concept of glorification in the FG? Can the concept of glorification also include the resurrection in the FG? What role do the Farewell Discourses play in the conception of resurrection in the FG? These and other questions seem to go against the orientation of giving too much importance to the cross at the cost of negating the resurrection event in the FG.

3.2.2. The Place of Resurrection in the FG

There are several reasons why one finds that the resurrection of Jesus occupied an important place in the FG and also in the Johannine community.

a) The reference to the resurrection occurs at the beginning of the gospel (Jn. 2:22),[71] emphasizing its importance. In Jn. 2:22 the FE states, "After he was raised from the dead, his disciples remembered that he had said this; and they believed the scripture and the word that Jesus had spoken" (Jn 2:22 NRSV). Jesus' body becomes the centre of worship with the fall of the Jerusalem Temple. The next reference, a veiled one to the resurrection, is in Jn. 12:16. The FE notes that the disciples did not understand the significance of Jesus riding on a young ass, but after Jesus was glorified his disciples remembered what had been written in the Scriptures. Here, most naturally when seen in relation to 12:16, glorification refers not to crucifixion but to resurrection.

b) Glorification cannot be restricted to the crucifixion alone. The resurrection of Jesus also played an important role in clarifying the significance of certain aspects of Jesus' life and ministry. Loader states in this connection, "Glorification has not just Jesus' death in mind but the total event of resurrection and return to the glory of the Father in mind."[72] Schneiders draws a theological distinction between the cross and the resurrection. She states, "...there is a subtle but significant distinction between *glorification*, that is what happened at the cross, and the *resurrection*, which is the communication of the effects of the significance of Jesus' glorification to the disciples."[73]

c) The story of the earthly life of Jesus is narrated from the perspective of the post-Easter Jesus. Loader notes, "The image of the Son's 'return/departure' to the Father seems in the first instance to be an image not of his death but of his resurrection/ascension. The Son who has come to earth to make the Father known 'departs' or 'returns' to the One from whom he came."[74] Brown too

---

[71] Rojas-Flores opines that Jn. 2:19 goes back to Jesus, who states it in order to attest his messianic authority, but is cast in Johannine symbolic language. G. Rojas-Flores, "From John 2.19 to Mark 15.29: The History of a Misunderstanding," *NTS* 56/1 (Ja. 2010): 23-24.

[72] Loader, *The Christology of the Fourth Gospel*, 10.

[73] Sandra M. Schneiders, "The Raising of the New Temple: John 20.19-23 and Johannine Ecclesiology," *NTS* 52/3 (Jl. 2006): 340.

[74] Martinus C. de Boer, "Jesus' Departure to the Father in John: Death or Resurrection," in *Theology and Christology in the Fourth Gospel: Essays by the Members of the Society for New*

states, "All the Gospels read the post-resurrectional situation back into the ministry ..."[75] Painter goes further than Brown in stating, "Only John shows *awareness* of doing this, and the evidence confirms that the extent and depth of transformation is significantly greater in John than in other gospels."[76]

d) There seems to be a merger of the past, present and future in the FG which makes one unsure of where Jesus is (Jn. 17:13).[77] In such case, any distinction between the significance of the cross and resurrection in the FG would interfer with the presentation of the FG.

e) de Boer rightly notes, "Resurrection was Jesus' greatest and culminating sign. This is supported by the placement of 20:30-31 immediately after the resurrection account."[78] So, also, Trites notes, "The resurrection is of juridical significance in that it constitutes Christ's last and greatest sign."[79]

f) Resurrection is part of the scriptural fulfilment as seen in 20:9. Martyn notes that Jesus' death is eclipsed by Jesus'signs which find their high point in his resurrection.[80]

g) Resurrection is closely tied with ascension. de Boer states,

> It is the ascension, not the death, which is the completion, for it is the ascension that completes the circle and brings the Son back to the one from whom he came. The 'passion' account is perhaps best characterized as a narrative interlude, it is not really integral to the portrait of Jesus as the Son of God sent into the world and departing to the Father... The Son will subsequently depart or ascend to the Father (20:17) thereby 'completing' his mission.[81]

Testament Study Johannine Writings Seminar, BETL 184, edited by G. Van Belle, J. G. Van der Watt and P. Maritz (Leuven: Leuven University Press, 2005), 1.

[75] Raymond E. Brown, *The Community of the Beloved Disciple* (New York: Paulist Press, 1979), 19.

[76] John Painter, "Memory Holds the Key: The Transformation of Memory in the Interface of History and Theology in John," in *John, Jesus and History*, vol. 1, *Crticial Appraisals of Critical Views*, edited by Paul N. Anderson, Felix Just, Tom Thatcher, SBLSS 44, edited by Victor H. Matthews (Atlanta: SBL, 2007), 242.

[77] It can be said that prolepsis is a common Johannine style. Gilbert van Belle, "Prolepsis in the Gospel of John," *NovT* 43/3 (O. 2001): 334-347.

[78] Martinus C. de Boer, *Johannine Perspectives on the Death of Jesus* (Kampen: Kok Pharos Publishing House, 1996), 86-87.

[79] Allison A. Trites, *The New Testament Concept of Witness*, SNTSMS 31 edited by Matthew Black (Cambridge: Cambridge University Press, 1977), 86.

[80] J. Louis Martyn, "Source Criticism and Religiongeschichte in the Fourth Gospel," in *The Interpretation of John*, edited by John Ashton (Edinburgh: T & T Clark, 1997), 110.

[81] de Boer, *Johannine Perspectives on the Death*, 139, 141, 144.

Even so Lincoln argues, "The climax of John's story about Jesus is neither his death itself nor his resurrection itself. Jesus is in a resurrected body to the Father. For the implied author, Jesus'death, his resurrection, and his ascension are all stages in the one event of glorification and together constitute the one hour of glory."[82] Thus, it can be said that glorification includes resurrection and ascension. Further, resurrection includes the ascension aspect. Lincoln also states, "The glory to be seen in Jesus' death does not obviate the need for his resurrection. But neither does the resurrection triumphalistically supersede his death."[83]

h) The resurrection narrative confirms what Jesus states in Jn. 5:21-29 – the two aspects of judgment and life that he possesses and also his equality with God. Jesus further states in Jn. 11:44 "I am the resurrection and the life."

i) Resurrection in Jn 20 also presents glimpses into the faith affirmation of Jesus' followers. Lincoln notes that the BD and Mary Magadalene are significant in the resurrection narrative; the former with the empty tomb and the latter with the resurrection appearance.[84]

j) Finally, the promises mentioned earlier in the Farewell Discourses find their fulfilment in the resurrection making it indispensable in the presentation of Jesus' life and ministry. John the Baptist sums up the mission of Jesus as one who will baptize with the Holy Spirit and this finds fufillment in Jn. 20. So, also the promises in the Farewell Discourses have their completion in Jn. 20.[85] In his farewell address, Jesus notes that he is going to the Father (14:12, 28; 16:5, 7, 10, 17: 17:11, 13). He also promises that he is "coming" to them (14:3, 18, 20, 23, 28).[86]

---

[82] Andrew T. Lincoln, ""I Am the Resurrection and the Life": The Resurrection Message of the Fourth Gospel" in *Life in the Face of Death: The Resurrection Message of the New Testament*, edited by Richard N. Longenecker (Grand Rapids, Michigan: William B. Eerdmans Publishing Company, 1998), 131.

[83] Lincoln, ""I Am the Resurrection and the Life,"" 131.

[84] Lincoln, ""I Am the Resurrection and the Life,"" 133.

[85] Berge has clearly presented the parallelism in the structure of the closing verse in the Farewell Discourses and Jn. 20:1-18. Paul S. Berge, "Easter to Trinity with the Gospel of John: Bearing Witness to Father, Son and Holy Spirit," *Word & World* 18/2 (Spring 1998): 207.

[86] This view is contrary to Bennema who notes, "Jesus' statements "I will not leave you orphaned; I am coming to you" (14:8) and "In a little while … you will see me" (14:9) do not refer to Jesus' resurrection appearances (otherwise the disciples would be orphaned again after ascension) or to the Parousia (otherwise the disciples would be orphans until then). Rather, they refer to Jesus' coming back to the disciples through the Spirit-Paraclete, whom he promised them in 14: 16-17." Cornelis Bennema, *Encountering Jesus: Character Studies in the Gospel of John* (Bangalore: Primalogue Publishing Media Private Limited, 2009), 165. It is true that the reference to the Spirit-Paraclete cannot be overruled in this text but Jn. 20 does indeed refer to the resurrection as his coming and explicitly fulfills what is pomised in Jn. 14.

Thus, it can be said that resurrection has an important place in the scheme of the FG, not just an added feature of the FG. Lincoln notes in this regard, "While all the Gospel accounts are written from a post resurrection perspective, the perspective in the FG is not only explicit in the narrator's asides (cf. 2:22; 7:39; 20:9) but also much more determinative for the shaping of the narrative than the synoptic Gospels."[87]

3.3. John 20: A Disclosure of Identity and Mission

The resurrection narrative in Jn. 20 can be discussed from the perspective of disclosure; it is a disclosure of the identity and mission of both Jesus and the Johannine community.

3.3.1. Context of John 20

Before considering the disclosure motif, it would be worthwhile to place Jn. 20 in the context of the FG. It would not be wrong to state that Jn. 1 and Jn. 20 form an *inclusio*. It forms a type of envelope in reaffirming the Christology stated in the prologue. Another way of looking at it is that the resurrection narrative becomes the guiding factor for the presentation of the prologue and thus the whole of the FG. In effect what is introduced or stated in the prologue (Jn. 1:1-18) takes place in Jn. 20.[88]

The aspect of identity and mission are expressed in chaps. 1 and 20. Jesus' identity as God is seen in (1:1; 1:18 and 20:28) and in the concept of ascending. Jesus stands in relationship with the Father (1:1; 20:28-my Father and my God). The description of the Children of God is described in terms of relationship with the Father (my father and your father). The community is represented in both instances (1:14 we beheld the glory and blessed are those who have not seen and yet believe 20:29). The concept of seeing as Mary and the disciples see Jesus so also the community-Jn. 1:14). Darkness as not overcoming the light (begins in darkness but light dawns in the case of Mary Magdalene and the disciples). Further, in Jn. 1:19 the Pharisees question John the Baptist's identity – "Who are you?" The answer to the question of identity of the Messiah is seen in Jesus' commission to Mary (Jn. 20:17) so

---

[87] Lincoln, ""I Am the Resurrection and the Life," 122.

[88] Stibbe identifies some of the parallelisms: a) Jn. 1:19-28 is the description of Jesus by John the Baptist to the Pharisees is μέσος ὑμῶν ἕστηκεν (1:26), the same is used for risen Jesus who appears to the disciples in 20:19 and 20:26. b) There is a distinct but analogous relationship with the theme of the Holy Spirit in chaps. 1 and 20. c) There is also the reference to the 'turning around' in Jn. 1: 38 and 20:14, 16. The first reference deals with Jesus turning around to see the two disciples who follow him while the next refers to Mary Magdalene. d) In 1:38, the first words of Jesus are 'what are you seeking?' so also the words appear again in Jesus' question to Mary Magdalene in 20:15 – 'what are you seeking?' Mark W. G. Stibbe, *John* (Sheffield: JSOT Press, 1993), 198-199.

also in the confession of Thomas (Jn. 20:28).[89] The prologue ends (1:18) with the FE calling attention to the unique relationship that Jesus shares with the Father and chap. 20 describes the outworking of this relationship in terms of the identity and mission of the disciples. So, also the mission of Jesus (1:34) and the disciples (Jn. 20:22) have their origin from the Father. Again, both the turning around of the two disciples (1:38) and the turning around of Mary (20:16) are related to the understanding of Jesus' identity. In Jn. 1:38, they see the place where Jesus is staying while in Jn. 20:16, Mary understands that Jesus' residence is with the Father, another reminder of where Jesus is from. Lastly, the words of Jesus to the disciples 'What are you looking for?' are the words that echo throughout the gospel and finds their completion in the confession of Thomas. In fact, the whole of the FG can be termed as a search — a search for the identity of Jesus. There are several characters that look for Jesus and find him: John the Baptist (1:36), Andrew (1:41), and Nathanael (1:49). The search continues for the Jews and the Pharisees in chaps. 5-10.

Not only is Jn. 20 related to chap. 1 but also to all of the Farewell Discourse (13-17). In the Farewell Discourse, Jesus promises to return shortly as also to send the Spirit, and this finds its completion in Jn. 20 which is connected with the passion of Jesus. There is an immediate link with the previous verse that is 19:42, which mentions Jesus was laid in the tomb that was near because of the Jewish day of Preparation and 20:1 draws attention to the same tomb.[90] The same tomb is found empty which precipitates the search for the missing Lord.

The theme of self-disclosure is an important one in the FG. Disclosure of Jesus' identity predominantly figures in the discourses preceded by signs. What makes the resurrection narrative unique is that resurrection as the sign also has the disclosure element. The prologue discloses that the 'Word is God.' The Nicodemus discourse also draws a very clear line between Jesus and Nicodmeus in terms of above and below.[91] The conversation with the Samaritan woman continues the theme. In the discussion with the Jews in chapter 8, the issue of identity resurfaces. The cross is also a revelation of his identity.

Most importantly the resurrection narrative deals with the question, 'Where has he gone?' The question to Mary by Jesus in 20:15a (τίνα ζητεῖς;) brings to attention the theme of the quest for Jesus. Bennema notes in this

---

[89] Ressigue succinctly puts it: "The object of the disciples' quest in chapter 1 is clarified in chapter 20. The quest is for a person." James L. Resseguie, *Narrative Criticism of the New Testament: An Introduction* (Grand Rapids, Michigan: Baker Academic, 2005), 145.

[90] Stibbe, *John*, 198. Also refer F. F. Bruce, *The Gospel of John: Introduction, Exposition and Notes* (Basingstoke: Pickering & Inglis, 1983), 383.

[91] Hakola interprets Nicodemus as a "...deviant subtype for Johannine Christians." Raimo Hakola, "The Burden of Ambiguity: Nicodemus and the Social Identity of the Johannine Christians," *NTS* 55/4 (O. 2009): 454.

connection that the verbs 'to seek' and 'to find' denote the quest for life and salvation.[92] However, the quest is for more than life and salvation, rather, it is the quest for the person of Jesus, for it is in the very person of Jesus that life and wholeness is mediated. Jn 1:4 states, "In him was life and the life was the light of men." Therefore, life and wholeness rest in the person of Jesus who is identified as sharing a relationship with the Father. The crowd is described as in a wrong quest (6:24-26; 12:37) so also 'the Jews' are said to be on a wayward quest (5:18, 44; 7:1,18, 34).

3.3.2. Structure

Scholars[93] have tried to analyse the structure of Jn. 20 by looking at the different possible traditions that the FE has used. Even if there could be traditions used, it is probably difficult to trace them and more importantly, Jn. 20 presents a unified whole. Lindars notes that the FG uses the traditional material to make known the experience of the resurrection of Jesus in 20:1-31.[94] Each unit is interwoven together systematically. Beirne[95] notes, "In narrative terms, the Magdalene incident (20:1-2, 11-18) is woven around that involving Simon Peter and the beloved disciple (20:3-10) and indeed is the immediate cause for it (20:2)."[96] Vv. 17 and 18 narrate the commissioning of Mary Magadalene by Jesus to tell the 'brothers' that he is ascending. This prepares for the appearance to the brothers in vv. 19-23 (disciples excluding Thomas) and 24-29 (disciples including Thomas). The appearances to the disciples form the climax not just to the resurrection narrative (chap. 20) but also to the entire Farewell Discourses. V. 24 links vv. 19-23 and vv. 24-29 in addition to serving as the reason for the resurrection appearance to Thomas (vv. 24-29). Vv. 29-31 serves as a conclusion to the resurrection narrative as well as to the whole of the FG. The

---

[92] Bennema, *Encountering Jesus: Character Studies*, 197.

[93] Several scholars have tried to find out the traditions behind it. In this regard Barnabas Lindars gives the following possibility: Three traditions concerning the resurrection are used: a. the discovery of the empty tomb by the women (here Mary Magdalene alone); b. a visit of Peter to the empty tomb (vv. 3-10); c. the appearance of Jesus to the assembled apostles (vv. 19-23). In all of this John has amplified the basic tradition by bring to the fore a particular person who presents his interest "...in the nature of the act of faith." In the first instance John made use of his source to develop the story of the appearance of Jesus to Mary Magdalene (vv. 11-18). In the second instance, John has added the BD to the tradition of Peter. In the third instance, John uses the motif of the scepticism of the disciples as the basis of the story about Thomas (vv. 24-29). Barnabas Lindars, *The Gospel of John*, NCB, edited by Matthew Black (Grand Rapids, Michigan: William B. Eerdmans Publishing Company, 1972), 594-595. Also refer Barnabas Lindars, "The Composition of John 20," *NTS* 7/2 (Ja.1961): 142-147.

[94] Lindars, *The Gospel of John*, 594-595.

[95] Margaret M. Beirne, *Women and Men in the Fourth Gospel: A Genuine Discipleship of Equals* (London: T & T Clark International, 2004).

[96] Beirne, *Women and Men in the Fourth Gospel*, 196.

overching theme that runs through the narrative of Jn 20 and the whole of the FG is the motif of believing which plays a crucial role in the understanding of the Johannine community.[97]

There are several time references in 20:1, 19, and 26 that structure the chapter and provide the point of reference for 21:14.[98] A majority of scholars view the structure of vv. 1-31 under two heads: empty tomb/visit to the tomb and appearances.[99]

A fairly descriptive structure of chap. 20 is offered by Craig S. Keener.

Jesus' Resurrection (20:1-29) –

vv. 1-18 Mary at the Tomb:

1. The Empty Tomb (20:1-10) –
   - (1A) Mary's Discovery (20:1-2),
   - (1B) The Missing Body (20:1-7),
   - (1C) The Wrappings (20:5-7),
   - (1D) The BD, Peter, and Scripture (20: 2-10);

---

[97] Witherington III rightly notes that Jn. 20 also reflects the Johannine communit situation. He notes, "We have here most or all of the elements of early Christian worship – the first day of the week, a meeting of the gathered community in a disciple's house, the passing of the peace (three times!), the bestowal of the Spirit, the mentio of the forgiving or retaining o sins, the confession fo faith, and finally the act of worship, with Jesus in the midst." Ben Witherington III, *John's Wisdom: A Commentary on the Fourth Gospel* (Cambridge: The Lutterworth Press, 1995), 345.

[98] Andreas J. Köstenberger, *John*, BECNT (Grand Rapids, Michigan: Baker Academic, 2004), 559.

[99] Leon Morris: A. The Empty Tomb (20:1-10); B. Appearances (20: 11-29) begins with:1. The appearance to Mary (20:11-18); 2. The Appearance to the Ten (20: 19-23); 3. The Appearance to Thomas (20:24-29); and The Purpose of the Gospel (20:30-31). Leon Morris, *The Gospel according to John*, NICNT, edited by Ned B. Stonehouse, F. F. Bruce, Gordon D. Fee, Revised edition, (Grand Rapids, Michigan: William B. Eerdmans Publishing Company, 1995), 731ff. Beasley-Murray: The Resurrection of Jesus (vv. 1-31): vv. 1-10 Mary Magadelene and Two Disciples visit the Tomb of Jesus; vv 11-18 Jesus appears to Mary Magdalene; vv. 24-29 Jeus appears to Thomas; vv. 30-31- Conclusion. George R. Beasley-Murray, *John*, WBC 36, edited by Ralph P. Martin (Texas: Word Books, 1987), 364ff. Brown: The Risen Jesus (chap. 20) and have two scenes – a. Scene one: At the Tomb (20:1-18) and b. Scene two: Where the Disciples are Gathered (19-29); Conclusion to the Book of Glory (20: 30-31). Brown, *The Gospel according to John (xiii-xxii)*, 965. Andreas J. Köstenberger: Jesus' Resurrection and Appearances and the Commissioning of His Disciples (20:1-29) and the sub-parts are: 1. The Empty Tomb (20:1-10); 2. Jesus Appears to Mary Magadalene (20:11-18); 3. Jesus Appears to his Disciples (20:19-23); 4. Jesus Appears to Thomas (20:24-29); and the fourth Part – D. Conclusion: The Signs of the Messiah Witnessed by the New Messianic Community (20:30-31). Köstenberger, *John*, 11. Stibbe offers an interesting structure: A[1] 1-2 The Prologue, B[1] 3-10 The two disciples race to the tomb, B[2] 11-18 Mary Magdalene looks into the tomb, C[1] 19-23 The disciples meet the risen Jesus, C[2] 24-29 Thomas meets the risen Jesus, A[2] 30-31 The epilogue. Stibbe, *John*, 200. Lindars describes three traditions in the resurrection narrative: a) discovery of the empty tomb by Mary; b) visit of Peter to the empty tomb; c) Jesus' appearance to the apostles. Barnabas Lindars, *The Gospel of John*, 595.

2. Appearance to Mary (20:11-18)-
   - (2A) Resurrection Appearances (20:15-29),
   - (2B) The Angelic Testimony (20:11-13),
   - (2C) Recognizing Jesus (20:14-16),
   - (2D) Mary's Testimony (20:17-18),
   - (2E) The Ascension (20:17),
   - (2F) Women's Witness (20:18);

vv. 19-29 Appearances to the Disciples:

3. Appearance to the Ten (20:19-23) –
   - (1A) A Johannine Pentecost?
   - (1B) The Setting (20:19),
   - (1C) Jesus' Appearance (20:19d – 21a),
   - (1D) The Commissioning (20:21),
   - (1E) Empowerment for the Mission (20:22),
   - (1F) Authority for Forgiveness (20:23);
4. Appearance to Thomas (20:24-29)-
   - (2A) Thomas's Scepticism (20:24-25),
   - (2B) Jesus' Wounds (20:26-27),
   - (2C) The Climatic Christological Confession (20:28-29);

vv. 30-31 conclusion.[100]

The structures discussed above seem to have failed to consider the theme of disclosure,[101] especially in terms of disclosure of Jesus' identity and mission. More importantly, the structures failed to look at the empty tomb as a point of disclosure of Jesus' identity. Further, there seems to be a tendency to view vv. 29-31 as separate from the resurrection account; this need not be the case. It is possible to state that vv. 29-31 forms not just the conclusion of the FG, but it also serves as a conclusion of chapter 20; thus, confirming that the resurrection is also one of the signs in the FG.

The following structure is followed in the exegetical study:

vv. 1-10: Disclosure of the empty tomb

vv. 11-18: Disclosure of the Son's identity in the Father

vv. 19-23: Disclosure of mission in identity

vv. 24-31: Disclosure of the Lord's identity to the community

---

[100] Craig S. Keener, *The Gospel of John: A Commentary*, vol. 2 (Peabody: Hendrickson Publishers, 2003), 1178-1216.

[101] The theme of disclosure is hinted by Jerome Neyrey's structure of John 20: vv. 1-10 Many witnesses to an empty tomb; vv. 11-18 Now she knows "where"; vv. 19-23 Appearances as commissioning; vv. 24-31 demands, demands, demands. Neyrey, *The Gospel of John*, 315-332.

3.3.3. John 20:1-10: Disclosure of the Empty Tomb

Like the synoptics, the FG begins with the empty tomb narrative. There are three characters who visit the empty tomb (Mary Magdalene, Peter and the BD), and the narrator focuses on introducing one character after another. Along with the characters there are certain objects that are also introduced: the stone (taken away from the entrance of the tomb (v. 1), linen cloths (v. 5) and napkin (v. 7). The narrator puts the characters in relation to these objects and the readers. The question that is put across is whether the objects lead to a disclosure of the identity of Jesus. It is interesting to note that one character after another comes and goes; thus, a great deal of movement is described in vv. 1-10. Do these objects, together with the empty tomb, lead to a disclosure? The implied question is put by the narrator to have its intended effect on its readers.

3.3.3.1. Translation

1 On the first day of the week Mary Magadalene came[102] early,[103] while it was still dark,[104] to the tomb and she saw that the stone was taken away[105] from the entrance.[106]

2 So, she went running[107] to Simon Peter and the other disciple, whom Jesus loved and said to them, "They have carried away[108] the Lord from the tomb and we[109] do not know where they have put[110] him."

---

[102] Lit. ἔρχεταιι comes, here, probably a case of historic present.

[103] Πρωῒ is put after the verb to indicate its use as an adverb of time.

[104] This is a genitive absolute construction– σκοτίας ἔτι οὔσης.

[105] Βλέπει τὸν λίθον ἠρμένον (βλέπω with accusative and participle instead of a dependent clause) means "that the stone was taken away." Walter Bauer, William F. Arndt, F. Wilbur Gingrich and Fredrick W. Danker, *A Greek-English Lexicon of the New Testament and Other Early Christian Literature* (Chicago: University of Chicago Press, 1979), 143. Hereafter referred to as BAGD.

[106] Lit. "from the tomb" but as suggested by Newman and Nida, the results of archaeological studies indicate that the entrance to the burial tombs was at the ground level through a small entrance. Barclay M. Newman and Eugene A. Nida, *A Translator's Handbook on the Gospel of John*, Helps for Translators Series vols. (Stuttgart: United Bible Societies, 1980), 602.

[107] Newman and Nida translate it- "went running to Simon Peter," for the reason that v. 3 indicates that they went from the same place, which also implies that they were staying in the same place. Newman and Nida, *A Translator's Handbook on the Gospel of John*, 603. Instead of this, the RSV has "she ran, and went to Simon Peter". It is probable that Newman and Nida are right in their observation. There are several clues to this in this verse as well as in vs. 3, such as αὐτοῖς (v. 2) and ἐξῆλθεν (v. 3).

[108] The verb αἴρω means "(lift up and) carry away, remove lit." BAGD, 24.

[109] The use of plural (οἴδαμεν) by Mary Magdalene has been a point of discussion, which is taken up in the exegesis.

[110] The word ἔθηκαν is translated as "put" which goes along with ἦραν (taken away).

3 Peter and the other disciple came out[111] and they went toward[112] the tomb.

4 The two of them were running together and the other disciple ran ahead[113] of Peter and was the first one to come[114] to[115] the tomb,

5 and he stooped down to look in and saw[116] the linen cloths[117] lying (there)[118] though[119] he did not go in.

6 So, Simon Peter also came following him, and he entered inside the tomb, and he observed[120] the linen cloths lying (there),

7 and the napkin[121] which had been around[122] his head, was not lying (there) with linen cloths, but rolled up in[123] a place by itself.

---

[111] Lit. the use of singular (ἐξῆλθεν) means "Peter came out". But going by the similar use of verbal structure in Jn. 2:2, it is possible that the singular verb refers to both Peter and the BD; this is made use of in the translation. Beasley-Murray, *John*, 366.

[112] The preposition εἰς was used instead of προς in koine Greek. Max Zerwick and Mary Grosvenor, *A Grammatical Analysis of the Greek New Testament*, translated by Mary Grosvenor (Rome: Editrice Pontificio Istituto Biblico, 1988), 97. Blass, Debrunner and Funk note that εἰς could also be used to mean "to, toward." Friedrich Blass and Albert Debrunner, *A Greek Grammar of the New Testament and Other Early Christian Literature*, translated by Robert W. Funk (Chicago: The University of Chicago Press, 1961), 112. Hereafter referred to as BDF.

[113] Lit. ran faster than (ποέδραμεν τάχιον του). Newman and Nida term it as a redundant Greek expression. Newman and Nida, *A Translator's Handbook on the Gospel of John*, 604. BDF term this as pleonasm, that is, a "...repetition of an idea which has already been expressed in the sentence, not for any rhetorical purpose." BDF, 256.

[114] BAGD note in the case of a predicative adjective (καὶ ἦλθεν πρῶτος), an adverb may be used in English, in this case, "the first one." BAGD, 725.

[115] This is another example of εἰς used instead of προς.

[116] The phrase βλέπει κείμενα τὰ ὀθόνια is another example of accusative and participle instead of a dependent clause.

[117] Zerwick defines ὀθόνιον as diminutive of ὀθόνη. Zerwick and Grosvenor, *A Grammatical Analysis of the Greek New Testament*, 344.

[118] The word κείμενα when referring to cloths could mean "lie (there)" as in the case of Jn 20:5, 6, 7.

[119] The phrase οὐ μέντοι, as an adversative, means "though not." BAGD, 503.

[120] The verb θεωρέω means to look at, observe with an accusative of the thing and a particle that follows (θεωρεῖ τὰ ὀθόνια κείμενα). BAGD, 360.

[121] Σουδάριον is a loan word from Latin and could mean 'napkin.' Zerwick and Grosvenor, *A Grammatical Analysis of the Greek New Testament*, 344.

[122] Lit. 'which was on his head' (ὃ ἦν τῆς κεφαλῆς αὐτου). Εἰμ with ἐπί followed by a genitive (ἦν ἐπί τῆς κεφαλῆς αὐτου) means "be of something, of place, on the roof." BAGD, 225.

[123] Εἰς for ἐν. Zerwick and Grosvenor, *A Grammatical Analysis of the Greek New Testament*, 344.

8 Now[124] the other disciple, who had[125] first come to the tomb, also entered in, and he saw and believed;

9 for they did not yet understand[126] the Scripture (which said) that he must rise[127] from the dead.

10 Then the disciples went back home.[128]

3.3.3.2. Context

As noted earlier,[129] Jn. 20 can be seen in relation to chap. 1 as well as the Farewell Discourses. However, the context that is of immediate relevance is 19:31-42. There are several details that find their significance here: the body of Jesus is wrapped with spices (vv. 39-40), it was placed in the garden in a new tomb and the tomb was a nearby one.[130] The fact that Jesus was buried gives room for the search of his body, and the empty tomb narrative grows out of the burial of Jesus. The narrator uses the present tense to describe Mary's arrival and her observation unlike the burial episode (aorist tense) which signifies resurrection as a continuing impinging reality in the lives of the disciples.[131]

---

[124] BDF explain τότε οὖν has the fuller meaning of 'now,' meaning, in contrast to what has taken earlier. It is used to introduce a subsequent and does imply an event taking place at definite time. BDF, 240.

[125] Lit. "who came."

[126] Lit. "were not yet understanding," ᾔδεισαν pluperfect with imperfect meaning.

[127] Zerwick notes that ἀναστῆναι uses a middle voice to express an intransitive meaning. Zerwick and Grosvenor, *A Grammatical Analysis of the Greek New Testament*, xxxiii.

[128] Lit. πρὸς αὐτοὺς -to them (selves) i.e., home. Zerwick and Grosvenor, *A Grammatical Analysis of the Greek New Testament*, 344.

[129] Refer page 140 for further elaboration on the context.

[130] Bultmann states, "The burial described in v. 40 as concluded, not as provisional, and the narrative does not contain any premonition of the following Easter story." Rudolf Bultmann, *The Gospel of John: A* Commentary, translated by George R. Beasley-Murray (Philadelphia: The Westminster John Knox Press, 1971), 680.

[131] Wes Howard-Brook, *Becoming Children of God: John's Gospel and Radical Discipleship* (Maryknoll: Orbis Books, 1994), 441.

3.3.3.3. Structure

Scholars[132] have tried to trace the compositional history of vv. 1-10, which continues to remain elusive. Based on the narrative as it is,[133] the following

[132] Bultmann views 20: 1-18 as clubbing together of two portraits: a. the story of Mary Magdalene at the grave and b. the story of the Peter and the BD. The two stories originally were not united. The account of Mary is from the tradition that is also traced in the synoptics but the story about Peter and the BD (3-10) is a creation of the evangelist. Bultmann also considers v. 2 as an editorial composition created in order to connect with v. 3. In the process of editing the evangelist has shortened the source and has closed the narrative with the evangelist's own particular point of view (v. 3). Peter seeing the grave in vv. 6f., originally belonged to the story of Mary with the purpose of illustration. Bultmann also views vv. 14-18 also as entirely the view of the evangelist, which he takes as the commission motif (vv. 14-18). He notes that the source the evangelist followed was like that of a resurrection narrative of the synoptic tradition. But it differed from the synoptic tradition in that it did not give an account of several women, but only Mary Magdalene. For him, "originally the story was an independent narrative, even if in the source it was linked with the foregoing Passion narrative." Rudolf Bultmann, *The Gospel of John: A Commentary*, 681-683. Pierre Benoit assumes two traditions used by the evangelist: one was a non-synoptic story (20:1-10) and the other synoptic-like (20:11a. 14b-18). He notes that the synoptic-like was adapted by FE and Matthew to meet the "...contextual theological needs." Pierre Benoit, "Marie-Madeleine et les Disciples au Tombeau selon John 20, 1-18," in *Judentum, Urchristentum, Kirche. Festchrift für Joachim Jeremias*, edited by Walter Eltester (Berlin: Töpelmann, 1960), 141-152 cited in Reimund Bieringer, ""I am ascending to my Father and your Father, to my God and your God" (John 20:17): Resurrection and Ascension in the Gospel of John," in *The Resurrection of Jesus in the Gospel of John*, edited by Craig R. Koester and Reimund Bieringer, WUZNT 22 (Tübingen: Mohr Siebeck, 2008), 219. Brown finds behind 20:1-18 the hints of three narratives: two narratives that concern the visit to the empty tomb, and the narrative of appearance of Jesus to Magdalene. He notes that one is not sure whether these three narratives were put together by evangelist or the evangelist received it in partial or whole combination. The evangelist did use these traditions as means to articulate the theology about faith and the meaning of resurrection. Brown, *The Gospel according to John (xiii-xxi)*, 998. Frans Neirynck is of the view that the FG directly depended on the synoptics. Jn. 20:1-10 was from Lk. 24:12 and Jn. 20:11-18 from Matt. 28:9-10. The FE used these texts freely and creatively to compose his narratives. Frans Neirynck, "John and the synoptics: The Empty Tomb Stories," in *Evangelica II, 1982-1991: Collected Essays*, edited by Frans Van Segbroeck (Leuven: Leuven University Press and Peeters, 1991), 571-600 cited in Bieringer, ""I am ascending to my Father and your Father, to my God and your God" (John 20:17): Resurrection and Ascension in the Gospel of John," 220-221.

[133] Dodd also notes that the tradition underlying this *pericopé* has been totally recasted by the FE. C. H. Dodd, *Historical Traditions in the Fourth Gospel* (Cambridge: Cambridge University Press, 1963), 146. Neirynck makes a detailed study of the empty tomb stories in the synoptics and the FG and concludes by stating, "The synoptic influence I think, surpasses the limits of the so-called interpolations of 20.2-10…It may have been determinative for the whole composition of Jn. 20:1-18. The Johannine writer who depends on the Synoptics is not a secondary redactor but none other than the Fourth Evangelist." Frans Neirynck, "John and the Synoptics the Empty Tomb Stories," *NTS* 30/2 (April 1984): 161-187. However, Craig has highlighted the shortcomings of Neirynck's conclusion and is of the view that behind the interdependence of the empty tomb stories in Lk. 24: 12-24 and Jn. 20:2-10 there is a common tradition. William L. Craig, "The Disciples' Inspection of the Empty Tomb (Lk. 24:12-24; Jn.

structure[134] can be proposed taking into consideration the theme of disclosure: vv.1-2 – Mary's discovery of the removed stone; vv. 3-5 – BD's discovery from outside the tomb; vv. 6-7- Peter's discovery of the empty tomb; vv. 8-10 – Disclosure of the empty tomb to the BD.

There are two terms used here: 'discovery' and 'disclosure.' 'Discovery' is getting to know but without grasping the 'meaning,' and this can be applied to Mary and Peter. On the other hand,'disclosure' comprehends the meaning behind what is seen/made visible; this can be used for the BD, who alone seems to have believed. There is an aspect of revelation in disclosure.

3.3.3.4. Exegetical Notes

In the exegetical notes, an attempt is made to understand the use and interactions of different concepts, expressions, and their significance for comprehending the identity and mission.

3.3.3.4.1. Vv. 1-2: Mary's Discovery of the Removed Stone

The narrator begins the resurrection account with the phrase Τῇ δὲ μιᾷ τῶν σαββάτων;[135] this is similar to the synoptics but different from Paul, who states it as "the third day after the crucifixion." After drawing a time reference, the narrative moves on to introduce Mary Magdalene[136] who was last described as being present at the foot of the cross (19:25). Here she is described as coming[137] early to the tomb while it was still dark.[138] In Lee's words, Mary is "...a disciple who has shown herself faithful, who has seen Jesus' life giving

20:2-10)," in *John and the Synoptics*, edited by Adelbert Denaux, BETL (Leuven: Leuven University Press, 1992), 616-618, 619. One can probably agree with Schneiders who states, "...the Johannine tomb narrative is theologically original and cannot be interpreted in terms of Synoptic preoccupations." Sandra M. Schneiders, *Written That You May Believe: Encountering Jesus in the Fourth Gospel* (New York: The Crossroad Publishing Company, 1999), 181.

[134] There are others who have discussed the structure as well. Stibbe has this structure: a[1] 3 The two disciples run to the tomb, b[1] 4-5 The BD arrives first, sees but does not enter, c 6-7 Peter arrives second, enters first and sees, b[2] 8-9 The BD, having arrived first, enters second and sees, a[2] 10 The two disciples leave the tomb. Stibbe, *John*, 200.

[135] Howard-Brook notes here that the narrator makes "…temporal jump from the imminence of the great Passover sabbath to a new time… For the Johannine community the "first day of the week" describes about the beginning of a "new sacred time." There is a irony involved in stating that the resurrection took place on Sabbath when in fact it replaces "the Judean Sabbath."" Howard-Brook, *Becoming Children of God*, 439.

[136] The name 'Magdalene' suggests that she was from Magdala, located on the northwest shore of the Sea of Galilee, seven miles southwest of Capernaum. Köstenberger, *John*, 561.

[137] The narrator makes use of the historical present (ἔρχεται, βλέπει) in the narration of the story which vivdly presents the scene.

[138] For Barrett, this phrase means "early on Sunday morning" and does not refer to the beginning of the day in the Jewish conception of time. Barrett, *The Gospel according to St. John*, 467.

glory in death and whose fidelity has brought her to the tomb."[139] The term darkness is symptomatic for the FE[140] and moves beyond a mere description of the physical reality in the FG.

There is an interplay between darkness and light in the FG.[141] The motif of darkness sets in 13:30 where Judas is described as going into the night heralding an apparent victory of darkness (cf. Jn. 1:5)[142] and it intensifies in the Farewell Discourses signifying the state of the disciples (Jn. 14:1). This implies that darkness here is not just a physical reality in terms of absence of light, but also ignorance of Jesus' destiny, which is also his identity.[143] In this regard Ben Witherington III rightly remarks, "The followers of Jesus are still in the dark about his nature and destiny."[144] However, this aspect of darkness does not last long, and will soon be replaced by light (as early as Jn. 20:8) as suggested in the use of *πρωῒ* with *σκοτίας*.[145] Culpepper succinctly puts it:

---

[139] Dorothy Lee, "Resurrection and Life: Symbols of Easter" in *Flesh and Glory: Symbolism, Gender and Theology in the Gospel of John* (New York: The Crossroad Publising Company, 2002), 222.

[140] This is unlike the synoptics which indicate the time factor as λίαν πρωῒ (Mk. 16:2), τῇ ἐπιφωσκούσῃ (Matt. 28:1), ὄρθρου βαθέως (Lk. 24:1).

[141] Kelly and Moloney bring out this interplay in clear terms. Darkness has several connotations in the FG: darkness as opposed to light (8:12); b.as a sign of unbelief (1:5); c. deakness of the storm the disciples experience separation I6:17). The removal of the stone from the entrance gives a clue to the intervention of the divine action (20:1b). Anthony J. Kelly and Fancis J. Moloney, *Experiencing God in the Gospel of John* (New York: Paulist Press, 2003), 373.

[142] Painter notes that the dawning of a new day (20:1) represents that the light shines in the darkness. John Painter, """The Light Shines in the Darkness..." Creation, Incarnation, and Resurrection in John," in *The Resurrection of Jesus in the Gospel of John*, edited by Craig R. Koester and Reimund Bieringer, WUZNT 22 (Tübingen: Mohr Siebeck, 2008), 21. Wead disagrees that the term 'darkness' has a symbolic meaning here. David W. Wead, *The Literary Devices in John's Gospel*, ThDiss 4 (Basel: Friedrich Reinhardt Kommissionsverlag, 1970), 44.

[143] Ressigue notes that the temporal setting described as early and dark suggests Mary's inability to understand the resurrection. Darkness in the FG represents "unintelligibility or moving away from the light" (Jn. 3:2). Ressiguie further states, "Separation from Jesus is a form of darkness." Another possible meaning being, "Darkness represents coalition with darkness and rejection of light" (Jn. 13: 30). Resseguie, *Narrative Criticism of the New Testament: An Introduction*, 143.

[144] Witherington III, *John's Wisdom*, 323. There are other possible interpretations for the term σκοτία: a. Whitacre notes that here the light of the world was in the process of being made known in darkness. Rodney A. Whitacre, *John*, IVPNTC (Downers Grove: InterVarsity Press, 1999), cited in Keener, *The Gospel of John*, vol. 2, 1178. b. darkness signifying Mary's fear or highlighting her devotion to come as early as possible after the Sabbath. Keener, *The Gospel of John: A Commentary*, vol. 42, 1178. The symbolism of light and darkness runs through the FG and it becomes certain when the resurrection narrative is seen in terms of the disclosure motif.

[145] Howard-Brook, *Becoming Children of God*, 441.

"...sight becomes insight into the identity of Jesus" and "...a willingness to believe."[146] In fact, the dawning of light takes place from one character after another beginning with the BD, climaxing with the Thomas episode and going futher into the experience of the Johannine community.[147]

Depite being early and dark, Mary comes to the tomb and finds the stone had been removed from the entrance of the tomb.[148] Her inability to interpret the stone being removed from the entrance of the tomb leads her to surmise that the body has been robbed;[149] it is this misunderstanding[150] that takes the

---

146 R. Alan Culpepper, *Anatomy of the Fourth Gospel: A Study in Literary Design* (Philadelphia: Fortress Press, 1983), 191.

147 In fact the whole resurrection narrative has to be seen from the perspective of light and darkness. Each unit plays a significant part in unraveling the nature and destiny of Jesus: 20:1-10 – the BD comes to believe; 20:11-18 – Mary Magdalene comes to belive; 20:19-23 – the disciples come to believe and commissioned to continue the work of Jesus; 20:24-29- Thomas comes to believe; 20:30-31- the instruction to the Johannine community to believe. Thus light is getting to know the nature and destiny of Jesus which also means removal of darkness.

148 Barrett righlty notes that 19:38-42 do not mention the closing of the tomb and thus is dependent on a source. C. K. Barrett, *The Gospel according to St. John: An Introduction with Commentary and Notes on the Greek Text* (London: SPCK, 1965), 467. Robertson notes that perfect passive participle of αἴρω is a predicative accusative in apposition with tòν λίθον. Archibald Thomas Robertson, *Word Pictures in the New Testament The Fourth Gospel & The Epistle to the Hebrews*, vol. V (New York: Ray Long and Richard R. Smith, 1932), 308. Interestingly unlike the Lazarus incident (Jn. 11:36) where Jesus commands the stone to be taken away, here the stone has already been taken away. The use of passive probably denotes the divine involvement.

149 This is probably confirmed when this verse is interpreted with what follows. Grave robbery was a common phenomenon during that time as suggested in Matt. 27:62-66. Witherington notes that this was a common practice, chiefly if it was a tomb of a wealthy person. To stop this Claudius (41- 51 CE) passed a decree forbidding this activity. Witherington III, *John's Wisdom*, 324. Other than this, there are other possibilities as well: the Romans, the Judean leaders, or a generally referring to an object that takes the blame. Howard-Brook, *Becoming Children of God*, 442.

150 Culpepper notes the dynamic aspects of misunderstanding: a. Jesus makes a pronouncement which makes use of metaphor, ambiguity or double entendre; b. there is a failure to understand the message Jesus tried to communicate; and c. Jesus goes on to clarify the meaning of his message and thus clears the misunderstanding. Culpepper, *Anatomy of the Fourth Gospel*, 152. Köstenberger defines misunderstanding in clear terms: "A Johannine misunderstanding is a statement, normally involving ambiguity, metaphor, or double entendre, whose intended meaning is not properly identified by the original audience of the statement, which typically leads to a subsequent explication of its proper meaning by the person making the statement (most frequently Jesus) or the narrator." He further goes on to give a list of misunderstandings: Jn 2:20; 3: 4, 9; 4: 10, 15; 4: 31-34; 6:32-35, 52; 6:42; 7:27; 8:21-22, 27; 8:31-39; 8:51-53, 56-58; 9:40-41; 10:6; 11: 11-13; 12:13; 12: 16; 12:32-34; 13: 6-11; 13: 28-29; 13: 36-38; 14:5, 8; 16:17-18; 18:11; 20: 29; 20:14-15; 21:4). Andreas J. Köstenberger, *A Theology of John's Gospel and Letters: The Word, the Christ, the Son of God* (Grand Rapids, Michigan: Zondervan 2009), 143-144. Suprisingly Köstenberger seems to have left out the empty tomb as a means of misunderstanding probably because it is not a statement of Jesus but an event. Though, the

narrative forward and in a way gets the other characters involved: Peter and the BD.

The assumption propels Mary to run[151] to Peter and later to the disciple whom Jesus loved.[152] She tells them, "They have carried away the Lord."[153] The use of plural, ἦραν, has resulted in different interpretations.[154] Here, she initiates the task of communicating the information[155] acting as a link between the empty tomb and the disciples, and later between the risen Lord and the disciples.[156] Mary's statement here connects with v. 9. The use of "the Lord" by Mary Magdalene can be interpreted in two ways. The first is probably part of the tradition used by the FE. Simon J. Gathercole[157] in his study proposes a valuable insight. He states, "The pre-existence christology is already widespread among various individuals and in various different communities around the Mediterranean well before AD 70."[158] If this is viable, then, it was a part of the source. At the same time Mary Magadalene is also an individual who is yet to understand the significance of τὸν λίθον ἠρμένον ἐκ τοῦ μνημείου.

---

empty tomb should have disclosed the identity of Jesus but in this case becomes a vehicle of misunderstanding.

151 Τρέχει is also a vivid dramatic present. Robertson, *Word Pictures in the New Testament*, 308.

152 The Phrase "the disciple whom Jesus loved" occurs in 13:23-24; 19:25-27. The identity of the BD is a matter that continues to be debated. It is quite clear that for the Johannine community, he is a BD of Jesus. Further, this does not suggest that both stayed at different locations. Brodie takes the repetition of the preposition πρὸς to indicate that Peter and the BD were staying in different places. Brodie, *The Gospel according to St. John*, 561.

153 Howard-Brook succinctly puts it as "mixture of faith and doubt." Faith is seen in expressing the title but still mourns the missing body. Howard-Brook, *Becoming Children of God*, 442. Köstenberger sees it as an indication of Mary Magdalene's disturbed state and seeking for help. Köstenberger, *A Theology of John's Gospel*, 257.

154 Lindars interprets the active voice having a passive meaning- the body has been stolen. Barnabas Lindars, *The Gospel of John*, 600. Barrett suggests enemies of Jesus or tomb-robbers. Barrett, *The Gospel according to St. John*, 467. Minear supposes that this is a reference to "the Jews." Paul S. Minear, ""We Don't Know Where…" John 20:2," *Int.* 30/2 (Apr. 1976): 126.

155 Neyrey is of the view that Mary cannot be categorized as an apostle. He gives four reasons for this: a. usually only females spoke to the males of their respective kingship groups; b. Mary is commissioned only like the Samaritan woman; c. Mary is not commissioned to preach the gospel about Jesus but only a word, though an extraordinary revelation; d. unlike the apostles the role assigned to Mary continue on. Neyrey, *The Gospel of John*, 325. Neverthless Mary occupies an important place in the resurrection narrative as noted later in the section on 'theological interpretation.'

156 Howard-Brook, *Becoming Children of God*, 442.

157 Simon J. Gathercole, *The Preexistent Son: Recovering the Christologies of Matthew, Mark, and Luke* (Grand Rapids, Michigan: William B. Eerdmans Publishing Company, 2006).

158 Gathercole, *The Preexistent Son*, 23.

How does one interpret the visit of Mary Magadalene to the tomb? The stone having been removed from the tomb was a discovery, but it remained a discovery and did not move on to a disclosure. She communicates to Peter and the BD, yet it was only a communication of disclosure. The sign of the removed stone revealed the absence of her Lord, but the absence was interpreted as him being moved to another place. The narrative moves on with the assumption of the body being taken away. With this, Mary leaves the scene though she comes back later. Her place is now taken by the visit of Peter and the BD to the tomb, who like Mary run to the tomb.

3.3.3.4.2. Vv. 3-5: BD's Discovery from Outside the Tomb

Peter and the BD respond to Mary's report. The construction that makes use of a singular verb (Ἐξῆλθεν οὖν ὁ Πέτρος καὶ ὁ ἄλλος μαθητὴς) is unique to the FG. The connecting verb is put in the singular. But the plural in ἤρχοντο[159] suggests that they went to the tomb together and also that they probably stayed together. This section seems to be an interlude but still an important one.[160] Though both ran together,[161] the other disciple is said to have run ahead of Peter and arrived at the tomb first.[162] This description probably added to state the importance of the BD as a link with the community.[163] The prominence is further highlighted in what follows, especially through the pairs of contrast, which continue till v. 8.

---

[159] "The imperfect middle pictures the scene 'they were going.'" Robertson, *Word Pictures in the New Testament*, 309.

[160] Ridderbos states, "The report of the two disciples going to the tomb (vss. 3-10) is thus an interlude in which the Evangelist lets his readers know that, within the general framework of the events of that morning, which were undoubtedly familiar to them, something else took place, that, as the sequel will show…is of special significance for an understanding of everything that happened that morning." Herman Ridderbos, *The Gospel of John: A Theological Commentary* (Grand Rapids, Michigan: William B. Eerdmans Publishing Company, 1997), 629.

[161] Προέδραμεν τάχιον is a "pleonastic" expression conveying redundancy. Barrett, *The Gospel according to St. John*, 468.

[162] Πρῶτος is used in the sense of predicative nominative. Robertson, *Word Pictures in the New Testament*, 309. Witherington observes correctly here that there is not room for taking this as a reference to a contention between Jewish and Gentile expressions of Christianity. Witherington III, *John's Wisdom*, 324. It would be also hypothetical to conjecture from this that the BD "…was younger and fleeter of foot" as supposed by Bruce. Bruce, *The Gospel of John*, 385.

[163] It is still a matter of speculation what lies behind the description of the BD as outrunning Peter. Brodie sees it as a symbol of superior discipleship. Brodie, *The Gospel according to St. John*, 561. Beasley-Murray takes it as a reference to the BD's love for Jesus. Beasley-Murray, *John*, 371-372. Moloney notes that this suggests a stronger faith in the miracle that had taken place. Francis J. Moloney, *The Gospel of John*, SacPag 4, edited by Daniel J. Harrington (Minnesota: The Liturgical Press, 1998), 522.

In v. 5, there seems to be brevity in the description of what the BD sees compared to what Peter observes (θεωρεῖ τὰ ὀθόνια[164] καὶ τὸ σουδάριον) in vv. 6 and 7. Παρακύψας stands for a glance, which needs an inclination of the head.[165] The BD only sees[166] the linen strips and does not enter the tomb. The expression οὐ μέντοι εἰσῆλθεν is difficult to explain, especially in relation to v. 8 where he does enter the tomb. Though not the first to see the empty tomb (to which Mary is the first witness), the BD is the first to see τὰ ὀθόνια. Τὰ ὀθόνια carry evidence that the body had not been removed by robbers as they would not have left behind the expensive linen strips.[167] The narrator clearly notes that the BD οὐ τὰ ὀθόνια contrasts with what Peter did (v. 6 εἰσῆλθεν).[168] It could be that the BD followed the Jewish ritual of not polluting himself,[169] though this does not explain why he went in later. It probably refers to the intial reaction of the BD.

Regarding the motif of disclosure, there is also an interaction between the persons and the objects present. The object that is not mentioned earlier is the linen strips. The BD stoops down and looks into the tomb, something that Mary did not do. The linen strips could communicate something about what happened to the body of Jesus. It is possible that the BD could only see the linen strips from outside the tomb. Apart from the additional description of the linen strips there is progress in disclosure. The narrator now moves from the BD to Peter's view point of the empty tomb.

3.3.3.4.3. Vv. 6-7: Peter's Discovery of the Empty Tomb

Unlike the BD, Peter follows[170] him and enters the tomb. Peter observes the ὀθόνια and σουδάριον.[171] The description of the folded up napkin in a place

---

[164] The word ὀθόνιον is unique to the FG and could mean linen bandage as those used for wrapping a dead body. Barrett, *The Gospel according to St. John*, 465.

[165] Barrett, *The Gospel according to St. John*, 468.

[166] Here the narrator uses the present tense (βλέπει) whereas in v. 8 it is put in the past tense (εἶδεν). The change from present to aorist is used to signify that σουδάριον is a past event which is unavailable for the future disciples. Howard-Brook, *Becoming Children of God*, 445.

[167] Köstenberger, *John*, 563.

[168] Witherington rightly notes here that there is not enough room for taking this as a reference to a competition between Johannine or Petrine churches or Jewish and Gentile forms of Christianity. WitheringtonIII, *John's Wisdom: A Commentary on the Fourth Gospel*, 324.

[169] It could also be due to "a wall of fear or sacred awe or some other unnamed emotion has prevented the disciple…" Howard-Brook, *Becoming Children of God*, 443.

[170] 'Ακολουθῶν is an important verb in the FG. It is not meant to subordinate Peter to the BD. Rather than taking it as an instance of subordination, it could be taken as a natural fall out of the BD outrunning Peter. On this point, the researcher differs from Barrett, who argues otherwise. Barrett, *The Gospel according to St. John*, 468.

[171] It is a borrowed term from Latin and does not occur in the Septuagint. Luke uses it to mean "handkerchief" (Lk. 19:20; Acts 19:12). In the Targums it is used to describe the veil that

by itself, apart from the linen strips, is to indicate that the napkin was exactly in the same position when Jesus' body was interred.[172] In other words, the body is said to have passed through the cloths and left the strips of linen lying there.[173] This rules out any case of robbery, for, if it had been a robbery, the linen strips would not have been left behind.[174] Significantly, this suggests that Jesus came out from within rather than from the outside through removal of the clothes. Painter rightly notes, "...Johannine narrative portrays Jesus as the one in whom the life giving power of God was present and that life-giving power was indestructible even by death."[175] This view is confirmed in the light of Jesus' words in Jn. 10:17.[176]

However, the act of Jesus coming back to life in the resurrection is to be seen as one of joint operations of Jesus and the Father, as righlty pointed by Howard-Brook.[177] Resurrection is an act that confirms once again the unity that the Son shares with the Father, a further confirmation of (Jn. 1:1).[178] Here, the resurrection is not an individualized event but a community act, the involvement of the Father, the Son, and the Spirit. Jn. 10:18 is a veiled reference to the resurrection which states that Jesus has the power to lay down his life and the authority to take it back again, but Jesus also adds that this charge he has received from the Father.

There are two objects that are now described by the narrator: the linen strips and the napkin. Both of these are signs which convey certain aspects of

---

covered Moses' face when he appears before the people after speaking with God. Sandra M. Schneiders, "The Face Veil: A Johannine Sign (John 20: 1-10)," *BibThBul* 13/3 (Ja. 1983): 96.

[172] Köstenberger, *John*, 564. Ernst Haenchen, *John 2 : A Commentary on the Gospel of John Chapters 7-21*, translated by Robert W. Funk, Hermeneia, edited by Robert W. Funk and Ulrich Busse (Philadelphia: Fortress Press, 1984), 208. The contrast between the raising of Lazarus and the resurrection of Jesus is made very clear. Lazarus came out of the tomb bound in the σουδάριον and had to be freed by others whereas Jesus had left it behind. Howard-Brook, *Becoming Children of God*, 444.

[173] Barrett states that this incident is unlike the raising of Lazarus. He further notes that one is not sure how the FE conceived that the resurrection had taken place. Barrett, *The Gospel according to St. John*, 468.

[174] B. F. Westcott, *The Gospel according to St. John* (Grand Rapids, Michigan: William B. Eerdmans Publishing Company, 1958), 290.

[175] Painter, ""The Light Shines in the Darkness...:"" 44. Howard-Brooks also notes, "Jesus *actively participated* in his resurrection...the "lying" of the burial cloths represents the act of the Father releasing Jesus from death..." This is different from the Pauline and Lukan understanding of resurrection as something that happened to Jesus through God's grace (Rom. 6:4; Acts 3:15). Howard-Brook, *Becoming Children of God*, 445.

[176] Byrne notes that Jesus fulfills the statement in Jn. 10:17-18. Brendan Byrne, "The Faith of the Beloved Disciple and the Community in John 20," *JSNT* 23 (Feb. 1995): 88.

[177] Howard-Brook, *Becoming Children of God*, 445.

[178] Howard-Brook, *Becoming Children of God*, 445.

the effects of the resurrection event. It goes to confirm that a robbery has not taken place but that the body has passed through these cloths, an act in which the Father is also involved. Inspite of this, Peter is not attentive to the details. However, the narrator moves on to describe the climax of this unit with the second look into the tomb by the BD.

3.3.3.4.4. Vv. 8-10: Disclosure of the Tomb to the BD

The BD, unlike Peter, saw and believed. The description of the BD here differs from v. 5. Not only is there a change in tense, i.e., both the verbs (εἶδεν, ἐπίστευσεν) are in aorist tense whereas in v. 5 is present tense. In addition, a different verb (εἶδεν) is used. The question remains: What did the BD see? What did the BD believe? In v. 5, the BD looks from outside and sees, but here he enters, sees and believes.[179] The same verb, i.e., ὁράω is used by Mary when she reports to the disciple of having seen the Lord. The BD saw and believed that Jesus had risen from the dead[180] and thus moves beyond just seeing to understanding the significance of the σουδάριον, amply expressed in 'believed.'[181] Here there is a clear distinction between the BD who believes

---

[179] Schneiders sees the FE had two purposes in stating that the BD stood outside until Peter saw the cloths and the 'face veil.' They are a) the reason for faith is not the loss of Jesus' body or the cloths but the presence of the 'face veil;' b) the face veil is sign that Peter does not comprehend but the BD understands. Schneiders, *Written That You May Believe*, 185.

[180] Several scholars take this view: Carson, *The Gospel according to John*, 638; Schnackenburg, *The Gospel according to St John*, vol. 3, 312; Brown, *The Gospel according to John (xiii-xxi)*, 987; Bultman, *The Gospel of John*, 684; Beasley-Murray, *John*, 373; Barrett, *The Gospel according to St. John*, 468; Edwyn Clement Hoskyns, *The Fourth Gospel*, vol.2 (London: Faber and Faber Limited, 1940), 644. Schneiders calls the faith of the BD "...genuine paschal faith." Schneiders, *Written That You May Believe*, 183. Some scholars have difficulty in coming to this conclusion as the following verse explicitly states that the disciples did not comprehend that Jesus was to rise from the dead according to scripture. Thus Bennema argues that BD did not believe that Jesus had risen but that Jesus' body has been removed. He also notes that only here the BD does not match the model of discipleship expected of him. Cornelis Bennema, *Excavating John's gospel: A Commentary for Today* (Delhi: ISPCK, 2005), 213. This is higly unlikely as the BD serves as link to the community and plays an invaluable role in the FG. Witherington interprets it as referring to an inadequate faith, i.e., not understanding Jesus as the crucified and risen Messiah (cf. 2: 23-24; 12:42-43; 20:8). Further the BD believed more than Mary, and Peter, but even the BD's faith was on a pilgrimage which was not yet over. Witherington III, *John's Wisdom: A Commentary on the Fourth Gospel*, 325. In Jn. 21:7, the BD identifies the Lord and this seems to suggest that the BD did come to an understanding earlier.

[181] Most scholars agree with this view. Bultmann, *The Gospel of John: A Commentary*, 684; Brown, *The Gospel according to John (xiii-xxi)*, 987; Raymond E. Brown, "The Resurrection in John 20 - A Series of Diverse Reactions," *Worship* 64/3 (My. 1990): 197; Byrne, "The Faith of the Beloved Disciple:" 83-97. Köstenberger notes that here the evangelist tries to affirm the superiority of faith rooted on apostolic witness for the good understanding of the generations that come later. Köstenberger, *A Theology of John's Gospel*, 258. Beasley-Murray rejects the understanding that this signifies "an embryonic and incomplete faith" and argues for a case of

and Peter who does not understand its significance. The use of the singular verb (ἐπίστευσεν) rules out that Peter shared the same faith as the BD.[182] The BD sees the sign of Jesus' resurrection in the σουδάριον and believes. It is also a sign that Jesus was going back to the Father.[183]

The use of ὁράω is significant for the understanding of BD's belief. It has a wide range of meanings. It is largely used to refer to divine phenomenon. It also means to recognize, and due to the influence of OT it often means experience (Acts 2:27).[184] Though it can be said that ὁράω in the FG refers to 'seeing,' this meaning does not convey the total aspect and thus does not result in faith (6:36; 12: 40; 15:24). Yet it does also refer to "...faith-related perception of Jesus' glory in his signs (I Jn. 1:3f; cf. I Jn. 1:14)."[185] Interestingly, the term ὁράω is used to express Mary Magadalene's and the disciples' experience of having seen the risen Lord (v. 18, 25). Thus, the experience of the BD, Mary Magadalene and the disciples are on equal footing. This further lends to the understanding that the resurrection is also a sign.[186] Lindars notes the faith of

---

genuine faith, especially when πιστεύω is used absolutely (5:44; 6:47; 19:35; 20:29). Beasley-Murray, *John*, 373. There are also other views. Howard-Brooks takes it to mean, believing in the account of Mary that the body was stolen. He further argues that this clearly explains the fact that the disciples return to their respective places without any expression of feelings. Howard-Brook, *Becoming Children of God*, 446. A couple of arguments can be said against this view: a. the fact that the narrator has vividly described the neatly arranged grace cloths dissuades the account of Mary; b. secondly, most importantly the narrator has reserved the news of resurrection to the presence of Jesus, i.e., to Mary and later to the disciples. This could be the reason for a static description of the disciples.

182 Bultmann's argument does not seem to hold good. He opines that if the two disciples (Peter and the BD) were set against each other, the evangelist would have explicitly stated that Peter did not believe. He further argues that in the context of this verse what is meant is only faith in the resurrection of Jesus and can be signified by the absolute πιστεύειν. Bultmann, *The Gospel of John*, 684. Contrary to Bultmann, Haenchen argues that since Peter is not mentioned that he believed, it appears that only the BD believed. Haenchen, *John* 2, 208. Though it is true that the faith here refers to the resurrection faith, it does not include Peter also. The two uses of third person singular (εἶδεν, ἐπιστεύσεν) confirm this view point.

183 It is not clear whether a reference to Moses can be seen here. Howard-Brook finds the contrast with Moses here as Jesus will not require a hereafter as he is returning to God and will no longer be present with the disciples. Howard-Brook, *Becoming Children of God*, 444.

184 K. Kremer, "," in *Exegetical Dictionary of the New Testament*, vol. 2, edited by Hort Balz and Gerhard Schneider ὁράω (Grand Rapids, Michigan: William B. Eerdmans Publishing Company, 1981), 527.

185 Kremer, "ὁράω," 527.

186 Köstenberger lays out the following aspects of signs. There are six commonly accepted signs by scholars: a) the changing of water into wine (2:1-11); b. the healing of the nobleman's son (4:46-54); c. the healing of the lame man (5: 1-15); d. the feeding of the five thousand (6: 1-15); e. the healing of the blind man (chap. 9); f. the raising of Laszarus (chap. 11). He comes to such a conclusion based on the criteria on determining the signs, which are discussed below. Signs in the FG are presented to portray Jesus as the authentic representative of God and also

the BD, and he states, "*His* kind of faith will be commended by the risen Jesus himself in verse 29. This holds good in spite of the formal contrast between this verse ('saw and believed') and verse 29 ('have not seen and yet believe')."[187]

It is quite surprising to note that after having stated that the BD saw and believed, the FE mentions that they did not know (ᾔδεισαν Pluperfect active indicative 3rd person plural). There are several solutions proposed by scholars to deal with the seeming contradiction in vv. 9 and 10.[188]

The disciples' lack of understanding of the Scripture concerning the Messiah's redemptive work is also noted in the Emmaus story (Lk. 24:25-27, 32). What does "the scripture" denote? The singular indicates that a specific OT text is in view and this includes Ps. 16:10, Isa. 53:10-112 and Hos. 6:2 and probably Scripture in its entirety.[189] Beasley-Murray notes that the plural

---

a proof of the messiahship of Jesus. He defines sign as "... a symbol laden, but not necessarily 'miraculous,' public work of Jesus selected and explicitly identified as such for John for the reason that it displays God's glory in Jsus who is thus shown to be God's true representative (cf. 20: 30-31)." Three criteria are followed by him to determine whether it is a sign or not: a. a sign needs to be a part of Jesus' public ministry; b. it needs to be clearly identified as a "sign" in the FG; c. it needs to reval Jesus as God's true representative. Köstenberger seems to be limited in his understanding when he rules out resurrection as a sign because crucifixion and resurrection are the realities to which the signs point. He follows Brown's understanding and thus restricts signs to the first part of the gospel. He also notes that resurrection is not a sign for two more reasons: a. not a "public work of Jesus"; b. "not called a sign" in John. The first objection does not hold good as resurrection would hold significance only for those who believe according to the FG. The second objection is also not convincing as Jn. 2: 23 notes the resurrected body as the temple. But the basic question seems to be: If one takes resurrection as a sign, does it nullify the aspect of reality? Not necessarily so, ὑψόω has two meanings – as glorification and lifted up in a literal sense. The researcher would like to propose the view that resurrection is a reality as well as a sign, i.e., the relationship that Jesus shares with the Father. Köstenberger draws support from the raising up of Lazarus to substantiate his point of view. The view is that if raising Lazarus is a sign pointing to Jesus as "the resurrection and life" the Jesus resurrection cannot be logically seen as a sign. Andreas J. Köstenberger, *The Mission of Jesus and the Disciples according to the Fourth Gospel* (Grand Rapids, Michigan: Wm B. Eerdmans Publishing Company, 1998), 60-70. Here again, it must be noted that the raising up of Lazarus and the resurrection of Jesus are two distinct events which share continutites as well as discontinuities and the lattter outnumbers the former. The fact that both cannot be put on the same plane throws light on the unique identity of Jesus.

[187] Lindars, *The Gospel of John*, 602.

[188] For Lee, the BD's believing has no "narrative impact" as it does alleviate Mary Magdalene's grief and in fact she sees vv. 8-10 as a prolepsis, pointing forward to the meeting of the risen Jesus in chap. 21. Dorothy A. Lee, "Partnership in Easter Faith: The Role of Mary Magdalene and Thomas in John 20," *JSNT* 58 (Ja. 1995): 39-40. Ridderbos comments that the BD believed on the basis of seeing rather than believing from the Scripture. Ridderbos, *The Gospel of John*, 634. Bultmann takes it as scribal gloss. Bultmann, *The Gospel of John: A Commentary*, 685.

[189] Köstenberger, *John*, 565. Barrett also notes that it could refer to the Old Testament generally. Barrett, *The Gospel according to St. John*, 468.

(ᾔδεισαν) is a pointer that ignorance of the Scripture applied to both disciples.[190] This need not be the case. On the contrary, Schnackenburg rightly observes that v. 9 is part of the evangelist's source as the formula δεῖ αὐτὸν ἐκ νεκρῶν ἀναστῆναι is unknown in the FG but common in the synoptics, especially in the passion predictions in Mk. 8:31 and in Lk. 24:7, 25-26, 46.[191]

It is probable then, that the inclusion of the BD is a deliberate step taken by the narrator. The reason for such a conclusion is that nowhere in the other gospels is Peter seen along with the BD, and this is considered as one of the distinct features of the presentation of the FG. The view that the BD is also included along with Peter as those who did not understand the Scripture seems untenable.[192] Kanagaraj rightly notes, "But the fact that they did not know the Scripture explains only the unbelief of the disciples, not the faith of the beloved disciple referred to in verse 8."[193] The view that the BD did not believe seems to refute the larger picture concerning the BD presented in the FG. The BD takes on an invaluable role in the Johannine presentation of Jesus. Peter and the BD are presented as figures of contrast. In 13:21-26, the BD is portrayed in proximity with Jesus and has access to information that Peter does not have. The next role that the BD takes up is at the foot of the cross (19:26-27), a place where there is no mention of Peter and the other disciples. The last contrast is seen in the BD arriving at the tomb first. He doesn't enter at first, but later enters, sees and believes.

In the FG, the BD is primarily a model of faith for the Johannine community.[194] The contrast between Peter and the BD should not be seen as a

---

190 Beasley-Murray, *John*, 373.

191 Schnackenburg, *The Gospel according to St. John*, vol. 3, 313. Bultmann also considers it as "unJohannine." But his interpretation seems different from Schnackenburg. Instead of seeing it as disbelief, he notes that until now they had not believed the scriptures but now since now they have seen with their eyes, they have come to believe. Bultmann, *The Gospel of John*, 685. It seems that Jn. 20:10 does convey a negative notion and not a positive one.

192 Haenchen righlty notes in this regard, "…one disciple becomes a believer, the other doesn't. Haenchen, *John 2*, 208.

193 However, later he explains the faith of the BD as a superficial faith as it was not based on scripture. Jey J. Kanagaraj, *The Gospel of John: A Commentary with Elements of Comparison to Indian Religious Thoughts and Cultural Practices* (Secunderabad: Om Books International, 2005), 642.

194 Byrne brings out the structure in terms of faith:
BD Mary-Disciples-Thomas Later Commmunity
'Sign' faith '3-Stage' faith 'Sign' faith
(Believing, yet not (Seeing Jesus and believing) (Believing, yet not
seeing risen Jesus) seeing risen Jesus).

This presentation of faith is quite appealing. But to put the BD and the Later Community on the same plane would be a problem as the BD is not only a model of faith as well as a link with the traditions of the FG. Brendan Byrne, "The Faith of the Beloved Disciple:" 92.

rivalry. Bultmann goes to the extent of seeing Peter and John as representatives of Jewish and Gentile Christianity, though he does state that there is no hint of precedence of Jewish Christianity over Gentile Christianity as both represent readiness of faith.[195] Brown brings in the right perspective when he states that there is no rivalry set out between Peter and the BD, and both are presented as friends; further, Peter is commissioned to take care of the Lord's sheep. The BD takes a prominent role, a primacy of love but does not exclude Peter's role.[196] This is a significant point, i.e., the Johannine community did not see itself as against the other existent communities, but in relation with the other communities scattered throughout Asia Minor; therefore, although it was not an introverted community, it was a community which gave a significant place to the BD.

This pericope is unique to the FG.[197] One wonders as to the significance of the position of this incident — in between Mary Magdalene's discovery of the empty tomb and Jesus' appearance to Mary Magdalene. In fact, some scholars see the present narrative (Jn. 20:4-10) as a break in the continuity between vv. 3-11. It clearly highlights the significance of the pericope, though the pericope that follows it is also highly significant for the Johannine community. The 'believing' element is the most important element here, and thus it finds repeated emphasis throughout Jn. 20 which draws to its climax in the last verses of this chapter. Thus, v. 10 forms a transitional verse, preparing for Mary Magdalene's encounter with the risen Jesus. The expression πρὸς αὐτοὺς literally means "to them" i.e., that which belongs to them—their homes.[198]

The disclosure of meaning takes place in the BD's understanding: what Jesus had instructed to the disciples before his departure (Chaps. 13-17) has taken place. Peter and Mary Magdalene fail to connect the removed stone and the objects in the tomb (linen strips and the napkin). Peter gets another opportunity for disclosure along with the rest of the disciples (vv. 19ff.), and Mary continues the quest for the missing body of Jesus.

---

[195] Bultmann, *The Gospel of John*, 685.

[196] Brown, *The Gospel according to John (xiii-xxi)*, 1006-7. Mahoney shares the same view point with Brown. Robert Mahoney, *Two Disciples at the Tomb: The Background and Message of John 20:1-10* Theologie und Wirklichkeit 6, edited by Hans-Werner Bartsch et. al (Franfurt: Peter Lang, 1974), 250-60.

[197] Mahoney presents an interesting study of Peter and the BD. He is of the view that the evangelist has placed particular emphasis on their functions not on the persons. Peter's function is to "..notarize the facts" and the BD's is to see the facts and believe. Robert Mahoney, *Two Disciples at the Tomb: The Background and Message of John 20:1*-10, TW 6, edited by Hans-Werner Bartsch et.al. (Frankfurt: Peter Lang, 1974), 278.

[198] Barrett notes that the translation "went to their homes" seems impossible. This expression agrees with the "Aramaic ethic dative." However, Barrett cautions against supposing that the FE is translating thus. Barrett, *The Gospel according to St. John*, 469.

3.3.3.5. Theological Interpretation

Where[199] is Jesus? This is a crucial question in the FG and is certainly related to the issue of identity. Chennatu[200] seems to argue for this, when she states that "where" has not just a geographical significance but also a 'theological meaning.' The question "...concerning Jesus' whereabouts reminds the readers of the indwelling shared between Jesus and the Father."[201] In Jn. 8, where Jesus shares a dialogue with the Jews, Jesus tells them that they could not come where he was going. Then, Jesus goes on to note the essential difference between the Jews and himself—Jesus is from 'above' and they are from 'below.' 'Where he comes from' signifies the identity of the Messiah, and in the case of the resurrection it deals with 'where' Jesus is going. Both where he comes from and where he is going from are intricately related. The search in this pericope consists of two groups: the first group consists of Mary and the second consists of Peter and the BD.

In the case of the first group, Mary begins the search for Jesus and is unable to find out where Jesus has gone. A little later Peter and the BD also join the search. Mary takes all possible efforts to clear her misunderstanding of the identity of Jesus and this is very vividly presented by the FE in terms of her comings and going – Mary Magadalene comes (to the tomb early) ⟶ goes (to Peter and the BD) ⟶ comes back again to the tomb (this time Mary comes with Peter and the BD; though Mary's coming back again is not explicitly stated in the narrative, it is certainly assumed). However, the significance of Mary Magadlene in this pericope cannot be overlooked. Mary is the initator of the search for both Peter and the BD. Later on, she is commissioned by Jesus to convey the identity of Jesus as well as the disciples in the expression Jesus conveys to her – "my father and your father." Mary's search for the body is a search where the Lord[202] has gone.

In the case of the second group, Peter and the BD, unlike Mary, only come and go. Though both come and go, the BD is clearly marked out by the FE as one who saw and believed. Contrary to the opinion of some scholars,[203] this

---

[199] Mollat has noted that the adverbs ποῦ and ὅπου occur eighteen and thirty times respectively in the FG. Donatian Mollat, "La découverte du tombeau vide (Jn. 20, 1-9)," *Assemblées du Seigneur* 221 (1969): 90-100 cited in Schneiders, *Written that You May Believe*, 191.

[200] Rekha M. Chennattu, *Johannine Discipleship as a Covenant Relationship* (Massachusetts: Hendrickson Publishers, 2006).

[201] Chennattu, *Johannine Discipleship*, 143.

[202] The use of the title 'Lord' by Mary clearly attests the fact that it is written from a post-Easter perspective.

[203] Bennema is of the view that the BD faults in two places: BD lacks understanding in 13:28 and has an "indeterminate 'belief' in 20:8. Bennema, *Encountering Jesus*, 181. Bultmann includes not only the BD but also Peter among the ones who believed (Jn. 20:8). He supposes

seems to be a significant aspect in the resurrection narrative. It is not related to the verses that follow which describe the failure of the disciples to comprehend Jesus' resurrection from the dead. The BD, the leader of the community, holds great importance in the FG.[204] This can be vividly illustrated in the previous descriptions of the BD. In Jn. 13:21-26, the BD is described reclining in the bosom of Jesus, a description reserved for describing the relationship that Jesus shared with the Father as seen in Jn. 1:18. Neyrey rightly notes that the BD had "access to esoteric information."[205] So, also he states that the BD plays the "...role of shepherd to Peter's sheep," by helping Peter enter Annas' palace through the gatekeeper (18:15-18).[206] The BD stands near the cross while Peter had long before denied and left.[207] Lastly, the reference to the BD in Jn. 21 provides the clue for a better reading of Jn. 20:8. The narrator states in Jn. 21:4 ᾔδεισαν οἱ μαθηταὶ ὅτι Ἰησοῦς ἐστιν. However, later the narrator also notes of the BD saying to Peter ὁ κύριός ἐστιν. (Jn. 21:7). Thus, it makes particularly clear that the BD did believe that the Lord has risen. More importantly, here, the motif of disclosure finds its linchpin in the motif of believing. Here, the BD does not see Jesus but a sign i.e., τὰ ὀθόνια and τὸ σουδάριον which moves the BD to believe. For the BD, the search for the identity of where Jesus is finds its meaning in the sign (linen strips) and the BD believes in the true identity of Jesus. Schneiders states, "What the face veil reveals is the former, that Jesus, the new Moses, has ascended to God that he has gone away. This the Beloved Disciple believes."[208]

Believing plays a significant place in the FG. Most importantly, it is the aspect of believing that makes all the difference between experiencing the advantages of the physicality of resurrection and not experiencing it, so it can be said that the community is not at a disadvantage.

---

this on the basis that the text does not explicitly state that Peter did not believe. Bultmann, *The Gospel of John*, 681, 684.

[204] Lee notes, "Part of the evangelist's agenda throughout the Farewell discourse and passion narrative is to situate the beloved disciple in the places of honor, thus vindicating the Johannine tradition (13:23; 19:25-27)." Dorothy Lee, "Resurrection and Life," 220.

[205] Though, Neyrey does mention that the BD has unique access and information, but he seems to contradict himself when he states concerning Mary Magadelene "…she knows better than any other disciple in the narrative." Neyrey, *The Gospel of John* , 317. It is true that Mary is an informed disciple but the FG seems to have a unique place for the BD. Later, Neyrey seems to correct himself when he states, "Except for the Beloved Disciple, she (Mary Magadalene) can be said to have the highest status in the Gospel." Neyrey, *The Gospel of John*, 324.

[206] Neyrey, *The Gospel of John*, 317.

[207] Neyrey, *The Gospel of John*, 317.

[208] Schneiders, *Written That You May Believe*, 187.

The empty tomb, strips of linen, facecloth lying separate and rolled up by itself is evidence for the Johannine community of the resurrection of Jesus.[209] Nevertheless, it must be remembered that for the Johannine community these were not just pointers to the testimony of Jesus, but also the answer to the question of where Jesus was. The Johannine concept of 'seeing' is unique.[210] Mlakuzhyil rightly notes, "He had already left a simple but significant sign (the rolled up napkin: 20, 7) to help his loved ones to see and believe in his resurrection (20, 8)."[211]

The significance of (20:9) is then for Peter, Mary and the rest of the disciples, for whom the search where the Lord continues.[212] For the BD seeing has led to believing. In effect, there is a gradation of disclosure. The narrator gives a graphic description of the empty tomb, and bit by bit things are revealed resembling the action of a video camera scanning various images. At first it is Mary Magadalene who sees the stone rolled, which leads her to conclude that some people have taken the body of Jesus. This is followed by another discovery of the BD which concerns the ὀθόνια. Later on, Peter also discovers the τὸ σουδάριον, in addition to the τὰ ὀθόνια. All of this leads to the conclusion that the BD believed in the sign, and thus becomes the model for the community. Catchpole rightly notes that Peter enters the tomb first "...but the extra-specialness of the BD is carefully affirmed – he it is who sees and believes, whereas Peter only sees. In short, there is only one prototypical resurrection believer, and only one person to whom the evangelist and his community look back to provide legitimacy to their own resurrection belief. And that one person is not Peter!"[213] Ridderbos also states, "...what the Evangelist has in mind with this interlude about the two disciples, which

---

[209] Köstenberger, *A Theology of John's Gospel*, 257.

[210] Glasson notes some of the significant texts that deal with 'seeing': 1:14, 'we beheld his glory'; 1:29, 36, 'behold the lamb of God'; 1:39, 46, 'Come and see'; 1:50 f., 'Ye shall see the heaven opened, and the angels of God ascending and descending upon the Son of man'; 6:40, 'everyone that beholdeth the Son'; 12:21'Sir, we would see Jesus'; 14:9, 'he that hath seen me hath seen the Father'; 14:19, 'the world beholdeth me no mere but ye behold me'; 16:16, 'a little while and ye behold me no more...ye shall see me'; 17:24, 'that they may behold my glory'; 19:35, 'he that hath seen...hath testified'. T. F. Glasson, *Moses in the Fourth Gospel*, SBT (London: SCM Press Ltd., 1963), 34-35.

[211] George Mulakuzhyil, *The Christocentric Literary Structure of the Fourth Gospel* (Roma: Editrice Pontificio Istituto Biblico, 1987), 339.

[212] There is a better possibility that is suggested by Haechen. He notes that v. 9 states the reason for seeing the different things in the tomb as they did not know that the scriptures predicted the resurrection of Jesus. Haenchen, *John 2*, 208.

[213] Catchpole further elucidates the importance of the BD: a) representative person; b) the Johannine community bases the revelation on him, i.e., the BD is the foundation of the "theological and religious position;" c) the community looks for approval from the BD; d) the BD is higher than Peter. Catchpoe, *Resurrected People*, 168, 171.

precedes all the appearances of the resurrected Jesus is to highlight this unique character of the Easter event in the whole framework of Jesus' departure and ascension to his Father (cf. v.17)."[214]

The disclosure of an empty tomb did have the intended effect, but this is restricted to the BD. Resurrection is a sign, and the empty tomb is also a sign[215] within this sign. It is a sign because it points to something else and reveals the identity of Jesus which he described in chap. 14.

3.3.4. John 20:11-18: Disclosure of the Son's Identity in the Father

In the earlier episode, the empty tomb served as a point of disclosure for the BD. The disclosure was not essentially the revelation of the person of Jesus, yet it can also be termed as a disclosure—the disclosure of a sign. Jesus' identity is disclosed in several places. The community acknowledges Jesus' presence as that of the "only Son from the Father" (Jn.1:14). In the FG, there are also several occasions where Jesus' messiahship is affirmed: the encounter with the Samaritan woman (Jn. 4), the healing of the blind man (Jn. 9) and a discussion on the Messiah in Jn. 6. The FG moves beyond just messiahship to a Christology that acknowledges the Father-Son relationship. The language of coming and going which signifies the origin of Jesus, illustrates this unique relationship with the Father. The identity of the Son remains in the identity of the Father and this is very clearly presented in this episode.

3.3.4.1. Context

The previous section ended with the disciples going back to their homes. This indicates a completion of one disclosure and anticipates another disclosure with Mary Magadalene. The question of where Jesus is still remains unanswered. There were hints conveyed in the previous episode: the open entrance, the linen cloths, and the napkin. These function as only indicators which convey the effects of resurrection. The presence of Jesus still awaits an unveiling, and the narrator has built this into the narrative.

3.3.4.2. Structure

In line with the theme of the episode, the structure is as follows: vv. 11-13, Mary's distress and discovery of the angels; vv. 14-15, Mary's discovery of the 'gardener;' and vv. 16-18, the Master discloses the Father-Son relationship.

---

[214] Ridderbos, *The Gospel of John*, 635.

[215] Lee terms the empty tomb as the "...symbol of living, resurrected Jesus, also the angels seated in the tomb. In both cases, the absence becomes paradoxically a divine presence, indicated also by the garden which is a symbol of fecundity and life." Lee, "Resurrection and Life," 227.

3.3.4.3. Translation

11 But Mary stood outside near[216] the tomb crying. While she was weeping, she stooped to look into the tomb

12 and observed two angels in white, one at the head and the other at the feet, where Jesus' body had been lying.

13 They asked[217] her, "Woman, why are you crying?" She said to them, "Because they have taken away my Lord and I do not know where they have put him."

14 After saying this she turned round and saw Jesus standing[218] there, but she did not know that it was Jesus.

15 Jesus asked her, "Woman why are you weeping? Whom do you seek?" She[219] supposing that he was the gardener, said to him, "Sir, if you have carried him away, tell me where you have put him and I will go[220] and get him."[221]

16 Jesus said to her, "Mary!" She turned and said to him in Hebrew, "Rabboni!" (which means "Teacher.")

17 Jesus said to her, "Stop clinging on to me,[222] for I have not yet ascended to the Father; but go to my brothers and say to them, 'I am ascending[223] to my Father and your Father, to my God and your God.'"

18 Mary Magdalene went and announced to the disciples, "I have seen the Lord, and told them what[224] he had said to her.

---

[216] BDF note that πρὸς with dative case occurs only six times in the NT (Mk 5:11, Lk 19:37, Jn. 18:16; 20:11) and always local 'near, at, by.' BDF, 125.

[217] Lit. "they say to her" but since a question follows, it could be rendered as "they asked her." Newman and Nida, *A Translator's Handbook on the Gospel of John*, 608.

[218] Ἑστῶτα (perfect) used intransitively with present sense (standing). Zerwick and Grosvenor, *A Grammatical Analysis*, 345.

[219] Lit. ἐκείνη - that woman.

[220] Lit. "I will take him away" but Newman and Nida note that the action of "going" is implicit in the context. Newman and Nida, *A Translator's Handbook on the Gospel of John*, 610.

[221] The use of αὐτόν is termed by BDF as *Constructio ad sensum* with αὐτου. They note, "The 3rd person pronoun etc. is often used without formal agreement, i.e., without a noun present in the same gender and number to which it would refer." BDF, 147.

[222] Zerwick points that Μή with ἅπτου (present imperative) suggests stopping a continuing action. Zerwick and Grosvenor, *A Grammatical Analysis*, 345. BDF also note that it is an action "...already happened or has been attempted." BDF, 172.

[223] Fanning sees the present used here in a futuristic sense with "...only the *intention, pledge or expectation* to act in the present: both the process and its termination are future... The present is used here by extension...inasmuch as the act is regarded as already underway, even if only in its intention." Buist M. Fanning, *Verbal Aspect in New Testament Greek*, Oxford Monographs (Oxford: Clarendon Press, 1990), 223.

[224] Lit. these things (ταῦτα).

3.3.4.4. Exegetical Notes

3.3.4.4.1. Vv. 11-13: Mary's Distress and Discovery of the Angels

One is not sure when Mary came to the tomb after reporting the disappearance of Jesus' body to Peter and the BD.[225] It is reasonable to suppose that v.11 continues from v. 3, where Mary discovers the empty tomb. Though Mary was the first to discover the stone rolled away from the entrance of the tomb, she does not enter in, unlike Peter and the BD. Δέ indicates a contrast[226] between the disciples who went home and Mary who stood outside weeping (κλαίουσα).[227] The reason for weeping[228] is because Jesus' body is missing. Beasley-Murray notes that among the Jews of that time, desecration of the dead was an appalling event (ex. 1 Sam. 31:9-13).[229] Mary's focus seems to be on the missing body of Jesus. Like the BD, she too stoops down to observe (the BD stoops down to see) two angels sitting at the head and feet,[230] where the body of Jesus was. This is something that Peter and the BD had not seen, nor were provided with such an opportunity.[231] Like the σουδάριον this too is a sign. Mary's first appearance was at the foot of the cross (19:25), a typification of loyalty and the same loyalty continues in her search for the missing body

---

[225] The difficulties in reconciling the stories of Mary Magdalene at the grave and Peter and the BD have led Bultmann to conclude that the former comes from the traditions belonging to the synoptic accounts but the latter refers back to the Evangelist. Bultmann, *The Gospel of John*, 681. Though this may be the case, yet it is difficult to conclude on this possibility.

[226] Carson, *The Gospel according to John*, 639.

[227] The term stands for loud wailing distinctive to the people in the ancient Near East. Gerald L. Brochert, *John 12-21*, The New American Commentary 25B, edited by E. Ray Clendenen (Nashville: Broadman and Holman Publishers, 2002), 297-298.

[228] Mary's weeping comes possibly from her frustration and grief, which further prevents her from understanding the significance of resurrection. Lee, "Resurrection and Life," 223.

[229] The incident narrates of how the Philistines expose the bodies of Saul and his sons. The bodies are recovered and a fitting burial is given by the brave men of Jabesh-Gilead. Beasley-Murray, *John*, 374.

[230] The angelophany recalls the synoptic accounts: Mk. 16: 5 – has a young man dressed in white sitting on the right hand dressed in white robe; Matt. 28:2-3- the angel of the Lord descends from heaven and rolls back the stone and the appearance of the angel is described as like lightning and the clothing white as snow); Lk. 24:4 - two men in flashing clothing. Also the appearance of angels signals the event of God's intervention with people (cf. Lk. 1:26-38; Gen. 19:1). Köstenberger, *A Theology of John's Gospel*, 258. Saeed Hamid-Khani is of the view that the two angels signify the cherubim at the mercy seat. Saeed Hamid-Khani, *Revelation and Concealment of Christ: A Theologial Enquiry into the Elusive Language of the Fourth Gospel* WUZNT 2/120 (Tübingen: Mohr Siebeck, 2000), 71. Barrett is of view that the description of the angels sitting at the head and feet does not refer to an independent tradition. Barrett, *The Gospel according to St. John*, 469.

[231] Bennema is of the view that Peter and the BD were denied the opportunity to see the angels, though he does not dwell on the reasons for such a denial. Bennema, *Encountering Jesus*, 197.

of Jesus.[232] It is this search that enables her to see what Peter and the BD did not see. They went to the same place, at the same time (if one takes Mary as present while Peter and BD were at the tomb), but the difference lies in the aspect of seeking.

The sight of the angels[233] does testify that the powers of heaven are involved here.[234] This is a reasonable conclusion to the resurrection in the synoptics but not so with the FG. This reference to the angels could be part of the source that the evangelist makes use of, but it has much more significance than resurrection as an act of God. So, it indicates resurrection both as an invasion of God's power, and with angels as testifying to the activity of the Father, as stated by Carson,[235] and Schnackenburg;[236] they highlight the fact that Jesus is the Son of man, on whom the angels descend and ascend (Jesus' reply to Nathaniel Jn. 1:51).[237] The motif of fear commonly associated with heavenly visitation does not take place here. However, it does appear in Jn. 20:19 where the disciples are said to fear the Jews.

The angels do not relieve Mary's anguish (v. 13) as seen in the synoptic narratives: their reply is neither in the form of statements like in Mk. 16:6 and in Matt. 28:5 nor in the form of a question like in Lk. 24.[238] Instead of being messengers of the good news, they ask Mary the reason for her weeping. Ridderbos notes that the question by the angels to Mary is a hint for her to leave aside her anguish and recognize the reality of Jesus' return to life.[239] Unlike the BD, Mary is still not able to understand the significance of disappearance of the body of Jesus and the appearance of angels in the tomb. Beasley-Murray rightly affirms that the question by the angles is "to elucidate the quest for Jesus."[240] In other words: where does the Lord belong? The reply of Mary to

---

[232] Lee notes, "Behind her tears are love and determination as well as misunderstanding." Lee, "Resurrection and Life," 223.

[233] Angels are commonly depicted as dressed in white (Dan. 10:5-6; Ezek. 9:2; Rev. 15:6). Their appearance in pairs is a common description of heavenly visitations (Acts 1:10; 2 Macc. 3:26). Köstenberger, *John*, 567.

[234] Beasley-Murray, *John*, 374.

[235] Carson, *The Gospel according to John*, 640.

[236] Schnackenburg, *The Gospel according to St. John*, vol. 3, 315-316.

[237] Beasley-Murray enumerates that the presence of angels is a reminder of another order –"it witnesses that *God*, not robbers, has taken Jesus, for purpose yet to be revealed."Beasley-Murray, *John*, 374.

[238] Here, the reading in the *Nestle-Aland Novum Testamentum Graece* (Stuttgart: Deutsche Bibelgesellschaft, 2006) and not *The Greek New Testament*, 4th edition. The reason for taking the former and not the latter is that the former takes it as a question, which seems to be a reasonable proposition.

[239] Ridderbos, *The Gospel of John*, 636.

[240] Beasley-Murray, *John*, 374.

the angels is similar to her report to Peter and the BD in Jn. 20:2, but instead of οἴδαμεν (v. 2) she uses οἶδα (v. 13).[241] The puzzling feature is the shift to 1st person plural seen earlier in the use of οἴδαμεν. The most probable solution is that it is a veiled reference to the community.[242]

There is another aspect of disclosure, and this time it is in the form of the presence of the angels. Her desperation to find the body and not the person blinds Mary from seeing the significance behind the appearance of the angels. In effect, it spells out the unexpected nature of resurrection as seen in the synoptic gospels though there still remains a difference. The idea is resurrection as going back to the Father which is, resurrection in terms of the Father-Son relationship. Misunderstanding continues to be used by the narrator as a feature to present the situation and also leads the episode to a climatic point.

3.3.4.4.2. Vv. 14-15: Mary's Discovery of the 'Gardener'

Mary becomes aware of the presence of another near the tomb but like the other synoptic resurrection narratives, she fails to recognize the Lord (Lk. 24: 16 Matt. 28:17; Jn. 21:4). Despite her misunderstanding, she persists in her search.[243]

Jesus addresses Mary as woman, a neutral term which does not signify any disrespect, an address which is also directed to Jesus' mother in 2:4; 19:26. The question "why are you weeping"[244] is a repetition of the question asked by the angels, and also has an element of empathizing with Mary's grief. However, the second question "what do you seek?" relates to a question of identity. The question shares affinities with Lk. 24:5.[245] Schnackenburg notes that the question directs Mary's attention from herself to Jesus.[246] Bennema opines that

---

[241] Mary's use of ὅτι could imply a direct speech or a causative meaning, 'because.' Barrett, *The Gospel according to St. John*, 469.

[242] Köstenberger and others take it to refer that Mary was in the company of other women, especially when it was still dark and at a time Jerusalem was crowded with visitors during religious festivals. Köstenberger, *John*, 562. Carson notes that the plural denotes a mode of speech without a plural indicator. Carson, *The Gospel according to John*, 635. Barrett notes that it is not simply borrowed from the synoptic narrative as οἴδαμεν does not occur there and there is such report brought by women. Barrett, *The Gospel according to St. John*, 563. Howard-Brook suggests that "we" signifies the "...wonder about the mystery of the empty tomb." Howard-Brook, *Becoming Children of God*, 442. Haenchen notes of two possibilities: a) the redactor is drawing from the synoptic tradition; b) probably an "oriental manner of speaking." Haenchen, *John 2*, 209.

[243] Lee, "Partnership in Easter Faith:" 41.

[244] Carson takes the question as a mild rebuke. Carson, *The Gospel according to John*, 641. This need not be the case.

[245] Here, again the reading in the *Nestle-Aland Novum Testamentum Graece* (Stuttgart: Deutsche Bibelgesellschaft, 2006) and not *The Greek New Testament*, 4th edition.

[246] Schnackenburg, *The Gospel according to St. John*, vol. 3, 317.

unlike the synoptics, it is not the angels who reveal to Mary Magdalene the resurrection of Jesus but Jesus himself. This is because for the FE, "...Jesus is the Revealer *par excellence*."[247]

Mary's words to the gardener[248] reveal her misunderstanding.[249] She asks him[250] for the body so that it could relieve her from despair.[251] The irony is clear, Mary goes about looking for the dead body of Jesus whereas the body has resurrected. Moloney notes the irony in Mary's question. He states, "The one whose body she is seeking is asked for a solution to the mystery of the empty tomb."[252] It is probable that the newness of the tomb led Mary to the assumption that the gardener may have removed Jesus' body to another place without any enmity.[253] The repetition of Mary's complaint (earlier to the angels in 20:13) and now to Jesus intensifies the narrative, emphasizing Mary's distress as well as remedy to be provided by Jesus.[254]

3.3.4.4.3. Vv. 16-18: The Master Discloses the Father-Son Relationship

Jesus' address as Μαριάμ (v.16) clears her misunderstanding. The comment by the narrator on the disciples not knowing the Scripture also probably includes Mary (Jn. 20:9), as disciples in the FG are not limited to the twelve disciples. This confirms Jesus' words in 10:3 "My sheep know my voice."[255]

---

[247] Bennema, *Excavating John's Gospel*, 214.

[248] This term is considered as *Hapax legomenon* and can be translated as 'Sir.' Barrett, *The Gospel according to St. John*, 469.

[249] Hamid-Khani describes this as situational irony which has an element of unawareness. Hamid-Khani, *Revelation and Concealment*, 78.

[250] Wyatt makes a comparison between the garden mentioned in the resurrection narrative and the garden of Eden. He concludes, "As the first Man had been raised from the dust as the primordial King, now the second Man, also raised from the dust in resurrection, took up hid rightful place in the garden. Indeed, he now resumed the task, as gardener, of tilling the soil and caring for Eden, from which the first Man has been banished." Nicolas Wyatt, ""'Supposing Him to Be the Gardner" (John 20, 15): A Study of the Paradise Motif in John," *ZNW* 81/1-2 (1990): 21-38, especially 38.

[251] Haenchen notes of the unrealistic statement of Mary in v. 15: a) the question of how Mary will take the body; b) there is no mention of another grave that is prepared. Haenchen, *John 2*, 209. Bruce supposes from the statement of Mary that she was a wealthy woman who was able to pay the expenses involved. Bruce, *The Gospel of John*, 389.

[252] Moloney, *The Gospel of John*, 525. Barrett takes this as technique which the FE evangelist uses, i.e, "...his literary formula of enlightenment through initial misunderstanding; indeed this is the supreme example of the device, for it is not a metaphor but Jesus himself who is mistaken." Barrett, *The Gospel according to St. John*, 469.

[253] Beasley-Murray, *John*, 375.

[254] Schnackenburg, *The Gospel according to St. John*, vol. 3, 314, 317.

[255] Schnackenburg, *The Gospel according to St. John*, vol. 3, 317. Barrett, *The Gospel according to St. John*, 469.

Moloney notes that Mary's response conveys a deep sense of intimacy,[256] but Köstenberger views it as Mary's inability to still not understand the reality of Jesus' resurrection.[257] Ridderbos opines that the address has a "strong personal and affective component."[258] Beasley-Murray rightly notes, "All the love and faith and joy which her illuminated heart and mind were capable were poured into that word: *Teacher*."[259] Certainly the meeting with Jesus creates a deeper level of understanding in Mary, and this is seen in her act that follows her address to Jesus.[260]

V. 17 forms the climax of the revelation of identity of the resurrected Jesus. The evangelist deliberately has avoided using the angels as harbingers of the resurrected Jesus in order to leave the importance of revelation to Jesus himself.[261] There is much debate among scholars on the words of Jesus: Μή μου ἅπτου. The discussion among scholars centres around whether Mary had already touched Jesus or if she was about to do so? Those that say that Mary

---

[256] Moloney, *The Gospel of John*, 528.

[257] Köstenberger, *John*, 569. Gustaf Dalman, *The Words of Jesus: Considered in the Light of Post-biblical Jewish Writings and the Aramaic Langugage*, translated by D. M. Kay (Edinburgh: T & T Clark, 1902), 340. More importantly, as suggested by Lee, "…names in the ancient world having the power to evoke identity and presence, as well as relationship (20:16)." Lee, "Resurrection and Life," 223.

[258] Ridderbos, *The Gospel of John*, 637.

[259] Beasley-Murray, *John*, 375. This is contrary to Bultmann who sees that Mary still continues in her state of misunderstanding. Bultmann, *The Gospel of John*, 687.

[260] Schneiders connects the address of Mary to the context of the Johannine community. She states, "Here, Mary, symbolic representative of the New Israel, the Johannine community and the readers, makes the salvific choice: Jesus, Jesus alone, is the Teacher, even– according to John- for the Jews." Sandra M. Schneiders, "John 20:11-18: The Encounter of the Easter Jesus with Mary Magadalene- A Transformative Feminist Reading," in "*What is John?,*" vol. 1: *Readers and Readings of the Fourth Gospel*, SBL Symposium Series 3, edited by F. F. Segovia (Atlanta: Scholars Press, 1996), 164. One is not sure whether this reading of Schneiders is viable, chiefly for the reason that the identity of Jesus as well the identity of the Johannine community is communicated and affirmed in the words of Jesus that follow Mary's address. Rather she shared a relationship earlier which is reaffirmed in her recognition of Jesus' voice. It is on the basis of this relationship that Jesus commissions her. However, what was ratified in this encounter is the unique relationship that Jesus shared with the Father which makes possible a redrawing of relationship between the disciples and the Father and certainly Mary is included in this.

[261] Catchpole rightly notes, "The repetition of both the incorrect inference form the tomb's openness (vv. 2, 13, 15) and the question (vv. 13, 15) serves to shift all the attention towards meeting with Jesus…" Catchpole, *Resurrected People*, 158.

had already touched Jesus include Morris,[262] Schnackenburg,[263] and R. E. Brown.[264] On the contrary, Bultmann[265] and Beasley-Murray[266] hold that Mary did not touch Jesus but was about to do so. There are several questions that remain if one takes the prohibition to mean "do not touch me."[267] The most feasible view point on a grammatical level[268] (the use of present imperative) is that Mary on recognizing Jesus proceeded to cling on to Jesus[269] and Jesus forbids doing so. This goes on well with what Matthew describes of women to whom Jesus appears in Matt. 28:9: they seized the feet of Jesus and worshipped him.[270]

However, the grammatical level does not take into consideration the syntactical interpretations of 20:17. The different syntactical interpretations

262 Morris rightly notes that the use of the negative with present imperative is a command to stop doing an action and does not mean "Do not start something." Thus could mean "Stop clinging on to me" and not "Do not begin to touch me." Morris, *The Gospel according to John*, 742.

263 Schnackenburg translates the phrase as "Do not hold on to me any longer, let go!" Schnackenburg, *The Gospel according to St. John*, vol. 3, 318.

264 Brown, *The Gospel according to John (xiii-xxi)*, 992.

265 Bultmann, *The Gospel of John*, 687.

266 Beasley-Murray notes that Mary attempts to take hold of Jesus. Beasley-Murray, *John*, 376.

267 Bieringer opines that the questions could be: a. does this imply that after Jesus has ascended to the Father, Jesus may well be touched?; b. does not the fact that Jesus has not yet ascended to the Father be a reason that Jesus can still be touched?; c. Is the prohibition to do with Mary Magdalene than in Jesus?; d. when Thomas is invited to touch, does it mean that Jesus has ascended in between the appearance to Mary Magdalene and Thomas and therefore could now be touched? Bieringer, ""I am ascending to my Father and your Father," 210.

268 This viewpoint is also not without its share of questions. This would suggest that the risen Jesus' manner of existence is only temporary or transitory and the focus shifts to ascension. Theobald goes to the extent of taking the resurrection appearance only as a "…sign of Jesus' Easter reality." Michael Theobald, "Der johanneische Osterglaube und die Grenzen siener narrative Vermittlung (Joh 20)," in *Von Jesus zum Christus. Christologische Studien, Festgabe für Paul Hoffmann zum 65. Geburtstag*, edited by Rudolf Hoppe and Ulrich Busse (Berlin: de Gruyter, 1998), 93-123, cited in Bieringer, ""I am ascending to my Father and your Father," 211.

269 There are several viewpoints raised regarding this prohibition. Smith sees the prohibition because Jesus has not ascended and Thomas can do so because Jesus has ascended. D. Moody Smith, *John*, Abingdon New Testament Commentaries (Nashville: Abingdon Press, 1999), 378. Interestingly the word "touch" is not used in the Thomas episode. Both can be compared or contrasted. More plausible is the view it as a prohibition to cling on to Jesus.

270 Beasley-Murray takes the term κρατέω in Matt. 28:9 as synonymous with ἅπτομαὶ. He further notes, "It is even possible that Matthews' statement about the women generalizes the action of Mary." Beasley-Murray, *John*, 376. Neyrey opines that there is a gender issue in Mary of Bethany and Mary Magadlene being allowed to touch Jesus' feet which is a gesture of intimacy and high status. Neyrey, *The Gospel of John*, 325.

are detailed by Bieringer.[271] Six clauses can be inferred from v.17: 17a λέγει αὐτῇ Ἰησοῦς, 17b μή μου ἅπτου 17c οὔπω γὰρ ἀναβέβηκα πρὸς τὸν πατέρα· 17d πορεύου δὲ πρὸς τοὺς ἀδελφούς μου 17e καὶ εἰπὲ αὐτοῖς 17f ἀναβαίνω πρὸς τὸν πατέρα μου καὶ πατέρα ὑμῶν καὶ θεόν μου καὶ θεὸν ὑμῶν.[272]

The discussions among scholars revolve around the 'prohibition' in the second clause (Μή μου ἅπτου) and its relation with the other clauses. In other words, to which clause is the prohibition connected, though some would not take 17b as a prohibition.[273] Some scholars take γὰρ (17c) as a "marker of cause or reason" that introduces a clause which reason for the prohibition stated in v. 17b. This has the support of a great majority of scholars.[274] Michael Thombard takes v.17c as necessary in the context to state the reason why Mary Magdalene should not cling on to Jesus and rephrases 20:17 as: "Do not hold on to me, for I have not yet ascended to the Father (my mode of existence as *risen one* is not yet my actual mode of existence with the Father, but it is only provisional)."[275] Zerwick concurs that γὰρ introduces what follows but not with 17b but 17d. He proposes this translation: "Do not keep hold of me, for (I am not ascended to My Father) go rather to My brethren and tell them..."[276] Zerwick takes this as an example of μὲν γὰρ... δὲ construction in which case the actual reason is not stated in the immediate clause but the next clause (in this case).[277]

---

[271] The arguments of scholars on varied syntactical interpretation of 20:17 are noted by Bieringer, ""I am ascending to my Father and your Father," 210-217. But the researcher would differ from Bieringer on the concluding interpretation as it seems incongruent with Johannine understanding of the Father-Son relationship.

[272] Bieringer, ""I am ascending to my Father and your Father," 210.

[273] Bultmann, *The Gospel of John*, 687.

[274] Bieringer, ""I am ascending to my Father and your Father," 210.

[275] Michael Theobald, "Der johanneische Osterglaube," cited in Bieringer, ""I am ascending to my Father and your Father," 211. Mary's effort to grasp Jesus contains recalls with Song of Songs 3:1-3. Stibbe comments that the narrator is describing a "'comic romance.'" Stibbe, *John*, 205.

[276] Maxmilian Zerwick, *Biblical Greek. Illustrated by Examples*, Scripta Pontificii Instituti Biblici 114, edited by Joseph Smith (Rome: Biblical Institute, 1963), 160, cited in Bieringer, ""I am ascending to my Father and your Father," 211. Lee seems to take a similar meaning, when she notes tha the present imperative describes a continuing aspect, i.e., "do not go on touching me." Lee, "Resurrection and Life," 225.

[277] Zerwick, *Biblical Greek*, 159, cited in Bieringer, ""I am ascending to my Father and your Father," 212. Bieringer also notes the major drawback of this interpretation: 17c and 17d is very different from each other to be correlated in a μὲν... δὲ construction. Bieringer, ""I am ascending to my Father and your Father," 212.

McGehee[278] take γὰρ as anticipatory.[279] This implies that there is a full stop after v.17b and a new thought begins in v.17c. He rephrases v.17 as: "Don't cling to me. Since I have not ascended to the Father, go to my brothers and tell them I am ascending to my Father and your Father..."[280] The focus shifts from Jesus ascending to the Father to Mary Magdalene being commissioned to tell the disciples that Jesus is in the process of ascending. This view is also beset with limitations such as being "tautological" and there is no direct evidence of an anticipatory γὰρ in the New Testament.

Lagrange[281] sees the connection between γὰρ and δὲ but the former does not have a 'motivational meaning.' For him, δὲ does not apply to v. 17d but to v. 17f, and so v. 17d and v. 17e are taken as parenthetical. The emphasis falls on v.17f which takes the motivation for the prohibition in v. 17b. [282] The effectiveness of this view is that v. 17b goes well with 20:27 and the other resurrection narratives where Jesus allows Thomas to touch him.[283] But the danger of such a reading is that it "does violence to the text."[284]

A different understanding of v. 17c is provided by Sandra M. Schneiders, who takes v. 17c not as a declarative sentence but as a question. She paraphrases 17c as: "For I have already ascended to the Father, haven't I?" Thus, the prohibition points to a transition that is different; therefore, the previous conception of Jesus does not lend meaning.[285] The difficulty with this interpretation is that out of the four of the twenty-six examples in the NT used in questions expecting an answer "yes" (Mk. 4:40; 8:17; 8:21; Matt. 16:11), there is no occurrence of οὔπω with γὰρ. In Gen. 15:16 LXX, 2 Macc. 7:35, and Jn. 3:24 where it is used, there is no clear indication that it is used in questions. The immediate context also does not warrant such an interpretation

---

278 Michael McGehee, "A Less Theological Reading of John 20:17," *JBL* 105/2 (Je. 1986): 299-302.

279 McGehee, "A Less Theological Reading:" 299-302.

280 McGehee, "A Less Theological Reading:" 302.

281 M. J. Lagrange, *Evangile selon Saint Jean* (Paris: Gabalda, 1936), 512, cited in Bieringer, ""I am ascending to my Father and your Father," 213.

282 Lagrange, *Evangile selon Saint Jean*, cited in Bieringer, ""I am ascending to my Father and your Father," 213.

283 Barrett states, "A possible conclusion from these facts is that John believed that between vv. 17 and 22 the ascension, or at least the complete glorification, of Jesus had taken place. But it must be admitted that he does not say so..." Barrett, *The Gospel according to St. John*, 470.

284 Bieringer, ""I am ascending to my Father and your Father," 214.

285 Schneiders, *Written that you might Believe*, 198. She also notes, "...I would suggest that what Jesus us really doing is redirecting Mary's desire for union with himself from his physical or earthly body...to the new locus of his presence in the world, that is, the community of his brothers and sisters, the disciples." Schneiders, "John 20:11-18: The Encounter of the Easter Jesus," 164-165.

– if Jesus has already ascended, then the commissioning of Mary to tell the disciples that Jesus is ascending is incongruous.[286]

The syntactic interpretation does not seem to offer inroads into the understanding of prohibition in v. 17b and the clause that follows in v. 17c. In other words, how is the prohibition clause (v. 17b) related to v.17? Bieringer also analyses the tradition-critical and redaction-critical approaches to Jn. 20:17. Different approaches raise the question of whether v. 17b, 17c, and 17f present a view contrary to the rest of the FG or not.[287]

Bieringer tries to find the solution to the problem of prohibition by taking a 'compositional-critical approach' to Jn. 20:17. He notes that the exact wording of 20: 17c and 17f is absent elsewhere in the FG but the idea is implicit. He also agrees that in 20:17c the FE is describing a process of ascension that is yet to be completed. In order to express this idea, the FE chose ἀναβαίνω, a "durative *Aktionsart*." The specific meaning related to ἀναβαίνω is its relation to the Temple. He notes, "The going up to Jerusalem to the temple in pilgrimage is the model for Jesus going up to the Father through his crucifixion and resurrection. In doing so Jesus opens the access to God for the believers and God becomes their Father and their God."[288] He further notes that ἅπτομαι in the LXX means to touch (no evidence of it meaning to seize or to cling), and there are many instances where it implies draw near, to reach. Thus, for him, the negated present imperative does not command to stop an ongoing action in the immediate preceding context and does not suggest that Mary Magdalene actually touches Jesus. In the book of Numbers ἅπτομαι is used in a cultic context (3:10, 28; 17:28). Also there are many examples in Numbers where the word ἅπτομαι is used for touching objects both holy or unholy. Using these different insights, Bieringer proposes that 20:17[289] can be read as: "It is not me as the risen Christ whom you have to approach and worship, but I will open access to God. When I have made pilgrimage to the Father and have prepared a place in my Father's house for you, you will be able to make this

---

[286] Bieringer, "I am ascending to my Father and your Father," 215-216.

[287] For example, Hartman notes that the prohibition of touch and reference to the ascension has no parallels in the tradition that the evangelist used, especially the combination of Vanabai,nw with the Son of Man title. Gert Hartmann, "Die Vorlafge," cited in Bieringer, ""I am ascending to my Father and your Father," 218. Frans Neiyrnck is of the view that John transposed the theology of ascension in 20:17c on the basic Matthean structure (Matt. 28:0-10). Frans Neirynck, *Evanelica, Gospel Studies- Etudes d'évangile:Collected Essays* (Leuven: Leuven University Press, 1991), 571-600, cited in Bieringer, ""I am ascending to my Father and your Father," 221.

[288] Bieringer, ""I am ascending to my Father and your Father," 233.

[289] Loader notes, "Unlike the other usages which has εἰς following the verb "go up" (2:13; 5:1; 7:8; 7:14; 3:13) in John 20:17 uses the preposition προς after ἀναβαινειν." Loader, *The Christology of the Fourth Gospel*, 123.

pilgrimage also and in my Father's house we shall all together experience the new communion."[290]

For Bieringer, Jn. 20:17 is a correction of Matt. 28: 9-10 as even the risen Christ is not to be worshipped but God, the Father. Thus, he interprets v. 17 not as 'chronological' but from a 'theocentric perspective.'[291] This theological interpretation of Bieringer is innovative and does look into the different nuances of ἅπτομαι and ἀναβαίνω. Though Bieringer takes a theological interpretation, he does not represent well the entire Christology of the FG.[292] Jn. 9 narrates the healing of the blind and reactions of the Pharisees and the Jews to the healing on the Sabbath. The narrative takes the course of conflict, focusing on whether Jesus is God or not. The blind man says to the Jews, who question the very identity of Jesus, "If this man were not from God, he could do nothing." (9:33). Later Jesus finding the blind man reveals his identity and the blind man in turn replies "Lord, I believe;" and he worshiped him. (9:38). This text clearly refutes the theory of Bieringer that Jesus is not to be worshipped but God the Father alone. It is only in the FG (other than Hebrews) that Christ is God. The occurrences come at the beginning (Jn. 1:1 ὁ λόγος ἦν πρὸς τὸν θεόν) and at the end (if one takes chap. 21 as epilogue) in the confession of Thomas (Jn. 20:28 - ὁ κύριός μου καὶ ὁ θεός μου). Having noted this unique feature in the FG, there is no denying that there is a degree of mutuality involved in the

---

[290] Bieringer, ""I am ascending to my Father and your Father," 232.

[291] Bieringer, ""I am ascending to my Father and your Father," 222-232.

[292] However, it must be said that Christology in the FG has two sides: a. Jesus as one with the Father and also b. Jesus as the Son who is obedient to the Father. There is a great deal of discussion on what this essentially means. Barrett in his *Essays on John* discusses the theme 'Subordinationist Christology' in the New Testament. For him, 5:1-47 explains the Son does the things God does but in a secondary, dependent relationship. He qualifies this statement by noting that all the 'subordinationist' material that he has discussed (5:1-47; 10:22-39) cannot be interpreted in terms of eternal relations between the Person of the Trinity. It rather belongs within the setting the FE has provided for it, i.e., the historic ministry. Thus, Barrett concludes that the FE's "christocentricity is theocentric." C. K. Barrett, *Essays on John* (London: SPCK, 1982), 28, 32. Smalley is of the view that the FG states that Jesus shared the two natures but also pointed the way towards resolution which such a Christology involves. Stephen S. Smalley, *John: Evangelist and Interpreter* (New York: Thomas Nelson Publishers, 1984), 213. O'Grady takes a counter view. The author of the gospel does not solve the precise relationship between divinity and humanity but with careful progression leads from humanity to divinity without losing anything in the process. John F. O'Grady, "The Human Jesus in the Fourth Gospel," *BibThBul* 14/2 (Apr. 1984): 66. Beasley-Murray is of the view that in the FG the function and person are not separable. For him the functions of the Christ envisioned are expressive of his person. George R. Beasley-Murray, *Gospel of Life: Theology in the Fourth Gospel* (Massachusetts: Hendrickson Publishers, 1991), 32. Also refer Marinus de Jonge, *Jesus: Stranger from Heaven and Son of God: Jesus Christ and the Christians in Johannine Perspective*, translated by John E. Steeley (Montana: Scholars Press, 1977), 36; Barrett, *The Gospel according to St. John*, 54. All these discussions present the complexities involved in the Father-Son relationship and this is taken up in the next chapter.

Father-Son relationship, in which case the Father does nothing without the Son and vice versa.

The prohibition to Mary (to stop clinging on to Jesus) finds its meaning in ascending[293] to the Father.[294] Kanagaraj opines rightly, "Perhaps the best interpretation is one that takes the particle 'for' with Jesus' command, 'go to my brethren and say to them,' rather than with His statement, 'I have not yet ascended to the Father.' In other words Jesus was telling that it was not the time

[293] The use of ἀναβαίνω is significant in the FG.' Αναβαίνω occurs 82 times in the NT (9 in synoptics, 19 in Acts, 13 in John, 4 in Paul, 3 in Ephesians, and 13 in Revelation). It signifies a movement away from the speaker then it means *going up*, *climbing up* and if it is towards the speaker then of *coming out*, *coming up* and in the absolute use means *going up* or *rising* or *coming up*, *growing up*. Johannes Beutler, "ἀναβαίνω," in *EDNT*, vol. 1, edited by Horst Balz and Gerhard Schneider (Grand Rapids, Michigan: William B. Eerdmans Publishing Company, 1990), 75. Usually it is used with a sense implying movement and it acquires a cultic meaning when the destination is a sacred place. Colin Brown, "Heaven, Ascend, Above," in *NIDNTT*, vol. 2, edited by Colin Brown (Grand Rapids, Michigan: Zondervan Publishing House, 1976), 184-185. Liddell and Scott note the special usages: Mount a ship, go on board; of land journeys; also to ascend to a higher knowledge; of things and events to come to an end; and in the causal sense, make to go up. Henry George Liddell and Robert Scott, comps., *A Greek-English Lexicon: With a Supplement*, 9th ed. (Oxford: Clarendon Press, 1968), 84. It can be said that the primary meaning is spatial, i.e., "to rise from depths to the heights." Johannes Schneider, "ἀναβαίνω," in *TDNT*, vol. 1, edited by Gerhard Kittel and Gerhard Freidrich (Grand Rapids, Michigan: William B. Eerdmans Publishing Company, 1964), 519. In the LXX ἀναβαίνω mostly translates 'ālâh (go up, ascend, climb), especially used to refer to going up to the mountain of God, sancturary and Jerusalem (Ex. 34:4; I Sam. 1:3; 2 Ki. 19:14). Beutler, "ἀναβαίνω," 75. The cultic aspect of ἀναβαίνω is frequent in the FG (2:13; 5:1; 11:55). Schneider, "ἀναβαίνω," 519. In the FG ἀναβαίνω takes on the meaning of the ascent of the Son of man and its correlate καταβαίνω complements it. The chief meaning is Jesus goes from and to God. Brown notes, "In his descent Jesus is the revealer; in his ascent the perfecter through whom his people receive the fatherhood of God and the brotherhood of the Son (Jn. 20:17)." Brown, "Heaven, Ascend, Above," 185. The Son shares a permanent relationship with the Father as seen in description of the vision of ascend and descend of angels in 1:51 (cf. Gen. 28:12). The climax of ἀναβαίνειν in the religious realm is the ἀναβαίνειν εἰς τὸν οὐρανον. Schneider, "ἀναβαίνω," 520. In the construction of Christology in the FG ἀναβαίνειν along with καταβαίνειν occupies an important place. Christ has come down from heaven and therefore knows heavenly things (3:12f.) and will ascend to the place where Christ has been before (6:62). Hoskyns takes the prohibition to Mary because it signifies to the interval between the resurrection and ascension. Hoskyns, *The Fourth Gospel*, 647.

[294] Loader notes, "In contrast with other signs, which had been reinterpreted as the *inbreaking* of divine glory into the world, the resurrection has manifestly been reinterpreted as the departure of divine glory from the world." Loader, *The Christology of the Fourth Gospel*, 128-129. Schneiders notes in this regard, "Jesus redirects Mary's attempt to relate to him by pointing her to his presence in the community where she will touch him, encounter him, in a new way corresponding to his new mode of being and presence." Sandra M. Schneiders, "The Resurrection (of the Body) in the Fourth Gospel: A Key to Johannine Spirituality," in *Life in Abundance: Studies of John's Gospel in Tribute to Raymond E. Brown*, edited by John R. Donahue (Minnesota: Liturgical Press, 2005), 188.

to keep clinging to Him, but the time to go and announce the message of the ascension to His disciples."[295] There are five references in the context of Jesus ascending to the Father (1:51; 3:13; 6:62; 20:17(2)). Other than 20:17, all the three references have to do with the Son of Man. Jn.1:51 presents an allusion to the Danielic Son of Man where the angels are said to ascend and descend on him. Further, these references deal with the pre-existent aspect of Jesus. The verb ἀναβαίνω does not figure in the Farewell Discourse nor in the Passion Narrative;[296] but this does not mean that a change of conceptual understanding is implied in the resurrection. The FE attempts to show that the one who descends from heaven is identical with the one who returns to heaven. On completion of the earthly task, Christ returns to where he is from.[297] In 20:17, there are two references to ἀναβαίνω, one put in the negative (ἀναβέβηκα perfect Tense) and the other in the positive (ἀναβαίνω Present Tense). Here, the present tense (ἀναβαίνω) signifies a 'process of ascending.' Ridderbos rightly notes that ascension denotes that the process of Jesus' glorification has not finished.[298] The reason given to Mary by Jesus for disallowing her to cling on to him is that he has not ascended[299] to the Father. The ascension brings into fruition the benefits of his departure highlighted in the Farewell Discourses: a place in the Father's house (14:2); removal of sorrow and joy of reunion (14:18-19); a redrawing of relationship where the Father and the Son will abide with them (14:21-23); and most of all the giving of the Paraclete, who reveals Jesus to them and helps them in their mission.[300] Esler and Piper rightly note, "The descent-ascent motif, which permeates the story of Jesus in this Gospel (as the one who comes from above and who returns to the Father), contributes to the sense of separateness..."[301] However, it presents not only seperateness but also a relationship; a relationship that is rooted in love. In other words, as Lindars notes, "The desire to hold Jesus must be restrained, because it is an attempt to

---

[295] Kanagaraj, *The Gospel of John*, 647.

[296] In fact, there are other verbs which also describe the aspect of departure - ὑπάγω (7:33; 14:4, 28; 16:5, 17; 8:14, 21; 13:3, 33), πορεύομαι (14:12; 16:28), ἔρχομαι (17:11), and μεταβαίνω (13:1). There seems to be a concentration of the language of departure in the Farewell Discourses (chaps. 13-17), though there are other earlier references (7:33; 8:14, 21).

[297] Schneider, "ἀναβαίνω," 521.

[298] Ridderbos, *The Gospel of John*, 638. Beasley-Murray notes "..which has not happened but is on the way, relates especially to the *work* for which he dies and rises and ascends to the Father, has been made known to the disciples, especially in the Upper Room discourses." Beasley-Murray, *John*, 377.

[299] Haenchen is of the view that οὔπω γὰρ is stated to prepare for Thomas, who later on touches Jesus. Haenchen, *John 2*, 210.

[300] Beasley-Murray, *John*, 377.

[301] Philip F. Esler and Ronald Piper, *Lazarus, Mary and Martha: Social-Scientific Approaches to the Gospel of John* (Minneapolis: Fortress Press, 2006), 106.

recapture the conditions of incarnate life in place of the universal and abiding relationship which is the object of his mission."[302]

The latter half of v. 17 deals with the commission of Mary Magdalene by Jesus. She is asked to tell the brothers the news of Jesus' resurrection and ascension. The term probably does not imply biological brothers, but those of the disciples who are to share in the sonship with the Father.[303] It expresses the view that the disciples form "...as a new family of brothers of Jesus (cf. Matthew 12:46-50; 23:8)."[304] The ascension[305] creates a re-drawing of relationship in terms of πατέρα μου and πατέρα ὑμῶν and καὶ θεόν μου καὶ θεὸν ὑμῶν.[306] The use of genitive indicates the relationship that also points to a new identity because of the ascension that is to take place. This new relationship is also related to the giving of the Spirit. The distinctions in terms are not to be highlighted and thus create an unbridgeable divide. Brown notes, "The statement of the Johannine Jesus is one of identification and not of disjunction."[307] Moloney rightly notes that in the earlier part of the FG the disciples never relate to God as "*their Father*."[308] The new situation occasions God, the Father of Jesus, who will

---

[302] Lindars, *The Gospel of John*, 607.

[303] This view is contrary to Howard-Brook, who takes it to refer to the "...*unbelieving* brothers who left Jesus behind at Tabernacles (7:1-9)." Howard-Brook, *Becoming Children of God*, 452.The researcher is of the view that the FG presents Jesus, who breaks away from traditional constructions of boundaries; the example in Jn. 4 i.e, his conversation with the Samaritan woman is one such example. In this regard Barrett states that the term "brothers" refer not to the unbelievers of 7:5. Barrett, *The Gospel according to St. John*, 470. Lee takes the reference to brothers as generic. Lee, "Resurrection and Life," 225.

[304] Catchpole, *Resurrected People*, 157.

[305] Barrett notes that ascension in the FG is not described as "an observable incident." Barrett, *The Gospel according to St. John*, 471.

[306] Kanagaraj relates this with Merkabah tradition. In this tradition, he notes, "...the mystic is transformed into one among the angels, who constitute 'the celestial family' or 'his household in the height' (*3 En.* 12.5). This also echoes the 'communal mysticism' of Qumran by which the worshippers enjoyed a sense of union with the angels is transferred in John to the 'mystical' union with the angelomorphic Son of Man...not in the sense of absorption in him but in the sense of sharing the same relationship with God." Jey J. Kanagaraj, *'Mysticism' in the Gospel of John: An Inquiry into its Background*, JSNTSup 158 (Sheffield: Sheffield Academic Press, 1998), 211.

[307] Brown, *The Gospel according to John (xiii-xxi)*, 1016. Köstenberger take it as a distinction between Jesus and the disciples' relationship with God which is probable not warranted. Andreas J. Köstenberger, *The Mission of Jesus and the Disciples*, 49. The same view is espoused by Barrett. Barrett, *The Gospel according to St. John*, 471. Bultmann also states that here the emphasis is not on the divine sonship but on the aspect that the disciples are his brothers. Bultmann, *The Gospel of John*, 689. Haenchen also notes tha the distinction has been removed. Haenchen, *John 2*, 210.

[308] Moloney, *The Gospel of John*, 526.

now also be the God and the Father of Jesus' disiciples.[309] Lee righlty notes the term signifies "...the birthing imagery of the Prologue, where those who accept the incarnate Word become God's children (*tekna theou*, 1:12; also 3:3, 5) and therefore brothers and sisters to one another, and to Jesus (cf. 15:15)."[310] She also notes the covenantal aspect, which contains "...the symbol of community as the people of God, and as sisters and brothers, come to life in and through the Easter events...."[311] Culpepper rightly comments on Jn. 20:17, when he states, "The implication is clear. The disciples have now become his brothers. The new family has been constituted."[312]

In v. 18, Mary becomes the messenger announcing the words of Jesus to the disciples. The misunderstanding seems to have cleared from Mary. Her proclamation, that she has seen the Lord, uses exactly the same words the disciples mention to Thomas. She also communicates what has been entrusted to her unlike in Mk. 16:8 where the women keep silent about the message asking the disciples and Peter to go to Galilee given to them by the young man.[313] One is not very sure whether one can take the confession of Mary to the disciples as a movement in her character from the "the margins to the center;"[314] rather one could take Mary as a major witness to the resuurection event.[315] Schneiders describes Mary "…as the official Easter witness in and

---

[309] Catchpole takes the statement of Jesus, "my Father and your Father, my God and your God" as "…one of the most severely subordinationist formulae in the 4G…" He bases this view on the angelophany traditions states in Tobit 12:20. Catchpole, *Resurrected People*, 172-173. Though it is true that Jesus acknowledges the Father is the God, the emphasis here seems to be primarily on the redrawing of relationship in which the Father has a prominent role.

[310] Lee, "Resurrection and Life," 225.

[311] Lee, "Resurrection and Life," 225.

[312] R. Alan Culpepper, "The Designs for the Church in the Gospel Accounts of Jesus' Death," *NTS* 55/3 (Jl. 2005): 389.

[313] Howard-Brook notes that the author of the Jn. 20 conveys the "superior *apostleship* of women," though Mary Magadalene fails to convince the disciples of Jesus on Jesus' victory over the forces of darkness and this has two social function: a) Johannine egalitarianism in contrast to the "Petrine" Christian communities where "male hiearachical leadership" was prevalent and b) the challenge to arrogance to those who think they hold the truth. Howard-Brook, *Becoming Children of God*, 438.

[314] Resseguie further adds there is a movement "from courier to the originator of a new language, parallels changes in names and epithets: Narrator: Mary Magadelene (19:25); Narrator: Mary Magdalene (20:1); Narrator: Mary (20:11); Angels: Woman (20:13); Jesus: Woman (20:15); Jesus: Mary (20:16); Narrator: Mary Magadelene (20:18)." Resseguie, *Narrative Criticism of the New Testament*, 145.

[315] Perkins notes, "Mary's presence among those witnesses also corrects another perception, that women's faith is derivative or inferior to males…The women in the Fourth Gospel come to faith through their own encounter with Jesus." Perkins also notes that Mary should have a place along with other witnesses in the "creedal formulas." Pheme Perkins, ""I Have Seen the Lord" (John 20:18): Women Witnesses to the Resurrection," *Int.* 46/1 (Ja. 1992): 41.

to the Johannine community. She is symbolically presented, by means of Old Testament allusions, as the beloved of the lover in the Canticle of Canticle, the spouse of the new covenant mediated by Jesus in his glorification, the representative figure of new Israel, which emerges from the new creation."[316] Schneiders has rightly stated the importance of Mary, but seems to override the BD, who also shares an equally significant place in the Johannine community. Further, the intertextual link presented by Schneiders between Jn. 20:1-18 and Song of Songs is not without its share of problems, but this is the topic of another study.[317]

The section ends with a disclosure of the risen Jesus to Mary. It seems to have gone a full cycle. Mary once again becomes the messenger to the disciples, but this time with the news of disclosure. The presence of Jesus and the words of commissioning signify more than just the aspect of resurrection. It brings to light the Son's share in the identity with the Father.

3.3.4.5. Theological Interpretation

The theme of disclosure operates on a misunderstanding. It continues to shape this pericope with Mary Magadelene as another representative, the earlier one being the BD. In fact, the misunderstanding holds the narrative together. Dialogues thrive on misunderstandings throughout the FG. There are several

---

[316] Schneiders, *Written that You May Believe*, 201.

[317] Roberts-Winsor has engaged in an elaborate study on the relation between Song of Songs and the FG. A. Roberts-Winsor, *A King is Bound in the Tresses: Allusions to the Song of Songs in the Fourth Gospel*, Studies in Biblical Literature, 6 (New York: Lang, 1999), cited in S. Van Den Eynde, "Love, Strong as Death? An Inter- and Intratextual Perspective on John 20, 1-18," in *The Death of Jesus in the Fourth Gospel,* edited by G. Van Belle, BETL (Leuven: Leuven University Press, 2007), 901. There have been other studies which have dealt on the intertextual element. Fehribach has studied the Mary Magdalene episode using scenes from the Greek love-novels and phrases from Canticle of Canticles. She is of the view that the author of the FG presents Mary as spouse in search of her husband. In this portrayal, Jesus is presented as the 'messianic bridegroom' and Mary as the 'bride-figure.'Adeline Fehribach, *The Women in the Life of the Bridegroom: A Feminist Historical-Literary Analysis of the Female Characters in the Fourth Gospel* (Collegeville: The Liturgical Press, 1998), 142-167. Another work that deals with similar perspective is by McWhirter. She sees the corresponding aspects between Jn. 20:1-18 and Song of Songs 3:1-4 and notes that Mary takes the role of the Song's bride and thus represents the Church. She, however, notes that this interpretation cannot be applied to the FG's implied audience. Jocelyn McWhirter, *The Bridegroom Messiah and the People of God: Marriage in the Fourth Gospel*, SNTSMS 138 (Cambridge: Cambridge University Press, 2006), 88-105. McConvery also discusses the same aspect. Brendan McConvery, "Hippolytus' *Commentary on the Song of Songs and John 20*: Intertexual Reading in Early Christianity," *ITQ* 71/3-4 (Jl. 2006): 211-222. Den Eynde assess the significance of the intertextual reading thus, "All these suggested references are as such very weak indications of intertextuality: without direct terminological links, only vague and ironic similiarities remain, which are unconvincing if the main arguments on the turning and touching are refuted." Den Eynde, "Love, Strong as Death?," 909.

instances where dialogues operate on two levels based on the misunderstandings (Jn. 3, 4, 6, etc.). Misunderstandings however cannot be confined to the use of words.[318] One could also say that a misunderstanding arises out of events or happenings and this is vividly presented here. The Mary Magadalene episode has several parallels with Jesus' dialogue with the Samritan woman, especially in this technique of misunderstanding. For example, in the case of the dialogue with the Samaritan woman (Jn. 4), there is a gradual development in the understanding of the Samaritan of the identity of Jesus i.e., 'Ιουδαίος (4:9), Κύριε (4:11), προφήτης (4:19), Μεσσίας (4:25). There is a gradation in the revelation of Jesus' identity, each propelled by a misunderstanding. The climax of the misunderstanding is the revelation of Jesus' identity as the Messiah. The object of misunderstanding was "living water" that Jesus provides. Here, the object of misunderstanding is the body of Jesus.

Both find the Messiah, but the Mary episode supplies the right understanding of the Messiah i.e., the Messiah shares a relationship with the Father. Up to this point, the narrative is built on a misunderstanding beginning with the empty tomb, where she mistakenly believes that the body has been taken away; after that she sees the two angels in the tomb, but still the misunderstanding continues; finally, here, she mistakes Jesus for a gardener. The narrator has carefully built the theme of disclosure by juxtaposing it with several negatives[319] that Mary Magadalene states: *οὐκ οἴδαμεν ποῦ* (20:2), *οὐκ οἶδα ποῦ ἔθηκαν αὐτόν* (20:13), *εἰπέ μοι ποῦ* (20:15—the negative is not used here). The negatives do not convey a flaw in the character of Mary.[320] The negatives find their meaning in the positive statement in 20:18—*'Εώρακα τὸν κύριον*. In the case of both the Samaritan woman and Mary Magdalene, it is Jesus who removes their misunderstandings. However, Mary does occupy a significant place in the resurrection narrative. Catchpole brings this out clearly when he notes, "...Mary is the only one who is brought to recognise the risen one, not by sight or touch nor even by the sound of his voice (for

[318] Unfortunately, several scholars look at the misunderstanding only in terms of words. J. H. Bernard defines misunderstanding: "A saying of deep import is uttered by Jesus; His hearers misunderstand it, after a fashom that seems stupid; and then He repeats the saying in a slightly different form before Je explains it and draws out its lesson." He then goes on to give six texts which have this idea (Jn. 3:3; 4: 10, 32; 6:27, 41, 51). J. H. Bernard, *A Critical and Exegetical Commentary on the Gospel according to St. John, vol. 1* (New York: Scribner's, 1929), cxi. James L. Resseguie is of the view that misunderstanding takes place when one meaning for word is taken as thoroughgoing. Resseguie, *Narrative Criticism of the New Testament*, 65.

[319] Neyrey does state about Mary Magadelene discovering where Jesus is from and title 20:11-18 as "Now she knows 'where'" and the references to Mary not knowing. The researcher differs from Neyrey in seeing negative statement as means of drawing the theme of disclosure to a climax. Howard-Brook, *Becoming Children of God*, 438.

[320] Neyrey rightly notes that elsewhere in the FG "not knowing" is taken as a flaw. Neyrey, *The Gospel of John*, 318.

he speaks in v.15a) but by his naming personally (v. 16a)…And even more specialness can be detected: the message to the 'brother' is about the ascent to the Father… "[321] Further, Catchpole notes that Mary is the representative of the whole community (Jn. 10:3, 4).[322]

If one considers the resurrection narrative discussed so far, there is a clear progress in the revelation of the identity of Jesus, from strips of linen and napkin to angelophany, and now a Christophany: Jesus standing in their presence. This takes one to another vital aspect of disclosure in the FG, which is his presence in their midst.

The resurrection event is a disclosure of Jesus' presence; it is a theology of presence where the Father-Son and Spirit are present in the community. In this episode, Jesus is described as standing[323] (ἑστῶτα lit. had been standing-perfect tense) when Mary turns around. Among the several theological aspects of the NT usage of ἵστημι,[324] the one that is relevant to the FG, is the meaning

---

[321] Catchpole, *Resurrected People*, 159.

[322] Catchpole, *Resurrected People*, 160.

[323] Liddell and Scott suggest several connotations for ἵστημι: a. in the causal usage: make to stand, set up, set, place, of things or persons, bring to standstill, stay, check; b. Passive and intransitive tenses of Act: to be set or placed, stand, stand still, halt, stand also used metaphorically (stand firm), to set up, rise up. Liddell and Scott, *A Greek-English Lexicon*, 841. The verb ἵστημι is quite significant for the evangelist's description of the resurrected Jesus. The verb occurs in gospels: Matt. 21 times, Mk. 4 times, Lk. 26 times and in FG 20 times. Out of the 71 usages in gospels, it is used seven times in the resurrection narratives of the FG and Luke's gospel. Luke has two occurrences, i.e., in 24: 17, 36 but the reference to 'Jesus standing among them' is only once. On the contrary the FG has five occurrences (20:11, 14, 19, 26; 21:4) in the resurrection narrative (Jn. 20 & 21) and most of them, except in 20:11(refers to Mary standing near the tomb), all refer to the resurrected Jesus. When used intransitively in the perfect and pluperfect, it has the meaning *stand*, mostly of the same meaning as εἰμί (Matt. 13:2; 12:46) and also indicating bodily position (Matt. 6:5). Also ἵστημι indicates the end of a movement *stand still* (Matt. 2:9, *stop* (transitive Acts 8:38). As a contrast to πίπτω, ἵστημι is used in the meaning *stand firm, resist*. Ἵστημι also has a cultic aspect in the case of worshippers *standing* before or in the presence of God, especially of angels in the heavenly court (Rev. 7:11; 2 Chr. 18:18, etc). The priests and the cultic gathering are said to *stand* before God in the OT and Qumran literature (Josh. 24:1; I Kgs. 8:14); IQH 7:30f.). The meaning signified here is the place of holiness where Yahweh inhabits. Walter notes, "The manner of the appearance corresponds to this: The one who appears *stands* near to the one to whom the appearance is made (Lk. 1:11; 24: 36; Jn. 20:14, 19, 26, 21:14; Acts 1:30; 10:30; 11:13; 16:19; 27:23). The LXX uses ἵστημι with the διαθήκη, ὅρκς and λογος or ἐντολή of Yahweh. Walter Grundmann, "ἵστημι," in *TDNT*, vol. 7, edited by Gerhard Kittel and Gerhard Friedrich (Grand Rapids, Michigan: Wm. B. Eerdmans Publishing Company, 1971), 641.

[324] Grundmann notes other theological aspects: a. to put someone in a particular place implying authority or actual power; b. the establishment of the Law; c. that which lasts and is not prone to change or decay. Grundmann, " ἵστημι," 648-651.

of 'standing' that has a theological import. Jesus comes to the disciples as one from the Father.[325] Importantly, ἵστημι defines the bodily presence of Jesus.

Reference	**Occasion**	**Text**
Jn. 20:14	Jesus' appearance to Mary	θεωρεῖ τὸν Ἰησοῦν ἑστῶτα
Jn. 20:19	Jesus' appearance to the disciples	ἔστη εἰς τὸ μέσον
Jn. 20:26	Jesus' appearance to the disciples including Thomas	ἔστη εἰς τὸ μέσον
Jn. 21: 4	Jesus' appearance to the seven disciples on the shore	ἔστη ὁ Ἰησοῦς εἰς τὸν αἰγιαλόν

The theology of bodily presence becomes clearer when one sees it in comparison with the resurrection narratives in the synoptics and Paul. Here, it is not a case of 'appearance' but one of presence. Presence fufills the promise that Jesus made in the Farewell Discourses (14:18). The narrator has deliberately left out the angel's role in announcing the resurrection in order that the disclosure comes from the very presence of the person himself. The absence of the body is in actuality the presence of the Jesus now and later through the Spirit. This stems from the community's struggle to understand itself.

Mary Magadelene discovers where Jesus belongs, i.e., Jesus has come from the Father and is now going to the Father. The content of the disclosure is the mutual relationship that Jesus shares with the Father. Minear rightly remarks, "The ascent to the Father appears to have eliminated spatial or temporal distance, opening the way for reciprocal dwelling."[326] The ascent and the Father-Son relationship becomes the basis for the relationship between the Son and the disciples. The Father is the initator in the relationship and the One who makes possible for the disciples to share a relationship with the Son. Christology does not eliminate the role of the Father which is imminent and vital to the understanding of the Son's relationship with the Father. This aspect can also be illustrated in the imagery of the vine and the branches. Mary Coloe rightly notes that the entire metaphor concerning the vine and the branches is based on vine/vinedresser relationship.[327] The aspect of going back to the Father is asserting the relationship that the Son shares with the Father. It can be said that the community's Christology emerges out of the struggles of the Johannine community.

---

[325] Grundmann, " ἵστημι," 650.

[326] Minear, "We Don't Know:" 134.

[327] Mary L. Coloe, *Dwelling in the Household of God: Johannine Ecclesiology and Spirituality* (Minnesota: Liturgical Press, 1989), 158.

It is in this pericope that the disciples are called brothers, a term that is frequent in the Johannine epistles. In the Farewell Discourses, the disciples are called friends (Jn. 15:14). The term also anticipates what had been promised in the Farewell Discourses.

Mary understands the identity of Jesus and is asked to convey this to the disciples. The risen Jesus is described as 'standing,' embodying the presence of God in the midst of the community. Mary is sent chiefly not to convey that Jesus is risen from the dead but the fact that the resurrection of Jesus has occasioned a new status for the disciples that is as the "... children of God and as brothers and sisters of Jesus and one another."[328] In this new status, the Father and Son now dwell with them (14:23).

In the same line of thought, resurrection in the FG can be seen as glorification and glorification in terms of the residing presence. This would explain the confession of the community in 1:14. This point of view would further substantiate the use of ἵστημι to describe the presence of Jesus. One could thus say that the cross does not exhaust the aspect of glorification;[329] though it is one of the aspects. Resurrection is also an aspect of glorification and this is important for understanding the Christology of the FG. Resurrection makes possible the presence of Jesus; an aspect that Jesus very clearly elucidated in the Farewell Discourses. Bennema rightly argues that the FE maintains a separation of events in terms of the time framework. Jesus' glorification is not to be understood as one event but includes death, resurrection and ascension.[330]

The Johannine community had a specific understanding of the resurrection-ascension scheme relating to the giving of the Spirit through which Jesus is present in the community. The physicality of the resurrection and the theology of resurrection (i.e., ascension) are fused together in this

---

[328] Bennema, *Encountering Jesus*, 200.

[329] At this point the researcher would beg to differ from those scholars who rule out the significance of the resurrection in the FG. Brown and Schanckenburg view it as one continuum. A similiar view is held by Beasley-Murray – "the replacement of the language of resurrection with that of ascension is an indication that the two are fundamentally one, indissolubly bound with the death of Jesus." Beasley-Murray, *John*, 377.

[330] The researcher would differ from Bennema in terms of interpreting these events. He deduces that giving of the Spirit started once the process of Jesus' glorification was underway i.e., on the cross. Jesus' handing over the Spirit on the cross symbolizes the release of the Spirit and in 20:22 Jesus gives the Spirit as the Spirit of salvation and the giving of the Spirit as Paraclete does not take place in the FG as the FE does not describe it (16:7). He also distinguishes between Jn. 20:22 and Acts 2. The former indicating the Spirit is given *as the Spirit of salvation* and the latter is the Spirit given as *Paraclete.* He uses a chronological framework such as the cross (19:30), resurrection (20:22), ascension, Pentecost (Acts 2). Interesting framework as it sounds, it relies more on Luke-Acts framework rather than on treating the FG as a unique presentation of cross, resurrection and ascension. The FG's unique framework is lost by subserving it under the Lukan framework. The particular meaning of Paraclete also requires a different interpretation from Acts of the Apostles. Benema, *Excavating John's Gospel*, 215-219.

narrative. The disciples are yet to experience the fruits of his glorification—he is yet to fulfil his promise. The difficulty in understanding ascension arises only if it is seen in realtion to Luke-Acts. The concept of 'ascending' in the FG is unlike Luke-Acts: it signifies the unique relationship that Jesus shares with the Father and also makes possible the presence of the Son and Father with the 'brothers' of Jesus.

This unit (vv. 11-19) conveys many elements on how the community understood the resurrection of Jesus. Here, it is a disclosure of the bodily presence of Jesus, which again reinstates the relationship the Son shares with the Father. As a consequence, this also draws the identity of the disciples. Essentially this unit describes the identity of the presence, a presence signifying that Jesus is the Messiah who abides with the community forever.

3.3.5. John 20:19-23: Disclosure of Mission in Identity

The discussion of the previous unit centred on the motif of disclosure of the bodily presence of Jesus to Mary Magadalene which signified his identity. This unit is intricately connected to the previous unit in that Jesus' statement to Mary Magadalene is fulfilled and so also the aspects described in the Farewell Discourses. It also reinstates that the risen Jesus disclosed his presence not only to individuals but also to the group of disciples. The time indicators note that Jesus appeared to them on the same day as he appeared to Mary.

3.3.5.1. Context

The present pericope and the subsequent one (20:24-29) describe the appearance to a group of disciples, 'brothers,' to whom Mary Magdalene was commissioned to convey Jesus' words. In fact, v.17 has already prepared the reader for Jesus' appearance to the disciples. More importantly, the pericope is connected with the Farewell Discourses in fulfilling the promises Jesus gave to the disciples before his departure.

3.3.5.2. Structure[331]

The structure of the vv. 19-23 is delineated as follows: vv. 19-20 is the Disclosure of the Lord to his disciples; v. 21is the Disclosure of the mission of the Father-Son; v. 22-23 is the Disclosure of the 'abiding presence' of Jesus.

---

[331] 'Two tripartite sequences' are noted by Stibbe: vv. 19-20 – a. Jesus comes and shares his peace with the disciples; b. he shows his hands and side to them; c. the narrator describes the disciples' joy. Vv. 21-23- a. Jesus shares his peace; b. breathes the Holy Spirit on them; c. his disciples are given authority to forgive or retain people's sins. Stibbe, *John*, 201.

3.3.5.3. Translation

19 On the evening of that day, the first day of the week, when the doors were locked, where the disciples were, because of the fear of the Jews, Jesus came and stood among them[332] and said to them, "Peace to you!"

20 When he said this, he showed them his hands and his side. Then the disciples were glad having seen the Lord.

21Then he said to them again, "Peace to you! As the Father has sent me, I also am sending you."

22 After he said this he breathed on them[333] and said to them, "Receive (the)[334] Holy Spirit.

23 Whoever[335] sins you forgive, they remain forgiven them, whoever sins you hold back, they remain held back."

3.3.5.4. Exegetical Notes

3.3.5.4.1. Vv. 19-20: The Disclosure of the Lord to the Disciples

There is a close connection between Jn. 20:19-23 and Lk. 24:36-42. The setting, words and the manner in which Jesus reveals himself is similar, but there are also differences which do point to the theological emphasis.

	Lk. 24:36-42	Jn. 20:19-23
Setting	ἑσπέραν (v. 29)	ὀψίας (v.19)
Jesus' appearance	ἔστη ἐν μέσῳ (v. 36)	ἔστη εἰς τὸ μέσον (v. 19)
Greeting	Εἰρήνη ὑμῖν. (v. 36)	Εἰρήνη ὑμῖν (v.19)
Jesus reveals himself	ἔδειξεν αὐτοῖς τὰς χεῖρας καὶ τοὺς πόδας. (v. 40)	ἔδειξεν τὰς χεῖρας καὶ τὴν πλευρὰν αὐτοῖς (v. 20)

The setting closely parallels v. 1 (Τῇ δὲ μιᾷ τῶν σαββάτων), but with an addition of ὀψίας and ἐκείνῃ indicating the lapse of time. Cassien argues that the

---

[332] Εἰς τὸ μέσον- the phrase means "stood among them". Zerwick and Grosvenor, *A Grammatical Analysis of the Greek New Testament*, 345.

[333] Lit. "he breathed on and said to them". Newman and Nida note that it is possible for "them" to be the object of "breathed on" as well as the indirect object of "said". Newman and Nida, *A Translator's Handbook on the Gospel of John*, 615.

[334] Morris notes that the absence of the article may denote "the quality of the gift of the Holy Spirit rather than on the individuality of the Spirit." Leon Morris, *The Gospel according to John*, 747, f.n. 59.

[335] This verse has given rise to a lot of discussion. The Greek particle ἄν is commonly translated by an 'if' clause can also be equally rendered as "whosoever sins..." C. F. D. Moule, *An Idiom Book of New Testament Greek* (Cambridge: Cambridge University Press, 1968), 152.

phrase τῇ ἡμέρᾳ ἐκείνῃ is a special term in the Farewell Discourses (Jn. 13-17) to indicate Jesus' return in the future;[336] this does not leave out the chronological aspect as referring to the evening of Jesus' resurrection appearance. Διὰ points to the reason for the doors being locked,[337] namely, "the fear of the Jews." Köstenberger is of the view that Jerusalem was the place where the disciples had gathered and where Mary also comes to report what Jesus had told her (Lk. 24: 33).[338] The primary focus here is on "the fear of the Jews" and not so much on the ability of Jesus to pass through the doors.[339]

The phrase "the fear of the Jews" is unique to the FG and clearly presents the Johannine community's situation.[340] It occurs in two other texts (Jn. 7:13; 19:38) other than this one (20:19). In Jn. 7:13 the context is the Festival of Booths and there seems to be a division in the crowd regarding the identity of Jesus. The FE notes that those who desired to acknowledge Jesus' identity did not do so because of "the fear of the Jews." The other text is Jn. 19:38 in which Joseph of Arimathea secretly obtains permission from Pilate to take the body of Jesus, the reason for doing so is again given as "the fear of the Jews." "The fear of the Jews" is pitted against "peace." Jesus' appearance to the disciples is described as 'coming' and 'standing in their midst' (Jn. 20:19) (ἦλθεν ὁ Ἰησοῦς καὶ ἔστη εἰς τὸ μέσον). Εἰς possibly could mean a motion towards the disciples.[341] Jesus meeting with his disciples is a consummation of Jesus' promise to the disciples (15:11; 16:20-24; 17:13). Μαθηταὶ here is

---

[336] Archimandriate Cassien, *La Pentecôte Johannique* (Valencesur-Rhône, 1939), 43, cited in Joost van Rossum, "The "Johannine Pentecost": John 20:22 in Modern Exegesis and in Orthodox Theology," *StVTQ* 35/2-3 (1991): 151. van Joost rightly negates the view of Cassien, who restricts the phrase τῇ ἡμέρᾳ ἐκείνῃ as only referring to the fulfillment of Christ, and argues that it also includes the chronological aspect. van Rossum, «The «Johannine Pentecost»: John 20:22 in modern exegesis and in Orthodox theology,» 151. However, the researcher does not agree with the harmonizing the account of Pentecost in Jn. 20:22 and Acts 2:1. He does so by assuming that Pentecost in the FG is an incomplete one which finds its completion in Acts 2:1. This view seems to misread the Johannine theology and its significance for the community.

[337] The perfect tense κεκλεισμένων suggests not just shut but locked. Köstenberger, *John*, 572.

[338] Köstenberger, *John*, 572.

[339] Several scholars have noted the unusual aspect of Jesus' arrival- Ridderbos, *The Gospel of John*, 641; Carson, *The Gospel according to John*, 646. The mention of the plural θυρῶν, may refer to "...a door at the entrance to the entrance to the house and a door into the room." Morris, *The Gospel according to John*, 745, f.n. 50.

[340] Catchpole notes righlty, "...the term 'the Jews' does represent negatively the non-Christian community which has expelled the Christian Jews." Catchpole, *Resurrected People*, 177. Haenchen views this as not referring to Jews as a people but to a community that was incompatible to Christians. Haenchen, *John 2*, 210.

[341] Morris, *The Gospel according to John*, 745, f.n. 52. Barrett terms εἰς τὸ μέσον "a pregnant construction" and is the means the same as ἐν τῷ μέσῳ. Barrett, *The Gospel according to St. John*, 473.

probably not restricted to the group of disciples but includes others as well; though Köstenberger contends that it is not always clear if it referred to the disciples or to a larger circle of Jesus' followers.[342] Εἰρήνη ὑμῖν was a well known everyday greeting of Jews in Palestine;[343] this is repeated in 20:26 and also occurs in Lk. (24:19). Nonetheless this greeting has a special significance for the FG, i.e., Jesus came in their midst and set into motion of what was promised to them in the Farewell Discourses. It can also be taken as a formula of revelation as seen in Judg. 6:23 and Daniel 10:19.[344]

In v. 20 Jesus shows his hands and side[345] (and not his feet as in Lk. 24: 39-40) to the disciples. Morris sees this as conveying the completion of the process mentioned in Jn. 16:20-22.[346] There is no element of fear and doubt on seeing Jesus (unlike Luke 24:37 where the disciples mistake Jesus for a spirit) and the need for showing his hands and side seem unnecessary on the surface. Ridderbos explains that these are pointers, not only of suffering, but also of Jesus' victory.[347] In line with this interpretation, Moloney notes that Jesus' mere presence in the midst of the disciples was a proof of triumph.[348] Beasley-Murray observes that the disclosure of his hands and side (pierced by the soldier) was to let the disciples know that it is the crucified Lord who stood in their midst. This was vital for the church to assert that "the crucified is the risen Lord."[349]

---

[342] Köstenberger, *The Mission of Jesus and the Disciples*, 142-169. Barrett too contends that the group referred here is smaller group. Barrett, *The Gospel according to St. John*, 472.

[343] The actual greeting was Shālôm 'āleikhem. Bruce, *The Gospel of John*, 391. Barrett notes that the ususal meaning is ""May all be well with you," but εἰρήνη had acquired so full a sense in Christian usage (cf. 14:27; 16:33) that much more is intended here." Barrett, *The Gospel according to St. John*, 473.

[344] Brochert also mentions that there are several similarities of theophanies in the Old Testament with slight differences. The important elements are: a. fear; b. the calming word of "peace' or "do not be afraid" from God or Christ, and c. a word of commission for the task to be performed. In the present instance as the disciples are already gripped with fear, what was required was shalom. Brochert, *John 12-21*, 304-305. J. N. Suggit mentions of Eucharistic echoes in the text. He notes, "Perhaps John is expounding more clearly Luke's understanding of eucharistic fellowship." John N. Suggit, "The Eucharistic Significance of John 20:19-29," *JTSA* 16 (Sep. 1976): 52, f.n. 2.

[345] The mention of Jesus' side being peierced is unique to the FG's passion story. The flow of blood and water also has important sacramental importance. More so, Jesus showing his hands and side helps the disciples to relate the resurrection appearance of Jesus with the passion of Jesus. Schneiders interprets revealing the side as signifying 'Jesus as the New Temple.' She futher states, "He is presence of God's glory in their midst and the source of life-giving water of the Spirit." Schneiders, "The Raising of the New Temple:" 348.

[346] Morris, *The Gospel according to John*, 746.

[347] Ridderbos, *The Gospel of John*, 641.

[348] Moloney, *The Gospel of John*, 530-531.

[349] Beasley-Murray, *John*, 379.

The disciples rejoice at seeing the display of hands and side by Jesus. Morris notes that the use of aorist (ἐχάρησαν) here indicates the sudden outburst of joy.[350] The use of οὖν confirms that the hand and side did convince the disciples.[351] For the disciples, the occasion has come for turning their sorrow into joy (Jn. 16:20), and the aspect of joy is also seen in John the Baptist (3:29) and Abraham (8:56). The accusative of κύριος seems to be a significant one for the FG. Out of the 68 occurences of κύριον in the NT, there are only six occurrences (11:2; 20:2, 13, 18, 20, 25) in the FG and all of these are found in the context of resurrection, especially chap. 20 (with the exception of 11:2 which is a note made by the narrator). The vocative occurs 119 times in the NT, out of which seven occurrences (9:38; 11:12, 21, 27, 32, 34, 39) are in the FG. A majority of these occurrences take place in the raising up of Lazarus. The genitive occurs 177 times in the NT, out of which there are six occurrences (13:13, 14; 15:15; 20:28; 21:7 twice) in the FG. Three of these are on the lips of Jesus in the context of footwashing (Jn. 13) and one each by Thomas and the BD. The title Lord signifies the aspect of identity for the disciples. Köstenberger rightly notes, "...calling Jesus "Lord" in a christological sense frequently presupposes either hindsight (6:23; 11:2) or at least Jesus' resurrection having occurred (20:28; 21:7, 12), though there are occasional instances where disciples address Jesus as "Lord" during his earthly ministry (e.g., 9:38; 11:12, 21, 27, 32, 34, 39)."[352]

Jesus discloses his bodily presence and gives them the proof of his presence by showing his hand and side. The crucified one is present in the midst of them. It is not mentioned whether the disciples doubted or not. Probably the narrator wanted to make use of it in the next unit (vv. 24ff.). It is also the disclosure of a peaceful presence in the context of the troubled spirit of the disciples.

3.3.5.4.2. V. 21: The Disclosure of the Mission of the Father-Son

Jesus repeats the common greeting εἰρήνη ὑμῖν. The commissioning aspects are also seen in Mat. 28:16-20 and Lk. 24:46-49. Two significant connectives in Jn. 20:21 are καθὼς and κἀγὼ.

Ridderbos notes that this commissioning looks back at Jesus' words in 17:18 with the exception of κόσμον. This indicates for Ridderbos that the stress in the present text is on the disciples being authorized rather than the sphere of activity.[353] Though this is true, the sphere of activity of mission is certainly the κόσμον, especially if the Farewell Discourses are proleptic to the resurrection

[350] Morris, *The Gospel according to John*, 46, f.n. 54.

[351] Morris, *The Gospel according to John*, 746.

[352] Köstenberger, *John*, 573.

[353] Ridderbos, *The Gospel of John*, 643.

narrative. The commissioning is not unique to the FG, but certainly the basis of it is. Jesus as the sent one of the Father is the climax of the statement and forms the undergirding principle of the mission of the disciples. The mission of the Son now taken by the disciples (not restricted to the Twelve) is also the mission of the Father. The mission of the disciples continues the perpetual mission of the Son.

It is a worthwhile exercise to look into the possible background of the concept of 'sending' in the FG. One of the backgrounds traced of this concept is in *Hermetica*. It says God filled a great bowl with νοῦς and sends the bowl in charge of a messenger, who proclaims, "Immerse thyself in this bowl, O soul that art able, who believest that thou shalt ascend to Him who sent down the bowl, who knowst for what thou wert born."[354] All those who comprehended the proclamation and dipped themselves in νοῦς shared the knowledge "... and became perfect men receiving νοῦς."[355] Kanagaraj notes the difference in purpose and the result of sending in the FG from the *Hermetica*.[356] Peder Borgen notes the close parallel of sending in the *Halakah*, in which the FG's Christology and Soteriology are fused together on Jewish aspects of agency.

Borgen notes several affinities between the halakhic principles of agency and the concept of 'sending' in the FG: "(a) the unity between the agent and his sender, (b) the agent is subordinate, (c) the obedience of the agent to the will of the sender, (d) the task of the agent in the lawsuit, (e) his return and reporting back to the sender, and (f) his appointing of other agents as an extension of his own mission in time and space."[357] He further notes that the FG has no great distinction from that of Rabbinic and Hellenistic Judaism.[358] Meeks understands Jesus as the sent one of God is patterned on the traditions

---

[354] Nock and Festugiére (eds). *Corpus Hermeticum*, IV. 4, cited in C. H. Dodd, *The Interpretation of the Fourth Gospel* (Cambridge: Cambridge University Press, 1958), 26.

[355] Dodd, *The Interpretation of the Fourth Gospel*, 26.

[356] Kanagaraj notes that in *Hermetica* those who partake of the νους "... that God has sent by dipping themselves in the basin and such people see the good by rising themselves even to what lies beyond heaven; after seeing the good, however, they regard the earthly life as only a calamity." Unlike this understanding, the FG emphasizes on believing in the Son whom the Father has sent in order to have a share in eternal life here and now. Further, he concedes concept of sending in *Hermetica* only points to a common idea prevalent in the Hellenistic circles. Kanagaraj, *'Mysticism' in the Gospel of John*, 255, 256.

[357] Peder Borgen, "God's Agent in the Fourth Gospel," in *The Interpretation of John*, edited by John Ashton (Philadelphia: Fortress Press, 1986), 72.

[358] Borgen is of the view that Jewish Merkabah traditions influenced the gnostic movement and the gnostic agents do not actually explain the background of God's agent in the FG. Borgen, "God's Agent in the Fourth Gospel," 75.

of Moses' mission, especially in the fact that Moses was enthroned as king and sent to the people as revealer (prophet) and vice-regent (king).[359]

Marinus de Jonge notes the importance of sonship over the prophetic function in the mission of the Son in the FG.[360] Dodd too notes that the language of sending recalls that of the OT prophets. He states, "This description (referring to 4:34) of the status and function of the Son of God recalls the language of the Old Testament prophets."[361] He draws attention to the aspect of the prophet as the one being sent by Jehovah (Is. 6:8 paralleled in Jn. 10:36; Jer. 1:5) and one having delegated authority (Jer. 1:10).[362] However, Dodd is quick to note the distinguishing aspects in the Son and the Prophet, especially in the aspects of giving life and judgment.[363] Ashton tries to resolve the incompatible elements in the FG's Christology—equal divine status and the servant not being greater than the master—by bringing the analogy of the prophetic mission and law of agency.[364] Ashton notes the limitation of the law of agency, "The exceptional character of Jesus' relationship with God cannot be *explained* by the law of agency, although it may be partly expressed in a terminology originally elaborated to deal with more mundane matters."[365] Kysar also notes the limitation of agency Christology when he states that the agent in the FG is not just a prophet but is also the Son of Man.[366] Kanagaraj highlights several distinctive elements of the sending theme in the FG. First, sending is to make known the Father. Second, in the mission of the Son the Father is glorified which implies the Son reveals God's glory. Third, the fact bearing witness of the words that the Son had heard from the Father, the pre-existence of the Son is acknowledged. Fourth, the sending of the Son results in judgment. Fifth, in the mission of the Son, the Father speaks and bears witness.[367]

These aspects clearly demonstrate the oneness motif in the mission of the Son and it being creatively weaved together the aspects of identity and mission. Further, these features do not find parallels in the backgrounds discussed earlier. Gathercole also mentions the aspect of sending in the synoptics which are summaries of the goal of Jesus' ministry, especially the references of Jesus

---

[359] Wayne A. Meeks, "Moses as God and King," in *Religions in Antiquity: Essays in Memory of Erwin Ramsdell Goodenough*, edited by Jacob Neusner (Leiden: E. J. Brill, 1970), 354-371.

[360] de Jonge, *Jesus: Stranger from Heaven*, 57.

[361] Dodd, *The Interpretation of the Fourth Gospel*, 254.

[362] Dodd, *The Interpretation of the Fourth Gospel*, 254-255.

[363] Dodd, *The Interpretation of the Fourth Gospel*, 257.

[364] John Ashton, *Understanding the Fourth Gospel* (Oxford: Clarendon Press, 1991), 316.

[365] Ashton, *Understanding the Fourth Gospel*, 325.

[366] Robert Kysar, *John, the Maverick Gospel* (Atlanta: John Knox Press, 1970), 36.

[367] Kanagaraj, *'Mysticism' in the Gospel of John*, 260.

to the Father as "the one who sent me" (Mark 9:37, Matt. 10:40; Lk. 9:48; Lk. 10:46).[368]

There are two verbs mentioned in the present text regarding 'sending' - ἀποστέλλω and πέμπω. There are about twenty eight occurrences of ἀποστέλλω (1:6, 19, 24; 3:17, 28, 34; 4:38; 5:33, 36, 38; 6:29, 57; 7:29, 32; 8:42; 9:7; 10:36; 11:3, 42; 17:3, 8, 18 (2), 21, 23, 25; 18:24; 20:21),[369] of which seventeen usages (3,17, 34; 5:36, 38; 6:29, 57; 8:42; 10:36; 11:42; 17:3, 8, 21, 23, 25; 18:24; 20:21) emphasize that the Father sent Jesus.

It is interesting to note that in the majority of occurrences noted above, the phrase "sent me" occurs nine times (5:36; 7:29; 8:42; 11:42; 17:8, 21, 23, 25; 20:21). There is a reference to John the Baptist being sent by God (Jn. 1:6). This probably denotes the assertion of Jesus as the 'one who is sent' and signifies his identity. The sender who is the Father is described in various ways, such as God (3:17, 34), "the Father" (5:36), "this one" (5:38), "that one" (6:29; 8:42), "you" (11:42; 17: 8, 21, 23, 25). The phrase "the Father sent me" occurs twice other than 20:21, i.e., in 5:36 and 6:57. The purpose for which the disciples are sent is not mentioned at all. The clue lies in 5:36 (ἀπέσταλκέν με ὁ πατήρ) where exactly the same phrase is used as in 20:21. In 5:36, it is the works which the Father has assigned Jesus to do that testify the Father has sent Jesus. So, also here the disciples are to accomplish the works of Jesus.[370] This is not the only occurrence of Jesus sending the disciples; it also takes place in 4:38. The difference in the the context here is Jesus' return to the Father and the mission of doing the works of the Father entrusted to the disciples.

Πέμπω is another word used for 'sending' in the FG. There are in all about thirty two usages of πέμπω (1:22; 1:33; 4:34; 5:23, 24, 30, 37; 6:38, 39, 44; 7:16, 18, 28, 33; 8:16, 18, 26, 29; 9:4; 12:44, 45, 49; 13:16, 20 (2); 14:24, 26; 15:21, 26, 16:5, 7; 20:21) in the FG. The striking aspect is that there are twenty occurrences (4:34; 5:24, 30, 37; 6:39, 44; 7:16, 28; 8:16, 18, 26, 29; 9:4; 12:44, 45, 39; 13:20; 14:24; 16:5) in which Jesus asserts that the 'Father

---

[368] Gathercole, *The Preexistent Son*, 177.

[369] W. F. Moulton and A. S. Geden, eds., *A Concordance to the Greek Testament* (Edinburgh: T & T Clark, 1957), 100.

[370] Köstenberger has done an elaborate study on the mission of Jesus and the disciples in the FG. He notes that the disciples of Jesus are not instructed to do any "signs" or works (14:2 does mention about greater works which he interprets as the "works *of the exalted Christ* through the believers"). The task of the disciples includes being involved in the eschatological harvest by giving fruit and witnessing to Jesus with the Spirit and to forgive others their sins in Jesus' name. Köstenberger, *The Mission of Jesus*, 169-175. But the question that can be raised against this view – Do the works also include the signs, don't they? If so, then, 14:12 cannot be seen as a point of differentiation.

sent me,'[371] making use of an articular participle.[372] Like ἀποστέλλω here too, this usage establishes the identity and mission of Jesus.

Rengstorf states, "The formula ὁ πέμψας με is used to affirm the participation of God in His (Jesus') work in the action of His sending."[373] In this connection, Schnackenburg notes that if this view is correct, then, the same applies to Jesus in the case of the disciples.[374] In addition to referring to Christ, ὁ πέμψας με is also used for sending of the Paraclete and Christ sending the disciples (20:21). The two verbs (ἀποστέλλω and πέμπω) are probably used synonymously in the FG.[375] It is not possible to identify two types of sending i.e., "...one in which the person sent is a delegate with transferred authority

---

[371] Schnackenburg, *The Gospel according to St. John*, vol. 3, 324.

[372] BDF state, "The articular participle is striking in some instances where Attic usage would have preferred to express the attributive relationship by means of a relative clause." BDF, 212.

[373] Karl Heinrich Rengstorf, "ἀποστέλλω (πέμπω)et.al.," in *TDNT*, vol.1, edited by Gerhard Kittel and Gerhard Freidrich (Grand Rapids, Michigan: William B. Eerdmans Publishing Company, 1964), 405.

[374] Schnackenburg, *The Gospel according to St. John*, vol. 3, 324.

[375] There are some who view and differently. Wescott states that ἀποστέλλω means "depatch" and "envoy" and implies "special commission" and "delegated authority" in the one sent while ἀποστέλλω means "...immediate relation of the sender to the sent." Wescott, *The Gospel according to St. John*, 298; and also Schnackenburg, *The Gospel according to St John*, vol. 3, 324; Beasley-Murray, *John*, 379-380. There are others who view the verbs synonymously- Barrett, *The Gospel according to St.* John, 473; Brown, *The Gospel according to John*, 134; Gerard S. Sloyan, *John*, Interpretation, edited by Paul J. Achtemeier (Atlanta: John Knox Press, 1988), 224; Calvin Mercer, "'ΑΠΟΣΤΕΛΛΕΙΝ and ΠΕΜΠΕΙΝ in John," *NTS* 36/4 (O.1990): 619-624; Morris,*The Gospel according to* John, 204; Ridderbos, *The Gospel of* John, 641, f.n. 35; Köstenberger does an elaborate study on the two verbs related to sending (πέμπω, ἀποστέλλω) and concludes that the use of these two verbs are best explicated in terms of perefrence of one kind of grammatical form. Köstenberger, *The Mission of Jesus*, 106. Also refer Andreas J. Köstenberger, "The Two Johannine Verbs for Sending: A Study of John's Use of Words with reference to General Linguistic Theory," in *Linguistic and the New Testament: Critical Junctures*, edited by Stanley E. Porter and D. A. Carson (Sheffield: Sheffield Academic Press, 1999), 125-143. More recently, this has been refuted by Schneiders. She states, "'Αποστέλλω emphasizes the relation of the *sentto those whom one is sent* with the consequent insistence upon the content of the mission to be accomplished and the authority for its accomplishment whereas πέμπω emphasizes the relation of the *sent to the sender* or the representative character of mission." Schneiders, 'The Raising of the New Temple:" 350.

(ἀποστέλλειν), and one in which this is not so (πέμπειν)."[376] Here, the stress is not on the contrast but on the parallel aspects of mission.[377]

The concept of sending does not have an object here (Jn. 20:21). There is another reference to sending of the disciples, i.e., in 17:18, which has the 'world' as the object of sending. It is surprising why, after mentioning of the hatred the disciples will experience in the future (15:18ff.), Jesus authorizes and legitimizes the mission of the disciples to the world.[378] The disciples are hated because those who hate them do note that Jesus is sent from the Father (15:21). This is a clear indication that the hatred noted here is from the Jews. Jesus also describes overcoming the world, so the mission does not end on a pessimistic note.

Köstenberger correctly notes that the crucifixion and resurrection are the valuabe parts of the disciples' mission.[379] He has some interesting conclusions: "The disciples do not replace Jesus-his ministry continues and is effective in their ministry (14:12-14). Jesus is still the "Sent One" par excellence (cf. 9:7). It is still Jesus, the exalted, glorified, crucified, risen, and coming one, who forgives and who gives salvation and eternal life. The disciples have simply entered into his mission (cf. 4:38), a mission that Jesus has never abandoned."[380] He further notes, "The identities of Jesus and of the disciples are different thus they have different parts in God's mission... the disciples are identified with Jesus in the way they are sent (cf. 17:18; 20:21), and, by way of instrumentality, also in the purpose of his sending (cf., e.g., 20:31 and Jesus' giving of life elsewhere in the Fourth Gospel)." [381]

Köstenberger has stated some vital aspects of Jesus' mission and mission of the disciples in noting that identities of Jesus and the disciples are different. He seems to reduce the identity of the disciples to one of instrumentality. The choosing of the disciples is also termed as the work of the Father (6:37) and the

---

[376] Barrett, *The Gospel according to St. John*, 473. Ferreira though notes that there is no difference in meaning between the two terms, yet, argues for two separate traditions. He notes, "Apostello and Pempo statements in John represent two distinctively early traditions about sending. Apostello statements in synoptic gospels and Old Testament prophetic tradition represent about the prophet as the emissary of god. Pempo statements should be located in the early Gnostic myth about the sending of the Redeemer." Johan Ferreira, *Johannine Ecclesiology*, JSNT Supp. 160 (Sheffield: Sheffield Academic Press, 1998), 170.

[377] Barrett, *The Gospel according to St. John*, 474.

[378] Coye Still interprets Jn. 20:21 in the light of Jn.17:18 and infers that mission of the disciples involves sufferings. E. Coye Still, "Sent to be Scarred: John 20:19-23," *ExpTim* 113/6 (Mr. 2002): 190-191. Hägerland opines, "The disciples are sent on a prophetic mission." Tobias Hägerland, "The Power of Prophecy: A Septuagintal Echo in John 20:19-23," *CBQ* 71/1 (Ja. 2009): 95.

[379] Köstenberger, *The Mission of Jesus*, 195.

[380] Köstenberger, *The Mission of Jesus*, 196.

[381] Köstenberger, *The Mission of Jesus*, 196.

work of the Son is to give life to them. In the shepherd discourse, Jesus states that those who are chosen are in the hands of the Father (10:29). The mission of the Son is not confined to the work of the Son, and the involvement of the Father is clearly stated. So, also the mission of the disciples is not just the mission of Jesus but also the mission of the Father and the Holy Spirit as seen in Jn.15:26. It is both the mission of the Father as well as the mission of the Son (though they are the same) which the disciples are asked to accomplish. Köstenberger has reduced the role of the disciples considerably in order to put forward the unique aspect of the Son's identity. In this regard, Barrett rightly draws the complexities of the relation between the mission of Jesus and the disciples. He notes,

> It follows further that as Jesus in his ministry was entirely dependent upon and obedient to God the Father, who sealed and sanctified him (4:34; 5:19; 10:37; 17:4), and other passages: 6:27; 10:36), and acted in the power of the Spirit who rested upon him (1:32), so the Chruch is the apostolic Chruch, commissioned by Christ, only in virtue of the act that Jesus sanctified it (17:19) and breathed the Spirit into it (v. 22), and only so far as it maintains an attitude of perfect obedience to Jesus (it is here, of course, that the parallelism between the relation of Jesus to the Father and the relation of the Church to Jesus breaks down).[382]

The aspect of sending has a part to play in the disclosure of the risen Jesus. The previous unit (vv. 11-18) very clearly brought out the aspect of identity of the Father and Son. Here again, the identity is noted in drawing the aspect of the Son being sent. The doing aspect of mission comes out of identity. In several places in the FG, Jesus repeatedly affirms that he speaks and does what he has seen from the Father. Thus, mission is the extension of the relationship with the Father, and the disciples are instructed to extend the presence of Jesus—the resurrected presence of Jesus.

3.3.5.4.3. Vv. 22-23: The Disclosure of the 'Abiding Presence' of Jesus

V. 22 is a fulfilment of the promise made by Jesus before his departure in 15:26. Καὶ τοῦτο εἰπὼν links the saying to the commission in v. 21.[383] The Greek verb ἐνεφυσάω means "breathe on" rather than "breathed into;"[384] and this is unique to the FG.[385] There are three possible backgrounds to this term, namely, Gen.

---

[382] Barrett, *The Gospel according to St. John*, 474.

[383] Beasley-Murray, *John*, 380.

[384] Köstenberger, *John*, 575.

[385] The unusual term is attributed to the Evangelist's source so also πνεῦμα ἅγιον. Beasley-Murray, *John*, 380. Derrett has observed an interesting Indian parallel in the 'breath'

2:7, Wisdom of Solomon 15:11, and Ezek. 37: 9-10. In Genesis, God breathes into Adam his Spirit at creation which makes him a "living being," and in a similar vein Jesus constitutes the disciples as a 'new messianic community.'[386] However, a recurring idea that runs through all these texts is that God recreates through the act of breathing His Spirit.[387] The term, πνεῦμά, recalls Jn. 3:8 and attests the concept of regeneration.[388] Keener makes an important point: Jesus as the one who imparts the Spirit is a common motif in the FG from the beginning (1:33) and reaches its high point in this verse. Further, this also suggests that since he is the giver of God's gift, Jesus himself is God.[389] Loader too makes an important point here, when he notes,

> The messiah actually does remain forever, not as the risen one but, paradoxically as the Spirit of the Son who has *ascended* to the father from whom he came. Jesus' physical absence does not disconfirm Johannine messianic claims for Jesus; on the contrary, his bodily absence becomes the proof of his abiding presence in a different form. Since the gift of the "holy Spirit" is mentioned in 20:22, it is probably being assumed that believers become God's children, through the heavenly Father's spiritual begetting (1:12-13; 3:5-8), whereby they too brought into the presence of the Father.[390]

Commissioning and giving of the Spirit should be seen together.[391] The giving of the Spirit is to equip the community for the mission, and is not so

---

metaphor. He notes that the Upanishads (*Bṛhadāraṇyaka Upaniṣad* I.5.17-20 and *Kauṣītakī Upaniṣad* II.15) describe a ceremony in which domestic power of the patriarch is given to a chosen successor, a son, commonly, his effective duty. In this ceremony, one of the senses was also transferred, *prāṇa* meaning 'breath of life,' to the successor. The term 'breath' is a metaphor for perceptual powers that was given and received with respect. Derrett draws the parallel, "Jesus appointed his successors with obvious disciplinary powers, and as we should say, hands the latter over to them – he will not exercise them again." J. Duncan M. Derrett, "An Indian Metaphor in John's Gospel," *JRAS* 9/2 (Jl. 1999): 274-275.

[386] Köstenberger, *John*, 575.

[387] Bennema, *Excavating John's gospel*, 216. Thus it also has the aspect of new creation. Anthony Tyrrell Hanson, *The Prophetic Gospel: A Study of John and the Old Testament* (Edinburgh: T & T Clark, 1991), 230. Brown views this as the "…participation in the renewal of creation." Jeannine K. Brown, "Creation's Renewal in the Gospel of John," *CBQ* 72/2 (Apr. 2010): 277.

[388] Keener, *The Gospel of John: A Commentary*, vol. 2, 1204.

[389] Keener, *The Gospel of John: A Commentary*, vol. 2, 1205.

[390] Loader, *The Christology of the Fourth Gospel*, 130.

[391] der Rand brings out this aspect, when he states, "God's commitment with his world continues through the mission of the disciples, guided by the Paraclete/Spirit. It is clear that the protagonist's resurrection and the breathing of the Spirit on to his followers (Jn. 20:22) introduces a new beginning or at least the succession of God's salvational commitment to this

much about the imparting of life as in Gen 2:7 and Ezek. 37:9.[392] It is probably not plausible to harmonize the account in v. 22 with the Acts.[393] Scholars have attempted to do so by terming 20:22 as "...a symbolic promise of the soon-to-be given gift of the Spirit."[394] The reasons given are: (a) it is difficult to see the FE running in actual conflict with narrative in Acts 2; (b) Spirit is to be given only after glorification, which is interpreted as return to the Father; (c) the consequent behaviour of the disciples in 20:26 does not go well with the reception of the Spirit.[395] Though these seem valid arguments, they offer only a limited perspective on the FG. Some of the proposed arguments against this position are as follows: (a) the resurrection narrative is primarily set in the backdrop of the Farewell Discourses, a unique feature of the FG; (b) equally important is the fact that the FG was written for the Johannine community that was going through periods of unrest due to external factors; (c) glorification in the FG cannot be simplified on the basis of Acts as only a return to the Father-the works of Jesus especially culminating on the cross and leading on to resurrection are also extended images of glorification; (d) though the disciples still continue behind closed (v. 26), the phrase "the fear of the Jews" mentioned in 20:19 is omitted here.

Thus, it is possible to conceive that the FG as well as Lk. contains two different representations of the giving of the Holy Spirit.[396] In Luke, it is spaced out as forty days after the resurrection when the outpouring of the Spirit takes place at Pentecost whereas in the FG, the cross is seen as one aspect of

---

world through the mission of the disciples." Jan A. der Rand, "The Creation Motif in the Fourth Gospel: Perspectives on the Narratological Function within Judaistic Background," in *Theology and Christology in the Fourth Gospel: Essays by the Members of the Society for New Testament Study Johannine Writings Seminar*, BETL 184, edited by G. Van Belle, J. G. Van der Watt and P. Maritz (Leuven: Leuven University Press, 2005), 22-23.

[392] Bruce, *The Gospel of John*, 392.

[393] Barrett in this regard notes that it is impossible to harmonize the giving of the Holy Spirit with Acts 2. Barrett, *The Gospel according to St. John*, 475.

[394] Köstenberger, *John*, 574. Köstenberger, *A Theology of John's Gospel*, 258.

[395] Köstenberger, *John*, 574. The concept of "receiving the Spirit" usually denoted experience of new relationship (Rom. 8:15; I Cor. 2:12; 2 Cor. 11:4; Gal. 3:2, 14) or equipping for mission (Acts 1:8). John's use of λαμβάνω instead of δέχομαι is not very frequent and the use of imperative calls for an acceptance of the offer. Keener, *The Gospel of John*, vol. 2, 1206. Schneiders takes this to signify an establishment of a New Covenant with the disciples, the New Israel, and Jesus as the New Temple. Schneiders, "The Raising of the New Temple:" 351.

[396] Pryor arues that Jn. 20:22 corresponds with Acts 2. He goes on to give seven reasons. Refer John W. Pryor, *John Evangelist of the Covenant People: The Narrative and Themes of the Fourth Gospel* (London: Darton, Longman and Todd, 1992), 125-131.

glorification, while the other being resurrection, ascension, and the giving of the Spirit, also equally significant.[397]

In v. 23, the phrase ἀφῆτε τὰς ἁμαρτίας in the context of commissioning to forgive sins is unique in the whole of New Testament, especially as the act of forgiving sins is restricted to God and the Son of Man (Mk. 2:1-12).[398] The crucial aspect in this saying is the translation of the verb κρατέω. Some translators, notes Beutler, interpret it as "to refuse forgiveness" on the basis of Matt. 18:19.[399] Weidemann rejects this view as both the texts make use of different verbs.[400] The better rendering would be "if you retain sins of any, they are retained."[401]

Despite the fact that various background(s)[402] can be traced to this saying, Beutler sums up the Johannine characteristics in the saying in its present form. First, the use of double conditional ἄν at the beginning of two antithesis namely:

---

[397] The researcher would disagree with the understanding of Brown, Schnackenburg, Beasley-Murray who view death, resurrection, ascension as one. Haenchen also notes, "At this point Easter and Pentecost fall together." Haenchen, *John 2*, 211.

[398] Johannes Beutler notes that this has yielded much interest in recent scholars. Some of them noted by him are: Thomas R. Hatina, "John 20, 22 in Its Eschatological Context" *Bib* 74 (1993): 196-219; Steven E. Hanse, "Forgiving and retaining Sin: A Study of the Text and Context of John 20:23," *HBT* 19 (1997): 24-32. Johannes Beutler, "Resurrection and the Remission of Sins: John 20:23 Against Its Traditional Background," in *The Resurrection of Jesus in the Gospel of John*, edited by Craig R. Koester, WUZNT 22 (Tübingen: Mohr Siebeck, 2008), 237.

[399] Beutler, "Resurrection and the Remission of Sins," 241. Thomas connects footwashing with forgiveness of sins. He states, "In all probability, footwashing was practicised as a religious rite by the Johannine community signifying the cleansing of believers from post-conversion sin. Footwashing was probably observed in conjunction with the Eucharist. Footwashing would most easily fit at this point serving as a sign that confessed sins are forgiven." John Christopher Thomas, *Footwashing in John 13 and the Johannine Community*, JSNTSup. 61 (Sheffield: JSOT Press, 1991), 184-185.

[400] Matthew uses λύω whereas the FG uses κρατέω. Hans-Ulrich Weidemann, "Nochmals John 20, 23. Weitere philologische und exegetische Bemerkungen zu einer problematischen Bibleübersetzung," *MTZ* (Munchener Theologische Zeitschrift) 52 (2001): 121-127, cited in Beutler, "Resurrection and the Remission of Sins," 241.

[401] There are others suggestions. W. E. Seitz renders κρατέω as "overcoming" them and views in 20:23 a synthetic rather than antithetic parallelism. Weindelin Eugen Seitz, "Philologische Bemerkungen zu einer problematischen Bibelübesetzung: Joh 20, 22.23," *MTZ* 51 (2000): 55-61, cited in Beutler, "Resurrection and the Remission of Sins," 241. Schneiders takes ἄν τινων κρατῆτε in the sense of community "holding fast" its members. Sandra M. Schneiders, "The Raising of the New Temple:" 352-353; also Sandra M. Schnieders, "The Lamb of God and the Forgiveness of Sin(s) in the Fourth Gospel," *CBQ* 73/1 (Ja. 2011): 29. Beutler rejects this view as it is unlikely that the shift from a possessive pronoun ("of any") to a pronoun is used as the object of the verb (holding "any" persons fast). Beutler, "Resurrection and the Remission of Sins," 241.

[402] Beutler discusses about Matthew, Luke, OT and Jewish Traditions. Refer Beutler, "Resurrection and the Remission, 244-250.

ἄν τινων ἀφῆτε τὰς ἁμαρτίας ἀφέωνται αὐτοῖς and ἄν τινων κρατῆτε κεκράτηνται. Second, "forgiveness of sins" is found in the literary tradition, i.e., twice in I Jn. (1:9; 2:12). Finally, the use of the perfect (ἀφέωνται, κεκράτηνται) goes along with the major emphasis of Johannine eschatology which is salvation has come definitively in Christ.[403]

How does one interpret this saying? Many scholars take it to mean the Matthean saying in the light of the rabbinic use of the terms "binding" and "loosing" for ascertaining those "allowed" and "not allowed" by the Law and thus relating it to magisterial office.[404] There is also the view among scholars that 'loose' and 'bind'describe the activity of a judge. In this regard it would denote Peter's authority to declare people forgiven or condemned according to the response to the message. Jeremias notes, "...the authority of the messenger includes both the communication of salvation and the imposition of judgment."[405] He further notes, "It is the judge's authority to acquit and pronounce guilty that is described by the pair of opposites and the synonymous phrases 'bind and loose' and 'forgive and retain sins.'"[406] Though agreeing in principle, Köstenberger views the "new messianic community" as endowed with authority "...to affirm or deny acceptance into the believing (new) community..."[407] For Beutler, the Johannine community drew their identity from Jesus, and therefore all sins were culminated in one sin which is rejecting Jesus. And thus lies the cause- the not acceptance of the message which is the retaining of sins.[408] A more feasible interpretation could be that the presence of Jesus in and through his Spirit equips the disciples to be agents of reconciliation and life.[409]

---

[403] Beutler, "Resurrection and the Remission of Sins," 246.

[404] Beasley-Murray, *John*, 383. Köstenberger notes that in the Jewish context the terms "binding and loosing" referred to the activity of the judge who said to pronounce persons innocent or guilty ("bound or loosed"). Köstenberger, *John*, 575. Haenchen takes this as the redactor's attempt to familiarize with the synoptic tradition because Johannine view is different from Matthean view, in that it does not see the will of human beingimportant in becoming the disciples of Jesus. Haenchen, *John 2*, 211.

[405] Joachim Jeremias, *New Testament Theology*, Part 1: *The Proclamation of Jesus* (London: SCM Press Ltd, 1971), 238.

[406] Jeremias, *New Testament Theology*, 238.

[407] Köstenberger, *John*, 575-576.

[408] Beutler, "Resurrection and the Remission of Sins," 243. It could also refer to the practise of discipline in the early Christian communities. Hanson, *The Prophetic Gospel*, 231.

[409] Barrett righlty notes, "This joint work, of Christ in sending the Holy Spirit and of the Holy Spirit in bearing witness to Christ is exercised in and through the Church as represented by the disciples." Barrett, *The Gospel according to St. John*, 475.

3.3.5.5. Theological Interpretation

As the risen Jesus reveals himself to the disciples,[410] they understand the identity of Jesus. Here the identity of Jesus and the mission of Jesus are fused together, and the same applies to the disciples. There is a transfer of identity and mission to the disciples. The giving of the Spirit is not only to aid the disciples in their mission, but also to ensure that the presence of Jesus continues in the form of the Paraclete. The FG presents the mission of the disciples only after the resurrection, unlike in the synoptics (Mk. 6:7-13; Mt. 10:1, 5-15; Lk.9:1-6).[411]

The concept of sending is important in the FG. The FG begins with sending and ends with sending. The first occurrence[412] is John the Baptist being sent from God (Jn. 1:6), but his mission is restricted to "witnessing to the light" (Jn. 1:7). The focus instead for the FE is on "the true light" (Jn. 1:9), the central character of the Gospel. The second occurrence is when Jesus presents himself as the sent one of God (Jn. 3:17).[413] However, the mission of the Son is closely tied to the identity of the Son. The FE declares Jesus as the only Son who is in the bosom of the Father (Jn. 1:18), and in 3:13 Jesus describes himself as one descended from heaven. Thus, it is clear that Jesus is not only the one sent from God, but also the one who has come from God. The third occurrence is regarding the Samaritan woman. She is instructed to go and call her husband (Jn. 4:16). Though the verb ὑπάγω is used instead of ἀποστέλλω, it still involves mission as the narrator reports in Jn. 4:28. The fourth reference is made when the disciples are sent to reap for which they did not labour (4:38). Jesus in his prayer to the Father also notes that, just as he has been sent by the Father, the disciples are sent into the world (Jn. 17:18). Here, the aorist (ἀπέστειλα) tense seem to signify that they have been already sent into the world. The fifth reference is made when Judas is asked by Jesus to do quickly what he plans to do (Jn. 13: 27). The sixth reference is to the Paraclete who is sent by the Father in Jesus' name (Jn. 14: 26). The seventh reference

[410] Neyrey takes the appearances of Jesus as a part of the "call narratives." He delineates four aspects of the call narrative which are also seen in Jn. 20:19-25; 20: 26-29. They are: "a. introduction: who, where, when (Jn. 20: 19, 26); b. confrontation/reaction: Because heavenly beings may destroy as wellas build up, they are received with fear; reassurance in the form of "Be not afraid!" may be necessary (Jn. 20: 19-20, 26); c. commission (Jn. 20:21); d. objections: Not uncommonly, those commissioned object. Reassurances such as "Do not fear!" may occur again. Signs may be given as proof of both God's favour and power (Jn. 20: 27-28); e. conclusion: departure of God or angel (Jn. 20: 29)." Neyrey, *The Gospel of John*, 326-327.

[411] Stanley B. Marrow, *The Gospel of John: A Reading* (New York: Paulist Press, 1995), 362.

[412] The researcher has taken the lead from Neyrey although Neyrey discusses this in the context of commissioning of Mary and in terms of role and status; which is of less interest to the researcher. Neyrey, *The Gospel of John*, 322-323.

[413] The other references are: 3:34; 6:57; 11:42; 17:3, 8; 20:21.

is made when Mary Magdalene is commanded to go and tell the disciples that Jesus is ascending to the Father. The final reference is made when Simon is asked to feed the lambs and sheep (Jn. 21:15-17).

In the sending episodes discussed above, there are some significant points to be noted. There are only three who are authorized and sent by God: John the Baptist, Jesus and the Paraclete. The role of the Baptizer is restricted to witnessing concerning Jesus. Similarly, the role of the Paraclete is to teach and bring to remembrance all that Jesus taught the disciples. Further, the Paraclete is sent in Jesus' name. It is only Jesus who is sent by the Father as a representative of the Father and to do the Father's will. Jesus also authorizes and sends individuals and a group: Samaritan woman (Jn. 4:16); the disciples (4:38; 17:18; 13:15; 20:21-23); Judas (13:27); Mary Magdalene (20:17); and Simon Peter (21:15-17). In all of this, the sending of the disciples is unique because it is only here that the FE draws a parallel between Jesus as being sent from the Father and the disciples being sent by Jesus. The mission of Jesus finds its completion in the continuing misson of the disciples. Okure states, "…the emphasis focuses on the *right attitude* which should animate the disciples *in the exercise of mission*, namely, that though sent, they are wholly dependent on Jesus."[414]

One aspect of the mission of the disciples involves the forgiveness of sins. There has been a lot of discussion on what exactly it means for the disciples to forgive sins. The aspect of forgiveness of sins is stated after the Spirit is given, an indication that forgiveness is related to the Spirit. Secondly, this commissioning is given in the context of the community. This does not seem to be a case of mission being restricted within the community[415] because Jesus' mission is not restricted to the disciples or their mission. Neyrey notes that the disciples' commission is limited within the group (Jn. 1:29; 8:21, 24; 16:8).[416] O'Grady puts it lucidly, "Forgiveness is not a juridical process in this gospel but a proclamation of peace that looks to the future and a new existence."[417]

[414] Teresa Okure, *The Johannine Approach to Mission: A Contextual Study of John 4:1-42* (Tübingen: Mohr, 1988), 230.

[415] It seems difficult to agree with Neyrey on this matter. Neyrey interprets "forgiveness of sins" as applicable only to the disciples. He states, "…Jesus' commission in 20:22-23 would seem to extend only to in-group ritual behavior." He also notes that Thomas' sins are retained because he does not respond positively to call for repentance to join the group and to believe the good news told by the disciples. Neyrey, *The Gospel of John*, 328-329. Kieffer states, "… the forgiveness of sins is linked to the gift of the Holy Spirit and the disciples' missionary work." René Kieffer, "John," in *The Gospels*, The Oxford Bible Commentary, edited by John Muddiman and John Barton (Oxford: Oxford University Press, 2001), 238.

[416] Neyrey, *The Gospel of John*, 329.

[417] John F. O'Grady, *According to John: The Witness of the Beloved Disciple* (New York: Paulist Press, 1999), 114.

The resurrection of Jesus in the FG is through his power. It is through this same power that Jesus ascends to the Father, and returns to where he was before. This concurs with the description of Jesus as a heavenly person who descends from above and ascends back to heaven. The aspects of descending and ascending have to be seen in the light of the Father's plan. Neyrey rightly notes that the FE has compressed the resurrection event, "ascending to the Father" and "receive the Holy Spirit" into one day. He further notes that ascension gives the complete answer to the question of "where" he goes.[418]

3.3.6. John 20:24-31: Disclosure of the Lord's Identity to the Community

Disclosure of the identity of Jesus so far is seen by the BD, Mary Magadalene and the group of disciples other than Thomas. The present episode accentuates the disclosure of Jesus and its significance in the community. It combines the Lord's disclosure of his identity to the disciples and the narrator's disclosure to the community through the sign of resurrection, a sign he has just described (20:30-31).

3.3.6.1. Context

There seems to be a symmetry in the presentation of the resurrection account by the narrator. After having described the disclosure to two individuals and a group, disclosure to another group seems to be on the cards. The appearance of Jesus to the disciples (vv. 19-23) did not have any response from the disciples; it was more of a monologue. In a sense this alludes to the confession that Thomas makes. The present unit transcends the limitation of the resurrection appearance to those historically present, and thus the community also becomes a participant in the resurrection.

3.3.6.2. Structure

The structure followed in the study of the unit is:

vv. 24-25: disclosure longed by Thomas

vv. 26-27: an opportunity for Disclosure to Thomas

vv. 28-31: the Johannine community grasps the disclosure from the Lord.

3.3.6.3. Translation

24 Now Thomas, one of the twelve, one who was called "Twin," was not with them when Jesus came.

[418] Neyrey, *The Gospel of John*, 329.

25 So, the other disciples said[419] to him, "We have seen the Lord." But he said to them, "Unless I see in his hands the nail prints[420] and put my finger in the nail prints and put my hand in his side, I will never[421] believe."

26 Eight days later, his disciples were indoors, and Thomas was with them. The doors were locked, but Jesus came and stood among them and said "Peace to you!"

27 Then he said to Thomas, "Reach out your finger, and see my hands, and reach out your hands and put it in[422] my side, stop being[423] unbelieving but believing."

28 Thomas answered him, "My Lord and My God!"

29 Jesus said to him, "Do you[424] believe because you see me? Blessed are those who have not seen and yet have believed."[425]

---

[419] The use of imperfect tense has been discussed in this verse. Beasley-Murray translates ἔλεγον as "tried to tell," taking this as an example of an imperfect with conative force. Beasley-Murray, *John*, 367. This does not seem a correct rendering because according to Turner a conative imperfect is defined as "of incomplete or interrupted action, which sometimes softens the harshness of a remark or makes it more diffident..." Nigel Turner, *A Grammar of New Testament Greek*, vol. III: *Syntax*, edited by James H. Moulton (Edinburgh: T & T Clark, 1963), 65.

[420] The noun is singular in Greek (τὸν κύριον) but according to Newman and Nidda, the plural form such as "nail prints" is natural. Newman and Nida, *A Translator's Handbook on the Gospel of John*, 617.

[421] Turner classifies οὐ μὴ as an emphatic denial. Turner, *A Grammar of New Testament Greek*, 95-96.

[422] This another example of εἰς for ἐν. BDF, 111.

[423] Lit. Do not be unbelieving.

[424] Newman and Nida mention that the earliest of the Greek manuscripts have no punctuation and in this case it is not clear whether a question or a statement was implied. Newman and Nida, *A Translator's Handbook on the Gospel of John*, 619. Brown translates it as a statement. "You have believed because you have seen." Brown, *The Gospel according to John (xiii-xxi)*, 1019. This rendering is based on Young, who views the perfect (πεπίστευκας) as denoting a Perfect of Present State. He states, "Often the context, verbal idea, and perfect form will convey a present state of affairs with no antecedent action." Richard A. Young, *Intermediate New Testament Greek: A Linguistic and Exegetical Approach* (Nashville: Broadman & Holman Publishers, 1994), 128.

[425] RSV renders it as "yet believe," as a gnomic or timeless aorist. Brown is right when he notes that aorist does not denote a timeless element but rather the evangelist is referring to a group of his own situation who has not seen but has believed. Brown, *The Gospel according to John (xiii-xxi)*, 1027.

30 Indeed[426] Jesus did many other signs in the presence of the disciples, which are not written[427] in this book.

31 But these have been written that you may continue to believe[428] that Jesus is the Christ, the Son of God, that believing you may have life in his name.

3.3.6.4. Exegetical Notes

3.3.6.4.1. Vv. 24-25: Disclosure Longed by Thomas

This is the second appearance of Jesus to the group of disciples. The content of this pericope is unique to the FG, though the element of doubt is also seen in other resurrection accounts in the Gospels.[429] Vv. 24 and 25 prepare for Jesus' appearance to Thomas and his dialogue with Jesus. The introductory verses need not necessarily be seen as a contrast[430] but as a connective orienting the reader to a change in the situation. Thomas is described as "one of the twelve," an expression used of Judas Iscariot in 6:71.[431] Though the expressions are the same, there seems to be no negative connotation implied, rather it seems to be one of the ways the narrator uses to introduce a character. Δίδυμος, a Greek term (twin)[432] was also used as a proper noun. The FE often adds the detail

---

[426] Μὲν οὖν can be taken to mean "indeed." Zerwick and Grosvenor, *A Grammatical Analysis of the Greek New Testament*, 346.

[427] Ἔστιν γεγραμμένα is a Periphrastic Construction Perfect Passive.

[428] Both the textual witnesses are divided whether it should be read as aorist subjunctive (Alexandrinus, Byzantine tradition) or present subjunctive (Vaticanus, Sinaiticus*, Westcott, Aland Synopsis). The aorist could be translated "may come to faith" meaning that the readers have not come to faith. Brown also notes that in Jn. 13:15, the aorist is also used in the sense of strengthening one's faith. Brown, *The Gospel according to John (xiii-xxi)*, 1056. The UBS committee favours the aorist but the rating "C" indicates a considerable degree of doubt as to whether this or the other reading is to be preferred. Metzger, *A Textual Commentary on the Greek New Testament*, 219-220.

[429] Matt. 28:17; Mk. 16:14; Lk. 24:11, 25, 37, 41. Barrett, *The Gospel according to St. John*, 475.

[430] Moloney notes "The use of (now) to introduce the Thomas episode establishes a contrast between Thomas and the disciples present at the events described in vv. 19-23." Moloney, *The Gospel of John*, 538.

[431] Moloney, *The Gospel of John*, 577. Newman and Nidda state, "...v.24 intimates that it was the eleven rather than the larger group of followers." Barclay M. Newman and Eugene A. Nida, *A Translator's Handbook on the Gospel of John*, 617. Borchert rightly disagrees with Newman and Nidda and notes that here the reference is not to the size of the group; rather "... the twelve are symbolic representatives of the new people of God." Brochert, *John 12-21*, 311. What is more probable is that "twelve" adds to the authentication of tradition and its significance to the Johannine community.

[432] The term "twin" is not to be taken as double-mindedness. Brown states, "...it is romantic to maintain that the name is explained here in order to prepare for Thomas "two-minded" or doubting role." Brown, *The Gospel according to John (xiii-xxi)*, 1024. So also Borchert calls it as "irresponsible exegesis." Brochert, *John 12-21*, 312. Bennema also notes that the symbolic

"called Didymus" when he describes Thomas (20:24; 21:2). There seems to be a greater role for Thomas in the FG than in the other Gospels (Jn. 14:5; 20: 24-29; 21:2).[433]

Ἔλεγον can be taken as imperfect, not necessarily in a connotative sense, to suggest that the disciples were conveying Thomas that they have seen the Lord. The expression ἑωράκαμεν τὸν κύριον is the same one used by Mary in v. 18.[434] It is used to report that she saw the Lord, and it is also in terms of conveying the news to the disciples. Thomas was not a party to both these appearances and so refuses to believe. The refusal to believe is vividly brought out in οὐ μὴ πιστεύσω where μὴ πιστεύσω with the future indicative (πιστεύσω) is termed by BDF as "...the most definite form of negation regarding the future."[435] He refuses to believe without tangible evidence. Schnackenburg points to the progression in the demand for evidence: movement from "'seeing' 'placing' his finger 'placing' his hand in the wound in Jesus' side." [436] The use of βάλλω conveys a forceful impression and has the idea of 'throwing' rather than just 'placing.'[437] Thomas' verification of evidence, especially in the use of the term πλευρά, unique to the FG's description of the passion of Jesus (19:34), and occuring only once outside the FG (Act. 12:7), is used to tie together the passion and resurrection of Jesus (Jn. 20:20, 25, 27).

3.3.6.4.2. Vv. 26-27: An Opportunity for Disclosure to Thomas

The Thomas episode begins with the description of time— μεθ' ἡμέρας ὀκτὼ, one week after the appearance to the disciples. Köstenberger opines that the Feast of Unleavened Bread was over by this time and the disciples were soon to return home to Galilee. The difference from the previous appearance to the disciples is the inclusion of Thomas with them.[438] V. 26 shares two similarities with v.19: first, the description of the doors having been locked; second, the greeting Εἰρήνη ὑμῖν. However, there is one significant difference from v.19 i.e., there is no mention "because of the fear of the Jews." Thus to take the

---

interpretation of Thomas as a doubter does not hold ground if Thomas could be proved not as a doubter. Bennema, *Encountering Jesus*, 164.

433 Moloney, *The Gospel of John*, 331.

434 The use of double negative occurs seventeen times in the FG and more often than not it denotes a confirming an assurance with the exception of 13:8. Schnackenburg, *The Gospel according to St. John*, vol. 3, 330.

435 BDF, 184.

436 Schnackenburg, *The Gospel according to St. John*, vol. 3, 330.

437 Brown, *The Gospel according to John (xiii-xxi)*, 1025.

438 Moloney points that scholars have suggested "...the rhythmic reference to " Τῇ δὲ μιᾷ τῶν σαββάτων (v.1), ὀψίας τῇ ἡμέρᾳ ἐκείνῃ τῇ μιᾷ σαββάτων (v. 19), μεθ' ἡμέρας ὀκτὼ (v. 26) consciously situating all the events on the "...day of the Lord." Moloney, *The Gospel of John*, 537.

description τῶν θυρῶν κεκλεισμένων as implying the continuing fear of the disciples is not forthcoming; this is probably unlikely. Köstenberger has taken the contrary view in order to argue that Jn. 20:22 is only a symbolic gesture and not an imparting of the Spirit to the disciples.[439] As argued earlier, harmonizing the FC and Acts is by passing the unique presentation of the FG which emerges out of the situation of the Johannine community. The description τῶν θυρῶν κεκλεισμένων is used rather to highlight Jesus' miraculous manifestation to his disciples than the fear of the Jews.[440] Once again the FE makes use of the typical Johannine description of the resurrection appearance vividly presented in the phrase ἔστη εἰς τὸ μέσον. The greeting εἰρήνη ὑμῖν is the same as Jn. 20:19, 21.

In v. 27 Jesus' instruction to Thomas closely resembles what Thomas desired in v. 25. There are several imperatives used (φέρε (twice) ἴδε, βάλε and γίνου) by Jesus. There is also change in the word order from that of v. 25. Verse 25 had ἴδω βάλω τὸν δάκτυλόν βάλω μου τὴν χεῖρα but here it is φέρε τὸν δάκτυλόν σου ὧδε καὶ ἴδε τὰς χεῖράς μου βάλε εἰς τὴν πλευράν μου. The stress is on tangibility rather than sight, the sum substance of what Thomas desired (v. 25). Again the use of πλευράν recalls 19:34 and the passion of Jesus. There is a dramatic visualization in Jesus' words φέρε τὸν δάκτυλόν σου ὧδε.[441] Interestingly φέρε also has the meaning 'bearing' especially in the context of the Farewell Discourses (15:2, 4, 5, 8, 16). One is not sure whether a pun is implied here, especially taking into consideration the imperative in the last part μὴ γίνου ἄπιστος. If it is so, then the challenge is to bear fruits of believing and not be fruitless i.e., unbelieving. In this regard, some scholars[442] have rightly suggested that Thomas was never an unbeliever and Jesus instructs him to continue in a situation of belief.[443] The expressions unique to this text are to be

---

[439] Köstenberger, *The Mission of Jesus*, 578. Carson also takes the same view. Carson, *The Gospel according to John*, 657.

[440] Moloney rightly notes that there is no room for fear after vv. 19-23. Moloney, *The Gospel of John*, 539.

[441] Pamplaniyil brings out an interesting comment regarding the wounds of Jesus. He notes that the FE uses double entendre to describe Jesus' wounds. There are two levels at which this is described: a) at the literal level, the wounds testify to the human nature of Jesus, which also has apologetic motives; b) at the 'meta-narrative level,' "…Jesus's wounds function as the sign that discloses his true divinity." He further states, "…the same wounds that function as the revelatory sign that reveals Jesus' divinity and Lordship to Thomas (20, 27-28)." J. T. Pamplaniyil, "ΤΥΠΟΝ ΤΩΝ ΗΛΩΝ…" (Jn. 20, 25): Johannine Double Entendre of Jesus' Wounds," in *The Death of Jesus in the Fourth Gospel*, edited by G. Van Belle, BETL 200 (Leuven: Lueven University Press, 2007), 931, 942.

[442] Scholars such Wescott, Barrett, and others argue for this view. Wescott, *The Gospel according to St. John*, 296; Barrett, *The Gospel according to St. John*, 572.

[443] Stibbe opines that there is a gradation in the portrayal of Thomas i.e., from "false bravado" (Jn. 11:6), to misunderstanding (Jn. 14:5), and later on to 'unbelief.' Stibbe, *John*, 206.

understood as nouns and mean, "Show that you believe."[444] Riley is of the view that the FE is referring to unbelievers in the Thomas community, and Thomas is used as a literary device to exhort them to give up a false understanding of resurrection.[445] One is not sure whether such a community existed, and even if it did, its relevance for the Johannine community is not clear. The words of Jesus to Thomas do not negate the need for signs as this would go aganist 20:30-31 where signs are important avenues to believing. Mary and the disciples needed palpable evidence to confirm their faith. Bennema states rightly, "Thomas demands what others got— a first hand experience of the risen Jesus..."[446] Here there is a correlation between the resurrected Jesus and the incarnated Jesus.[447] Behind this episode is the attempt by the BD to bridge the gap between two periods: the time of Jesus' earthly ministry and the time of the BD's testimony. The evidence now available to the Johannine community still remains tangible through the BD's testimony.

3.3.6.4.3. Vv. 28-31: The Community Grasps the Disclosure

There is no indication in the text that Thomas verified his evidence.[448] The challenge of faith leads to Thomas' confession "my Lord and my God."[449] Schnackenburg corroborates that the double use of μου conveys a personal tone but in so doing does not remove the effectiveness of the statement.[450] Thomas'

---

444 Barrett, *The Gospel according to St. John*, 476.

445 He also affirms, "The conclusion of the Thomas pericope is not for the Thomas community alone, but for all who would read or hear this Gospel, and be asked to rely upon only the witness of John." Gregory J. Riley, *Resurrection Reconsidered: Thomas and John in Controversy* (Minneapolis: Fortress Press, 1995), 119-125.

446 Bennema, *Encountering Jesus*, 167.

447 Haenchen, *John 2*, 211.

448 Barrett opines that v. 29 suggests sight but was enough and therefore Thomas did not verify it. Barrett, *The Gospel according to St. John*, 476.

449 Ridderbos views the confession of Thomas as revealing "...shame and reverence at seeing Jesus' divine glory..." Ridderbos, *The Gospel of John*, 647. Bultmann states, "By means of these words ὁ θεός μου, the last confession spoken in the Gospel makes it clear that Jesus, to whom it refers, is the Logos who has now returned to the place where he was before the Incarnation, and who is glorified with the glory that he had with the Father before the world was (17:5); he is now recognized as the θεός that he was from the beginning (1:1)." Bultmann, *The Gospel of John*, 695. Bruce rightly notes that it is possibly wrong to differentiate between κύριός μου καὶ ὁ θεός μου as did Dodd; the former referring to Jesus before death and the latter as the risen Jesus. C. H. Dodd, *Interpretation of the Fourth Gospel*, 430, f.n. 2. cited in Bruce, *The Gospel of John*, 394.

450 Schnackenburg, *The Gospel according to St. John*, vol. 3, 333. van Belle gives three grammatical explanations for Thomas' reaction: "A. predicative explanation of ὁ θεός μου introduces two possibilities- a. Artemonius – Thomas' use of "my God" referred to God the Father and "my Lord" to Jesus (Artemonius cited by J. A. Bengel, *Gnomon Novi Testamenti in quo exnativa verborum vi simplicitas, profunditas, concinnitas, aslubritas sensum, coelestium*

confession sums up the Christological emphasis of the entire FG evidenced in the titles ὁ κύριός καὶ ὁ θεός. Scholars are divided on how to view the relation between v. 28 and v. 29. If v. 28 is taken separately, then, it can be seen as the climax of the Christological pronouncement of the FG. Brown notes, "In chap.1 the first disciples gave many titles to Jesus, and we have heard still others throughout the ministry: Rabbi, Messiah, Prophet, King of Israel, Son of God. In the post-resurrection appearances Jesus has been hailed as the Lord by Mary Magdalene … But it is Thomas who makes clear that one may address Jesus in the same language in which Israel addresses Yahweh..."[451]

Another way of viewing the Christological statement of Thomas is in relation to v. 29, not as a climax, but to denote a quality of faith that goes beyond Thomas' confession. Bultmann notes, "The answer of Jesus (v. 29) by all means confirms that in the statement of Thomas faith speaks; but at the same time the answer puts him to shame..."[452] However, for the Johannine community, the resurrection is an important climax of the self-revelation of Jesus. Ridderbos rightly notes, "Jesus' resurrection is the end and climax of that historical revelation."[453]

The combination of κύριός and θεός have allusions to OT forms of expression.[454] It is probably the result of the evangelist's reflection and possibly

---

indicator Tübingen); b. E. A. Abott paraphrased the confession as follows; "My dear Lord- is actually none other than my God." E. A. Abott, *Johannine Grammar: A Comparison of the Words of the Fourth Gospel with those of the Three* (London: Adam and Charles Black, 1906), 94. B. If Thomas' reaction is taken as exclamatory (My Lord and by God! One is faced with two possibilities: a. Thomas referred to God the Father: "praise (or) glory be to my Lord and my God (M. J. Harris, *Jesus as God: The New Testament use of Theos in Reference to Jesus* (Grand Rapids, Michigan: Baker Book House, 1992), 106-111). b. also maintain that Thomas addressed himself to Jesus and paraphrase the reaction together with F.C. Burkitt: "It is Jesus Himself and Now I recognize Him as Divine" (F. C. Burkitt, *Christian Beginnings* (London: University of London Press, 1924), 48). C. One can also translate the reaction of Thomas as vocative. Thomas responded to Jesus with "My Lord and my God" as a term of address. This represents the most commonly accepted explanation. The confession of Thomas was neither predicative nor exclamatory. The formula in v.28 clearly indicates that the following expression should be understood as a response to Jesus' invitation in vs. 27 and not so much as an exclamation." Gilbert van Belle, "Christology and Soteriology in the Fourth Gospel: The Conclusion to the Gospel of John Revisited," in *Theology and Christology in the Fourth Gospel: Essays by the Members of the Society for New Testament Study Johannine Writings Seminar*, BETL 184, edited by G. Van Belle, J. G. Van der Watt and P. Maritz (Leuven: Leuven University Press, 2005), 454-455.

[451] Brown, *The Gospel according to John (xiii-xxi)*, 1047.

[452] Bultmann, *The Gospel of John: A Commentary*, 695.

[453] Ridderbos, *The Gospel of John*, 648.

[454] Schnackenburg, *The Gospel according to St. John*, vol. 3, 333.

an aspect of primitive Christian liturgy. Further, it is a gibe at the emperor cult where both these terms occur.[455]

Jesus' response to Thomas' confession has led to much discussion about whether it is a statement or a question. Schnackenburg takes it as a statement, though in 1:50 and 16:31, it is a question.[456] Barrett notes, Jesus "...does not ask questions but declares the truth."[457] It is possible to take it as a question expecting an answer 'yes.' However, it does not seem to be a rebuke[458] as those described earlier also benefited from seeing Jesus. The focus of this saying is more on the second part. Thomas' meeting with the risen Jesus is summarized in ἑώρακάς. Ἑώρακάς here signifies seeing beyond the temporal to the actual identity of Jesus, i.e., Jesus is both κύριός and θεός, a confession that Thomas had made in v. 28. Thomas acknowledges that Jesus is "equal to God" as "... he has two powers: ("God") and eschatological ("Lord")."[459] in the sense of power to lay down life and take it again. It is a belief that issues from seeing.

Nonetheless, there is no scope for a contrast here between 'seeing and believing' and 'believing without seeing.' The second part of the saying begins with *μακάριοι*; a clear indication that comparison is not implied. There are a number of beatitudes in the synoptics as well in Acts (20:35), but the FG has only one other beatitude (13:17). Also, faith that is based on seeing the risen

---

455 Schnackenburg, *The Gospel according to St. John*, vol. 3, 333. Witherington III notes that emperor Domitian took over "...the address "*Dominus et Deus noster*," meaning "Our Lord and God."" Witherington III, *John's Wisdom*, 349.

456 Schnackenburg gives four reasons: a. "The high-minded confession of the disciple who (distinct form Nathanael) is already a long-time follower of Jesus, does not, as such, permit of any doubt; b. in this situation after Jesus' resurrection, the evangelist scarcely still casts doubt the faith of the disciple; c. the perfect of πιστεύειν signifies a firm faith (cf. 6:69; 11:27) – the two other passages have the perfect tense; d. the connection to what follows is also better: the statement is followed by the blessing of those who, without seeing, summon up this faith." Schnackenburg, *The Gospel according to St. John*, vol. 3, 334.

457 Barrett, *The Gospel according to St. John*, 573. There are others scholars who also take it as a statement: Schnackenburg, *The Gospel according to St. John*, vol. 3, 334; Carson, *The Gospel according to John*, 659-660; Beasley-Murray, *John*, 386. Kanagaraj, *The Gospel of John*, 662.

458 Köstenberger takes the response to Thomas as a mild rebuke. Köstenberger, *John*, 580. Two works note that this particular incident reported in the FG is to correct the view held by Thomas Christians. The presupposition being that Jesus in the FG rebukes Thomas. The two works are: a) E. Pagels, *Beyond Belief: The Secret Gospel of Thomas* (New York: Random Book House, 1998); and b) J. Riley, *Resurrection Reconsidered*. Pagels states, "John's Jesus rebukes Thomas for lacking in faith and tells him to believe "*Do not be faithless, but believe*." Pagels, *Beyond Belief*, 32. Judge rightly critiques the faulty position presented in these works by noting, "The evangelist acknowledges the struggle with doubt – it is in fact constitutive of faith. But his story is about more than doubt and gets beyond rebuke." P. J. Judge, "John 20, 24-29: More Than Doubt, Beyond Rebuke," in *The Death of Jesus in the Fourth Gospel*, edited by G. Van Belle, BETL 200 (Leuven: Leuven University Press, 2007), 919.

459 Neyrey, *The Gospel of John*, 331.

Jesus is not to be seen as a limited faith[460] or an inferior faith. Brown rightly notes, "...the use of visible is an indispensable condition of the Word's having become flesh. As long as Jesus stood among men, one had to come to faith through the visible."[461] He also states the change of situation that has taken place, the passing away of witnesses but the presence of Jesus in the person of the Spirit.[462] Thus, though being in the second generation, who now have to rely on the words of the apostles, the community is not at a disadvantage, but from rather benefits from the blessing. It is in this sense that the term μακάριοι has to be understood. Brown again rightly notes that the saying of Jesus here is "...certainly not a rejection of the value of signs for faith."[463] This is contrary to the view of Haenchen who states, "He thereby also rejects as imperfect that tradition which attempts to overcome doubt by palpable proof of the visible, as in Luke 24:36-43."[464]

In v. 30, the use of μὲν οὖν[465] points to a continuity with the Thomas episode.[466] The continuity is clearly brought out by Howard-Brook when he says, "The narrator suggests that the offer to let Thomas touch his risen body was itself a sign: a physical act that invites the conclusion that Jesus is from God, to those eyes to see."[467] The FE also adds that Jesus did many other signs in the presence of the disciples. Σημεῖα is a significant term in the FG. It points to the reality beyond the visible. Signs are a manifestation of Jesus' glory. The term occurs seventeen times in the FG (2:11, 18, 23; 3:2; 4:48, 54; 6:2, 14, 26, 30; 7:31; 9:16; 10:41; 11:47; 12:18, 37; 20:30).[468] To what do σημεῖα (signs) refer to here? For Bultmann, they refer to the entire content of the FG i.e, both sign and word. Bultmann also notes that for the

---

[460] Köstenberger does not see Thomas' faith as inferior for the confession of Thomas has a climatic value in the Johannine narrative. However, he does see it as a limitation of a faith in Jesus based on seeing him rise. Köstenberger, *John*, 580.

[461] Brown, *The Gospel according to John (xiii-xxi)*, 1050

[462] Brown, *The Gospel according to John (xiii-xxi)*, 1050.

[463] Brown, *The Gospel according to John (xiii-xxi)*, 1051. Ridderbos, *The Gospel of John*, 649.

[464] Haenchen, *John 2*, 212.

[465] Brown describes some of the characteristics of Lucan style found in this verse: a. μὲν οὖν other than this only seen in 19:24 whereas occurs 26 times in Acts; b. the use of καὶ subsequent to Πολλα to introduce an adjective is a Lucan characteristic; c. ἐνώπιον occurs only in v.30 but is common in Luke/Acts. Brown, *The Gospel according to John (xiii-xxi)*, 1055. The origin of the passage need not "…be doubted as the peculiarities can also be explained in other ways." Schnackenburg, *The Gospel according to St. John*, vo. 3, 336.

[466] Köstenberger, *John*, 581.

[467] Howard-Brook, *Becoming Children of God*, 463.

[468] Moulton and Geden, eds., *A Concordance to the Greek Testament*, 891.

FE, "σημεῖα and ῥήματα flow together."[469] The context here does not call for including discourses in the signs. Brown rightly notes that σημεῖα include not only the signs of chaps. 1-12, but also the appearances to the disciples in 20:1-28[470] that led the disciples to acknowledge Jesus' lordship.[471] Nicol states, "The concept of *sēmeion* is widened to include appearances...(it) has acquired striking elasticity."[472] However, he is against the view that death[473] and resurrection[474] are also σημεῖα. Barrett is correct here when he states, "… in death and resurrection of Jesus, sign and its meaning coincide."[475] Death and resurrection are σημεῖα,[476] one such reference is in 2:21 where he refers to his body as the temple. In this regard Nicol notes, "John never directly says the resurrection is also a σημεῖον, but it is significant that when the Jews ask Jesus for a σημεῖον in 2:18, he answers by referring to his resurrection."[477] But if the signs are taken not only to refer to acts of Jesus but also occasions in which Jesus manifested his glory,[478] then, resurrection can also be taken as a sign.

The purpose of describing the signs is to inculcate belief. There is a lot of discussion on whether πιστεύ[σ]ητε is an aorist subjunctive or present subjunctive. Those that advocate the present argue for continuing in faith whereas those that advocate the aorist argue for coming to the faith. It is not very clear, and Carson notes, "...John elsewhere in his Gospel can use *either* tense to refer to *both* coming to faith[479] and continuing in the faith."[480] He further notes that in the FG the aorist subjunctive after ἵνα occurs approximately eighty eight times and with the present subjunctive it occurs approximately forty seven times. On syntactical basis, Carson argues that the question is, "Who is the Messiah?" He then concludes that aorist subjunctive meant coming to faith.[481] Taking into account the situation in which it was written

---

469 Bultmann, *The Gospel of John: A Commentary*, 452.

470 Beasley-Murray also supports this view. Beasley-Murray, *John*, 387.

471 Brown, *The Gospel according to John (xiii-xxi)*, 1058.

472 W. Nicol, *The Sēmeia in the Fourth Gospel: Tradition and Redaction* Supplements to Novum Testamentum 32 (Leiden: E. J. Brill, 1972), 115.

473 Lightfoot notes, "The crucifixion was to St. John doubtless the greatest sign of all." R. H. Lightfoot, *St. John's Gospel: A Commentary* (Oxford: Clarendon Press, 1957), 336.

474 Barrett notes at first "…the death and resurrection are the supreme revelation." Barrett, *The Gospel according to St. John*, 78.

475 Barrett, *The Gospel according to St. John*, 78.

476 Carson states, "…greatest sign of them all is the death, resurrection and exaltation of the incarnate word." Carson, *The Gospel according to John*, 661.

477 Nicol, *The Sēmeia in the Fourth Gospel*, 115.

478 This is the view of Ridderbos. Ridderbos, *The Gospel of John*, 651.

479 Witherington III, *John's Wisdom*, 346; Carson, *The Gospel according to John*, 662.

480 Carson, *The Gospel according to John*, 662.

481 Carson, *The Gospel according to John*, 662.

and the circumstances related to it, especially in the context of the Johannine community, it is more feasible to take it as an exhortation to continue in faith.[482] Schnackenburg clearly spells out this aspect when he states that the messianic question pertains to the conflict between the Johannine community and the contemporary Judaism and thus, it is written to retort the Jewish objections and inculcate faith in Jesus the Messiah.[483] de Jonge also rightly argues on similar lines, when he states, "The FG was primarily written for the instruction and inner strengthening of the Johannine community. The Johannine view of Jesus and the union between belivers and the Son of God came into being in a long process of internal discussion and collective meditation. Internal discussions had spurred by debate with group outside the community."[484]

V. 31 also expresses the Christological aspects of the FG in the use of the titles Messiah and Son of God. Ridderbos rightly notes that the title 'Son of God' signifies "...the preexistent ontological relation to God that underlies this all embracing function of the Son of man...One cannot, therefore, simply view "Son of God" in 20:31 as synonymous with "Messiah,"..."[485] The purpose of the FG is stated in terms of *ζωὴν ἔχητε ἐν τῷ ὀνόματι αὐτοῦ*. The expression *τῷ ὀνόματι αὐτοῦ* means "...on and in his person (3:18)."[486] Here *ζωὴν* refers to "all-embracing salvation" ...to which faith in Jesus as the only-begotten of the Father gives access..."[487] Lee describes the concept of life in the FG succinctly, "The great paradox, for John, is that the one who is the source of life of creation has become incarnate, entering into the natural world and transfiguring its life with divine glory."[488]

---

[482] Ridderbos, *The Gospel of John, 652.*

[483] Schnackenburg, *The Gospel according to St. John*, vol. 3, 339.

[484] Marinus de Jonge, "Christology, Controversy and Community in the Gospel of John," in *Christology, Controversy and Community: New Testament Essays in Honour of David R. Catchpole*, NovTSup 99, edited by David G. Horrell and Christopher M. Tuckett (Leiden: Brill, 2000), 226.

[485] Ridderbos, *The Gospel of John*, 653. Schnackenburg also argues on similar lines, when he states, "But for the evangelist, it has become the most exalted expression of his Christology and has taken up into itself the full significance of the 'Son'-revelation." Schnackenburg, *The Gospel according to St. John*, vol. 3, 339.

[486] Schnackenburg, *The Gospel according to St. John*, vol. 3, 339.

[487] Ridderbos, *The Gospel of John*, 653. Neyrey and Rohrbaugh note in this regard, "This Gospel has been written to mediate and maintain life in John's antisocietal group and to whomever this group might include within its membership." Bruce J. Malina and Richard L. Rohrbaugh, *Social-Science Commentary on the Gospel of John* (Minneapolis: Fortress Press, 1998), 286

[488] Lee, "Resurrection and Life," 213.

3.3.6.5. Theological Interpretation

The Thomas episode has figured in a lot of discussion on the relation between seeing and believing, especially in the context where Jesus discourages people's need for signs and wonders in 4:48. In line with this, some scholars take Thomas' belief as inferior while others defend Thomas' demand for proof. Dodd states, "John, it appears, has brought out this contrast of belief and unbelief by making Thomas the spokesman of the incredulous, and representing him as having been absent when Christ appeared to his disciples..."[489] Köstenberger uses the incident involving Thomas recorded by the FE against the gnostic understanding that Jesus only appeared to be human as in the case of Jn. 1:14.[490] Whatever said and done, this pericope is significant for two reasons, both of which are related to each other. The first reason being, it is important because of the Christological title Lord and God confessed by Thomas, and the second reason is the significance of these titles to the Johannine community. The title 'God' is significant in the FG and remains as one of the prominent titles that describes Jesus' identity in the FG. In Jn. 12:28, Jesus says, "For I spake not from myself; but the Father which sent me, he hath given me a commandment, what I should say, and what I should speak...the things therefore which I speak, even as the Father who said unto me, so I speak." The usual emphasis on Jesus doing things in the Father's name relates to the prophecy, "my words which he will speak in my name" (Deut. 18:19).[491]

What is vitally important concerning the Thomas episode is the fact that the Johannine community viewed it extremely important that their believing is based on the testimony of the BD who stands behind the tradition. This becomes the tangible evidence of their understanding of Jesus' identity and in turn the community's own identity. The identity of Jesus emphasized by the community is that the risen Jesus is both Lord and God. In fact there is a movement from the understanding 'Lord' to 'God.' The community in affirming the risen Jesus as God brings to a close what has been stated in the prologue. The whole FG is an attempt by the FE to convince the readers that Jesus shares a relationship with God. Most probably the community understood the significance of the resurrection of Jesus not just as the risen Son of God but God himself; a title unparalleled in the other canonical gospel accounts. The confession of Thomas seems to be out of the ordinary, but it is not so when seen in the light of Jn. 14:5. Jesus instructs Thomas saying that knowing him is to know the Father (Jn. 14:7). Believing becomes the cornerstone of the

---

[489] Dodd, *Historical Traditions in the Fourth Gospel*, 145.

[490] Köstenberger, *The Mission of Jesus*, 578.

[491] Glasson, *Moses in the Fourth Gospel*, 30.

community's embracing of the BD's testimony regarding Jesus' identity. This distinguishes the community from those outside the community.

Just as Jesus reveals the Father to the disciples, the BD reveals Jesus is God to the Johannine community. Thus, there seems to be a symmetry between the role of Jesus to the disciples and the role of the BD in the Johannine community.

There is ground for stating this view. In Jn. 1:18, Jesus is described as the Son who is in the bossom of the Father who makes known the Father and in Jn 13:23 the BD is described as reclining in the bossom of Jesus. Bennema in this regard notes, "As the Father and Jesus have an intimate relationship characterized by love (1:18; 3:35; 5:20; 14:31; 15:9), so the BD enjoys an especially close relationship with Jesus, which the other disciples apparently did not share..."[492] The BD certainly not only shares a close relationship with Jesus, but also knows things which the other disciples know. However, in the FG the knowledge of Jesus surpasses that of the BD as he lacks understanding in knowing the person who will betray Jesus (13:28).

The placement of the purpose of the FG immediately after the resurrection narrative highlights the significance of the resurrection narrative. The resurrection narrative is also a sign that is meant to convey the identity of Jesus. The disciples at various levels understand the identity of Jesus as one who has ascended and is now ascending to the place that he came from. The presence of Jesus now takes the form of the Paraclete, and the benefits of Jesus' ascension are now made available to all the 'brothers' of Jesus who extend beyond the disciples to the Johannine community.

Conclusion

The resurrection narrative in Jn. 20 describes varied events of disclosure. These are not to be pitted against each other. It is a well constructed narrative disclosing, at different stages, the identity and mission of Jesus and the disciples. What is the identity of Jesus that this narrative attempts to present? How can this be seen as the key to understanding the identity of Jesus in the rest of the gospel? In the resurrection narrative, the identity of Jesus is stated through different titles and relationships. The titles include: Lord (20:2, 13, 18, 20, 25, 28 (my Lord)), teacher (v. 16), God (vv. 17, 28), Christ (v. 31) and lastly Son of God (v. 31). All these titles find their significance in the Father-Son relationship. Incidentally, the Father-Son relationship comes at two crucial points in the narrative; v. 21 describes the identity of Jesus with the Father,

---

[492] Bennema goes on to characterize the BD as one who follows Jesus and remains with Jesus (18: 15-27; 19: 26; 21: 20-22); one who is perceptive (19:27; 21: 7); He further states, "...the Beloved Disciple is an ideal and unique eyewitness to Jesus' ministry because he enjoys a privileged position, is perceptive, and remains with Jesus from the start in 1:29 to the end in 21:22. Bennema, *Encountering Jesus*, 171-172, 172-174.

and in v. 21 which sets the mission of the disciples. Identity is born out the relationship which the Son shares with the Father. Therefore, the coming of the Son into the world (1:14) was an opportunity for the disciples to see the glory of God in the Son, and the coming also implies a return to the Father, a return to the relationship with the Father. This would complete the circle but not in terms of engagement with the community which necessitates coming again in the Spirit. It is the last two i.e., the going back to the Father and the coming again as Spirit to reside among the disciples that are clearly brought out in the resurrection narrative of Jn. 20.

The resurrection narrative presents the glorification of the Son which can be termed as one of presence i.e., being in the presence of the Father and being present among the disciples. The presence of the Spirit given to the disciples is at one and the same time the presence of the Father as well as the Son. The disciples experience the community's presence (Father, Son and the Spirit) and it is in this bonding that the disciples engage in mission, which is the extension of the presence of Jesus. Jesus' unique characteristics serve as a basis for his unique identity and mission.[493] It can be better explained as:

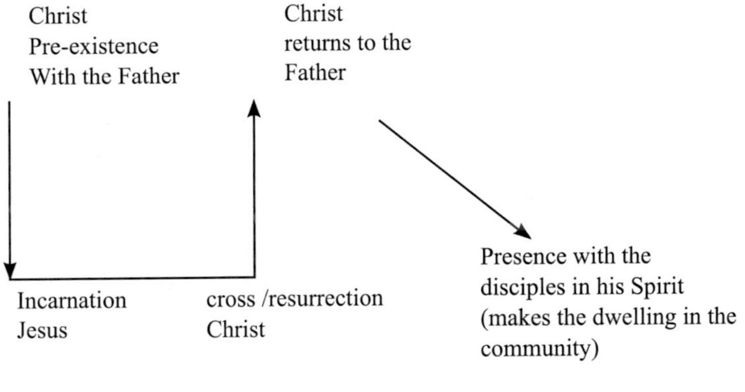

Resurrection in the FG is also a sign— a sign that describes the journey back to the Father, and also a return in order to be present among the disciples. This sign reiterates the relationship that Jesus shares with the Father.

[493] Köstenberger takes the unique identity as the basis for a unique mission. Köstenberger, *The Mission of Jesus*, 50. The researcher would like to take the unique characteristics of the Messiah as the basis for the unique identity and mission. In other words, the identity and mission remain inseparable and the same is true with the disciples of Jesus.

Chapter 4

John 20: Paradigm of the Johannine Community's Identity and Mission

Introduction

The resurrection narrative in Jn. 20 defines the identity and mission of Jesus and the disciples in precise terms. Interestingly, identity and mission in the FG are not separate aspects but are conjoined with each other. They converge at the Father-Son relationship. The FG essentially is a revelation of this relationship and its importance. The present chapter takes the discussion further on identity and mission by viewing the significance of Jn. 20 to the FG as a whole and the Johannine community in particular. In other words, this chapter attempts to look at Jn. 20 from the perspective of the Johannine community's identity and mission. Some of the queries of importance include: What were the factors that went into the making of identity and mission of the Johannine community? How did these factors reorient the Johannine community's understanding of identity and mission? What metaphor did the Johannine community use to assert its identity and mission? These issues are taken up for discussion in this chapter.

4.1. Context of the Johannine Community

Identity formation does not take place in a vacuum. In most cases, identity formation is related to social, religious, political, and economic factors. Mikael Tellbe defines identity as a social construct.[1] Though this social construct is

[1] Tellbe notes, "..."identity" is basically a social concept." Mikael Tellbe, "The Prototypical Christ-believer: Early Christian Identity Formation in Ephesus," in *Exploring Early Christian Identity*, edited by Bengt Holmberg (Tübingen: Mohr Siebeck, 2008), 120. This was noted also by Richard Jenkins, who states, "...all human identities are by definition

of immense importance, yet in the context of the first century,[2] in which the Johannine community took shape, religious expression cannot be isolated from the social.[3] The understanding of God did affect the perception of society and vice versa. van der Watt rightly notes, "Language is a social phenomenon. Texts express social conventions and are also embedded in social contexts."[4] This is true in the case of the Johannine community where Christology is reinterpreted in terms of the experiences of the community.

There are two issues involved here: the experiences of the Johannine community, and how these led to a reinterpretation of Christology. Dunn rightly opines that the developed form of the FG, in comparison with the synoptics, pertains to the social and religious context in which the FG took shape.[5] Thus, one could assume that the FG's Christology essentially presents an interpretive Christology with its catalyst being the social context of the Johannine community. The identity of Christ is mediated through the context and the needs of the community, which in turn provides the probable key to the

---

social identities. Identifying ourselves or others is a matter of meaning, and meaning always involves interaction: agreement and disagreement, convention and innovation, communication and negotiation." Richard Jenkins, *Social Identity* (London: Routledge, 2004), 4.

[2] Nickelsburg brings out this idea clearly when he states, "Ancient religious texts are historical artifacts, created in time and place. Their conceptions and ideologies responded to specific historical circumstances and functioned in particular social locations. If our interpretation is to do these texts justice, we must try to identify their time, circumstances, and locations to the extent that this is possible." George W. E. Nickelsburg, *Ancient Judaism and Christian Origins: Diversity, Continuity, and Transformation* (Minneapolis: Fortress Press, 2003), 191.

[3] LaFrague notes, "The important aspect of early Christian history does not lie in the moral tales we can tell of concrete struggles between Jewish and Christian groups. The reconstruction of social setting is important because human consciousness is thoroughly a social reality." Michael LaFargue, "The Authority of the Excluded: Mark's Challenge to a Rational Hermeneutics," in *Religious Propaganda and Missionary Competition in the New Testament World: Essays Honouring Dieter Georgi*, NovTSup 74, edited by Lukas Bormann, Kelly Del Tredici and Angela Standhartinger (Leiden: E. J. Brill, 1994), 255. Brown states, "*Primarily*, the gospels tell us how an evangelist conceived of and presented Jesus to a Christian community in the last third of the first century, a presentation that gives us an insight into that community's life at the time when the gospel was written." Raymond E. Brown, "The Johannine Ecclesiology-the Community's Origins," *Int*. 31/4 (O. 1977): 380.

[4] Jan G. van der Watt, "The Father Shows the Son Everything. The Imagery of Education in John 5:19-23," *APB* 18 (Ja. 2007): 263.

[5] James D. G. Dunn, "John and the Synoptics as a Theological Question," in *Exploring the Gospel of John in Honor of D. Moddy Smith*, edited by R. Alan Culpepper and C. Clifton Black (Westminster: John Knox Press, 1996), 307. Wenham and Walton ascertain that though the issue of identity is seen in Matthew, Mark, and Luke, John has the primary focus on the identity of Jesus. The FG deals with question of who Jesus is and this begins in the very first chapter of John's gospel (Jn 1: 41, 49). David Wenham and Steve Walton, *Exploring the New Testament: A Guide to the Gospels and Acts*, vol. 1 (London: SPCK, 2001), 245.

understanding of the Christology in the FG.[6] This does not deny the historical aspect of the FG or the traditions behind it; or makes a value judgment on the historic element of the FG.[7]

The community setting has a vital role in comprehending the Christology of the FG; this has been noted by several scholars. Weder notes, "The Johannine community was not facing the question on how one might conceive God's presence in the world but rather, the question of how one might appropriately understand the experience with Jesus of Nazareth. The Logos hymn originated in the experiences that were to be had with Jesus of Nazareth and with his own words, as well as words about him."[8] de Jonge also notes, "Christology developed in the Fourth Gospel is meant for and function within a particular "Johannine" community. This is ... of a particular community: orienting itself towards the testimony of the disciples and guided by the Spirit of Truth (14-16)."[9] O'Day puts it succinctly, "Literary style of the Gospel of John works in partnership with its theology to tell its story of Jesus. The gospel is crafted to foreground the inseparability of the event and interpretation, story and theology. To try to separate what happened in the life of Jesus from its meaning is a false pursuit for this gospel...Jesus' life and ministry lies in their theological significance …and not in the events in and of themselves."[10]

---

[6] Coloe notes, "The hermeneutical paradigm that emerged throughout the last century and continues to be used in most Johannine criticism- this paradigm understands the text as the product of a particular community; it therefore addresses the needs of that community and to some extent reflects the community's life and concerns. This paradigm presumes that the gospel uses the language, images, conventions, perceptions, and theological understanding of its historical situation in order to communicate to people living within that situation." Mary L. Coloe, *Dwelling in the Household of God: Johannine Ecclesiology and Spirituality* (Minnesota: Liturgical Press, 2007), 172-173. However, it must be noted that Judith Lieu would disagree with this point. For Lieu, the text constructs rather than reflects social realities. Judith M. Lieu, *Christian Identity in the Jewish and Graeco-Roman World* (Oxford Oxford University Press, 2004), 11. Though this is true, there is the other side as well. Tellbe notes "The text should be regarded as vehicle, which may not only construct the self-understanding of reader/s (individual and social identities) but which may also reflect the existing realities (both relating to the author and to the community of the addressees)." Tellbe, "The Prototypical Christ-believer," 119.

[7] Bauckham discusses elaborately the historiographical characteristics of the gospel in terms of topography, chronology, etc. Richard Bauckham, "Historiographical Characteristics of the Gospel of John," *NTS* 53/1 (Ja. 2007): 17-36.

[8] Hans Weder, "*Deus Incarnatus*: On the Hermeneutics of Christology in the Johannine Writings," in *Exploring the Gospel of John: in Honor of D. Moddy Smith*, edited by R. Alan Culpepper and C. Clifton Black (Westminster: John Knox Press, 1996), 329.

[9] Marinus de Jonge, "Christology, Controversy and Community in the Gospel of John," in *Christology, Controversy and Community: New Testament Essays in Honour of David R. Catchpole*, NovTSup 99, edited by David G. Horrell and Christopher M. Tuckett (Leiden: Brill, 2000), 222.

[10] Gail R. O' Day, "The Word Become Flesh: Story and Theology in the Gospel of John," in "*What is John?*", vol. 2: *Literary and Sociological Readings of the Fourth Gospel*, edited by

Thatcher also argues, "The Christology of the Johannine literature becomes coherent only when viewed against the backdrop of the "social crisis" that led to the composition of these books."[11]

If it is supposed that the Johannine community radically reinterpreted Christology by drawing resources from its context, it becomes mandatory to investigate the factors that facilitated this reinterpretation.

4.1.1. Defining the Context of the Johannine Community

In discerning the defining factors that helped the Johannine community to articulate its identity and mission, context plays a pivotal role. What was the setting of the Johannine community? The *Birkat ha-Minim* has been taken as one of the primary contexts of the Johannine community.[12] Nevertheless, this is a matter of debate in the current scholarly discussion.[13] This does not negate the notion that the Johannine community underwent conflicts with the synagogue, which led to the expulsion of the community, though their expulsion can be defined in various ways.[14] Nevertheless, a situation of

---

Fernando F. Segovia, SBL Symposium Series 7 (Atlanta: Scholars Press, 1998), 67.

[11] Tom Thatcher, "Remembering Jesus: John's Negative Christology" in *The Messiah in Old and New Testaments*, edited by Stanley E. Porter, McMaster NT Studies (Grand Rapids, Michigan: William B. Eerdmans Publishing Company, 2007), 175. Cameron and Miller in their description of the Christian origins use the terms "myth making" and "social formation;" these categories would be helpful in understanding Johannine Christology and Johannine Community. Ron Cameron and Merrill P. Miller, "Conclusion: Redescribing Christian Origins" in *Redescribing Christian Origin*, SBL Symposium Series 28, edited by Ron Cameron and Merrill P. Miller (Leiden: Brill, 2004), 513.

[12] For further details refer Chapter III where various views were exchanged and evaluated concerning the formation, composition and the nature of the Johannine community.

[13] van der Watt states, "The exact nature, situation, stage and locale of the conflict between the Johannine community and synagogue Judaism are still open to debate, but that does not negate the fact that there most probably was such a conflict and that the material in the Gospel relates to such a conflict. The ethical material does relate to a situation of conflict and that the emphases found in the Gospel are even determined by such a conflict." Jan G. van der Watt, "Radical Social Redefinition and Radical Love: Ethics and ethos in the Gospel according to John," in *Identity, Ethics and Ethos in the New Testament*, edited by Jan G. van der Watt (Berlin: Walter de Gruyter, 2006), 128.

[14] Charlesworth certainly argues for the Johannine community's expulsion from the synagogue services and this according to him is seen when the gospel is looked at in the light of the Jewish festivals (chapters 7-9). "…John mirrors the fact that…once cherished opportunities are no longer possible to the Jews in Johannine school." Charlesworth further notes on the rifts that took place in the community: a. the separation from the synagogue; b. some of the community members leave and the author denounces them as the antichrists (I Jn. 2:19); c. the polemic between the Johannine group and the followers of John the Baptist. James H. Charlesworth, "The Dead Sea Scrolls and the Gospel according to John," in *Exploring the Gospel of John in Honor of D. Moody Smith*, edited by R. Alan Culpepper and C. Clifton Black (Westminster: John Knox Press, 1996), 76-77.

conflict was inevitable towards the end of the first century CE,[15] especially in the wake of the destruction of the Jerusalem Temple, where communities—the Johannine and Jewish communities—were involved in articulating the finer points of their separate identities.[16] The conflict with the synagogue and the consequent fractured relationship is an argument that can also be inferred from the other canonical gospels such as Matthew and Luke. This presupposition is a needed prerequisite for understanding identity and mission in the FG. The fractured relationship did make room for diverse experiences of the Johannine community.

4.1.1.1. Consequences of the Fractured Relationship

The experiences of the Johannine community are inferred from the FG, especially by looking at some of the Christological aspects of the FG, and the texts that deal with the situation of the community. The assumption supposed here is that the text is born out of the context, and Christology as enumerated in the FG is an interpretative Christology. The exclusion could be seen as expulsion from the synagogal service, but this does not rule out the social consequences. Stegemanns (Ekkehard and Wolfgang) note, "Initially only a question of the exclusion of Christ-confessors from the synagogal worship service, that this could also involve social consequences too…"[17] Loader too notes, "The dislocation was at once social and religious."[18]

4.1.1.1.1. Loss of Sacred Space

The loss of sacred space began with the expulsion of the Johannine community from the synagogue but became more acute in the light of the events that followed. Here, sacred space had to do with the community's question about who Christ is. What place did Christ occupy in the monotheistic framework of the Jewish faith? The Father-Son relationship with its diversified conceptual framework of unity and functionality is an attempt to deal with this question.

Related to the discussion on the identity of Christ, there also arose a debate between the Johannine community and the synagogue on the place of Jewish leaders. What role does Christ have in relation to the leaders of Jewish faith?

---

[15] "The Christian church was in conflict with the Jewish synagogue throughout much of the first century: Christians claimed to be the successors of Israel, and seemed to the synagogue to be poaching its members. The confrontation is quite clear, John writes to stress on Jesus' messiahship, an aspect denied by the Jews." Wenham and Walton, *Exploring the New Testament: A Guide to the Gospels and Acts*, 261.

[16] Robert Kysar, *John, the Maverick Gospel* (Atlanta: John Knox Press, 1970), 16.

[17] Ekkehard W. Stegemann and Wolfgange Stegemann, *The Jesus Movement: A Social History of the First Century*, translated by O. C. Dean (Minneapolis: Fortress Press, 1995), 239.

[18] William Loader, *The Christology of the Fourth Gospel: Structure and Issues*, BBET 23, edited by Jürgen Becker and Henning Graf Reventlow (New York: Peter Lang, 1989), 57.

Texts in the FG however, exclusively deal with the role of Moses,[19] Abraham,[20] Jacob,[21] and their relation to Christ. Jesus in his conversation with the Samaritan woman states, "But the hour is coming, and now is, when the true worshipers will worship the Father in spirit and truth, for such the Father seeks to worship him" (Jn. 4:23). Köstenberger rightly explains this statement, "…the crucified and resurrected Christ would serve as a substitute for the Jerusalem Temple as the new center of worship for God's people- (Jn. 19-22)."[22] Unlike the worship of "the father," the expression used by the Samaritan woman (Jn. 4:20), Jesus uses her response to stress the worship of "the father" (Jn. 4:21c).[23] This brings a valuable insight into the Johannine community: the Johannine community understood worship as rightly belonging to the Father and not the leaders of Israel. It expresses an inclusive aspect of worship, which accommodates rather than excludes. Swanson brings out a meaningful point when he notes, "The link that Jesus establishes between the fathers and the Father implies a relationship between two kinds of space: the patriarchal homelands and the Father's House, that spaceless place in which all who worship the Father worship neither on the Samaritan Gerazim nor on the Judaioi Mt. Zion but "in spirit and in truth."[24]

The apocalyptic and merkabah mysticism also claimed direct knowledge of heavenly mysteries, and were represented by Enoch, Abraham and others.[25] The identity of these leaders is redefined in the light of the identity of Christ. Thatcher notes, "According to John, Jesus is not what the Jews say that he is; he is far superior, not only to their claims about him, but also to the entire religious system."[26] However, it was not just the leaders, but also the Scriptures

---

[19] Refer Thatcher, "Remembering Jesus," 177-183. Some of the texts that deal with Moses include: Jn. 1:17; 1:45; 3:14; 5:45; 6:32; 7:19; 7:22-23; 8:5; 9:28. Jn. 1:17 can be taken to mean "…Christ has revealed God in a more intimate fashion than even Moses." Robert Kysar, "Christology and Controversy: The Contribution of the Prologue of the Gospel of John to New Testament Christology and their Historical Setting," *CurTM* 5/6 (Dec. 1978): 356. There seem to be an emphasis on the "greater than Mose" motif in these texts. Minear compares Dt. 34 and Jn. 20 and sees the latter as an indication of the Johannine community's assertion of knowing 'where' Jesus has gone. Paul S. Minear, ""We Don't Know Where…" John 20:2," *Int.* 30/2 (Ap. 1976): 138-139.

[20] The discussion on Abraham is seen in Jn. 8:33-58.

[21] Jn. 4: 5, 6, 12.

[22] Andreas J. Köstenberger, *John*, BECNT (Grand Rapids, Michigan: Baker Academic, 2004), 155.

[23] Francis J. Moloney, *The Gospel of John*, SacPag 4, edited by Daniel J. Harrington (Minnesota: The Liturgical Press, 1998), 128.

[24] Tod D. Swanson, "To Prepare a Place: Johannine Christianity and the Collapse of Ethnic Territory," *JAAR* 62/2 (Summer 1994): 256.

[25] James D. G. Dunn, *The Parting of the Ways: Between Christianity and Judaism and their Significance for the Character of Christianity*, 2nd ed. (London: SCM Press, 2006), 295.

[26] Thatcher, "Remembering Jesus," 177.

that played a vital role in defining the Jewish identity.[27] In this regard, the question could have been: How do the Scriptures determine the identity of Christ? Unlike the view of the *Torah* that he is the embodiment of Wisdom, as enunciated by Rabbinic Judaism, Jesus takes the place of "*self-revelation of God himself*"[28] for the Johannine community. Thus, the Johannine community's loss of sacred space, as a result of strained relationship with the synagogue, necessitated the need for defining the identity of Christ.

4.1.1.1.2. Loss of Physical Space

The Johannine community seems to have also experienced a loss of physical space. Stibbe's view is of significance here, he notes, "The Johannine Christians, no doubt facing the social and psychological bereavement of alienation from the family of Judaism as well as from their own natural families, such an adoption would have provided consolation."[29] Jn. 14 contains some pointers to this fact; both in the use of the term ὀρφανούς (Jn. 14:18) and Jesus' statement πορεύομαι ἑτοιμάσαι τόπον ὑμῖν (Jn.14:2). Of great importance is the use of the term μοναὶ. One of the ways of interpreting is to emphasize the presence, the reality of Christ's presence, in their midst, especially in the context of fear (7:13; 9:22; 12:42; 16:2; 20:19). However, the emphasis on the present eschatology need not negate the aspects of future eschatology in the FG.

4.1.1.1.3. Loss of Communal Space

The loss of communal space can be seen in the emphasis on the term 'love' in the FG.[30] It is modelled on the relationship between the Father-Son (Jn. 3:35; 5:20; 10:17;14:21, 23, 28, 31; 15:9, 10; 17:23, 24, 26), and is often defined in the FG in terms of a collective relationship (3:16;13:1, 34, 35; 14:23; 15:9, 12, 17; 17:23). One of the primary outworkings of the community in their relationship with one another is through 'love.' Love is also termed in relation to mission—mission of witness (13:35). Jn. 13 defines love in terms of serving one another which was exhibited in the washing of feet when the community

[27] Pryor states, "Johannine theology does indeed share 'the basic constellation of beliefs' of the Judaism out of which it emerges and with which it is in dispute: belief in God of Israel, his gift of Law, use of the Scriptures, the hopes of the messiah and so on." John W. Pryor, *John Evangelist of the Covenant People: The Narrative and Themes of the Fourth Gospel* (London: Darton, Longman and Todd, 1992), 166.

[28] This view is expressed by Dunn. He further notes that for the FE Jesus is "the self-revelation of God himself" and not a second divine being; and this is within the limits of Jewish monotheistic understanding. Dunn, *The Parting of the Ways*, 299.

[29] Mark W. G. Stibbe, *John as Storyteller: Narrative Criticism and the Fourth Gospel.* SNTS 73, edited by G. N. Stanton (Cambridge: Cambridge University Press, 1992), 166.

[30] Ἀγάπη occurs in 5:42; 13:35; 15:9, 10, 13; 17:26; ἀγαπάω in 3:16, 19, 35; 8:42; 10:17; 11:5; 12:43; 13:1, 23, 34; 14:15, 21, 23, 24, 28, 31; 15:9, 12, 17; 17:23,24, 26; 19:26; 21:7, 15, 16, 20; φιλέω in 5:20; 11:3, 36; 12:25; 15:19; 16:27; 20:2; 21:15, 16, 17.

gathered for a collective meal.[31] The community redefines the communal space in terms of caring for one another and participating in the fellowship of the Father, Son and Spirit. Love is also juxtaposed with hatred in the FG (Jn. 15:19).

These losses need not be seen as a 'parting of the ways' between the Johannine community and the synagogue. It is quite likely that the community continued dialogue with the synagogue[32] and some of the issues included the role of Christ in the Jewish monotheistic framework, the identity of Christ in relation to Moses, Abraham, Jacob, and most importantly, who constituted the family of God. The Johannine community also viewed the Jewish religion and the Law in terms of repudiation of the Jewish patrimony. This is evident in Jn. 8:56, where Jesus states, Ἀβραὰμ ὁ πατὴρ ὑμῶν and also in Jn. 10:34, γεγραμμένον ἐν τῷ νόμῳ ὑμῶν. The interpretative aspects certainly led to conflict.

The community's reflection was not just shaped by the setting. Shared memories and recollection of the traditions concerning the life and ministry of Jesus also played an influential role. The FG mentions the events of recollection on two occasions (2:22; 12:16); both of them have vital interpretative significance. Byrskog defines the usefulness of social memory: "The social memory approach has a focus which highlights that groups usually rely on shared memory to claim and negotiate identity... identifying with its collective past ...acquiring social identity."[33] Mary Cole also asserts this point, "The gospel not only reflects the tradition originating with the life of Jesus but also the ongoing experience of a Christian community living now with the indwelling of the Father, Jesus and the Spirit...the remembrance of the community impacts on their continued living in creative dialectic."[34]

---

[31] van der Watt, "Radical Social Redefinition," 129.

[32] McHugh infers from Nicodemus's willingness to speak in favour of Jesus (Jn 7:50) as suggesting that the Johannine community was engaged in debate or dialogue with Pharisaism. John McHugh, "In Him was Life," in *Jews and Christians: The Parting of Ways A.D. 70 to 135*, The Second Durham- Tübingen Research Symposium on Earliest Christianity and Judaism, edited by James D. G. Dunn (Michigan: William B. Eerdmans Publishing Company, 1992), 157.

[33] Samuel Byrskog, "Memory and Identity in the Gospels: A New Perspective," in *Exploring Early Christian Identity,* edited by Bengt Holmberg (Tübingen: Mohr Siebeck, 2008), 57.

[34] Coloe, *Dwelling in the Household of God*, 91.

4.1.2. Remembrance and Context

Remembrance for the Johannine community had to do primarily with the Christ-event.[35] The Christ-event, which included the passion and resurrection, defined the identity of the community. Byrskog notes, "Christology has to do with Christian identity. The early Christians nourished a sense of belonging to the Christ event—an identity."[36] Unfortunately, there has been undue emphasis on the passion in the FG with the neglect of the role of the resurrection. The resurrection has been undervalued by some Johannine scholars. Smith affirms the importance of the resurrection event in the experiences of the Johannine community. He notes,

> Yet the entire Gospel is written, and could only have written, from the standpoint of a distinctly Christian and *postresurrection* perspective. But the interpreter should not lose sight of the *historical* perspective of this highly theological Gospel...has, however two dimensions, the obvious one of the earthly, historical Jesus, but also the no less important historical dimension of the Johannine community, represented by Jesus' disciples. Thus, the historical and postresurrection perspectives actually merge. Jesus, who was historically real, is now truly known only in the light of his death and resurrection and in the struggles of the community of his followers.[37]

In a similar vein, Tidball states, "Certainly all the threads get their purpose in the report of the resurrection appearances. And all the early claims made in the Gospel's grand opening words find their approval there too."[38] Thatcher also vividly brings out this idea, "In Johannine terms "Christology" is the

---

[35] Keith argues that the gospels present the remembered Jesus. Chris Keith, "The Claim of John 7.15 and the Memory of Jesus' Literacy," *NTS* 56/1 (Ja. 2010): 55. There are many other works that argue for a relation between memory and history in Early Christian community. Some of these scholars include John Painter, *John: Witness and Theologian* (London: SPCK, 1975); James D. G. Dunn, *Jesus Remembered: Christianity in the Making*, vol. I (Grand Rapids, Michigan: William B. Eerdmans Publishing Company, 2003); Tom Thatcher, "Why John Wrote a Gospel: Memory and History in an Early Christian Community," in *Memory, Tradition, and Text: Uses of the Past in Early Christianity*, edited by Alan Kirk and Tom Thatcher, Semeia Studies 52 (Atlanta: SBL, 2005), 79-97.

[36] Samuel Byrskog, "Christology and Identity in an Intertextual Perspective: The Glory of Adam in the Narrative Substructure of Paul's Letter to the Romans," in *Identity Formation in the New Testament*, edited by Bengt Holmberg and Mikael Winninge (Tübingen: Mohr Siebeck, 2008), 1.

[37] D. Moody Smith, *The Theology of the Gospel of John* (London: Cambridge University Press, 1995), 102.

[38] Derek Tidball, "Completing the Circle the Resurrection according to John," *ERT* 30/2 (Apr. 2006): 183.

image that emerges when a Christian interprets events from Jesus' life through the lens of resurrection against the backdrop of the Hebrew Bible ..."[39]

In order to cope with experiences of expulsion from the synagogue, the Johannine community found it necessary to define both its identity of Christ and the community. The FG, especially the resurrection narrative, presents the identity of the Johannine community as well as the community's understanding of the identity of Christ.

4.2. Models of Identity and Mission

Two scholars in recent times have articulated the identity of the Johannine community: Jan G. van der Watt[40] and Mary L. Cole.[41] Their works deal with the identity motif from the perspective of Christology as well as the Johannine community.

4.2.1. van der Watt: Family of the King and Dynamics of Metaphor in the Gospel According to John

In his work,[42] van der Watt explores the metaphoric family in the FG, the "family of the King." The family imagery is used as a launching pad for the description of "analogous reality."[43] He notes, "Family imagery provides the major description of the relationship between God, Jesus and the believers in this gospel. There are several other images: the image of a king and his people; forensic activities, slavery, servants or friendship."[44] For him, the references to birth in the FG are mingled with the concept of Kingdom of God. God is the Father as well as the King. Thus, the FG illustrates not a normal birth but a descent into a King's family.[45] Throughout his work, van der Watt unearths and delineates various aspects of the family in conjunction with the family in the Mediterranean context.

First is the notion of birth, which signifies the family to which one belongs. Birth defines one's identity. Here, the father was under the obligation to take care of his children. In a reciprocal manner, the children were obliged to obey and respect their parents, thus honouring their parents.[46] On the metaphorical

---

[39] Thatcher, "Remembering Jesus," 174-175.

[40] Jan G. van der Watt, *Family of the King: Dynamics of Metaphor in the Gospel according to John*, BIS 47, edited by R. Alan Culpepper and Rolf Rendtorff (Leiden: Brill, 2000).

[41] Mary L. Coloe, *God Dwells with Us: Temple Symbolism in the Fourth Gospel* (Minnesota: The Liturgical Press, 2001); *Dwelling in the Household of God.*

[42] van der Watt, *Family of the King: Dynamics of Metaphor in the Gospel according to John.*

[43] van der Watt, *Family of the King*, 264.

[44] van der Watt, *Family of the King*, 359.

[45] van der Watt, *Family of the King*, 381.

[46] van der Watt, *Family of the King*, 167.

level, the birth into the family of the King is determined by God the Father, who is the author of birth.[47]

The second notion is related to the education that takes place in the family. The Father plays a crucial role in the education of the son.[48] Jn. 5:19-30 describes the Father educating the Son, so the Son could do what the Father does. Obedience played a significant role in defending the honour of the family. Children were under their parents' authority and there was a shared relationship between the members of the family.[49] The content of the learning process comprised of giving life (5:20-21) and executing judgment (5:22, 29-30).[50] van der Watt is of the view that, in the metaphorical usage, the Father is replaced with God and the Son by Jesus. Jesus does what the Father does and thus reflects that he is from God, which also implies that the Son is to be honoured.[51] In the FG, the Father educates the Son (5:17-30). The model of learning seen here is that of apprenticeship like a father teaching the trade to his son. In the learning process not only is knowledge mediated, but also "... the power and authority to do these things are mediated (5:21)."[52] van der Watt also notes that the education process of the Son goes back to a period before the Son's incarnation, and there is a bit of a "mystery with this relationship."[53] The Son, educated by the Father, carries on the process of guidance by instructing the children of the Father and by making the Father known (17:3).[54] The aspect of education of the children is taken up by the *Paraclete* (6:8; 4:26) after the departure of Jesus.[55]

The learning process also extends to mission in the FG. The sender i.e., the Father, updates and trains his agent, the Son, and gives everything into his hand (3:35). The mission of the Father is to bestow eternal life and not judgment (3:17).[56] The coming of the Son is founded on the Son being sent; this underlines the basis of his coming, and the impetus for his actions.[57] As

---

[47] van der Watt uses Jn. 8 to illustrate this point. Chapter 8 delineates two families: the family of God and family of Satan. He notes a person's behaviour indicates also his/her origin. This was an accepted view in the Mediterraean context. Drawing from this idea, the Jewish behaviour does not authenticate as belonging to the same family as Jesus. van der Watt, *Family of the King*, 180, 189.

[48] van der Watt, *Family of the King*, 267.

[49] van der Watt, *Family of the King*, 271-272.

[50] van der Watt, *Family of the King*, 208.

[51] van der Watt, *Family of the King*, 209.

[52] van der Watt, *Family of the King*, 275.

[53] van der Watt, *Family of the King*, 277.

[54] van der Watt, *Family of the King*, 278.

[55] van der Watt, *Family of the King*, 283.

[56] van der Watt, *Family of the King*, 298.

[57] van der Watt, *Family of the King*, 299.

an agent of the Father, the Son does the will of the one who sent him and also reports to the Father after completing the task (17:1-50). The consequence of the Son's mission is the creation of the family.[58] van der Watt notes, "It is not just a mission but a mission of a family for the sake of the family…"[59] The image of the agent continues in that the agent is allowed to appoint a third person to carry out the mission. In this case, Jesus instructs the disciples to continue the mission he began (14:12; 17:18).[60]

Third, the FG also enunciates expressions of family unity i.e., being in the family implies participating in life and being exempt from judgment, as God is not only a Father but also a king.[61] van der Watt notes that the metaphor of the family is strengthened by incorporating other metaphors such as life and light. Jesus is the dispenser of the life he received from the Father, but life is given in the family context.[62]

Fourth, the family imagery in the FG illustrates the expression of love. van der Watt notes, "Love functions within the metaphorical context of familial relations." Love functions within the limits of obedience; obedience results in receiving the love of the Father (14:21). This aspect is another significant characteristic of the ancient Mediterranean society.[63] van der Watt infers a few propositions from the portrayal of love in the FG: The foundation of love from the lowest levels upwards (i.e., movement from Son to the Father and believers to the Son) is by means of obedience. The foundation of love from above i.e., Father to Son and Son to a believer is by dispensing gifts and obedience to commands (15:10, 12). The Father has absolute authority over the children.[64] Reciprocity in love forms the core of ethics in the FG. Love functions for the wellbeing of the family members and this takes ethics beyond legal stipulations. [65]

Finally, the father is responsible for the care and protection of the family in the ancient Mediterranean world. Thus, in Jn. 6, the Father provides food and drink. Jesus is personified as the food come down from heaven to grant eternal life.[66] In case of conflict between heavenly and earthly, the former takes precedence over the latter (2:1, 12; 7:3-10).[67] van der Watt, in the concluding

---

[58] van der Watt, *Family of the King*, 300.

[59] van der Watt, *Family of the King*, 301.

[60] van der Watt, *Family of the King*, 300.

[61] van der Watt, *Family of the King*, 212.

[62] van der Watt, *Family of the King*, 243, 259.

[63] van der Watt, *Family of the King*, 307

[64] van der Watt, *Family of the King*, 311.

[65] van der Watt, *Family of the King*, 311.

[66] van der Watt, *Family of the King*, 336.

[67] van der Watt, *Family of the King*, 243.

part of his work, relates the family imagery with the situation of the Johannine community. In the context of being rejected by the synagogue (15:18-16:4), the community saw the family imagery as a way of "resocialization."[68] He also notes:

> They do not have to be concerned about rejection on earthly social level. They have a heavenly family that is significant. In this family God is Father and King, and he loves his children. He is present with them and will protect them and care for them. They have a place in his house. Interpreted in this light, their symbolic universe is adjusted to cope with their situation of rejection by their own kinsman. It is also clear that they were quite dependent on one another. Love, service and unity of mind and behaviour bound them together. These qualities drew their social boundaries for them and strengthened their group feeling. Although rejected by their own people, they became a community with a mission, which was fulfilled in the power of God and his *Paraclete*. The content of this mission is Jesus, the Son of God, who is Lord and God. This seems to be part of the nature of the Johannine community, or at least their supposed nature.[69]

van der Watt's study on the concept of the family in the FG is meticulous. However, there are some aspects that need some more exploration, especially relating the Johannine community with the concept of the family in the FG. Van der watt seems to have limited this discussion to the closing part of his work. Correlating the social situation of the Johannine community with the concept of the family could help formulate a better understanding of the concept of the family. Some of the points of discussion could be: How is the family imagery related to the Christology of identity? How is the concept of the family of God relevant in defining the community in relation to the religious environment, especially Judaism, with which they were in a dialogue? How does the family imagery of Father-Son address the issue of monotheism? How does the family imagery cater to the necessity of expressing their identity and mission of the community? A discussion on the family of God helps address these issues.

Another area of difficulty with van der Watt is in the concept of kingship and the FG's presentation of the family of the King. Combining kingship and family is probably an innovative way of describing the primary metaphor, but in the context of the first century, especially the struggles of the Johannine community, the concept of family does not seem to comply with the concept of the family of the King. The reason is that the family image seems to

[68] van der Watt, *Family of the King*, 432.

[69] van der Watt, *Family of the King*, 432.

accommodate the identity of Christ better than the concept of the family of the King. The debate with the Jews figured on the deity of Christ and the place he shared in the monotheistic framework (Jn. 8:31-58). The struggle for space for the community was more important than whether it was a royal family or not. Further, the concept of kingship does seem to suggest a hierarchical model with those under him as subjects, and this does seem to go well with the community model presented in the FG where there is a place for everyone. Also, the FG seems to avoid the terminology of kingship, unlike the synoptics, probably to accommodate everyone.

Yet another area of difficulty is van der Watt's concept of hierarchy followed in the principle of love. While there is an element of movement from the higher to lower portrayed in the love of the Father to the Son, yet the principles of mutuality and reciprocity seem to suggest the opposite, and thus create a sense of balance. Further, the Father's love is also present in the love shared by the Son to the disciples. The relationship of love seems to move in the FG in concentric circles rather than in a linear manner or simple development as suggested by van der Watt.

A further difficulty is that van der Watt states that the content of the mission of the Johannine community is the Son, which is true to some extent. But the mission has to do with the entire family of God, which includes the Father also and not just the Son. In effect what the Son reveals is the Father and not just himself.

So, how does one evaluate the family imagery and its impact in the presentation of the theology/Christology of the FG? It must be noted that, at certain points, the family imagery seems to be incongruent and breaks the continuity. This has to do with the fact that metaphors do communicate reality, but fall short of describing reality. One such example has to do with the process of education in the first century context.

4.2.2. Mary Coloe: God Dwells with Us and Dwelling in the Household of God

In her former work, *God Dwells with Us*, Coloe focuses on the view that Christ is God, who dwells with us. She presupposes that the Temple is an essential Christological image in the FG,[70] and provides the catalyst for understanding the FG's portrait of Jesus and his mission—to build a new Temple where God dwells in the world.

[70] Coloe, *God Dwells with Us*, 4. Köstenberger has also made an elaborate study on the relation between the destruction of the Jerusalem Temple and the composition of the FG. Refer Andreas J. Köstenberger, "The Destruction of the Second Temple and the Composition of the Fourth Gospel," *TrinJ* 26/2 (Fall 2005): 205-242.

The prologue of the FG affirms that in Christ God is accessible.[71] This is further evidenced in the Temple cleansing scene where the motif seems to be "Jesus is the Temple, the new dwelling place of God in human history."[72] The Temple motif bridges the Jewish tradition and the community's faith in Jesus in the context of the painful rejection from the synagogue i.e., the post-70 Judaism scenario.[73] She notes,

> Because of the intimacy between *Logos* and *Theos* (1:1), Jesus is the new locus of God's dwelling (1:14) and so he can rightly say "Destroy this temple, and in three days I will raise it up" (2:19); the narrator then adds, "He spoke of the temple of his body" (2:21). John 2 is the hermeneutical key to understand both Jesus' identity and his mission in the Fourth Gospel. The rest of the narrative show how a Temple is destroyed by "the Jews" and raised by Jesus. If the text does not show this, then its claim to truthfulness (19:350 has no foundation.[74]

Jn. 2:21 notes the notion that Israel's temple, which used to be the place where God dwells, is now Jesus, who becomes the dwelling place of God.[75] The idea of building a personal relationship is also seen by Coloe in 14:2, where the reference is to Father's household.[76] The phrase "many dwellings" (14:2) is interpreted as referring to the interpersonal relationships between the Father, Jesus, the Paraclete and believers. She rejects the notion that the phrase refers to the place where believers would reside at a future time. The rationale for taking this viewpoint seems to be that a future union does not provide any consolation in the event of Jesus' departure.[77]

Coloe also elucidates two aspects in *God Dwells with Us*: "i) The Temple, as the dwelling place of God, points to the identity and role of Jesus;[78] ii) The

---

[71] Coloe, *God Dwells with Us*, 11.

[72] Coloe, *God Dwells with Us*, 12.

[73] Coloe, *God Dwells with Us*, 2.

[74] Coloe, *Dwelling in the Household of God*, 106.

[75] Mary L. Coloe, "Temple Imagery in John," *Int.* 63/ 4 (Oct. 2009): 368. Hoskins notes that Jesus fulfills as well as replaces the Temple. Paul M. Hoskins, *Jesus as the Fulfillment of the Temple in the Gospel of John*, PBM, edited by I. H. Marshall, et.al. (Colorado Springs: Paternoster, 2006), 193.

[76] Coloe, "Temple Imagery in John:" 375. The Greek is clearer on this. The μοναὶ of Jn. 14:2 becomes the μοναὶ of the Father, Son and Spirit in 14:23.

[77] Coloe, "Temple Imagery in John:" 375.

[78] Neyrey also associates Jesus body as the temple: one that was destroyed but raised up in the resurrection. Jesus showing his hand and side is a proof that the temple was destroyed and re-established. Jerome H. Neyrey, *The Gospel of John in Cultural and Rhetorical Perspective* (Grand Rapids, Michigan: William B. Eerdmans Publishing Company, 2009), 71.

imagery of the Temple is transferred from Jesus to the Christian community, indicating its identity and people."[79] In the understanding of the community, the Temple gave "...a clear sense of identity and a way of sustaining faith in the absence of Jesus."[80]

In her later work, *Dwelling in the Household of God: Johannine Ecclesiology and Spirituality*, contrary to van der Watt, Coloe used the motif "household of God" to discuss the identity of the Johannine community. The reason for using the term 'household' for 'family' is the lack of the term family in the Bible.[81] The former expresses in a definite way the cultural situation of the Johannine theology, and occurs twice in the gospel (2:16; 14:2).[82] Coloe relates the community identity in relation to the identity of Christ. The community becomes the dwelling place of God. She notes, "The unique Johannine vision draws together the life of Jesus and the life of the community."[83] For her, the household represents a reasonable metaphor of the Johannine community. The community understood itself as living in Jesus' presence, mediated through the Spirit, which is also the place of God's dwelling.[84] The physical body of Jesus can be called the Temple as Jesus shared a unique relationship with the Father, so also the community shared the experience of the Father, Jesus and Spirit (14:10, 27, 23, 25).[85] She categorically states, "The new Temple/household of God is the Johannine community,[86] in whom the Risen Christ dwells through the mediation of the Spirit."[87]

In her interpretation of the resurrection narrative, Coloe rightly understands resurrection in the FG, not as vindication, but the reality of the

---

[79] Coloe, *God Dwells with Us*, 3.

[80] Coloe, *God Dwells with Us*, 3.

[81] Coloe argues, "The bible does not have a word for family. The closest expression in the MT to what we understand as family is the *beth 'abh* ("father's house") or in the LXX, *oikos tou patrou*." Coloe, *Dwelling in the Household of God*, 140.

[82] Coloe, *Dwelling in the Household of God*, 140. This to her is the only criticism of van der Watt. The concept of family is not alien to the Bible. The Old Testament portrays Israel as the family of God and in the New Testament the picture of the family of God includes the Jews and Gentiles. The Father-Son language in the FG is clear affirmation of the family language. However, it must be stated, Coloe draws interesting lesson from the term household of God – She states, ""The spirituality of dwelling in God' *oikos* offers a rich biblical and thoroughly Christian dimension to human desire to live in harmony with all creation in a fragile ecology of our planet." Coloe, *Dwelling in the Household of God*, 199.

[83] Coloe, *Dwelling in the Household of God*, 91.

[84] Coloe, *Dwelling in the Household of God*, 102.

[85] Coloe, *Dwelling in the Household of God*, 102.

[86] Coloe seems to have failed to note that the indwelling is not only communal but also personal.

[87] Coloe, *Dwelling in the Household of God*, 112.

"house/hold of God," forecast by the narrative plot.[88] John 20:24-25 is seen as the "narrative hinge" echoing the Eucharistic occasions of later "household believers."[89] The text also represents the element of early Christian worship in the presence of Jesus with the community. Jesus' invitation to Thomas to touch his pierced side is taken by Coloe as a reference to the destruction of the Temple, i.e., a symbolic reference to the Temple, and "...bringing to birth the new Temple/household of God."[90] Coloe rightly draws the importance of the Thomas episode. The confession of Thomas is not just an acknowledgement of the community's faith in Jesus' identity, but as also the community's self-identity.[91] The community becomes the "new house of God."[92]

Coloe's conceptual framework does address the context of the Johannine community and the community's attempt to understand itself in terms of the identity of Christ. However, there are some areas where difficulties arise. First, the term household signifies a model of hierarchy in terms of masters and subordinates; defined according to different social groupings.[93] This was probably not so with the Johannine community, where the use of the term "brothers" (Jn. 20:17) suggests a certain degree of fluidity. Second, the Johannine community does not exhaust the presence of God. Third, the term 'family' is not alien to the OT, as noted by Coloe. The term בַּיִת also implies the concept of *pater familias*, though it denotes a larger family in terms of household.[94] Fourth, Coloe interprets "many dwellings" (14:2) as referring to the interpersonal relationships between the Father, Jesus, the Paraclete and believers. This view is not without its share of problems. Her

---

[88] Coloe, *Dwelling in the Household of God*, 168.

[89] Several parallels are noted by her: "1. The day of both gatherings is the Sunday; 2. The disciples gather inside a house; 3. The doors are shut; 4. Jesus comes to them; 5. Jesus shows the disciples and Thomas signs of the crucifixion; 6. Jesus greets them with "Peace"; 7. There is a response of faith." Coloe, *Dwelling in the Household of God*, 172.

[90] Coloe, *Dwelling in the Household of God*, 178.

[91] Coloe, *Dwelling in the Household of God*, 191.

[92] Coloe, *Dwelling in the Household of God*, 191.

[93] Coloe, however, clarifies that the image of household in describing Johannine ecclesiology does not imbibe the patriarchal household of the first century but rather "...the divine household governed by the singular dynamic of self-giving love, even unto death." Coloe, *Dwelling in the Household of God*, 164. Horrell looks at the same idea from the perspective of Pauline Churches. "...this change as one from the model of an egalitarian community of ἀδελφοί toward the model of a hierarchical household-community, a community with masters and subordinates, structured according to the relative positions of different social groups." David G. Horrell, "From ἀδελφοὶ to οἶκος θεοῦ: Social Transformation in Pauline Christianity," *JBL* 120/2 (Summer 2001): 310.

[94] Harry A. Hoffner, "בַּיִת *bayith*," in *TDOT*, vol. 2, edited by G. Johannes Botterweck and Helmer Ringgren, translated by John T. Willis, Revised edition (Grand Rapids, Michigan: William B. Eerdmans Publishing Company, 1977), 113.

interpretative framework seems to lead to an over-emphasis on the present eschatology.[95] Though the present position eschatology is widely acclaimed by Johannine scholars and is also attested in the FG, the future aspect cannot be overlooked.[96] There seems to be a correlation between the Word coming and going back to the Father.[97] The use of terms ἄνωθεν (Jn. 3:31;19:11), ὑάγω και ἔρχομαι (Jn. 14:12, 28; 16:5, 6), carry an indication of space and thus cannot be subsumed by present emphasis. While the Johannine community can be termed as the place of God's presence, it cannot replace the presence of God. True worship in spirit and truth (Jn. 4:24) transcends the minimalistic notions of the community.

4.3. Paradigm of the Johannine Community's Identity and Mission: Family of God and Witness

The two models elucidated earlier have their limitations. In fact, there are several models in the FG that represent the expression of identity; these include master- slave, shepherd-sheep, vine-branches, etc. Even so, taking into consideration the context of the Johannine community and the fall out of the relationship with synagogue, the family model[98] seems to be a plausible model that glues together the identity and mission of Christ, as well as the identity and mission of the Johannine community.

In the ensuing discussions, an attempt is made to argue for a family of God paradigm. This model is vividly presented in Jn. 20:17 where the risen Christ states to Mary: πρὸς τὸν πατέρα μου καὶ πατέρα ὑμῶν καὶ θεόν μου καὶ θεὸν ὑμῶν, communicating the expression of identity; and in Jn. 20:21 the risen Christ commissions the disciples: καθὼς ἀπέσταλκέν με ὁ πατήρ, κἀγὼ πέμπω

---

[95] Coloe notes, "…the eschatology of the Fourth Gospel is primarily realized…" Coloe, *Dwelling in the Household of God*, 101.

[96] O'Donnell rightly brings out in the study of Jn. 5:19-30, "…the speech's rhetorical framework also challenges Johannine Christians to widen their own vision by moving from a common ground in realized eschatology into a broader understanding that places the Son's life-giving and judging activities in the future as well as in the present." Tim O'Donnell, "Complementary Eschatologies in John 5:19-30," *CBQ* 70/4 (O. 2008): 759.

[97] Coloe interprets the notion of "going to prepare a place" – "The Father's house will no longer be a construction of stones, but will be a household of many relationships, *many dwellings*, where the Divine Presence can dwell within believers." Coloe, *Dwelling in the Household of God*, 112. This interpretation seems to be farfetched because the particular emphasis of the FG seems to be on the overlapping of relationships between the Father, Son and the Spirit. The family works together not in terms of individuality.

[98] Culpepper in his study of the prologue identifies a chiastic structure in the prologue (Jn. 1:1-18) with 12b ἔδωκεν αὐτοῖς ἐξουσίαν τέκνα Θεοῦ γενέσθαῖ as its centre. Further, he relates the aspect of being the children of God with Jn. 8:31-38, where the debate centers on belonging to Abraham's family. Culpepper notes that this describes the 'self-understanding' of the Johannine community. R. Alan Culpepper, "The Pivot of John's Prologue," *NTS* 27/1 (Oc. 1980): 1, 28, and 31.

ὑμᾶς. However, here, there is no merging of identities but a placing together of both the identities i.e., the identity of Christ and identity of the Johannine community. Both Christ and the Johannine community are part of the Family of God though in a different sense. It is one family, the Divine Family, that makes possible the other— the Metaphorical Family of God.

Mission in this regard is primarily one of witness, witness in the Family of God. This is true with the Divine Family where the Son is the witness of the Father and the Spirit is also the witness of the Father. It is a community of witness and the Johannine community is instructed to continue this in their existence. The community aspect helped the Johannine community to cope with the distress they found themselves in.

4.3.1. Family in the First Century CE

Before considering the Family of God's paradigm, it would be beneficial to excogitate the nuances of the family in the first century context, both the Jewish and Greco-Roman conceptions. The Johannine community borrowed some of the nuances of the Family of God from the prevailing understanding of the family. At the same time, the community was aware of the inadequacy of the family metaphor to describe the understanding of theology i.e., the relationship shared between the Father, Son and the Spirit.

Families and households are an integral part of the social units of the Mediterranean society.[99] The family had considerable importance in terms of economic and social functioning, particularly in terms of participating in religious and cultural ethos. Thus to leave one's family meant also leaving the community with its share of consequences. Neyrey notes: "It did imply not only losing the support system of the household, but also leaving the authority of one's father, as well as the authority of tradition and the association with lineage and ethnic identity."[100]

The family was also considered as the main source of honour and therefore, it was necessary for its members to act in a manner befitting the family honour.[101] So, also the family was the primary means by which a person is integrated into social life and thus played an extremely powerful role in defining the identity of the individual. Santiago notes, "To be born into a

---

[99] Dennis C. Duling, "The Matthean Brotherhood and Marginal Scribal Leadership," in *Modelling Early Christianity: Social-Scientific Studies of the New Testament in its Context*, edited by P. F. Esler (London: Routledge, 1995), 156.

[100] Jerome Neyrey, "Loss of Wealth, Loss of Family and Loss of Honor," in *Modelling Early Christianity: Social-Scientific Studies of the New Testament in its Context,* edited by P. F. Esler (London: Routledge, 1995), 139-158.

[101] Halvor Moxnes, "What is Family? Problems in Constructing Early Christian Families," in *Constructing Early Christian Families: Family as a Social Reality and Metaphor*, edited by Halvor Moxnes (New York: Routledge, 1997), 28.

certain family was a decisive factor, because family was the depository of 'honour' and of position in society.... 'What family do you come from?' The answer will tell us his or her position on the social scale, possible way of life, religious attitudes, and so on. Every piece of information about a person's family can help gain a better understanding of that person."[102]

4.3.1.1. Terminology

The LXX translates the Hebrew *bayiṯ*[103] with οἶκός and οἰκία. Hebrew lacks an adequate term to refer to the family, and in the process of usage in the LXX, בַּיִת acquired the connotation of household. The term בַּיִת acquired has often been translated as "home," "dwelling," or "family."[104]

There are several terms used in the OT to describe the concept of 'family.' Some of them are discussed below.

Maṭṭeh ("Tribe"): This constituted the main division of Israel's territorial structure.[105] Out of the 252 occurrences in the OT, *maṭṭeḥ* ("Tribe"): is commonly used with a sociological meaning,[106] i.e., a term "...under which all the members of a group are subsumed, but also because of the image of the different branches which belong to the same tree trunk..."[107]

Mišpāḥâ ("Clan"): The term meant many large families and its importance lay in defining kinship and territorial identity (Jos. 3-16). It functioned to protect and restore the household as in the case of "kinsman-redeemer."[108] The clan also had the aspect of "communal culpability," i.e., the consequences of the evil or the good done by a member affects the whole clan.[109] The term was also used to explain Israel's uniqueness as the people of God.[110]

---

[102] Santiago Gujarro, "The Family in First-Century Galilee," in *Constructing Early Christian Families: Family as a Social Reality and Metaphor*, edited by Halvor Moxnes (New York: Routledge, 1997), 62.

[103] Hoffner states, "Frequently it has to be translated "home," "dwelling," or "family." It would hardly be possible to show that *bayith* had an earlier original meaning other than "house."" Hoffner, "בַּיִת *bayith*," 108.

[104] Hoffner, "בַּיִת *bayith*," 108.

[105] C. J. H. Wright, "Family," *ABD*, vol. 2, edited by David Noel Freedman (New York: Doubleday, 1992), 762-763.

[106] H. Simian-Yofre, "מַטֶּה *maṭṭeh*" in *TDOT*, vol. 8, edited by G. Johannes Botterweck, Hlemer Ringgren, and Heinz-Josef Fabry, translated by Douglas W. Stott (Grand Rapids, Michigan: William B. Eerdmans Publishing Company, 1997), 241.

[107] Simian-Yofre, " *maṭṭeh*," 245.

[108] Wright, "Family," 762-763.

[109] H. J. Zobel, "*mišpāḥâ*" in *TDOT*, vol. 9, edited by G. Johannes Botterweck, Hlemer Ringgren, and Heinz-Josef Fabry, translated by David E. Green (Grand Rapids, Michigan: William B. Eerdmans Publishing Company, 1998), 83.

[110] Zobel, "מִשְׁפָּחָה *mišpāḥâ*," 85.

Father's House: The married daughters, slaves, and labourers were excluded from the list. It signified territorial identity and functioned as the means of inheritance and self-sufficiency.[111]

The use of diverse terms to explain the concept of the family in the OT seems to indicate that 'family' was a multifaceted and a dominant concept; this is also the case with the NT.

There seems to be no adequate term either in the NT or the Greek literature to explain the term 'family.'[112] Further, the term 'family' as understood today does not have its counterpart in the Greek or Latin, especially, in the sense of the nuclear family.[113] The NT primarily uses two terms to describe the family and its related constructs. The first is *πατριά*, to signify an ancestry in terms of descent (Lk. 2:4). The second is *οἴκός* (plural *οἰκία*) which is used frequently to refer to the household, equal to *bayith*;; in the OT.[114] Οἴκός also could mean "family," or "estate."[115]

Beginning with Homer, the term *οἴκός* acquired the following meanings: house/building, household/family, and possessions/belongings.[116] Οἴκός is interchangeably used with *οἰκία* in the NT; though initially the former was used to describe the whole house which included the property and those who stayed in the house.[117] The latter referred only to one's place of stay.[118] Thus, the common meaning of *οἴκός* and *οἰκία* remains house.[119]

---

[111] Wright, "Family," 762.

[112] Moxnes, "What is Family?," 29. Peskowtiz defines family as a "plural concept." Futher, "Family is a cultural concept, a set of social values, a symbolic code for all sorts of social relations." Mirian Peskowitz, "Family/ies in Antiquity: Evidence from Tannaitic Literature and Roman Galilean Architecture," in *The Jewish Family in Antiquity,* edited by Shaye J. D. Cohen (Atlanta: Scholars Press, 1993), 14, 18-19.

[113] Moxnes, "What is Family?," 18.

[114] Wright, "Family," 768.

115 Sarah B. Pomeroy, "Some Grek Families: Production and Reproduction," in *The Jewish Family in Antiquity*, edited by Shaye J. D. Cohen (Atlanta: Scholars Press), 155.

[116] P. Weigandt, "οἶκός" in *EDNT*, vol. 2, edited by Horst Balz and Gerhard Schneider (Michigan: William B. Eerdmans Publishing Company, 1991), 500.

[117] Wright notes, "...the *oikos* was comparable social unit to the Israelite *bêt-'āb*. It included not only blood relatives of the head of the house, but also other dependents – slaves, employees and the peculiarly Roman phenomenon known as "clients" (i.e., freedmen, friends, and other who looked to the head of the house for patronage, protection, or advancement)." Wright, "Family," 768.

[118] J. Goetzmann, "House," in *NIDNT*, vol. 2, edited by Colin Brown (Grand Rapids, Michigan: Zondervan Publishing House, 1976), 247. Pomeroy also notes that the term was larger term than family as it included members of family, "...movable and immovable property, including slaves, animals, the house itself, land and all that was produced, consumed, disbursed by its members." Pomeroy, "Some Grek Families," 155.

[119] J. Goetzmann, "House," 248.

When one compares the connotation of both Father's House and *οἶκός*, there seems to be the influence of LXX on the term *οἶκός*. Wright rightly notes, "The emphasis on sharing, meeting needs, equality, and generosity strongly recalls the economic ethic of the OT and has roots in its household ethics. As Israel could be called the *bêt-Yahweh*, "house/family of Yahweh" (Num. 12:7; Jer. 12:7; Hos. 8:1), so the Church... could be called the οἰκεῖοι τοῦ Θεοῦ (Eph. 2:19; Gal. 6:10; Heb. 3:2-6; I Tim. 3:15; I Pet 4:17)."[120] Though this is the case, there seems to be one distinction, i.e., the NT describes the community as the Temple of God (I Cor. 3:16; 6:19), which seems to be only reserved for the Temple in the OT.[121] Philo describes a pure individual soul as that which becomes God's house, but this does not refer to the community.[122] This thought is analogous to the Qumran community's understanding of itself (I QS 5:6; CD 3:19).[123]

Terms cannot be understood in isolation, and they reach their meaning and significance in the social context in which they are used; thus, one has to look into how these terms functioned in the Jewish and Hellenistic background. Further, looking at the Jewish and Hellenistic concepts of the family helps in evaluating how the family was conceived in the first century context, and specifically, how the Johannine community conceived the concept of the Family of God.

4.3.1.2. Family in the Jewish Setting

The family defined the social, religious, political and economic aspects of Jewish life and the Jewish faith permeated all these aspects. The family as a social unit was a critical part of channelling, training and strengthening the Jewish faith. Barclay notes, "The family constituted the key arena for the socialisation ...it was as 'ancestral custom' *(ta patria ethnê)* that the Jewish tradition was preserved, it was natural that the family ...be the principal carrier of Judaism."[124] Wright too notes, "...it (the family) was of central importance in the experience and preservation of the covenant relationship with Yahweh."[125]

---

[120] Wright, "Family," 768.

[121] Weigandt , "οἶκός:" 501.

[122] Otto Michel, "οἶκος,οἰκία, et.al." in *TDNT*, vol. 5, edited by Gerhard Friedrich, translated by Geoffrey W. Bromiley (Grand Rapids, Michigan: William B. Eerdmans Publishing Company, 1967), 126.

[123] Weigandt , "οἶκός," 501.

[124] John M. G. Barclay, "Family as the Bearer of Religion in Judaism and Early Christianity," in *Constructing Early Christian Families: Family as a Social Reality and Metaphor*, edited by Halvor Moxnes (New York: Routledge, 1997), 68.

[125] Wright, "Family," 765.

Education formed a vital part of preserving the Jewish faith and the home formed the backdrop of the first education.[126] Religious identity in terms of faith, history (in terms of reminding the children of events, institutions) and traditions of the nation were transmitted in the family. In this context, the role of the father attains considerable importance. The father was required to teach the Law to his children. This was not just a necessary obligation, but it also brought blessing in the form of extended life span (Deut. 6:7; 11: 19; 32: 46f).

There are texts that establish the fact that the family served as the epicentre of Israel's relationship with Yahweh.[127] In 4 Maccabees 18:10f, the mother reminds the seven sons about their father's teaching at a time when they are about to be killed:

> (10) ...He used to teach you, while he was with you, the law, the prophets. (11) He used to read to you about Abel, slain by Cain, and Isaac being offered as a sacrifice, and Joseph in prison. (12) He used to speak to you about the zealous Phinehas, and he used to teach you about Hananiah, Azariah, and Mishael in the fire, (13) and he used to glorify Daniel in the pit of lions, whom he called favored. (14) And he would call to mind also the writing of Isaiah that says, 'Even if you pass though fire, a flame will not consume you.' (15) He would sing to you David the psalmist who said, 'Many are the trials of the just.' (16) He made proverbial [the saying of] Solomon, who said 'There [or, He] is a tree of life for the ones who keep doing His will.' (17) He used to confirm Ezekiel, who said 'will these dry bones live?' (18) For he did not neglect teaching you the song which Moses taught, that says, (19) 'I will kill and I will cause to live. This is your life and the length of days.'[128]

The quote suggests that the Father taught the children both the Law and the prophets. Philo also notes that the children were instructed by their Jewish parents at an unusually young age: "...who had been taught in a manner from their very swaddling-clothes by their parents, and teachers, and instructors, and even before that by their holy laws, and also by their unwritten maxims and

[126] O. Larry Yarbrough, "Parents and Children in the Jewish Family of Antiquity," in *Jewish Family in Antiquity*, edited by Shaye J. D. Cohen (Atlanta: Scholars Press, 1993), 42.

[127] Wright, "Family," 765.

[128] David de Silva, *4 Maccabees: Introduction and Commentary on the Greek Text in Codex Sinaiticus*, Septuagint Commentary Series, edited by Stanley E. Porter, Richard S. Hess, and John Jarick (Leiden: E. J. Brill, 2006), 61.

customs, to believe that there was but one God, their Father and the Creator of the world;…."[129]

Philo asserts that the purpose of teaching the children was to determine the Jewish faith in terms of monotheistic understanding. Josephus describes how children were instructed in Law at a remarkably young age: "…but beginning immediately from the earliest infancy, and the appointment of everyone's diet, he left nothing of the very smallest consequence to be done at the pleasure and disposal of the person himself."[130] The book of *Jubilees* also mentions that fathers taught their sons writing at an extremely young age.[131] Furthermore, *The Testament of Levi* 13:2 notes, "Teach your children letters also, so that they might have understanding throughout all their lives as they ceaselessly read the law of God."[132] Children are to be taught to write in order that they might study the Law.

In conclusion, Philo, Josephus and 4 Maccabees, and others, demonstrate that in the Jewish family children were taught at a young age by the father who instructed them from the Law and the prophets.

The role of fathers was not only to educate, but also to discipline their children (Prov. 13:24; 19:18; 22:15; 23:13-14).[133] *The Letter to Aristeas*, 248, notes,

> On the following day (the King) seized the opportunity and asked the guet, "what is the worst (type of) neglect?" To this he replied, "If a man were neglectful of children, and did not use every endeavour to bring them up. For we continually pray to God for ourselves and also for our children, that all blessings may rest upon them. The

[129] Again he notes "…for all men are eager to preserve their own customs and laws, and the Jewish nation above all others; for looking upon their laws as oracles directly given to them by God himself, and having been instructed in this doctrine from their very earliest infancy they bear in their souls the images of the commandments contained in these laws as sacred;…" "On the Embassy to Gaius: The First Part on the Treatise on Virtues," in *The Works of Philo: Complete and Unabriged*, translated by C. D. Yonge (Peabody: Hendrickson Publishers, 1993), 115, 210.

[130] Josephus, "Falvius Josephus Agaisnt Apion," in *The Works of Josephus: Complete and Unabridged in One Volume*, translated by William Whiston (Peabody: Hendrickson Publishers, 1987), 2.18.

[131] Jubilee 8:2 "The son grew, and his father taught him writing …." in *The Lost Books of the Bible: Great Rejected Texts* by Joseph B. Lumpkin (Blountsville: Fifth Estate Publishers, 2009).

[132] "The Testament of Levi," translated by by H. C. Kee, in *The Old Testament Pseudepigrapha*, vol. 1: *Apocalyptic Literature and Testaments*, edited by James H. Charlesworth (New York: Doubleday, 1993).

[133] Yarbrough, "Parents and Children," 45.

> petition that children may have some discretion is something which comes to pass only by the power of God." [134]

Here, education is seen in the wider perspective of taking care of the children; thus, parents who did not educate children were guilty of immense neglect. Philo sees education as a task which goes along with the advantage of being the creators with God. He notes, "...but those who beget or bring forth a child are in some sense the causes and producers of the child which is begotten or brought forth,..."[135] Philo also qualifies the privilege in terms of parents being compared with God in the idea of bringing forth even though they are mortal. He postulates, "because they have engendered other beings, and have brought what did not exist into existence: for, in my opinion, what God is to the world,..."[136] Parents engage in the process of education as parents are older and bear of the children. Philo ascertains,

> ...they stand in the light of teachers, inasmuch as all that they know themselves they teach to their children from their earliest infancy, and they not only exercise and train them in the supernumerary accomplishments, impressing reasonings on the minds of their children when they come to their prime, but they also teach them those most necessary lessons which refer to choice and avoidance, the choice, that is to say, of virtues, and the avoidance of vices, and of all the energies in accordance with them.[137]

To sum up, the role of Jewish parents as teachers included an emphasis on moral and religious education, including teaching them the scriptures, the Law and moral code. They were also responsible for imparting a trade so children could support themselves.[138] In addition to all these, the disciplining aspect was also equally important as children were seen as a reflection of their parents.

The responsibility of the father in the Jewish family has been thus established. The other side is the response of the children to the care given by the parents; reciprocity was demanded from the children. As a matter of

---

[134] "The Letter of Aristeas," translated by R. J. H. Shutt, in *The Old Testament Pesuepigrapha*, vol. 2: *Expansion of the "Old Testament" and Legends, Wisdom and Philosophical Literature, Prayers, Psalms and Odes, Fragment of Judeo-Hellenistic Works*, edited by James H. Charlesworth, (New York: Doubleday, 1993).

[135] Philo, "The Special Laws," II, 228, in *The Works of Philo.*

[136] Philo, "The Special Laws," II, 225, in *The Works of Philo.*

[137] Philo, "The Special Laws," II, 228, in *The Works of Philo.*

[138] The father teaching his son the trade also had to do with the fact that economy played a great role in the relationship between parents and children.Yarbrough, "Parents and Children," 48, 58.

reciprocity, children were obliged to honour their parents (Ex. 20:12; Deut. 5:16; Lev. 19:13a) and obey them. The Old Testament gives considerable emphasis on honour and obedience required from children (Ex. 20:12; Deut. 21:18-21).[139] Sirach 3:3ff. states,

> 3 'He that honoureth his father "maketh atonement for sins"'",
> 4 And as one that layeth up treasure is he that honoureth his mother.
> 5 He that honoureth his father shall have joy of his children,
> And what time he prayeth he shall be heard.
> 6 He that giveth glory to his father shall have length of days,
> And he that '"giveth rest to" his mother' shall receive reward from God.
> 7 "He that feareth the Lord honoureth his father",
> 'And serveth his parents as masters'.
> My son", in word and in deed honour thy father'",
> That "every blessing" may overtake thee.
> 9 The blessing of a father establisheth (his) seed",
> But the curse of a mother rooteth up the ""young plant"".
> 10 Glorify not thyself in the dishonour of thy father.
> For that is no glory to thee?.
> 11 A man's glory is the glory of his father,
> And he that dishonoureth his mother "multiplieth sin'
> 12 My son', 'help thy father in his old age',
> "And "grieve him" not "all the days of his"" life;"[140]

Philo justifies the commandment to honour the parents. The first reason is because parents share the 'immortal essence' – "by reason of the similarity of the act of generation to God the Father of the universe."[141] The second reason is because of priority (in terms of time) they share over their children.[142] Finally, parents have enabled their children "not only to live, but also to live

[139] Wright, "Family," 766.

[140] "Sirach" in *The Apocrypha and Pseudepigrapha of the Old Testament in English,* vol. I, *Pseudepigrapha*, edited by R. H. Charles (Oxford: Clarendon Press, 1913).

[141] Philo, "The Decalogue," 107, in *The Works of Philo*. The same aspect is also stated in "The Special Laws," II: 225– "For parents themselves are something between divine and human nature, partaking of both; of human nature, inasmuch as it is plain that they have been born and that they will die; and of divine nature, because they have engendered other beings, and have brought what did not exist into existence: for, in my opinion, what God is to the world, that parents are to their children; since, just as God gave existence to that which had no existence, they also, in imitation of his power, as far at least as they were able, make the race of mankind everlasting." "The Special Laws," in *The Works of Philo*.

[142] Philo in "The Special Laws," II: 226 discusses on several priorities in terms of older and younger, teacher and pupils, etc. "The Special Laws," in *The Works of Philo*.

well."[143] For Philo, honouring parents included respect, obedience and fear. Honouring parents was not meritorious because in doing so one was obeying the law; he notes: "Therefore the law says, "Honour thy father and thy mother next after God;"...assigning to them the second place in honour, on the same principle as nature herself has ranked them in her decision of their proper place and duties."[144] The foundation for children obeying their parents was based on the fact that parents do not think much on their advantage but the contrary for the "virtue" and "excellence" of their children.[145]

Honouring parents also includes fear. In this regard, Philo stresses, "For the law says, "Let each man fear his father and his mother," *Leviticus 19:3*; enjoining fear rather than affection, not as being more advantageous and profitable with reference to the present occasion..."[146] Reinhartz notes for Philo, "the parent-child relationship is informed by three fundamental features: the presence of an indissoluble bond of love and kinship between child and parent; the inherent superiority of parent to child; the hierarchy of male and female."[147] Thus, children are to reciprocate by honouring "in word and in deed."[148] The duties of children also included obedience, a significant motif in the wisdom tradition as evidenced in Prov.1:8 and 6:20.[149] *The Testament of the Twelve Patriarchs* also attests to the importance of obedience to parents.[150] The author of *4 Maccabees* argues for the importance of Law over obedience to parents.[151]

Wright neatly sums up three ways in which the family functioned in Israelite kinship. The first way was that family was the basic unit in terms of providing social backdrop with judicial and military underpinnings. Next, it was also an economic unit in which rights and functions were exercised.

---

[143] Philo, "The Special Laws," II, 229, in *The Works of Philo*.

[144] Philo, "The Special Laws," II, 235, in *The Works of Philo*.

[145] Philo, "The Special Laws," II, 236, in *The Works of Philo*.

[146] Philo, "The Special Laws," II, 239, in *The Works of Philo*.

[147] Adele Reinhartz, "Parents and children: a Philonic Perspective," in *The Jewish Family in Antiquity*, edited by Shaye J. D. Cohen (Atlanta: Scholars Press, 1993), 86.

[148] "Sirach," 3:8 and this is explained further in terms of helping the father in the old age and being considerate to him. "Sirach," 3: 12-13, in The *Apocrypha and Pseudepigrapha of the Old Testament in English*.

[149] Yarbrough, "Parents and Children," 51.

[150] *The Testament of Reuben* 4:5 states: "So then my children, observe all the things that I command you and do not sin..." *The Testament of Issachar* 4: 1 notes: "Now, listen to me, children, and live in integrity of heart, for in it I have observed everything that is well-pleasing to the Lord." In "Testament of the Twelve Patriarch," translated by H. C. Kee, *The Old Testament Pseudepigrapha*, vol. 1: Apocalyptic Literature & Testaments, edited by James H. Charlesworth (New York: Doubleday, 1983).

[151] *4 Maccabees* 4:10 states, "For the law even restrains good will toward parents, not betraying virtue on their account" in de Silva, *4 Maccabees*.

Finally, it was an essential aspect in the knowledge, nurturing and maintaining a relationship with Yahweh.[152]

The concept of 'family' needs to be therefore seen in terms of the kinship structure also. Kinship played a pivotal role, both in the cultural and social position, in stating the collective identity. It bridged a person belonging to a household with the community and the people.[153] Not just that, honour was distributed on the basis of belonging to a kinship group. One became a part of a kinship group through the ancestral line, i.e., through genealogies. Kinship defined one's identity, power and status,[154] but the negative side is that it was also used as a way of exercising social control. The Jewish kinship group defined itself against the outsiders with the role of Abraham as the father of the Jews. The Jewish nation was divided into twelve tribes stemming from sons of Jacob with their convergence in Abraham.[155]

4.3.1.3. Family in the Greco-Roman Setting

In the Roman tradition, the family formed the backbone of society. There was wide respect given to the Roman family. The Roman *familia* were governed by *paterfamilias*.[156] The father exerted influence over the members of his *familia*. The parents were to provide care for their children of which their principal responsibility was providing food.[157] Of the parents, the father had the responsibility of being the one who provided, nurtured and took care of the children.[158] The father-son relationship had deeper social underpinnings than that of a master-slave relationship. Essentially the Roman family structure was hierarchical.[159]

The concept of the father-figure was also used for military commanders who rescued the Roman people in time of war. Caesar was given the title 'Father of the Fatherland' for having saved his country.[160] The family metaphor

---

[152] Wright, "Family," 765.

[153] Moxnes, "What is Family?," 24.

[154] Moxnes, "What is Family?," 28. This aspect is also seen in the Roman emperors' attempt to associate with gods and goddesses.

[155] Moxnes, "What is Family?," 29.

[156] Eva Marie Lassen, "The Roman Family: Ideal and Metaphor" in *Constructing Early Christian Families: Family as a Social Reality and Metaphor*, edited by Halvor Moxnes (New York: Routledge, 1997), 104.

[157] Moxnes, "What is Family?," 33.

[158] Moxnes, "What is Family?," 33.

[159] Lassen, "The Roman Family," 114.

[160] S. Weinstock, *Divus Julius* (Oxford: Clarendon Press, 1971), 200, cited in Lassen, "The Roman Family," 112.

was also used elsewhere to show the "authority of God over humans, senior officials over junior officials and state leaders over subject."[161]

Honouring one's parents was also a significant concept in the Roman world, like the Jewish world. Pempelus notes:[162] "Every one, therefore, endued with intellect should honour and venerate his parents, and should dread their execrations and [unfavourable] prayers, as knowing that many of them frequently take effect."[163] Here, Pempelus asserts that parents need to be honoured. Elsewhere[164] he also states that if a person has the least amount of wisdom, he/she would not ignore his/her parents. Here, again, as in the Jewish understanding, honouring the parents had the impression of taking care of the parents. This also echoes Aristoxenus, who notes: "After divinity and demons, the greatest attention should be paid to parents and the laws; not fictitiously, but in reality…"[165]

Plato also seems to put parents in line with gods, when he states: "…we could not possess any statue more honourable in the eyes of the gods than a father or forefather in their old age, or mothers having the like capacity, and when one takes delight in them with honours, the god rejoices."[166]

Hellenistic moralistic literature emphasized the duty of children to obey their parents. Greek and Roman philosophers debated whether the father needs to be always obeyed.[167] Plutarch notes, "…that one ought to reverence the gods, to honour one's parents, to respect one's elders, to be obedient to the laws, to yield to those in authority…"[168] Though the parents are to be obeyed, there seems to have been a debate on whether the parents need to be obeyed on every occasion. Aulus Gellius[169] notes three difficulties according to the Greeks: a. "…whatever a father commands are to be done" b. "he is

---

[161] Lassen, "The Roman Family," 114.

[162] "From the Treatise of Pempelus on Parents," in *The Political Fragments of Archytas, Charondas, Zalecus, and Other Ancient Pythagoreans by Stobaeus and also Ethical Fragments of Hierocles*, translated by Thomas Taylor (London: C. Whittingham, 1908), 67.

[163] "From Treatise of Pempelus on Parents," 68.

[164] "From Treatise of Pempelus on Parents," 67.

[165] "On the Reverence Due to Parents" *From the Apophthegms of Aristoxenus, The Tarentine* in *The Political Fragments of Archytas, Charondas, Zalecus, and Other Ancient Pythagoreans by Stobaeus and also Ethical Fragments of Hierocles*, translated by Thomas Taylor (London: C. Whittingham, 1822), 65.

[166] "Plato's Laws XI," in *The Laws of Plato*, translated by Thomas L. Pangle (Chicago: University of Chicago Press, 1990), 931d.

[167] Yarbrough, "Parents and Children," 54.

[168] Plutarch, "The Education of Children" in *Plutarch's Moralia,* vol. 1, translated by Frank Cole Babbitt (London: William Heinemann Ltd., 1928), 10.

[169] The dating ca. 123-169 CE, though it echoes the thought of the family in antiquity. Yarbrough, "Parents and Children," 54.

to be obeyed at home, in others not" c. "it is not at all necessary to obey the father."[170] Gellius eschews a middle position i.e., a father is to be obeyed only in some cases."[171] Epictetus notes that one's duties are evaluated on the basis of relation, in this he notes the responsibility of a son to the Father: "Is a man a father? The precept is to take care of him, to yield to him in all things, to submit when he is reproachful, when he inflicts blows."[172] The Athenian laws, Solon's law notes, "enacted a law that no son who had not been taught a trade should be compelled to support his father."[173]

From the above discussion, one could conclude along with Yarbrough that essentially there seems to be no difference between Jewish and Hellenistic family life in terms of parents' duty to their children and vice versa; this aspect was a common feature of the ancient world.[174]

4.3.1.4. Family as a Metaphor in the Early Christian Practice

Family as a metaphor is seen commonly in the New Testament, both in the gospels and the epistles of Paul, but in what role did it function? Lakoff and Johnson note, "The primary function of metaphor is to provide a partial understanding of one kind of experience in terms of another kind of experience. This may involve preexisting isolated similarities, the creation of new similarities, and more."[175] The above statement notes that the family as understood in Jewish and Roman categories was used to explain the family of God.

The Fatherhood of God and Israel as the family of God were well known categories in the Jewish conception of God. The early Christian community differed from the Jewish conception of the family of God because they broke away from the ethnic conception of the family of God. One of the chief reasons for this was the inclusion of the Gentiles into the Christian community. This necessitated the need to break away from the ethnic constraints of the family as the community consisted of Jews and Gentiles. Barclay describes the change that defined the Christian community from that of the Jewish family

---

[170] Aulus Gellius, *The Attic Nights of Aulus Gellius*, translated by W. Beloe, vol. 1 (London: St. Paul's Church Yard, 1795), 2.7.1.

[171] Gellius, *The Attic Nights of Aulus Gellius,* vol. 1, 2.7.1. This is contrary to the view that Philo has concerning the Father. Philo notes, "…for a father will never teach his child anything which is inconsistent with virtue or with truth." Philo, "The Special Laws II" *The Works of Philo*, 236.

[172] Epitectus, *Enchiridion or the Manual*, translated by George Long (Mineola, New York: Dover Publications, 2004), 30.

[173] "Solon," in *Plutarch's Lives*, vol. 1: Thesesu and Romulus, Lycurgus and Nume, Solon and Publicola, translated by Bernadotte Perrin (London: William Heinemann Ltd., 1967), 22.3.

[174] Yarbrough, *Jewish Family in Antiquity*, 56.

[175] G. Lakoff and M. Johnson, *Metaphors We Live By* (Chicago: Chicago University Press, 1980), 154.

as "the rupture of ethnic tradition."[176] In Galatians 3:15-29, Paul gives to a new level by constituting a 'fictive kinship' that includes the non-Jews also. Thus, a different kinship relationship is established there which went beyond the family relations. This feature of going beyond family relations can be seen in two ways: moving beyond ethnic traditions, but also beyond blood relations. With regards to the latter, the term 'brother/sister' was redefined to accommodate those outside the horizon of blood relations. The term 'brother,' is a metaphor or a 'fictive kinship,' a term used to by the members of the Christian community to address each other though they come from different families and ethnic communities. Jesus' discipleship programme (Lk. 14:26-27; Matt. 10:37-38) also implied lesser importance to kinship and household connections.[177] Duling likens this to "surrogate family language in Graeco-Roman associations."[178]

The family was defined in terms of the Family of God in the early Christian practice. It can be termed as a metaphor which had resemblance to the family as seen in the first century context. A metaphor describes the unknowable through the knowable, and in this case it is the the Family of God seen in the light of the first century context. However, the concept of the Family of God was in some ways different from the notion of the household in the Roman family system. Unlike hierarchical power relations in the Greco-Roman household, the family of God moved towards embracing equality (Gal. 3:28) and creating a sense of belonging: belonging to God and superseded belonging to an earthly family.

---

[176] Barclay, "Family as the Bearer of Religion," 73. Esler deals with the aspect of Family Imagery and Christian Identity in Gal. 5:13 to 6:10. There are five ways in which Paul establishes the group identity: a. the members of the congregation have known God as a father. Through Jesus they have become adopted sons (4:1-7); b. through Christ, the seed of Abraham (3:16), they are also sons of Abraham (3:7) and seed of Abraham (3:29); c. Paul actually describes the church at Galatia as his children (4:19-20); d. they are also children of promise made to Sarah (4:21-31); e. this "ancestor-descendant relationships" becomes the foundation for Paul addressing them as brothers (1:2; 3:15; 4:12). Philip F. Esler, "Family Imagery and Christian Identity in Gal. 5:13 to 6:10," in *Constructing Early Christian Families: Family as a Social Reality and Metaphor*, edited by Halvor Moxnes (New York: Routledge, 1997), 131.

[177] Barton notes, "...the anti-family' material in the Gospels is primarily a rhetorically powerful metaphorical way of calling for the displacement of every obstacle to true discipleship of Jesus in the light of the imminent coming of the kingdom of God." Stephen C. Barton, "The Relativisation of Family Ties in Jewish and Graeco-Roman Traditions," in *Constructing Early Christian Families: Family as a Social Reality and Metaphor*, edited by Halvor Moxnes (New York: Routledge, 1997), 81.

[178] Duling, "The Matthean Brotherhood," 159. Neusner describes of a pharisaic *Haburoth* where a similar fictive kinship was practized; though one is not sure whether it existed at an early time. Jacob Neusner, "The Fellowship (chbwrh) in the Second Jewish Commonwealth," *HTR* 53/2 (Ap. 1960): 125-142.

The transition from family with all its associations to the family of God was not particularly smooth. Sandnes notes that the usage of 'family' in the New Testament is an intersection of the old structure which consisted of the household model i.e., a patriarchal model and the new structures where the brotherhood/sisterhood aspect is integrated.[179] Sandnes further notes, "The New Testament bears evidence of the process by which new structures emerged from within the household structures. What we see in the New Testament is not an egalitarian community which is being replaced by patriarchal structures; the brotherhood-like nature of the Christian fellowship is in the making, embedded in household structures."[180] In other words, Sandnes is of the view that the household continued to have effect on the Christian community but in a modified sense, accepting the "eschatological equality" among believers.[181] Unlike this view of Sandnes, Lassen argues that Christian communities in some cases practised the hierarchical nature of the Roman household. Lassen states, "As, in the first three centuries AD, the Christian religion expanded within the Roman world, …and the use of family metaphors in Christian communities opened up new developments. In some areas the Christian message would maintain its original content, emphasising equality. In other areas, it would be distorted, eventually adopting the hierarchical nature of pagan Rome."[182] This view of Lassen seems difficult to perceive; the chief reason being in the early Christian movement, the practice of equality was one of the major attractions, especially among the groups that were negated by the society.

4.3.2. Family of God in the FG: Identity of the Johannine Community

Several varieties of families are mentioned in the FG. In this regard, Campbell discusses two kinship groups evidenced in the FG: the natural family of Jesus and the adopted family of Jesus.[183] One could go a step further and add one more family to these groups—the Divine family consisting of the Father, Son and the Spirit. The FG begins with the description of the eternal family i.e., the family of God in the opening verses of the prologue (1:1-2). Thus, there

---

[179] Karl Olav Sandnes, "Equality within Patriarchal Structures: Some New Testament Perspective on the Christian Fellowship as a Brother – or Sisterhood and a Family," in *Constructing Early Christian Families: Family as a Social Reality and Metaphor*, edited by Halvor Moxnes (New York: Routledge, 1997).

[180] Sandnes concludes the essay by noting, "The Christian fellowship as a family consisting of brother and sisters was articulated and incarnated in dialogue with the cultural forces of a patriarchal society." Sandnes, ""Equality within Patriarchal Structures," 151, 163.

[181] Sandnes, "Equality within Patriarchal Structures," 163.

[182] Lassen, "The Roman Family," 115.

[183] Joan Cecelia Campbell, *Kinship Relations in the Gospel of John*, CBQMS 42 (Washington: The Catholic Biblical Association of America, 2007), 1.

are three families represented in the FG: the Divine Family, b. the Earthly Family, and the Metaphorical Family of God. The first one affects the third; it consequently creates a tension between the second and third families. In the second category, the Earthly Family, the FG describes not only Jesus' brothers but also other families such as the blind man and his parents, Lazarus and his sister, and so on.

4.3.2.1. Divine Family: The Father, Son, and Spirit

The notion of the Divine Family embraces the aspect of working in conjunction with each other, especially in relation to the disciples. The Father and Son make their abode in the disciples (14:23) and so also the Spirit. The family aspect also gives room for understanding the shared relationship that exists between the Father, Son and the Spirit. Duraisingh rightly notes, "In John, all traditional attributes of God are expressed not as adjectives but as adverbial modifiers of divine social relationship to all else; that is, divine attributes in John are divine modes of relation, love being the supreme mode...Johannine Christ as God's self-revelation of himself exemplifies the structure of authentic sociality and the self-giving situational mode of social relation."[184]

4.3.2.1.1. The Role of the Father

In the design of the Divine Family, the description of God as Father plays a prominent place in the FG;[185] though this was a familiar concept in the first century CE.[186] The FE uses Father as an equivalent for God emphasizing Jesus'

---

[184] Christopher Duraisingh, "The Gospel of John and the world of India Today" in *India's Search for Reality and the Relevance of Gospel of John: Papers from a conference held in Pune in February 1974*, edited by Christopher Duraisingh and Cecil Harreaves (Delhi: ISPCK, 1975), 50.

[185] A cursory look at the FG would attest this fact. Πατὴρ is mentioned 414 times in the NT (Jn (136), Matt. (63), Mk (19), Lk (56), Acts (35), Paul (40), I Jn. (14), Hebrew (9)). Jesus describes God as Father in Jn. 100 times (Mk (3), Q & L (4), Matt. (31). O. Michel, "πατὴρ et.al.," in *EDNT*, vol. 3, edited by Horst Balz and Gerhard Schneider (Grand Rapids, Michigan: William B. Eerdmans Publishing Company, 1990), 53.

[186] In the OT God assumes a fatherly role in terms of love, care and instruction (Jer. 31:9; 2 Sam 7:14; Ps. 2:7). In the biblical conception, the Father-Son relationship is accompanied by necessity to obey and stay faithful (Deut. 14:1). Michel, "πατὴρ et.al.," 53. In Hellenistic Judaism, the relationship with God as father is the privilege of a righteous person (Wis. 2:13-20; Tob. 13:4). The Palestinian conception of world as consisting of the angelic world is seen as the upper family and the human world as the lesser family and both these worlds are ruled by God as Father and Lord. Paul addresses God as "God the Father of our Lord Jesus Christ" (Rom. 1:7; I Cor. 1:3; 2 Cor. 1:2; Gal. 1:3). "This doctrinal form is bipartite where confession of God as Father is expanded to include Jesus' lordship. Michel, "πατὴρ et.al.," 53, 55. In the religions of ancient orient and classical Greece and Rome the expression for God was founded upon mythical concept of physical descent of all men from God in a natural sense. Otfried Hofius, "πατὴρ," in *NIDNTT*, vol. 1, edited by Colin Brown (Grand Rapids, Michigan: Zondervan

unique relationship to the Father (Jn. 6:57; 10:30; 14:10f.);[187] and Jesus, the Son who has complete knowledge of God (3:35; 10:15a; 16:15a) and reveals the Father (1:18; 8:26-29). One of the common characterizations of God[188] in the FG is "the Father[189] who sent me." For O'Day, the "Father" in the FG is "not simply a preferred name for God...it is the Gospel's primary metaphor for shaping theological discourse."[190] D' Angelo notes that the FG uses "father" and "God" alternatively and in similar contexts.[191] For Lee, the term "Father" is a symbolic act rather than a literal act describing divine substance.[192] For Thompson, this phrase has several aspects: a. the Father is known by the activity of sending the Son; b. how is the Father to be identified and known?[193] c. the unique relationship that Jesus shares with the Father;[194] d. Father is identified as the "subject and initiator of the Son's activity."[195] The uniqueness of Jesus' filial relationship with God is seen in terms of "the uniqueness of God's paternal relationship with Jesus...the relationship implies at one and the same time an indissoluble unity and a clear separateness."[196] The Father is the author of life and a foundational principle of Jewish monotheism.[197] D' Angelo "Father" is the favoured title of the divine in the FG and it has the theological

Publishing House, 1976), 616. God as Father is only used for relationship with people of Israel (Deut. 32:6; Isa. 63:16); not to any individual or to humankind in general. Here, Fatherhood is understood not in biological terms but in terms of salvation; divine election and redemption. In Rabbinic Judaism the use of the name Father began to be widely used. In the early Christian theology God as Father was also an important concept. The expression in Paul, "God and Father of our Lord Jesus Christ" (Rom. 8:14-17) stresses that God has manifested himself as Father in Jesus Christ and thus recognized in this way. Hofius, "πατὴρ," 617, 620.

[187] Hofius, "πατὴρ," 619.

[188] There are other adjectives uses in the Fourth Gospel as well: "the only God" (5:44); "God the Father" (6:27; 8:41, 42); "the only true God" (17:3); "my Father and your Father, my God and your God" (20:17); "my Lord and my God" (20:28).

189 The term "Father" occurs approximately 120 times and "God" 108 times. The expression "the Father" is used over 85 times by Jesus. Marianne Meye Thompson, *The God of the Gospel of John* (Grand Rapids, Michigan: William B. Eerdmans Publishing Company, 2001), 57.

[190] Gail R. O'Day, "Show Us the Father, and We Will Be Satisfied" (John 14:8)," *Semeia* 85 (1999): 16.

[191] Mary Rose D'Angelo, "Intimating Deity in the Gospel of John: Theological Language and "Father" in "Prayers of Jesus,"" *Semeia* 85 (1999): 64.

[192] Dorothy Ann Lee, "The Symbol of Divine Fatherhood," *Semeia* 85 (1999): 177.

[193] Thompson, *The God of the Gospel of John*, 51.

[194] The only other one sent by the Father according to Thompson is the Paraclete. Thompson, *The God of the Gospel of John*, 92. Thompson seems to have left out John the Baptist (Jn. 1:6); though the term Father is not used there.

[195] Thompson, *The God of the Gospel of John*, 93.

[196] Thompson, *The God of the Gospel of John*, 71-72.

[197] Thompson, *The God of the Gospel of John*, 72.

scheme suggesting the deity as the origin and destiny of Jesus.[198] The difficulty lies in Jesus' claim that he is part of the meaning of God, a relationship that does not begin with the incarnation and is always maintained in the state of continuity. Jesus' relationship with the Father is unique; thus, the phrase "the Father who sent me" (5:23, 30, 3, 37; 6:38; 7:29; 8:16, 26, 42; 10:36; 11:42; 16:5), functions not only as a metaphor but conveys revelation.[199] The Father in the FG seems to recede to the background, though the Father exerts his pervasive influence.[200] However, the Father is often described from the perspective of the Son, i.e., in terms of the relationship between the Son and the Father.

The description of the Father-Son relationship is one of the most puzzling aspects of the FG. Jesus states that the Father is greater (14:28), but at the same time notes that he and the Father are one (Jn. 10:13; 17:11). Down through the centuries intriguing discussions have evolved over this. Ellis notes that there is a certain degree of autonomy shared by the Son in terms of judging and giving life. Nonetheless, the sent one is lower and fulfils the works of the Father. He opines that the filial union denotes a 'subordinationist Christology.'[201] For Barrett, sonship includes more than a physical relationship. Barrett argues, "The charge that Jesus, by claiming to be the Son of God and to work continuously with him, makes himself equal to God, is never rebutted. John does not mean to rebut it."[202] Barrett further notes that in the FG sonship includes "moral likeness" (obedience to the Father) and "essential identity."[203]

Sadananda[204] holds a contrary view to Barrett. The standpoint from which he considers the Christology of the FG is, in his own words, "Today *God* has become a captive of Christology. To liberate God from the church's Christological captivity, in fact to liberate our language of God, the time has come to re-read, to re-hear the New Testament witness in their struggle to liberate the God-language from Judaism's racial/political Theology."[205] To the question "Is Jesus God?," he is of the view, "A theocentric Jesus cannot himself

---

198 D'Angelo, "Intimating Deity in the Gospel of John:" 77.

199 Michel, "πατὴρ et.al.," 54.

200 R. Alan Culpepper, *The Anatomy of the Fourth Gospel: A Study in Literary Design* (Philadelphia: Fortress Press, 1983), 113.

201 E. Earle Ellis, "Background and Christology of John's Gospel: Selected Motifs," *SWJT* 31/1 (Fall 1988): 30.

202 C. K. Barrett, *The Gospel according to St. John: An Introduction with Commentary and Notes on the Greek Text*, translated by D. M. Smith (London: SPCK, 1965), 60.

203 Barrett, *The Gospel according to St. John*, 60.

204 Daniel Rathnakara Sadananda, *The Johannine Exegesis of God: An Exploration into the Johannine Understanding of God*, BZNW (Berlin: Walter de Gruyter, 2004).

205 Sadananda, *The Johannine Exegesis of God*, 5.

become God!"[206] He argues that the confession of Thomas, ὁ κύριός μου καὶ ὁ θεός μου (Jn. 20:28) is only a "...worshiping confession of joy for God's vindication of His Son, the Sent One, through the sign of the resurrection."[207] He also notes that the Evangelist does not treat this confession of Thomas as absolute because it is followed up with editorial notes of beatitude (Jn. 20:29). The emphasis is rather on the instruction to believe in the 'Sent One' (Jn. 20:31).[208] This view of Sadananda does require a hearing, but it seems to be more inclined to the synoptics' view of passion rather than the FG, for the FG does not seem to present resurrection merely as a vindication of passion. Sadananda discusses another pertinent question: "Is Jesus equal to God?" (Jn. 5:17-30). He notes, "The evangelist identifies the continuous working of God in Jesus...In doing this he does not create ditheism, or make Jesus God, instead he unfolds in front of us the relationship of the Father and the Son through a phenomenon which we may call God's self-emptying reciprocated by the Son's obedience and dependence."[209] It is true that the struggle to define the role of the Son's relationship with the Father is to tread on slippery ground. Even the FG seems to have an ambiguous view on this. Moloney rightly notes, "God is the Father of the Son, Jesus Christ. The Father sends and loves the Son and the Son loves the Father. The gift of the Paraclete is intimately linked with the continuation of the ministry of the absent Jesus... However, the Fourth Gospel never attempts to resolve the nature of this relationship."[210]

---

[206] Sadananda, *The Johannine Exegesis of God*, 44.

[207] Sadananda, *The Johannine Exegesis of God*, 44.

[208] Sadananda, *The Johannine Exegesis of God*, 44.

[209] Sadananda, *The Johannine Exegesis of God*, 79-80, 116, 119, 123, 216-217. Sadanada also deals with other questions: a) "Is Jesus pre-existent?" (Jn. 8:12-59). He notes, "...Jesus as pre-existent, which is in fact an affirmation of the eternity of God's universal salvific pupose." b) "Are Jesus and the Father One?" (Jn. 10: 22-39). He notes that the Paristic writings interpretation of oneness in terms of essence or of will and love is anachronistic and thus oneness is seen "... not only as the shepherd who gives life (10:10) or as judge ... or as the redeemer-liberator, but as their 'oneness in self-emptying.'" Futher, he states, "Oneness is a network of relationship based on the principle of self-giving of the Father and the Son. Therefore, 'oneness' is soteriological/ eschatological existence." In order to accomadate this understanding, Sadanada states, "Logos is the relational face of God....the unique Son-Jesus through his historical existence gives us an exegesis of God." Blomberg rightly argues about Sadanada's views, "His work *does* provide an important corrective to works that see John's "high christology" as directly equating Jesus with God in text after text...But the final verdict on his more specific claims about the subordination of christology to theology must remain *non liquet*." Craig L. Blomberg, review of *The Johannine Exegesis of God: An Exploration in the Johannine Understanding of God* by Daniel Rathnakar Sadananda, *CBQ* 69/3 (Jl. 2005): 541.

[210] Moloney, *The Gospel of John*, 21. Cowan also notes this aspect, he states, "...one need not choose between the two, if evidence for both exists in the text." Christopher Cowan, "Father and Son in the Fourth Gospel: Johannine Subordination Revisited," *JETS* 49/1 (Mr. 2006): 135. Bauckham is of the view that the FG "...redefines Jewish monotheism as Christological

Further, Köstenberger and Swain seem to bring out the right perspective to the obedience of the Son to the Father, when they note, "He obeys the Father because the Father's will *is* his will and because obedience to the Father is the truest *personal* expression of his *filial* unity with the Father."[211]

Difficulty still remains on how to interpret Jesus' relationship with God. However, the later Christological developments need not be read into the Christology of the FG, as clearly stated by Pollard.[212] Related with the understanding of Jesus' relationship with God is the understanding of whether

---

monotheism." R. Bauckham, "Monotheism and Christology in the Gospel of John," in *Contours of Christology in the New Testament* (Grand Rapids, Michigan: William B. Eedrmans Publishing Company, 2005), 165, cited in Andreas J. Köstenberger and Scott R. Swain, *Father, Son and Spirit: The Trinity and John's Gospel*, NSBT 24, edited by D. A. Carson (Illinois: InterVarsity Press, 2008), 44. Hurtado notes that monotheism in the first century Greco-Roman Jewish religion emphasized: a) "universal sovereignity and uniqueness of the one God of Israel...;" b) "...reservation of cultic devotion to this one God...;" c) "...refusal to offer cultic honours to other gods or even to the divine agents..." Larry W. Hurtado, "First-Century Jewish Monotheism," *JSNT* 71 (Summer 1998): 25. Köstenberger and Swain take the view that the Christology in the FG is a '*trinitarian* Christology.' Köstenberger and Scott R. Swain, *Father, Son and Spirit*, 111. Schnackenburg and Barrett ascribe deity to Jesus without seeing it as a challenge to Jewish monotheism. Schnackenburg argues that Jesus is not only one with the Father in his doing but also in terms of his essence. Schnackenburg, *The Gospel according to St. John*, vol. 3, 333. Barrett, *The Gospel according to St. John*, 156. There are also others who take this perspective: Beasley-Murray, *John*, 11; F. F. Bruce, *The Gospel of John: Introduction, Exposition and Notes* (Basingstoke: Pickering & Inglis, 1983), 31. Cho enumerates on the 'prophet Christology' of the FG. For him, this was used to encourage Jewish Christians, who believed in Jesus as the prophet, to believe in Jesus as the Son of God. Sukmin Cho, *Jesus As Prophet in the Fourth Gospel*, SNTSMS 15, edited by Stanley E. Porter (Sheffield: Sheffield Phoenix Press, 2006), 277.

[211] Köstenberger and Swain, *Father, Son and Spirit*, 124.

[212] Pollard warns against misreading the term "essential identity" that Jesus shares with the Father. He states, "The use of such terminology from a later stage of christological development must not be allowed to carry all the implications of its later meaning. Difficult though it may be to avoid speaking in terms like 'essence', 'essential', 'ontology', etc., we must not transform St John into a fourth-century Father." T. E. Pollard, *Johannine Christology and the Early Church* SNTMS 13, edited by Matthew Black (Cambridge: Cambridge University Press, 1970), f.n. 4, 17. Meyer also notes, " It would be anarchronistic to project back onto the Gospel a coherence and homogeneity among its diverse christological strands that were attained only in later interpretation and reflection." Paul W. Meyer, ""The Father": The Presentation of God in the Fourth Gospel," in *Exploring the Gospel of John in Honor of D. Moddy Smith*, edited by R. Alan Culpepper and C. Clifton Black (Westminster: John Knox Press, 1996), 262.

Jesus was human[213] or divine,[214] or both.[215] The deity of Jesus was affirmed in the early Christian context. Hurtado contends on three interconnected ideas: a) "...the devotion to Jesus was not a late development;" b) "... devotion to Jesus was exhibited in an unparalleled intensity and diversity of expression, for which we have no true analogy on the religious environment of the time;" c) "...intense devotion to Jesus, which includes reverencing him as divine, was offered and articulated characteristically within a frame stance of exclusivist monotheism, ...that anticipated and helped to establish mainstream ...Christianity."[216] He also opines, "...Jesus is not reverenced as another deity of independent origin or significance; instead his divine significance is characteristically expressed in terms of his relationship to the one God."[217] This feature of relationship is better explained in terms of family relationship.

The family relationship between the Father and the Son include obedience to the Father (the Son is described as being obedient to the Father), defending

---

[213] Bultmann takes the view that Jesus was only human and not divine. In his comment on Jn. 1:14 he notes, "...the Revealer is nothing but a man." He makes further comments in f.n. 4 "To see the ἐγένετο as a miraculous process, that it is a physiological miracle, is to do violence to the main theme of the Gospel, that the Revealer is a man." Rudolf Bultmann, *The Gospel of John: A Commentary*, translated by G. R. Beasley-Murray (Philadelphia: The Westminster Press, 1971), 62.

[214] Käsemann went to the other extreme of stating that Jesus as only divine. Käsemann denies that the central concept of the prologue is the incarnation of the divine logos. For him, the FE is interested only in the divinity of Jesus. Käsemann gives importance to 1:14b and states that the second part of vs.14 gives the incarnation its proper content. He further states that in the FG there is no trace of truly human Jesus persecuted and exposed to human suffering but only "*God striding over the earth.*" The FE is controlled by dogmatic reflection and the FG can no longer offer a picture of the historical Jesus. Ernst Käsemann, *The Testament of Jesus: A Study of the Gospel of John in the Light of Chapter 17*, translated by Gerhard Krodel (London: SCM Press Ltd, 1968), 9, 44.

[215] Schnackenburg argues for the two natures of Christ with a soteriological orientation. Schnackenburg comments on ἐγένετο in Jn. 1: 14 "The ἐγένετο announces a change in the mode of being of the Logos: hitherto he was in glory with his Father (cf. 17:5, 24), now he takes on the lowliness of human, earthly existence; formerly he was "with God" (1:1b), now he pitches his tent among men, and in human form, in the full reality of the , to attain once more the glory of his heavenly mode of being after his return to the Father (17:5). This is a history-centred view of salvation, which finds expression in terms of the descent and ascent of the Son of Man (3:13, 31; 6:62). Rudolf Schnackenburg, *The Gospel according to St. John*, translated by Kevin Smyth, vol. I (New York: The Crossroad Publishing Company, 1982), 267. Paddison notes, "...Jesus is *concurrently* divine and human in one person, and he brings what is divine and human into a renewed and mutual communion." Angus Paddison, "Engaging Scripture; Incarnation and the Gospel of John," *SJT* 60/2 (2007): 152.

[216] L. W. Hurtado, *Lord Jesus Christ: Devotion to Jesus in Earliest Christianity* (Grand Rapids, Michigan: William B. Eerdmans Publishing Company, 2003), 2-3.

[217] Hurtado, *Lord Jesus Christ*, 52.

the honour of the family (the Son glorifying the Father through his works) and learning the trade from the Father (Jesus as hearing from the Father and doing what he has seen from the Father).[218] In effect, the FE in describing Jesus as the Son of the Father does not seem to break away from the concept of Jewish monotheism. Köstenberger and Swaim rightly argue, "…John does not violate exclusivist Jewish monotheism by attributing divinity and pre-existence to Jesus, because he understands Jesus as belonging to the identity of God rather as second, separate, distinct God, resulting in his portrayal of Jesus as Son of the Father."[219]

However, caution needs to be exercised here as not all the complexities of the Father-Son relationship can be explained in terms of father-son relationship in the first century scenario. To a large extent the FG presents the Father-Son as a unique relationship. The Divine Family certainly alludes to a human family but moves beyond it. Some of the considerable difficulties could be: a. the father in the family is superior to the son in terms of age and experience (this could describe Jesus' statement that the Father is greater than he)[220] but there is no parallel in the understanding that the Father and the Son are one; b. the Father and Son partake in giving life and judgment. Thompson makes a valid comment on the Life given by the Father to the Son, "Jesus is not a second deity,[221] not a second source of life, standing alongside of the Father... the Gospel has in view neither an ultimate dualism of power tantamount to die-theism nor an arbitrary attribution of life-giving power to the Son as one possible agent ..."[222] c. the Father-Son relationship cannot be understood in terms of subject-object relationship. In some cases, the Father is the subject which the Son reveals (Jn. 8:38, 40) but in some other cases, the subject is not the Father but the Son. The Son is also the locus of revelation, especially Jesus' saying that seeing the Son is seeing the Father (Jn.14:9). There is a blurring of the subject-object relationship, which describes the complexity of the Father-Son relationship. In other words, the description of the Father-Son relationship has continuities as well as discontinuities with the representation of family in the first century context.

As noted earlier, the Father has an invaluable role in the ministry of the Son. The Son's ministry is based on what is heard (Jn. 8:26, 40, 47; 15:15), and

---

[218] van der Watt states, "The educational process not only exists in mediating knowledge, but also the power, the authority and the ability to do these things are mediated." van der Watt, "The Father shows the Son:" 265.

[219] Köstenberger and Swain, *Father, Son and Spirit*, 33.

[220] This statement cannot also be taken to mean that the Son does not fully exhaust the Father.

[221] Fennema had echoed this view in stating "Logos is not a second Deity who stands beside the Father God…" D. A. Fennema, "John 1:18: 'God the Only Son'," *NTS* 31/1 (Ja. 1985): 131.

[222] Thompson, *The God of the Gospel of John*, 78-79.

seen (Jn. 8:38) from the Father. The Father is always present in the ministry of the Son (Jn. 8:29; 16:32), sustains the Son's ministry (6:57),[223] glorifies (Jn. 13:32; 10:15), and justifies the Son against the conviction of the world (Jn. 16:10). The works (10:32; 4:36; 5:36), judgment (5:22), life (5:26), authority (5:27), drawing individuals to Jesus (10:29; 6:44, 65), instructions (8:28), life (5:16), power (5:19), knowledge (8:16),message (7:16), mission (7:28), glory (17:24), and love (10:17), are all given by the Father. The Son in turn completes the will of the Father (5:30) and the work of the Father (Jn. 17:4), thus glorifying the Father (17:2). The Father is with the Son though everyone leaves the Son (16:32). The Father loves the world (Jn. 3:16) and also provides for the world (5:17). The Father is also described by the Son as living Father (Jn. 6:57), righteous Father (Jn. 17:25), vinegrower (Jn. 15:1), who gives bread from heaven (6:32), worthy of worship (Jn. 4:23) and honour (Jn. 5:23).

The task of making known the Family of God has been given to the Son, the one who reveals the Father. Revelation pertains to what the Son has heard and seen from the Father (Jn. 8:38, 40), and thus reveals the Family of God. The Son becomes the authentic representative of making known the Family of God because the Son has descended from as well as is ascending to the Father (Jn.10:28). The Son shares a prior relationship with the Father (Jn. 1:18) and revelation proceeds from the communion that already exists in the Divine Family. The descent-ascent scheme (14:12) reveals the Father as well as the Son i.e., in terms of identity.[224]

---

[223] Jn. 6:31-58 is often compared with Qumran *pesharim* but Witmer argues that though there are similiarities yet the differences suggest that the former is not a *pesher* exegesis. Stephen E. Witmer, "Approaches to Scripture in the Fourth Gospel and the Qumran *Pesharim*," *NovT* 48/4 (O. 2006): 313-328.

[224] Several backgrounds have been suggested for the descent-ascent schema in the FG. Bultmann asserts that the language recalls the Gnostic redeemer myth. He notes, "Jesus as the Revealer of God *reveals nothing but that he is the* Revealer...In the Gnostic myth, whose language John uses as his means of expression, it suffices that the Revelation consists of nothing more than the bare fact of it (its *Dass*) i.e., the proposition that the Revealer has come and gone, has descended and been re-exalted. For even though Gnosticism speaks at length in cosmogonic and soterilogical speculation about the content of the Revelation, nevertheless the decisive thing for it is the bare fact of Revelation." Rudolf Bultmann, *Theology of the New Testament*, translated by Kendrick Grobel, vol. 2 (New York: Charles Scribner's Sons, 1955), 66-67. Bultmann's gnostic myth has been rejected for several reasons. Talbert give four problems related to the Gnostic redeemer myth: a. The sources for the Gnostic myth are quite late; b. a redeemer myth is not basic to Gnosticism and it is not a necessity; c. the Gnostic myth describes of an ontological unity which does not exist in the case of the FG; d. the myth of descending-ascending redeemers was a common factor in the Mediterranean world before and during the time of the origins of Christianity. Charles H. Talbert, *Reading John: A Literary and a Theological Commentary on the Fourth Gospel and the Johannine Epistles* (New York: SPCK, 1992), 266.

4.3.2.1.2. The Role of the Son: The Descent-Ascent Motif

The role of the Son cannot be isolated from the relationship with the Father. As discussed above, the Father-Son relationship is one of the intriguing aspects of the FG. The identity of the Son is both an expression of the identity of the Son as well as the identity of the Father. Christological identity probably needs to be seen in relation to theology; this issue is discussed later. There are several terms used in the FG to describe the aspect of sonship:[225] μονογενής,[226] τοῦ υἱοῦ τοῦ Θεοῦ,[227] τὸν υἱὸν τοῦ ἀνθρώπου,[228] ὁ υἱὸς.[229]

The Christological identity proceeds from the understanding that Jesus not only represents the Divine Family of God but is also part of the Divine Family of God. In the family image, "father' has the rights of inheritance and "son" shares the duty of obligation and honour to the father.[230] One of the significant aspects of the Father-Son relationship is that it is characterized by

---

[225] In the discussion that follows, sonship is dealt generally without taking the difference in the terminologies. The most significant aspect in the use of the Son title is the "...the special claims for the identity and function of Jesus are made." Robert Kysar, "The Gospel of John," *ABD*, edited by David Noel Freedman, vol. 3 (New York: Doubleday, 1992), 924. Dahms notes that the use of the term does not suggest the 'idea of generation.' John V. Dahms, "The Johannine use of *Monogenēs* Reconsidered," *NTS* 29/2 (Apr. 1983): 222. Pendrick argues for the meaning of the term μονογενής is 'unique' or 'only,' 'single.' Gerard Pendrick, "ΜΟΝΟΓΕΗΣ" *NTS* 41/4 (O. 1995): 587-600.

[226] It occurs in Jn. 1:18; 3:16, 18. Köstenberger and Swain assert that it signifies Jesus' uniqueness as both the human and the divine Son of God. Köstenberger and Swain, *Father, Son and Spirit*, 77.

[227] The phrase is mentioned eight times (19:7; 1:49; 20:31; 3:18; 11:27; 5:25; 10:36; 11:4). For Kysar, this describes the special position of Jesus in relation to God. Kysar, *John, the Maverick*, 33.

[228] There are thirteen references to the term 'Son of Man' in the FG (1:51; 3:13, 14; 5:27; 6:27, 62; 8:28; 9:35; 12:23, 34 (2); 13:31). Moloney after a careful study of the use of τὸν υἱὸν τοῦ ἀνθρώπου concludes that the title is a distinct use and presents the Son of man as the locus of revelation and consequently the one who judges the world. Francis J. Moloney, *The Johannine Son of Man*, BSR 14 (Rome: LAS, 1976). Kysar opines that the Son of Man is closely related to the Father-Son relationship. Kysar, *John, the Maverick*, 35. The terms ὑψόω (Jn. 3:14; 12:34) and δοξάζω are used chiefly with Son of Man to describe Jesus' death as exaltation. George W. Nickelsburg, "Son of Man," *ABD*, vol. 6 (New York: Doubelday, 1992), 146. Ashton rightly notes that the ascending-descending conception is not related to the Gnostic myth. Instead he introduces a new proposal, which is a combination of two distinct developments: a) "...the tradition of Jesus as a visionary seer;" b) "...the outcome of a long debate with 'the disciples of Moses' that originated with the synagogue." John Ashton, "The Johannine Son of Man: A New Proposal," *NTS* 57/4 (O. 2011): 527-528.

[229] It is a commonly used titles for Jesus in the FG and occurs seventeen times (5:19 (2), 20, 21, 22, 23 (2), 26; 6:40; 8:36; 14:13; 17:1 (2); 3:17, 35, 36 (2)). Fossum opines that the title is mostly lined with the understanding of God as the Father. Jarl Fossum, "Son of God," *ABD*, vol. 6, edited by David Noel Freedman (New York: Doubleday, 1992), 136.

[230] Thompson, *The God of the Gospel of John*, 23.

love. The Father loves the Son (3:35; 5:20; 10:17) and has given all things to the Son. The Father's love and life are present in the Son, and through the Son into the community that grows out of the Son. The command to love is an extension of relationship of the Father and the Son.[231]

There are two possible ways in which the identity of the Son is mediated in the FG: first in the use of the descent-ascent motif; second, in the sending motif.[232]

The FG uses several terms to describe the ascent of Christ ἀναβαίνω (1:51; 3:13; 6:62; 10:1; 20:17), ἔρχομαι (17:11, 13) μεταβαίνω (13:1), ὑπάγω (7:33; 8:14; 8:21, 22; 13:3, 33; 14:4, 5, 28; 16:5, 10, 17), πορεύομαι (7:35; 14:2, 3,12, 28; 16:7, 28), ἀπέρχομαι (16:7); but here the focus is on ἀναβαίνω,[233] the term used in the resurrection narrative (Jn. 20). The verb indicates movement away, or towards a speaker, or in absolute use of going up; [234] and in the "technical" sense of ascent to the Temple mountain, sanctuary (Exod. 34:4; 1 Sam. 1:3; 2 Ki. 19:14) or in terms of Jesus' exaltation and ascension.[235]

The FG uses ἀναβαίνω as a common expression to denote the ascent of the Son of Man, and used along with καταβαίνω, descent.[236] The emphasis is more on Jesus' departure from and back to God. The ascent language, as Meeks notes, is a part of the foundational description of Jesus: "descended from heaven and at the end of his mission reascends to the Father."[237] The ascent language is also significantly used in the FG to affirm the identity of Christ.

In what way does the descent-ascent language affirm the identity of Christ? Schneiders notes that "location" and "origins" pervade the FG.[238]

---

[231] Thompson, *The God of the Gospel of John*, 100.

[232] This motif is taken in the next section dealing with the Family of God and mission of the community.

[233] The term comes from the root *bainō* meaning "to go," "to walk. The other cognates of *bainō* are: *metbainō* (pass over) and *katabainō* (eschatological arrival of the kyrios). Colin Brown, "Heaven, Ascend, Above," in *NIDNT*, vol. 2, edited by Colin Brown (Grand Rapids, Michigan: Zondervan Publishing House, 1976), 184-185. Ἀναβαίνω figures about 82 times in the NT (Matt. (9), Mk. (9), Lk. (9), Acts (19), Jn. (13), Paul (4), Eph. (3), Rev. (13). Johannes Beutler, " ἀναβαίνω,» in *EDNT*, vol.1, edited by Horst Balz and Gerhard Schneider (Grand Rapids, Michigan: William B. Eerdmans Publishing Company, 1990), 74.

[234] Beutler, " ἀναβαίνω,» 75.

[235] Brown, "Heaven, Ascend, Above." 184.

[236] Brown, "Heaven, Ascend, Above." 185.

[237] Wayne A. Meeks, "Man from heaven in Johannine Sectarianism," *JBL* 91/1 (Mr. 1972): 44.

[238] Sandra M. Schneiders, "To See or Not to See: John 9 as a Synthesis of the Theology and Spirituality of Discipleship," in *Word, Theology and Community in John*, edited by John Painter, R. Alan Culpepper, and Fernando F. Segovia (Missouri: Chalice Press, 2002), 199.

She considers the word "where" a "leitmotif."[239] "To know where Jesus is from is to know *who* he is."[240] In other words as Schneiders suggests, the "where" signifies the identity of Christ. Neyrey[241] also has commented on the import of "whence"[242] and "whither"[243] in enumerating the Christology of the FG. For Neyrey, those who are termed as "outsiders" by the Evangelist interpret "whence" in terms of a village or region where Jesus stayed. The "whither" is misunderstood by the "outsiders" as going to the "dispersion among the Greeks." (Jn. 7:35).[244] However, for the evangelist the reference to "whence" and "whither," when Jesus is the reference point, moves beyond the geographical places. Neyrey concludes: "the spatial data relate to the FG's high christology and membership in the group, not to the geographical places."[245] Neyrey has rightly observed that the terms "whence" and "whither" move beyond the geographical references.[246] However, one of the drawbacks of Neyrey's argument is to view the disciples as "insiders" which defines them as all knowledgeable while the term "outsiders" conveys that they are ignorant of what these terms signify.[247] The disciples as far as the FG is concerned are repeatedly not in 'the know.' Jn. 20:9 is an example of this; they are ignorant that Christ will rise from the dead.

Taking the discussion of Neyrey further, the descent-ascent scheme highlights Jesus' identity and the resurrection narrative is a clear indicator of this, though the "whence" aspect is not stated in the resurrection but assumed. Gaventa notes that Jesus' descent from the Father creates the possibility of 'narration' as well as 'closure;' probably referring to Jesus' return to the Father

---

[239] Schneiders, "To See or Not to See," 199. Schneiders also goes on to state that in Jn. 9 one sees "...the postresurrection Johannine community struggling with the synagogue over the messianic identity of Jesus." Schneiders, "To See or Not to See: John 9 as a Synthesis of the Theology and Spirituality of Discipleship," 206.

[240] Schneiders, "To See or Not to See," 199.

[241] Neyrey notes that the problem of "whence" and "where" can be seen in these texts: 3:6; 6:41-42; 7:27-29; 7:41-42, 52; 8:14; 9:29-30, 33. Neyrey, *The Gospel of John in Cultural*, 73.

[242] Neyrey notes "whence" in reality denotes that Jesus has come from the realm of God." Neyrey, *The Gospel of John in Cultural*, 73.

[243] "Whither" means the "bosom of God" Neyrey, *The Gospel of John in Cultural*, 74.

[244] Neyrey, *The Gospel of John in Cultural*, 58.

[245] Neyrey, *The Gospel of John in Cultural*, 59.

[246] Neyrey goes further in arguing for the symbolic references to "Galilee" and "Judea". The former represents loyalty and obedience to Jesus while the latter is devoid of it. For Neyrey they constitute not a "topological space" but a "social space." Neyrey, *The Gospel of John in Cultural*, 65.

[247] Neyrey notes the disciples have the correct understanding of exalt Jesus and they are drawn by the Father; they from a group of "enlightened membership." Neyrey, *The Gospel of John in Cultural*, 73.

suggested by Jn. 20.[248] Jesus' ascent sets up for the bestowal of gifts such as peace, joy, the Spirit, and forgiveness.[249] Jesus' ascent is described in terms of benefit for the community: "to prepare a place for them" and further notes ἐν τῇ οἰκίᾳ τοῦ πατρός μου μοναὶ πολλαί εἰσιν.[250] It also signals the coming of the Paraclete. There has been intriguing discussions on the use of the term μοναὶ.[251] Does the term signify only a present and realized aspect? Or does it relate more than this? The term is quite significant for the community. The phrase μοναὶ πολλαΐ (Jn. 14:2) could signify the Temple with many rooms.[252] This is significant for the community that has lost its space to worship and now is offered a space as a result of the resurrection of Jesus. In this regard, the phrase "going to prepare" refers to the benefits of being a part of the worshipping community of God.

The descent-ascent language has a far-reaching effect in comprehending the family of God. Jesus' messiahship is rejected on the basis that his family is known only to those who are around him. Identity is attached to one's family. In Jn. 6:42, Jesus' identity is seen in terms of his incarnation, the localizing of the divine presence. The earthly associations of Jesus cancel his connections in the family of God for those around him. However, this seems ironical to the evangelist who vividly affirms Jesus' origin is not from the earthly sphere.

---

[248] Beverly Roberts Gaventa, "The Archive of Excess: John 21 and the Problem of Narrative Closure," in *Exploring the Gospel of John in Honor of D. Moddy Smith*, edited by R. Alan Culpepper and C. Clifton Black (Westminster: Westminster John Knox Press, 1996), 248-249.

[249] Beutler, "ἀναβαίνω," 75.

[250] Jn. 14:2.

[251] For Aalen Sverre, "house of the Father" denotes the kingdom of God. Aalen Sverre, "'Reign' and 'House' in the Kingdom of God in the Gospels" *NTS* 8/3 (1962): 238. James McCaffey contends that "house' and "rooms" need to be understood in the light of the porches, chambers, etc of the Jerusalem Temple. He takes this stand by taking 14:2 as a parallel expression of 2:16. James McCaffey, *The House with Many Rooms: The Temple Theme of Jn. 14: 2-3* (Rome: Pontifical Biblical Institute, 1988), 67-70 cited in Neyrey, *The Gospel of John in Cultural*, 75. For Gundry dwelling denotes a present experience (14:10, 17 also 15:4-7, 9-10). Therefore he concludes, "Father's house is no longer heaven but God's household or family." R. H. Gundry, "In my Father's House are many *Monai*," *ZNW* 58, no. 1/2 (1967): 70. Neyrey in this connection notes that since the "new temple" refers to Jesus, then, it implies that being part of the household of the Father. The phrase "many rooms" for Neyrey "is fluid space which is only occasionally realized in time and place when the disciples father in the name of the risen Jesus." Further, this has significance in the context of being excluded from the synagogue. Neyrey, *The Gospel of John in Cultural*, 76.

[252] Here, it is described in terms of temple imagery but certainly transcends it. Thus Counet rightly states, "John's gospel can be read as an example of text which is aware of the fact that language is essentially inadequate to verbalise certain experiences." Patrick Chatelion Counet, *John, a Postmodern Gospel: Introduction to Deconstructive Exegesis Applied to the Fourth Gospel*, BInS 44 (Leiden: Brill, 2000), 12.

Location defines the identity of Jesus, but for the evangelist and his community Jesus' location is in the divine realm. The location of Jesus is further limited to Galilee (Jn. 7:41), and Galilee is termed as the place where no prophet is said to have originated (Jn. 7:52). 'The Jews' conversation with the blind man, seem to unconsciously state the obvious – they state in Jn. 9:29 "We know that God has spoken to Moses, but as for this man, we do not know where he comes from."

The journey of the Son makes the intersection between the divine family and the earthly family. The FE seems to present that the intersection makes the opponents of Jesus focus on earthly aspect of Jesus and in the process leave out his heavenly origin. The Son bears witness to the Family of God in the event of his incarnation. The identity of the Son remains in the Divine Family.

What significance does the descent-ascent scheme hold for the Johannine community? For the community, the scheme defines the identity of Christ. By implication, in becoming part of the family of Jesus, they also become part of the family of God. There is a movement beyond their present status of being rejected to becoming members in the Family of God. This idea is conveyed when Jesus describes the new relationship as 'my father' and 'your father' (Jn. 20:17).

4.3.2.1.3. The Role of the Spirit

The third member in the Divine Family is the Spirit. The Spirit proceeds from the Father and is sent in the name of Jesus (Jn. 14:26). Thus, the Spirit is not just an individual entity but is seen in relation to the Father and the Son. The role of the Spirit is described as the extension of Jesus' being and work (Jn. 20:22; 14:16-17).[253] The Paraclete bears witness to Jesus' teaching and reminds them of all that Jesus said (Jn. 14:26). The Paraclete also continues the function of judging that comes from the revelation of God, a function attributed to Jesus (5:27).[254] It is interesting to note that the mission of the Paraclete is to bear witness to Jesus just as Jesus witnessed to what he has heard and seen from the Father (Jn. 14:26). Moloney notes, "Neither Jesus nor the Paraclete is the ultimate source of the revelation they communicate."[255] There is a sense of continuity and unity in witnessing which reiterates the aspect of family.

The Divine Family is an adequate description when one considers the relationship between the Father, Son and Spirit. There is an aspect of continuity in the work of the Father and the Son,[256] and the Spirit. The FG presents a

---

[253] Smith, *The Theology of the Gospel of John*, 79.

[254] Moloney, *The Gospel of John*, 440.

[255] Moloney, *The Gospel of John*, 441.

[256] Barrett states of a "..complete continuity between the work of the Father and work of the Son. The life however of the Son is dependent upon that of the Father. This does not

creative tension between independence (Jn. 5:28-29; 6:57) and dependence of the Son on the Father (Jn. 5:30; 8:28) and so also the Spirit (Jn. 14:26). In this regard, the family image gives scope for continuity and discontinuity. Like in the first century context, the Father in the FG is acknowledged as the source of all things. The family aspect is also seen in terms of the fellowship of the Father and Son with the believers. Stephen C. Barton notes, "In John, unity has a communicative dimension. It is a unity of presence, of love, of work, of will, of gift, of the Spirit. It also provides the grounds for the transformation of the people of God in a new unity."[257] He further notes, "The oneness of the communicative activity of the Father and the Son in the Spirit who by the same Spirit brings into being a new oneness of the people of God on earth."[258] The concept of the family also helps in explaining the understanding of Christology in relation to monotheism. The term θεος has an important place in the understanding of the identity of Jesus and God in the FG.[259] The Son as being part of the family shares the unique aspects of judging and giving life (Jn. 8:16; 5:26), which are the prerogatives of God.

The concept of family goes a long way in describing the identity of God in relational aspects. Köstenberger and Swain in this regard state, "God thus transcends one-dimensional conceptions of human identity."[260] As noted earlier, the Divine Family cannot be fully explained in earthly categories. There is a certain aspect of mystery in defining the Divine Family; and this has to be acknowledged, as the family concept is only a metaphor and if one takes it thus, then, it is only a means of describing reality. Köstenberger and Swain encapsulate the relationship of the Father, Son and Spirit thus: "One divine action is executed on the stage of the Fourth Gospel, the singular action *of* the Father *through* his obedient, incarnate Son (Jn. 10:37-38; 14:10-11) in the power of the Spirit."[261]

The FG describes not just the Divine Family but also the Earthly Family; this is of importance for the FE as it details the movement of the Word from the eternal world to the physical world, and opens up the possibility of the Johannine community becoming part of the Family of God.

---

contradict the words of the Prologue, since the giving is not a temporal act but describes the eternal relation of the Father and the Son." Barrett, *The Gospel according to St. John*, 218.

[257] Barton, "Christian community in the light of the Gospel of John," 294.

[258] Barton, "Christian community in the light of the Gospel of John," 301.

[259] Thompson, *The God of the Gospel of John*, 20.

[260] Köstenberger and Swain, *Father, Son and Spirit*, 37.

[261] Köstenberger and Swain, *Father, Son and Spirit*, 127.

4.3.2.2. Earthly Family of Jesus: Jesus' Brothers and Mother

Incarnation necessitates a description of the earthly family of Jesus. The FE attempts to bring together the two families: the Divine Family and the Earthly Family of Jesus. In doing so, it creates a complex situation, which often leads to conflict and displeasure. The question that needs to be addressed is: What role does the Earthly Family of Jesus play in ascertaining his association with the divine family? Does one override the other? Are both given equal importance? Jesus' mother and brothers are discussed in the FG, especially in relation to the task entrusted to him by the Father.

The role of Jesus' mother is not clear at the beginning, i.e., at the wedding feast (Jn. 2:1-11).[262] The difficult aspect in the narrative is Jesus' question to her mother: "Woman, what concern is that to you and to me?.. Several views have been proposed to deal with the difficult rendering of Jesus.[263] However, the place of Jesus' mother in his passion (Jn. 19:26-27) is quite significant for the Johannine community. This scene is unique to the FG, different from the synoptics, which further explains its importance. One of the differences is that the women are mentioned after Jesus' death[264] (Mt. 27:55-56; Mk. 15:40-41; Lk. 23:48-49), unlike Jn. 19: 25.[265] Another difference is that the narrator adds an insightful comment after Jesus entrusts the 'son' and the 'mother,' "And from that hour the disciple took her to his own home" (Jn 19:27 RSV), which notes the gravity of the preceding scene.[266] The scene begins in v. 26 with Jesus addressing his mother, "Woman, behold, your son!" and this followed by Jesus' address to the BD, "Behold, your mother!" (v. 27).[267]

---

[262] One of the puzzling aspects is the anonymity of Jesus' mother in the FG. Lieu ascribes this to the tradition used by the FE. Judith Lieu, "The Mother of the Son in the Fourth Gospel," *JBL* 117/1 (Spring 1998): 63.

[263] Brown opines that Jesus distanced from his mother until she appears at the foot of the cross where she becomes a model for believers. Raymond E. Brown, et al., eds., *Mary in the New Testament* (Philadelphia: Fortress Press, 1978), 194. Leon Morris is of the view that Jesus distances between his mother and him. Leon Morris, *The Gospel according to John* (Grand Rapids, Michigan: William B. Eerdmans Publishing Company, 1995), 159. Williams is of the view that though Jesus' words to her mother indicate the tension between Jesus and his mother; they do not communicate a refusal or rebuke. Ritva H. Williams, "The Mother of Jesus at Cana: A Social-Science Interpretation of John 2:1-12," *CBQ* 59/4 (O. 1997): 692.

[264] Brown, *The Gospel according to John*, 922.

[265] Bultmann is of the view that the FE deliberately altered the source as seen in Mk. 15:40 in order to relate it with vv. 26f. Bultmann, *The Gospel of John*, 671.

[266] Brown, *The Gospel according to John*, 922.

[267] Culpepper calls this "performative language." R. Alan Culpepper, "The Quest for the Church in the Gospel of John," *Int.* 63/4 (O. 2009): 352.

This incident can be seen as an instance of adoption, but Brown rightly discredits it.[268] There are several other interpretations of this episode.[269] However, what is of importance is Mary's maternal role in the Johannine community.[270] There is a liberative dimension brought out here. Brown brings out this aspect when he states, "The sorrowful scene at the foot of the cross represents the birth pangs by which the spirit of salvation is brought forth (Isa. 26:17-18) and handed over (John 19:30). In becoming the mother of the Beloved Disciple (the Christian), Mary is symbolically evocative of Lay Zion who, after the birth pangs, brings forth a new people in joy (John xv:11; Isa. xlix:20-22, liv, lxvi:7-11)..."[271] He also notes, "...the Johannine picture of Jesus' mother becoming the mother of the Beloved Disciple seems to evoke the OT themes of Lady Zion's giving birth to a new people in the messianic age, and of Eve and her offspring."[272] There is also the other dimension i.e., the redrawing of the earthly family with the BD described as the 'son.'[273] This is a clear example of how the earthly categories are suspended to accommodate the

---

[268] Brown notes that the Scripture commonly uses the "you are" phrase to describe adoption (Ps. 2:7, I Sam. 18:21) but here is more in the sense of "here is." Brown, *The Gospel of John*, 907.

[269] Schnackenburg discusses four major interpretations: a) "A historicizing interpretation," a view adopted by the Church Fathers to drive home the point that Jesus' brothers and sisters are only distant relatives and have no connection in flesh; b) "A typological-symbolic exegesis understands Mary as a model of the Church, a view which, since the twelfth century, is found in many variations throughout the Church's exegesis;" c) "The Mariological exegesis in the narrower sense, that is, the installations of Mary in a personal role which has a theological relevance or one for salvation history, is also found to any degree only since the twelfth century;" d) Bultmann takes the symbolic meaning thus: "The mother of Jesus, who tarries by the cross, represents Jewish Christianity that overcomes the offence of the cross. The beloved disciple represents Gentile Christianity, which is charged to honour former as its mother from whom it has come, even as Jewish Christianity is charged to recognize itself as "at home" within Gentile Christianity..." Bultmann, *The Gospel of John*, 673. In this regard, Schnackenburg rightly notes that the symbolic interpretations do not seem to be based on the text. Schnackenburg, *The Gospel according to St. John*, vol. 3, 279-281. A common interpretation is that the text describes the duties of Jesus to his mother. Ridderbos, *The Gospel of John*, 612; see also Neyrey, *The Gospel of John*, 309-310; Köstenberger, *John,* 549.

[270] Ridderbos takes the contrary view, i.e., the emphasis is not on Mary but on the disciple who takes the role of Jesus in caring for his mother. However, he does note, "Both Mary his mother and the disciples whom he loves represent in the most authentic manner this new community: Mary will from this moment on step back as his mother and uniquely reflect the image of the community that remains behind on earth." Herman Ridderbos, *The Gospel of John: A Theological Commentary* (Grand Rapids, Michigan: William B. Eerdmans Publishing Company, 1997), 613. The same view is also seen in Neyrey, *The Gospel of John*, 310.

[271] Brown, *The Gospel according to John*, 925.

[272] Brown, *The Gospel according to John*, 926.

[273] Moloney in this connection states, "...from the moment of the cross a new family of Jesus has been created. The Mother of Jesus, a model of faith, and the disciple whom Jesus

community of faith, in this case, the Johannine community. In addition to this aspect, Kanagaraj infers from the mention of male and female persons at the cross by the FE as communicating a new community where men and women have "...equals roles to play."[274]

The other natural kinship of Jesus constitutes his brothers (2:12; 7:3, 5, 10). Here, there seem to be different views on Jesus' relationship with his brothers. Campbell notes that there are two primary possibilities: Jesus and his brothers form the sons of Joseph and Mary, or the brothers of Jesus are sons of Joseph but not of Mary. The first reference is seen in Jn. 2:12. Does the reference to Jesus' brothers allude to his followers? The use of ἔμειναν in Jn. 2:12 could be taken in a local sense of residing in Capernaum or as a term for discipleship.[275] Campbell rightly states that the possibility of Jesus' brothers being termed as his followers cannot be sidelined.[276] The second reference to Jesus' brothers in 7:1-10 does affect the plot of the story. Destro and Pesce argue that the brothers of Jesus were part of the Jesus movement. Their words seem to highlight the need for Jesus to do this in order to get back the disciples who deserted him.[277] How does one interpret the words of the disciples? Can they be likened to the scepticism of the disciples? Kilpatrick[278] and Painter[279] note that the brothers of Jesus are not different from the disciples on this occasion.

---

loved and held close to himself are one as the disciple accepts the Mother..." Moloney, *The Gospel of John*, 504.

[274] Jey J. Kanagaraj, "The Profiles of Women in John: House-bound or Christ-bound?," *ERT* 27/1 (Ja. 2003): 31.

[275] Dorothy A. Lee, "Abiding in the Fourth Gospel: A Case-Study in Feminist Biblical Theology" *Pacifica* 10 (1997): 127 cited in Campbell, *Kinship Relations in the Gospel of John*, 58. Brown notes that this was inserted by the "disciple-editor." Raymond E. Brown, "Problem of Historicity in John," *CBQ* 24/1 (Ja. 1962): 13. Keener is doubtful whether the continuance of the disciples could refer to the relationship Jesus shared with his followers. Craig S. Keener, *The Gospel of John: A Commentary*, vol. 1 (Massachusetts: Hendrickson Publishers, 2003), 518.

[276] Campbell, *Kinship Relations in the Gospel of John*, 58.

[277] Adriana Destro and Mauro Pesce, "Kinship, Discipleship, and Movement: An Anthropological Study of John's Gospel," *BI* 3/3 (O. 1995): 274-275.

[278] Kilpatrick notes, "...in principle the family seems to have accepted Jesus in the terms of the disciples. This reconciliation has been read back into the Gospel story in John where the only hint of a breach occurs in J.vii.2-5,10, where *v.5* reveals a scepticism in Jesus' brothers comparable to the scepticism in most of his disciples, vi.60-71." George Dunbar Kilpatrick, "Jesus, his family and his disciples," *JSNT* 15 (Jl. 1982): 16.

[279] Painter notes, "Here the brothers use the more positive term *works* which, in John, also covers the signs but frequently draws attention to Jesus' relation to the Father. Further, the use of the imperfect tense with *oude* suggests that "not even his brothers were believing in him." This lacks the definitive sense of unbelief that can be communicated with the aorist tense. It also implies that the suggestion of the brothers that Jesus go to Judea so that his disciples (there?) may see the works he does should not be understood in a cynical sense." John Painter, "Who Was James? Footprints as a Means of Identification," in *The Brother of Jesus: James the Just*

Campbell rightly notes, though the disciples fail to understand his identity (21:24) yet they make statements of faith (2:11, 22; 6:69; 9:38; 11:27; 17:8; 20:28) which is not the case with brothers of Jesus.[280] Campbell concludes by explaining that, at the narrative level, the relationship between Jesus and his mother conveys loyalty and respect while hostility seems to have continued between the brothers of Jesus, and Jesus and the disciples.[281]

The FG seems to play down earthly or natural relationships.[282] This is done possibly for two reasons. The first reason could be in order to assert the identity of Jesus in the Divine Family. The second reason could be to make clear its significance for the Johannine community – emphasis on the divine family helps in moving beyond the particularistic or reductionist understanding of the Family of God. In this way, the scope becomes universal, and it becomes possible to accommodate the Johannine community. For the Johannine community members that faced conflicts with the synagogue, the understanding that they too were part of the Family of God, gave them space to draw their own identity. There is certainly a movement beyond the temporal, space bound, and limited nature of an earthly family to an accommodative characteristic of the Family of God. The phrase used by Jesus in Jn. 20:17: "My father and your father" captures this paradigm.

4.3.2.3. Metaphorical Family of God: The Johannine Community

Language plays an invaluable role in shaping social relationships,[283] and the FG is studded with the language of kinship. 'Family of God' is a concealed metaphor used by the FE. Here, metaphorical language takes over to describe the identity and mission of Jesus and the community. Metaphors create space for interaction with living reality, but also assist in transcending it.

The term "Metaphorical Family of God" is used here to signify something other than the natural representation of the family of God, which in the first century Jewish context implies Israel. It is metaphorical because it also

---

and His Mission, edited by Bruce Chilton and Jacob Neusner (London: Westminster John Knox Press, 2001), 27.

[280] Campbell, *Kinship Relations in the Gospel of John*, 59-60. Bauckham sees this as a narrative opportunity, another occasion where a misunderstanding leads to clarification Jesus' understanding and intentions. Richard Bauckham, "James and Jesus," in *The Brother of Jesus: James the Just and His Mission*, edited by Bruce Chilton and Jacob Neusner (London: Westminster John Knox Press, 2001), 107-108.

[281] Campbell, *Kinship Relations in the Gospel of John*, 65.

[282] Seim rightly notes this in discussing the role of Jesus' mother, "The two scenes (referring to Jn. 2:1-12 and 19: 25-27) in which the mother of Jesus appears constitute a pattern that is a special Johannine version of how the *families dei* takes the place of a family relationship defined by the flesh." Turid Karlsen Seim, "Descent and Divine Paternity in the Gospel of John: Does the Mother Matter?," *NTS* 51/3 (Jl. 2005): 368.

[283] Horrell, "From ἀδελφοὶ to οἶκος θεοῦ:" 294

represents those outside the earthly family of Jesus. The prologue highlights the tension that exists between the earthly family and the metaphorical family of God. In Jn 1:11, the narrator states, "He came to his own home, and his own people received him not." It is a rejection by the earthly association but this occasions a creation of the metaphorical family of God as stated in the following verses (v.12-13). The phrase ἐκ θεοῦ ἐγεννήθησαν clearly indicates that the metaphorical family is the work of God and thus transcends the earthly relationship. The whole of the FG illustrates the point of the Metaphorical Family of God. Jesus' use of the phrase γεννηθῇ ἄνωθεν (3:3) in his conversation with Nicodemus further illustrates that metaphorical family is the result of the work of God. Crump rightly notes, "...John has more to say about the mutual indwelling of the Father, Son and disciple than he does the Father, Son and Spirit."[284]

Vellanickal's study[285] on divine sonship in the Johannine writings throws light on the Metaphorical Family. He notes that there are two terms used to describe the divine sonship of human beings: τέκνα Θεοῦ (Jn. 1:12; 11:52) and γεννηθῆναι τοῦ Θεοῦ (I Jn. 2:29; 3:9; 4:7; 5:1, 4, 18).[286] He rightly distinguishes the sonship of Christ from the rest. He notes, "...the "υἱὸς τοῦ Θεου" who was the son of God by virtue of a strictly natural generation, is clearly differentiated by John from the "τέκνα τοῦ Θεου" who are by natural generation men, and become children of God through a supernatural generation."[287] Sonship is further explained by the differences in terms of 'children of God' and 'children of the devil.' The former is the result of "begetting," where God is active and ascertains the nature of the children of God, while the latter is the result of influence.[288] Thus, for Vellanickal, "...divine sonship of Christians is more than a mere moral relationship and is based on a supernatural endowment, a communication of the Life of God, and therefore destined to growth and development to full maturity."[289] Divine sonship is a change of state from 'not being the children' to a state of 'being children of God' and the chief aspect in this is 'faith,' i.e., appropriation of allegiance to the person of Christ.[290] The Father is the source of the divine life and Christ is the mediator of

[284] Crump systematically argues from the FG that the aspect of indwelling of the Spirit is not mentioned in the FG, instead the disciples are said to indwell in the Father and Son (Jn. 17:21). David Crump, "Re-examining the Johannine Trinity: Perichoresis or Deification?," *SJT* 59/4 (2006): 395-412, especially 398.

[285] Matthew Vellanickal, *The Divine Sonship of Christians in the Johannine Writings*, AnBib 72 (Rome: Biblical Institue Press, 1977).

[286] Vellanickal, *The Divine Sonship of Christians*, 90.

[287] Vellanickal, *The Divine Sonship of Christians*, 93.

[288] Vellanickal, *The Divine Sonship of Christians*, 102.

[289] Vellanickal, *The Divine Sonship of Christians*, 103.

[290] Vellanickal, *The Divine Sonship of Christians*, 160-161.

it.[291] Vellanickal stresses on the responsibility of sonship in terms of 'doing righteousness,' and the impetus for this comes from the divine life that remains an active force in the children of God.[292] Vellanickal has thrown great light on the aspect of sonship but has glossed over the sociological aspect, especially the hostility between the Johannine community and synagogue.[293]

The Divine Family of God does not exclude but rather embraces outsiders; the inclusion of the Samaritans in Jn. 4 reiterates this point, especially in 4:30 where the narrator notes, "They went out of the city and were coming to him." Another characteristic is that it engages in acts of liberation. Jesus is questioned by his opponents for having healed the invalid man on the Sabbath. Jesus' reply underlines a unity of action in the family engaged in liberation. He states in 5:17, "My Father is working still, and I am working." The expression "My Father" reinforces the relationship Jesus shares with the Father. Moloney rightly notes, "It is as the incarnate Son of the Father that Jesus is also working."[294] Further, the addition of "...and I am working" points to the unity of action in the Divine Family of God. A similar act of liberation is also narrated in the healing of the blind man (Jn. 9). He is termed as *ἐν ἁμαρτίαις σὺ ἐγεννήθης* and the narrator notes *ἐξέβαλον αὐτὸν ἔξω* (Jn. 9: 34). The narrator vividly brings in the speech of the interlocutors of the blind man, two allegiances pitted against each other: *σὺ μαθητὴς εἶ ἐκείνου, ἡμεῖς δὲ τοῦ Μωϋσέως ἐσμὲν μαθηταί* (Jn. 9:28). There is an attempt to exclude the blind man from their fellowship. The blind man who was cast out is now invited into the Family of God (Jn. 9:35).

The Family of God is sustained by the living bread, which is taking part in the very flesh of the Son of Man (Jn. 6). While Jesus' ministry did emphasize the aspect of the Family of God, both in terms of his relationship with the Father and his relationship with those under the Fatherhood of God, the actualizing of the family relationship is seen in his engagement with the disciples. The relationship with the disciples gets redefined from a master-slave relationship (Jn. 15:15) to a level of friendship (Jn.15:5) and finally culminating in a relationship of kinship and family in the resurrection narrative.

---

[291] Vellanickal, *The Divine Sonship of Christians*, 355.

[292] Vellanickal, *The Divine Sonship of Christians*, 356.

[293] R. Alan Culpepper, "Review of *The Divine Sonship of Christians*, by Matthew Vellanickal" *JBL* 98/3 (Sep. 1979): 447-449.

[294] Moloney, *The Gospel of John*, 170. Philo too argues that God does not rest on the Sabbath, "...For God never ceases from making something or other; but, as it is the property of fire to burn, and of snow to chill, so also it is the property of God to be creating. And much more so, in proportion as he himself is to all other beings the author of their working. (6) Therefore the expression, "he caused to rest," is very appropriately employed here, not "he rested." For he makes things to rest which appear to be producing others, but which in reality do not effect anything; but he himself never ceases from creating..." "Allegorical Interpretations," in *The Works of Philo: Complete and Unabridged*, translated by C. D. Yonge (Peabody: Hendrickson Publishers Inc., 1993), I.5-6.

In Jn. 20:17, Jesus' words to Mary 'to go and tell his brothers'- highlights the language of kinship, one that did contribute to the shaping of a social relationship within the Johannine community. The term "...in its varied contexts reflects the existence or, the desire for, a sibling-like bond between speaker and addressee(s). The term itself conveys no sense of hierarchy or superiority though that may of course be assumed or stated elsewhere in the context where it appears."[295] It possibly states the kinship of Jesus with the community or the Johannine community's belonging to the metaphorical Family of God. This is evident in the description of Jesus' relationship with the Father as well as the disciples' relationship with the Father.

There are two ways of looking at the phrase, "my father and your father, and my God and your God." The first way is to state that there is a clear line of distinction between Jesus' relationship with the Father and the disciples' relation with the Father. The second way of looking at it is to recognize that though the distinction can be seen, the focus is on the emergence of a metaphorical family which accommodates those outside the purview of the Family of God. The latter deserves careful attention.

In Jn. 8:31-59,[296] there is a compelling dialogue between Jesus and "the Jews." The allegiance to different families is acknowledged in the course of Jesus' discussions with "the Jews." The discussions dwell on the questions concerning the father of Jesus and the father of "the Jews."[297] The opponents of Jesus ("the Jews") arrogate the physical lineage with Abraham (vv. 33, 37,

---

[295] David G. Horrell,"From a|del foi| to oi|ko~ qeou:" 293-311.

[296] The dialogue begins in v.12. Talbert makes an observation of the pattern seen in different units: it begins with an intriguing statement by Jesus, which is followed up by a response from the Jews that precipitates a response from Jesus in the form of a monologue or dialogue (vv. 12-20; vv. 21-30; vv. 31-40; vv. 51-59). Talbert, *Reading John*, 152. Poirier locates the context of chap. 8 in the Hanukah festival and not Sukkoth. John C. Poirier, "Hanukah in the Narrative Chronology of the Fourth Gospel," *NTS* 54/4 (O. 2008): 475-476.

[297] The interpretation of Motyer concerning the phrase "You are of your Father the devil" (Jn. 8:44) in terms of warning and persuasion, does not seem go with the context, which is one of conflict. Motyer states, "Far from being an insulting and denigrating, this passage would have served as a powerful appeal to Jews in the late first century to believe in Jesus the Christ. "You are of your father the devil" would not have been heard as a designation of Jewish ontology, but as a serious *warning* about the real nature of certain course of action. Hearing such a warning, the late-first century reader must decide what attitude he/she will take to the Christ faith." Stephen Motyer, *Your Father the Devil? A New Approach to John and 'the Jews'* PBTM (Carlisle: Paternoster Press, 1997), 209. This interpretation seems innovative but one is not sure whether negative orientation can serve as an appeal. Griffth states, "The language of *diabolization* is restricted to those who have once been followers of Jesus and is appropriate to them alone." Terry Griffth, ""The Jews Who Had Believed in Him" (John 8:31) and the Motif of Apostasy in the Gospel of John," in *The Gospel of John and Christian* Theology, edited by Richard Bauckham and Carl Mosser (Grand Rapids, Michigan: William B. Eerdmans Publishing Company, 2008), 191.

39, 40, 52, 52, 53, 56, 57, 58). Jesus states a counter argument to this claim by noting that in rejecting the revelation of God in the person of Jesus, they have conducted themselves contrary to what Abraham did (v. 39, 40).[298] Jesus is here appealing to the fact that there seems to be a certain amount of givenness in belonging to a particular family. Actions characterize the family to which one belongs. The opponents of Jesus seem to characterize actions contrary to that of belonging to the family of Abraham, which is termed as that of killing Jesus. Unlike the opponents, Abraham received the revelation and responded to it in obedience.[299] Meanwhile, though the Jews profess Abraham as their father, they do not mirror his character because they did not obey God by receiving the revelation of Jesus.

The opponents of Jesus repudiate the charge of not belonging to the family of Abraham by accusing Jesus of being the offspring of an illegitimate birth.[300] In addition to this, they insist on having a relationship with the one God. The association with Abraham passes on to asserting their belonging to God as their Father. Moloney notes that on the basis of the covenant made between *YHWH* and a people, they were considered as God's children (Exd. 4:22; Deut. 14:1; 32:6; Jer. 3:4, 19).[301] Thus, the argument moves from belonging to the family of Abraham to belonging to the Family of God, especially in terms of belonging to God as their Father. The answer of the Johannine community is given in the words of Jesus, who refutes this by stating that if the opponents belonged to God they would have received Jesus as the one who has come from God. More than the thought of preexistence, their focus would have been on the aspect of belonging to the family. Moloney puts it succinctly, "...children of the same father love one another."[302] In other words, Jesus' belongingness to the Divine Family of God is evidenced in the relationship that he shares with God.

There is yet another family that is introduced that has the devil as its father. This father is characterized as doing contrary deeds of God. Jesus again appeals to the idea of children of the family behaving according to the family.

---

[298] Schanckenburg states, "All their claims, descent from Abraham and descent from God, break against the fact that they want to kill him (vv. 37, 40). Rudolf Schnackenburg, *The Gospel according to St.* John, translated by Cecily Hastings, Francis McDonagh, David Smith, et.al., vol. 2 (London: Burns and Oats, 1980), 212.

[299] Jesus uses the rabbinic style of argumentation here. The rabbis commonly described Abraham as a paradigm to be followed by the Jews. But Abraham is contrasted to the works of Balaam. Köstenberger, *John*, 264.

[300] Köstenberger notes that the Jews in v. 41 seem to suggest the "illegitimacy of Jesus' birth." Köstenberger, *John*, 265. A similar view is also taken by Moloney. Francis J. Moloney, *The Gospel of John*, SacPag, edited by Daniel H. Harrington (Minnesota: The Liturgical Press, 1998), 279.

[301] Moloney, *The Gospel of John*, 279.

[302] Moloney, *The Gospel of John*, 279.

The opponents of Jesus do not hear and believe the words of Jesus and thus do not qualify either as the family of Abraham or the Family of God but as the family of the devil (8:44). The basis for such a proposition is that the "the Jews" do not acknowledge Jesus' identity in the Divine Family of God because they do not believe or hear him. The opponents speak and reflect their ancestry.[303] Jesus also asserts his union with God the Father by challenging the opponents to accuse him of sin.[304]

In 8:39-47, Jesus lays emphasis on certain characteristics of being in the family of God i.e., hearing and doing. In other words, not hearing and doing disqualifies one from belonging to the family. While Jesus hears and does, which proves his belonging to the Divine Family of God, the opponents do not hear and do, thus acting contrary to what they profess. Here, the issue is one of Jewish monotheism.[305] There is a clear indication of the argument taking the form of a dialogue between the Johannine community and the Jewish interlocutors. For the Johannine community, Jesus finds a place in the Divine Family.

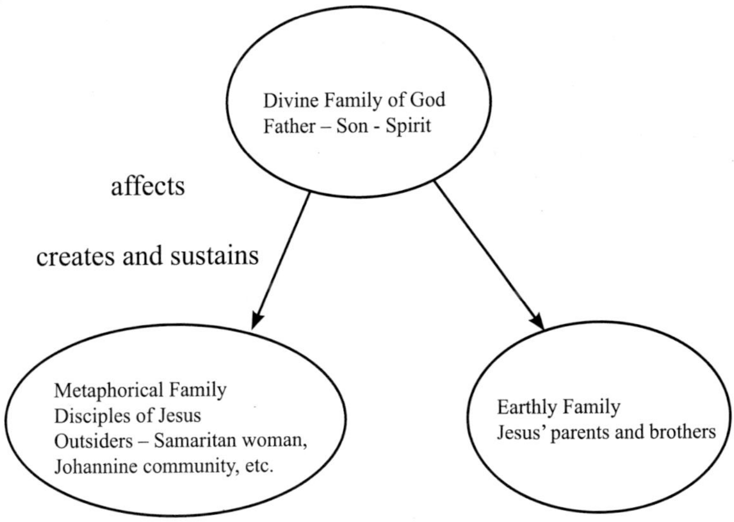

[303] Moloney, *The Gospel of John*, 279.

[304] Köstenberger, *John*, 267.

[305] Köstenberger, *John*, 265.

Processes	Natural Family	Family of God - Disciples/ Community
Birth	Natural birth	In opposition to natural birth
Sharing resources	Eligible but do not share	Ineligible but indeed share in the resources
Sharing relationship	Not clear	Fictive kinship with the Father, Son and Spirit
Boundaries	Exclusive	Inclusive – ever expanding

Further, the concept of the Family of God as a paradigm of the Johannine community's identity can be located in the context of the community, especially in the context of their struggles.

As seen earlier, the fractured relationship with the synagogue resulted in the loss of space in terms of religious, physical and communal space. It is in this context that the concept the Family of God became a paradigm of the Johannine community's identity. There are several implications that can be drawn from this understanding: The concept of the Family of God helped the Johannine community come to terms with their tumultuous relationship with the synagogue. Though considered by others as not being part of the Family of God, they sought to define it in terms of Christology. Christology helps the Johannine community in defining the basis of the Family of God. However, Christology is not to be seen in isolation from theology. For the Johannine Community, Christology works in relation to the Father and this is important for the community's claim to be a part of the Family of God. In the dialogue between "the Jews" and the Jewish Christians of the synagogue, the question of who constitutes the Family of God certainly figured; the discussion in Jn. 8 was an outcome of this.

"The Jews" rejected Jesus' messiahship because they 'knew' where he was from. (Jn. 7:27-28), but ironically they rejected exactly what they had been looking for i.e., Jesus' divine origin. In other words, what they were looking for, a Messiah whose origin is unknown, is clearly represented in Jesus, but they failed to grasp it. They rejected the very claim of the person they were seeking –Jesus' discourse was aimed at driving home the point that his origin is different from the physical descent. By refusing to accept it, they only further proved that his origin was unknown to them. Thus, Jesus' identity is established on 'un-knowness.'

This has lot to do with the community's perception of itself; the fact that the community was not recognized defined its identity. It is thus an identity of 'un-knowness.' 'Un-knowness' has aspects of the known and the unknown. 'Knowness' is a social category which leads to a rejection or acceptance of identity. The emphasis on "no one has ever seen God" (Jn. 1:18) has a polemic aspect to it. Menken notes that in the first century Judaism there was a belief that Moses' ascent of Mount Sinai (Exod. 20:21; 24:18) was an ascent into heaven where he saw God and received revelations.[306] *Apocalypse of Abraham* 16:2-8 also describes the ascent of Abraham:

> And the angel took me with his right hand and set me on the right wing of the pigeon and he himself sat on the left wing of 3 the turtledove, (both of) which were as if neither slaughtered nor divided. And 4 he carried me up to the edge of the fiery flames. And we ascended as if (carried) 5 by many winds to the heaven that is fixed on the expanses. And I saw on the air 6 to whose height we had ascended a strong light which cannot be described. And behold, in this light a fiery Gehenna was enkindled/ and a great crowd in the 7 likeness of men. 8 They all were changing in aspect and shape, running and changing form and prostrating themselves and crying aloud words I did not know.[307]

For the Jews with whom the Johannine community was engaged in controversy, it was one of rejection of identity. 'Knowness' is also a political aspect which points to how power is maintained and permeated. It is the cliquishness that defines their identity.

The Father plays an important part in the metaphorical Family of God in terms of working out the aspects of fatherhood. Culpepper rightly notes some of these aspects: a) the Father does not leave the disciples as orphans but along with Jesus abides with them (Jn. 14:23); b) he educates the children through his Son (Jn. 17:8, 14); c) the Johannine community has received the tradition of Jesus' teaching from the BD.[308] Thus, the Father exercises the essentials of Fatherhood not only with the Son but through the Son to the wider Family of God.

4.3.3. Mission in the FG: Witness of the Johannine Community[309]

Just as identity comes out of a shared relationship between the Father and the Son in the FG, so does mission. One of the more appropriate ways of looking

---

[306] Maarten J. J. Menken, "Observations on the Significance of the Old Testament in the Fourth Gospel," in *Theology and Christology in the Fourth Gospel: Essays by the Members of the Society for New Testament Study Johannine Writings Seminar*, BETL 184, edited by G. van Belle, J. G. van der Watt, and P. Maritz (Leuven: Leuven University Press, 2005), 158.

[307] James H. Charlesworth, ed., *The Old Testament Pseudepigrapha: Apocalyptic Literature and Testaments*, vol. 1 (New York: Doubleday, 1983), 696.

[308] Culpepper, "The Pivot of John's Prologue:" 29.

[309] Mission in the FG is a vast subject. Here, the discussion on mission is restricted to the resurrection narrative in Jn. 20, especially the aspect of sending the disciples. However, the

at mission in the FG is to consider it from the perspective of the family. The Family imagery is amalgamated with the agent imagery, and one enriches the other. In other words, the family identity i.e., the Son's relationship with the Father, is a paradigm for the understanding of mission in the FG. The agency motif has been a matter of debate, especially in terms of defining the relationship of the Son to the Father. It is necessary to first consider the agency motif before elaborating on the aspect of mission in the context of the Family of God.

4.3.3.1. Witness in the Divine Family

The mission motif in the context of the resurrection narrative in Jn. 20 has been dealt with elsewhere.[310] Here, the focus is on comprehending mission in the FG from the perspective of witness, particularly witness in the Family of God.

As seen earlier, the Father can be seen as the originator of the mission of the Son as well as the mission of the Spirit. The latter has been neglected in the discussion on mission. If mission can be seen in terms of sending, then, the Spirit has also an indispensable part in mission. It remains to be seen what role witness plays in the mission of the Divine Family.

The term 'witness' constantly recurs in the FG; in fact, the gospel can be seen from the perspective of witness.[311] What is of importance of course is that witness entails an object in the FG—the revelation of the Father by the Son. The Son witnesses to the things he has seen and heard from the Father (Jn. 8:38, 40, 47). All these aspects are subsumed under the notion of knowing the Father. Knowing the Father authenticates the witness of the Son (Jn. 15:15) and the identity of the Son because he shares a relationship with the Father.

---

sending of the disciples cannot be seen in isolation from the sending of the Son by the Father.

[310] Refer to Chapter IV the exegetical comments on 20:21.

[311] Trites views the FG from the point of view of witness: a) testimony of John the Baptist (1:6-8, 15, 19-34); b) testimony of the first disciples (1:35-51); c) testimony of the first sign (2:1-11); d) testimony of the resurrection (2:12-25); e) final testimony of John the Baptist (3:22-30); f) testimony of the Samaritans (4:1-42); g) the testimony of the Second sign (4:46-54); h) the testimony of the third sign (5:1-47); i) testimony of the fourth and fifth signs (6:1-71); j) testimony of the sixth sign (9:1-41); k) testimony of the seventh sign (11:1-57), etc. Trites looks at witness in the FG primarily from the lens of Isa. 40-55. He notes that like in Isa. 40-55 "God incarnate has a lawsuit with the world." The world he considers as referring to the unbelieving Jews and the subject of debate concerns "messiahship and divine sonship of Jesus." Allison A. Trites, *The New Testament Concept of Witness*, SNTSMS 31, edited by Matthew Black (Cambridge: Cambridge University Press, 1977), 91-109, 79. But one could move further and also see witness not only in terms of divine sonship, i.e., identity but also unraveling of the Father's mission.

4.3.3.1.1. The Agency Motif

The aspect of sending is not unique to the FG.[312] Peder Borgen[313] has compared the aspect of sending with the Jewish aspect of agency.[314] He highlights the Halakhic principle of agent, especially the principle that notes, "The agent is like the one who sent him."[315] Borgen ascertains six similarities between the halkahic principles of agency and the concept of 'sending' in the FG. First, there is the unity between the agent and his sender. Second, the agent is subject to the sender. Third, it is required of the agent to be obedient to the will of the sender. Fourth, the agent's task is in the lawsuit. Fifth, the agent returns and reports to the sender. Lastly, the agent also makes use of others to fulfill the agent's mission."[316]

Though the agency motif is not unique to the FG, there are many differences in its exposition in the FG. The use of an agency model is insufficient

---

[312] O'Brien notes that even in Luke's gospel "...the basic foundational mission is that of Jesus, who has been sent by God." This aspect is clearly mentioned in Lk. 4:16-30 and Acts 3:20, 26. Peter T. O'Brien, "Mission, Witness and the coming of the Spirit," *BBR* 9 (Ja. 1999): 203-214.

[313] Peder Borgen, "God's Agent in the Fourth Gospel," in *Religions in Antiquity: Essays in Memory of Erwin Ramsdell Goodenough*, edited by Jacob Neusner (Leiden: E. J. Brill, 1970), 137-148. It could be noted that the book by J. –A Bühner *Der Gesandte und sein Weg im 4. Evangeliuum,* WUNT 2/2. Reihe (Tübingen: Mohr Siebeck, 1977), cited in A. E. Harvey, "Christ as Agent," in *The Glory of Christ in the New Testament: Studies in Christology In Memory of George Bradford Caird*, edited by L. D. Hurst and N. T. Wright (Oxford: Oxford Clarendon Press, 1987), 241, was the first major study on the relation between Jewish law of agency and the New Testament. Harvey notes that this work helps in understanding the language in the FG is "...drawn from juridical practice." Harvey, "Christ as Agent," 241. Talbert finds two currents in ancient Judaism that makes use of descent-ascent pattern: a) the wisdom tradition seen in Sirach 24, Baruch 3:27-4:4; b) the Wisdom of Solomon; c) Jewish angelology, which is seen in *mal'ach* Yahweh and also the archangels. Talbert, *Reading John*, 267-268.

[314] Voowinde attributes the view taken up by Borgen as an offshoot of Bultmann's interpretation of Johannine Christology of in terms of Gnostic Redeemer-myth. Stephen Voorwinde, *Jesus' Emotions in the Fourth Gospel Human or Divine?* (London: T & T Clark, 2005), 8. The myth notes that in order to redeem those creatures of light that fell into the power of darkness the Father sends the Redeemer to impart knowledge of true origin and being those that fell into the power of darkness. On completing the task of redemption, the Redeemer ascends again. Bultmann, *The Gospel of John*, 8.

[315] Berakoth 5:5 notes, "If he that says the *Tefillah* falls into error it is a bad omen for him; and if he was the agent of the congregation it is a bad omen for them that appointed him, because a man's agent is like to himself." *The Mishnah*, translated by Herbert Danby (Oxford: Oxford University Press, 1933). There is also the view that the Jewish *Shaliah* institution is of a late origin. 33. Sean Freyne, "Apostle, Apostolicity" in *NDCT*, edited by Alan Richardson and John Bowden (London: SCM Press, 1983).

[316] Borgen also goes further in combining the halakahic principle and mystical thought, especially the early stages of *merkabah* mysticism. Borgen, "God's agent in the Fourth Gospel," 144.

to describe the Christology in the FG. Wenham notes that Jesus is more than an agent signified in the words, "Before Abraham was, I am" (Jn. 8:58).[317] The aspect of giving life and judging (Jn. 5:26-27), which are divine prerogatives, cannot be subsumed in the concept of agency. Unlike the agency model in rabbinic writings, "John tends to stress that the one who sends is greater than the one who is sent (13:16; 14:28) …it is as the origin of the Son's very being that "the Father is greater than I."" [318] The agency motif does not accommodate motifs such as: "...descent and ascent of the Son of Man, the use of "Logos," Jesus' function of teaching and illumination, or the Gospel's emphasis on *seeing* the Father in the Son... the limitation duration of the commission is a chief deficiency."[319] Dunn summarizes the limitation by noting,

> The commissioning formula is too narrow a base to sustain such a thesis. John's language grew out of this kind of talk of divine commissioning of the prophet, but his christology is neither constrained in nor explained by it-particularly, once again, his emphasis on a *pre-existence* that is cosmic (as in 8:25 and 17:5), or his emphasis on a *unity* between the Father and Son (as in 1:18 and 10:30) which goes beyond the identity of the sender and sent on the *šālîaḥ* model.[320]

Köstenberger and Swain rightly opine, "*The kind of agency exhibited by Jesus in John's Gospel is a distinctly divine-filial agency.*"[321]

The crucial aspect of agency in the FG, however, is not so much dependent on the parallel backgrounds,[322] but on how the agency motif describes the relation between the Father and the Son. In other words, what role does the

---

[317] David Wenham and Steve Walton, *Exploring the New Testament: A Guide to the Gospels & Acts*, vol. 1 (Illinois: InterVarsity Press, 2001), 247.

[318] Thompson, *The God of the Gospel of John*, 94. Keener opines that the Father is 'greater in rank' and has no reference to equality in being. Craig S. Keener, "Is Subordination within the Trinity Really Heresy? A Study of John 5:18 in Context," *TrinJ* 20/1 (Spring 1999), 40.

[319] For Thompson Wisdom serves better because the concept can fit the aspects of "... heavenly origin, cosmic pre-existence, unity with God, and embodiment of divine presence." Thompson, *The God of the Gospel of John*, 127-128.

[320] James D. G. Dunn, "Let John Be John: A Gospel for Its Time," in *The Gospel and the Gospels*, edited by Peter Stuhlmacher (Grand Rapids, Michigan: William B. Eerdmans Publishing Company, 1991), 313.

[321] Köstenberger and Swain, *Father, Son and Spirit*, 121. Neyrey considers the role of Jesus in terms of 'patron-client-broker relations' where Jesus belongs to two worlds: 'world of God-Patron' and 'disciples-clients.' Jerome H. Neyrey, ""I am the Door" (John 10:7, 9): Jesus the Broker in the Fourth Gospel," *CBQ* 69/2 (Apr. 2007): 272.

[322] Talbert presents three limitations of the descending-ascending saviour personality originating from the Gnostic redeemer myth. They are: a) the sources of the Gnostic myth come from a later period; b) redeemer myth is not vital to Gnosticism; c) the ontological identity is

agency motif play in describing the function of the Son? There seems to be a wide range of opinions among scholars regarding this subject.

For Thompson, the use of *Shaliah* terminology helps in describing the relationship of Jesus to the Father: the unity of the work of the Father and the Son (5:17-18; 10:29-30); the obedience, and even "subordination," of the agent to the sender, or of the Son to the Father; the call to honour the Son as one would the Father (5:23); and the language of sending (6:29, 38, 44, 57). Harvey opines that Jewish Christians used agency to describe the functional identity between Jesus and God.[323] Anderson sees the Father's[324] actions in the FG as expressed in the mission of the Son and this leads him to see the "Prophet-like-Moses typology" based on the agency motif described in Deut. 18:15-22.[325] The phrase "the having-sent-me one" is used to authenticate the mission of Jesus.[326] Anderson further notes, "Jesus' egalitarian and subordinate relations to the Father are *two sides of the same coin*- and agency schema rooted in Deut. 18:15-22."[327] For Köstenberger and Swain, the terminology explains three aspects in the Father-Son relationship: the concept of not honouring the Son is also not honouring the Father; the idea of coming in the Father's name; and those who hate the Son, hate the Father also (Jn. 15:23-25).[328] The views expressed here cover a wide range of understanding of the role of the agency

---

absent in the relationship between Christ and believers as in Gnosticism; d) the descent-ascent schema is not unique to Gnosticism. Talbert, *Reading John*, 265-266.

[323] Harvey states this understanding developed among the Jewish Christians in order to extend the "exclusive" use of 'god.' And this scenario changed when the Greeks took it for granted that Jesus should be called 'god.' Harvey, "Christ as Agent," 249-250.

[324] Anderson is of the view that the presentation of the Father in the FG has both primitive (the Prophet-like-Moses presentation of Jesus' ministry) and developed tradition (it represents a Johannine construct). Paul N. Anderson, "The Having-Sent-Me Father: Aspects of Agency, Encounter, and Irony in the Johannine Father-Son Relationship," *Semeia: God the Father in the Gospel of John* 85 (1999): 36.

[325] Anderson identifies eight themes of Deut. 18:15-22 explained in the FG: a. Deut. 18: 15a, 18a – i. Jesus identified as being a Prophet like Moses (6: 14-15), ii. The term prophet is used by the Samaritan woman (4:19), the Jews (7:40) and the blind man (9:17); b. Deut 18: 15b - the Son bears witness to that which he has *seen and heard* from the Father; hearing implies believing and knowing his voice (10: 3-4); c. 18b – Yahweh will put his words in his (the prophet's) mouth; d. 18c – He shall speak everything Yahweh commands him; e. The one who does not pay attention to the prophet who speaks in Yahweh's name, will be held accountable; f. 20 – If the prophet speaks whatever does not take place that prophet shall die; g. 22a – If a prophet speaks in the name of the Lord and the word does not take place or does not occur, that is a message the Lord has not spoken; h. 22b – If the prophet has spoken presumptuously no one shall fear him. Anderson, "The Having-Sent-Me Father:" 34, 37-40.

[326] Anderson, "The Having-Sent-Me Father," 36.

[327] Anderson, "The Having-Sent-Me Father," 41.

[328] Köstenberger and Swain, *Father, Son and Spirit*, 65-66, 72.

motif. It ranges from viewing it as an expression of subordination[329] to seeing it as expressing both egalitarian and subordinate relations.

One of the ways to comprehend the agency motif is to understand the purpose of the agency motif. Does it have to do with defining the identity of the Father or the Son, or both in terms of the Family of God?

Some scholars, who view the agency model, assert the Christological identity of the FG. Brown notes, "The Gospel is not so much interested in the God who sent Jesus as it is in the Jesus whom God sent."[330] For Ronald A. Piper, "It is hardly an exaggeration to claim that everything in the Fourth Gospel revolves around christology."[331] There seems to be truth in what is said by Brown and Piper. Meyer opines that the evangelist mentions that the Father has placed all things into the Son's hands and this implies: "God is known and God's presence felt only because the Son alone "presents" God to the world, is wholly transparent to God, and is the only reliable vehicle for God's presence and action in the world. The only "presentation of God" in the Fourth Gospel is the self-presentation of Christ in the narratives and discourses."[332]

Though Christology seems to define the Johannine understanding of agency, there is another side to it. Meyer notes, "Everything in the Gospel's presentation of Christ is also a "presentation" of God. In confronting Jesus people are dealing with the Father (8:16) and they see the Father (14:7)..."[333] Thus, the overemphasis on the "Christocentric" aspect of agency does not seem to present the whole picture explicated in the FG. Thompson notes:

> ...to label the Gospel of John "Christocentric" is inadequate and imprecise: *inadequate* because the label diverts our attention from the theocentric framework of the Fourth Gospel; *imprecise* because it ignores the prior question of the function and referent of John's Christology and because it obscures important observations

---

[329] Segovia is of the view that Jn. 1: 3-17 highlights three subordinate relationships between the Word and the World: a. Word and world of creation (1:3); b. Word and human beings in the world (1:4-13); Word and those human beings who welcome the world (1:14-17). Fernando F. Segovia, "John 1:1-18 as Entrée into Johannine Reality: Representation and Ramifications," in *Word, Theology and Community in John*, edited by John Painter, R. Alan Culpepper, and Fernando F. Segovia (Missouri: Chalice Press, 2002), 39.

[330] Raymond Bryan Brown, "Distinctives of John's Gospel," *SWJT* 8/1 (O. 1965): 28.

[331] Ronald A. Piper, "Satan, Demons and the absence of Exorcisms in the Fourth Gospel," in *Christology, Controversy and Community: New Testament Essays in Honour of David R. Catchpole*, NovTSup 99, edited by David G. Horrell and Christopher M. Tuckett (Leiden: Brill, 2000), 253.

[332] Meyer, ""The Father": The Presentation of God," 255.

[333] Meyer, ""The Father": The Presentation of God," 256.

> about the text that might lead us to rethink and reformulate our understanding of Johannine theology.[334]

Keck notes, "...even though every statement about Christ implicates God, beginning with the designation of Jesus as the Anointed. This neglect of the theological correlate has constricted Christology and skewed Christianity as a whole..."[335] Barrett also states, "John clarifies the relation of Jesus to God."[336] Christology in the FG does not overshadow its theology. Thompson rightly states, "...the Gospel would better be termed "theocentric," in that it directs our attention to God, and this designation is particularly apt in the light of the fact that Johannine Christology itself regularly, comprehensively...seeks to relate Jesus to God."[337] Thompson also makes a valid point, "It is highly unlikely that John intends the reader to understand that at some point the Father and Son simply "collapse" into one...the identity of Jesus...as the manifestation and revelation of God."[338] In this regard, Meyer notes that the presentation of God in the FG is not to be "...treated as an independent *locus* in the evangelist's theology but neither can it be simply suppressed and ignored."[339] He uses the term "theocentric Christocentricity"[340] to describe the theology of the FG.

The movement from a purely Christological emphasis of the FG to a more theocentric understanding helps in situating the understanding of agency in the FG better. Jesus commonly refers to himself as the one sent by the Father (5:23, 30, 3, 37; 6:38; 7:29; 8:16, 26, 42; 10:36; 11:42; 16:5). Jesus is defined as part of the meaning formation of God. Wenham notes, "Jesus is God made audible and visible."[341] As Meyer succinctly puts it, ""the Father who sent me" or "he who sent me" is God's name."[342] In this connection, Thompson explains

---

[334] Thompson, *The God of the Gospel of John*, 11.

[335] Leander E. Keck, "Towards the Renewal of New Testament Theology," *NTS* 32/3 (Jl. 1986): 363.

[336] Barrett, *The Gospel according to St. John*, 54.

[337] Thompson, *The God of the Gospel of John*, 227. Thompson also notes: "Barrett, Dahl, Dunn, Keck and others have argued convincingly that christology is indeed as aspect of theology and only in that perspective properly grasped." Thompson, *The God of the Gospel of John*, 14.

[338] Thompson, *The God of the Gospel of John*, 235.

[339] Meyer, ""The Father": The Presentation of God," 257.

[340] Meyer, ""The Father": The Presentation of God," 257.

[341] Wenham and Walton, *Exploring the New Testament*, 247.

[342] Meyer sees the concept: "the Father who sent me" as the reason for the cross or the resurrection being portrayed as vindication. He opines, ""The "presentation of God as Father" in this Gospel is as the Vindicator and Authorizer of Jesus. Unlike Paul God is the *eschatological* Vindicator, whose aspect "in power" in the resurrection provides the *ex post facto* warrant, backing, and justification of Jesus. But here in the "presentation of God as Father" eschatology has been replaced by *protology*. Jesus stands in no need of an eschatological vindication. He

that Jesus' identity has its "origin and destiny in God."[343] The language of sending reveals that the origin and decisions come from outside the one who is being sent, thus theology is not collapsed into Christology.[344] The Father is not only the originator of all that Jesus says and does, including Jesus' mission to the disciples.[345] Thus in one sense, Father has an all important role and is implicated in the sending of the Son, i.e., the mission of the Son and mission in the FG originates from the Father.

There are several texts in the FG that attest that the Father has sent the Son (3:17, 34; 5:36, 38; 6:29, 57; 7:29; 8:42; 10:36; 11:42; 17:3, 8,18, 23, 25; 18:24; 20:21), and also that the Son comes and goes to the Father, the point of origin (13:1; 10:28; 14:12, 28; 16:5,6). Thompson notes, "…the Father as *the one who sends*, makes the Father the subject and initiator of the Son's activity and once again identifies the Father by means of his action with respect to the Son."[346] Köstenberger and Swain also note, "…chapters 5-10 characterize God as the Father of Jesus, who initiated an authorized Jesus' mission and who bears witness to him."[347] The works the Son does pertain to the Father and have been entrusted to him by the Father (Jn. 5:36; 9:4; 10:25, 32, 37).

The mission of the Son cannot be isolated from the identity of the Son. The phrase "the Father who sent me" also affirms the identity of the Son, in terms of his deity. It can be stated that Johannine Christology with reference to God is both functional[348] and relational.[349] Tonstad rightly states, "The identity of the agent and the purpose of his coming into the world are indissolubly linked."[350] Brown argues that the NT certainly affirms Jesus' divinity on three

---

does not need to come again "in power". He is "right" because God is "the Father who has sent me."" Meyer, ""The Father": The Presentation of God in the Fourth Gospel," 264-265.

343 Thompson, *The God of the Gospel of John*, 237.

344 Meyer, ""The Father": The Presentation of God," 261.

345 Meyer, ""The Father": The Presentation of God," 264.

346 Thompson, *The God of the Gospel of John*, 93.

347 Köstenberger and Swain, *Father, Son and Holy Spirit*, 68.

348 Thompson defines *functional christology*: "… A functional christology is a "high christology," particularly when the functions exercised are seen as unique divine prerogatives." Thompson, *The God of the Gospel of John* 47.

349 In this regard Thomson notes, "The whole gospels elaborates the one "who is "with God" and who "is God."" Thompson, *The God of the Gospel of John*, 53. Weder notes that "Wisdom theology" helps in explaining the relationship between God and Jesus of Nazareth and one of the ways is that wisdom is both a present in the reality to the world of the flesh at the same time belongs to God so it is with Christ. Weder also notes, "Jesus of Nazareth reveals God precisely in the sense that he becomes an event of God." Unlike the Wisdom theology here the concern is on the ministry of Jesus. Weder, "*Deus Incarnatus*: On the Hermeneutics of Christology in the Johannine Writings," 330-332.

350 Sigve K. Tonstad, ""The Father of Lies," "the Mother of Lies," and the Death of Jesus (John 12: 20-33)," in *The Gospel of John and Christian Theology*, edited by Richard

occasions (Jn. 1:1; 20:28; Heb. 1:8-9), and probably on five others (Jn. 1:18; Rom. 9:5; Tit. 2, 13; 2Pet. 1:1; 1 Jn. 5:20).[351] Fennema concludes on the study of Jn. 1:1-2 and 1:14: "Thus, John perceives the Logos/Son and the Father/God as two distinct beings, yet ascribes the identical deity to both. This paradoxical assertion that Father and Son together are 'the only God,' John has expanded the traditional Jewish, monotheistic conception of deity. The one true God is now to be recognized as both God the Father and God the Logos/Son."[352] This possibly provides the clue: the FG's Christology emerged out of the Johannine community's dialogue with the synagogue and its pursuit of defining the identity and mission of Jesus. de Jonge states that the FG is different from the "monotheist confession of faith in the first century," and the difference lies in the Johannine Christology – "christology is John's way of speaking of God at those points where the understanding of God is being transformed... the change is – new hermeneutic which recognizes a new centre from which all is viewed. John's christology constitutes a new centre for understanding God, the purpose of God, the destiny of creation and the meaning of faith."[353]

The phrase "the Father who sent me" is at once an affirmation of the mission of the Son and identity of the Son, and this needs to be seen in relation to the mission and identity of the Father. In other words, it needs to be seen as the mission and identity of the Divine Family. If the identity of the Family of God is all-embracing and not self-restricting in terms of circumscribing the identity of ethnic descent such as Moses, Abraham, etc., what does the mission in the Family of God involve? Mission in the Family of God can be termed as witnessing i.e., witnessing in the Family of God.

4.3.3.2. Witness: An Outcome of Family Relationship

Jesus underlines that he is educated by the Father (Jn. 8:28), stressing the unity of action between Father and the Son. The aspect of hearing ἤκουσα in 8:26 is further described in 8:28 as ἐδίδαξέν. It reveals that what he speaks is the outcome of having been taught by the Father. Here, the doing and the speaking of the Son is the result of sharing intimacy with the Father. Keener notes, "Jesus speaks to the world some of the things which he has heard from the Father which reveals his intimacy."[354] There are other texts (Jn. 10:18; 12:49)

Bauckham and Carl Mosser (Grand Rapids, Michigan: William B. Eerdmans Publishing Company, 2008), 204.

[351] Raymond E. Brown, "Does the New Testament Call Jesus God?," *TS* 26/4 (Dec. 1965): 561f. There are others who agree to this view. Fortna does a redaction critical analysis of the FG and notes that the FE emphasizes on the divinity of Jesus. Robert T. Fortna, "Christology in the Fourth Gospel: Redaction-Critical Perspectives," *NTS* 21/4 (Jl. 1975): 494.

[352] Fennema, "John 1:18: 'God the Only Son:'" 131.

[353] de Jonge, "Christology, Controversy and Community," 233, 235.

[354] Keener, *The Gospel of John*, vol. 1, 745.

in the FG where Jesus is said to have received the command or charge from the Father. Jesus notes in 10:18 that he has received the command (τὴν ἐντολὴν) to lay down life and take it up again from the Father. The sacrifice of the Son is in obedience to the Father's command.[355] Here, the text denotes unity both in command and obedience. This aspect is made clear in 12:48 where Jesus states that Father has instructed him on what to say and what to speak.

The Son does not speak independently of the Father (3:34-35; 5:19-20; 7:16-18; 8:26-29; 12:47-50), and neither does the Spirit. Jn.16:13 (ἀλλ' ὅσα ἀκούσει λαλήσει) closely parallels with Jn. 8:26 (κἀγὼ ἃ ἤκουσα παρ' αὐτοῦ); the former deals with Spirit who speaks what the Spirit hears and the latter, the Son speaking what he has heard from the Father. It is not clear from whom the Spirit hears, but taking the clue from what follows, it can be said that the Spirit hears from the Son. Köstenberger opines, "...the Spirit will speak only what he hears – his dependence on Jesus enacting the pattern set by Jesus in relation to the Father..."[356] The Spirit speaks what he hears from the Son but even what he hears from the Son comes from the Father. The next verses (Jn. 16:14-15) seem to convey this idea. In essence, the revelation goes back to the Father. Carson notes, "...the content of *what is mine* is nothing less than the revelation of the Father himself, for Jesus declares, *All that belongs to the Father is mine* (v.15)."[357] The pattern seems to be:

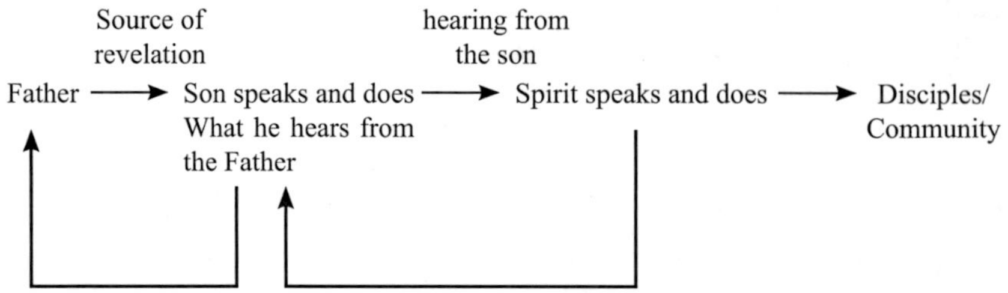

This pattern reinforces that the FG does not eliminate the role of theology, but rather Christology is to be seen in the light of theology. However, what is more important here is that the pattern does support the metaphor of the family where the Father takes a significant place. The family concept conveys the idea of unity in message and action.

4.3.3.3. Witness as Unity in Doing

The Mission aspect of witnessing in the FG can be seen as one of "doing," and this is attached to the relationship that the Son shares with the Father. The notion of incarnation does convey a movement from one sphere to the

[355] Herman Ridderbos, *The Gospel of John*, 365.

[356] Köstenberger, *John*, 473.

[357] Carson, *The Gospel according to John*, 541.

other. The aspect of "doing" is not to be detached or seen independently as "doing" of the Son. Köstenberger and Swain rightly explain, "…the action to be undertaken involves not the imposition of the will of the one upon the other, but where the action to be undertaken must be understood as a common cause, and a common cause because it is family business."[358] This is seen clearly in the healing of the invalid person on the Sabbath, which ignites a controversy with the Jewish opponents.

The context of 5:19-20 is provided by the narrator, who notes the Jewish opposition to Jesus' words in v.18, which implied that Jesus not only broke the Sabbath but also made himself equal to God (5:19). Here, Keener rightly notes the issue of Jesus calling God "Father" was not the real problem, but asserting an unequalled relationship, different from what the Jews shared, that disturbed the Jewish opponents.[359] He also notes that the phrase "equal to God" was used by rabbis to mean "...to make oneself independent from God, similar to a phrase applied to a son who casts off the yoke of his parents."[360] Contrary to the meaning of independence, v.18 asserts the dependence on the Father in doing what he has seen from the Father. The Son validates the action of healing the invalid man on the Sabbath by noting that he is doing what he has seen from the Father (Jn. 8:38). In other words, the Son does not work independently but only in terms of what he has seen the Father doing. Thus, the works of the Son are witnesses of what the Father is doing. This interpretation goes in line with what Jesus says in 5:17: Ὁ πατήρ μου ἕως ἄρτι ἐργάζεται, κἀγὼ ἐργάζομαι. It reinforces the fact that Jesus is dependent and obedient to the Father who sent him. Schnackenburg is of the view that Jesus' participation in the healing of the invalid man means, he is doing what is in congruence with what the Father has instructed him.[361] Mission of the Son thus seems to embrace what he has seen the Father doing.

The narrator not only provides the context of Jesus' saying (Jn. 5:19) in v. 18, but also gives a clue to the situation faced by the Johannine community where the community had to answer regarding Jesus' place in the Jewish monotheistic understanding. Ridderbos rightly notes that here the issue of Sabbath has been overshadowed by the issue of Jesus' relationship with the

---

[358] Köstenberger and Swain, *Father, Son and Spirit*, 122.

[359] Keener, *The Gospel of John*, vol. 1, 646. McGrath notes an interesting aspect, though it is a reiteration of Odberg's view, he states, "…to make oneself equal to one's father, in the sense of claiming for oneself the unique prerogatives or honour which belonged to one's father, would have been understood as making oneself a rebellious son, one who was behaving in a way inappropriate to a son." James F. McGrath, "A Rebellious Son? Hugo Odeberg and the Interpretation of John 5:18," *NTS* 44/3 (Jl. 1998): 472.

[360] Keener, *The Gospel of John*, vol. 1, 647.

[361] Schnackenburg, *The Gospel according to St. John*, vol. 2, 103.

Father in the ensuing discussion.[362] Keener notes that v.18 more likely presents the Jewish opponents as affirming the "Christian claims," and the charge against the Jewish Christians for worshipping two gods.[363]

Jesus retorts to the charge that he is making himself equal to God by bringing together two concepts: the dependence of the Son on the Father i.e., doing what he has seen the Father doing; and the nature of the Father showing his deeds to the Son based on the principle of love. The latter aspect further explains the relationship that is shared by the Father and the Son. Carson notes that the use of γάρ explicates how the Son's action is congruent with the Father's action. He also notes, "The love of the Father for the Son is displayed in the continuous disclosure of all he does to the Son (here in v. 20); the love of the Son for the Father is displayed in the perfect obedience that issues in the cross (14:31)."[364] In the verses that follow, the Father entrusts the aspect of giving life and judging to the Son (5:21-23). The Son's responsibility of judging is again not independent of the Father. There are two texts that clearly affirm this understanding: καθὼς ἀκούω, κρίνω (Jn. 5:30) and κἀγὼ ἃ ἤκουσα παρ' αὐτοῦ (Jn. 8:26). Jesus hears from his Father and thus makes judgment according to the Father's will.[365] It exemplifies Jesus' submission to the Father.[366]

The 'doing' aspect of the mission of the Son possibly cannot be limited to the aspect of 'seeing' from the Father. It comes from being educated and being commanded by the Father. Thus, the witness of the divine family clearly expresses the loss of individualized will in order that the community is expressed. Witnessing is the effect of moving out of the confines of the Divine Family in order that those outside could also become part of the family.

4.3.3.4. Witness in the Johannine Community

The entire FG is written from the perspective of witness. It is the witness of the BD presented in a narrative form (Jn. 21:24). It can also be said that the gospel was narrated and adapted by the BD with a view to eliciting a specific response from the readers –"These are written..." However, embedded also in the FG is the Johannine community's witness to the family relationship shared by the Father, Son and the Spirit. Witness in this regard is a witness of identity i.e., witnessing to the Family of God. Here there are two aspects to witness in the FG. First, the Johannine community is a witness to the Divine family

---

[362] Ridderbos, *The Gospel of John*, 196.

[363] Keener, *The Gospel of John*, vol. 1, 647.

[364] D. A. Carson, *The Gospel according to John* (Michigan: William B. Eerdmans Publishing Company, 1991), 251.

[365] Keener, *The Gospel of John*, vol. 1, 655.

[366] Carson, *The Gospel according to John*, 259.

relationship. Moreover, the community has to exemplify the witness both within the community as well as without i.e., engaging in acts of liberation.

4.3.3.5. Witness the 'Within-Without' Dimension

The identity of the Son is prescribed in relation to the Father.[367] In several ways, κἀγὼ ἃ ἤκουσα παρ' αὐτοῦ the FG expounds that Jesus' identity comes from his relationship with the Father. First, the ministry of the Son comes from the relationship with the Father. The Son does everything he has seen and heard from the Father (Jn. 5:19-20), receiving instructions from the Father (Jn. 8:28), and thus completing the work of the Father (5:36). In effect, the Father has shown πάντα (Jn. 5:20) to the Son, that which the Father is doing. Thus, the Son shares the intimate knowledge of the Father about what the Father is doing. This is a reiteration of what the FE has stated in the prologue about Jesus sharing an intimate relationship with the Father with the use of the expression: ὢν εἰς τὸν κόλπον τοῦ πατρός (Jn. 1:18; 6:46). Second—and this is related to the first point—the Son has been authorized by the Father. There are several indicators of this aspect: the Son has come in the Father's name (5:43); the Father has set the seal on the Son (6:27); the Son is sanctified and sent by the Father (10:36); and the Father remains in the Son and does the works (Jn. 14:10). This idea moves beyond the Father as a mere authorizer of the Son's works. Third, the Father also acknowledges the work of the Son by glorifying the Son (Jn. 10:15; 13:32), and bearing witness to the Son (Jn. 5:30, 37; 8:18). The identity of the Son is also asserted in describing the total dependence of the Son on the Father because whatever the Son has belongs to the Father (Jn. 17:7). Fourth, the aspects of going and coming, a description of the Son's identity, have the Father as the reference point (13:1; 14:12; 10:28; 16:5, 6). Fifth, the Father-Son relationship is one characterized by love. The Father loves the Son before the πρὸ καταβολῆς κόσμου. Sixth, there is the aspect of oneness shared by the Father and Son (17:21). This oneness[368] is explained in judgment, where the Father is present in the judgment of the Son (Jn. 8:16); in honouring, not honouring the Son is not honouring the Father (5:23); in the

[367] The relationship between the Father and the Son in the FG is "…thoroughly and inextricably intertwined," according to Köstenberger and Swain. They note that this is seen in the use of 'just as' in 5:21, 23, 26; 6:57; 8:28; 10:15; 12:50; 17:18; 20:21; and also the description of the "Jesus 'in' the Father and the Father in him" (10:38; 14:11, 20). Köstenberger and Swain, *Father, Son and Spirit*, 74.

[368] Jesus categorically states in Jn. 10:30, 'Εγὼ καὶ ὁ πατὴρ ἕν ἐσμεν. This has been differently interpreted by scholars. Köstenberger and Swain infer that there is not only a 'unity of works' but also 'ontological unity.' Köstenberger and Swain, *Father, Son and Spirit*, 67. Heath notes that the use of term 'goodness' (Jn. 7:12b) for Jesus points to a shared "…relationship of Jesus to God in which their shared 'goodness' becomes both a theological and ethical challenge." In other words, it affirms "…Jesus' unity with God." J. Heath, "'Some were saying, "He is good"' (John 7:12b)" 'Good' Christology in John's Gospel?," *NTS* 56/4 (O. 2010): 513,535.

presence of the Father in the ministry of the Son (8:29); in the Son knowing the Father and the Father knowing the Son (10:15); in the mutual indwelling (10:38; 14:10, 11; 17:21), the indwelling of the Son in the Father also extends to the Son's relationship with the disciples (14:20); in the Son sharing the name of the Father (17:11); in serving the Son, the Father is honoured (12:26); believing the Son is also believing the one who sent the Son (12:44); knowing the Son is knowing the Father (14:7); seeing the Son is also seeing the Father (14:9), loving and hating the Son is loving and hating the Father (14:21; 15:23); eternal life is knowing the Father and the Son (17:3).

These aspects of the Father-Son relationship can be understood as witness in the context of a family relationship, especially the expression used by Jesus in Jn. 10:38.[369] Even the Spirit's role in the FG is one of witness; the Spirit witnesses to the Son (15:26). The Father, the Son and the Spirit bear witness to each other. Witness in the FG is not presented as individual witness, but as witness of the Divine Family. Thus, by extension the Johannine community primarily bears witness to the Divine Family i.e., the relationship that exists in the Divine Family. Jesus states that besides the Spirit of Truth, the disciples themselves are a testimony of who Jesus is (Jn. 15:27). It is interesting to note that in Jn. 14:7 Jesus recognises the Spirit of Truth as already dwelling in the disciples.

There are two ways in which the Johannine community is said to witness to the Divine Family. First, witness has community implication of relating with one another and this can be termed as witness within the community. Second, and more importantly, witness has an external dimension, which calls for engaging in factors that promote fullness of life; those outside the fold also need to participate in situations that enhance life.

Witness in the FG has an internal dimension where the disciples as a community are asked to represent the love of the Son within the community (Jn. 15:10). This love exemplified in the Son is better viewed against the backdrop of the love that exists in the Father-Son relationship i.e., the Divine Family, and more specifically, the love of the Father for the Son. Ridderbos rightly notes, "The love in which the disciples must remain does not begin with Jesus but has its source and energy in the love with which the Father has loved his Son..."[370] The Father's love is expressed in two places.[371] The first, πάντα δέδωκεν ἐν τῇ χειρὶ αὐτοῦ (Jn. 3:35). For Schnackenburg, the expression refers to the "...Johannine way of expressing the authority and "equipment" of the

[369] Köstenberger and Swain rightly suggests that this denotes "…a very close personal family relationship." Köstenberger and Swain, *Father, Son and Spirit*, 71.

[370] Ridderbos, *The Gospel of John*, 519.

[371] Father's love for the Son is stated in several places: 5:20. 15:9f.; 17:23f., 26.

revealer and redeemer as he is sent into the world."[372] However, here, mission of the Son is seen as an outcome of the love of the Father (3:16). Ridderbos, in this regard rightly notes, "In him and in his mission God is present in the world as the God of love." [373] The second, πάντα δείκνυσιν αὐτῷ ἃ αὐτὸς ποιεῖ (Jn. 5:20). The Father shows everything to the Son that emerges out of the richness of that love.[374]

Lee's comment on fatherhood in the FG is worth mentioning. Lee notes that the patriarchal fatherhood is dissimilar in two ways. First, the Johannine father-symbol functions in the context of surrender of power as seen in the example of handing over to the Son (5:22; 13:3; 16:5), unlike the Roman-Hellenistic *paterfamilias*. Second, there is also a restructuring of the patriarchal structure in terms of intimacy ruling out superiority or power structure.[375] Here, the love of the Divine family for the Johannine community is what solidifies the community's internal brother/sister hood to withstand the attacks from the world (Jn. 15:20ff.). Further, this love principle is what transfers the community from its insular viewpoint to take up its commission and engage the world. It is thus changed from its narrow perspective (flight from the world) to a full-fledged religious community (world-embracing body).

The expression of love in the FG is presented in the family context. This is true especially in texts where the Son reciprocates the love of the Father by keeping the Father's commandments (15:10). Obeying the commands of the Father in the FG is related to the concept of sending, especially in terms of doing the will of the sender (4:34; 6:38; 8:29, 55; 10:17-18). However, sometimes the relationship between the Father and the Son moves beyond the confines of the family structure in accommodating authority with obedience (10:17). Schnackenburg notes, "Both concepts are inseparably tied up with and dialectically related to each other."[376] What is of importance here, however, is that there is a certain sense of reciprocity within the family, i.e., in the Father-Son relationship. However, it does not end here; the Father's love is further exemplified in the Son's love for the disciples. It is interesting to note that love moves beyond the boundaries of the family to embrace the disciples. The

---

[372] Schnackenburg, *The Gospel according to St. John*, vol. 1, 388.

[373] Ridderbos, *The Gospel of John*, 151.

[374] Schnackenburg observes that here the use of the verb φιλειν instead of ἀγαπαν elsewhere to denote the love of the Father for the Son, suggests that personal love is stressed here. It is doubtful whether differences in meaning are implied here. Schnackenburg, *The Gospel according to St. John*, vol. 2, 105.

[375] Lee, "The Symbol of Divine Fatherhood:" 180-181.

[376] Schnackenburg, *The Gospel according to St. John*, vol. 2, 300-301. This is contrary to the understanding of Ridderbos who is of the view that the self-giving and the taking back of life is based on the authority that the Father has given to the Son. Ridderbos, *The Gospel of John*, 365.

imagery of the family is broken to create space for accommodating the disciples into the family. Keener rightly notes, "The Father's enormous love for the Son (3:35) becomes the Johannine measure of God's love for the disciples (17:23), as Christ's sacrifice attests (3:16)."[377]

The disciples are recipients of the Son's love, which is the continuation of the Father's love to the Son. The aspect of love builds with a conditional clause that requires the disciples to keep the commandments (Jn. 15:10). Furthermore, keeping the commandments is defined as loving one another (Jn 15:12). Brown conceptualizes this graphically as the "chain of love."[378] There is certainly a movement that is described here: Father-Son-disciples-community. Moloney captures the development in vv. 12-17 by identifying three parts to it.[379] First, the commandment to love as Jesus loved (vv.12-14): here Moloney notes that there is an interplay of tenses, in v. 12a ἀγαπᾶτε (present subjunctive) suggests that the love required from them is to be persistent and lasting, and in v.12b (aorist) describes the bench mark of love for one another which is the exemplary love of Jesus for them. Second, Jesus' love creates a new relationship (15-16). Moloney notes that Jesus in giving his life for them reverses the relationship from servants to friends.[380] Finally, there is a reciprocity implied in the commandment to love (v.17) because the disciples are to love one another as friends and not as servants.

The aspect of loving one another in the FG is probably not an end in itself but involves bearing fruit; it thus has an active dimension of mission. Mission involves the expression of love for one another as friends to the extent of giving one's life. Moloney notes, in his comment on 13:34, "Both the example and the commandment are closely associated with Jesus' demand that his disciples follow him not a loving self-gift in death."[381] Schnackenburg rightly notes that fruit-bearing manifests the depth of love. He states, "The fruit of being a disciple of Jesus grows in the soil of love, as a gift of Jesus' love, and is essentially love itself as Jesus demonstrated it."[382] Thus, there is a connection between mission, bearing fruit and love for one another. This is the reiteration of what was said in 13:35 where love for one another is linked with witness; however, this needs to be seen in relation to what is said earlier in v. 34. The

---

[377] Keener, *The Gospel of John*, vol. 1, 583.

[378] Brown, *The Gospel according to John (xiii-xii)*, 682.

[379] Moloney, *The Gospel of John*, 424.

[380] Barrett notes, "The eternal divine love reached its complete and unsurpassable expression in the death of Christ, which was at the same time the death of a man for his friends." Barrett, *The Gospel according to St. John*, 476.

[381] Moloney, *The Gospel of John*, 386.

[382] Schnackenburg, *The Gospel according to St. John*, vol. 3, 103.

prominent emphasis[383] seems to be καθὼς ἠγάπησα ὑμᾶς. The use of καθὼς is significant here. Schnackenburg also correctly observes that the καθὼς phrase does not just state the law of loving one another, but is also the basis for it. He also notes, "...καθὼς here means not so much a comparative 'as' as a motivating 'according to the way in which' or 'because' ....is the consequence of the reason for and the norm of Jesus' love."[384] Moloney notes, "A unique quality of love, inspired by the love Jesus had for his own..."[385] For Brown, it stresses "...that Jesus is the source of the Christians' love for one another. (Only secondarily does it refer to Jesus as the standard of Christian love)."[386] The kinship relation between the Father and Son has mutual love as the basis (3:35; 5:20; 10:17), and also becomes the foundation for the many claims that Jesus makes including the authority to judge and to give life.[387]

The love for another has an aim which is expressed in γνώσονται πάντες (Jn. 13: 35). The phrase suggests a broader perspective that moves beyond the faith community. Schnackenburg notes, "This implies not a renunciation of the neighbourly love that is owed to all men, but certain, though not exclusive restriction of that love to fellow-Christians."[388] Legrand too notes that mission in the FG pertains to the community's witness of the fellowship with one another (17:21-23; 13:35).[389] Love moves beyond the boundaries to embrace those that are neglected and ostracized. Thus, witness has not just a 'within' function but also a 'without' aspect.

---

[383] There are other issues of concern such as: a. vv. 34-35 is part of the editorial additions – a. Schnackenburg states seven reasons why the commandment to love is an editorial addition; b. the meaning of the phrase ''εντολήν ήν καινήν; Schnackenburg rightly notes that the καινὴν aspect is not to be seen as opposite of the Old Testament but connotes a distinctive stress given in his service for others and the lay down of lie in death. Schnackenburg, *The Gospel according to St. John*, vol. 3, 54. For Brown, the newness of love relates to "... the generosity of God's love could not be fully known until He had given His own Son, in another way Christian concept of love stemming from Jesus is new." Brown, *The Gospel according to St. John (xii-xxi)*, vol., 614.

[384] Schanckenburg, *The Gospel according to St. John*, vol. 3, 54.

[385] Moloney, *The Gospel of John*, 386.

[386] Brown, *The Gospel according to John (xii-xxi)*, 612.

[387] Thompson, *The God of the Gospel of John*, 70.

[388] Schnackenburg, *The Gospel according to St. John*, vol. 3, 55. This view is contrary to Brown who takes "love for one another" as a love that is shared among Christians because for Brown the 'fatherhood of God' and 'the brotherhood of man' in the FG is not universal in scope. He argues, "For John, God is a Father only to those who believe in His Son and who are begotten as God's children by the Spirit in Baptism." Brown, *The Gospel according to John (xii-xxi)*, 613. However, the appeal of Jesus to the fact of the Father as working does signify a universal scope of God's mission.

[389] L. Legrand, *Mission in the Bible* (Pune: Ishvani Publications, 1992), 118-119.

'Sending' in the resurrection narrative (Jn. 20:21) assumes the 'without' aspect. Jesus' acts of healing in Jn. 5 and 9 end up in him having to bear the brunt from the Jews. These events took place against the backdrop of the Sabbath. More importantly, Jn. 5:17 occasions a weighty statement from Jesus. There are two aspects involved, intricately related though, the first being the identity of Jesus seen in relation to the Father; the second, but equally important one is the work of God bringing things to wholeness as in the case of the blind man. The Father is involved with the agents of transformation, wholeness, and creating space for human beings to participate in the fullness of life (Jn. 20:31). Namitha states, "The Johannine emphasis is on the life-giving mission rather than the salvific ... Thus, it seems undeniable that life giving is the ultimate force of Jesus' mission in John."[390] Jesus' mission involved fulfilling the works of the Father, which is also the will of the Father. This meant engaging in acts that allowed human beings to experiencing the fullness of life. Besides Jn. 5 and 9, Jesus' dialogue with the Samaritan woman in Jn. 4 also demonstrates the liberative dimension of mission. Irudaya notes that Jesus' action "…reveals his liberative attitude to transcend dehumanizing outlook and … and to treat the Samaritan woman as a person worthy of dignity and honour of the children of God."[391] Here, mission is the extension of the Family of God to those who are in the sidelines. Thus, the Father sending the Son espouses the liberative aspect of mission which is the ongoing mission of the Father.

If one takes the Father sending the Son as the source of the mission of the disciples, then, by implication it means that the disciples are also sent to participate in the liberation mission of the sender, thus fulfilling the mission of the Son as well as the Father. Jn. 15:20 reiterates this in bringing the imagery of the servant and the master. The disciples are no better than their master who endured suffering in carrying out his mission, and it presents not just a probability but an inevitable situation that the disciples cannot avoid.[392] It assumes that the disciples would encounter hatred because they continue the mission of the sender.[393] As Schnackenburg explains, the love for one another is juxtaposed with the hatred from the world.[394] There seems to be an "inexcusable

[390] Namitha, *A New Paradigm for Evangelisation in the Third Millennium: In the Light of Mission in the Gospel according to St. John and the Early Upanishads* (Bangalore: St. Peter's Pontifical Institute Publications, 2000), 50, cited in Raj Irudaya, *Mission to the Marginalized: A Subaltern, Feminist and Interreligious Reading of John 4:1-42* (Bangalore: Asian Trading Corporation, 2007), 116.

[391] Raj Irudaya, *Mission to the Marginalized*, 166.

[392] The mention of Εἰ ὁ κόσμος ὑμᾶς μισεῖ in Jn. 15:18 probably is not referring to a probability but a reality. Ridderbos, *The Gospel of John*, 523-24.

[393] Ridderbos, *The Gospel of John*, 523.

[394] Schnackenburg, *The Gospel according to St. John*, vol. 3, 113.

character"[395] in the hostility theme. Jesus' reminder about expecting hatred is to urge them to continue the aspect of bearing witness of the Father just as he did. They are asked to "...to carry out the same task and go the same way as Jesus."[396]

The Paraclete is also included in the mission as the one who bears witness. It is interesting to note that in Jn. 15:26, 27, the witness of the Paraclete and the disciples are described separately but as Schnackenburg notes that this is to "... be regarded as a single, unified and carefully reflected formulation."[397] In Jn. 15:27, Jesus explicitly states that the disciples are also pertinent witnesses as they have been with him from the beginning. Here, it denotes that the disciples become the reference point to their later proclamation. The sufferings of the disciples will happen after the departure of Jesus where the Paraclete has a vital role. Moloney notes, "The disciples, directed, reminded, and strengthened by the Spirit, give witness to Jesus in the midst of the hostile world."[398] However, the witness of the disciples is seen within the context of the edifying and imparting role of the Paraclete.[399]

The mission of the disciples can be further understood with reference to Jn. 15:26-27. There is no mention of the object of mission in Jn. 20:21, but here it is made clear that the disciples are asked to engage in the mission of Jesus. Though the disciples are not part of the world by virtue of belonging to the Family of God, yet this does not set them free from their mission towards their fellow human beings.[400] The Family of God exists for the benefit of others, not for itself. It is an existence for the involvement in the liberative mission of Jesus which is also the mission of the Father.

A pertinent query in this regard is: how did the Johannine community understand the task of witnessing? The community certainly had a fractured relationship with the synagogue though it continued its dialogue with it. It is also probable that the Johannine community moved on and faced opposition from the Gentile world as well. The community saw itself faced with opposition on the grounds of belongingness to Christ. The proximity that the community had with Christ was the cause for hatred suggested in Jn. 15:21. In such a context, the community saw the importance of binding itself together. Here the

---

395 Ridderbos, *The Gospel of John*, 523.

396 Schnackenburg, *The Gospel according to St. John*, vol. 3, 114.

397 Schnackenburg, *The Gospel according to St. John*, vol. 3, 118-119. He further notes, "The bearing witness by the disciples follows that of the Spirit; it is not contrasted with it ('but also...'), rather, because of the καὶ δὲ, means closely connected with ('and also...).

398 Moloney, *The Gospel of John*, 430.

399 Schnackenburg, *The Gospel according to St. John*, vol. 3, 120.

400 Schnackenburg, *The Gospel according to St. John*, vol. 3, 115.

command of Jesus to love one another had great significance.[401] Nevertheless, it would probably be wrong to interpret this witnessing in terms of loving one another as a purely introverted one. The Johannine community as the Family of God had to engage in the liberative mission of Jesus by breaking away from their own exclusive domain. The hatred from the world was also the consequence of engaging in mission. Schnackenburg brings in a valid point here when he states, "…the Johannine community cannot be accused of turning away from the world as the Gnostic communities did…the world continued to be the object of God's love (3:16)."[402] Though faced with the problem of rejection, the Johannine community is urged to continue its mission and not to set it aside. Even here mission is related to identity. Schnackenburg observes that the Johannine community took the essential aspects of the eschatological discourse (Mk. 13:3), and used it to face difficult situations.[403]

Conclusion

The Johannine community suffered a fractured relationship with the synagogue. In such a context, it was crucial for the community to understand where it belonged. Here, belonging meant defining the community's identity, and its belief defined its belonging. Its Christology helped it to formulate an understanding of its belonging/identity. Its answers to the questions of Christ's own identity, origin, the source of his words and actions and his place in the Jewish belief system defined not just its understanding of Christ, but also shaped the community's own sense of belonging/identity. This was not a passive role of belonging, but rather an active form of belonging, which comes from believing. Believing engages in action and witnesses to belonging as in seen in the debate detailed in Jn. 8:31-37. There the question of belonging is related to action; the action of the Jews showed they did not really belong to Abraham's family. Every member in the Divine Family acts in congruence to belonging to the family. Further, the actions associated with belonging center on liberation and promotion of life or 'life embracing.' The Johannine community, in associating with the Divine Family, is also asked to involve themselves in such liberative actions that foster life and wholeness. The involvement is prone to face resistance and hatred. It is an inevitable result of engaging in and being agents of life and wholeness. Jesus' incarnation is a prime example of promotion of life, risking in order that life may be made manifest. Here, the mission of promotion of life originates with the Father, but continues in the

[401] Saldanha opines that the differences in the mission emphasis in all the four gospels and Paul had to do with "...the interaction of the local church with diverse situations and the variety of missionary praxis which these gave rise to." Julian Saldanha, *Mission Today: Themes and Issues* (Bangalore: Claretian Publications, 2006), 71.

[402] Schnackenburg, *The Gospel according to St. John*, vol. 3, 114.

[403] Schnackenburg, *The Gospel according to St. John*, vol. 3, 116.

work of the Son and the Spirit where the Father is also present. The result is a community of witness engaging in liberative, life-giving acts. The Johannine community, drawing its resources from the Divine Family, is asked to imitate this with acts of liberation.

The Family of God paradigm which surfaced out of the struggles of the Johannine community becomes a useful model for communities that go through struggles of alienation and rejection, especially the oppressed ones in the Indian context. The reality of belonging to the Family of God attains significance in their struggle to define their identity and purpose.

Conclusion

The study has attempted to unearth the identity and mission of Jesus and the Johannine community in John 20. The identity and mission were a response to the situation that the Johannine Community underwent. Thus the central point of this research is: The resurrection narrative in John 20 reflects the Johannine Community's identity and mission, particularly, in terms of the Family of God.

The situation of post 70 CE can only be understood in relation to the period before, i.e., the destruction of Jerusalem and the Temple. The period before 70 CE period witnessed diversity, especially in the practice of Judaism. Scholars have brought to light this aspect through various studies. There were also reactions against the Jewish establishment for having joined hands with the Roman administration. The harshness and cruelty of some of the Roman administrators coupled with famine and social disparity dampened the situation further. There was a slow build up of resistance to the Roman rule coming from the common people. The Roman instance on taxes and the effects of double taxation took a heavy toll on the common people. The first Jewish revolt was more of a resistance against the insensitivity of Rome and the Jewish authorities to the plight of the common people. The resistance took the shape of popular movements and uprisings, which also had the tinge of nationalism. The Jewish revolt had the aspect of inevitability in it. Looking at the revolt itself, one could identify two groups: one group that did not want to wage a war against Rome – a strong reason for this was the benefits that this group shared with the Roman administration and the other being, the so-called invincibility of Rome. The other groups, consisting of the common masses, saw there was no means to make their ends meet except through active resistance to Rome. The first Jewish revolt brought with it a trail of consequences in political, economic, social and religious spheres. Stringent measures were adopted by Rome to arrest any further incidents of revolt. On the religious side, several groups such as the Sadducees, Qumran community and others made their exit.

Further, one of the important developments after the Jewish revolt was the retrospection on the reasons for the destruction of the Jerusalem Temple. It goes without saying that the Jerusalem Temple played an invaluable role in holding together the Jewish expression of faith; it formed the cultic centre of the Jewish faith. This occasioned two reactions: a) a retrospective deliberation on what caused the destruction of the Temple, which were described, among other sources, in the apocalyptic writings. Along with the Jewish deliberations from different quarters also came the Christian interpretations of God's vindication of Christ through the destruction of the Temple. This possibly made further inroads into the already strained Jewish-Christian relationship. b) The destruction of the Jerusalem Temple also meant that there need to be a centre in the absence of the a Temple, which earlier acted as the centre. The Law in this regard was taken as substitute and facilitated in defining the cohesive factor of the Jewish community. In this regard, the Pharisaic movement with its emphasis on the Law was at a vantage position and thus was able to tide over the crisis that resulted from the absence of the Temple.

Nonetheless, the upsurge of Pharisaism need not necessarily imply that this was the only existing group after 70 CE. In fact, before and after 70 CE were periods of considerable diversity. On the flipside, Christians in the wake of the absence of the Temple articulated the Christological positions that did not augur well in the Jewish-Christian relations. Thus, there was in all possibility a movement towards defining identity, which gave way to rivalry, conflicts, and competitions, though these were still in its formative stage. Hence, the notion of a wider ban or excommunication coming from a normative Judaism seems to be out of question. This period presents a difficult time for both Judaism and Christianity. Both were involved in defining the relationship with each other and their own respective identities. In the process of consolidation there is bound to be measures to define one's boundaries, though there is much truth in arguing for a fluid stage in the post 70 CE contexts. These measures to keep the boundaries could have sparked of inter-Jewish conflicts in the synagogues where the Christian communities belonged. Though a generalized ban cannot be safely argued, each localized synagogue had its own rules of functioning.

In this connection, the *Birkat ha-Minim* could be taken as one such effect on the ever growing separation between Judaism and Christianity. Also, it is in this light that the testimonies of the Church Fathers should be taken into consideration. The *Birkat ha-Minim* did not signal a parting of the ways of Judaism and Christianity since neither of them was normative or orthodox in their approaches at this stage. Also there was considerable diversity in their expression of faith. But this does not prevent one from taking the view that there were conflicts and rivalry in localized situations. So, though the parting of the ways cannot be looked at as a phenomenon which had wide implications in terms of the Jewish-Christian relationships, yet there were instances of strained relationship and conflicts in certain locations. The Johannine community seems to be a part of one such location and the FG evidences to many such conflicts between Jesus and "the Jews."

The Johannine Community hypothesis aids in a meaningful interaction with the FG. Objections have been raised recently to such a conception by Richard Bauckham. The areas of objection deal with the understanding of the gospel genre, which is said to have a wider audience in mind and also the notion that the gospel communities were in touch with other communities as well. Though these propositions seem to have some truth, yet the distinct presentation of Christology, the special use of language and the ambiguous presentation of 'Jews' lead to affirming the Johannine Community hypothesis. There are many scholars who affirm the Johannine Community hypothesis – Martyn, Brown, Fugsleth, Meeks, Lieu, and others. There are certain indicators for the community aspect in the FG. Some of these include: use of plural language (1:14, 16; 3:11; 21:24), editorial comments (1:15, 2:22; 11:49), implicit reference to a group (9:22), and ecclesiological metaphors and allusions. Attempts have been made to draw the contours of the Johannine Community, especially beginning with J. Louis Martyn and later on by R. E. Brown.

However, one of the drawbacks of these constructions is that they rely so much on *Birkat ha-Minim* as a wider phenomenon, which has been questioned by recent Johannine scholars. The intra-Jewish dispute factor as defining the conflict presented in the FG still presents a possibility. The suggested contours of the Johannine Community could be as follows: a) it began with the followers of John the Baptist; b) the members did have a dialogue with the Jews; c) one of the clear aspects of the conflict had to do with the messiahship of Jesus, messiahship related with the identity of Jesus; d) at a particular stage the community was separated from the synagogue, which leading to a further self-understanding of the community; e) as a result of separation the community looks at its identity in familial lines, i.e., in terms of the children of God and having a place to share in the Father's house; and f) the community retraced its traditions to the BD who served as a link with Jesus.

Before considering the resurrection narrative in John 20 and its perception by the Johannine Community it would be necessary to look at the resurrection narrative itself and its presentation of Jesus' identity and mission. For the resurrection narrative is at once the identity and mission of Jesus as well as the identity and mission of the Johannine Community. There are some common elements that the FG shares with the other resurrection narratives in Paul, Mark, Matthew, and Luke. These aspects include the motif of unexpectedness, the empty tomb, the presence of the angels, the appearance tradition, and the element of doubt on the part of the disciples. However, one of the unique aspects of the FG has to do with the emphasis on the Father-Son relationship and its effect on the identity and mission of the disciples. Some of the Johannine Scholars, such as Brown, Schnackenburg, Lindars and Moody Smith, have overlooked the importance of the resurrection aspect and have given a secondary role to it. The underlying reason further is the cross in the FG has paved way for glorification and therefore there is no place for the resurrection in the FG. How does one evaluate this lop-sided emphasis?

There are a few aspects that go against this understanding. First, as like the other gospels and letters in the New Testament, the FG is primarily written from the post-Easter perspective. This would then mean that resurrection is the linchpin from which the FG is written. There are some indicators of this in the FG. John 2:12 and 12:16 emphasize the role of resurrection in the interpretative tradition of the Johannine Community. Second, the resurrection has not only an interpretative role, but also the structure of the FG is arranged in such a way that the resurrection completes what is stated in the prologue. In effect, John 1 and 20 form an *inclusio* in describing the identity of Jesus, the divinity of Jesus, relationship with the Father, concept of seeing, etc. The resurrection narrative also is a completion of what is foretold in the Farewell Discourses (13-17). In other words, the resurrection propels towards fulfilling the events proleptically described in the Farewell Discourses. Third, most importantly, resurrection is a sign that reveals the identity of Jesus, i.e., the relationship that Jesus shares with the Father.

In connection with a resurrection as a sign, it can be said that the resurrection is not only a sign but also a sign that has the element of disclosure in it. The resurrection narrative in John 20 can be divided into parts: the first part dealing with the question 'where has he gone' and the second part unravels the mystery of 'where he has gone.' In other words, it is a disclosure of the identity of Jesus. But the disclosure needs to be seen in relation to the discovery that many characters make in the course of the narrative. The two terms 'disclosure' and 'discovery' are those that are related but do not mean the same thing. The former moves beyond the physical sight to comprehending where Jesus has gone, i.e., the identity of Jesus whereas the latter stays on the physical sight but is not able to understand the deeper significance of the discovered things. For a better understanding of these concepts, it is important to dwell deeper.

In the resurrection narrative, Mary Magdalene discovers the stone rolled from the entrance of the empty tomb in her first visit but in her second visit she notices two angels and later mistakes Jesus for the gardner. Her discovery does not lead her anywhere as she looks from the perspective of the body of Jesus being stolen. It is only when Jesus calls her Mary that she responds by calling him *Rabboni*. But even here the discovery is again in terms of Jesus as the teacher. Jesus draws her attention to his true identity in the words, οὔπω γὰρ ἀναβέβηκα πρὸς τὸν πατέρα (Jn 20:17). Identity is born out of the relationship – the relationship which the Son shares with the Father. Mary is told that Jesus is in the process of ascending to the Father. Thus, while the coming of the Son into the world (1:14) was an opportunity for the disciples to see the glory of God in the Son, the coming also implies also a return to the Father, a return to the relationship with the Father. The relationship with the Father is further defined in terms of the disciples' Father and Jesus' Father, disciples' God and Jesus' God. Here, the underlying meaning is that Mary is taken far beyond discovering things (empty tomb, stone rolled, etc) and beings (angels, Gardner), to a disclosure of the identity of Jesus. There is a mutuality in relationship in terms of "my Father and your Father," "my God and your God." These expressions need not be seen as Jesus distinguishing himself from the disciple but rather he is here stressing the mutuality of relationship shared by both Jesus and the disciples with the Father.

In addition, the resurrection also sets in motion a new form of relationship for the disciples, i.e., God as their Father and the disciples as the brothers of Jesus. Sandwiched between Mary's discovery and the disclosure given to Mary is the episode of the BD and Peter. Like Mary, the BD comes to the tomb and sees the linen clothes but later enters the tomb, sees and believes. The BD sees and believes but it is not so with Peter who though sees the linen clothes and the napkin in the tomb, is not part of the disclosure. For Peter, it still remains only a discovery, and it is only in the next episode – the appearance of Jesus to the disciples – that Peter is able to move from the discovery stage of comprehending Jesus' identity. As far as The BD is concerned, he has already seen the sign and believed in the identity of Jesus and the fulfillment of what was propleptically mentioned by Jesus in the Farewell Discourses. This further reiterates the understanding that the resurrection is a sign, which Peter failed to grasp.

In the resurrected Jesus' appearance to the disciples, there is no time interval between seeing Jesus and the disclosure given to them. The episode uses contrast; on the one hand the narrator mentions that the disciples feared Jews, the evidencing a clue of the Johannine Community, and the imparting of peace by the risen Jesus. The resurrection narrative presents the glorification of the Son which can be termed one of presence, i.e., being in the presence of the Father and being present among the disciples. The presence of the Spirit given to the disciples is at one and the same time the presence of the Father as well as the Son. So, the disciples experience the community's presence (Father, Son and the Spirit), and in this bonding the disciples engage in mission, which is the extension of the presence of Jesus. Jesus' unique characteristics serve as a basis for his unique identity and mission. By showing his hands and side Jesus stresses the connection between the passion and resurrection in the FG. More importantly, this episode combines the identity and mission of Jesus with the identity and mission of the disciples/Johannine Community. Jesus' words, *καθὼς ἀπέσταλκέν με ὁ πατήρ, κἀγὼ πέμπω ὑμᾶς* (Jn 20:21b), notes the continuation of the identity and mission of the disciples with the identity and mission of Jesus. The resurrection affirms the identity of Jesus and this identity enables the disciples to share a relationship with the Father. The bestowing of the Spirit by Jesus highlights the forthcoming absence of Jesus from the disciples and equipping for the ministry the disciples are to engage in, which involves the ministry of forgiveness.

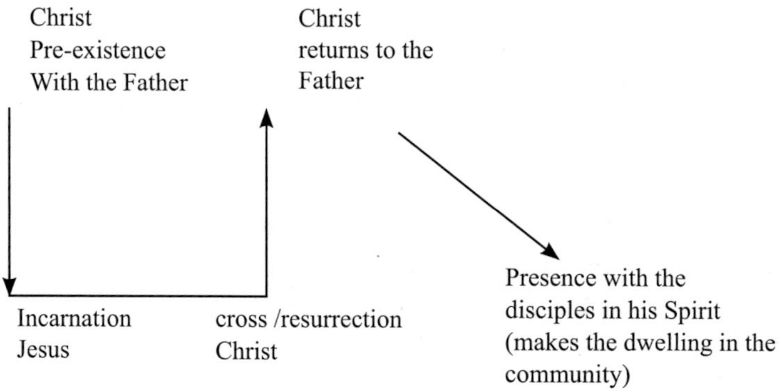

There is a continuity between the mission of Jesus and the mission of the disciples, in the sense that both derive their source from the Father. Jesus' words, καθὼς ἀπέσταλκέν με, is a statement of identity and mission of Jesus.

The last episode in John 20, deals with Jesus' appearance to the disciples along with Thomas. Like Mary, the disciples testify to Thomas ἑωράκαμεν τὸν κύριον (John 20:25), suggesting a movement from discovery to disclosure. But Thomas fails to grasp the disclosure element and awaits Jesus' disclosure to him. This episode is not to denigrate Thomas for the lack of faith but rather to further explain the identity of Jesus: i.e., the relationship he shares with the Father, the fact that he has come from the Father, and most importantly, Jesus is Lord and God. Moreover, Jesus' words "…Blessed are those who have seen and yet believe." (Jn. 20:29b), is a reaffirmation of the Johannine Community who are not at a disadvantage for not having witnessed the resurrection appearance of Jesus. However, the community has a link in their relationship with Jesus through the testimony of the BD. The BD reduces the time interval between Jesus' ministry and their acceptance of the testimony of Jesus. Thus, in the resurrection narrative in John 20, the identity of Jesus is stated through different titles and relationships. The titles include: Lord/ my Lord (vv. 2, 13, 18, 20, 25, 28, teacher (v. 16), God (vv. 17, 28), Christ (v. 31) and lastly Son of God (v. 31).

As discussed above the resurrection narrative in John 20 presents the identity and the mission of the Johannine community. There is, however, another issue worth discussing: how can one see the resurrection narrative in John 20 as a paradigm of the Johannine community's identity and mission? Identity formation emerges out of the social, economic, and religious context.

So also is the case with the Johannine community, where Christology is reinterpreted in the light of the community's experiences. In other words, identity is mediated through the context of the community and the needs of the community. It can be assumed that the Johannine community suffered three kinds of losses. First, it was the loss of sacred space. The loss of the Jerusalem temple and the fractured relationship with the synagogue occasioned the need for the Johannine community to define the identity of Christ, especially the place of Christ in the monotheistic framework and also in relation to the leaders of the Jewish faith. Second, there was a loss of physical space. The fractured relationship also resulted in the loss of the physical space and this is evident in the use of μοναὶ (Jn. 14:2). Third, the community suffered a loss of communal space as well. This is clear from the fact that the Fourth Gospel repeatedly emphasizes the aspect of love, love as a collective relationship. The interpretative Christology in the Fourth Gospel is an interaction between the shared memories, i.e., the memories of the life and ministry of Jesus, the link being provided by the BD and the memories of the fractured relationship with the synagogue. There are evidences of memory aiding in the interpretation of the Johannine community in John 2:22 and 12:6.

If the FG is an interpretative Christology, how is the identity and mission presented in it? The study proposes that the Fourth Gospel presents the Family of God as the expression of identity for both Jesus and the Johannine community. If the identity can be explained in terms of the Family of God, then, mission is a witness to the Family of God. Moving beyond Campbell who proposes that there are two families exemplified in the Fourth Gospel, the natural family and the adopted family of Jesus, I would like to propose that in fact there are three families: divine family, earthly family, and the metaphorical family. The divine family is expressed in earthly family categories but yet transcends it. Further, the divine family creates the the metaphorical family and thus results in the tension between the earthly and the metaphorical family.

The Divine Family consists of the Father, Son and the Holy Spirit. The Father plays an important place in the Divine Family. The Father is seen as the initiator of the action, and at the same time, grants autonomy to the Son. One of the puzzling points in the FG pertains to the Father-Son relationship. The Son reveals the Father, and the revelation of the Son is based on the relationship that the Son shares with the Father. The Son reveals the Father but this need not be seen as a subject-object relationship as in some cases the Son also becomes the locus of revelation. To some extent the Father-Son relationship in the FG can be explained in earthly categories of the father-Son relationship but the imagery breaks down at a certain point. For example, the expression "I and the Father are one," cannot be explained in earthly categories. There is another description of the person in the Divine Family, who is the Spirit. The Spirit's mission is to witness to Jesus just as Jesus witnesses to the Father. The source of the witness remains the Father.

Like the Divine Family, the FG also presents the Earthly Family. Incarnation of the Son necessitates the description of the Earthly Family. However, the Earthly Family relationship of Jesus is played down for two reasons: a) to assert the identity and origin of Jesus in the Divine Family; b) the Johannine Community's attempt to move beyond the reductionist understanding of the family of God in narrower terms. Thus, the brothers of Jesus do not find great importance in the FG and in their place the disciples are taken as brothers of Jesus. The earthly category here is superseded by the metaphorical category.

The third family described in the FG is the Metaphorical Family. In this conception of the family there are no ethnic categories and the family embraces outsiders and is engaged in acts of liberation. The Johannine Community understands itself as a part of the Metaphorical Family of God. In the context of having a fractured relationship with the synagogue, the Family imagery gave the Johannine Community its distinguished status. This aspect is clearly indicated in the resurrection narrative, especially in the phrase, "My Father and your Father and my God and your God" (John 20: 17).

The mission in the Family of God is witness to the Family of God. Here, the FG uses the agency motif to describe the witnessing aspect of the Son. The Son witnesses to what was heard from the Father. Here again, identity and mission are mutually related. The Johannine Community witnesses to the Divine Family by relating with one another and engaging in acts that promote life. The Johannine community witnesses to Divine Family that sheds the boundaries of exclusivism in order to accommodate the Johannine community as a part of the Family of God. The community on its part bears witness to the characteristics of the Divine Family not just in its relationship within but also without. The Family of God thus emerged out of the context of the Johannine community, which was a context of struggle and a search for identity.

Bibliography

Tools and References

Abott, Edwin A. *Johannine Vocabulary: A Comparison of the Words of the Fourth Gospel with those of the Three*. London: Adam and Charles Black, 1906.

Aland, Barbara, Kurt Aland and Johannes Karavidopoulos, et.al., eds. *Novum Testamentum Graece*. 27th edition. Stuttgart: Deutsche Bibelgesellschaft, 2006.

Aland, Kurt, Matthew Black and Carlo Maria Martini, et.al., eds. *The Greek New Testament*. 4th edition. Stuttgart: Deutsche Bibelgesellschaft, 2001.

4 Baruch. Translated by Jens Herzer. Edited by Abraham J. Malherbe. Atlanta: SBL, 2005.

Balz, Horst and Gerhard Schneider, eds. *EDNT*. Vols.1, 2, 3. Grand Rapids, Michigan: William B. Eerdmans Publishing Company 1990.

Bauer, Walter, William F. Arndt and F. Wilbur Gingrich, et.al. *A Greek-English Lexicon of the New Testament and Other Early Christian Literature*. Chicago: University of Chicago Press, 1979.

Blass, Friedrich and Albert Debrunner. *A Greek Grammar of the New Testament and Other Early Christian Literature*. Translated by Robert W. Funk. Chicago: The University of Chicago Press, 1961.

Botterweck, G., Johannes Hlemer Ringgren and Heinz-Josef Fabry, eds. *TDOT*. Vols. 2 & 8. Grand Rapids, Michigan: William B. Eerdmans Publishing Company, 1977, 1997.

Brown, Colin, ed. *NIDNTT*. Vols. 1, 2. Grand Rapids, Michigan: Zondervan Publishing House, 1976.

Capps, E., ed. *Eusebius: The Ecclesiastical History*. The Loeb Classical Library. Vol. 1. Translated by Kirsopp Lake. London: William Heineman, 1926.

Charles, R. H. *The Apocrypha and Pseudepigrapha of the Old Testament in English*. Vol. 1: *Pseudepigrapha*. Oxford: Clarendon Press, 1913.

Charlesworth, James H., ed. *The Old Testament Pseudepigrapha: Apocalyptic Literature and Testaments*. Vols. 1 & 2. New York: Doubleday, 1983.

Epitectus. *Enchiridion or the Manual*. Translated by George Long. Mineola, New York: Dover Publications, 2004.

Freedman, David N., ed. *ABD*. Vols. 2, 3, 5, 6. New York: Doubleday, 1992.

"From the Treatise of Pempelus on Parents." In *The Political Fragments of Archytas, Charondas, Zalecus, and Other Ancient Pythagoreans by Stobaeus and also Ethical Fragments of Hierocles*. Translated by Thomas Taylor. London: C. Whittingham, 1908.

Horbury, W., W. D. Davies, and J. Sturdy, eds. *The Cambridge History of Judaism*. Vol. 3: *The Early Roman Period.* Cambridge: Cambridge University Press, 1999.

Josephus. *The Works of Josephus: Complete and Unabridged in One Volume*. Translated by William Whiston. Peabody: Hendrickson Publishers, 1987.

Kittel, Gerhard and Gerhard Freidrich, eds. *TDNT*. Vols. 1, 5, 7. Grand Rapids, Michigan: William B. Eerdmans Publishing Company, 1964.

Liddell, Henry George and Robert Scott, comps. *A Greek-English Lexicon: With a Supplement*. 9th ed. Oxford: Clarendon Press, 1968.

Lumpkin, Joseph B. *The Encyclopaedia of Lost and Rejected Scriptures: The Pseudepigrapha and Apocrypha*. Atlanta: Fifth Estate Publishers, 2010.

Metzger, Bruce M. *A Textual Commentary on the Greek New Testament.* London: UBS, 2001.

Moule, C. F. D. *An Idiom Book of New Testament Greek*. Cambridge: Cambridge University Press, 1968.

Moulton, W. F., A. S. Geden and Harold Keeling Moulton, eds. *A Concordance to the Greek Testament*. Edinburgh: T & T Clark, 1957.

Moulton, James H. and Nigel Turner. *A Grammar of New Testament Greek*. Vol. 3: *Syntax*. Edited by James H. Moulton. Edinburgh: T & T Clark, 1963.

Newman, Barclay M. and Eugene A. Nida. *A Translator's Handbook on the Gospel of John*. Helps for Translators Series vols. Stuttgart: UBS, 1980.

"On the Reverence Due to Parents." *From the Apophthegms of Aristoxenus, The Tarentine*. In *The Political Fragments of Archytas, Charondas, Zalecus, and Other Ancient Pythagoreans by Stobaeus and also Ethical Fragments of Hierocles*. Translated by Thomas Taylor. London: C. Whittingham, 1822.

Philo. *The Works of Philo: Complete and Unabridged.* Translated by C. D. Jonge. Peabody: Hendrickson Publishers, 1993.

Plutarch. *Plutarch's MoraliaI.* Vol. 1. Translated by Frank Cole Babbitt. London: William Heinemann Ltd., 1928.

Roberts, Alexander and James Donaldson, eds. *The Ante-Nicene Fathers.* Vols. 1 & 3. Grand Rapids, Michigan: William B. Eerdmans Publishing Company, 1996.

"Sayings of Simeon the Righteous." In *The Fathers according to Rabbi Nathan.* YJS 10. Translated by Judah Goldin. New Haven: Yale University Press, 1955.

Schaff, Philip and Henry Wace, eds. *Nicene and Post-Nicene Fathers.* Vol 1. Reprint. Massachusetts: Hendrickson Publishers, 1999.

Schürer, Emil. *A History of the Jewish People in the Time of Jesus Christ.* Vol. 2. Second Division. Translated by Sophia Taylor and Peter Christie. Edinburgh: Hendrickson, 1998.

"Sirach." In *The Apocrypha and Pseudepigrapha of the Old Testament in English.* Vol. I: *Pseudepigrapha.* Edited by R. H. Charles. Oxford: Clarendon Press, 1913.

Skolnik, Fred, ed. *EncJud.* Vols. 3, 16, 17, 18. New York: Keter Publishing House, 2007.

"Solon." In *Plutarch's Lives.* Vol. 1: Thesesu and Romulus, Lycurgus and Nume, Solon and Publicola. Translated by Bernadotte Perrin. London: William Heinemann Ltd., 1967.

Tacitus the Histories. Vol. II. Translated with Introduction and Notes by W. Hamilton Fyfe. Oxford: Clarendon Press, 1912.

The Mishnah. Translated by Herbert Danby. Oxford: Oxford University Press, 1933.

Thomas, Archibald. *Word Pictures in the New Testament The Fourth Gospel & The Epistle to the Hebrews.* Vol. V. New York: Ray Long and Richard R. Smith, 1932.

Vermes, G. *The Dead Sea Scrolls in English.* 2nd ed. New York: Penguin, 1975.

Young, Richard A. *Intermediate New Testament Greek: A Linguistic and Exegetical Approach.* Nashville: Broadman & Holman Publishers, 1994.

Zerwick, Max and Mary Grosvenor. *A Grammatical Analysis of the Greek New Testament.* Translated by Mary Grosvenor. Rome: Editrice Pontificio Istituto Biblico, 1988.

Commentaries, Books and Articles

Alexander, Philip S. ""The Parting of the Ways" From the Perspective of Rabbinic Judaism." In *Jews and Christians: The Parting of the Ways*

A. D. 70 to 135. Edited by James D. G. Dunn. Grand Rapids, Michigan: William B. Eerdmans Publishing Company, 1992.

Anderson, Paul N. "The Having-Sent-Me Father: Aspects of Agency, Encounter, and Irony in the Johannine Father-Son Relationship." *Semeia: God the Father in the Gospel of John* 85 (1999): 33-57.

Andrews, C. F. *The Renaissance in India: Its Missionary Aspect*. London: Church Missionary Society, 1912.

Ashton, John. "The Identity and Function of ΙΟΥΔΑΙΟΙ in the Fourth Gospel." *NovT* 27/1 (Ja. 1985): 40-75.

__________. "The Johannine Son of Man: A New Proposal." *NTS* 57/4 (O. 2011): 508-529.

__________. *Understanding the Fourth Gospel*. 2nd ed. Oxford: Oxford University Press, 2007.

__________. *Understanding the Fourth Gospel*. Oxford: Clarendon Press, 1991.

Atkinson, Kenneth and Jodi Magness. "Josephus' Essenes and the Qumran Community." *JBL* 129/2 (Summer 2010): 317-342.

Attridge, Harold W. "Christianity from the Destruction of Jerusalem to Constantine's Adoption of the New Religion: 70-312 CE" In *Christianity and Rabbinic Judaism: A Parallel History of their Origins and Early Development*. Edited by Hershel Shanks. London: SPCK, 1993.

Aune, David E. "On the Origins of the 'Council of Javneh' Myth." JBL 110/3 (Fall 1991): 491-493.

Barclay, John M. G. "Family as the Bearer of Religion in Judaism and Early Christianity." In *Constructing Early Christian Families: Family as a Social Reality and Metaphor*. Edited by Halvor Moxnes. New York: Routledge, 1997.

Barker, Margaret. *The Great Angel: A Study of Israel's Second God*. Kentucky: Westminster John Knox Press, 1992.

Barrett, C. K. *Essays on John*. London: SPCK, 1982.

Barrett, C. K. *The Gospel according to St. John: An Introduction with Commentary and Notes on the Greek Text*. London: S. P. C. K, 1955, 1965.

__________. The Gospel of John and Judaism. Translated by D. M. Smith. Philadelphia: Fortress Press, 1975.

Barton, Stephen C. "Christian Community in the Light of the Gospel of John." In *Christology, Controversy and Community: New Testament Essays in Honour of David R. Catchpole*. NovT Supp 99. Edited by David G. Horrell and Christopher M. Tuckett. Leiden: Brill, 2000.

__________. "The Relativisation of Family Ties in Jewish and Graeco-Roman Traditions." In *Constructing Early Christian Families: Family as a Social Reality and Metaphor*. Edited by Halvor Moxnes. New York: Routledge, 1997.

Basser, Herbert W. *Studies in Exegesis: Christian Critiques of Jewish Law and Rabbinic Responses, 70-300 CE.* The Brill Reference Library of Ancient Judaism. Vol. 2. Edited by Jacob Neusner. Leiden: Brill, 2000.

Bauckham, Richard. "For Whom Were Gospels Written?" In *The Gospels for All Christians: Rethinking the Gospel Audience*. Edited by Richard Bauckham. Grand Rapids, Michigan: William B. Eerdmans Publishing Company, 1998.

__________. *Gospel Women: Studies of the Named Women in the Gospels*. Grand Rapids, Michigan: William B. Eerdmans Publishing Company, 2002.

__________. "Historiographical Characteristics of the Gospel of John." *NTS* 53/1 (Ja. 2007): 17-36.

__________. "Introduction." In *The Gospels for All Christians: Rethinking the Gospel Audience*. Edited by Richard Bauckham. Grand Rapids, Michigan: William B. Eerdmans Publishing Company, 1998.

__________. "James and Jesus." In *The Brother of Jesus: James the Just and His Mission*. Edited by Bruce Chilton and Jacob Neusner. London: Westminster John Knox Press, 2001.

__________. "John for Readers of Mark." In *The Gospels for All Christians: Rethinking the Gospel Audience*. Edited by Richard Bauckham. Grand Rapids, Michigan: William B. Eerdmans Publishing Company, 1998.

__________. "Response to Esler." SJT 51/2 (Jan. 1998): 249-253.

__________. "The Audience of the Fourth Gospel." In *Jesus in Johannine Tradition*. Edited by Robert T. Fortna and Tom Thatcher. London: Westminster John Knox Press, 2001.

__________. "The Beloved Disciple as Ideal Author." JSNT 49 (Mr. 1993): 21-44.

Baumgarten, Albert I. "The Name of the Pharisees," *JBL* 102/3 (Summer 1983): 411-428.

__________. "Marcel Simon's Verus Israel as a Contribution to Jewish History." *HTR* 92/4 (O. 1999): 465-478.

Beasley-Murray, George R. *Gospel of Life: Theology in the Fourth Gospel*. Massachusetts: Hendrickson Publishers, 1991.

__________. *John*. WBC 36. Edited by Ralph P. Martin. Texas: Word Books, 1987.

Beirne, Margaret M. *Women and Men in the Fourth Gospel: A Genuine Discipleship of Equals*. London: T & T Clark International, 2004.

Bennema, Cornelis. "The Sword of the Messiah and the Concept of Liberation." *Bib* 86/1 (2005): 35-58.

__________. *Encountering Jesus: Character Studies in the Gospel of John*. Bangalore: Primalogue Publishing Media Private Limited, 2009.

__________. *Excavating John's Gospel: A Commentary for Today*. Delhi: ISPCK, 2005.

Berge, Paul S. "Easter to Trinity with the Gospel of John: Bearing Witness to Father, Son and Holy Spirit." *Word & World* 18/2 (Spring 1998): 207-216.

Bernard, J. H. *A Critical and Exegetical Commentary on the Gospel according to St. John*. Vol. 1. New York: Scribner's, 1929.

Beutler, Johannes. "Resurrection and the Remission of Sins: John 20:23 Against Its Traditional Background." In *The Resurrection of Jesus in the Gospel of John*. Edited by Craig R. Koester. WUZNT 22. Tübingen: Mohr Siebeck, 2008.

__________. *Judaism and the Jews in the Gospel of John*. SubBi 30. Rome: Editrice Pontifico Instituto Biblico, 2006.

Bickerman, Elias J. "The Civic Prayer for Jerusalem." *HTR* 55/3 (Jl. 1962): 163-185.

Bieringer, Reimund. ""I am ascending to my Father and your Father, to my God and your God" (John 20:17): Resurrection and Ascension in the Gospel of John." In *The Resurrection of Jesus in the Gospel of John*. Edited by Craig R. Koester and Reimund Bieringer. WUZNT 22. Tübingen: Mohr Siebeck, 2008.

Bird, Mike. "Bauckham's The Gospel for All Christians Revisited." *EuroJTh* 15/1 (Apr. 2006): 5-13.

Blenkinsopp, Joseph. "Interpretation and the Tendency to Sectarianism: An Aspect of Second Temple History." In *Jewish and Christian Self-Definition*. Vol. 2: *Aspects of Judaism in the Greco-Roman Period*. Edited by E. P. Sanders, Albert I. Baumgarten and Alan Mendelson. Philadelphia: Fortress Press, 1981.

Blomberg, Craig L. Review of *The Johannine Exegesis of God: An Exploration in the Johannine Understanding of God* by Daniel Rathnakar Sadananda. *CBQ* 69/3 (Jl. 2005): 540-541.

__________. *The Historical Reliability of John's Gospel: Issues and Commentary*. Downers Grove: InterVarsity Press, 2001.

Bock, Darrell L. *Luke 9:51-24:53*. BECNT. Edited by Mosés Silva. Grand Rapids, Michigan: Baker Academic, 1996.

Bolt, Peter G. "Mark 16:1-8: The Empty Tomb of a Hero?" *TynBul* 47/1 (My. 1997): 27-37.

Boomershine, Thomas E. and Gilbert L. Bartholomew. "The Narrative Technique of Mark 16:8." *JBL* 100/2 (Ja. 1981): 213-223.

Borgen, Peder. "God's Agent in the Fourth Gospel." In *Religions in Antiquity: Essays in Memory of Erwin Ramsdell Goodenough*. Edited by Jacob Neusner. Leiden: E. J. Brill, 1970.

Boring, M. Eugene. "The Influence of Christian Prophecy on the Johannine Portrayal of the Paraclete and Jesus." *NTS* 25/1 (O. 1978): 113-123.

Bouyer, Louis. *Eucharist: Theology and Spirituality of the Eucharistic Prayer*. Translated by Charles Underhill Quinn. London: Notre Dame Press, 1968.

Bowker, J. *Jesus and the Pharisees*. Cambridge: Cambridge University, 1973.

Boyarin, Daniel. "A Tale of two Synods: Nicaea, Yavneh, and Rabbinc Ecclesiology." *Exemplaria* 12/1 (2000): 21-62.

__________. *Dying for God: Martyrdom and the Making of Christianity and Judaism*. Stanford: Stanford University Press, 1999.

__________. "Justin Martyr Invents Judaism." *CH* 70/3 (Sep. 2003): 427-461.

__________. "Semantic differences; or, "Judaism"/"Christianity."" In *The Ways that Never Parted: Jews and Christians in Late Antiquity and the Early Middle Ages*. Edited by Adam H. Becker and Annette Yoshiko Reed. Minneapolis: Fortress Press, 2007.

__________. "The *Ioudaioi* in John and the Prehistory of "Judaism."" In *Pauline Conversations in Context: Essays in Honour of Calvin J. Roeztel*. Edited by J. C. Anderson, et.al. Sheffield: Sheffield Academic Press, 2002.

Brochert, Gerald L. *John 12-21*. The New American Commentary 25B. Edited by E. Ray Clendenen. Nashville: Broadman and Holman Publishers, 2002.

Brodie, Thomas L. *The Gospel according to St. John: A Literary and Theological Commentary*. New York: Oxford University Press, 1993.

Broer, Ingo. "Knowledge of Palestine in the Fourth Gospel?" In *Jesus in Johannine Tradition*. Edited by Robert T. Fortna and Tom Thatcher. Louisville: Westminster John Knox Press, 2001.

Broshi, Magen and Hanan Esher. "Qumran and the Dead Sea Scrolls: The Contention of Twelve Theories." In *Religion and Society in Roman Palestine: Old Questions, New Approaches*. Edited by Douglas R. Edwards. New York: Routledge, 2004.

Brown, Jeannine K. "Creation's Renewal in the Gospel of John." *CBQ* 72/2 (Apr. 2010): 275-290.

Brown, Raymond Bryan. "Distinctives of John's Gospel." *SWJT* 8/1 (O. 1965): 25-34.

Brown, Raymond E. *An Introduction to the New Testament.* AB Reference Library. Edited by David Noel Freedman. Bangalore: TPI, 2009.

__________. "Does the New Testament Call Jesus God?" *TS* 26/4 (Dec. 1965): 545-573.

__________. "Johannine Ecclesiology: The Community's Origins" *Int.* 31/4 (O. 1977): 379-393.

__________. *Mary in the New Testament.* Bangalore: Theological Publications in India, 2008.

__________."Not Jewish and Gentile Christianity but Types of Jewish/ Gentile Christianity." *CBQ 45/1*(Ja. 1983): 74-79.

__________. "Problem of Historicity in John." *CBQ* 24/1 (Ja. 1962): 1-14.

__________. *The Community of the Beloved Disciple* (New York: Paulist Press, 1979).

__________. *The Gospel according to John.* The AB Series 29 A & B. 2 vols. New York: Doubleday & Company, Inc., 1966.

__________. "The Resurrection in John 20- A Series of Diverse Reactions." *Worship* 64/3 (My. 1990): 194-206.

Brown, Schuyler. "The Matthean Community and the Gentile Mission." *NovT* 22/3 (Jl. 1980): 193-221.

Brownlee, William Hugh. "The Wicked Priest, the Man of Lies and the Righteous Teacher- the Problem of Identity." *JQR* 73/1 (Jl. 1982): 1-37.

Bruce, F. F. *The Gospel of John: Introduction, Exposition and Notes.* Basingstoke: Pickering & Inglis, 1983.

Bultmann, Rudolf. *The Gospel of John: A Commentary*. Translated by G. R. Beasley-Murray. Philadelphia: The Westminster John Knox Press, 1971.

__________. *Theology of the New Testament.* Translated by Kendrick Grobel. Vol. 2. New York: Charles Scribner's Sons, 1955.

Burge, Gary M. "Situating John's Gospel in History." In *Jesus in Johannine Tradition.* Edited by Robert T. Fortna and Tom Thatcher. Louisville: Westminster John Knox Press, 2001.

Burkett, Delbert. *An Introduction to the New Testament and the Origins of Christianity*. Cambridge: Cambridge University Press, 2002.

Byrne, Brendan. "The Faith of the Beloved Disciple and the Community in John 20." *JSNT* 23 (Fall 1985): 83-97.

Byrskog, Samuel. "Christology and Identity in an Intertextual Perspective: The Glory of Adam in the Narrative Substructure of Paul's Letter to the Romans." In *Identity Formation in the New Testament*. Edited by Bengt Holmberg and Mikael Winninge. Tübingen: Mohr Siebeck, 2008.

__________. "Memory and Identity in the Gospels: A New Perspective." In *Exploring Early Christian Identity*. Edited by Bengt Holmberg. Tübingen: Mohr Siebeck, 2008.

Cadbury, Henry Joel. "The Meaning of John 20:23, Matthew 16:19, and Matthew 18:18." *JBL* 58/3 (1939): 251-254.

Cameron, Ron and Merrill P. Miller. "Conclusion: Redescribing Christian Origins." In *Redescribing Christian Origin*. SBL Symposium Series 28. Edited by Ron Cameron and Merrill P. Miller. Leiden: Brill, 2004.

Campbell, Joan Cecelia. *Kinship Relations in the Gospel of John*. CBQMS 42. Washington: The Catholic Biblical Association of America, 2007.

Carson, D. A. *The Gospel according to John*. Grand Rapids, Michigan: William B. Eerdmans Publishing Company, 1991.

Casey, Maurice. *The Solution to the 'Son of Man' Problem*. New York: T & T Clark International, 2009.

Catchpole, David. *Resurrection People: Studies in the Resurrection Narratives of the Gospels*. Sarum Theological Lectures. London: Darton, Longman and Todd Ltd., 2000.

Charlesworth, James H. *Beloved Disciple Whose Witness Validates the Gospel of John?* Valley Forge: Trinity Press International, 1995.

__________. "Christians and Jews in the First Six Centuries." In *Christianity and Rabbinic Judaism: A Parallel History of their Origins and Early Development*. Edited by Hershel Shanks. London: SPCK, 1993.

__________. "The Dead Sea Scrolls and the Gospel according to John." In *Exploring the Gospel of John in Honor of D. Moody Smith*. Edited by R. Alan Culpepper and C. Clifton Black. Westminster: Westminster John Knox Press, 1996.

Chatterji, Saral K. "Some Aspects of Dalit Ideology." In *Towards a Common Dalit Ideology*. Edited by Arvind P. Nirmal. Madras: Gurukul LutheranTheological College & Research Institute, 1989.

Chennattu, Rekha. M. *Johannine Discipleship as a Covenant Relationship*. Massachusetts: Hendrickson Publishers, 2006.

Chester, Andrew "The Parting of the Ways: Eschatology and Messianic Hope." In *Jews and Christians: The Parting of Ways A.D. 70 to 135*. The Second Durham-Tübingen Research Symposium on Earliest Christianity and Judaism. Edited by James D. G. Dunn. Grand Rapids, Michigan: William B. Eerdmans Publishing Company, 1999.

Cho, Sukmin. *Jesus as Prophet in the Fourth Gospel*. SNTSMS 15. Edited by Stanley E. Porter. Sheffield: Sheffield Phoenix Press, 2006.

Cohen, Shaye J. D. "Crossing the Boundary and Becoming a Jew." *HTR* 82/1 (Ja. 1989): 13-33.

__________. *From the Maccabees to Mishnah*. 2nd ed. London: Westminster John Knox Press, 2006.

__________. "The Significance of Yavneh: Pharisees, Rabbis, and the End of Jewish Sectarianism." *HUCA* 55 (Ja. 1984): 27-53.

Coloe, Mary L. *Dwelling in the Household of God: Johannine Ecclesiology and Spirituality*. Minnesota: Liturgical Press, 2007.

__________. "Temple Imagery in John." *Int.* 63/ 4 (O. 2009): 368-381.

__________. *God Dwells with Us: Temple Symbolism in the Fourth Gospel*. Minnesota: The Liturgical Press, 2001.

Counet, Patrick Chatelion. *John, a Postmodern Gospel: Introduction to Deconstructive Exegesis Applied to the Fourth Gospel*. BInS 44. Leiden: Brill, 2000.

Cowan, Christopher. "Father and Son in the Fourth Gospel: Johannine Subordination Revisited." *JETS* 49/1 (Mr. 2006): 115-135.

Craig, William L. "The Disciples' Inspection of the Empty Tomb (Lk. 24:12-24; Jn. 20:2-10)." In *John and the Synoptics*. Edited by Adelbert Denaux. BETL. Leuven: Leuven University Press, 1992.

Crenshaw, James L. *Defending God: Biblical Responses to the Problem of Evil*. Oxford: Oxford University Press, 2005.

Crump, David. "Re-examining the Johannine Trinity: Perichoresis or Deification?" *SJT* 59/4 (2006): 395-412.

Cullmann, Oscar. *The Johannine Circle*. Translated by John Bowden. London: SCM Press Ltd, 1976.

Culpepper, R. Alan. "An Introduction to the Johannine Writings." In *The Johannine Literature*. Edited by Barnabas Lindars, Ruth B. Edwards and John M. Court. Sheffield: Sheffield Academic Press, 2000.

__________. "Anti-Judaism in the Fourth Gospel as a Theological Problem for Christian Interpreters." In *Anti-Judaism and the Fourth Gospel: Papers of the Leuven Colloquim, 2000*. Edited by Reimund Bieringer, Didier Pollefeyt and Frederique Vandecasteele-Vanneuville. Assen: Royal van Gorcum, 2001.

__________. *The Anatomy of the Fourth Gospel: A Study in Literary Design*. Philadelphia: Fortress Press, 1983.

__________. *John: The Son of Zebedee: The Life of a Legend*. Columbia: The University of South Carolina, 1994.

__________. "Review of *The Divine Sonship of Christians* by Matthew Vellanickal." *JBL* 98/3 (Sep. 1979): 447-449.

__________. "Seeing the Kingdom of God: The Metaphor of Sight in the Gospel of Luke." *CurTM* 21/6 (Nov. 1994): 434-443.

__________. "The Designs for the Church in the Gospel Accounts of Jesus' Death." *NTS* 55/3 (Jl. 2005): 376-392.

__________. "The Gospel of John and the Jews." *RevExp* 84/2 (Spring 1987): 273-288.

__________. *The Johannine School: An Evaluation of the Johannine-School Hypothesis Based on an Investigation of the Nature of Ancient Schools*. SBL Dissertation Series 26. Montana: Scholars Press, 1975.

__________. "The Pivot of John's Prologue." *NTS* 27/1 (O. 1980): 1-31.

__________. "The Quest for the Church in the Gospel of John." *Int.* 63/4 (O. 2009): 341-354.

Dahms, John V. "The Johannine use of *Monogenēs* Reconsidered." *NTS* 29/2 (Apr. 1983): 222-232.

Dalman, Gustaf. *The Words of Jesus: Considered in the Light of Post-biblical Jewish Writings and the Aramaic Langugage*. Translated by D. M. Kay. Edinburgh: T & T Clark, 1902.

D'Angelo, Mary Rose. "Intimating Deity in the Gospel of John: Theological Language and "Father" in "Prayers of Jesus."" *Semeia* 85 (1999): 59-82.

Daniel, Ayub. "Approaches of Mission and Churches towards the Indian Caste-System." *RelSoc* (Ja. 1995): 42:5-10.

Davies, Margret. *Rhetoric and Reference in the Fourth Gospel*. JSNTSup 69. Sheffield: JSOT Press, 1992.

de Boer, Martinus C. "Jesus' Departure to the Father in John: Death or Resurrection." In *Theology and Christology in the Fourth Gospel: Essays by the Members of the Society for New Testament Study Johannine Writings Seminar*. BETL 184. Edited by G. Van Belle, J. G. Van der Watt and P. Maritz. Leuven: Leuven University Press, 2005.

__________. *Johannine Perspectives on the Death of Jesus*. Kampen: Kok Pharos Publishing House, 1996.

de Jonge, Marinus. "Christology, Controversy and Community in the Gospel of John." In *Christology, Controversy and Community: New Testament Essays in Honour of David R. Catchpole*. NovTSup 99. Edited by David G. Horrell and Christopher M. Tuckett. Leiden: Brill, 2000.

__________. *Jesus: Stranger from Heaven and Son of God: Jesus Christ and the Christians in Johannine Perspective*. Translated by John E. Steeley. Montana: Scholars Press, 1977.

__________. "The Use of the word 'Anointed' in the time of Jesus" *NovT* 8/2-4 (Apr.-O. 1966): 132-148.

der Rand, Jan A. "The Creation Motif in the Fourth Gospel: Perspectives on the Narratological Function within Judaistic Background." In *Theology and Christology in the Fourth Gospel: Essays by the Members of the Society for New Testament Study Johannine Writings Seminar*. BETL 184. Edited by G. Van Belle, J. G. Van der Watt and P. Maritz. Leuven: Leuven University Press, 2005.

Derrett, J. Duncan M. "An Indian Metaphor in John's Gospel." *JRAS* 9/2 (Jl. 1999): 271-286.

de Ruyter, B.W. J. *The Community of John the Evangelist: Its Polemic and Its History*. Delft: Eburon, 1998.

de Silva, David. *4 Maccabees: Introduction and Commentary on the Greek Text in Codex Sinaiticus*. Septuagint Commentary Series. Edited by Stanley E. Porter, Richard S. Hess, and John Jarick. Leiden: E. J. Brill, 2006.

Destro, Adriana and Mauro Pesce. "Kinship, Discipleship, and Movement: An Anthropological Study of John's Gospel." *BI* 3/3 (O. 1995): 266-284.

Devasahayam, V. "Theological Reflections on Charting a New Course for Churches in Dalit Struggles." *NCCR* (Apr. 2004) 124/4: 297-316.

Dewey, Arthur J. "The Eyewitness of History: Visionary Consciousness in the Fourth Gospel." In *Jesus in Johannine Tradition*. Edited by Robert T. Fortna and Tom Thatcher. Louisville: Westminster John Knox Press, 2001.

Divakar, Paul. "What Can the Churches Do to Support the Movements?" *NCCR* (Jl. 2002) 122/6: 589-601.

Dodd, C. H. *Historical Traditions in the Fourth Gospel*. Cambridge: Cambridge University Press, 1963.

__________. *The Interpretation of the Fourth Gospel*. Cambridge: Cambridge University Press, 1958.

Duling, Dennis C. "The Matthean Brotherhood and Marginal Scribal Leadership." In *Modelling Early Christianity: Social-Scientific Studies of the New Testament in its Context*I. Edited by P. F. Esler. London: Routledge, 1995.

Dunn, James D. G. "John and the Synoptics as a Theological Question." In *Exploring the Gospel of John in Honor of D. Moddy Smith*. Edited by R. Alan Culpepper and C. Clifton Black. Westminster: Westminster John Knox Press, 1996.

__________. "Concluding Summary." *Jews and Christians: The Parting of Ways, A.D. 70 to 135*. The Second Durham-Tübingen Research Symposium on Earliest Christianity and Judaism. Edited by James D.

G. Dunn. Grand Rapids, Michigan: William B. Eerdmans Publishing Company, 1999.

__________. *Jesus Remembered: Christianity in the Making*. Vol. I. Grand Rapids, Michigan: William B. Eerdmans Publishing Company, 2003.

__________. "Let John Be John: A Gospel for Its Time." In *The Gospel and the Gospels*. Edited by Peter Stuhlmacher. Grand Rapids, Michigan: William B. Eerdmans Publishing Company, 1991.

__________. *The Parting of the Ways: Between Christianity and Judaism and their Significance for the Character of Christianity*. 2nd ed. London: SCM Press, 2006.

__________. "The Question of Anti-Semitism in the New Testament Writings of the Period." In *Jews and Christians: The Parting of the Ways, A. D. 70 to 135*. Edited by James D. G. Dunn. Grand Rapids, Michigan: William B. Eerdmans Publishing Company, 1992.

Duraisingh, Christopher. "The Gospel of John and the World of India Today." In *India's Search for Reality and the Relevance of Gospel of John: Papers from a conference held in Pune in February 1974*. Edited by Christopher Duraisingh and Cecil Harreaves. Delhi: ISPCK, 1975.

Edwards, Douglas R. "Constructing the World of Roman Palestine: An Introduction." In *Religion and Society in Roman Palestine: Old Questions, New Approaches*. Edited by Douglas R. Edwards. New York: Routledge, 2004.

Ellis, E. Earle "Background and Christology of John's Gospel: Selected Motifs." *SWJT* 31/1 (Fall 1988): 24-31.

Esler, Philip Francis and Ronald Piper. *Lazarus, Mary and Martha: Social-Scientific Approaches to the Gospel of John*. Minneapolis: Fortress Press, 2006.

Esler, Philip Francis. "Community and Gospel in Early Christianity: A Response to Richard Bauckham's Gospels for All Christians." SJT 51/2 (1998): 235-248.

__________. "Family Imagery and Christian Identity in Gal. 5:13 to 6:10." In *Constructing Early Christian Families: Family as a Social Reality and Metaphor*. Edited by Halvor Moxnes. New York: Routledge, 1997.

Evans, Craig F. *Resurrection and the New Testament*. SBT. Second Series 12. London: SCM Press Ltd., 1970.

Eynde, S. Van Den. "Love, Strong as Death? An Inter- and Intratextual Perspective on John 20, 1-18." In *The Death of Jesus in the Fourth Gospel*. Edited by G. Van Belle. BETL 200. Leuven: Leuven University Press, 2007.

Fanning, Buist M. *Verbal Aspect in New Testament Greek*. Oxford Monographs. Oxford: Clarendon Press, 1990.

Fehribach, Adeline. *The Women in the Life of the Bridegroom: A Feminist Historical-Literary Analysis of the Female Characters in the Fourth Gospel*. Collegeville: The Liturgical Press, 1998.

Fennema, D. A. "John 1:18: 'God the Only Son.'" *NTS* 31/1 (Ja. 1985): 124-135.

Ferreira, Johan. *Johannine Ecclesiology*. JSNTSup 160. Sheffield: Sheffield Academic Press, 1998.

Finkel, Asher. "Yavneh's Liturgy and Early Christianity." *JES* 18/2 (Spring 1981): 231-250.

Forkman, Goran. *Limits of the Religious Community: Expulsion from the Religious Community within the Qumranic Sect, within Rabbinic Judaism and within Primitive Christianity*. Translated by Pearl Sioelamder. ConBNT 5. Sweden: CWK Gleerup Lund, 1972.

Fortna, Robert T. "Christology in the Fourth Gospel: Redaction-Critical Perspectives." *NTS* 21/4 (Jl. 1975): 489-504.

Fredriksen, Paula. "What was the "Parting of the Ways"? Jews, Gentiles, and the Ancient Mediterranean City." In *The Ways that Never Parted: Jews and Christians in Late Antiquity and the Early Middle Ages*. Edited by Adam H. Becker and Annette Yoshiko Reed. Minneapolis: Fortress Press, 2007.

Freed, Edwin D. "Did John Write His Gospel Partly to Win Samaritan Converts?" *NovT* 12/3 (Jl. 1970): 241-256.

Frend, W. H. C. *Martyrdom and Persecution in the Early Church: A Study of a Conflict from the Maccabees to Donatus*. Grand Rapids, Michigan: Baker Book House, 1965.

Frey, Jörg "Eschatology in the Johannine Circle." In *Theology and Christology in the Fourth Gospel: Essays by the Members of the Society for New Testament Study Johannine Writings Seminar*. BETL 184. Edited by G. Van Belle, J. G. Van der Watt and P. Maritz. Leuven: Leuven University Press, 2005.

Freyne, Sean. "Apostle, Apostolicity." In *NDCT*. Edited by Alan Richardson and John Bowden. London: SCM Press, 1983, 33-35.

Fuglseth, Kåre Sigvald. *Johannine Sectarianism in Perspective: A Sociological, Historical, and Comparative Analysis of Temple and Social Relationships in the Gospel of John, Philo and Qumran*. NovTSup 116. Edited by M. M. Mitchell and D. P. Moessner. Brill: Leiden, 2005.

Fuller, R. H. *The Formation of the Resurrection Narratives*. New York: The Macmillian Company, 1971.

Gafni, Isaiah. "The Historical Background." In *Jewish Writings of the Second Temple Period: Apocrypha, Pseudepigrapha, Qumran Sectarian Writings, Philo, Josephus*. Edited by Michael E. Stone. Philadelphia: Fortress Press, 1984.

__________. "The Historical Background." In *The Literature of the Sages*. Part One. CRINT 3. Edited by Shmuel Safari. Philadelphia: Fortress Press, 1987.

Gager, John G. "Jews, Christians, and the Dangerous Ones in Between." In *Interpretation in Religion*. Edited by Shlomo Biderman and Ben-Ami Scharfstein. Leiden: Brill, 1992.

Gary M. Burge. *The Anointed Community: The Holy Spirit in the Johannine Tradition*. Grand Rapids, Michigan: William B. Eerdmans Publishing Company, 1987.

Gathercole, Simon J. *The Preexistent Son: Recovering the Christologies of Matthew, Mark, and Luke*. Grand Rapids, Michigan: William B. Eerdmans Publishing Company, 2006.

Gaventa, Beverly Roberts. "The Archive of Excess: John 21 and the Problem of Narrative Closure." In *Exploring the Gospel of John in Honor of D. Moddy Smith*. Edited by R. Alan Culpepper and C. Clifton Black. Westminster: Westminster John Knox Press, 1996.

Gellius, Aulus. *The Attic Nights of Aulus Gellius*. Translated by W. Beloe. Vol. 1. London: St. Paul's Church Yard, 1795.

Georgi, Dieter "The Early Church: Internal Migration or New Religion?" *HTR* 88/1 (Ja. 1995): 35-68.

Glasson, T. F. *Moses in the Fourth Gospel*. SBT. London: SCM Press Ltd., 1963.

Goodman, Martin. "Diaspora Reactions to the Destruction of the Temple." In *Jews and Christians: The Parting of Ways, A.D. 70 to 135*. The Second Durham-Tübingen Research Symposium on Earliest Christianity and Judaism. Edited by James D. G. Dunn. Michigan: William B. Eerdmans Publishing Company, 1999.

__________. "Modeling the "Parting of the Ways."" In *The Ways that Never Parted: Jews and Christians in Late Antiquity and the Early Middle Ages*. Edited by Adam H. Becker and Annette Yoshiko Reed. Minneapolis: Fortress Press, 2007.

Grayston, Kenneth. "The Translation of Matthew 28: 17." *JSNT* 21 (Ja. 1984): 105-109.

Green, Joel B. *The Gospel of Luke*. NICNT. Edited by Need B. Stonehouse, F. F. Bruce and Gordon D. Fee. Grand Rapids, Michigan: William B. Eerdmans Publishing Company, 1997.

Green, Wiliam Scott. "What's in a Name? The Problematic of Rabbinic "Biography."" In *Approaches to Ancient Judaism: Theory and Practice*. Edited by William Scott Green. Montana: Scholars Press, 1978.

Griffth, Terry. ""The Jews Who Had Believed in Him" (John 8:31) and the Motif of Apostasy in the Gospel of John." In *The Gospel of John and Christian* Theology. Edited by Richard Bauckham and Carl Mosser. Grand Rapids, Michigan: William B. Eerdmans Publishing Company, 2008.

Gujarro, Santiago. "The Family in First-Century Galilee." In *Constructing Early Christian Families: Family as a Social Reality and Metaphor*. Edited by Halvor Moxnes. New York: Routledge, 1997.

Gundry, Robert H. "In my Father's House Are Many *Monai*." *ZNW* 58/1/2 (1967): 68-72.

___________. *A Survey of the New Testament*. 4th edition. Grand Rapids, Michigan: Zondervan Publishing House, 2003.

Gurtner, Daniel M. *Second Baruch: A Critical Edition of the Syriac Text with Greek and Latin Fragments, English Translation, Introduction and Concordances*. Jewish and Christian Texts in Contexts and Related Studies. Edited by James H. Charlesworth. New York: Continuum International, 2009.

Haenchen, Ernst. *John 2: A Commentary on the Gospel of John Chapters 7-21*. Translated by Robert W. Funk, Hermeneia. Edited by Robert W. Funk and Ulrich Busse. Philadelphia: Fortress Press, 1984.

Hägerland, Tobias. "John's Gospel: A Two-Level Drama?" *JSNT* 25/3 (Mr. 2003): 309-322.

___________. "The Power of Prophecy: A Septuagintal Echo in John 20:19-23." *CBQ* 71/1 (Ja. 2009): 84-103.

Hakola, Raimo. *Identity Matters: John, the Jews and Jewishness*. NovTSup 118. Edited by M. M. Mitchell and D. P. Moessner. Leiden: Brill, 2005.

___________. "The Burden of Ambiguity: Nicodemus and the Social Identity of the Johannine Christians." *NTS* 55/4 (O. 2009): 438-455.

___________. "The Johannine Community as Jewish Christians? Some Problems in Current Scholarly Consensus." In *Jewish Christianity Reconsidered: Rethinking Ancient Groups and Texts*. Edited by Matt Jackson-Mc Cabe. Minneapolis: Fortress Press, 2007.

Hamid-Khani, Saeed. *Revelation and Concealment of Christ: A Theologial Enquiry into the Elusive Language of the Fourth Gospel*. WUZNT 2/120. Tübingen: Mohr Siebeck, 2000.

Hamilton, Neill Q. "Resurrection Tradition and the Composition of Mark." *JBL* 84/4 (Dec. 1965): 415-421.

Hanson, Anthony Tyrrell. *The Prophetic Gospel: A Study of John and the Old Testament*. Edinburgh: T & T Clark, 1991.

Harrington, Daniel J. *The Gospel of Matthew*. SacPag 1. Edited by Daniel J. Harrington. Minnesota: Liturgical Press, 2007.

Harvey, A. E. "Christ as Agent." In *The Glory of Christ in the New Testament: Studies in Christology In Memory of George Bradford Caird*. Edited by L. D. Hurst and N. T. Wright. Oxford: Oxford Clarendon Press, 1987.

Heath, J. "'Some were saying, "He is good"' (John 7:12b)" 'Good' Christology in John's Gospel?" *NTS* 56/4 (O. 2010): 513-535.

Hengel, Martin. *Four Gospels and One Gospel of Jesus Christ: An Investigation of the Collection and Origin of the Canonical Gospels*. London: SCM Press, 2000.

__________. *The Johannine Question*. London: SCM Press, 1989.

__________. *The Zealots: Investigation into the Jewish Freedom Movement in the Period from Herod I until 70 A.D.* Translated by David Smith. Edinburgh: T & T Clark, 1989.

Hirshman, Marc G. *A Rivalry of Genius: Jewish and Christian Biblical Interpretation in Late Antiquity*. Translated by Batya Stein. Albany: SUNY Press, 1996.

Horbury, William. *Jews and Christians in Contact and Controversy*. Edinburgh: T & T Clark, 1998.

__________. "The Benediction of the *Minim* and Early Jewish-Christian Controversy." *JTS* 33/1 (Apr. 1982): 19-61.

Horrell, David G. "From ἀδελφοὶ to οἶκος θεοῦ: Social Transformation in Pauline Christianity." *JBL* 120/2 (Summer 2001): 293-311.

Horsley, Richard A., John S. Hanson. *Bandits, Prophets and Messiahs: Popular Movements in the Time of Jesus*. Pennsylvania: Trinity Press International, 1999.

__________. ""Messianic" Figures and Movements in First-Century Palestine." In *The Messiah: Developments in Earliest Judaism and Christianity*. Edited by James H. Charlesworth. Minneapolis: Fortress Press, 1992.

__________. "Popular Messianic Movements around the Time of Jesus." CBQ 46/3 (Jl. 1984): 471-495.

__________. "Popular Prophetic Movements in the time of Jesus: Their Principal features and Social Origins." *JSNT* 26 (Feb. 1986): 3-27.

__________. *The Covenant Economics: A Biblical Vision of Justice for All*. Kentucky: Westminster John Knox Press, 2009.

Hoskins, Paul M. *Jesus as the Fulfilment of the Temple in the Gospel of John*. PBM. Edited by I. H. Marshall, et.al. Colorado Springs: Paternoster, 2006.

Hoskyns, Edwyn Clement. *The Fourth Gospel*. Vol. 2. London: Faber and Faber Limited, 1940.

Howard-Brook, Wes. *Becoming Children of God: John's Gospel and Radical Discipleship*. Maryknoll: Orbis Books, 1994.

Humbert, Jean-Baptiste. "An Essene Identity at Qumran." *NEA* 63/3 (Sep. 2000): 172-174.

Hurtado, Larry W. "First-Century Jewish Monotheism." *JSNT* 71 (Summer 1998): 3-26.

__________. *Lord Jesus Christ: Devotion to Jesus in Earliest Christianity*. Grand Rapids, Michigan: William B. Eerdmans Publishing Company, 2003.

__________. "Pre-70 CE Jewish Opposition to Christ-Devotion." *JTS* 50/1 (Apr. 1999): 35-58.

Instone-Brewer, David. "The Eighteen Benedictions and the Minim before 70 CE." *JTS 54/1* (Apr. 2003): 25-44.

Irudaya, Raj. *Mission to the Marginalized: A Subaltern, Feminist and Interreligious Reading of John 4:1-42*. Bangalore: Asian Trading Corporation, 2007.

Jenkins, Richard. *Social Identity*. London: Routledge, 2004.

Jeremias, Joachim. *Jerusalem in the Time of Jesus: An Investigation into the Economic and Social Conditions during the New Testament Period*. Translated by F. H. and C. H. Cave. Philadelphia: Fortress Press, 1969.

Jeremias, Joachim. *New Testament Theology*. Part 1: *The Proclamation of Jesus*. London: SCM Press Ltd, 1971.

Johnson, Luke Timothy. *The Gospel of Luke*. SacPag 3. Edited by Daniel J. Harrington. Minnesota: Liturgical Press, 1991.

Jones, Kenneth R. *Jewish Reactions to the Destruction of the Jerusalem Temple in A.D. 70: Apocalypses and Related Pseudepigrapha*. JSJSup 151. Edited by Hindy Najman. Boston: Leiden, 2011.

Judge, P. J. "John 20, 24-29: More than Doubt, Beyond Rebuke." In *The Death of Jesus in the Fourth Gospel*. Edited by G. Van Belle. BETL 200. Leuven: Leuven University Press, 2007.

Kanagaraj, Jey J. *'Mysticism' in the Gospel of John: An Inquiry into its Background*. JSNTSup 158. Sheffield: Sheffield Academic Press, 1998.

__________. *The Gospel of John: A Commentary with Elements of Comparison to Indian Religious Thoughts and Cultural Practices*. Secunderabad: Om Books International, 2005.

__________. "The Profiles of Women in John: House-bond or Christ-bound?" *ERT* 27/1 (Ja. 2003): 27-46.

Karris, Robert J. *Jesus and the Marginalized in John's Gospel*. Zacchaeus Studies: NT. Edited by Mary Ann Getty. Collegeville: The Liturgical Press, 1990.

Käsemann, Ernst. *The Testament of Jesus: A Study of the Gospel of John in the Light of Chapter 17*. Translated by Gerhard Krodel. London: SCM Press Ltd, 1968.

Katz, Steven T. "Issues in the Separation of Judaism and Christianity after 70 CE: A Reconsideration." *JBL* 103/1 (Mr. 1984): 43-76.

Kazen, Thomas. "Sectarian Gospels for Some Christians? Intention and Mirror Reading in the Light of Extra-Canonical Texts." *NTS* 51/4 (O. 2005): 561-578.

Keck, Leander E. "Towards the Renewal of New Testament Theology." *NTS* 32/3 (Jl. 1986): 362-367.

Kee, Howard Clark. "The Transformation of the Synagogue after 70 CE: Its Import for Early Christianity." *NTS* 36/1 (Ja. 1990): 1-24.

Keener, Craig S. *The Gospel of John: A Commentary*. Vol. 1 & 2. Massachusetts: Hendrickson Publishers, 2003.

__________. "Is Subordination within the Trinity Really Heresy? A Study of John 5:18 in Context." *TrinJ* 20/1 (Spring 1999): 39-51.

Keith, Chris. "The Claim of John 7.15 and the Memory of Jesus' Literacy." *NTS* 56/1 (Ja. 2010): 44-63.

Kelly, Anthony J. and Fancis J. Moloney. *Experiencing God in the Gospel of John*. New York: Paulist Press, 2003.

Kendall, Daniel and Gerald O' Collins. "Mary Magdalene as Major Witness to Jesus' Resurrection." TS 48/4 (Dec. 1987): 631-646.

Kessler, Edward. *An Introduction to Jewish-Christian Relations*. Cambridge: Cambridge University Press, 2010.

Kieffer, René "John." In *The Gospels*. The Oxford Bible Commentary. Edited by John Muddiman and John Barton. Oxford: Oxford University Press, 2001.

Kierspel, Lars. *The Jews and the World in the Fourth Gospel*. Tübingen: Mohr Siebeck, 2006.

Kilpatrick, George Dunbar. "Jesus, his Family and his Disciples." *JSNT* 15 (Jl. 1982): 3-19.

Kimelman, Reuven. "*Birkat Ha-Minim* and the Lack of Evidence for an Anti-Christian Jewish Prayer in Late Antiquity." In *Jewish and Christian Self-Definition*. Vol. 2: *Aspects of Judaism in the Greco-Roman Period*.

Edited by E. P. Sanders, Albert I. Baumgarten and Alan Mendelson. Philadelphia: Fortress Press, 1981.

Kingsbury, Jack Dean. "The Composition and Christology of Matt 28:16-20." *JBL* 93/4 (Dec. 1974): 573-584.

Kinzig, Wolfram. "'Non-Separation:' Closeness and Co-operation between Jews and Christians in the Fourth Century." *VigChr* 45/1 (Mr. 1991): 27-53.

__________. Review of *Anti-Judaism and Early Christina Identity: A Critique of the Scholarly Consensus*, by Miriam S. Taylor. *JTS* 48/2 (O. 1997): 643-649.

Klauck, Hans-Josef. "Community, History, and Text(s): A Response to Robert Kysar." In *Life in Abundance: Studies of John's Gospel in Tribute to Raymond E. Brown*. Edited by John R. Donahue. Minnesota: Liturgical Press, 2005.

Klink III, Edward W. "The Gospel Community Debate: State of the Question." CBR 3/1 (O. 2004): 60-85.

Knox, Wilfred Lawrence. "The Ending of St. Mark's Gospel." *HTR* 35/1 (Ja. 1942): 13-23.

Koester, Helmut. "Ephesos in Early Christian Literature." In *Ephesos: Metropolis of Asia: An Interdisciplinary Approach to Its Archaeology, Religion and Culture*. HTS 41. Edited by Helmut Koester. Valley Forge: Trinity Press International, 1995.

Kohler, Kaufmann. "The Origin and Composition of the Eighteen Benedictions with a Translation of the Corresponding Essene Prayers in the Apostolic Constitutions." *HUCA* 1 (Jan. 1924): 387-425.

Köstenberger, Andreas J. *A Theology of John's Gospel and Letters: The Word, the Christ, the Son of God*. Grand Rapids, Michigan: Zondervan Publishing House, 2009.

__________ and Scott R. Swain. *Father, Son and Spirit: The Trinity and John's Gospel*. NSBT 24. Edited by D. A. Carson. Illinois: InterVarsity Press, 2008.

__________. *John*. BECNT. Grand Rapids, Michigan: Baker Academic, 2004.

__________. *The Mission of Jesus and the Disciples according to the Fourth Gospel*. Grand Rapids, Michigan: William B. Eerdmans Publishing Company, 1998.

__________. "The Destruction of the Second Temple and the Composition of the Fourth Gospel." *TrinJ* 26/2 (Fall 2005): 205-242.

__________. "The Two Johannine Verbs for Sending: A Study of John's Use of Words with reference to General Linguistic Theory." In *Linguistic and the New Testament: Critical Junctures*. Edited by Stanley E. Porter and D. A. Carson. Sheffield: Sheffield Academic Press, 1999.

Kraft, Robert A. "The Weighing of the Parts: Pivots and Pitfalls in the Study of Early Judaisms and their Early Christian Offspring." In *The Ways that Never Parted: Jews and Christians in Late Antiquity and the Early Middle Ages*. Edited by Adam H. Becker and Annette Yoshiko Reed. Minneapolis: Fortress Press, 2007.

Krauss, S. "The Jews in the Works of the Church Fathers." *JQR* Old Series 5/1 (O. 1892): 122-157.

Küng, Hans. *Judaism: The Religious Situation of Our Time*. Translated by John Bowden. London: SCM Press Ltd., 1992.

Kulik, Alexander. *Retroverting to Slavonic Pseudepigrapha: Towards the Original of Apocalypse of Abraham*. TCS 3. Edited by James R. Adair. Atlanta: SBL, 2004.

Kurian, Sunil Geoge. "Struggle for Survival – Experience of Christian Dalits (inVijayapuram Diocese) in Kerala." *RelSoc* (Ja. 1995) 42/2: 11- 24.

Kysar, Robert. "Christology and Controversy: The Contribution of the Prologue of the Gospel of John to New Testament Christology and their Historical Setting." *CurTM* 5/6 (Dec. 1978): 348-364.

___________. *John, the Maverick Gospel*. Atlanta: Westminster John Knox Press, 1970.

___________. "The Expulsion from the Synagogue: The Tale of the Theory." In *Voyages with John: Charting the Fourth Gospel*. Texas: Baylor University Press, 2005.

___________. "The Whence and Whither of the Johannine Community." In *Life in Abundance: Studies of John's Gospel in Tribute to Raymond E. Brown*. Edited by John R. Donahue. Minnesota: Liturgical Press, 2005.

LaFargue, Michael. "The Authority of the Excluded: Mark's Challenge to a Rational Hermeneutics." In *Religious Propaganda and Missionary Competition in the New Testament World: Essays Honouring Dieter Georgi*. Edited by Lukas Bormann, Kelly Del Tredici and Angela Standhartinger. Leiden: E. J. Brill, 1994.

Lakoff, G. and M. Johnson. *Metaphors We Live By*. Chicago: Chicago University Press, 1980.

Lane, William. *The Gospel of Mark*. NICNT. Edited by Ned B. Stonehouse, F. F. Bruce, and Gordon D. Fee. Grand Rapids, Michigan: William B. Eerdmans Publishing Company, 1974.

Larbeer, P. Mohan. "Deconstruction and Reconstruction of the first Murder – A Dalit Perspective." *NCCR* (Apr. 2002) 122/3: 311-322.

Lassen, Eva Marie. "The Roman Family: Ideal and Metaphor." In *Constructing Early Christian Families: Family as a Social Reality and Metaphor*. Edited by Halvor Moxnes. New York: Routledge, 1997.

Last, Richard. "Communities that Write: Christ-Groups, Associations, and Gospel Communities." *NTS* 58/2 (Apr. 2012): 173-198.

Lee, Dorothy Ann. "Partnership in Easter Faith: The Role of Mary Magdalene and Thomas in John 20." *JSNT* 58 (Ja. 1995): 37-49.

__________. "Resurrection and Life: Symbols of Easter." In *Flesh and Glory: Symbolism, Gender and Theology in the Gospel of John*. New York: The Crossroad Publising Company, 2002.

__________. "The Symbol of Divine Fatherhood." *Semeia* 85 (1999): 177-187.

Legrand, L. *Mission in the Bible*. Pune: Ishvani Publications, 1992.

Lenowitz, Harris. *The Jewish Messiahs: From Galilee to the Crown Heights*. Oxford: Oxford University Press, 1998.

Levine, Lee I. "Judaism from the Destruction to the End of the Second Jewish Revolt: 70-135 CE" In *Christianity and Rabbinic Judaism: A Parallel History of their Origins and Early Development*. Edited by Hershel Shanks. London: SPCK, 1993.

__________. "The Nature and Origin of the Palestinian Synagogue Reconsidered." *JBL* 115/3 (Fall 1996): 425-448.

Lieu, Judith M. *Christian Identity in the Jewish and Graeco-Roman World*. Oxford: Oxford University Press, 2004.

__________. *The Theology of the Johannine Epistles*. Cambridge: Cambridge University Press, 1991.

__________. "Temple and Synagogue in John." *NTS* 45/1 (Ja. 1999): 51-69.

__________. "'Impregnable Ramparts and Walls of Iron': Boundary and Identity in Early 'Judaism' and 'Christianity.'" *NTS* 48/3 (Jl. 2002): 297-313.

__________. "The Mother of the Son in the Fourth Gospel." *JBL* 117/1 (Spring 1998): 61-77.

__________. ""The Parting of the Way:" Theological Construct or Historical Reality." JSNT 56 (Dec. 1994): 101-119.

__________. *The Second and Third Epistles of John: History and Background*. Edinburgh: T & T Clark, 1986.

Lightfoot, R. H. *St. John's Gospel: A Commentary*. Oxford: Clarendon Press, 1957.

Lincoln, Andrew T. ""I Am the Resurrection and the Life": The Resurrection Message of the Fourth Gospel." In *Life in the Face of Death: The Resurrection Message of the New Testament*. Edited by Richard N.

Longenecker. Grand Rapids, Michigan: William B. Eerdmans Publishing Company, 1998.

___________. "The Beloved Disciple as Eyewitness and the Fourth Gospel as Witness." *JSNT* 24/85 (Jl. 2002): 3-26.

Lindars, Barnabas. *John.* NT Guides. Sheffield: JSOT Press, 1990.

___________. "John." In *The Johannine Literature.* Edited by Barnabas Lindars, Ruth B. Edwards and John M. Court. Sheffield: Sheffield Academic Press, 2000.

___________. "The Composition of John 20." *NTS* 7/2 (Ja. 1961): 142-147.

___________. "The Son of Man in the Johannine Christology." In *Essays on John.* SNTA 17. Edited by Christopher M. Tuckett. Leuven: Leuven University Press, 1992.

___________. *The Gospel of John.* NCB. Edited by Matthew Black. Grand Rapids, Michigan: William B. Eerdmans Publishing Company, 1972.

Ling, Timothy J. M. *The Judean Poor and the Fourth Gospel.* Cambridge: Cambridge University Press, 2006.

Lingad, Celestino G. *The Problems of Jewish Christians in the Johannine Community.* TGST 73. Rome: Gregorian University Press, 2001.

Loader, William. *The Christology of the Fourth Gospel: Structure and Issues.* BBET 23. Edited by Jürgen Becker and Henning Graf Reventlow. New York: Peter Lang, 1989.

Lourduswamy, S. "The Church and Dalit Christians." *NCCR* (Jl. 2002) 122/6: 579-588.

Lowe, Malcolm. "Who were ̓ΙΟΥΔΑΙΟΙ?" *NovT* 18/ 2 (April 1976): 101-130.

Lüdemann, Gerd. "The Successors of Pre-70 Jerusalem Christianity: A Critical Evaluation of the Pella-Tradition." In *Jewish and Christian Self-Definition.* Vol. 1: *The Shaping of Christianity in the Second and Third Centuries.* Edited by E. P. Sanders. Philadelphia: Fortress Press, 1980.

Mahoney, Robert. *The Two Disciples at the Tomb: The Background and Message of John 20:1-10.* Frankfurt: Peter Lang, 1974.

Maile, John F. "The Ascension in Luke-Acts." *TynBul* 37 (Ja. 1986): 29-59.

Malina, Bruce J. and Richard L. Rohrbaugh. *Social-Science Commentary on the Gospel of John.* Minneapolis: Fortress Press, 1998.

Mann, Jacob. "Genizah Fragments of the Palestinian Order of Service." *HUCA* 2 (Ja. 1925): 269-338.

Manns, Fréderic. *John and Jamnia: How the Break Occurred between Jews and Christians, ca. 80-100 A.D.* Translated by Mildred Dual and Marina Riadi. Jerusalem: Franciscan Printing Press, 1988.

Mar Poulose, Poulose. "Witnessing to Life in the Midst of Death – A Reluctant Critique on the Life of the Church." *IndJT* 31/2 (Apr.-Ja. 1982): 96-102.

Marcus, Joel. "*Birkat Ha-Minim*: Revisited." *NTS* 55/4 (O. 2009): 523-551.

Marxsen, Willi. *The Resurrection of Jesus of Nazareth*. Translated by Margaret Kohl. Philadelphia: Fortress Press, 1972.

Marrow, Stanley B. *The Gospel of John: A Reading*. New York: Paulist Press, 1995.

Martin, Vincent. *A House Divided: The Parting of the Ways Between Synagogue and Church*. New York: Paulist Press, 1995.

Martyn, J. Louis. *History & Theology in the Fourth Gospel*. Nashville: Abingdon Press, 1968.

___________. *The Gospel of John in Christian History: Essays for Interpreters*. New York: Paulist Press, 1978.

Mason, Steve. "Jews, Judeans, Judaizing, Judaism: Problems of Categorization in Ancient History." *JSJ* 38/ 4-5 (Nov. 2007): 457-512.

Massey, James. "Prophetic Witness and Subaltern Struggle for Justice." In *Edinburgh 2010: Witnessing to Christ Today in India*. Edited by James Massey and Wati Longchar. West Bengal: BTESSC/SATHRI/SCEPTRE, 2011.

___________. "The Role of the Churches in whole Dalit Issue." *NCCR* (My.-Ja. 1996), 116/5: 325-333.

___________. *Dalits in India: Religion as a Source of Bondage or Liberation with Special Reference to Christians*. New Delhi: ISPCK, 1995.

McConvery, Brendan. "Hippolytus' *Commentary on the Song of Songs and John 20*: Intertexual Reading in Early Christianity." *ITQ* 71/3-4 (Jl. 2006): 211-222.

McGehee, Michael. "A Less Theological Reading of John 20:17." *JBL* 105/2 (Ja. 1986): 299-302.

McGrath, James F. "A Rebellious Son? Hugo Odeberg and the Interpretation of John 5:18." *NTS* 44/3 (Jl. 1998): 470-473.

___________. *John's Apologetic Christology: Legitimation and Development in Johannine Christology*. SNTMS 111. Edited by Richard Bauckham. Cambridge: Cambridge University Press, 2004.

McHugh, John. "In Him was Life." In *Jews and Christians: The Parting of Ways, A.D. 70 to 135*. The Second Durham-Tübingen Research Symposium on Earliest Christianity and Judaism. Edited by James D. G. Dunn. Michigan: William B. Eerdmans Publishing Company, 1992.

McKay, Kenneth L. "The Use of *hoi de* in Matthew 28: 17: A Response to K. Grayston." *JSNT* 24 (Ja. 1985): 71-72.

McWhirter, Jocelyn. *The Bridegroom Messiah and the People of God: Marriage in the Fourth Gospel*. SNTSMS 138. Cambridge: Cambridge University Press, 2006.

Meeks, Wayne A. "Breaking Away: Three New Testament Pictures of Christianity's Separation from the Jewish Communities." In *"To See Ourselves as Others See Us": Christians, Jews and "Others" in Late Antiquity*. Edited by Jacob Neusner and Ernst Frerichs. California: Scholars' Press, 1985.

___________. " Man from heaven in Johannine Sectarianism." *JBL* 91/1 (Mr. 1972): 44-72.

___________. "Moses as God and King." In *Religions in Antiquity: Essays in Memory of Erwin Ramsdell Goodenough*. Edited by Jacob Neusner. Leiden: E. J. Brill, 1970.

___________. *The Prophet-King Moses Traditions and the Johannine Christology*. NovTSup 14. Leiden: Brill, 1967.

Mendels, D. "Pseudo-Philo's *Biblical Antiquities*, "The Fourth Philosophy," and the Political Messianism of the First Century CE" In *The Messiah: Developments in Earliest Judaism and Christianity*. Edited by James H. Charlesworth, et.al. Minneapolis: Fortress Press, 1992.

Menken, Maarten J. J. "Observations on the Significance of the Old Testament in the Fourth Gospel." In *Theology and Christology in the Fourth Gospel: Essays by the Members of the Society for New Testament Study Johannine Writings Seminar*. BETL 184. Edited by G. van Belle, J. G. van der Watt and P. Maritz. Leuven: Leuven University Press, 2005.

Mercer, Calvin. "'ΑΠΟΣΤΕΛΛΕΙΝ and ΠΕΜΠΕΙΝ in John." *NTS* 36/4 (O. 1990): 619-624.

Meyer, Paul W. ""The Father": The Presentation of God in the Fourth Gospel." In *Exploring the Gospel of John in Honor of D. Moddy Smith*. Edited by R. Alan Culpepper and C. Clifton Black. Westminster: Westminster John Knox Press, 1996.

Minear, Paul S. """We Don't Know Where..." John 20:2." *Int.* 30/2 (Apr. 1976): 125-139.

Mitchell, Margaret M. "Patristic Counter-Evidence to the Claim that the 'The Gospels Were Written for All Christians." *NTS* (Ja. 2005) 51/1: 36-79.

Moloney, Francis J. "The Fourth Gospel and the Jesus of History." *NTS* 46/1 (Ja. 2000): 42-58.

___________. *The Gospel of John*. SacPag 4. Edited by Daniel J. Harrington. Minnesota: The Liturgical Press, 1998.

___________. *The Johannine Son of Man*. BSR 14. Rome: LAS, 1976.

Moore, George Foot. *Judaism in the First Centuries of the Christian Era: The Age of the Tannaim*. Vol. 1. Cambridge: Harvard University Press, 1950.

Morris, Leon. *The Gospel according to John*. NICNT. Edited by Ned B. Stonehouse, F. F. Bruce, Gordon D. Fee. Revised edition. Grand Rapids, Michigan: William B. Eerdmans Publishing Company, 1995.

Motyer, Stephen. "Jesus and the Marginalized." In *Mission and Meaning: Essays Presented to Peter Cotterell*. Edited by A. Billington, et.al. Carlisle: Paternoster Press, 1995.

__________. *Your Father the Devil? A New Approach to John and 'the Jews'* PBTM. Carlisle: Paternoster Press, 1997.

Moulton, W. F. and A. S. Geden, eds. *A Concordance to the Greek Testament*. Edinburgh: T & T Clark, 1957.

Moxnes, Halvor. "What is Family? Problems in Constructing Early Christian Families." In *Constructing Early Christian Families: Family as a Social Reality and Metaphor*. Edited by Halvor Moxnes. New York: Routledge, 1997.

Mulakuzhyil, George. *The Christocentric Literary Structure of the Fourth Gospel* Roma: Editrice Pontificio Istituto Biblico, 1987.

Nielsen, Jesper Tang. "The Narrative Structures of Glory and Glorification in the Fourth Gospel." *NTS* (Jl. 2010): 343-366.

Neirynck, Frans. "John and the Synoptics the Empty Tomb Stories." *NTS* 30/2 (Apr. 1984): 161-187.

Neusner, Jacob. *A Life of Yohanan Ben Zakkai, Ca. 1-80 CE.* 2nd ed. Leiden: E. J. Brill, 1970.

__________. *Ancient Israel after Catastrophe: The Religious World View of the Mishnah*. Charlottesville: University Press of Virginia, 1983.

__________. *Development of a Legend: Studies on the Tradition Concerning Yohanan Ben Zakkai*. SPB 6. Leiden: E. J. Brill, 1970.

__________. *From Politics to Piety: The Emergence of Pharisaic Judaism*. New Jersey: Prentice-Hall, Inc., 1973.

__________. *Judaism in the Beginning of Christianity*. London: SPCK, 1984.

__________. "Preface." In *Judaism and their Messiahs at the Turn of the Christian Era*. Edited by Jacob Neusner, William Scott Green, Ernest S. Frerichs. Cambridge: Cambridge University Press, 2003.

__________. "The Fellowship (chbwrh) in the Second Jewish Commonwealth." *HTR* 53/2 (Apr. 1960): 125-142.

__________. "The Formation of Rabbinic Judaism: From the Mishnah's Philosophy to the Talmud's Religion." *ComViatI* 44/1 (2002): 19-43.

Newman, Hillel. *Proximity to Power and Jewish Sectarian Groups of the Ancient Period: A Review of Lifestyle, Values and Halakah in the Pharisees, Sadducees, Essenes and Qumran*. Edited by Ruth Ludlam.

Brill Reference Library of Judaism 25. Edited by Allen J. Avery-Peck and William Scott Green. Leiden: Brill, 2006.

Neyrey, Jerome H. ""I am the Door" (John 10:7, 9): Jesus the Broker in the Fourth Gospel." *CBQ* 69/2 (Apr. 2007): 271-291.

___________. "Loss of Wealth, Loss of Family and Loss of Honor." In *Modelling Early Christianity: Social-Scientific Studies of the New Testament in its Context*. Edited by P. F. Esler. London: Routledge, 1995.

___________. *The Gospel of John in Cultural and Rhetorical Perspective*. Grand Rapids, Michigan: William B. Eerdmans Publishing Company, 2009.

___________. *The Gospel of John*. NCBC. Edited by Ben Witherington III. Cambridge: Cambridge University Press, 2007.

Nickelsburg, George W. E. *Ancient Judaism and Christian Origins: Diversity, Continuity, and Transformation*. Minneapolis: Fortress Press, 2003.

___________. "Revolt-Destruction- Reconstruction." In *Jewish Literature between the Bible and the Mishnah: A Historical and Literary Introduction*. 2nd edition. Minneapolis: Fortress Press, 2005.

Nicol, W. *The Sēmeia in the Fourth Gospel: Tradition and Redaction*. NovTSup 32. Leiden: E. J. Brill, 1972.

Nielsen, Jesper Tang. "The Narrative Structures of Glory and Glorification in the Fourth Gospel." *NTS* (Jl. 2010): 343-366.

Nir, Rivka. *The Destruction of the Jerusalem Temple and the Idea of Redemption in the Syriac Apocalypse of Baruch*. EJL 20. Edited by John C. Reeves. Atlanta: Society of Biblical Literature, 2003.

North, Wendy E. Sproston. "John for Readers of Mark? A Response to Richard Bauckham's Proposal." JSNT 25/4 (Ja. 2003): 449-468.

O'Brien, Kelli S. "Written That You May Believe: John 20 and Narrative Rhetoric." *CBQ* 67/2 (Apr. 2005): 284-302.

O'Brien, Peter T. "Mission, Witness and the coming of the Spirit." *BBR* 9 (Ja. 1999): 205.

O'Collins, Gerald. *The Resurrection of Jesus Christ*. Pennsylvania: Judson Press, 1973.

O'Day, Gail R. "Show Us the Father, and We Will Be Satisfied" (John 14:8)." *Semeia* 85 (1999): 11-17.

___________. "The Word Become Flesh: Story and Theology in the Gospel of John." In "*What is John?" * Vol. 2*: Literary and Sociological Readings of the Fourth Gospel*. Edited by Fernando F. Segovia. SBL Symposium Series 7. Atlanta: Scholars Press, 1998.

O'Donnell, Tim. "Complementary Eschatologies in John 5:19-30." *CBQ* 70/4 (O. 2008): 750-765.

O'Grady, John F. *According to John: The Witness of the Beloved Disciple*. New York: Paulist Press, 1999.

__________. "The Human Jesus in the Fourth Gospel." *BibThBul* 14/2 (Apr. 1984): 63-66.

Okure, Teresa. *The Johannine Approach to Mission: A Contextual Study of John 4:1-42* Tübingen: Mohr, 1988.

Okure, Teresa. "The Significance Today of Jesus' Commission to Mary Magdalene." *IRM* 81/322 (Apr. 1992): 177-188.

Osborne, Grant R. *The Resurrection Narratives: A Redactional Study*. Grand Rapids, Michigan: Baker Book House, 1984.

Overman, J. Andrew. *Matthew's Gospel and Formative Judaism: The Social World of the Matthean Community* (Minneapolis: Fortress Press, 1990).

Paddison, Angus. "Engaging Scripture; Incarnation and the Gospel of John." *SJT* 60/2 (2007): 144-160.

Pagels, E. *Beyond Belief: The Secret Gospel of Thomas*. New York: Random Book House, 1998.

Painter, John. *John: Witness and Theologian*. London: SPCK, 1975.

__________. "Memory Holds the Key: The Transformation of Memory in the Interface of History and Theology in John." In *John, Jesus and History*. Vol. 1: *Crticial Appraisals of Critical Views*. Edited by Paul N. Anderson, Felix Just, Tom Thatcher. SBLSS 44. Edited by Victor H. Matthews. Atlanta: SBL, 2007.

__________. """The Light Shines in the Darkness..." Creation, Incarnation, and Resurrection in John." In *The Resurrection of Jesus in the Gospel of John*. Edited by Craig R. Koester and Reimund Bieringer. WUZNT 22. Tübingen: Mohr Siebeck, 2008.

__________. "The Point of John's Christology: Christology, Conflict and Community in John." In *Christology, Controversy and Community: New Testament Essays in Honour of David R. Catchpole*. NovT Sup 99. Edited by David G. Horrell and Christopher M. Tuckett. Leiden: Brill, 2000.

__________. *The Quest for the Messiah: The History, Literature and Theology of the Johannine Community*. Edinburgh: T & T Clark, 1993.

__________. "Who Was James? Footprints as a Means of Identification." In *The Brother of Jesus: James the Just and His Mission*. Edited by Bruce Chilton and Jacob Neusner. London: Westminster John Knox Press, 2001.

Palumbo, Arthur E. *The Dead Sea Scrolls and the Personages of Early Christianity*. New York: Algora, 2004.

Pamment, Margaret. "The Son of Man in the Fourth Gospel." *JTS* 36/1 (Apr. 1985): 56-66.

Pamplaniyil, J. T. "ΤΥΠΟΝ ΤΩΝ ΗΛΩΝ..." (Jn. 20, 25): Johannine Double Entendre of Jesus' Wounds." In *The Death of Jesus in the Fourth Gospel*. Edited by G. Van Belle. BETL 200. Leuven: Leuven University Press, 2007.

Pancaro, Severino. "The Relationship of the Church to Israel in the Gospel of John." *NTS* 21/3 (Apr. 1975): 396-405.

Parkes, James. *The Conflict of the Church and the Synagogue: A Study in the Origins of Anti-Semitism*. New York: The Word Publishing Company, 1961.

Patty, Paul. "The Beloved Disciple and Apostle Thomas." *BibBh* 27/3 (Sep. 2001): 161-173.

Pendrick, Gerard. "ΜΟΝΟΓΕΝΗΣ" *NTS* 41/4 (O. 1995): 587-600.

Perkins, Pheme. ""I Have Seen the Lord" (John 20:18): Women Witnesses to the Resurrection." *Int*. 46/1 (Ja. 1992): 31-41.

Perrin, Norman. *The Resurrection Narratives: A New Approach*. London: SCM Press Ltd, 1977.

Peskowitz, Mirian. "Family/ies in Antiquity: Evidence from Tannaitic Literature and Roman Galilean Architecture." In *The Jewish Family in Antiquity*. Edited by Shaye J. D. Cohen. Atlanta: Scholars Press, 1993.

Petersen, Norman R. *The Gospel of John and the Sociology of Light: Language and Characterization in the Fourth Gospel*. Valley Forge: Trinity Press International, 1993.

Piper, Ronald A. "Satan, Demons and the Absence of Exorcisms in the Fourth Gospel." In *Christology, Controversy and Community: New Testament Essays in Honour of David R. Catchpole*. NovT Sup 99. Edited by David G. Horrell and Christopher M. Tuckett. Leiden: Brill, 2000.

Poirier, John C. "Hanukah in the Narrative Chronology of the Fourth Gospel." *NTS* 54/4 (O. 2008): 465-478.

Pollard, T. E. *Johannine Christology and the Early Church*. SNTMS 13. Edited by Matthew Black. Cambridge: Cambridge University Press, 1970.

Pomeroy, Sarah B. "Some Greek Families: Production and Reproduction." In *The Jewish Family in Antiquity*. Edited by Shaye J. D. Cohen. Atlanta: Scholars Press.

Prabhakar, M. E. "Caste-Class and Status in Andhra Churches and Implications for Mission Today: Some Reflections." *RelSoc* (Sep. 1981) 28/3: 9-35.

Pryor, John W. *John Evangelist of the Covenant People: The Narrative and Themes of the Fourth Gospel*. London: Darton, Longman and Todd, 1992.

Purvis, James D. "The Fourth Gospel and the Samaritans." *NovT* 17/3 (Jl. 1975): 161-198.

Raj, Antony. "Disobedience: A Legitimate Act for Dalit Liberation." In *Toward A Common Dalit Ideology*. Edited by Arvind P. Nirmal. Madras: Gurukul Lutheran Theological College & Research Institute, 1989.

Raj, M. C. and Jyothi Raj. *Dalitology: The Book of the Dalit People*. Tumkur: Ambedkar Resource Centre, 2001.

Rajaratnam, K. "The Indian Church and the Dalits of India – New Agenda for the Church in India Dalit Liberation." *NCCR* (Apr. 2002) 122/3: 291-298.

Reed, Annette Yoshiko and Adam H. Becker. "Introduction: Traditional Models and New Direction." In *The Ways that Never Parted: Jews and Christians in Late Antiquity and the Early Middle Ages*. Edited by Adam H. Becker and Annette Yoshiko Reed. Minneapolis: Fortress Press, 2007.

Regev, Eyal. "Where the Early Christians Sectarians?" *JBL* 130/4 (Winter 2011): 771-793.

Reinhartz, Adele. "Parents and children: a Philonic Perspective." In *The Jewish Family in Antiquity*. Edited by Shaye J. D. Cohen. Atlanta: Scholars Press, 1993.

__________. "The Johannine Community and Its Jewish Neighbors: A Reappraisal." In *"What is John?"* Vol. 2: *Literary and Social Readings of the Fourth Gospel*. SBL Symposium Series 7. Edited by Fernando F. Segovia. Georgia: Scholars Press, 1998.

Rensberger, David. *Overcoming the World: Politics and Community in the Gospel of John*. London: SPCK, 1989.

Resseguie, James L. *Narrative Criticism of the New Testament: An Introduction*. Grand Rapids, Michigan: Baker Academic, 2005.

Riches, John K. *A Century of New Testament Study*. Cambridge: The Lutterworth Press, 1993.

Ridderbos, Herman. *The Gospel of John: A Theological Commentary*. Grand Rapids, Michigan: William B. Eerdmans Publishing Company, 1997.

Riley, Gregory J. *Resurrection Reconsidered: Thomas and John in Controversy*. Minneapolis: Fortress Press, 1995.

Ringe, Sharon H. *Wisdom's Friends: Community and Christology in the Fourth Gospel*. Louisville: Westminster John Knox Press, 1999.

Rivkin, Ellis. "Defining the Pharisees: the Tannaitic Sources." *HUCA* 40-41 (1969-1970): 205-249.

Robinson, John A. T. *The Priority of John*. London: SCM Press Ltd, 1983.

Roetzel, Calvin J. ""As Dying, and Behold We Live:" Death and Resurrection in Paul's Theology." *Int.* 46/1 (Ja. 1992): 5-18.

Rojas-Flores, G. "From John 2.19 to Mark 15.29: The History of a Misunderstanding." *NTS* 56/1 (Ja. 2010): 22-43.

Rowe, C. Kavin. "Literary Unity and Reception History: Reading Luke-Acts as Luke and Acts." *JSNT* (Ja. 2007) 29/4: 449-457.

Rowland, Christopher. "The Parting of the Ways: The Evidence of Jewish and Christian Apocalyptic and Mystical Material." In *Jews and Christians: The Parting of Ways, A.D. 70 to 135*. The Second Durham-Tübingen Research Symposium on Earliest Christianity and Judaism. Edited by James D. G. Dunn. Michigan: William B. Eerdmans Publishing Company, 1999.

Rubenstein, Richard L. "What was at Stake in the Parting of the Ways between Judaism and Christianity?" *Shofar* 28/3 (2010): 78-102.

Rutgers, Leonard Victor. "Archaeological Evidence for the Interaction of Jews and non-Jews in Late Antiquity." *AJA* 96/1 (Ja. 1992): 101-118.

Sadananda, Daniel Rathnakara. *The Johannine Exegesis of God: An Exploration into the Johannine Understanding of God*. BZNW. Berlin: Walter de Gruyter, 2004.

Saldanha, Julian. *Mission Today: Themes and Issues*. Bangalore: Claretian Publications, 2006.

Saldarini, Anthony J. *Pharisees, Scribes and Sadducees in Palestinian Society: A Sociological Approach*. The Biblical Resource Series. Grand Rapids: William B. Eerdmans Publishing Company, 2001.

Sanders, E. P. *Judaism Practice and Belief 63 BCE-66 CE*. London: SCM Press, 1992.

___________. *Paul and Palestinian Judaism*. Philadelphia: Fortress Press, 1977.

Sandmel, Samuel. *Judaism and Christian Beginnings*. New York: Oxford University Press, 1978.

Sandnes, Karl Olav. "Equality within Patriarchal Structures: Some New Testament Perspective on the Christian Fellowship as a Brother – or Sisterhood and a Family." In *Constructing Early Christian Families: Family as a Social Reality and Metaphor*. Edited by Halvor Moxnes. New York: Routledge, 1997.

Schams, Christine. *Jewish Scribes in the Second-Temple Period*. JSOT Sup 291. Edited by David J. A. Clines and Philip R. Davies. Sheffield: Sheffield Academic Press, 1991.

Schechter, S. "Genizah Specimens." *JQR* Old Series 10/4 (Jl. 1898): 654-659.

Schiffman, Lawerence H. "Halakhah and Sectarianism in the Dead Sea Scrolls." In *The Dead Sea Scrolls in their Historical Context*. Edited by Timothy H. Lim, Larry W. Hurtado, A. Graeme Auld and Alison Jack. London: T & T Clark International, 2000.

__________. "At the Crossroads: Tannaitic Perspectives on the Jewish-Christian Schism." In *Jewish and Christian Self-Definition.* Vol. 2: *Aspects of Judaism in the Greco-Roman Period.* Edited by E. P. Sanders, Albert I. Baumgarten, and Alan Mendelson. Philadelphia: Fortress Press, 1981.

Schnabel, Eckhard J. Review of *Beyond the Essene Hypothesis: The Parting of the Ways between Qumran and Enochic Judaism* by Gabriele Boccaccini. *JBL* 120/2 (Summer 2001): 372-373.

Schnackenburg, Rudolf. *The Gospel according to St. John.* Vol. 1. Translated by Kevin Smith. Kent: Burns & Oates, 1990.

__________. *The Gospel according to St.* John. Vol. 2. Translated by Cecily Hastings, et.al. London: Burns and Oats, 1980.

__________. *The Gospel according to St. John.* Vol. 3. Translated by David Smith and G. A. Kon. New York: The Crossroad Publishing Company, 1982.

Schneiders, Sandra M. ""Because of the Woman's Testimony...": Reexamining the Issue of Authorship in the Fourth Gospel." *NTS* 44/4 (O.1988): 513-535.

__________. "John 20:11-18: The Encounter of the Easter Jesus with Mary Magadalene- A Transformative Feminist Reading." In *"What is John?* Vol. 1: *Readers and Readings of the Fourth Gospel.* SBL Symposium Series 3. Edited by F. F. Segovia. Atlanta: Scholars Press, 1996.

__________. "The Face Veil: A Johannine Sign (John 20: 1-10)." *BibThBul* 13/3 (Ja. 1983): 94-97.

__________. "The Lamb of God and the Forgiveness of Sin(s) in the Fourth Gospel." *CBQ* 73/1 (Ja. 2011): 1-29.

__________. "The Raising of the New Temple: John 20.19-23 and Johannine Ecclesiology." *NTS* 52/3 (Jl. 2006): 337-355.

__________. "The Resurrection (of the Body) in the Fourth Gospel: A Key to Johannine Spirituality." In *Life in Abundance: Studies of John's Gospel in Tribute to Raymond E. Brown.* Edited by John R. Donahue. Minnesota: Liturgical Press, 2005.

__________. "To See or Not to See: John 9 as a Synthesis of the Theology and Spirituality of Discipleship." In *Word, Theology and Community in John.* Edited by John Painter, R. Alan Culpepper, and Fernando F. Segovia. Missouri: Chalice Press, 2002.

__________. *Written that You May Believe: Encountering Jesus in the Fourth Gospel.* New York: The Crossroad Publishing Company, 1999.

Schnelle, Udo. *Antidocetic Christology in the Gospel of John.* Minneapolis: Fortress Press, 1987.

Schremer, Adiel. *Brothers Estranged: Heresy, Christianity, and Jewish Identity in Late Antiquity*. Oxford: Oxford University Press, 2010.

Segal, Alan F. *Rebecca's Children: Judaism and Christianity in the Roman World*. Cambridge: Harvard University Press, 1986.

__________. *The Other Judaisms of Late Antiquity*. BJS 127. Atlanta: Scholars Press, 1987.

__________. *Two Powers in Heaven: Early Rabbinic Reports about Christianity and Gnosticism*. Leiden: Brill, 1977, 2002.

Segovia, Fernando F. "John 1:1-18 as Entrée into Johannine Reality: Representation and Ramifications." In *Word, Theology and Community in John*. Edited by John Painter, R. Alan Culpepper, and Fernando F. Segovia. Missouri: Chalice Press, 2002.

Seim, Turid Karlsen. "Descent and Divine Paternity in the Gospel of John: Does the Mother Matter?" *NTS* 51/3 (Jl. 2005): 361-375.

Sell, Canon. *The Talmud, Mishnah and Midrash*. Madras: SPCK, 1928.

Shiri, Godwin. "Churches and Dalits: Few Historical-critical Reflections on the Churches' Role in Dalit Liberation." *NCCR* (Jl. 2002): 567-577.

Shoemaker, Stephen J. "Let Us Go and Burn her Body:" The Image of the Jews in Early Dormition Traditions." *CH* 68/4 (Dec. 1999): 775-823.

Sicker, Martin. *Between Rome and Jerusalem: 300 Years of Roman-Judaean Relations*. London: Praeger, 2001.

Sigal, P. *The Emergence of Contemporary Judaism*. Vol. I. *The Foundation of Judaism from Biblical Origins to the Sixth Century AD*. Pittsburgh: Pickwick, 1980.

Sim, David C. *Apocalyptic Eschatology in the Gospel of Matthew*. SNTSMS 88. Edited by Margret E. Thrall. Cambridge: Cambridge University Press, 1996.

__________. "The Gospels for all Christians? A Response to Richard Bauckham." JSNT 84 (Dec. 2001): 3-27.

__________. *The Gospel of Matthew and Christian Judaism*. SNTW. Edited by John Barclay, Joel Marcus and John Riches. Edinburgh: T & T Clark, 1998.

Simon, Marcel. *Verus Israel: A Study in the Relation between Christians and Jews in the Roman Empire (135-425)*. Translated by H. McKeating. Oxford: Oxford University Press, 1986.

Sloyan, Gerard S. *John*. Interpretation. Edited by Paul J. Achtemeier. Atlanta: Westminster John Knox Press, 1988.

Smalley, Stephen S. *John: Evangelist and Interpreter*. New York: Thomas Nelson Publishers, 1984.

Smallwood, E. Mary. *The Jews under Roman Rule: From Pompey to Diocletian*. SJLA 20. Edited by Jacob Neusner. Leiden: E. J. Brill, 1976.

Smiga, George M. *Pain and Polemic: Anti-Judaism in the Fourth Gospel*. New York: Paulist Press, 1992.

Smith, D. Moody "Johannine Christianity: Some Reflections on Its Character and Delineation." *NTS* 21/2 (Ja. 1975): 222-248.

__________. *John*. Abingdon New Testament Commentaries. Nashville: Abingdon Press, 1999.

__________. *The Theology of the Gospel of John*. London: Cambridge University Press, 1995.

Sorek, Susan. *The Jews against Rome: War in Palestine, AD 66-73*. London: Continuum, 2008.

Stanton, G. N. "Early Christian-Jewish Polemic and Apologetic." *NTS* 31/3 (Jl. 1985): 377-92.

__________. "Gospel of Matthew and Judaism." BJRL 66/2 (Spring 1984): 264-284.

__________. "Matthew's Christology and the Parting of the Ways." In *Jews and Christians: The Parting of Ways, A.D. 70 to 135*. The Second Durham- Tübingen Research Symposium on Earliest Christianity and Judaism. Edited by James D. G. Dunn. Grand Rapids, Michigan: William B. Eerdmans Publishing Company, 1999.

Stegemann, Ekkehard W. and Wolfgange Stegemann. *The Jesus Movement: A Social History of the First Century*. Translated by O. C. Dean. Minneapolis: Fortress Press, 1995.

Stein, Robert H. *Mark*. BECNT. Edited by Robert W. Yarbrough and Robert H. Stein. Grand Rapids, Michigan: Baker Academic, 2008.

Stemberger, Günter. *Jews and Christians in their Holy Land: Palestine in the Fourth Century*. Edinburgh: T & T Clark, 2000.

Stibbe, Mark W. G. *John as Storyteller: Narrative Criticism and the Fourth Gospel*. SNTS 73. Edited by G. N. Stanton. Cambridge: Cambridge University Press, 1992.

__________. *John*. Sheffield: JSOT Press, 1993.

Still, E. Coye. "Sent to be Scarred: John 20:19-23." *ExpTim* 113/6 (Mr. 2002): 190-191.

Stoutenburg, Dennis. Review of *Qumran and the Essenes: A Re-Evaluation of the Evidence, Texte und Studien zum Antiken Judentum 60* by Lena Cansdale. Διδασκαλία 13/2 (Spring 2002): 108-110.

Stuhlmacher, Peter. "Understanding of Christ in the Pauline Tradition: A Sketch." In *Jews and Christians: The Parting of Ways, A.D. 70 to 135*. The Second Durham-Tübingen Research Symposium on Earliest Christianity and Judaism. Edited by James D. G. Dunn. Grand Rapids, Michigan: William B. Eerdmans Publishing Company, 1999.

Suggit, John N. "The Eucharistic Significance of John 20: 19-29." *JTSA* 16 (Sept. 1976): 52-59.

Sugirtharaj, Felix N. "Developing a Common Dalit Ideology: Is it a Myth or Reality?" In *Towards a Common Dalit Ideology*. Edited by Arvind P. Nirmal. Madras: Gurukul Lutheran Theological College & Research Institute, 1989.

Sverre, Aalen. "'Reign' and 'House' in the Kingdom of God in the Gospels." *NTS* 8/3 (Jl. 1962): 215-240.

Swanson, Tod D. "To Prepare a Place: Johannine Christianity and the Collapse of Ethnic Territory." *JAAR* 62/2 (Summer 1994): 241-263.

Talbert, Charles H. *Reading John: A Literary and a Theological Commentary on the Fourth Gospel and the Johannine Epistles*. New York: SPCK, 1992.

__________. "The Place of Resurrection in the Theology of Luke." *Int.* 46/2 (Ja. 1992): 19-30.

Taylor, Joan E. *The Holy Places: The Myth Making Jewish-Christian Origins*. Oxford: Clarendon Press, 1997.

Taylor, Miriam S. *Anti-Judaism and Early Christian Identity: A Critique of the Scholarly Consensus*. Leiden: E. J. Brill, 1995.

Tellbe, Mikael. "The Prototypical Christ-believer: Early Christian Identity Formation in Ephesus." In *Exploring Early Christian Identity*. Edited by Bengt Holmberg. Tübingen: Mohr Siebeck, 2008.

Tenney, Merril C. *John: The Gospel of Belief. An Analytic Study of the Text*. Grand Rapids, Michigan: William B. Eerdmans Publishing Company, 1976.

Thatcher, Tom. "Remembering Jesus: John's Negative Christology." In *The Messiah in Old and New Testaments*. McMaster NT Studies. Edited by Stanley E. Porter. Grand Rapids, Michigan: William B. Eerdmans Publishing Company, 2007.

__________. "The Legend of the Beloved Disciple." In *Jesus in Johannine Tradition*. Edited by Robert T. Fortna and Tom Thatcher. Lousiville: Westminster John Knox Press, 2001.

__________. "Why John Wrote a Gospel: Memory and History in an Early Christian Community." In *Memory, Tradition, and Text: Uses of the Past in Early Christianity*. Edited by Alan Kirk and Tom Thatcher. Semeia Studies 52. Atlanta: SBL, 2005.

Thomas, John Christopher. *Footwashing in John 13 and the Johannine Community*. JSNTSup. 61. Sheffield: JSOT Press, 1991.

Thompson, Marianne Meye. *The God of the Gospel of John*. Grand Rapids, Michigan: William B. Eerdmans Publishing Company, 2001.

Tidball, Derek. "Completing the Circle the Resurrection according to John." *ERT* 30/2 (Apr. 2006): 169-183.

Tonstad, Sigve K. ""The Father of Lies," "the Mother of Lies," and the Death of Jesus (John 12: 20-33)." In *The Gospel of John and Christian* Theology. Edited by Richard Bauckham and Carl Mosser. Grand Rapids, Michigan: William B. Eerdmans Publishing Company, 2008.

Trebilco, Paul R. *Jewish Communities in Asia Minor*. SNTS 69. Edited by G. N. Stanton. Cambridge: Cambridge University Press, 1991.

___________. *The Early Christians in Ephesus from Paul to Ignatius*. WUZNT 166. Edited by Jörg Frey Tübingen: Mohr Siebeck, 2004.

Trites, Allison A. *The New Testament Concept of Witness*. SNTSMS 31. Edited by Matthew Black. Cambridge: Cambridge University Press, 1977.

Turner, David L. *Matthew*. BECNT. Edited by Robert W. Yarbrough and Robert H. Stein. Grand Rapids, Michigan: Baker Academic, 2008.

Vallianippuram, Thomas. *New Society in John's Gospel*. Thrissur: National Printing Press, 2008.

van Belle, Gilbert. "Prolepsis in the Gospel of John." *NovT* 43/3 (O. 2001): 334-347.

van der Horst, Pieter W. "Once More: The Translation of οἱ δε, in Matthew 28:17." *JSNT* 27 (Ja. 1986): 27-30.

___________. "The *Birkat Ha-Minim* in Recent Research." *ExpTim* 105/12 (Sep. 1994): 363-368.

van der Watt, Jan G. *Family of the King: Dynamics of Metaphor in the Gospel according to John*. BIS 47. Edited by R. Alan Culpepper and Rolf Rendtorff. Leiden: Brill, 2000.

___________. "Radical Social Redefinition and Radical Love: Ethics and Ethos in the Gospel according to John." In Identity, Ethics and Ethos in the New Testament. Edited by Jan G. van der Watt. Berlin: Walter de Gruyter, 2006.

___________. "The Father Shows the Son Everything: The Imagery of Education in John 5:19-23." *APB* 18 (Ja. 2007): 263-276.

van Rossum, Joost. "The "Johannine Pentecost": John 20:22 in Modern Exegesis and in Orthodox Theology." *StVTQ* 35/2-3 (1991): 149-167.

van Tilborg, Sjef. *Reading John in Ephesus*. New York: E. J. Brill, 1996.

Varenda, Pere Villalba I. *The Historical Method of Josephus*. ALGHJ 19. Leiden: E. J. Brill, 1986.

Vellanickal, Matthew. *The Divine Sonship of Christians in the Johannine Writings*. AnBib 72. Rome: Biblical Institue Press, 1977.

von Harnack, Adolf. *The Mission of Early Christianity*. Translated by J. Moffat. Vol. 1. New York: G. P. Puttnam's Sons, 1908.

von Wahlde, Urban C. "The Johannine 'Jews': A Critical Survey." *NTS* 28/1 (Jan. 1982): 33-60.

___________. "The Terms for Religious Authorities in the Fourth Gospel: A Key to Literary-Strata? " *JBL* 98/2 (Ja. 1979): 231-253.

Voorwinde, Stephen. *Jesus' Emotions in the Fourth Gospel Human or Divine?* London: T & T Clark, 2005.

Wardle, Timothy Scott. *Continuity and Discontinuity: The Temple and Early Christian Identity*. PhD dissertation. Duke University, 2008.

Wead, David W. *The Literary Devices in John's Gospel*. ThDiss 4. Basel: Friedrich Reinhardt Kommissionsverlag, 1970.

Weaver, Dorothy Jean. "Matthew 28:1-10." *Int.* 46/4 (O. 1992): 398-402.

Weder, Hans "*Deus Incarnatus*: On the Hermeneutics of Christology in the Johannine Writings." In *Exploring the Gospel of John: in Honor of D. Moddy Smith*. Edited by R. Alan Culpepper and C. Clifton Black. Westminster: John Knox Press, 1996.

Wenham, David and Steve Walton. *Exploring the New Testament: A Guide to the Gospels & Acts*. Vol. 1. Illinois: InterVarsity Press, 2001.

___________. "The Resurrection Narratives in Matthew's Gospel." *TynBul* 24 (Ja. 1973): 21-54.

Wescott, B. F. *The Gospel according to St. John*. Grand Rapids, Michigan: William B. Eerdmans Publishing Company, 1959.

Williams, Ritva H. "The Mother of Jesus at Cana: A Social-Science Interpretation of John 2:1-12." *CBQ* 59/4 (O. 1997): 679-692.

Wilson, B. *Magic and the Millennium: A Sociological Study of Religious Movements of Protest among Tribal and the Third-World Peoples*. London: Heinemann, 1973.

Wilson, Stephen G. *Related Strangers: Jews and Christians, 70-170 CE*. Minneapolis: Fortress Press, 1995.

Wise, Michael O. "Dating the Teacher of Righteousness and the Floruit of his Movement." *JBL* 122/1 (Spring 2003): 53-87.

Witherington III, Ben. *John's Wisdom: A Commentary on the Fourth Gospel*. Cambridge: The Lutterworth Press, 1995.

Witmer, Stephen E. "Approaches to Scripture in the Fourth Gospel and the Qumran *Pesharim*." *NovT* 48/4 (O. 2006): 313-328.

Wright, N. T. *The Resurrection of the Son of God*. London: SPCK, 2003.

Wyatt, Nicolas. ""Supposing Him to Be the Gardner" (John 20, 15): A Study of the Paradise Motif in John." *ZNW* 81/1-2 (1990): 21-38.

Yarbrough, O. Larry "Parents and Children in the Jewish Family of Antiquity." In *Jewish Family in Antiquity*. Edited by Shaye J. D. Cohen. Atlanta: Scholars Press, 1993.

Yuval, Israel Jacob. *Two Nations in Your Womb: Perceptions of the Jews of Christians in Late Antiquity and the Middle Ages*. California: University of California Press, 2008.